Learn and Live SM

The New American
Heart Association
Cookbook

Seventh Edition

American Heart Association®

*Learn and Live*sm

The New American
Heart Association
Cookbook

Seventh Edition

Clarkson Potter/Publishers
New York

Published by Clarkson Potter/Publishers, New York, New York.
Member of the Crown Publishing Group, a division of Random House, Inc.
www.crownpublishing.com

CLARKSON N. POTTER is a trademark and POTTER and colophon are registered trademarks of Random House, Inc.

Earlier editions of this work were published in 1973, 1975, 1979, 1984, 1991 and 1998. The seventh edition was originally published in 2004 by Clarkson Potter/ Publishers and is reprinted here in slightly different form.

Your contribution to the American Heart Association supports research that helps make publications like this possible. For more information, call 1-800-AHA-USA1 (1-800-242-8721) or contact us online at www.americanheart.org.

Printed in the United States of America

Design by Laura Palese

Library of Congress Cataloging-in-Publication Data
The new American Heart Association cookbook / American Heart Association—7th ed.
    1. Heart—Disease—Diet therapy—Recipes. 2. Low-cholesterol diet—Recipes.
    I. American Heart Association.
RC684.D5A44   2004
641.5'6311—dc22   2004011239

ISBN 978-0-307-35205-7

10 9 8 7 6 5 4 3 2 1

Seventh Edition

Back cover (from left): Winter Fruit Salad with Spinach and Gorgonzola (page 106), Chocolate Crème Brûlée (page 609), Sun-Dried Tomato and Kalamata Olive Chicken (page 224). Spine: Sweet Corn Soup with Crab and Asparagus (page 74).

Preface

In the more than thirty years since the American Heart Association published its first cookbook, we have seen many changes. Each subsequent edition of the *American Heart Association Cookbook* has reflected important updates in nutritional science, new trends in the marketplace, and the consumer's growing commitment to eat with good health in mind. At the same time, it has always been true that the way things *taste* drives people to choose, prepare, and eat particular foods. For that reason, taste is still the number one factor in all our recipes.

These days, we are all increasingly aware that what we eat directly affects our health. More and more of us are actively seeking guidance on how to take better control of our diets and our well-being. Much of the information thrown at us, however, is conflicting, if not downright confusing. Furthermore, for better or for worse, the wide array of foods now available gives us more choices than ever before.

We are happy to say that you can use this cookbook with confidence as you sort through those choices. Remember that the American Heart Association has been spreading the word about heart health for more than fifty years. We've translated the latest and most grounded scientific information about diet and heart health into a practical and comprehensive resource that's easy to use.

This seventh edition of *The New American Heart Association Cookbook*—or "Big Red," as we affectionately call it—offers you a broad-based, commonsense approach to eating well while taking care of your heart. Always staying within the guidelines for good heart health, we show you how to prepare favorite dishes like those Grandma used to make and contemporary foods designed to become new favorites. We've developed 150 brand-new recipes to make it even easier to find something you will just have to try tonight!

We think you'll find yourself turning to this book again and again for delicious and satisfying food that you know will be good for you. We are excited to share with you what we have learned. Celebrate with us as we enjoy the best of the past and look forward to a healthy future.

Acknowledgments

American Heart Association Consumer Publications
    Director: Linda S. Ball
    Managing Editor: Deborah Ann Renza
    Senior Editor: Janice Roth Moss
    Science Editor: Jacqueline Fornerod Haigney
    Assistant Editor: Roberta Westcott Sullivan
    Senior Marketing Manager: Bharati Gaitonde
Recipe Developers for This and Previous Editions
    Claire Criscuolo
    Patricia E. Dahl
    Sarah Fritschner
    FRP
    Gail Greene
    Nancy S. Hughes
    Ruth Mossok Johnston
    Carol Ritchie
    Marjorie Steenson
    Linda Foley Woodrum
Nutrition Analyst
    Tammi Hancock, R.D.

Contents

Introduction:
A Wealth of Possibilities

Good food and good health go hand in hand. With this new edition of our flagship cookbook, the American Heart Association renews its commitment to bring you the best of what we do best. We offer sensible dietary recommendations based on reliable scientific consensus. We give you tips and information to help you translate those recommendations into your daily life. And, of course, there are the recipes—more than 600 of them—to make it easy to eat wisely and eat well, whatever the occasion.

Balance and variety are the keys to a healthful and satisfying eating plan. The American Heart Association's approach, reflected in these recipes, provides ample opportunity for both. You are not limited to a narrow regimen; rather, we encourage you to experiment within the full range of foods that make up a healthful diet.

Lifelong health does not come from quick-fix diets or fads. It is an investment in the future, for young and old and everyone in between. This book offers an eating plan for the whole family. That plan is based on sound nutritional principles, backed by careful consideration from the world's scientific community. Common sense and the enduring appeal of absolutely delicious food make an unbeatable combination.

We invite you now to explore the wealth of possibilities open to you. Try different foods and combinations, use new cooking techniques, and enjoy the many benefits of eating well for good health.

Dietary Recommendations

The American Heart Association dietary recommendations help you make wise choices about the foods you eat. By following these recommendations, which apply to all healthy people over age two, you will enjoy the best of nature's bounty, and at the same time, you may reduce your risk for heart disease and stroke.

SIMPLE STEPS TO GOOD HEALTH

1. Use up at least as many calories as you take in.
2. Aim for at least 30 minutes of physical activity on most days, if not all.
3. Eat a wide variety of nutrient-rich foods.
   - Eat a diet rich in vegetables and fruits.
   - Choose whole-grain, high-fiber foods.
   - Eat fish, especially oily fish, at least twice a week.
4. Eat less of the nutrient-poor foods.
   - Limit how much saturated fat, trans fat, and cholesterol you eat.
   - Choose lean meats and poultry without skin and prepare them without added saturated and trans fats.
   - Select fat-free and low-fat dairy products.
   - Cut back on beverages and foods with added sugars.
   - Choose and prepare foods with little or no salt.
   - If you drink alcohol, drink in moderation.
5. Follow the American Heart Association recommendations when you eat out.

For more information on the dietary and lifestyle recommendations from the American Heart Association, visit www.americanheart.org.

Heart disease and stroke are concerns for people of all ages, not just those in their forties, fifties, and beyond. Teaching children good eating habits at home will help promote a lifetime of good health.

As you use this book to plan your daily meals, you'll find that it offers you a rich variety—from mouthwatering appetizers to delectable desserts and all the courses in between. To help you make good choices, every recipe has been carefully analyzed so you will know how it fits into your overall plan of healthful eating.

BALANCE + VARIETY = GOOD HEALTH

The more research uncovers about food and health, the more it confirms the wisdom of emphasizing balance and variety in your diet. We continue to learn more about the various nutrients and the roles they play in maintaining good health. Each food group makes an important contribution to the overall equation. You can and *should* enjoy the many different grains, vegetables, fruits, and fat-free and low-fat dairy products available to you. See Appendix A, "Shopping with Your Health in Mind" (page 636), for tips on how to choose wisely from each food group.

Complex, Not Complicated: Carbohydrates

The cornerstone of a balanced diet, complex carbohydrates—such as whole grains, vegetables, and fruits—provide important vitamins, minerals, and both soluble and insoluble fiber. Soluble fiber, as part of a low-saturated-fat, low-cholesterol diet, has been shown to help lower blood pressure and blood levels of the "bad" low-density lipoprotein, or LDL, cholesterol that can increase your risk of heart disease. Insoluble fiber is digested slowly, so it also may help stabilize levels of glucose in the blood.

The term "carbohydrate" can be confusing these days. Be careful to distinguish between the complex carbs that your body needs and the simple carbs, such as table sugar, corn syrup, and other processed sugars. Simple carbs provide no nutrients and are high in calories. They are sources of the "empty" calories that add up to excessive caloric intake, which can lead to overweight, obesity, or even diabetes. High intake of carbohydrates has been linked to lowered blood levels of the "good" high-density lipoprotein, or HDL, cholesterol, again increasing the risk of heart disease.

Complex carbohydrates are excellent hunger-busters and can replace foods that are high in calories and saturated or trans fats. Sample the wide variety of grains, whole-grain breads and cereals, legumes, brown and wild rices, oats, and quinoa.

One Serving =

1 slice whole-wheat bread

½ cup oatmeal, wheat cereal, or polenta

1 cup flaked cereal

½ cup cooked brown rice, whole-grain pasta, or whole grain

Vegetables and Fruits

Be sure to explore the many vegetables and fruits you'll find in the produce section. Look for a wide variety of colors to be sure you get a broad range of nutrients. Include one serving of citrus fruit or a vegetable high in vitamin C and one serving of dark green, leafy vegetables or deep yellow vegetables every day. Frozen or canned produce is as healthful as fresh, as long as no fats, salt, or high-calorie sauces are added in processing.

One Serving =

1 medium apple, banana, orange, or pear
   (about the size of a baseball)
½ cup fresh, frozen, or canned fruit
1 cup raw leafy greens
½ cup chopped raw or cooked vegetables
½ cup fruit juice or vegetable juice

Dairy Products

Another component of a well-rounded diet, dairy products such as fat-free or low-fat milk, cheeses, and yogurt provide calcium, protein, and other vital nutrients. It's very important to realize how much difference there is between fat-free or low-fat and whole-milk products. You can start by comparing the values for calories and saturated fat (see page 640). Fortunately, many healthful dairy alternatives, ranging from fat-free half-and-half to fat-free and low-fat frozen yogurt, are now available.

One Serving =

1 cup fat-free or low-fat milk or yogurt
1½ ounces fat-free or low-fat cheese
½ cup fat-free or low-fat cottage cheese

Proteins

Protein, the body's construction material, is required for growth and tissue repair. You may not realize, however, that most adults eat more than they actually need.

Excellent protein sources include lean meats, skinless poultry, seafood, fat-free and low-fat dairy products, soy protein, dried beans, grains, and nuts and seeds.

Seafood is a particularly valuable protein choice. Research suggests that eating fish that contain omega-3 fatty acids may reduce the risk for coronary events and heart disease. These fish include salmon, halibut, tuna, and mackerel. The American Heart Association recommends that you eat at least two servings of fish, especially oily fish, per week.

Eggs are another economical source of protein. Remember, however, that the yolk from a single large egg contains between 213 and 220 mg of cholesterol, which is very close to the recommended daily limit of 300 mg. Eggs can fit into a heart-healthy diet if you keep your intake of other dietary cholesterol low. Egg whites and egg substitutes have no cholesterol, so you can enjoy them freely.

Nuts and seeds contain no cholesterol and are a healthful addition to your diet. They're good sources of protein and, to some degree, can replace other high-protein foods. Most nuts and all seeds are high in the beneficial unsaturated fats. If you're watching your weight, remember that nuts are also high in calories.

One Serving =

3 ounces cooked (4 ounces raw) lean meat, poultry, or seafood (about the size of a deck of cards or a computer mouse)

¼ cup canned tuna, sardines, or salmon (packed in water)

½ cup cooked beans or lentils

2 tablespoons peanut butter

⅓ cup or 1½ ounces nuts

USING COMMON SENSE: FATS, CHOLESTEROL, AND SODIUM

You may hear a lot of contradictory information these days about the "right" diet and the "wrong" foods. Amid all the confusion, it seems best to use a little common sense. Once you understand the roles that different substances play in determining your overall health, you will be better armed to make wise dietary choices.

Fats

Fat has become a "dirty word" in recent years, but it is an essential part of good nutrition. Eliminating fat completely from your diet would be impossible, since fat occurs naturally in many foods, including grains, vegetables, and fruits. The idea is to keep the harmful saturated and trans fats to a minimum and to replace them with the more helpful unsaturated fats.

The three main types of fat in the foods you eat are called saturated, trans, and unsaturated fat. (In this book, the term "saturated fat" is used as shorthand for the more accurate term "saturated fatty acid." Likewise, we refer to monounsaturated and polyunsaturated fats versus fatty acids.) Unsaturated fat is either polyunsaturated or monounsaturated. Eating saturated and trans fats tends to raise the level of cholesterol in your blood. Polyunsaturated and monounsaturated fats, on the other hand, tend to lower the level of blood cholesterol when the saturated fat content of the diet is low. This is why you want to reduce the amounts of saturated and trans fats in your diet and replace them with unsaturated fats.

Saturated fats are found in meat, poultry, whole-milk dairy products (such as cream, butter, and cheese), lard, and tropical vegetable oils, such as coconut, palm, and palm kernel oils. Saturated fats stay solid at room temperature.

Trans fats are found in vegetable oils that have gone through a process called hydrogenation to make them more solid. The amount of trans fat is especially high in commercial products that contain hydrogenated or partially hydrogenated vegetable oils. These products include vegetable shortenings, stick margarines, and many fried foods and baked goods such as cookies and crackers.

Unsaturated fats include
- Polyunsaturated fats, found in corn oil, safflower oil, walnuts, and fish
- Monounsaturated fats, found in olives, olive oil, canola oil, peanut oil, and avocados

Unsaturated fats are the best ones to use in your diet, especially in place of saturated and trans fats. Most unsaturated oils and fats include both polyunsaturated and monounsaturated fats, in varying percentages.

Cholesterol

Excess cholesterol in your blood can accumulate on the inner walls of your arteries and clog them, which can lead to a heart attack. We now know that much of the harmful cholesterol that develops in your body actually results from a diet high in saturated fat. (See page 660 for more information on cholesterol and diet.) If you are actively trying to lower your blood cholesterol, it is of primary importance to limit your intake of saturated and trans fats. Even so, it still makes sense to watch out for foods that are highest in cholesterol, such as egg yolks, organ meats, animal fats, and shellfish. Remember that dietary cholesterol comes only from animal products. Vegetable-based foods contain no cholesterol.

Sodium

Sodium is vital in maintaining the complicated balance of fluids and electrolytes in your body, but most Americans consume more sodium than they need. The American Heart Association recommends no more than 2,300 milligrams of sodium per day for most adolescents and adults. For the most benefit, your goal should be even lower. Some people— African Americans, middle-aged and older adults, and people with high blood pressure—need less than 1,500 milligrams.

Research has shown that, for many people, reducing the amount of sodium in the diet may lower high blood pressure and the risks of heart disease and stroke that come with it.

High-sodium foods include salt (which is about half sodium), soy sauce, Worcestershire sauce, pickles, and canned soups.

Alcohol

Alcohol has no nutritional value. Although a small amount of wine has been shown to protect against heart disease, too much alcohol can lead to high blood pressure and an increased risk of stroke. If you do drink alcohol, do so in moderation. This means one drink per day for a woman and two drinks per day for a man. (A drink is 12 ounces of beer, 4 ounces of wine, 1.5 ounces of 80-proof spirits, or 1 ounce of 100-proof spirits.) If you don't drink, don't start.

STAY FIT TO STAY WELL

The importance of maintaining a balance between the calories you eat and your level of physical activity cannot be overstated.

Calories

Calories measure energy—the energy your body uses and the energy stored in the foods you eat. You need enough calories each day to support your body's various functions. If you eat more calories than your body uses, you gain weight. If you eat fewer, you lose weight. The chart below shows how many calories you use per pound of body weight, based on how active you are on average. Your doctor can help you determine your ideal weight and whether you should reduce, increase, or maintain your caloric intake.

ACTIVITY LEVEL	CALORIES REQUIRED PER POUND OF BODY WEIGHT	
	Men	Women
Sedentary	16	14
Light	18	16
Moderate	21	18
Active	26	22

* Sedentary is occupations that involve sitting most of the day.
* Light is activities that involve standing most of the day.
* Moderate includes walking, gardening, and housework.
* Active includes dancing, skating, and manual labor.

Overweight and Obesity

There is much concern about the growing problem of obesity in adults and children alike. Excess weight can lead to high levels of blood cholesterol, high blood pressure, and diabetes. People who are overweight or obese are more likely to have heart disease and stroke even if no other risk factors are present. That's why it's important for anyone carrying excess weight to eat fewer calories and burn more calories in physical activity.

Physical Activity

Regular physical activity is crucial to good health. It makes you feel better and gives you energy. It strengthens the heart's pumping power and may lower blood pressure. Exercise also protects against heart disease by increasing the protective HDL cholesterol. In some people, exercise reduces harmful levels of LDL cholesterol.

We recommend that you get 30 to 60 minutes of moderate exercise on most days of the week. If you are over 40 or if you have medical problems, see your doctor before you start an exercise program.

Have fun! Be sure to find an activity that you enjoy. People who make physical activity a regular part of their lives succeed because they like what they are doing. Remember that you will benefit from even moderate levels of regular low-intensity physical activity, such as walking and gardening. Set reasonable goals for yourself. As you achieve them, reward yourself for doing a great job by going to the movies or buying a new sweater.

How to Use These Recipes

To help you with meal planning, we have carefully analyzed each recipe in this cookbook to provide useful nutrition information. If you're on a restricted diet, read the analyses and choose your recipes carefully. For example, if you're on a low-sodium diet, concentrate on recipes with less sodium. If you're trying to lose weight, select recipes lower in calories.

INGREDIENTS USED IN THE ANALYSES

Each analysis is based on one serving of the dish, unless otherwise indicated, and includes all the ingredients listed. Optional ingredients and garnishes, however, are not analyzed unless otherwise noted; neither are foods suggested as accompaniments.

We've made every effort to provide accurate nutrition information. Because of the many variables involved in analyzing foods, however, these values should be considered approximate.

- When a recipe lists ingredient options, such as ½ cup fat-free or low-fat Cheddar cheese, we analyzed the first one.
- Ingredients with a range—for example, a 2½- to 3-pound chicken —were analyzed using the average of the range.

- Values except for fats are rounded to the nearest whole number. Fat values are rounded to the nearest 0.5 gram. The values for saturated, monounsaturated, and polyunsaturated fats may not add up to the total fat in the recipe because total fat also includes other fatty substances and glycerol.
- When the recipe calls for "acceptable" vegetable oil, we used canola oil for the analysis. You can use canola or any other oil that is low in saturated fat, such as olive, safflower, sunflower, corn, sesame, soybean, walnut, or almond.
- When selecting an "acceptable" stick margarine, choose the one that is lowest in saturated and trans fats. We used corn oil stick margarine for the analysis.
- Values for ground beef are based on meat that is 90 percent fat free.
- After you brown ground beef without seasonings, you can wash away some of the fat by rinsing the beef under hot running water. Our recipes tell you to do this when it's practical, and this is how the beef was analyzed in those cases.
- If meat, poultry, or seafood is marinated and the marinade is discarded, we include the amount of sodium in the marinade to account for its possible absorption.
- The specific ingredients listed in each recipe were analyzed. For instance, we used both fat-free and low-fat cream cheese in this collection of recipes, depending on the taste and texture desired. In each case, the type listed was used for the nutrition analysis. If you prefer a different variety, use it. Of course, the fat values will change with such substitutions. Other nutrient values, such as sodium, may change as well. On the other hand, if you want to substitute reconstituted lemon juice for fresh, or white onions for yellow, the substitutions won't change the ingredient analyses enough to matter.
- When no quantity is listed for an ingredient in a recipe, that ingredient cannot be figured into the analysis. For example, we don't list a quantity for the small amount of flour used to prepare a surface for kneading dough. Therefore, we don't include it in the analysis.
- If a recipe calls for alcohol, we estimate that most of the alcohol calories evaporate during the cooking process.

- Because products in the marketplace often are reformulated, the terminology on their labels may change. Therefore, to avoid confusion, we use the terms "fat-free" for both "fat-free" and "nonfat," and "low-fat" for both "low-fat" and "light."
- We use the abbreviations "g" for gram and "mg" for milligram.

A WORD ON SODIUM AND SALT

We try to keep the sodium values low in most recipes, and we use salt sparingly. You may wish to add a little salt to the recipes until your tastebuds adjust to the change. The small amount of salt you add will not raise the sodium level as much as if you used a prepared food product processed with salt. That's why, for example, we use canned no-salt-added tomato sauce plus a small amount of salt instead of regular tomato sauce.

Some high-sodium canned items are not available (or are hard to find) without added salt. These items include capers, clams, chiles, and some beans. If a recipe calls for such an item, we probably say to rinse it to reduce the sodium content.

The products listed below typically also are high in sodium. In our analyses, we use the lowest-sodium products that are widely available. If the sodium in the products you use differs from these amounts, adjust the analyses accordingly.

Barbecue sauce = 210 mg sodium per 2 tablespoons

Fat-free, no-salt-added beef broth = 74 mg sodium per 1 cup

Fat-free, low-sodium chicken broth = 60 mg sodium per 1 cup

Fat-free flour tortillas = 340 mg sodium per 8-inch tortilla

Low-fat, lower-sodium ham = 235 mg sodium per ounce

Light Italian salad dressing = 270 mg sodium per 2 tablespoons

No-salt-added ketchup = 3 mg sodium per 1 tablespoon

Salsa = 140 mg sodium per 2 tablespoons

Low-salt soy sauce = 390 mg sodium per 1 tablespoon

Fat-free, low-sodium spaghetti sauce = 168 mg sodium per ½ cup

Steak sauce = 90 mg sodium per 1 tablespoon

Light teriyaki sauce = 280 mg sodium per teaspoon

No-salt-added vegetable broth = 47 mg sodium per 1 cup

Very low sodium Worcestershire sauce = 7 mg sodium per 1 teaspoon

SHOPPING EQUIVALENTS

The specific amounts of the ingredients listed, not the amounts sometimes shown in parentheses, were analyzed. The amounts in parentheses
are guidelines to help you decide how much of an ingredient you need to
buy. For example, when a recipe calls for 5 cups sliced fresh peaches
(about 3 pounds), we analyzed the 5 cups, not the 3 pounds. The paren-
thetical amounts are only estimates, based on the best information we
have. For your convenience, we've listed the most common shopping
equivalents on pages 662–663.

We developed the following recipes with your enjoyment and
good health in mind. As you take this book into your kitchen,
choose freely from the wealth of possibilities that eating wisely
can offer, and enjoy every bite!

recipes

appetizers, snacks, and beverages

Mexican Bean Dip

Serves 16; 2 tablespoons per serving

A colorful array of garnishes, such as cilantro, radishes, tomatoes, green and red onions, and jalapeño peppers, would be a perfect finishing touch for this creamy dip.

2 teaspoons very low sodium beef bouillon granules
1/4 cup hot water
15.5-ounce can no-salt-added kidney beans, rinsed and drained
1/2 cup no-salt-added tomato sauce
1/2 cup chopped onion

1/4 cup chopped green bell pepper
2 1/2 tablespoons fresh lime juice
2 medium garlic cloves, minced
1/4 teaspoon cayenne, or to taste
1/4 teaspoon ground cumin (optional)
1 tablespoon olive oil (extra-virgin preferred)

Put the bouillon granules in a food processor or blender. Pour the hot water over the granules, stirring to dissolve.

Add the remaining ingredients except the oil. Process until smooth.

To serve at room temperature, stir in the olive oil (don't process it). To serve warm, heat the dip in a small saucepan over medium heat for 5 to 6 minutes, stirring frequently. Remove from the heat and stir in the oil.

Cook's Tip on Decorative Veggie Bowls

When entertaining, halve butternut and acorn squash lengthwise and remove seeds. Put a different garnish in each squash half. For the dip, cut the top off a large acorn squash and remove the seeds, or use a decorative bowl. Arrange the garnish-filled squash halves around the dip.

calories 38
protein 2 g
carbohydrates 6 g
 fiber 1 g
 sugars 1 g
cholesterol 0 mg
total fat 1.0 g
 saturated 0.0 g
 polyunsaturated 0.0 g
 monounsaturated 0.5 g
sodium 5 mg

dietary exchange
1/2 starch

Spicy Taco Dip

Serves 8; 2 tablespoons per serving

Try this with baked tortilla chips or crunchy vegetables or as a baked potato topper.

½ cup fat-free or light sour cream
¼ cup plus 2 tablespoons fat-free
    or light mayonnaise dressing
3 tablespoons no-salt-added ketchup
2 teaspoons balsamic vinegar

1 teaspoon salt
½ teaspoon sugar
½ teaspoon ground cumin
½ teaspoon red hot-pepper sauce

In a small bowl, whisk together the ingredients. Serve immediately or cover with plastic wrap and refrigerate for up to two days.

calories 37
protein 1 g
carbohydrates 7 g
  fiber 0 g
  sugars 4 g
cholesterol 3 mg
total fat 0.0 g
  saturated 0.0 g
  polyunsaturated 0.0 g
  monounsaturated 0.0 g
sodium 401 mg

dietary exchange
½ other carbohydrate

Smoked Salmon
Party Dip

Serves 20; 2 tablespoons per serving

A hollowed-out red cabbage bowl makes a striking container for this dip, especially when you surround it with strips of brilliantly colored bell peppers. What a great way to lure your guests to take a heart-healthy dip!

1 cup fat-free or low-fat cottage cheese
1 cup fat-free or light sour cream
4 ounces smoked salmon, chopped

4 medium green onions (green and white parts), finely chopped
2 teaspoons fresh lemon juice
1/4 teaspoon garlic powder

In a food processor or blender, process the cottage cheese for 30 seconds, or until smooth. Transfer to a medium bowl.

Stir in the remaining ingredients. Cover and refrigerate until ready to serve.

calories 41
protein 4 g
carbohydrates 6 g
  fiber 1 g
  sugars 2 g
cholesterol 4 mg
total fat 0.5 g
  saturated 0.0 g
  polyunsaturated 0.0 g
  monounsaturated 0.0 g
sodium 163 mg

dietary exchange
1/2 starch

Cucumber
and Yogurt Dip

Serves 11; 2 tablespoons per serving

A tasty dip, this dish is also an excellent sauce for chilled poached or grilled salmon.

1 medium unpeeled cucumber, seeded and diced

4 to 5 medium green onions (green and white parts), finely chopped

½ cup fat-free or light plain yogurt

⅓ cup fat-free or light mayonnaise dressing

¼ cup shredded or grated Parmesan cheese

2 medium garlic cloves, minced

1 teaspoon white wine Worcestershire sauce

In a medium bowl, stir together the ingredients. Cover and refrigerate for at least 1 hour.

calories 25
protein 2 g
carbohydrates 3 g
  fiber 0 g
  sugars 2 g
cholesterol 2 mg
total fat 0.5 g
  saturated 0.5 g
  polyunsaturated 0.0 g
  monounsaturated 0.0 g
sodium 106 mg

dietary exchange
Free

Artichoke Dip

Serves 14; 2 tablespoons per serving

Surround a bowl of this dip with low-fat crackers or baked chips.

9-ounce package frozen artichoke hearts, thawed

4 ounces fat-free or light cream cheese, at room temperature

$1/2$ cup fat-free or light plain yogurt

2 medium green onions (green part only), thinly sliced

$1/2$ tablespoon cream sherry

1 teaspoon salt-free Italian seasoning

$1/8$ teaspoon garlic powder

$1/8$ teaspoon salt

Using paper towels, pat the artichokes dry. Chop the artichokes into small pieces.

In a medium bowl, whisk together the remaining ingredients.

Stir in the artichokes. Cover and refrigerate for at least 1 hour. Stir before serving.

calories 23
protein 2 g
carbohydrates 3 g
 fiber 1 g
 sugars 1 g
cholesterol 2 mg
total fat 0.0 g
 saturated 0.0 g
 polyunsaturated 0.0 g
 monounsaturated 0.0 g
sodium 78 mg

dietary exchange
Free

Spinach Dip

Serves 12; 2 tablespoons per serving

Use a variety of fresh vegetables as dippers for this peppery appetizer.

10-ounce package frozen chopped spinach
5 medium green onions (green and white parts), coarsely chopped
1/2 cup watercress, stems removed, or arugula
1/4 cup fresh parsley, stems removed
8 ounces fat-free or light plain yogurt

1 medium avocado, chopped
1 1/4 teaspoons salt-free garlic seasoning
1/8 teaspoon pepper
1/8 teaspoon salt
1/8 teaspoon red hot-pepper sauce, or to taste

Prepare the spinach using the package directions, omitting the salt and margarine. Drain well and squeeze dry.

In a food processor or blender, process the spinach, green onions, watercress, and parsley until just blended; the mixture should be coarse. Transfer to a colander to drain.

Put the remaining ingredients in the processor or blender. Process until smooth. Transfer to a medium bowl.

Stir the spinach mixture into the yogurt mixture. Cover and refrigerate for at least 1 hour.

Cook's Tip

For chunkier avocado in this dip, mash it with a fork instead of processing it. Stir the avocado into the yogurt mixture when you add the spinach.

calories 48
protein 2 g
carbohydrates 5 g
  fiber 2 g
  sugars 2 g
cholesterol 0 mg
total fat 2.5 g
  saturated 0.5 g
  polyunsaturated 0.5 g
  monounsaturated 1.5 g
sodium 62 mg

dietary exchange
1 vegetable
1/2 fat

Apricot Dip

Serves 16; 2 tablespoons per serving

Is this dish better as a dip for fresh fruits, such as strawberries, bananas, and apple slices, or as a sauce over angel food cake? Try it both ways and decide for yourself.

1 cup fresh orange juice
1/2 cup finely chopped dried apricots
   (3 to 4 ounces)
1/2 cup unsweetened applesauce

1/4 teaspoon ground cinnamon
2 dashes ground nutmeg
8 ounces fat-free or light vanilla
   yogurt

In a small nonaluminum saucepan, stir together the orange juice and apricots. Bring to a boil over medium-high heat. Reduce the heat and bring to a simmer, stirring frequently. As the apricots become tender, mash them with the back of a wooden spoon. Simmer for about 20 minutes, or until all the liquid is absorbed. Transfer to a medium bowl.

Stir in the applesauce, cinnamon, and nutmeg. Cover and let cool.

Stir the yogurt into the cooled mixture. Cover and refrigerate for at least 1 hour.

Cook's Tip on Cutting Sticky Foods

To cut dried apricots or other sticky foods easily, use kitchen shears lightly sprayed with vegetable oil spray.

calories 35
protein 1 g
carbohydrates 8 g
  fiber 1 g
  sugars 7 g
cholesterol 0 mg
total fat 0.0 g
  saturated 0.0 g
  polyunsaturated 0.0 g
  monounsaturated 0.0 g
sodium 11 mg

dietary exchange
1/2 fruit

Fire-and-Ice
Cream Cheese Spread

Serves 4; 3 tablespoons per serving

Easy but elegant, this cream cheese spread is spiced with hot red pepper and cooled with the sweet taste of apricots. Serve with low-fat cracked-pepper crackers and fresh pear slices.

$1/4$ cup fat-free whipped cream cheese (in tub)

$1/4$ cup fat-free or light sour cream

$1/4$ cup all-fruit apricot spread

$1/4$ teaspoon crushed red pepper flakes

2 tablespoons finely chopped red bell pepper

In a small mixing bowl, using an electric mixer, beat the cream cheese and sour cream until well blended.

Line a 6-ounce ramekin or small bowl with plastic wrap. Spoon the cream cheese mixture into the container. Press the mixture lightly to get rid of any air pockets. Smooth the surface with a rubber scraper. Cover and refrigerate for at least 30 minutes to firm slightly.

Meanwhile, in a small saucepan, cook the fruit spread and red pepper flakes over medium heat for 3 minutes, or until the spread just begins to melt, stirring occasionally. Remove from the heat.

Stir in the bell pepper. Let cool to room temperature.

To serve, if using a ramekin, top the cream cheese mixture with the apricot mixture. If using a bowl, invert the mixture onto a serving plate, remove the plastic wrap, and top the cream cheese mixture with the apricot mixture.

calories 59
protein 4 g
carbohydrates 10 g
  fiber 1 g
  sugars 7 g
cholesterol 5 mg
total fat 0.0 g
  saturated 0.0 g
  polyunsaturated 0.0 g
  monounsaturated 0.0 g
sodium 115 mg

dietary exchange
1 fruit

Herb Cream Cheese Spread

Serves 8; 2 tablespoons per serving

So few ingredients, so incredibly easy to make, and so much flavor!

4 ounces fat-free cream cheese
4 ounces low-fat cream cheese
2 sprigs of fresh parsley, snipped
1/2 teaspoon pepper

1 medium garlic clove, mashed
1/4 teaspoon dried thyme, crumbled
1/4 teaspoon dried chervil, crumbled

In a food processor or blender, process the ingredients for 10 seconds, scraping the side of the bowl once or twice if using a food processor. Transfer the mixture to a small bowl. Cover and refrigerate for at least 1 hour.

Cook's Tip on Chervil

An herb of the parsley family, chervil is available fresh and dried. With its delicate aniselike flavor, it gives a lightly zesty touch to sauces for vegetables and when sprinkled on salads, soups, lamb, veal, and pork.

calories 49
protein 4 g
carbohydrates 2 g
  fiber 0 g
  sugars 2 g
cholesterol 10 mg
total fat 2.5 g
  saturated 1.5 g
  polyunsaturated 0.0 g
  monounsaturated 0.5 g
sodium 112 mg

dietary exchange
1 fat

Mock Boursin
Cheese Spread

Serves 8; 2 tablespoons per serving

You'll need to begin making this spread the day before you want it so the yogurt has time to thicken and the flavors have time to meld.

12 ounces fat-free or low-fat plain yogurt without gelatin
1/4 cup fat-free or light sour cream
2 teaspoons minced fresh parsley
1/2 teaspoon dried basil, crumbled
1/4 teaspoon dried rosemary, crushed
1/4 teaspoon dried thyme, crumbled

1/4 teaspoon dried tarragon, crumbled
1/4 teaspoon dried sage, crumbled
1/4 teaspoon sugar
1/2 small garlic clove, crushed, or 1/8 teaspoon garlic powder
1 teaspoon pepper, or to taste (freshly ground preferred)

Line a rustproof colander with a double-thick layer of fine-mesh cheesecloth or paper coffee filters. Put the colander in a deep bowl. (The colander must not touch the bottom of the bowl.) Pour the yogurt into the colander. Cover with plastic wrap and refrigerate for at least 8 hours. Discard the watery liquid (whey) that drains into the bowl.

In a small bowl, whisk together the drained yogurt and sour cream.

Whisk in the remaining ingredients except the pepper.

Pour the mixture into a serving bowl. Sprinkle generously with the pepper. Cover the bowl and refrigerate for at least 8 hours.

calories 35
protein 3 g
carbohydrates 5 g
  fiber 0 g
  sugars 4 g
cholesterol 2 mg
total fat 0.0 g
  saturated 0.0 g
  polyunsaturated 0.0 g
  monounsaturated 0.0 g
sodium 39 mg

dietary exchange
1/2 skim milk

Roasted-Pepper Hummus

Serves 16; 2 tablespoons per serving

Roasted bell pepper not only boosts the flavor of this creamy chick-pea spread but adds color as well. Serve with toasted pita bread pieces, heart-healthy crackers, or vegetable dippers.

2 tablespoons sesame seeds
1/2 cup diced roasted red bell pepper, rinsed and drained if bottled
15- or 16-ounce can no-salt-added chick-peas, rinsed and drained

1/4 cup water
2 tablespoons fresh lime juice
1 medium garlic clove, minced
1/4 teaspoon salt
1/8 teaspoon pepper

In a small nonstick skillet, dry-roast the sesame seeds over medium heat for 2 to 3 minutes, or until golden, stirring the pan occasionally.

In a food processor or blender, process the sesame seeds for 30 seconds.

Add the remaining ingredients. Process until smooth. Serve at room temperature or refrigerate in an airtight container and serve chilled.

calories 59
protein 3 g
carbohydrates 9 g
  fiber 3 g
  sugars 2 g
cholesterol 0 mg
total fat 1.5 g
  saturated 0.0 g
  polyunsaturated 0.5 g
  monounsaturated 0.5 g
sodium 48 mg

dietary exchange
1/2 starch
1/2 very lean meat

Torta with Chèvre Cheese and Sun-Dried Tomatoes

Serves 12; 2 tablespoons per serving

Chèvre (SHEHV-ruh), or goat cheese, lends its unique tart flavor to this attractive layered spread.

3 ounces fat-free cream cheese, softened
2 ounces low-fat cream cheese, softened
3 ounces soft goat cheese
1 cup water
1/2 cup dry-packed sun-dried tomatoes
1 teaspoon dried oregano

1 medium garlic clove, minced
1/4 teaspoon dried basil
1/8 teaspoon pepper
1 to 2 teaspoons water (optional)
1/4 cup snipped fresh parsley
1/4 teaspoon paprika
1 tablespoon pine nuts

In a medium mixing bowl, beat the cream cheese and goat cheese for 1 to 2 minutes, or until smooth. Cover and refrigerate for 30 minutes.

Meanwhile, in a small saucepan, bring the 1 cup water to a boil. Stir in the tomatoes. Turn off the heat. Let soak for 10 to 15 minutes. Using a slotted spoon, transfer the tomatoes to a small bowl. Let cool for 5 minutes.

Coarsely chop the tomatoes. Squeeze out and discard the excess liquid.

In a food processor or blender, process the tomatoes, oregano, garlic, basil, and pepper for 20 to 30 seconds, or until the desired consistency. For a smoother texture, add 1 to 2 teaspoons water. Cover and refrigerate for 30 minutes.

Line a 1 1/2-cup round container with plastic wrap. Spread one third of the cheese mixture in the container. Press the mixture lightly to get rid of any air pockets. Smooth the surface with a rubber scraper. Top with one half of the tomato mixture. Repeat the layers. Top with the remaining cheese mixture. Cover with plastic wrap and refrigerate for at least 30 minutes.

To serve, uncover and invert the torta onto a plate. Remove the plastic wrap. Press the parsley onto the sides of the torta. Sprinkle with the paprika and pine nuts.

calories 49
protein 3 g
carbohydrates 3 g
 fiber 0 g
 sugars 1 g
cholesterol 7 mg
total fat 2.5 g
 saturated 1.5 g
 polyunsaturated 0.0 g
 monounsaturated 0.5 g
sodium 77 mg

dietary exchange
1/2 lean meat
1/2 fat

Cold Veggie Pizza Snacks

Serves 20; 1 piece per serving

Need a new way to entice the kids to eat their veggies? This dish may be the answer!

Vegetable oil spray
10-ounce package refrigerated pizza dough (in tube)
8 ounces fat-free or light cream cheese, softened
1/2 cup fat-free or light sour cream
2 tablespoons fat-free or light ranch salad dressing

4 cups chopped or thinly sliced fresh vegetables (broccoli, carrots, radishes, mushrooms, cucumbers, seeded and drained cherry tomatoes, celery, red onion, or any combination)

calories 64
protein 4 g
carbohydrates 10 g
  fiber 1 g
  sugars 2 g
cholesterol 3 mg
total fat 0.5 g
  saturated 0.0 g
  polyunsaturated 0.0 g
  monounsaturated 0.0 g
sodium 176 mg

dietary exchange
1/2 starch

Preheat the oven using the package directions on the dough. Lightly spray a 13 × 9 × 2-inch baking pan or a baking sheet with vegetable oil spray.

Pat the dough over the bottom of the pan or pat it into a 13 × 9-inch rectangle on the baking sheet.

Bake the dough using the package directions. Let cool for 10 to 15 minutes.

In a small mixing bowl, beat the cream cheese and sour cream until smooth. Stir in the salad dressing. Spread over the cooled crust.

Arrange the vegetables on top. Cover with plastic wrap and refrigerate until ready to serve.

To serve, cut into 20 pieces.

Apple Dessert Pizza Snacks
Replace the salad dressing with a mixture of 1/2 cup firmly packed light brown sugar and 1/2 teaspoon vanilla extract, and replace the vegetables with 2 medium chopped apples mixed with 1 tablespoon fresh lemon juice. Serves 20; 1 piece per serving.

apple dessert pizza snacks

calories 86
protein 3 g
carbohydrates 16 g
  fiber 1 g
  sugars 9 g
cholesterol 3 mg
total fat 0.5 g
  saturated 0.0 g
  polyunsaturated 0.0 g
  monounsaturated 0.0 g
sodium 158 mg

dietary exchange
1 starch

Creamy Pepperoni Cucumber Rounds

Serves 4; 4 pieces per serving

A nice break from the typical herbed cream cheese, and packed with pepperoni flavor, too!

2 ounces fat-free or light cream cheese, softened
2 tablespoons fat-free milk
10 turkey pepperoni slices, finely chopped

2 tablespoons minced green onion (green and white parts)
$1/8$ teaspoon garlic powder
1 medium cucumber

In a small bowl, using a rubber spatula, stir together the cream cheese and milk until well blended.

Stir in the remaining ingredients except the cucumber. Cover and refrigerate for at least 4 hours.

To serve, cut the cucumber into sixteen $1/4$-inch slices. Spread 1 teaspoon cream cheese mixture on top of each cucumber slice.

Cook's Tip

You can make the cream cheese mixture up to 24 hours in advance. You can also use it to stuff celery sticks for variety.

calories 64
protein 7 g
carbohydrates 5 g
  fiber 1 g
  sugars 3 g
cholesterol 20 mg
total fat 1.5 g
  saturated 0.5 g
  polyunsaturated 0.5 g
  monounsaturated 0.5 g
sodium 330 mg

dietary exchange
1 vegetable
1 lean meat

Plum Tomatoes
with Blue Cheese

Serves 8; 3 pieces per serving

This colorful appetizer features tomatoes topped with a spicy blue cheese mixture and chopped green onions.

1½ ounces blue cheese

1 tablespoon plus 2 teaspoons fat-free milk

¼ teaspoon red hot-pepper sauce

12 medium Italian plum tomatoes

2 tablespoons finely chopped green onions

calories 40
protein 2 g
carbohydrates 5 g
  fiber 1 g
  sugars 3 g
cholesterol 4 mg
total fat 2.0 g
  saturated 1.0 g
  polyunsaturated 0.0 g
  monounsaturated 0.5 g
sodium 85 mg

dietary exchange
1 vegetable
½ fat

In a medium mixing bowl, using an electric mixer, beat the cheese, milk, and hot-pepper sauce until completely blended, scraping the side of the bowl with a rubber scraper. Transfer to a small container. Cover and refrigerate for 30 minutes to 24 hours.

Cut the tomatoes in half lengthwise. Top each half with the cheese mixture. Sprinkle with the green onions. Serve at room temperature or cover and refrigerate for up to 1 hour.

plum tomatoes with feta cheese

calories 41
protein 2 g
carbohydrates 5 g
  fiber 1 g
  sugars 3 g
cholesterol 6 mg
total fat 2.0 g
  saturated 1.0 g
  polyunsaturated 0.0 g
  monounsaturated 0.5 g
sodium 91 mg

dietary exchange
1 vegetable
½ fat

Plum Tomatoes with Feta Cheese
Substitute 2 ounces feta cheese for the blue cheese. Substitute fat-free or light plain yogurt for the milk.

Red Potatoes with Feta Cheese and Basil

Replace the tomatoes with eight 1¹/₂-ounce red potatoes, cut in half lengthwise. Steam for 10 minutes. Plunge the potatoes into a bowl of ice water for 2 minutes. Drain well on paper towels. Top each piece with the feta cheese mixture in Plum Tomatoes with Feta Cheese. Sprinkle with 2 tablespoons finely chopped fresh basil leaves or green onions.

red potatoes with feta cheese and basil
calories 52
protein 2 g
carbohydrates 7 g
fiber 1 g
sugars 1 g
cholesterol 6 mg
total fat 1.5 g
saturated 1.0 g
polyunsaturated 0.0 g
monounsaturated 0.5 g
sodium 85 mg
dietary exchange
½ starch
1 vegetable

Tortilla Pinwheels

Serves 20; 2 pieces per serving

You can vary the heat of this Tex-Mex finger food with the type of salsa you choose.

8 ounces fat-free or light cream cheese, softened
15-ounce can no-salt-added black beans, rinsed, drained, and mashed
1 medium red bell pepper, finely chopped
1/2 cup salsa
2 medium green onions (green and white parts), thinly sliced
1/2 teaspoon ground cumin
1/4 teaspoon salt
10 6-inch corn tortillas

Preheat the oven to 350°F.

In a medium bowl, beat the cream cheese until smooth. Stir in the remaining ingredients except the tortillas.

Wrap the tortillas in aluminum foil. Bake for 5 minutes, or until warmed through. Remove the tortillas from the oven.

Put a tortilla on a cutting board, leaving the others wrapped. Spread 1/4 cup bean mixture over the entire top of the tortilla. Roll up jelly-roll style and place with the seam side down on the cutting board. Insert four toothpicks about 1 inch apart into the tortilla roll. Using a sharp knife, slice between the toothpicks to make 4 pieces. Leaving the toothpicks in place, arrange the pieces on a platter. Repeat with the remaining filling and tortillas.

calories 49
protein 3 g
carbohydrates 8 g
  fiber 1 g
  sugars 1 g
cholesterol 1 mg
total fat 0.5 g
  saturated 0.0 g
  polyunsaturated 0.0 g
  monounsaturated 0.0 g
sodium 131 mg

dietary exchange
1/2 starch

Tortilla Stacks
with Cumin Sour Cream

Serves 4; 3 wedges per serving

Pile seasoned sour cream, tomatoes, black olives, and cilantro on crisp tortilla wedges for a tasty treat.

2 8-inch fat-free or low-fat flour tortillas
1/2 teaspoon chili powder
1/4 cup fat-free or light sour cream
1 teaspoon ground cumin
1/4 to 1/2 teaspoon red hot-pepper sauce

1/3 cup seeded and finely chopped tomato
9 medium black olives, each cut into 4 slices
1/4 cup snipped fresh cilantro or parsley

Preheat the oven to 475°F.

Cut each tortilla into 6 triangles. Sprinkle the tortillas with the chili powder. Put on a baking sheet.

Bake for 3 minutes, or until the edges of the tortillas begin to brown.

In a small bowl, stir together the sour cream, cumin, and hot-pepper sauce. Spread over the tortilla wedges.

Sprinkle the wedges with the tomato, olives, and cilantro. Serve immediately.

Cook's Tip

Don't worry if the tortillas puff up while baking. They'll give your tortilla stacks an extra bit of character.

Cook's Tip on Flour Tortillas

Fat-free and low-fat tortillas can be high in sodium. When shopping, select the ones with the lowest sodium value or substitute corn tortillas.

calories 95
protein 3 g
carbohydrates 17 g
  fiber 2 g
  sugars 2 g
cholesterol 3 mg
total fat 1.5 g
  saturated 0.0 g
  polyunsaturated 0.0 g
  monounsaturated 1.0 g
sodium 275 mg

dietary exchange
1 starch

Jalapeño Poppers

Serves 24; 1 piece per serving

Charring jalapeños imparts a smoky flavor and helps the coating adhere.

Vegetable oil spray
12 large fresh jalapeños
1/4 cup all-purpose flour
Egg substitute equivalent
to 2 eggs, or 2 large eggs
1/3 cup plain dry bread crumbs

1 teaspoon salt-free all-purpose
seasoning
8 ounces fat-free or light cream
cheese, softened
1/2 cup shredded fat-free or low-fat
Cheddar cheese
1 teaspoon ground cumin

Preheat the broiler. Lightly spray the broiler rack and pan and a large baking sheet with vegetable oil spray.

Wearing rubber gloves, cut the jalapeños in half vertically. Discard the stems and seeds. Place the jalapeños with the cut side down on the broiler rack.

Broil 2 inches from the heat for 3 to 4 minutes, or until slightly charred. Using tongs, turn the jalapeños. Broil for 2 to 3 minutes, or until tender-crisp. Remove from the broiler.

Put the flour and egg substitute in separate shallow bowls. In a third shallow bowl, stir together the bread crumbs and all-purpose seasoning. Set the bowl with the flour, the bowl with the egg substitute, the bowl with the bread crumb mixture, and the baking sheet in a row, assembly-line fashion.

In a medium bowl, beat the cream cheese until smooth. Stir in the Cheddar and cumin.

Preheat the oven to 400°F.

Wearing rubber gloves, spoon about 1 tablespoon cream cheese mixture into the jalapeños. Lightly coat each jalapeño on both sides with flour, then egg substitute, then bread crumbs. Place with the stuffed side up on the baking sheet.

Bake for 8 to 10 minutes, or until golden brown and warmed through. Put the baking sheet on a cooling rack. Let cool for 3 to 4 minutes.

calories 33
protein 3 g
carbohydrates 4 g
  fiber 1 g
  sugars 1 g
cholesterol 2 mg
total fat 0.0 g
  saturated 0.0 g
  polyunsaturated 0.0 g
  monounsaturated 0.0 g
sodium 87 mg

dietary exchange
1 vegetable

Coconut Halibut Bites

Serves 12; 2 pieces per serving

You'll be delighted with these tempting morsels of halibut, served with a triple-citrus sweet-and-sour dipping sauce.

1/4 cup all-purpose flour
1/4 cup sweetened coconut
    Egg substitute equivalent to 1 egg, or 1 large egg, lightly beaten
1/2 teaspoon dried dillweed
1/8 teaspoon pepper
1 pound halibut fillets

Sweet-and-Sour Dipping Sauce

1/2 cup sweetened orange marmalade
1 tablespoon fresh lemon juice
1 teaspoon grated lime zest
1 tablespoon fresh lime juice

Preheat the oven to 400°F.

In a shallow bowl, stir together the flour and coconut. In a separate shallow bowl, whisk together the egg substitute, dillweed, and pepper.

Rinse the fish and pat dry with paper towels. Cut the fish into 1-inch cubes. Place the fish in the egg mixture, turning to coat. Using a slotted spoon, remove the fish in batches and place in the flour mixture, turning to coat. Shake off any excess flour. Place the fish on the baking sheet, spacing the cubes slightly apart so they brown evenly.

Bake for 7 to 8 minutes, or until the fish flakes easily when tested with a fork.

Meanwhile, in a small serving bowl, stir together the sauce ingredients.

To serve, place the bowl of sauce in the middle of a platter and arrange the fish cubes around it.

calories 95
protein 9 g
carbohydrates 12 g
  fiber 0 g
  sugars 10 g
cholesterol 12 mg
total fat 1.5 g
  saturated 0.5 g
  polyunsaturated 0.5 g
  monounsaturated 0.5 g
sodium 42 mg

dietary exchange
1 fruit
1 very lean meat

Orange Chicken
Lettuce Wraps

Serves 16; 1 lettuce wrap per servings

A great conversation piece for your next party, these cool and crisp lettuce cups filled with warm stir-fried orange chicken and vibrant vegetables will delight your guests. To use this dish as an entrée for four instead of as an appetizer, serve four wraps per person.

2 heads iceberg lettuce
1 teaspoon grated orange zest
1/4 cup fresh orange juice
1/4 cup fat-free, low-sodium chicken broth, such as on page 45
1 tablespoon plain rice vinegar
2 teaspoons low-salt soy sauce
1/2 tablespoon cornstarch
1/2 teaspoon toasted sesame oil
1 pound boneless, skinless chicken breasts, all visible fat discarded

1 teaspoon acceptable vegetable oil
1 medium bell pepper, diced (yellow preferred)
1 cup broccoli slaw or 1 cup chopped broccoli florets
1/2 cup sliced canned water chestnuts, rinsed and drained
2 medium green onions (green and white parts), thinly sliced

Cut each head of lettuce in half vertically. Remove the cores. Carefully peel off four outside layers from each half. Set aside.

In a small bowl, stir together the orange zest, orange juice, chicken broth, vinegar, soy sauce, cornstarch, and sesame oil. Set aside.

Cut the chicken into 1/2-inch cubes.

Heat a nonstick wok or large nonstick skillet over medium-high heat. Pour the vegetable oil into the wok and swirl to coat the bottom. Cook the chicken for 3 to 4 minutes, or until lightly browned and no longer pink in the center, stirring constantly.

Stir in the bell pepper. Cook for 1 to 2 minutes, or until tender-crisp, stirring constantly.

calories 47
protein 7 g
carbohydrates 3 g
 fiber 1 g
 sugars 1 g
cholesterol 16 mg
total fat 1.0 g
 saturated 0.0 g
 polyunsaturated 0.0 g
 monounsaturated 0.5 g
sodium 39 mg

dietary exchange
1 very lean meat

Stir in the broccoli slaw, water chestnuts, and green onions. Cook for 1 to 2 minutes, or until the vegetables are tender-crisp and the water chestnuts are warmed through.

Stir in the reserved orange zest mixture. Reduce the heat and simmer for 2 to 3 minutes, or until the sauce is thickened, stirring occasionally.

To serve, spoon the mixture into a serving bowl. Place the bowl in the center of a platter. Arrange the lettuce leaves around the bowl. Let each diner spoon about $1/4$ cup chicken mixture into a piece of lettuce and gently roll the lettuce to enclose the filling.

Cook's Tip on Reducing the Sodium in Canned Broth

If you don't want to make your own broth and can't find the fat-free, low-sodium canned variety, replace a little more than half the low-sodium broth called for with regular broth and use water for the rest.

Crumb-Crusted
Mushrooms with Lemon

Serves 4

Coat whole mushrooms with yogurt and a crust of seasoned bread crumbs, bake them for a few minutes, and watch them disappear!

2 slices bread (whole-wheat preferred)
2 teaspoons acceptable stick margarine
4 medium garlic cloves, minced
1 teaspoon salt-free Italian seasoning, crumbled

$^1/_8$ teaspoon salt-free lemon pepper (optional)
1 tablespoon grated lemon zest
   Vegetable oil spray
8 ounces small button mushrooms
$^1/_3$ cup fat-free or light plain yogurt
   Paprika
   Lemon wedges

Tear the bread into pieces. In a food processor or blender, process until the consistency of packaged bread crumbs.

In a large nonstick skillet, melt the margarine over medium-high heat. Cook the bread crumbs, garlic, Italian seasoning, and lemon pepper for 6 minutes, or until golden brown, stirring frequently. Remove from the heat.

Stir in the lemon zest.

Preheat the oven to 450°F. Lightly spray a baking sheet with vegetable oil spray.

In a large bowl, gently stir together the mushrooms and yogurt to coat. Arrange a single layer of mushrooms about $^1/_4$ inch apart on the baking sheet.

Sprinkle the mushrooms with the bread crumb mixture, then with the paprika.

Bake for 5 minutes.

To serve, gently place the mushrooms on a platter. Sprinkle the mushrooms with any bread crumbs remaining on the baking sheet. Garnish with the lemon wedges.

calories 82
protein 4 g
carbohydrates 12 g
 fiber 2 g
 sugars 3 g
cholesterol 0 mg
total fat 2.5 g
 saturated 0.5 g
 polyunsaturated 0.5 g
 monounsaturated 1.5 g
sodium 115 mg

dietary exchange
$^1/_2$ starch
1 vegetable

Crumb-Crusted Tomato Slices

Lightly spray a 9-inch square baking pan with vegetable oil spray. Substitute 2 tomatoes (about 8 ounces each) for the mushrooms. Cut the tomatoes into 4 slices each. Place the tomatoes in the pan. Spoon the yogurt over each slice. Top with the crumb topping. Bake at 450°F for 20 minutes, or until soft. Serves 4.

crumb-crusted tomato slices

calories 92
protein 4 g
carbohydrates 15 g
  fiber 2 g
  sugars 5 g
cholesterol 0 mg
total fat 3.0 g
  saturated 0.5 g
  polyunsaturated 0.5 g
  monounsaturated 1.5 g
sodium 123 mg

dietary exchange
½ starch
1 vegetable

Stuffed Mushrooms

Serves 6; 3 mushrooms per serving

Savor these plump mushrooms as an appetizer or jazz up your next spaghetti dinner by placing them on the pasta and sauce.

18 medium mushrooms with stems (about 1 pound)
2 teaspoons olive oil
3 medium garlic cloves, minced
1/4 medium red bell pepper, diced
1/4 medium yellow bell pepper, diced
2 medium green onions (green and white parts), sliced

3/4 cup fresh soft whole-wheat bread crumbs
Egg substitute equivalent to 1 egg, or 1 large egg, lightly beaten
2 tablespoons shredded or grated Parmesan cheese
1/2 teaspoon salt-free Italian seasoning, crumbled

Remove and mince the mushroom stems. Put the caps in a 13 × 9 × 2-inch baking dish. Set aside.

Preheat the oven to 425°F.

Heat a medium nonstick skillet over medium heat. Pour the oil into the skillet and swirl to coat the bottom. Cook the mushroom stems and garlic for 5 minutes, stirring occasionally.

Stir in the bell peppers. Cook for 2 to 3 minutes, or until soft.

Stir in the green onions. Cook for 2 minutes.

Remove the pan from the heat. Stir in the remaining ingredients. Spoon the filling into the mushroom caps, packing the mixture lightly.

Bake for 25 minutes, or until heated through.

calories 68
protein 5 g
carbohydrates 8 g
  fiber 2 g
  sugars 2 g
cholesterol 1 mg
total fat 2.5 g
  saturated 0.5 g
  polyunsaturated 0.5 g
  monounsaturated 1.5 g
sodium 90 mg

dietary exchange
1/2 starch
1/2 fat

Sweet-and-Sour
Spring Rolls

Serves 4; 3 spring rolls per serving

These vegetarian spring rolls are pan-fried, then glazed with sweet-and-sour sauce.

½ teaspoon acceptable vegetable oil
1½ cups shredded cabbage
4 medium garlic cloves, minced
4 medium green onions (green and white parts), chopped
8-ounce can bamboo shoots, rinsed and drained

2 teaspoons low-salt soy sauce
⅛ teaspoon pepper
3 sheets frozen phyllo dough, thawed
Vegetable oil spray
½ teaspoon acceptable vegetable oil
1 tablespoon plus 1 teaspoon bottled sweet-and-sour sauce

Heat a large nonstick skillet over medium-high heat for 1 minute. Pour ½ teaspoon oil into the skillet and swirl to coat the bottom. Cook the cabbage and garlic for 3 minutes, stirring constantly.

Stir in the green onions and bamboo shoots. Cook for 30 seconds, stirring constantly. Remove from the heat. Stir in the soy sauce and pepper.

Keeping the unused phyllo covered with a damp dish towel to prevent drying, lightly spray one sheet of dough with vegetable oil spray. Working quickly, cut the dough into fourths. Put three of the quarter-sheets under the towel. On the fourth piece, put 1 rounded tablespoon cabbage mixture 2 to 3 inches from one end. Fold that end over the filling, then fold in the sides. Roll tightly. Set aside with the seam side down. Repeat with the remaining phyllo and filling.

Pour ½ teaspoon oil into the skillet and swirl to coat the bottom. Heat over medium-high heat for 1 minute. Cook the spring rolls for 6 minutes, turning occasionally.

To serve, brush with the sweet-and-sour sauce.

calories 83
protein 3 g
carbohydrates 14 g
  fiber 2 g
  sugars 3 g
cholesterol 0 mg
total fat 2.0 g
  saturated 0.5 g
  polyunsaturated 0.5 g
  monounsaturated 1.0 g
sodium 175 mg

dietary exchange
½ starch
1 vegetable

Skewered Chicken Strips
with Soy-Peanut Marinade

Serves 16; 2 skewers per serving

This flavorful chicken strip appetizer will be the talk of your next party. (See the Cook's Tip on Skewered Food on page 245 for how to make a festive presentation.) Or try this recipe for dinner, using unsliced chicken breast halves.

4 boneless, skinless chicken breast halves (about 4 ounces each), all visible fat discarded

Soy-Peanut Marinade
2 tablespoons fresh lime juice
1 tablespoon peanut butter
1 tablespoon low-salt soy sauce

1 tablespoon plain rice vinegar
2 medium garlic cloves, minced
1/2 teaspoon ground cumin
1/2 teaspoon toasted sesame oil
1/4 teaspoon pepper

❖

Vegetable oil spray

Put the chicken with the smooth side up between two pieces of plastic wrap. Using a tortilla press, the smooth side of a meat mallet, or a rolling pin, lightly flatten the breasts, being careful not to tear the meat. Cut each piece lengthwise into 8 strips.

In a small nonmetallic bowl, whisk together the marinade ingredients. Pour the marinade into a resealable plastic bag.

Add the chicken. Seal the bag and turn to coat. Refrigerate for 30 minutes to 8 hours, turning the bag occasionally.

Meanwhile, soak 32 wooden skewers in cold water for at least 10 minutes. Lightly spray the grill rack with vegetable oil spray. Preheat the grill on medium-high.

Thread one strip of chicken on each skewer. Grill for 2 to 3 minutes on each side, or until no longer pink in the center.

Serve hot or cover and refrigerate to serve chilled.

calories 31
protein 7 g
carbohydrates 0 g
  fiber 0 g
  sugars 0 g
cholesterol 16 mg
total fat 0.5 g
  saturated 0.0 g
  polyunsaturated 0.0 g
  monounsaturated 0.0 g
sodium 50 mg

dietary exchange
1 very lean meat

Meatballs
in Beer Sauce

Serves 16; 2 meatballs per serving

You can make the sauce while these easy-to-prepare meatballs bake.

Vegetable oil spray

Meatballs
2   slices whole-wheat bread, cut into cubes
4   ounces beer (light or nonalcoholic)
1   pound lean ground beef
1/2 cup shredded fat-free or part-skim mozzarella cheese
1/2 teaspoon pepper, or to taste

Sauce
1   teaspoon light tub margarine
1/2 cup chopped onion
1   tablespoon all-purpose flour
8   ounces beer (light or nonalcoholic)
2   tablespoons light brown sugar
2   tablespoons cider vinegar
2   tablespoons fat-free, no-salt-added beef broth, such as on page 44

Preheat the oven to 350°F. Lightly spray a baking sheet with vegetable oil spray.

In a medium bowl, soak the bread cubes in 4 ounces beer for 2 to 3 minutes.

Add the remaining meatball ingredients. With clean hands or a spoon, thoroughly mix the ingredients. Form the mixture into 32 meatballs. Place on the baking sheet.

Bake for 15 minutes.

Meanwhile, in a small skillet, melt the margarine over medium-high heat and swirl to coat the bottom. Cook the onion for 2 to 3 minutes, or until soft, stirring occasionally.

Stir in the flour. Cook for 1 to 2 minutes, stirring constantly.

Stir in the remaining sauce ingredients. Reduce the heat and simmer for 10 minutes.

When the meatballs are done, drain on paper towels to remove the fat. Add the meatballs to the sauce. Simmer for 20 minutes.

calories 82
protein 7 g
carbohydrates 5 g
  fiber 1 g
  sugars 2 g
cholesterol 17 mg
total fat 3.0 g
  saturated 1.0 g
  polyunsaturated 0.0 g
  monounsaturated 1.0 g
sodium 85 mg

dietary exchange
1/2 starch
1 lean meat

Spinach and Cheese
Mini Quiches

Serves 24; 2 per serving

For occasions from bridal showers to brunch parties, these delicious mini quiches are the perfect size. They freeze well, so you can make them in advance.

Vegetable oil spray

16 ounces fat-free or low-fat cottage cheese

10-ounce package frozen chopped spinach, thawed and squeezed dry

1 cup shredded fat-free or low-fat Swiss cheese

Egg substitute equivalent to 3 eggs, or 3 large eggs

1/2 cup low-fat all-purpose baking mix

2 medium green onions (green and white parts), thinly sliced

2 tablespoons shredded or grated Parmesan cheese

2 tablespoons fat-free half-and-half

1 tablespoon olive oil

1 tablespoon fresh snipped dillweed or 1 teaspoon dried, crumbled

1/4 teaspoon pepper

Preheat the oven to 350°F. Lightly spray two 24-cup mini muffin pans with vegetable oil spray.

In a large bowl, stir together the remaining ingredients until the baking mix is just moistened (don't overmix). Spoon a heaping tablespoon of the batter into each muffin cup.

With the pans on separate oven racks, bake for 25 to 30 minutes, or until a cake tester or toothpick inserted in the center comes out clean, switching the pans from top to bottom after 15 minutes of cooking time. Transfer the pans to a cooling rack. Let cool for 5 minutes. Using a thin spatula, loosen and remove the quiches. Transfer to a platter.

calories 44
protein 5 g
carbohydrates 4 g
  fiber 1 g
  sugars 1 g
cholesterol 2 mg
total fat 1.0 g
  saturated 0.0 g
  polyunsaturated 0.0 g
  monounsaturated 0.5 g
sodium 158 mg

dietary exchange
1 very lean meat

Pita Crisps

Serves 18; 2 wedges per serving

Excellent as snacks, these herb-flecked bread wedges also complement soups and salads.

3 6-inch whole-wheat pita breads	³/₄ teaspoon dried basil, crumbled
¹/₄ cup very finely snipped fresh parsley	¹/₂ teaspoon dried rosemary, crushed
2 green onions (green and white parts), finely chopped	1 medium garlic clove, minced
	Olive oil spray
1 teaspoon olive oil	2 tablespoons grated or shredded Parmesan cheese

Preheat the oven to 350°F.

Separate each pita bread into 2 layers.

In a small bowl, stir together the parsley, green onions, olive oil, basil, rosemary, and garlic. Spread the mixture on the pitas.

Lightly spray the tops with olive oil spray. Sprinkle with the Parmesan. Cut each pita half into 6 wedges. Put the wedges on an ungreased baking sheet.

Bake for 12 minutes, or until crisp. Serve warm.

Cook's Tip

Store any leftovers in an airtight container for up to one week.

calories 33
protein 1 g
carbohydrates 6 g
  fiber 1 g
  sugars 0 g
cholesterol 0 mg
total fat 0.5 g
  saturated 0.0 g
  polyunsaturated 0.0 g
  monounsaturated 0.5 g
sodium 64 mg

dietary exchange
¹/₂ starch

Nibbles

Serves 16; ½ cup per serving

Serve this snack warm, or cool it thoroughly and store in an airtight container.

5 cups dry cereal (such as rice squares, wheat squares, oat circles, or puffed corn, or a combination)
2 cups unsalted pretzel sticks, broken in half
¼ cup fat-free tub margarine
2 teaspoons low-sodium Worcestershire sauce

1 teaspoon celery flakes
1 teaspoon onion powder
½ teaspoon garlic powder
½ cup raw peanuts or other unsalted raw nuts

Preheat the oven to 275°F.

In a large bowl, stir together the cereal and pretzel sticks.

In a small saucepan, melt the margarine over low heat. Stir in the remaining ingredients except the nuts. Stir into the cereal mixture.

Stir in the nuts. Transfer the mixture to a shallow roasting pan.

Bake for 1 hour, stirring every 10 minutes.

Southwestern Nibbles
Add ½ teaspoon ground cumin, ½ teaspoon chili powder, and ⅛ teaspoon red hot-pepper sauce to the melted margarine with the other seasonings.

Cook's Tip on Dry-Roasting Nuts

One way to dry-roast nuts is to heat them in an ungreased skillet over medium heat for 3 to 4 minutes, stirring occasionally. If you prefer, put them in a shallow baking pan and roast them in a 350°F oven for 10 to 15 minutes, stirring occasionally. For dry-roasted nuts ready at a moment's notice, prepare extras for storing in an airtight container in the freezer. You don't even need to thaw the nuts before using them.

calories 81
protein 3 g
carbohydrates 12 g
  fiber 1 g
  sugars 1 g
cholesterol 0 mg
total fat 2.5 g
  saturated 0.5 g
  polyunsaturated 1.0 g
  monounsaturated 1.0 g
sodium 91 mg

dietary exchange
1 starch

Animal Crackers in My Fruit

Serves 16; ¼ cup per serving

The classic song "Animal Crackers in My Soup" inspired this snack. Kids of all ages will enjoy the stirring action of this stovetop recipe.

²/₃ cup walnut halves
2¼ cups animal crackers (about 48)
    Vegetable oil spray
½ teaspoon ground cinnamon

⅛ teaspoon ground nutmeg
12 ounces dried mixed fruit, such as apricots, pears, figs, or plums

In a large nonstick saucepan or skillet, dry-roast the walnuts over medium heat for 3 to 4 minutes, or until golden brown, stirring occasionally.

Stir in the animal crackers. Remove from the heat. Lightly spray the mixture with vegetable oil spray (being careful not to spray near a gas flame). Return to the heat.

Sprinkle the mixture with the cinnamon and nutmeg. Dry-roast for 1 minute, or until the cookies are slightly warmed, stirring constantly.

Stir in the dried fruit. Remove from the heat. Spread the mixture on a baking sheet or large platter to cool.

Store in an airtight container, plastic sandwich bags, or wax paper bags (see the Cook's Tip) and refrigerate for up to five days.

Cook's Tip

To serve in wax paper bags, cut sixteen 12-inch wax paper squares. Place ¼ cup mixture in the center of one square. Bring the edges up and twist to enclose the mixture. Secure with a twist-tie or ribbon. Repeat with the remaining mixture and wax paper.

calories 97
protein 1 g
carbohydrates 17 g
  fiber 2 g
  sugars 9 g
cholesterol 0 mg
total fat 3.0 g
  saturated 0.5 g
  polyunsaturated 2.0 g
  monounsaturated 0.5 g
sodium 47 mg

dietary exchange
1 starch
½ fat

Frozen Fruit Slush

Serves 6

No matter your age, you never outgrow the love of frozen fruit concoctions on a stick. These treats will bring back sweet childhood memories.

½ cup water
¼ cup frozen limeade concentrate
½ 16-ounce bag unsweetened frozen
   mixed fruit, slightly thawed

1 tablespoon plus 1 teaspoon sugar
2 cups ice cubes

In a food processor or blender, process half of each ingredient until smooth. Pour into three ⅓-cup molds. Repeat with the remaining ingredients.

Freeze for 4 hours, or until firm.

calories 50
protein 0 g
carbohydrates 13 g
   fiber 1 g
   sugars 10 g
cholesterol 0 mg
total fat 0.0 g
   saturated 0.0 g
   polyunsaturated 0.0 g
   monounsaturated 0.0 g
sodium 2 mg

dietary exchange
1 fruit

Summer Slush

Serves 4

With its fruit, fruit juice, and yogurt, this drink is a fine way to start your morning or give yourself a lift midday.

2 cups frozen unsweetened strawberries or unsweetened peaches

1½ cups pineapple-orange juice

1 large banana, sliced

6 ounces fat-free or light vanilla or fruit-flavored yogurt

2 tablespoons sugar

¼ to ½ teaspoon coconut extract

In a food processor or blender, process the ingredients until smooth. Pour into 12-ounce glasses.

Cook's Tip

For an even colder treat, place your glasses in the freezer at least 30 minutes before serving.

calories 166
protein 3 g
carbohydrates 39 g
  fiber 2 g
  sugars 34 g
cholesterol 1 mg
total fat 0.5 g
  saturated 0.0 g
  polyunsaturated 0.0 g
  monounsaturated 0.0 g
sodium 37 mg

dietary exchange
2 fruit
½ skim milk

Berry Good
Smoothie

Serves 2

Drink your dessert and get more fresh fruit into your diet at the same time.

1 cup fresh strawberries, hulled and
   halved, or raspberries
1 medium banana, cut into large
   pieces

1 cup fresh orange juice

In a food processor or blender, process the ingredients until smooth.

Cook's Tip

If your food processor or blender can crush ice, add $1/2$ to 2 cups ice to make a sherbetlike dessert.

calories 132
protein 2 g
carbohydrates 32 g
  fiber 3 g
  sugars 27 g
cholesterol 0 mg
total fat 1.0 g
  saturated 0.0 g
  polyunsaturated 0.0 g
  monounsaturated 0.0 g
sodium 3 mg

dietary exchange
2 fruit

Cherry Limeade Punch

Serves 12

This refreshing sweet-tart punch features maraschino cherries hidden in pineapple-juice ice cubes.

24 whole maraschino cherries
1½ cups pineapple juice
    2-liter bottle lemon-lime soda
    12-ounce can frozen limeade concentrate

½ cup maraschino cherry juice
1 teaspoon grated lime zest
1 medium lime, cut into thin slices

Put a maraschino cherry in each compartment of two ice cube trays. Pour the pineapple juice over the cherries to fill the compartments. Freeze for 4 hours to 2 weeks.

To serve, in a large punch bowl, stir together the remaining ingredients except the lime slices. Add the pineapple-cherry ice cubes. Garnish with the lime slices.

calories 176
protein 0 g
carbohydrates 46 g
  fiber 0 g
  sugars 42 g
cholesterol 0 mg
total fat 0.0 g
  saturated 0.0 g
  polyunsaturated 0.0 g
  monounsaturated 0.0 g
sodium 41 mg

dietary exchange
3 other carbohydrate

Peppermint Coffee Chiller

Serves 4

If you love the gourmet coffee shops but want to cut the calories, the fat grams, and the cost, enjoy this delicious treat instead.

2 cups fat-free or low-fat chocolate
ice cream
1 cup water
1 cup fat-free milk

2 tablespoons sugar
1 tablespoon instant coffee granules
1 teaspoon vanilla extract
¼ teaspoon peppermint extract

In a food processor or blender, process the ingredients until smooth.

Fill four 12-ounce glasses with ice cubes. Pour the mixture into each glass.

calories 151
protein 6 g
carbohydrates 33 g
  fiber 0 g
  sugars 24 g
cholesterol 1 mg
total fat 0.0 g
  saturated 0.0 g
  polyunsaturated 0.0 g
  monounsaturated 0.0 g
sodium 99 mg

dietary exchange
2 other carbohydrate

Sparkling
Cranberry Cooler

Serves 4

Chill your prettiest glasses for serving this festive drink.

1½ cups unsweetened cranberry juice
1 cup purple grape juice
½ cup burgundy or other dry red wine
(regular or nonalcoholic)

2 teaspoons fresh lime juice
1½ cups sugar-free lemon-lime soda

In a glass pitcher, stir together all the ingredients except the soda. Refrigerate for at least 1 hour, or until well chilled.

To serve, stir in the soda. Add ice, if desired. Serve immediately.

Orange Juice Cooler
Replace the cranberry juice with orange juice, the purple grape juice with white grape juice, and the burgundy with dry white wine (regular or nonalcoholic).

calories 83
protein 0 g
carbohydrates 15 g
  fiber 0 g
  sugars 13 g
cholesterol 0 mg
total fat 0.0 g
  saturated 0.0 g
  polyunsaturated 0.0 g
  monounsaturated 0.0 g
sodium 14 mg

dietary exchange
1 fruit

orange
juice cooler

calories 103
protein 1 g
carbohydrates 20 g
  fiber 0 g
  sugars 19 g
cholesterol 0 mg
total fat 0.0 g
  saturated 0.0 g
  polyunsaturated 0.0 g
  monounsaturated 0.0 g
sodium 5 mg

dietary exchange
1½ fruit

soups

Beef Broth

Chicken Broth

Vegetable Broth

Greek Egg and Lemon Soup

Creamy Asparagus Soup

Quick Cream of Broccoli Soup

Broccoli Soup with Sour Cream

Creamy Cauliflower Soup

Cucumber Watercress Soup

Herbed Mushroom Soup
with Red Wine

Fresh Mushroom Soup

Onion Soup

Spinach Pasta Soup

Thai-Style Lemon and Spinach Soup

Summer Squash Soup

Winter Squash Soup

Flavorful Tomato Bouillon

Tomato Corn Soup

Gazpacho

Vegetable Soup

Minestrone

Five-Minute Soup

Any-Season Fruit Soup

Yogurt Fruit Soup

Minted Cantaloupe Soup
with Fresh Lime

Black Bean Soup

European Cabbage
and White Bean Soup

White Bean Soup with Tarragon

Lentil Chili Soup

Split Pea Soup

Sweet Corn Soup with
Crab and Asparagus

Southwestern Cod Soup

Shrimp Gumbo

Shrimp and Tomato Soup with
Chipotle Peppers

Chicken and Vegetable Soup

Chicken, Greens, and Potato Soup

Chile-Chicken Tortilla Soup

Vietnamese Beef and
Rice Noodle Soup

Beef Barley Soup

Beef Broth

Makes 3½ quarts

Roasting the bones is the key to making this beef broth so flavorful.

Vegetable oil spray
6 pounds beef bones
1 teaspoon acceptable vegetable oil
2 large carrots, sliced
2 large leeks (white and green parts), sliced

2 medium ribs of celery, including leaves, coarsely chopped
1 large onion, cut into large pieces
5 quarts water
8 whole peppercorns
6 to 8 sprigs of fresh parsley
3 sprigs of fresh thyme

Preheat the oven to 400°F.

Lightly spray a large baking pan with vegetable oil spray. Put the beef bones in the baking pan.

Brown the bones in the oven for 40 minutes to 1 hour.

Meanwhile, heat a large stockpot over medium-high heat. Pour the oil into the pot and swirl to coat the bottom. Cook the carrots, leeks, celery, and onion for 6 minutes, stirring occasionally. Reduce the heat to medium. Cover and cook for 15 to 20 minutes, or until the leeks are limp.

Stir in the browned bones and remaining ingredients. Increase the heat to high and bring to a boil. Reduce the heat and simmer, covered, for 4 to 5 hours. Strain the broth and discard the solids. Cover the broth and refrigerate for 6 to 8 hours. Discard the congealed fat on the surface.

1 cup of broth

calories 10
protein 2 g
carbohydrates 1 g
 fiber 0 g
 sugars 0 g
cholesterol 0 mg
total fat 0.0 g
 saturated 0.0 g
 polyunsaturated 0.0 g
 monounsaturated 0.0 g
sodium 30 mg

dietary exchange
Free

Cook's Tip on Freezing Broth

Freeze broth in covered plastic containers for future use. For smaller amounts, freeze broth in a muffin tin or ice cube trays. Remove the frozen portions from the container and store them in a resealable plastic freezer bag. Thaw the broth for several hours in the refrigerator or by heating in the microwave.

Chicken Broth

Makes 4 quarts

Homemade broth is so much more flavorful—and so much lower in sodium— than canned that it really is worth taking the time to make your own. You can omit the roasted bones, but they definitely add flavor. (See the Cook's Tip on Freezing Broth, page 44, for how to always have a supply of home- made broth on hand.)

Vegetable oil spray
4 pounds chicken bones
1 teaspoon acceptable vegetable oil
2 medium carrots, sliced
2 medium leeks (white and green parts), sliced
1 medium rib of celery, including leaves, coarsely chopped

1 large onion, quartered
2 cups dry white wine (regular or nonalcoholic)
5 quarts water
6 to 8 sprigs of fresh parsley
3 sprigs of fresh thyme
8 whole peppercorns
1 bay leaf

Preheat the oven to 400°F.

Lightly spray a large baking pan with vegetable oil spray. Put the chicken bones in the baking pan.

Brown in the oven for 1 hour. (If you prefer a lighter- colored broth, brown the bones for only 30 to 40 minutes.)

Meanwhile, heat a large stockpot over medium-high heat. Pour the oil into the pot and swirl to coat the bottom. Cook the carrots, leeks, celery, and onion for 5 minutes, stirring occasionally. Cover and cook for 10 minutes.

Stir in the wine. Increase the heat to high and bring to a boil. Boil, uncovered, for 5 to 10 minutes, or until the wine evaporates.

Stir in the remaining ingredients, including the browned bones. Bring to a boil over high heat. Reduce the heat and simmer, covered, for about 5 hours. Strain the broth and discard the solids. Cover the broth and refrigerate for about 8 hours. Discard the congealed fat on the surface.

1 cup of broth
calories 10
protein 2 g
carbohydrates 1 g
fiber 0 g
sugars 0 g
cholesterol 0 mg
total fat 0.0 g
saturated 0.0 g
polyunsaturated 0.0 g
monounsaturated 0.0 g
sodium 25 mg
dietary exchange
Free

Vegetable Broth

Makes 1¾ quarts

Aromatic vegetables are the base for this versatile broth. Use it in other soups and in vegetarian dishes. It's great for moistening Corn Bread Dressing (page 479) and as a substitute for water when cooking rice. (See the Cook's Tip on Freezing Broth, page 44, for how to always have a supply of homemade broth on hand.)

1 teaspoon acceptable vegetable oil	3 medium ribs of celery, including leaves, coarsely chopped
2 medium onions, quartered	
2 large leeks (white and green parts), sliced	3 or 4 sprigs of fresh thyme
	3 large sprigs of fresh parsley
9 to 10 cups water	12 whole peppercorns
2 medium carrots, sliced	1 bay leaf

1 cup broth

calories 7
protein 1 g
carbohydrates 1 g
  fiber 0 g
  sugars 0 g
cholesterol 0 mg
total fat 0.0 g
  saturated 0.0 g
  polyunsaturated 0.0 g
  monounsaturated 0.0 g
sodium 20 mg

dietary exchange
Free

Heat a heavy stockpot over medium-high heat. Pour the oil into the pot and swirl to coat the bottom. Cook the onions and leeks for 4 to 5 minutes, stirring occasionally.

Stir in the remaining ingredients. Increase the heat to high and bring to a boil. Reduce the heat and simmer for 1¼ to 1½ hours, or until reduced to 8 cups. Strain the broth and discard the solids. Cover the broth and refrigerate. Discard any congealed fat on the surface.

1 cup vegetable bouillon

calories 14
protein 2 g
carbohydrates 1 g
  fiber 0 g
  sugars 0 g
cholesterol 0 mg
total fat 0.0 g
  saturated 0.0 g
  polyunsaturated 0.0 g
  monounsaturated 0.0 g
sodium 40 mg

dietary exchange
Free

Vegetable Bouillon
Simmer the cooked broth for 20 to 30 minutes, or until reduced by half. Use the reduction when a recipe calls for canned bouillon.

Greek Egg and Lemon Soup

Serves 4

Avgolemono (ahv-goh-LEH-moh-noh) is the Greek name for this simply delicious soup. It's fun to stir in the egg-lemon mixture and watch it create an interesting texture and appearance.

4 cups fat-free, low-sodium chicken
   broth, such as on page 45
¼ cup uncooked rice

Egg substitute equivalent to 3 eggs,
   at room temperature
¼ cup fresh lemon juice

Pour the broth into a large stockpot and bring to a boil over medium-high heat.

Stir in the rice. Reduce the heat and simmer, covered, for 15 to 20 minutes, or until the rice is tender. Remove from the heat.

In a medium bowl, whisk together the egg substitute and lemon juice. Whisk about half the broth, a little at a time, into the egg mixture. Pour the egg mixture back into the remaining broth, whisking well.

Reduce the heat to low. Cook for 4 to 5 minutes, or just until the soup has thickened, stirring constantly. Don't let the soup boil.

calories 74
protein 7 g
carbohydrates 11 g
 fiber 0 g
 sugars 1 g
cholesterol 0 mg
total fat 0.0 g
 saturated 0.0 g
 polyunsaturated 0.0 g
 monounsaturated 0.0 g
sodium 119 mg

dietary exchange
1 starch
½ very lean meat

Creamy Asparagus Soup

Serves 4

Pureed rice adds creaminess to this simple-to-make soup.

1 tablespoon fat-free, low-sodium chicken broth, such as on page 45
1 small onion, chopped
1 medium rib of celery, chopped
4 cups fat-free, low-sodium chicken broth, such as on page 45

10-ounce package frozen asparagus spears, thawed
¼ cup uncooked rice
Dash of white pepper
Dash of ground nutmeg

In a large saucepan, heat 1 tablespoon broth over medium-high heat. Cook the onion and celery for 2 to 3 minutes, or until the onion is soft, stirring occasionally.

Stir in 4 cups broth. Increase the heat to high and bring to a boil.

Meanwhile, trim the tips off the asparagus and set aside. Cut the stalks into 1-inch pieces.

When the broth is boiling, stir in the asparagus pieces (not the tips) and rice. Reduce the heat and simmer, covered, for 15 minutes, or until the rice is tender.

In a food processor or blender, process the broth mixture until completely smooth. Return to the pan.

Stir in the asparagus tips, pepper, and nutmeg. Heat until warmed through.

Cook's Tip on Rice

Throughout this cookbook, the cooking times given are for white rice unless another variety, such as brown, is specified. Feel free to substitute, adjusting the cooking time as needed.

calories 76
protein 5 g
carbohydrates 15 g
 fiber 2 g
 sugars 3 g
cholesterol 0 mg
total fat 0.0 g
 saturated 0.0 g
 polyunsaturated 0.0 g
 monounsaturated 0.0 g
sodium 45 mg

dietary exchange
½ starch
1 vegetable

Quick Cream of Broccoli Soup

Serves 4

If you want a steaming bowl of soup with minimal effort, try this.

^{1}/$_3$ cup water

2 cups frozen cut broccoli

2 cups frozen bell pepper strips or 2 cups chopped red bell pepper
10.75-ounce can low-fat, reduced-sodium condensed cream of chicken soup

1 cup fat-free half-and-half

^{1}/$_2$ cup finely chopped green onions (green and white parts)

^{1}/$_8$ teaspoon cayenne

^{1}/$_2$ cup finely shredded fat-free or low-fat sharp Cheddar cheese

In a large saucepan, bring the water to boil over high heat. Stir in the broccoli and bell peppers. Reduce the heat and simmer, covered, for 5 minutes, or until the broccoli is tender-crisp.

Stir in the soup and half-and-half. Simmer, covered, for 10 minutes, or until the vegetables are tender. Remove from the heat.

Stir in the green onions and cayenne.

To serve, ladle the soup into bowls. Top with the cheese.

calories 153
protein 13 g
carbohydrates 24 g
  fiber 3 g
  sugars 9 g
cholesterol 9 mg
total fat 1.5 g
  saturated 0.5 g
  polyunsaturated 0.0 g
  monounsaturated 0.0 g
sodium 480 mg

dietary exchange
2 vegetable
1 skim milk
^{1}/$_2$ very lean meat

Broccoli Soup
with Sour Cream

Serves 4

Serve this as a first course in place of a salad when entertaining, especially on a cold, blustery night.

1³/₄ cups fat-free, low-sodium chicken broth, such as on page 45

14-ounce package frozen broccoli florets

1 large onion, chopped

1 medium rib of celery, thinly sliced

1 medium carrot, thinly sliced

1 cup fat-free half-and-half

¹/₂ teaspoon salt

¹/₈ teaspoon ground nutmeg

¹/₈ teaspoon cayenne

¹/₂ cup fat-free or light sour cream

In a large saucepan, bring the broth to a boil over high heat.

Stir in the broccoli, onion, celery, and carrot. Return to a boil. Reduce the heat and simmer, covered, for 20 minutes, or until the carrot is tender.

In a food processor or blender, process 1 cup soup until smooth. Transfer to a large bowl. Repeat with the remaining soup in 1-cup increments. Return the soup to the saucepan.

Stir in the remaining ingredients except the sour cream. Cook over medium heat until heated through.

To serve, ladle the soup into bowls or mugs. Top each serving with sour cream.

calories 135
protein 11 g
carbohydrates 26 g
 fiber 5 g
 sugars 12 g
cholesterol 5 mg
total fat 0.5 g
 saturated 0.0 g
 polyunsaturated 0.0 g
 monounsaturated 0.0 g
sodium 427 mg

dietary exchange
2¹/₂ vegetable
1 skim milk

Creamy Cauliflower Soup

Serves 4

With its subtle, rich flavors, this elegant soup is a perfect starter for your next dinner party.

4 cups cauliflower florets (about
  ¹/₂ large head)
¹/₂ cup chopped onion
1 tablespoon fresh lemon juice
¹/₄ cup fat-free milk
2 tablespoons all-purpose flour

2³/₄ cups fat-free milk
1 medium garlic clove, minced
2 tablespoons light tub margarine
¹/₄ cup chopped fresh basil leaves
  (optional)
³/₄ teaspoon salt

Put the cauliflower and onion in a steamer basket. Sprinkle with the lemon juice. Steam for 8 minutes, or until the cauliflower is very tender. Drain well.

Meanwhile, in a small jar with a tight-fitting lid, combine ¹/₄ cup milk with the flour. Cover. Shake until completely blended.

Return the cauliflower and onion to the saucepan. Stir in 2³/₄ cups milk, the flour mixture, and garlic. Bring just to a boil over medium-high heat, stirring occasionally. Reduce the heat and simmer for 3 minutes, or until thickened.

Using a wire whisk or potato masher, mash the cauliflower mixture to thicken slightly. Remove from the heat. Stir in the remaining ingredients.

calories 133
protein 9 g
carbohydrates 19 g
  fiber 3 g
  sugars 13 g
cholesterol 4 mg
total fat 3.0 g
  saturated 0.5 g
  polyunsaturated 0.5 g
  monounsaturated 1.5 g
sodium 607 mg

dietary exchange
¹/₂ skim milk
2 vegetable
¹/₂ fat

Cucumber
Watercress Soup

Serves 4

Dainty cucumber and watercress sandwiches are popular at high tea, and this soup combines the same mellow cucumber with peppery watercress. Serve it chilled at everything from tea to picnics.

1 large unwaxed cucumber, unpeeled
1 tablespoon fat-free, low-sodium chicken broth, such as on page 45
1 large onion, finely chopped
4 cups fat-free, low-sodium chicken broth, such as on page 45
2 large bunches watercress, leaves only (about 2 cups, packed)

2 tablespoons uncooked rice
1/4 teaspoon white pepper
1 tablespoon finely snipped fresh dillweed or 1 teaspoon dried, crumbled
1/4 cup fat-free or light plain yogurt
1 Italian plum tomato, thinly sliced (optional)

Cut the cucumber in half lengthwise. Using a spoon (a grapefruit spoon works well), scoop out and discard the seeds. Dice the cucumber.

In a large saucepan, heat 1 tablespoon broth over medium-high heat. Cook the onion for 2 to 3 minutes, or until soft.

Reduce the heat to medium. Stir in the cucumber, 4 cups broth, watercress, rice, and pepper. Cook for 15 to 20 minutes, or until the rice is tender.

Stir in the dillweed. Cook for 2 minutes.

In a food processor or blender, process the soup in batches until smooth. Cover and refrigerate until chilled.

Just before serving, whisk in the yogurt. Garnish with the tomato slices.

calories 113
protein 7 g
carbohydrates 19 g
  fiber 2 g
  sugars 8 g
cholesterol 0 mg
total fat 0.5 g
  saturated 0.0 g
  polyunsaturated 0.0 g
  monounsaturated 0.0 g
sodium 224 mg

dietary exchange
1/2 starch
1/2 skim milk
1 vegetable

Herbed Mushroom Soup
with Red Wine

Serves 4

The concentrated, deep flavors of onion, wine, and herbs are brought together in this any-occasion soup.

Vegetable oil spray
2 large onions, chopped
1 pound sliced button mushrooms
1 medium garlic clove, minced
2 cups water
3/4 cup dry red wine (regular or nonalcoholic)
1 tablespoon very low sodium beef bouillon granules

1 teaspoon dried thyme, crumbled
2 teaspoons low-sodium Worcestershire sauce
1/2 tablespoon sugar
1/2 teaspoon salt
1/4 teaspoon pepper
1/2 cup finely snipped fresh parsley
2 tablespoons light tub margarine

Heat a Dutch oven over medium-high heat. Remove from the heat and lightly spray with vegetable oil spray (being careful not to spray near a gas flame). Cook the onions for 4 minutes, stirring frequently.

Add the mushrooms and garlic. Lightly spray the vegetables with vegetable oil spray. Cook for 4 minutes, or until the mushrooms are tender, stirring frequently.

Stir in the water, wine, bouillon granules, and thyme. Increase the heat to high and bring to a boil. Reduce the heat and simmer, covered, for 15 minutes, or until the onions are very soft.

Stir in the Worcestershire sauce, sugar, salt, and pepper. Simmer, covered, for 10 minutes. Remove from the heat.

Stir in the parsley and margarine.

Cook's Tip

Adding the sugar near the end makes the taste of the onions a bit sweeter and richer.

calories 140
protein 5 g
carbohydrates 19 g
 fiber 4 g
 sugars 10 g
cholesterol 0 mg
total fat 2.5 g
 saturated 0.0 g
 polyunsaturated 0.5 g
 monounsaturated 1.5 g
sodium 361 mg

dietary exchange
4 vegetable
1/2 fat

Fresh Mushroom Soup

Serves 4

Try a variety of mushrooms to make your soup exotic. Among the choices are shiitake, portobello, oyster, golden Italian, and, of course, button.

1 teaspoon light tub margarine
4 ounces fresh mushrooms, finely chopped
4 ounces fresh mushrooms, sliced
1 large onion, chopped
2 medium garlic cloves, minced
3½ cups fat-free, low-sodium chicken broth, such as on page 45
5-ounce can fat-free evaporated milk
⅓ cup all-purpose flour
1½ tablespoons finely snipped fresh parsley
1 tablespoon dry sherry
½ teaspoon grated lemon zest
1 teaspoon fresh lemon juice
¼ teaspoon salt
⅛ teaspoon white pepper

Heat a large saucepan over medium heat. Melt the margarine in the pan and swirl to coat the bottom. Cook the mushrooms, onion, and garlic, covered, for 8 minutes, stirring occasionally. Increase the heat to high and cook, uncovered, for 2 to 3 minutes, or until the moisture evaporates.

In a medium bowl, whisk together the broth, milk, and flour. Immediately whisk the broth mixture into the mushroom mixture. Bring to a boil over medium-high heat, stirring occasionally. Cook for 3 to 5 minutes, or until thickened, stirring occasionally.

Stir in the remaining ingredients.

Cook's Tip

If you can't immediately add the broth mixture to the mushroom mixture, stir the broth mixture to keep the flour from settling to the bottom of the bowl.

calories 122
protein 6 g
carbohydrates 16 g
  fiber 2 g
  sugars 4 g
cholesterol 2 mg
total fat 2.5 g
  saturated 1.0 g
  polyunsaturated 0.5 g
  monounsaturated 1.0 g
sodium 306 mg

dietary exchange
½ starch
1 vegetable
½ lean meat

Onion Soup

Serves 6

Caramelized onions give this soup its rich flavor. Once you master the technique of caramelizing onions, you can use them to enhance the flavor of other dishes. For starters, try them in casseroles, in quiches, and on pizzas.

12 slices French bread (baguette) (about ¹/₃ ounce each)

¹/₄ cup shredded or grated Parmesan cheese

1 teaspoon light tub margarine

1 teaspoon acceptable vegetable oil

3 cups thinly sliced onions

¹/₂ teaspoon sugar

¹/₄ teaspoon salt

6 cups fat-free, no-salt-added beef broth, such as on page 44

¹/₂ cup dry white wine (regular or nonalcoholic)

1 bay leaf

¹/₄ teaspoon dried thyme, crumbled

¹/₄ teaspoon pepper, or to taste

¹/₈ teaspoon ground nutmeg

Preheat the oven to 350°F.

Put the bread slices on a baking sheet. Bake for 10 minutes, or until toasted.

Sprinkle the Parmesan over the bread. Bake for 1 to 2 minutes, or until the cheese melts. Set aside.

Heat a large saucepan over medium-high heat. Melt the margarine and heat the oil in the pan. Swirl to coat the bottom. Cook the onions for 2 minutes. Reduce the heat to low. Cook, covered, until the onions are soft, about 5 minutes.

Stir in the sugar and salt. Increase the heat to medium-high. Cook, uncovered, for 15 to 20 minutes, or until the onions are golden brown, stirring occasionally. After the first 10 minutes, stir more often to prevent the onions from sticking and burning.

Stir in the remaining ingredients. Bring to a boil. Reduce the heat and simmer, partially covered, for 15 minutes.

To serve, ladle the soup into bowls. Put 2 toasted bread slices in each bowl.

calories 78
protein 6 g
carbohydrates 14 g
 fiber 3 g
 sugars 1 g
cholesterol 0 mg
total fat 0.5 g
 saturated 0.0 g
 polyunsaturated 0.0 g
 monounsaturated 0.0 g
sodium 227 mg

dietary exchange
¹/₂ starch
1 vegetable

Spinach Pasta Soup

Serves 4

Very easy to make and attractive as well, this soup will fast become a favorite.

4 cups fat-free, low-sodium chicken broth, such as on page 45	8 ounces fresh spinach, leaves chopped, or 1/2 10-ounce package frozen chopped spinach, thawed and well drained
1/2 cup water	
1/4 cup plus 1 tablespoon no-salt-added tomato paste	2 medium green onions (green and white parts), sliced
1/2 teaspoon grated lemon zest (optional)	1/4 teaspoon pepper
1/4 cup dried orzo or pastina	1/4 teaspoon salt

In a medium saucepan over medium-high heat, whisk together the broth, water, tomato paste, and lemon zest until smooth. Bring to a boil.

Stir in the pasta. Reduce the heat to medium and cook for 5 to 7 minutes, or until the pasta is tender.

Stir in the spinach and green onions. Cook for 2 to 3 minutes.

Stir in the pepper and salt.

Cook's Tip on Orzo

Orzo looks like, and is a good substitute for, rice. Actually, it's very small pasta, so look for it in your supermarket's pasta section.

Cook's Tip on Pastina

Pastina, or tiny pasta, is frequently used in soups. If you cannot find pastina, crush any type of macaroni.

calories 91
protein 6 g
carbohydrates 17 g
  fiber 3 g
  sugars 8 g
cholesterol 1 mg
total fat 0.5 g
  saturated 0.0 g
  polyunsaturated 0.0 g
  monounsaturated 0.5 g
sodium 64 mg

dietary exchange
1/2 starch
1 1/2 vegetable

Thai-Style Lemon and Spinach Soup

Serves 4

So quick, so easy, so versatile! This soup is great as a starter and to accompany grilled chicken or fish.

3 cups fat-free, low-sodium chicken broth, such as on page 45

2 ounces dried vermicelli, broken into thirds

1 cup coarsely chopped spinach leaves (about 1 ounce)

1/2 cup finely chopped green onions (green and white parts)

1/2 cup finely snipped cilantro

4 lemon slices

1/2 teaspoon grated peeled gingerroot

1/8 teaspoon crushed red pepper flakes

In a large saucepan, bring the broth to a boil over high heat. Stir in the pasta. Return to a boil. Reduce the heat and simmer, covered, for 8 minutes, or until the pasta is tender.

Stir in the remaining ingredients. Increase the heat to high and bring just to a boil. Remove from the heat and ladle into bowls.

calories 67
protein 4 g
carbohydrates 13 g
  fiber 1 g
  sugars 1 g
cholesterol 0 mg
total fat 0.5 g
  saturated 0.0 g
  polyunsaturated 0.0 g
  monounsaturated 0.0 g
sodium 29 mg

dietary exchange
1 starch

Summer Squash Soup

Serves 5

With summer squash available all year round, you can enjoy this comforting thyme-flavored soup anytime.

1 large onion, chopped	2 tablespoons uncooked rice
1 teaspoon light tub margarine	1 teaspoon dried thyme, crumbled
2 medium yellow summer squash, zucchini, or a combination, diced	2 cups fat-free, low-sodium chicken broth, such as on page 45
2 cups fat-free, low-sodium chicken broth, such as on page 45	1 medium carrot, grated
	1/2 cup fat-free or light plain yogurt

Heat a medium saucepan over medium-high heat. Melt the margarine in the pan and swirl to coat the bottom. Cook the onion for 2 to 3 minutes, or until soft.

Stir in the squash. Cook for 5 minutes. Remove and set aside 1 cup of the mixture.

Stir 2 cups broth, rice, and thyme into the pan. Reduce the heat to medium and cook for 20 minutes, or until the rice is tender.

In a food processor or blender, process the soup in batches until smooth.

Return the soup to the pan. Stir in 2 cups broth and the carrot. Cook over medium-high heat for 5 minutes, stirring occasionally. Reduce the heat to low. Stir in the reserved squash mixture. Cook for 1 to 2 minutes, stirring occasionally.

Stir in the yogurt. Cook for 1 to 2 minutes, or until warmed through.

Cook's Tip

Don't rinse the extra starch off the rice. It will help thicken the soup.

calories 32
protein 2 g
carbohydrates 8 g
  fiber 1 g
  sugars 6 g
cholesterol 0 mg
total fat 0.0 g
  saturated 0.0 g
  polyunsaturated 0.0 g
  monounsaturated 0.0 g
sodium 24 mg

dietary exchange
1 1/2 vegetable

Winter Squash Soup

Serves 6

*It's very easy to transform leftover cooked winter squash or sweet pota-
toes into this creamy dish.*

2 cups mashed winter squash (any variety) or sweet potatoes, cooked if fresh, thawed if frozen, or drained if canned	1 teaspoon onion powder
	1/2 teaspoon garlic powder
	1/2 teaspoon ground cumin
	1/2 teaspoon salt
3 cups fat-free, low-sodium chicken broth, such as on page 45	1/4 teaspoon pepper
	1 cup fat-free half-and-half

In a medium saucepan, bring all the ingredients except
the half-and-half to a simmer over medium-high heat,
stirring occasionally. Reduce the heat and simmer,
covered, for 6 to 8 minutes, or until the flavors have
blended.

Stir in the half-and-half. Cook for 2 to 3 minutes, or
until the soup is warmed through, stirring occasionally.

Cook's Tip

*For 2 cups mashed roasted acorn squash, cut a 2-pound
acorn squash in half lengthwise. Discard the seeds and
strings. Place the squash on a nonstick baking sheet with
the cut side up. Bake for 50 to 60 minutes, or until tender.
Scoop out the flesh and mash. For 2 cups mashed sweet
potatoes, cook 1 1/2 pounds sweet potatoes in boiling water
for 30 minutes, or until tender. Discard the skins. Mash the
flesh with a potato masher.*

Cook's Tip on Winter Squash

*Some raw winter squash, such as butternut, are difficult to
cut. To make the job easy, pierce the squash several times
with a fork and place on a microwave-safe plate. Microwave
on 100 percent power (high) for 1 to 2 minutes. Let stand
for 5 minutes before cutting. Using a large, sturdy knife, cut
off the stem end. Then cut vertically from the stem end
through the root end. Discard the seeds and strings.*

calories 68
protein 5 g
carbohydrates 14 g
  fiber 2 g
  sugars 8 g
cholesterol 0 mg
total fat 0.0 g
  saturated 0.0 g
  polyunsaturated 0.0 g
  monounsaturated 0.0 g
sodium 248 mg

dietary exchange
1 starch

Flavorful Tomato Bouillon

Serves 8

A variety of herbs and spices transforms basic tomato juice and beef broth into a soothing bouillon. Serve some today and freeze the rest for other uses, such as flavoring vegetables, poached fish, and pasta.

46-ounce can no-salt-added tomato juice
2 cups fat-free, no-salt-added beef broth, such as on page 44
2 to 3 tablespoons snipped fresh dillweed or 2 teaspoons dried, crumbled
6 whole cloves
2 bay leaves
1/2 teaspoon dried basil, crumbled
1/2 teaspoon dried marjoram, crumbled
1/2 teaspoon dried oregano, crumbled
1/2 teaspoon sugar
1/4 to 1/2 teaspoon pepper
8 thin slices lemon (optional)

Pour the tomato juice and broth into a medium saucepan.

Stir in the remaining ingredients except the lemon. Bring to a boil over medium-high heat. Reduce the heat and simmer for 30 minutes. Remove the cloves and bay leaves.

Ladle the soup into soup bowls or mugs. Top each serving with a slice of lemon.

Microwave Method
Put all the ingredients except the lemon in a 3-quart microwave-safe baking dish. Cover and bring to a boil on 100 percent power (high). Reduce the power to 50 percent (medium), and cook for 7 to 8 minutes. Let the soup rest for 5 minutes, then serve topped with slices of lemon.

calories 167
protein 8 g
carbohydrates 34 g
 fiber 3 g
 sugars 14 g
cholesterol 2 mg
total fat 2.0 g
 saturated 0.5 g
 polyunsaturated 0.5 g
 monounsaturated 1.0 g
sodium 224 mg

dietary exchange
1 1/2 starch
1/2 skim milk
1 vegetable

Tomato Corn Soup

Serves 4

You can quickly put this comforting soup together with ingredients you usually have on hand.

1 teaspoon olive oil	2 cups fat-free milk
1/2 cup chopped onion	1/2 teaspoon bouquet garni (optional)
14.5-ounce can no-salt-added whole tomatoes, undrained	1/2 teaspoon salt-free all-purpose seasoning
17-ounce can no-salt-added cream-style corn	1/4 teaspoon salt

Heat a large, heavy saucepan over medium heat. Pour the oil into the pan and swirl to coat the bottom. Cook the onion for 5 minutes, stirring occasionally.

In a food processor or blender, process the onion and undrained tomatoes until smooth. Pour the mixture back into the pan.

Process the corn until smooth. Add to the tomato mixture. Increase the heat to medium-high and bring to a boil. Reduce the heat and simmer for 20 minutes.

Stir in the remaining ingredients. Increase the heat to medium-high and bring the mixture just to the boiling point.

Cook's Tip on Bouquet Garni

Traditionally, a bouquet garni (French for "garnished bouquet") consists of parsley, thyme, and a bay leaf, tied together by their stems or tied in cheesecloth, to be cooked in soups or stews. Make your own bouquet garni or buy it—with different herbs—in a jar at the supermarket.

calories 85
protein 3 g
carbohydrates 19 g
  fiber 4 g
  sugars 12 g
cholesterol 0 mg
total fat 1.0 g
  saturated 0.0 g
  polyunsaturated 0.5 g
  monounsaturated 0.0 g
sodium 29 mg

dietary exchange
4 vegetable

Gazpacho

This cold soup is versatile as well as refreshing. Make it part of a late-night supper with a sandwich or low-fat cheese and crackers, use it as a salsa for dipping baked chips, or top grilled chicken or fish with it.

Soup
- 6 cups chopped tomatoes (peeled if desired) or canned no-salt-added Italian plum tomatoes, undrained
- 1 medium onion, coarsely chopped
- 1/2 medium green bell pepper, coarsely chopped
- 1/2 cup coarsely chopped cucumber (peeled if skin is tough)
- 1 medium garlic clove, minced
- 2 cups no-salt-added tomato juice
- 1/4 cup red wine vinegar
- 1/2 teaspoon sugar
- 1/2 teaspoon ground cumin (optional)
- 1/8 to 1/4 teaspoon pepper

Garnishes
- 1 cup finely chopped tomato
- 1 small to medium onion, finely chopped
- 1/2 medium green bell pepper, finely chopped
- 1/2 cup finely chopped cucumber

In a food processor or blender, process the 6 cups tomatoes, medium onion, 1/2 bell pepper, 1/2 cup cucumber, and garlic in batches until smooth. Pour each batch into a large bowl.

Stir the remaining soup ingredients into the tomato mixture. Cover and refrigerate for at least 30 minutes.

Meanwhile, put the garnishes in individual dishes.

To serve, ladle the soup into bowls. Let each diner choose desired garnishes.

calories 86
protein 4 g
carbohydrates 18 g
  fiber 4 g
  sugars 5 g
cholesterol 0 mg
total fat 0.5 g
  saturated 0.0 g
  polyunsaturated 0.0 g
  monounsaturated 0.0 g
sodium 145 mg

dietary exchange
1/2 starch
2 vegetable

Vegetable Soup

Serves 9

Vegetables processed until smooth thicken this soup. Add or substitute other vegetables, such as squash or leeks, to vary the flavor.

6 cups fat-free, no-salt-added beef broth, such as on page 44
2 cups peeled, diced potatoes (2 to 3 medium)
4 medium carrots, diced
4 ounces fresh green beans
2 medium ribs of celery, diced
1 large onion, chopped

1 cup shredded cabbage
6-ounce can no-salt-added tomato paste
1 teaspoon dried thyme, crumbled
1/4 teaspoon pepper
1/4 teaspoon salt
1/3 cup finely snipped fresh parsley

In a large stockpot, bring all the ingredients except the parsley to a boil over medium-high heat. Reduce the heat and simmer for 20 minutes, or until the vegetables are tender.

Transfer 3 cups vegetables and broth to a food processor or blender. Process until smooth. Return the processed soup to the pot.

Stir in the parsley. Heat to warm through.

calories 158
protein 7 g
carbohydrates 30 g
 fiber 7 g
 sugars 7 g
cholesterol 1 mg
total fat 1.5 g
 saturated 0.5 g
 polyunsaturated 0.0 g
 monounsaturated 1.0 g
sodium 75 mg

dietary exchange
1½ starch
2 vegetable

Minestrone

One of the best things about a recipe like this is that almost anything works. The combination of vegetables can be different each time you make the soup.

2 teaspoons olive oil
1 medium onion, chopped
2 medium carrots, chopped
2 medium ribs of celery, including leaves, chopped
2 medium garlic cloves, chopped
4 cups low-sodium vegetable broth, such as on page 46, or fat-free, no-salt-added beef broth, such as on page 44
1 large potato, peeled and cubed
1/2 pound fresh green beans, cut into 1-inch pieces

15-ounce can no-salt-added navy beans, rinsed and drained
15-ounce can no-salt-added diced tomatoes, undrained
1 small zucchini, cubed
1/2 cup whole-wheat dried elbow macaroni or shells
1 tablespoon dried basil, crumbled
1 teaspoon dried oregano, crumbled
1 teaspoon pepper, or to taste
1 medium garlic clove, whole
1 to 2 cups water (optional)
2 tablespoons shredded or grated Parmesan cheese

Heat a stockpot over medium-high heat. Pour the oil into the pot and swirl to coat the bottom. Cook the onion, carrots, celery, and chopped garlic for 2 to 3 minutes, or until the onion is soft, stirring occasionally.

Stir in the broth, potato, green beans, navy beans, undrained tomatoes, zucchini, macaroni, basil, oregano, pepper, and whole garlic clove. Reduce the heat and simmer for 45 minutes. Add the water if the soup is too thick.

Slightly mash the soup ingredients with a potato masher to thicken. Stir.

To serve, ladle the soup into bowls. Sprinkle with the Parmesan.

calories 40
protein 5 g
carbohydrates 3 g
  fiber 1 g
  sugars 1 g
cholesterol 9 mg
total fat 1.0 g
  saturated 0.0 g
  polyunsaturated 0.5 g
  monounsaturated 0.5 g
sodium 37 mg

dietary exchange
1 very lean meat

Five-Minute Soup

Serves 6

Serve this quick-cooking soup immediately after preparing it, while the vegetables are fresh and colorful.

4 cups fat-free, low-sodium chicken broth, such as on page 45, heated

2 cups shredded fresh spinach, cabbage, or lettuce

1 medium zucchini, very thinly sliced

1/2 cup shredded cooked chicken without skin or shredded cooked lean meat, cooked without salt, all visible fat discarded

4 medium button mushrooms, sliced

1 medium tomato, cubed

Put the ingredients in a large saucepan. Bring to a boil over medium-high heat. Reduce the heat and simmer for 5 minutes.

calories 157
protein 2 g
carbohydrates 41 g
  fiber 4 g
  sugars 31 g
cholesterol 0 mg
total fat 0.5 g
  saturated 0.0 g
  polyunsaturated 0.0 g
  monounsaturated 0.0 g
sodium 12 mg

dietary exchange
3 fruit

Any-Season Fruit Soup

Serves 8

Because it's made with dried fruit, you can enjoy this fruit soup any time of the year.

2 quarts water
1 cup pitted dried plums
1 cup dried apricot halves
1 cup golden or dark raisins

1 cinnamon stick, about 3 inches long
2 tablespoons cornstarch
¼ cup cold water

In a large saucepan, stir together the water, prunes, apricots, raisins, and cinnamon stick. Bring to a boil over medium-high heat. Reduce the heat and simmer, covered, for about 15 minutes, or until the fruit is tender but not falling apart. Discard the cinnamon stick.

Put the cornstarch in a cup. Add the water, stirring to dissolve. Stir the cornstarch mixture into the fruit. Cook for 2 to 3 minutes, or until thickened, stirring constantly.

Serve hot or cover and refrigerate to serve cold.

calories 141
protein 8 g
carbohydrates 28 g
  fiber 3 g
  sugars 25 g
cholesterol 2 mg
total fat 0.5 g
  saturated 0.0 g
  polyunsaturated 0.0 g
  monounsaturated 0.0 g
sodium 89 mg

dietary exchange
1 fruit
1 skim milk

Yogurt Fruit Soup

Serves 4

Chilled soup is a wonderful way to begin a brunch or luncheon.

2 cups peeled and cubed fresh peaches (about 4 medium)
16 ounces fat-free or light plain yogurt
1 cup fresh strawberries, stems discarded

$^1/_2$ cup fresh orange juice
$^1/_2$ cup water
1 tablespoon honey
Sprigs of fresh mint (optional)

In a food processor or blender, process all the ingredients except the mint leaves until well blended.

Pour into a glass bowl. Cover and refrigerate for at least 3 hours.

To serve, garnish with the mint leaves.

Variation
Try a wide variety of fruits in place of the fresh peaches and strawberries. Substitute unsweetened frozen peaches, blueberries, or mixed fruit for fresh peaches, or use 1 to 2 medium bananas instead of the strawberries.

calories 107
protein 5 g
carbohydrates 23 g
 fiber 2 g
 sugars 20 g
cholesterol 1 mg
total fat 0.5 g
 saturated 0.0 g
 polyunsaturated 0.0 g
 monounsaturated 0.0 g
sodium 61 mg

dietary exchange
1 fruit
$^1/_2$ skim milk

Minted Cantaloupe Soup
with Fresh Lime

Serves 4

Delicately sweetened melon blended with vanilla, mint, and lime—what a refreshing treat on a hot summer day!

8 ounces fat-free or light vanilla
   yogurt
4 cups diced cantaloupe
1 tablespoon plus 1 teaspoon sugar

$^1/_4$ cup chopped fresh mint leaves
$1^1/_2$ to 2 tablespoons fresh lime juice
   Sprigs of fresh mint (optional)

Put the yogurt, cantaloupe, sugar, and $^1/_4$ cup mint, in the order listed, in a food processor or blender. Process until smooth. Pour into a large stainless steel or glass bowl. Cover with plastic wrap and refrigerate until well chilled, at least 1 hour.

To serve, stir in the lime juice. Pour the soup into bowls and garnish with mint leaves. Serve immediately.

Variation
For a taste of the Caribbean, add 1 teaspoon grated peeled gingerroot and 3 tablespoons frozen orange-pineapple concentrate to the food processor or blender and process with the yogurt mixture.

Time-Saver
To chill the soup quickly, put it in the freezer for 20 to 25 minutes, or until very cold, occasionally stirring at the edges with a rubber scraper. Chill the soup bowls at the same time.

calories 128
protein 5 g
carbohydrates 28 g
   fiber 2 g
   sugars 25 g
cholesterol 1 mg
total fat 0.5 g
   saturated 0.0 g
   polyunsaturated 0.0 g
   monounsaturated 0.0 g
sodium 34 mg

dietary exchange
$1^1/_2$ fruit
$^1/_2$ skim milk

Black Bean Soup

Serves 8

Use an assortment of small bowls for the optional garnishes—cilantro, green onions, cucumber, and orange sections—suggested for this soup. They'll dress up your table setting while letting each person select his or her favorite toppings.

1 teaspoon olive oil
1 medium onion, chopped
2 medium garlic cloves, minced
1½ quarts water
3 15-ounce cans no-salt-added black beans, undrained
  8-ounce can no-salt-added tomato sauce
¼ cup dry sherry
1 teaspoon dried oregano, crumbled
1 teaspoon dried thyme, crumbled

1 teaspoon white vinegar
1 bay leaf
1 sprig of fresh parsley
¾ teaspoon salt
⅛ teaspoon ground cloves (optional)
2 tablespoons dry sherry (optional)
  Snipped cilantro, thinly sliced green onions, chopped cucumber, and/or peeled and seeded orange sections (optional)
  Red hot-pepper sauce (optional)

Heat a stockpot over medium-high heat. Pour the oil into the pot and swirl to coat the bottom. Cook the onion and garlic for 3 to 4 minutes, or until soft, stirring occasionally.

Stir in the water, beans with liquid, tomato sauce, ¼ cup sherry, oregano, thyme, vinegar, bay leaf, parsley, salt, and cloves. Bring to a simmer. Reduce the heat and simmer, covered, for 30 minutes. Stir in the remaining sherry.

For a smooth soup, in a food processor or blender, process the soup in batches. For a thick soup, mash some of the beans right in the pot.

Ladle the soup into bowls. Let each person choose a garnish or two and add the red hot-pepper sauce as desired.

calories 164
protein 9 g
carbohydrates 29 g
  fiber 7 g
  sugars 8 g
cholesterol 0 mg
total fat 0.5 g
  saturated 0.0 g
  polyunsaturated 0.0 g
  monounsaturated 0.5 g
sodium 234 mg

dietary exchange
1½ starch
1 vegetable
1 very lean meat

European Cabbage and White Bean Soup

Serves 8

Be sure to have plenty of hard-crusted bread on hand for dunking!

1 tablespoon olive oil

3 medium leeks (white and pale green parts), coarsely chopped (about 2 cups)

1 large sweet onion, such as Texas Sweet, coarsely chopped

3 19-ounce cans reduced-sodium Great Northern beans or cannellini beans

6 cups water

2 cups fat-free, low-sodium chicken broth, such as on page 45

2 bay leaves

3 dried juniper berries, crushed with mortar and pestle

6 cups shredded green cabbage

4 medium ribs of celery, including leaves, cut into ¹/₂-inch pieces

1 cup coarsely chopped fresh Italian, or flat-leaf, parsley

¹/₂ cup frozen cut green beans

2 tablespoons fresh basil leaves

1 tablespoon finely chopped fresh thyme or 1 teaspoon dried, crumbled

1 tablespoon fresh rosemary or 1 teaspoon dried, crushed

1 tablespoon fresh lemon juice

¹/₂ teaspoon salt

¹/₂ teaspoon pepper, or to taste

1 cup fresh basil leaves

Heat a large stockpot over medium-low heat. Pour the oil into the pot and swirl to coat the bottom. Cook the leeks and onion, covered, for 10 minutes, stirring occasionally.

Stir in the undrained beans, water, broth, bay leaves, and juniper berries. Cover. Increase the heat to high and bring to a boil. Reduce the heat and simmer, covered, for 30 minutes.

Stir in the remaining ingredients except 1 cup basil. Simmer, covered, for about 45 minutes, or until the celery is tender, stirring occasionally. Add hot water if needed.

Ladle 1¹/₂ to 2 cups of soup into a food processor or blender. Add the basil. Process until smooth. Pour the processed mixture into the soup. Stir well.

calories 212
protein 12 g
carbohydrates 37 g
  fiber 10 g
  sugars 9 g
cholesterol 0 mg
total fat 2.0 g
  saturated 0.5 g
  polyunsaturated 0.5 g
  monounsaturated 1.5 g
sodium 423 mg

dietary exchange
1¹/₂ starch
2 vegetable
1 very lean meat

White Bean Soup
with Tarragon

Serves 4

Adding tarragon gives this traditionally mild comfort soup a touch of sophistication.

Vegetable oil spray
1 large onion, chopped
2 medium ribs of celery, thinly sliced
2 medium carrots, finely chopped
2 medium garlic cloves, minced
16-ounce can no-salt-added navy beans, rinsed and drained
1³/4 cups fat-free, low-sodium chicken broth, such as on page 45

¹/2 cup water
1 teaspoon ground cumin
¹/2 teaspoon dried tarragon, crumbled
¹/2 cup finely chopped green onions (green and white parts)
¹/4 cup finely snipped fresh parsley
2 teaspoons olive oil (extra-virgin preferred)

Heat a Dutch oven over medium-high heat. Remove from the heat and lightly spray with vegetable oil spray (being careful not to spray near a gas flame). Put the onion, celery, carrots, and garlic in the Dutch oven. Lightly spray the vegetables with vegetable oil spray. Cook for 3 to 4 minutes, or until the onions are soft, stirring occasionally.

Increase the heat to high. Add the beans, broth, water, cumin, and tarragon. Bring to a boil. Reduce the heat and simmer, covered, for 15 minutes, or until the carrots are tender. Remove from the heat.

Stir in the remaining ingredients.

calories 170
protein 9 g
carbohydrates 29 g
  fiber 7 g
  sugars 10 g
cholesterol 0 mg
total fat 2.5 g
  saturated 0.5 g
  polyunsaturated 0 g
  monounsaturated 1.5 g
sodium 53 mg

dietary exchange
1 starch
3 vegetable
¹/2 very lean meat

Lentil Chili Soup

Serves 7

This robust soup gets its full-bodied flavor from beer and a variety of seasonings.

1 teaspoon acceptable vegetable oil
2 medium onions, chopped
1 medium green bell pepper, finely chopped
3 medium garlic cloves, minced
3½ cups fat-free, low-sodium chicken broth, such as on page 45
1½ cups light beer or water
1¼ cups water
1½ cups dried lentils, sorted for stones and shriveled lentils and rinsed

6-ounce can no-salt-added tomato paste
2½ to 3 tablespoons chili powder
½ tablespoon ground cumin
1 teaspoon salt-free all-purpose seasoning
1 teaspoon sugar
¼ teaspoon cayenne
½ cup grated fat-free or low-fat Cheddar cheese
3 or 4 medium green onions (green and white parts), thinly sliced

Heat a heavy stockpot over medium-high heat. Pour the oil into the pot and swirl to coat the bottom. Cook the onions, bell pepper, and garlic for 10 minutes, stirring frequently.

Stir in the broth, beer, 1¼ cups water, lentils, tomato paste, chili powder, cumin, all-purpose seasoning, sugar, and cayenne. Increase the heat to high and bring to a boil. Reduce the heat and simmer, partially covered, for 35 to 40 minutes, or until the lentils are tender, stirring occasionally. Add water as necessary.

To serve, ladle the soup into bowls. Sprinkle with the Cheddar and green onions.

calories 278
protein 20 g
carbohydrates 45 g
  fiber 19 g
  sugars 8 g
cholesterol 2 mg
total fat 2.0 g
  saturated 0.5 g
  polyunsaturated 1.0 g
  monounsaturated 0.5 g
sodium 152 mg

dietary exchange
2 starch
3 vegetable
1½ very lean meat

Split Pea Soup

Serves 4

Easy to prepare, homemade split pea soup is lower in sodium than its canned cousin. Our version is flavorful even without the usual ham.

1 cup dried split peas, sorted for stones and shriveled peas and rinsed	1 medium carrot, chopped
	1/2 cup snipped fresh parsley
	1 teaspoon pepper, or to taste
1 teaspoon light tub margarine	1/2 teaspoon dried marjoram
1 small onion, chopped	1/2 teaspoon dried thyme, crumbled
4 cups water	1/2 teaspoon dried basil, crumbled
3 medium ribs of celery, including leaves, chopped	1/2 teaspoon celery seeds
	1 bay leaf

Soak the split peas using the package directions.

Heat a large saucepan over medium-high heat. Melt the margarine in the pan and swirl to coat the bottom. Cook the onion for 5 minutes, or until lightly browned.

Stir in the peas and remaining ingredients. Reduce the heat and simmer, covered, for 1 to 1½ hours, or until the peas are tender, stirring occasionally.

Cook's Tip

If you like soup with lots of texture, serve as is. For a little less texture, use a potato masher to blend the ingredients. For an even smoother texture, process the soup in batches in a food processor or blender until the desired consistency.

calories 198
protein 13 g
carbohydrates 36 g
  fiber 15 g
  sugars 7 g
cholesterol 0 mg
total fat 1.0 g
  saturated 0.0 g
  polyunsaturated 0.5 g
  monounsaturated 0.5 g
sodium 60 mg

dietary exchange
2 starch
1 vegetable
1 very lean meat

Sweet Corn Soup with
Crab and Asparagus

Serves 8

This Cantonese-style soup is practically a meal in itself. Serve with Easy Refrigerator Rolls (page 532) and one of our fruit desserts, such as Baked Ginger Pears (page 621), to round out your dinner. (See photo on book spine.)

1$\frac{1}{2}$ pounds fresh asparagus
$\frac{1}{4}$ cup water
4 cups fat-free, low-sodium chicken broth, such as on page 45
15-ounce can no-salt-added cream-style corn
2 teaspoons low-salt soy sauce
$\frac{1}{2}$ teaspoon salt
2 tablespoons cornstarch

2 tablespoons cold water
Egg substitute equivalent to 3 eggs, or 3 large eggs
2 6-ounce cans crabmeat, rinsed and drained
$\frac{1}{2}$ teaspoon toasted sesame oil
6 medium green onions (green part only), finely chopped
Chili garlic sauce to taste (optional)

Trim the asparagus and cut into 1-inch pieces. Put in a microwave-safe dish with $\frac{1}{4}$ cup water. Microwave, covered, on 100 percent power (high) for 5 minutes, or until tender-crisp. Don't overcook. Drain well.

In a large saucepan, bring the broth to a boil over high heat. Stir in the corn, soy sauce, and salt. Return to a boil.

Meanwhile, put the cornstarch in a cup. Add 2 tablespoons water, stirring to dissolve. Pour into the broth mixture, stirring constantly.

Pour the egg substitute into the boiling soup in a thin stream. Remove from the heat.

To serve, spoon $\frac{1}{2}$ cup asparagus into each bowl. Ladle the broth mixture over each serving. Top with the crabmeat and sesame oil. Sprinkle the green onions over each serving.

Serve the chili garlic sauce on the side.

calories 138
protein 15 g
carbohydrates 17 g
  fiber 3 g
  sugars 5 g
cholesterol 38 mg
total fat 1.0 g
  saturated 0.0 g
  polyunsaturated 0.5 g
  monounsaturated 0.5 g
sodium 278 mg

dietary exchange
1 starch
1 vegetable
1$\frac{1}{2}$ very lean meat

Sweet Corn Soup with Chicken and Asparagus
Substitute 2 cups chopped cooked skinless chicken breasts, cooked without salt, for the crabmeat.

Cook's Tip on Asparagus

An asparagus spear has a natural bending point where the tough stem ends. Holding a spear of asparagus at the top and the bottom, bend the spear; snap at the bending point. Discard the tough part, or save it to use in making broths and other soups.

---

sweet corn soup with chicken and asparagus

calories 154
protein 15 g
carbohydrates 17 g
  fiber 3 g
  sugars 5 g
cholesterol 26 mg
total fat 3.0 g
  saturated 0.5 g
  polyunsaturated 1.0 g
  monounsaturated 1.0 g
sodium 269 mg

dietary exchange
1 starch
1 vegetable
1½ very lean meat

Southwestern Cod Soup

Serves 4

The mild flavor of cod marries well with the intense flavors of the Southwest, including green chiles, cumin, and cilantro. This dish is great any time of year, but it's especially comforting as the weather turns colder.

2 cups fat-free, low-sodium chicken broth, such as on page 45
14.5-ounce can no-salt-added diced tomatoes, undrained
6 small red potatoes, halved (about 6 ounces)
1 medium carrot, sliced
4-ounce can chopped green chiles, rinsed and drained

1 teaspoon ground cumin
2 medium garlic cloves, minced
1/4 teaspoon salt
8 ounces cod fillets
2 tablespoons snipped fresh cilantro
1 teaspoon grated lime zest
1 teaspoon fresh lime juice

In a large saucepan, stir together the broth, undrained tomatoes, potatoes, carrot, green chiles, cumin, garlic, and salt. Bring to a simmer over medium-high heat, stirring occasionally. Reduce the heat and simmer, covered, for 15 minutes, or until the vegetables are tender.

Meanwhile, rinse the fish and pat dry with paper towels. Cut the fish into 3/4-inch cubes. Stir the fish and the remaining ingredients into the broth mixture. Simmer, covered, for 5 minutes, or until the fish flakes easily when tested with a fork.

calories 118
protein 14 g
carbohydrates 16 g
  fiber 4 g
  sugars 6 g
cholesterol 24 mg
total fat 0.5 g
  saturated 0.0 g
  polyunsaturated 0.0 g
  monounsaturated 0.0 g
sodium 332 mg

dietary exchange
1/2 starch
1 1/2 vegetable
1 1/2 very lean meat

Cook's Tip

Found at gourmet shops and some grocery stores, a crinkled-edge garnishing tool makes attractive, wavy-edged slices of various foods. Use it when you want to dress up your veggies, such as the carrots in this soup. You'll be pleased at how it perks up the presentation.

Shrimp Gumbo

Serves 6

For a great, warming winter meal, try this thick gumbo.

1 teaspoon acceptable vegetable oil
2 cups sliced fresh okra (about
   1 pound) or 10-ounce package
   frozen sliced okra
1 large onion, chopped
1/2 medium green bell pepper,
   chopped
1 medium rib of celery, chopped
3 medium garlic cloves, minced
1/2 teaspoon pepper, or to taste
2 cups fat-free, low-sodium chicken
   broth, such as on page 45

14.5-ounce can no-salt-added
   diced tomatoes, undrained
2 bay leaves
1 cup uncooked rice
1 tablespoon cornstarch
2 tablespoons water
1 pound peeled raw medium shrimp
1 tablespoon gumbo filé powder
   (optional)
1/4 teaspoon salt
1/8 teaspoon red hot-pepper sauce, or
   to taste

Heat a large stockpot over medium-high heat. Pour the oil into the pot and swirl to coat the bottom. Cook the okra, onion, bell pepper, celery, garlic, and pepper for 5 minutes, stirring frequently.

Stir in the broth, undrained tomatoes, and bay leaves. Increase the heat to high and bring to a boil. Reduce the heat and simmer, covered, for 45 minutes.

Meanwhile, prepare the rice using the package directions, omitting the salt and margarine. Set aside.

Put the cornstarch in a cup. Add the water, stirring to dissolve. Add to the okra mixture. Cook for 1 minute, or until thickened, stirring constantly.

Stir in the shrimp. Increase the heat to high and bring to a low boil. Reduce the heat and simmer, covered, for 3 to 5 minutes, or until the shrimp turns pink and opaque. Don't overcook, or the shrimp will become rubbery.

Discard the bay leaves. Stir in the filé, salt, and hot-pepper sauce.

To serve, spoon the rice into soup bowls. Ladle the gumbo over the rice.

calories 215
protein 16 g
carbohydrates 35 g
  fiber 3 g
  sugars 5 g
cholesterol 111 mg
total fat 1.5 g
  saturated 0.0 g
  polyunsaturated 0.5 g
  monounsaturated 0.5 g
sodium 273 mg

dietary exchange
1½ starch
2 vegetable
2 very lean meat

Shrimp and Tomato Soup
with Chipotle Peppers

Serves 4

The mild, smoky heat of chipotle peppers is a nice balance with tomatoes, as this soup proves.

1 medium chipotle pepper
  Vegetable oil spray
1 large onion, finely chopped
1 medium green bell pepper, chopped
1³/₄ cups fat-free, low-sodium chicken broth, such as on page 45
  14.5-ounce can diced tomatoes with bell peppers and onions, undrained

1 pound raw medium shrimp in shells, peeled
1 tablespoon olive oil (extra-virgin preferred)
1 medium lime, quartered
¹/₄ cup fat-free or light sour cream
¹/₄ cup snipped fresh cilantro

Wearing gloves, discard the seeds and ribs of the chipotle pepper. Mash the pepper.

Heat a Dutch oven over medium-high heat. Remove from the heat and lightly spray with vegetable oil spray (being careful not to spray near a gas flame). Cook the onion and bell pepper for 4 minutes, or until the onion is soft, stirring frequently.

Stir in the broth, tomatoes, and chipotle pepper. Increase the heat to high and bring to a boil. Reduce the heat and simmer, covered, for 20 minutes, or until the bell pepper is tender.

Stir in the shrimp. Simmer, covered, for 5 minutes, or until the shrimp is opaque in the center, stirring frequently. Remove from the heat. Stir in the oil.

To serve, ladle into bowls. Squeeze the juice of a lime wedge over each serving. Top each with a dollop of sour cream. Sprinkle with the cilantro.

calories 201
protein 22 g
carbohydrates 18 g
  fiber 3 g
  sugars 11 g
cholesterol 168 mg
total fat 4.5 g
  saturated 0.5 g
  polyunsaturated 0.5 g
  monounsaturated 2.5 g
sodium 608 mg

dietary exchange
3 vegetable
3 lean meat

Chicken and Vegetable Soup

Serves 4

Although the amount of Parmesan used is small, the cheese makes this entrée soup complete.

1 pound boneless, skinless chicken breasts, all visible fat discarded	1/2 teaspoon dried thyme, crumbled
Vegetable oil spray	4 or 5 medium green onions (green and white parts), finely chopped (about 1/2 cup)
1 medium zucchini, thinly sliced	
1 medium red bell pepper, chopped	1/4 cup finely snipped fresh parsley
1 3/4 cups fat-free, low-sodium chicken broth, such as on page 45	1 tablespoon olive oil
	1/2 teaspoon salt
2 ounces dried no-yolk egg noodles	1/4 teaspoon pepper
1/2 cup frozen whole-kernel corn	2 tablespoons shredded or grated Parmesan cheese
1/2 cup water	

Cut the chicken into bite-size pieces.

Heat a Dutch oven over medium-high heat. Remove from the heat and lightly spray with vegetable oil spray (being careful not to spray near a gas flame). Cook the chicken for 2 to 3 minutes, or until no longer pink on the outside, stirring constantly. Transfer the chicken to a plate.

Lightly spray the Dutch oven with vegetable oil spray (no need to wipe clean first). Cook the zucchini and bell pepper for 2 minutes, or until just beginning to brown lightly on the edges, stirring constantly.

Stir in the broth, noodles, corn, water, and thyme. Increase the heat to high and bring to a boil. Reduce the heat and simmer, covered, for 10 minutes.

Stir in the chicken and any accumulated juices. Cook for 3 minutes, or until the chicken is no longer pink in the center. Remove from the heat.

Stir in the remaining ingredients except the Parmesan.

To serve, ladle into bowls. Sprinkle with the Parmesan.

calories 268
protein 31 g
carbohydrates 21 g
  fiber 4 g
  sugars 4 g
cholesterol 68 mg
total fat 6.0 g
  saturated 1.5 g
  polyunsaturated 1.0 g
  monounsaturated 3.0 g
sodium 436 mg

dietary exchange
1 starch
1 vegetable
3 lean meat

Chicken, Greens, and Potato Soup

Serves 4

Adding chicken and mustard greens or spinach turns this potato soup into a main dish. Leeks, dillweed, and thyme make a good thing even better.

3 medium potatoes, peeled and cut into ¹/₂-inch pieces (about 3 cups)

2¹/₂ cups fat-free, low-sodium chicken broth, such as on page 45

10 ounces boneless, skinless chicken breasts or turkey breasts
Vegetable oil spray

1 medium leek, sliced (white part only) (about 1 cup), or 9 medium green onions (green and white parts), sliced

4 medium garlic cloves, minced

12-ounce can fat-free evaporated milk

¹/₂ 10-ounce package frozen mustard greens or chopped spinach, thawed and drained

1 teaspoon snipped fresh dillweed or ¹/₄ teaspoon dried, crumbled

1 teaspoon chopped fresh thyme or ¹/₄ teaspoon dried, crumbled

¹/₄ teaspoon salt

¹/₈ teaspoon pepper

In a Dutch oven, bring the potatoes and broth to a boil over medium-high heat. Reduce the heat and simmer, covered, for 20 minutes, or until tender. Don't drain. Let cool slightly.

Meanwhile, cut the chicken into bite-size pieces.

In a food processor or blender, process the potato mixture until smooth.

Wipe the Dutch oven with paper towels. Lightly spray with vegetable oil spray (being careful not to spray near a gas flame). Cook the leek over medium heat for 5 minutes, stirring occasionally.

Stir in the garlic. Cook for 1 minute, stirring occasionally.

Stir in the chicken. Cook for 5 minutes, or until the chicken is tender and no longer pink in the center, stirring often.

Stir in the potato mixture and remaining ingredients. Cook over low heat for 2 to 3 minutes, or until heated through, stirring occasionally.

calories 263
protein 27 g
carbohydrates 36 g
fiber 4 g
sugars 12 g
cholesterol 41 mg
total fat 1.0 g
saturated 0.5 g
polyunsaturated 0.5 g
monounsaturated 0.5 g
sodium 336 mg

dietary exchange
1¹/₂ starch
1 skim milk
1 vegetable
2 very lean meat

Chile-Chicken Tortilla Soup

Serves 8

This is a terrific soup for using up leftover chicken or turkey.

2 fresh Anaheim chile peppers, diced
1 teaspoon acceptable vegetable oil
1/2 cup chopped onion
2 medium garlic cloves, minced
4 cups fat-free, low-sodium chicken broth, such as on page 45
15-ounce can no-salt-added pinto beans, rinsed and drained
14.5-ounce can no-salt-added whole tomatoes, crushed, undrained
1 cup cubed cooked skinless chicken or turkey breast, cooked without salt

1 teaspoon ground cumin
1 teaspoon chili powder
1/2 teaspoon dried oregano, crumbled
1/4 teaspoon salt
1/8 teaspoon pepper
Vegetable oil spray
8 6-inch corn tortillas
1/2 teaspoon chili powder
2 medium green onions (green and white parts), thinly sliced

Wearing gloves, discard the seeds and ribs of the chile peppers. Dice the peppers.

Heat a large nonstick saucepan over medium heat. Pour the oil into the pan and swirl to coat the bottom. Cook the onion and garlic for 2 to 3 minutes, or until the onion is soft, stirring occasionally.

Stir in the broth, beans, undrained tomatoes, chicken, chile peppers, cumin, 1 teaspoon chili powder, oregano, salt, and pepper. Bring to a boil over medium-high heat. Reduce the heat and simmer, covered, for 20 to 25 minutes, stirring occasionally.

Meanwhile, preheat the oven to 350°F. Lightly spray a baking sheet with vegetable oil spray.

Cut the tortillas in half, then into 1/4-inch strips. Place in one layer on the prepared baking sheet. Lightly spray with vegetable oil spray. Sprinkle with 1/2 teaspoon chili powder.

Bake for 10 minutes, or until crisp.

To serve, ladle the soup into bowls. Sprinkle with the tortilla strips and green onions.

calories 137
protein 10 g
carbohydrates 19 g
 fiber 4 g
 sugars 4 g
cholesterol 13 mg
total fat 2.5 g
 saturated 0.5 g
 polyunsaturated 0.5 g
 monounsaturated 1.0 g
sodium 168 mg

dietary exchange
1 starch
1 vegetable
1 very lean meat

Vietnamese Beef
and Rice Noodle Soup

Serves 6

Tender beef in a flavorful broth and a spike of lime just before serving characterize this classic Vietnamese soup. You can dress it up with bonus garnish ingredients, such as matchstick-size strips of fresh snow peas and shredded carrots.

4 cups water (if using rice noodles)
4 ounces dried rice noodles or dried angel hair pasta (whole-wheat or regular)
3 cups fat-free, no-salt-added beef broth, such as on page 44
2 cups fat-free, low-sodium chicken broth, such as on page 45
2 1/4-inch-thick slices unpeeled gingerroot

1 teaspoon grated lime zest
1/4 teaspoon sugar
1/8 teaspoon ground allspice
1 pound boneless sirloin steak, all visible fat discarded, cut into thin slices
1 teaspoon toasted sesame oil
1/3 cup loosely packed coarsely chopped fresh cilantro or mint
1 large lime, cut into 6 wedges

In a medium saucepan, bring the water to a boil over high heat. Stir in the noodles. Remove from the heat and let the noodles soak in the hot water for 3 to 4 minutes, or until tender. (If using the angel hair pasta, prepare using the package directions, omitting the salt and oil.) Drain in a colander. Set aside.

Rinse any noodle residue from the pan. Stir together the beef broth, chicken broth, gingerroot, lime zest, sugar, and allspice in the pan. Bring to a simmer over medium-high heat. Reduce the heat and simmer for 2 to 3 minutes, or until the broth is infused with ginger flavor, stirring occasionally.

Stir in the meat and sesame oil. Simmer for 2 to 4 minutes, or until the meat reaches the desired doneness. Discard the gingerroot slices.

To serve, spoon the noodles into large soup bowls. Ladle the broth mixture over the noodles. Garnish each serving with a scant 1 tablespoon cilantro and a squeeze of lime juice (or let guests squeeze the lime into their soup at the table).

calories 193
protein 19 g
carbohydrates 17 g
  fiber 0 g
  sugars 0 g
cholesterol 45 mg
total fat 5.0 g
  saturated 1.5 g
  polyunsaturated 0.5 g
  monounsaturated 2.0 g
sodium 76 mg

dietary exchange
1 starch
2½ lean meat

Beef Barley Soup

Serves 6

With crisp salad topped with Ranch-Style Herb Dressing (page 139) and Whole-Wheat Muffins (page 538), this filling soup makes a meal that will help drive away the winter chill.

1 pound bottom round steak
Vegetable oil spray
1 medium onion, chopped
4 cups fat-free, no-salt-added beef broth, such as on page 44
4 cups water
1/2 cup uncooked pearl barley
1 bay leaf
3/4 teaspoon salt

1/4 teaspoon pepper
2 medium potatoes, peeled and diced (about 3 cups)
3 medium carrots, sliced
2 medium ribs of celery, thickly sliced on the diagonal
2 teaspoons dried thyme, crumbled
1/2 teaspoon salt

Discard all the visible fat from the meat. Cut the meat into bite-size pieces.

Heat a Dutch oven over medium heat for 2 to 3 minutes. Remove from the heat. Lightly spray with vegetable oil spray (being careful not to spray near a gas flame). Cook the meat for 10 minutes, or until brown, stirring occasionally.

Stir in the onion. Cook for 2 to 3 minutes, or until soft, stirring occasionally.

Stir in the broth, water, barley, bay leaf, 3/4 teaspoon salt, and pepper. Increase the heat to high and bring to a boil. Reduce the heat and simmer, covered, for 1 hour, or until the meat is tender.

Stir in the remaining ingredients. Increase the heat to medium-high and bring to a boil. Reduce the heat and simmer, partially covered, for 20 to 25 minutes, or until the vegetables are tender.

Remove the bay leaf before serving the soup.

calories 244
protein 20 g
carbohydrates 32 g
  fiber 6 g
  sugars 4 g
cholesterol 45 mg
total fat 4.0 g
  saturated 1.5 g
  polyunsaturated 0.5 g
  monounsaturated 1.5 g
sodium 567 mg

dietary exchange
2 starch
2 very lean meat

salads and salad dressings

Hot and Spicy Watercress and Romaine Salad

Salad Greens with Oranges and Strawberries

Wilted Baby Spinach with Pear and Goat Cheese

Spinach-Chayote Salad with Orange Vinaigrette

Artichoke and Hearts of Palm Salad

Marinated Fresh Asparagus, Tomato, and Hearts of Palm Salad

Brussels Sprouts Caesar-Style

Marinated Green Beans

Tomato-Basil Salad with Balsamic Dressing

Roasted Beet and Orange Salad

Dijon-Marinated Vegetable Medley

Tossed Vegetables in Creamy Vinaigrette

Tangy Cucumbers

Asian Coleslaw

Confetti Coleslaw

Parsnip Salad with Jícama and Apple

Carrot Salad with Jícama and Pineapple

Berry Explosion Salad

Fresh Fruit Salad Romanoff

Winter Fruit Salad with Spinach and Gorgonzola

Cranberry Orange Salad

Herbed Tomato Orzo Salad

Parsley Potato Salad

Zesty Corn Relish

Tabbouleh

Wild Rice Salad with Cranberry Vinaigrette

Italian Rice Salad with Artichokes

Sixteen-Bean Salad

Marinated Pasta Salad

Greek Pasta Salad

Salmon and Orzo Salad

Fresh Salmon Salad

Salade Niçoise

Curried Tuna Salad

Picante Shrimp with Broccoli and Snow Peas

Mexican Shrimp Salad

Curried Chicken Salad

Chicken Vegetable Salad

Cajun Chicken Salad

Asian Chicken and Rice Salad

Island Chicken Salad with Fresh Mint

Turkey on a Bed of Sliced Tomatoes

Grilled Flank Steak Salad with Sweet-and-Sour Sesame Dressing

Warm Orzo Salad with Black Beans and Ham

Southwestern Pork Salad

Double Spinach Tortellini Salad

Marinated White Beans and Cucumber with Basil

Curried Rice and Bean Salad

Curried Quinoa Salad with Cranberries and Almonds

Couscous Salad

Zesty Tomato Dressing

Chunky Cucumber and Garlic Dressing

Ranch-Style Herb Dressing

Poppy Seed Dressing with Kiwifruit

Lemon Dressing

Hot and Spicy Watercress and Romaine Salad

Serves 4

This salad combines jícama, also called Mexican potato, with peppery watercress, crunchy romaine, and several staples of Asian cooking. The result? Greens with an attitude.

Dressing

1¹/₂ tablespoons low-salt soy sauce
1 tablespoon white wine vinegar
2¹/₂ teaspoons toasted sesame oil
¹/₂ tablespoon sugar
1 teaspoon chili oil

Salad

1 head romaine, torn into pieces
2 bunches watercress, stems discarded and leaves torn into pieces
6 medium radishes, thinly sliced
¹/₂ cup matchstick-size jícama strips
4 medium green onions (green and white parts), thinly sliced

In a small bowl, whisk together the dressing ingredients.

In a large bowl, toss the salad ingredients.

Pour the dressing over the salad. Toss lightly. Serve immediately.

calories 82
protein 3 g
carbohydrates 9 g
  fiber 4 g
  sugars 4 g
cholesterol 0 mg
total fat 4.5 g
  saturated 0.5 g
  polyunsaturated 2.0 g
  monounsaturated 2.0 g
sodium 174 mg

dietary exchange
2 vegetable
¹/₂ fat

Salad Greens with Oranges and Strawberries

Serves 4

When it's sizzling outside, this salad is a must—cool and refreshing!

Citrus Dressing
- 1/3 cup fresh orange juice
- 3 tablespoons sugar
- 2 tablespoons cider vinegar
- 1 1/2 tablespoons low-salt soy sauce
- 1/2 tablespoon grated orange zest
- 1 1/4 teaspoons ground cumin
- 1/4 teaspoon crushed red pepper flakes

Salad
- 6 cups mixed salad greens (spring greens preferred)
- 1 cup strawberries, quartered
- 2 medium oranges, sectioned
- 1/2 cup thinly sliced red onion
- 3 tablespoons slivered almonds, dry-roasted

In a small bowl, whisk together the dressing ingredients until the sugar dissolves.

In a large bowl, toss together the salad ingredients except the almonds.

To serve, pour the dressing over the salad. Toss gently to coat. Sprinkle with the almonds.

calories 135
protein 4 g
carbohydrates 26 g
  fiber 5 g
  sugars 19 g
cholesterol 0 mg
total fat 3.0 g
  saturated 0.5 g
  polyunsaturated 1.0 g
  monounsaturated 1.5 g
sodium 170 mg

dietary exchange
1 fruit
1 vegetable
1/2 fat

Wilted Baby Spinach with Pear and Goat Cheese

Serves 6

A warm, fruity dressing slightly wilts tender baby spinach, which is topped with pear slices and goat cheese. This dish is perfect for "fussy" entertaining without the fuss!

6 cups baby spinach leaves (4 to 6 ounces)
1/2 cup thinly sliced red onion

Vinaigrette
3 tablespoons dry white wine (regular or nonalcoholic)
2 tablespoons red wine vinegar
2 tablespoons all-fruit seedless raspberry spread

2 teaspoons sugar
2 teaspoons toasted sesame oil
1/4 teaspoon salt

❖

1 small pear, thinly sliced
1 1/2 ounces soft goat cheese, cut into small pieces

In a large salad bowl, toss together the spinach and onion.

In a small saucepan, stir together the vinaigrette ingredients. Bring to a boil over high heat, stirring constantly. Remove from the heat. Immediately pour over the spinach mixture. Toss gently to coat.

To serve, place the spinach mixture on plates (tongs work well for this). Arrange the pear slices and goat cheese on each.

calories 80
protein 2 g
carbohydrates 10 g
  fiber 2 g
  sugars 7 g
cholesterol 3 mg
total fat 3.0 g
  saturated 1.5 g
  polyunsaturated 0.5 g
  monounsaturated 1.0 g
sodium 147 mg

dietary exchange
1/2 fruit
1/2 fat

Cook's Tip on Goat Cheese

If the goat cheese is too soft to cut easily, put it in the freezer for a few minutes to chill slightly.

Spinach-Chayote Salad with Orange Vinaigrette

Serves 10

If you've wondered how to use the pale-green, pear-shaped chayote, this no-cook salad is the answer.

Dressing
- ½ teaspoon grated orange zest
- ½ cup fresh orange juice
- 3 tablespoons acceptable vegetable oil
- 2 tablespoons sugar
- 2 tablespoons white wine vinegar
- 1 tablespoon fresh lemon juice

Salad
- 1 chayote (about 8 ounces), peeled, seeded, and thinly sliced
- 6 to 8 ounces fresh spinach or other greens, stems discarded, torn into bite-size pieces
- 11-ounce can mandarin oranges in water or light syrup, drained
- 1 small cucumber, thinly sliced
- 2 tablespoons sliced green onion (white and green parts)

In a small bowl, whisk together the dressing ingredients until the sugar is dissolved.

Put the chayote in a large bowl. Stir in 2 tablespoons dressing. Let stand for 5 to 10 minutes.

To assemble, add the remaining salad ingredients to the chayote. Toss well. Pour the remaining dressing over the salad. Toss lightly.

Cook's Tip on Chayote

The chayote (chy-OH-tay or ky-OH-tay) is a mild-flavored summer squash, also called mirliton and christophene. A vegetable peeler works well to remove the skin except at the puckered end—you'll need a sharp knife for that. After peeling the squash, cut it in half lengthwise to remove its one seed. Use chayote raw in salads, cook it like other summer squash, or stuff and bake it like acorn squash.

calories 76
protein 1 g
carbohydrates 9 g
fiber 1 g
sugars 7 g
cholesterol 0 mg
total fat 4.5 g
saturated 0.5 g
polyunsaturated 1.5 g
monounsaturated 2.5 g
sodium 17 mg

dietary exchange
½ fruit
1 fat

Artichoke and
Hearts of Palm Salad

Serves 4

Here's a salad with lots of heart—tender hearts of artichoke, palm, and romaine—all gently tossed with fresh citrus juices and cilantro leaves.

1/2 14-ounce can quartered artichoke hearts, rinsed and drained
1/2 cup thinly sliced red onion
1/2 cup chopped red bell pepper
1/4 cup snipped fresh cilantro
1/4 cup fresh orange juice
2 tablespoons fresh lime juice

1 tablespoon fresh lemon juice
1 1/2 tablespoons sugar
2 teaspoons acceptable vegetable oil
1/8 teaspoon crushed red pepper flakes
1/2 14-ounce can hearts of palm
4 romaine heart leaves

In a medium bowl, stir together the artichokes, onion, bell pepper, cilantro, orange juice, lime juice, lemon juice, sugar, oil, and red pepper flakes, tossing gently to coat.

Rinse and drain the hearts of palm. Cut into 1/2-inch pieces. Gently stir into the artichoke mixture.

To serve, put a romaine leaf on each plate. Spoon 1/2 cup artichoke mixture on each serving.

Cook's Tip

If you have a favorite, you can use one whole can of artichokes or hearts of palm instead of half of each.

Cook's Tip on Romaine Hearts

Romaine hearts are the smaller, more delicately flavored leaves close to the center of the head. You can either buy a head of romaine and use the outer layers of leaves for tossed or Caesar salad or buy a bag of the hearts.

calories 86
protein 3 g
carbohydrates 15 g
 fiber 3 g
 sugars 8 g
cholesterol 0 mg
total fat 3.0 g
 saturated 0.0 g
 polyunsaturated 1.0 g
 monounsaturated 1.5 g
sodium 278 mg

dietary exchange
2 vegetable
1/2 other carbohydrate
1/2 fat

Marinated Fresh Asparagus, Tomato, and Hearts of Palm Salad

Serves 6

This colorful and inviting salad is popular at any dinner party or buffet.

8 ounces fresh asparagus, trimmed and cut into 2-inch pieces

1 pound Italian plum tomatoes, cut into ¼-inch slices

14-ounce can hearts of palm, rinsed and drained

¼ cup thinly sliced yellow onion

¼ cup red wine vinegar

2 tablespoons dry red wine (regular or nonalcoholic)

2 teaspoons sugar

¼ teaspoon pepper

Steam the asparagus for 3 minutes, or until tender-crisp. Immediately put the asparagus in a shallow glass baking dish.

To assemble the salad, place the tomatoes on the asparagus. Top with the hearts of palm, then with the onion.

In a small bowl, whisk together the remaining ingredients until the sugar is dissolved. Pour over the vegetables. Cover the dish and refrigerate for 30 minutes, stirring occasionally.

Cook's Tip

You can make this salad up to 24 hours in advance, but don't add the hearts of palm until about 30 minutes before serving. They become discolored from the wine if added sooner.

Cook's Tip on Hearts of Palm

Hearts of palm, which really do come from palm trees, taste somewhat like artichokes. Sometimes the outer stem of the larger pieces is a bit tough. Make a small slit in the tough layer and peel it off before using the tender part.

calories 54
protein 3 g
carbohydrates 10 g
  fiber 3 g
  sugars 5 g
cholesterol 0 mg
total fat 0.5 g
  saturated 0.0 g
  polyunsaturated 0.5 g
  monounsaturated 0.0 g
sodium 267 mg

dietary exchange
2 vegetable

Brussels Sprouts
Caesar-Style

Serves 4

Vitamin-rich brussels sprouts are teamed with a Caesar-style dressing, crispy homemade croutons, and juicy slices of Italian plum tomatoes. This twist on a classic might convince even the most finicky eaters to eat their brussels sprouts!

4 ounces fresh or frozen brussels sprouts (about 10)

1 slice whole-wheat bread, cut into ³/₄-inch cubes

Vegetable oil spray (olive oil spray preferred)

¹/₄ teaspoon garlic powder

Caesar-Style Dressing

1 tablespoon shredded or grated Parmesan cheese

¹/₂ tablespoon Dijon mustard

¹/₂ tablespoon fresh lemon juice

¹/₂ tablespoon low-sodium Worcestershire sauce

¹/₂ tablespoon white wine vinegar

1 teaspoon olive oil

¹/₂ teaspoon sugar

¹/₈ teaspoon pepper

❖

2 medium Italian plum tomatoes, thinly sliced

Preheat the oven to 350°F.

If using fresh brussels sprouts, trim the ends. Remove the outer leaves if necessary. Cut the sprouts in half lengthwise. Fill a medium saucepan half-full of water. Bring to a boil over high heat. Add the brussels sprouts. Reduce the heat and simmer for 10 to 12 minutes, or until tender. If using frozen brussels sprouts, prepare using the package directions, omitting the salt and margarine. Drain well. Let the cooked sprouts cool slightly. Cut in half vertically.

Meanwhile, put the bread cubes on a nonstick baking sheet. Lightly spray the tops with vegetable oil spray. Sprinkle with the garlic powder.

Bake for 5 minutes, or until golden brown. Put the baking sheet on a cooling rack.

In a small bowl, whisk together the dressing ingredients.

calories 58
protein 3 g
carbohydrates 9 g
  fiber 2 g
  sugars 3 g
cholesterol 1 mg
total fat 2.0 g
  saturated 0.5 g
  polyunsaturated 0.5 g
  monounsaturated 1.0 g
sodium 109 mg

dietary exchange
1¹/₂ vegetable
¹/₂ fat

To assemble, arrange the tomatoes in one layer on a platter. Arrange the brussels sprouts on top. Drizzle the dressing over the vegetables. Sprinkle with the toasted bread cubes.

Cook's Tip on Brussels Sprouts

Miniature versions of cabbage, brussels sprouts provide significant amounts of vitamin C and beta carotene and are a good vegetable source of protein. Choose sprouts that are heavy for their size and have compact heads without yellow outer leaves. For more even cooking, choose sprouts of about the same size. Select small brussels sprouts, or halve or quarter larger ones. Cook the sprouts quickly—overcooking makes them smell strong, lose vitamins, and become mushy. When the sprouts are just tender enough to be pierced easily with a skewer or the point of a knife when tested at the stem end, they are ready.

Marinated Green Beans

Serves 4

To stay in tune with today's busy schedules, we shortened the marinating time for this classic dish.

8 ounces fresh green beans, trimmed	¹/₄ teaspoon salt
¹/₄ cup thinly sliced red onion	¹/₄ teaspoon pepper
2 tablespoons cider vinegar	2 tablespoons finely snipped fresh parsley
2 tablespoons sugar	

In a medium saucepan, steam the beans for 6 minutes, or until just tender-crisp. Using a slotted spoon, immediately transfer the beans to a baking sheet. Arrange in a single layer to cool quickly, about 5 minutes.

Transfer the beans to a medium bowl. Add the remaining ingredients except the parsley. Toss gently to coat. Refrigerate for 30 minutes, tossing occasionally.

To serve, add the parsley. Toss gently.

Cook's Tip

This salad is best if eaten within 1 hour of combining the ingredients.

calories 47
protein 1 g
carbohydrates 12 g
  fiber 2 g
  sugars 8 g
cholesterol 0 mg
total fat 0.0 g
  saturated 0.0 g
  polyunsaturated 0.0 g
  monounsaturated 0.0 g
sodium 150 mg

dietary exchange
1 vegetable
¹/₂ other carbohydrate

Tomato-Basil Salad
with Balsamic Dressing

Serves 6

Serve as a complement to Greek Fish Fillets (page 186) or Spaghetti with Perfect Pesto (page 354).

4 medium tomatoes, sliced
2 tablespoons chopped fresh basil or 2 teaspoons dried, crumbled
2 tablespoons balsamic vinegar
1 tablespoon olive oil (extra-virgin preferred)

$1/2$ teaspoon sugar
$1/4$ teaspoon pepper
2 tablespoons shredded fat-free or part-skim mozzarella cheese
2 teaspoons shredded or grated Parmesan cheese

Arrange the tomato slices on a large, flat plate. Sprinkle with the basil.

In a small bowl, whisk together the vinegar, oil, sugar, and pepper. Pour over the tomatoes.

Sprinkle with the mozzarella and Parmesan. Cover and refrigerate until serving time.

Cook's Tip on Slicing Tomatoes

If you slice tomatoes vertically instead of horizontally, they'll lose less of their juice.

calories 50
protein 2 g
carbohydrates 6 g
  fiber 1 g
  sugars 4 g
cholesterol 1 mg
total fat 2.5 g
  saturated 0.5 g
  polyunsaturated 0.5 g
  monounsaturated 1.5 g
sodium 47 mg

dietary exchange
1 vegetable
$1/2$ fat

Roasted Beet
and Orange Salad

Serves 8

The sweet-savory flavor of roasted beets meets the tang of oranges and lime in this attractive salad.

Vegetable oil spray
2 pounds fresh beets

Dressing
3 tablespoons white wine vinegar
1 tablespoon acceptable vegetable oil
1 tablespoon fresh orange juice or water
2 teaspoons maple syrup or honey

1 teaspoon grated lime zest
❖
8 small lettuce leaves
11-ounce can mandarin oranges in water or light syrup
3 tablespoons slivered almonds, dry-roasted
Sprigs of fresh mint (optional)

Preheat the oven to 350°F. Lightly spray a shallow baking pan with vegetable oil spray.

Cut off all but 1 to 2 inches of the stems from the beets. Put the beets in a single layer on the baking pan. Lightly spray the beets with the vegetable oil spray.

Roast the beets for about 1 hour, or until they can be pierced easily with a knife. Let cool slightly, then remove the skins. Coarsely chop the beets (you should have about 3 cups). Put in a bowl with a lid.

In a small bowl, whisk together the dressing ingredients. Pour over the beets, tossing gently to coat. Cover and let marinate in the refrigerator for 2 to 24 hours.

To serve, place a lettuce leaf on each salad plate. Rinse and drain the oranges. Gently stir into the beet mixture. Using a slotted spoon, transfer the beet mixture onto the lettuce leaves. Sprinkle each serving with the almonds. Garnish with the mint.

Time-Saver

Fresh roasted beets give this salad a delicious concentrated beet flavor. However, if you don't have time to roast fresh beets, you can use two 16-ounce cans or jars of diced beets, rinsed and drained, instead.

calories 85
protein 2 g
carbohydrates 13 g
  fiber 3 g
  sugars 9 g
cholesterol 0 mg
total fat 3.0 g
  saturated 0.0 g
  polyunsaturated 1.0 g
  monounsaturated 2.0 g
sodium 62 mg

dietary exchange
½ fruit
1½ vegetable
½ fat

Dijon-Marinated Vegetable Medley

Serves 4

Picnic-perfect, this easy-to-make salad offers a rainbow of color to brighten any lunch or dinner.

Salad
- ³/₄ cup frozen whole-kernel corn
- ³/₄ cup frozen cut green beans
- ³/₄ cup no-salt-added canned black beans
- 2 cups chopped, seeded tomatoes
- ¹/₂ cup chopped red onion

Dressing
- ¹/₄ to ¹/₂ cup balsamic vinegar, plus water to make ³/₄ cup
- 2 tablespoons Dijon mustard
- 2 tablespoons chopped fresh basil or 2 teaspoons dried, crumbled
- 1 tablespoon olive oil (extra-virgin preferred)
- 1 teaspoon sugar
- 1 tablespoon chopped fresh thyme
- 2 medium garlic cloves, minced
- ¹/₄ teaspoon white pepper

❖

- 4 lettuce leaves

Rinse the corn, green beans, and black beans in a colander. Drain well. Put in a large bowl.

Stir in the tomatoes and onion.

In a medium bowl, whisk together the dressing ingredients. Pour over the salad and toss gently. Cover and refrigerate for 4 to 8 hours, stirring occasionally. Drain, discarding the dressing.

To serve, line plates with the lettuce. Spoon the vegetable mixture over the lettuce.

calories 104
protein 5 g
carbohydrates 22 g
 fiber 5 g
 sugars 7 g
cholesterol 0 mg
total fat 0.5 g
 saturated 0.0 g
 polyunsaturated 0.5 g
 monounsaturated 0.0 g
sodium 197 mg

dietary exchange
1 starch
1¹/₂ vegetable

Tossed Vegetables
in Creamy Vinaigrette

Serves 8

Take this dish on a picnic or enjoy it at home on a hot summer day.

Dressing
- 1/4 cup fat-free or light plain yogurt
- 2 tablespoons white wine vinegar
- 1 tablespoon Dijon mustard
- 1 teaspoon sugar
- 1 teaspoon acceptable vegetable oil
- 1/2 teaspoon coarsely ground pepper
- 1/4 teaspoon salt

❖

- 2 large carrots, sliced
- 8 ounces fresh green beans, trimmed and cut into 1 1/2-inch pieces
- 4 ounces medium button mushrooms, quartered
- 2 medium tomatoes, each cut into 8 wedges
- 3 to 4 medium green onions (green part only), thinly sliced

In a medium bowl, whisk together the dressing ingredients.

Steam the carrots and green beans for 3 to 4 minutes, or until tender-crisp. Plunge them into a bowl of ice water to stop the cooking. Drain, pat dry with paper towels, and put in a shallow glass bowl.

Add the mushrooms, tomatoes, and green onions.

Pour the dressing over all. Toss gently. Cover and refrigerate for 30 minutes to 4 hours.

calories 49
protein 2 g
carbohydrates 9 g
  fiber 3 g
  sugars 5 g
cholesterol 0 mg
total fat 1.0 g
  saturated 0.0 g
  polyunsaturated 0.5 g
  monounsaturated 0.5 g
sodium 133 mg

dietary exchange
2 vegetable

Tangy Cucumbers

Serves 4

These sweet-and-sour cucumbers are good with or without the sauce.

Marinade
- ¹/₂ cup cider vinegar
- 4 medium green onions (green and white parts), chopped
- ¹/₄ cup sugar
- ¹/₄ cup snipped fresh parsley
- ¹/₂ teaspoon pepper

❖

- 3 medium cucumbers
- 1 medium red onion, sliced (about 1 cup)

Yogurt Sauce (optional)
- ¹/₂ cup fat-free or light plain yogurt
- 1 teaspoon sugar
- 1 teaspoon fresh lemon juice
- ¹/₂ teaspoon dry mustard

In a large bowl, whisk together the marinade ingredients. Cover and refrigerate.

Peel the cucumbers if desired. Cut in half lengthwise and scrape out the seeds. Cut the cucumbers crosswise into thin slices.

Stir the cucumbers and red onion into the marinade. Cover and refrigerate for 1 to 2 hours.

If using the sauce, whisk together the ingredients in a small bowl.

Drain the vegetables and serve plain or mixed with the sauce.

Cook's Tip on Seeding Cucumbers

A grapefruit spoon is a good tool for seeding cucumbers. It's sharper than a regular spoon, so the job goes more quickly.

---

calories 93
protein 1 g
carbohydrates 23 g
  fiber 3 g
  sugars 17 g
cholesterol 0 mg
total fat 0.5 g
  saturated 0.0 g
  polyunsaturated 0.0 g
  monounsaturated 0.0 g
sodium 12 mg

dietary exchange
1½ vegetable
1 other carbohydrate

---

with yogurt sauce

calories 117
protein 3 g
carbohydrates 26 g
  fiber 3 g
  sugars 20 g
cholesterol 1 mg
total fat 0.5 g
  saturated 0.0 g
  polyunsaturated 0.0 g
  monounsaturated 0.0 g
sodium 35 mg

dietary exchange
2 vegetable
1 other carbohydrate

Asian Coleslaw

Serves 10

You can make this salad a day ahead, and there's no mayonnaise to worry about—perfect picnic or potluck fare.

Slaw
- 1 small head napa cabbage, thinly sliced (about 2 pounds)
- 2 medium carrots, coarsely grated
- 2 medium green onions (white and green parts), thinly sliced on diagonal
- 1 medium red bell pepper, thinly sliced

Dressing
- 2 tablespoons low-salt soy sauce
- 2 tablespoons plain rice vinegar
- 1 tablespoon finely grated peeled gingerroot or 1 teaspoon ground ginger
- 2 teaspoons toasted sesame oil or acceptable vegetable oil
- 1 medium garlic clove, finely chopped
- 1/4 teaspoon crushed red pepper flakes

In a large bowl, toss together the slaw ingredients.

In a small bowl, stir together the dressing ingredients. Pour over the slaw. Toss well. Serve at room temperature or cover and refrigerate until needed, tossing again just before serving.

Cook's Tip on Napa Cabbage

Napa, or Chinese, cabbage has long, crinkly, cream-colored leaves with pale green tips. It's delicious in salads, soups, and stir-fries. You can store napa cabbage in the vegetable bin of your refrigerator for up to five days.

Time-Saver

Use a food processor for the slicing and grating. The salad won't be as pretty, but the preparation will be fast.

calories 40
protein 2 g
carbohydrates 5 g
  fiber 2 g
  sugars 3 g
cholesterol 0 mg
total fat 1.0 g
  saturated 0.0 g
  polyunsaturated 0.5 g
  monounsaturated 0.5 g
sodium 97 mg

dietary exchange
1 vegetable

Confetti Coleslaw

Serves 12

Bursting with color and flavor, this tangy coleslaw is excellent with barbecued chicken or beef.

Dressing
- 1/3 cup white wine vinegar
- 1/4 cup sugar
- 1 tablespoon acceptable vegetable oil
- 1 tablespoon honey
- 1/4 teaspoon salt
- 1/4 teaspoon coarsely ground pepper
  ❖

- 3/4 pound green cabbage, shredded (about 4 cups)
- 1/2 pound red cabbage, shredded (about 3 cups)
- 4 medium green onions (green and white parts), thinly sliced
- 1/2 medium red bell pepper, diced
- 1/2 medium green bell pepper, diced

In a large bowl, whisk together the dressing ingredients.

Add the remaining ingredients. Toss well. Cover and refrigerate for at least 30 minutes.

calories 51
protein 1 g
carbohydrates 10 g
  fiber 1 g
  sugars 7 g
cholesterol 0 mg
total fat 1.5 g
  saturated 0.0 g
  polyunsaturated 0.5 g
  monounsaturated 0.5 g
sodium 58 mg

dietary exchange
1/2 other carbohydrate

Parsnip Salad with
Jícama and Apple

Serves 4

Jícama contributes a nutty flavor to this unusual slawlike salad.

1/3 cup fat-free or light sour cream
    Juice of 1/2 medium lemon
1 tablespoon snipped fresh parsley
3/4 teaspoon sugar
3 medium parsnips, peeled and shredded

1 cup matchstick-size jícama strips
1 tablespoon finely chopped onion
1 unpeeled medium apple (Delicious preferred)
1/3 cup golden raisins (optional)

---

calories 125
protein 3 g
carbohydrates 29 g
  fiber 7 g
  sugars 11 g
cholesterol 3 mg
total fat 0.5 g
  saturated 0.0 g
  polyunsaturated 0.0 g
  monounsaturated 0.0 g
sodium 27 mg

dietary exchange
1 starch
1 fruit

---

with raisins

calories 167
protein 3 g
carbohydrates 40 g
  fiber 7 g
  sugars 20 g
cholesterol 3 mg
total fat 0.5 g
  saturated 0.0 g
  polyunsaturated 0.0 g
  monounsaturated 0.0 g
sodium 29 mg

dietary exchange
1 starch
1 1/2 fruit

In a large bowl, whisk together the sour cream, lemon juice, parsley, and sugar.

Stir in the parsnips, jícama, and onion. Cover and refrigerate for 2 hours.

Just before serving, chop the apple. Stir the apple and raisins into the salad. Serve immediately.

Carrot Salad with
Jícama and Pineapple

Serves 6

A longtime favorite gets an update with the refreshing crunch of jícama.

Dressing
- ¼ cup fat-free or light plain yogurt
- 2 tablespoons fat-free or light mayonnaise dressing
- 2 tablespoons fresh lemon juice
- 1 teaspoon sugar

❖

- 2 cups shredded carrots
- ½ cup diced jícama
- ½ cup drained pineapple tidbits canned in their own juice
- ¼ cup golden raisins

In a large bowl, whisk together the dressing ingredients.

Stir in the remaining ingredients.

Cook's Tip on Jícama

A Mexican vegetable, jícama (HEE-kah-mah) looks like a fat turnip in a potato skin. Peeled and sliced or diced, it looks and tastes something like apple, although not so sweet, and something like potato, although not so bland, and even something like cucumber. Either raw or cooked, jícama adds a nice crunchy texture. For an easy appetizer, cut jícama into sticks and sprinkle with fresh lime juice and cayenne.

calories 64
protein 1 g
carbohydrates 15 g
  fiber 2 g
  sugars 12 g
cholesterol 0 mg
total fat 0.0 g
  saturated 0.0 g
  polyunsaturated 0.0 g
  monounsaturated 0.0 g
sodium 65 mg

dietary exchange
½ fruit
1 vegetable

Berry Explosion Salad

Serves 5

Big, bold flavors are infused in this salad featuring summer fruit. Every bite "explodes" with freshness: The dynamic combinations of the best seasonal fruit, toasted almonds, and fresh mint are brought to life by grains of light brown sugar, a hint of lemon zest, and a topping of vanilla-yogurt dressing enhanced with kiwifruit.

2 cups sliced fresh berries, such as strawberries, blueberries, raspberries, or blackberries

1/2 medium mango, cubed

4 fresh mint leaves

1 tablespoon light brown sugar

1/2 medium green kiwifruit, peeled and cut crosswise

1/2 cup fat-free or light vanilla yogurt

1/2 teaspoon grated lemon zest

1/8 cup sliced almonds, dry-roasted

Put the berries and mango in a large bowl.

Using a mortar and pestle, combine the mint and brown sugar until the mint is bruised and the flavor is released. Add to the berry mixture. Using two spoons, toss gently to coat.

Put the kiwifruit in a small bowl. Mash with a fork. Stir in the yogurt and lemon zest.

To serve, sprinkle the almonds on top of the salad. Spoon the vanilla-yogurt dressing on top or serve on the side.

calories 91
protein 2 g
carbohydrates 19 g
  fiber 3 g
  sugars 16 g
cholesterol 0 mg
total fat 1.5 g
  saturated 0.0 g
  polyunsaturated 0.5 g
  monounsaturated 1.0 g
sodium 21 mg

dietary exchange
1 fruit
1/2 fat

Cook's Tip

The mortar and pestle and the coarse grains of brown sugar help to "bruise" the mint, bringing out its full flavor. If you do not have a mortar and pestle, finely chop the mint and stir together with the brown sugar in a bowl, mashing the mixture together with the back of a spoon.

Fresh Fruit Salad Romanoff

Serves 4

Serve this delectable salad as a side dish or for dessert. It's especially good when served in chilled bowls.

Fruit Salad
- 2 medium fresh peaches, peeled and chopped
- 1 cup honeydew melon cubes or balls
- 1/2 cup fresh blueberries
- 1/2 cup sliced fresh strawberries
- 20 red grapes, halved

Topping
- 3 tablespoons fresh orange juice
- 2 tablespoons light brown sugar
- 1/2 cup fat-free or light sour cream or fat-free or light plain yogurt
- 2 tablespoons light brown sugar

In a large bowl, gently stir together the fruit salad ingredients.

In a small bowl, stir together the orange juice and 2 tablespoons brown sugar. Sprinkle over the fruit. Toss gently. Cover and refrigerate for about 2 hours, or until thoroughly chilled.

To serve, in a small bowl, stir together the sour cream and 2 tablespoons brown sugar. Spoon the fruit into glass dessert bowls. Top with the sour cream mixture.

calories 162
protein 3 g
carbohydrates 38 g
  fiber 3 g
  sugars 32 g
cholesterol 5 mg
total fat 0.5 g
  saturated 0.0 g
  polyunsaturated 0.0 g
  monounsaturated 0.0 g
sodium 37 mg

dietary exchange
1 1/2 fruit
1 other carbohydrate

Winter Fruit Salad with
Spinach and Gorgonzola

Serves 6

The beauty of this salad lies not only in the presentation but also in the fact that you can prepare the fruit mixture ahead, then assemble the salad quickly at the last minute. The juices of the cooked fruit mingle with the raspberry vinegar for a simple yet sensational dressing. (See photo on back cover.)

2 medium Granny Smith or Gala apples, thinly sliced

2 medium Bosc or Bartlett pears, thinly sliced

¼ cup unsweetened cranberry juice

2 tablespoons light brown sugar

4 cups baby spinach leaves

2 tablespoons crumbled Gorgonzola cheese

3 tablespoons walnut halves, dry-roasted

3 tablespoons raspberry vinegar or red wine vinegar

¼ teaspoon pepper

In a medium saucepan, bring the apples, pears, cranberry juice, and brown sugar to a simmer over medium-high heat. Reduce the heat and simmer, covered, for 5 to 6 minutes, or until the fruit is tender. Transfer the fruit with juices to a medium bowl and let cool for 5 to 10 minutes.

To assemble the salad, put the spinach in a large bowl or on a platter. Spoon the fruit mixture with juices over the spinach. Sprinkle with the cheese, walnuts, vinegar, and pepper.

calories 110
protein 2 g
carbohydrates 21 g
  fiber 3 g
  sugars 16 g
cholesterol 2 mg
total fat 3.0 g
  saturated 0.5 g
  polyunsaturated 1.5 g
  monounsaturated 0.5 g
sodium 50 mg

dietary exchange
1½ fruit
½ fat

Cranberry Orange Salad

Serves 8

Get out your prettiest glass serving plate, line it with dark green romaine, and serve this salad on it for a holiday buffet.

0.3-ounce box sugar-free or 3-ounce box regular lemon gelatin (small box)
1 cup boiling water
1 cup fresh orange juice, chilled

12- or 16-ounce container cranberry-orange relish
1 medium apple, chopped
1/4 cup chopped pecans, dry-roasted
Vegetable oil spray

Pour the gelatin into a medium bowl. Pour in the water. Stir constantly until the gelatin is dissolved.

Stir in the orange juice. Cover and refrigerate for 30 minutes, or until almost jelled.

In a small bowl, stir together the remaining ingredients except the vegetable oil spray. Fold into the gelatin mixture.

Lightly spray a 1-quart mold with vegetable oil spray. Pour the mixture into the mold. Cover and refrigerate for 1 hour, or until firm.

Cook's Tip on Unmolding Gelatin

Insert a spatula or knife between the mold and the gelatin in several places. Set the mold in hot water up to 1/4 inch from the top. Leave the mold in the water for only a couple of seconds, remove the mold from the water, and dry it. Rinse a serving plate in cold water; dry the plate. Center the plate over the mold and invert both together. The salad should drop out. If it doesn't, shake the mold. Still no luck? Repeat the process. Whatever you do, don't leave the mold in the hot water for long, or your salad may start to melt.

calories 129
protein 1 g
carbohydrates 26 g
  fiber 1 g
  sugars 24 g
cholesterol 0 mg
total fat 3.0 g
  saturated 0.5 g
  polyunsaturated 1.0 g
  monounsaturated 1.5 g
sodium 40 mg

dietary exchange
1 fruit
1/2 other carbohydrate
1/2 fat

Herbed Tomato Orzo Salad

Serves 4

Flecks of red, purple, black, and green add visual appeal to this fresh-tasting salad.

2 ounces dried orzo
1 medium tomato, seeded, diced
1/3 cup finely chopped red onion
8 kalamata olives, finely chopped
1/2 tablespoon cider vinegar
1/2 medium garlic clove, minced

1 teaspoon dried basil, crumbled
1/2 teaspoon dried oregano, crumbled
1 ounce fat-free or low-fat feta cheese, crumbled
1/8 teaspoon salt

Prepare the orzo using the package directions, omitting the salt and oil. Drain in a colander. Run it under cold water until completely cooled. Drain well.

Meanwhile, in a medium bowl, stir together the tomato, onion, olives, vinegar, garlic, basil, and oregano.

Add the orzo to the tomato mixture. Toss gently to blend.

Add the feta and salt. Toss gently.

Cook's Tip

Be sure to remove the seeds and liquid center before chopping the tomato so they don't water down the intense flavors of this salad.

calories 95
protein 4 g
carbohydrates 15 g
  fiber 1 g
  sugars 3 g
cholesterol 0 mg
total fat 2.5 g
  saturated 0.5 g
  polyunsaturated 0.5 g
  monounsaturated 1.5 g
sodium 309 mg

dietary exchange
1 starch

Parsley Potato Salad

Serves 6

Great flavor, crunch, and color—this salad has them all!

2 cups diced cooked red potatoes (about 3 medium)
1 medium rib of celery
2 tablespoons snipped fresh parsley
1 tablespoon chopped onion
1 tablespoon chopped red bell pepper
$1/2$ tablespoon cider vinegar
1 teaspoon dry mustard

$1/2$ teaspoon celery seeds
$1/4$ teaspoon salt
$1/8$ teaspoon pepper
$1/4$ cup fat-free or light mayonnaise dressing
Pimiento or red bell pepper strips (optional)

In a large bowl, lightly toss together the potatoes, celery, parsley, onion, bell pepper, vinegar, mustard, celery seeds, salt, and pepper.

Stir in the mayonnaise. Cover and refrigerate for several hours.

To serve, garnish with the pimiento.

Mustard Potato Salad
Reduce the salt to $1/8$ teaspoon, reduce the mayonnaise to 2 tablespoons, and add 2 tablespoons prepared mustard.

calories 93
protein 2 g
carbohydrates 19 g
  fiber 2 g
  sugars 3 g
cholesterol 0 mg
total fat 0.5 g
  saturated 0.0 g
  polyunsaturated 0.0 g
  monounsaturated 0.0 g
sodium 194 mg

dietary exchange
1½ starch

mustard potato salad

calories 92
protein 3 g
carbohydrates 19 g
  fiber 2 g
  sugars 2 g
cholesterol 0 mg
total fat 0.5 g
  saturated 0.0 g
  polyunsaturated 0.0 g
  monounsaturated 0.0 g
sodium 160 mg

dietary exchange
1½ starch

Zesty Corn Relish

Serve this corn and bell pepper combination on leaf lettuce as a salad, or use small portions as a condiment with ham or turkey. Although cilantro and coriander usually are not interchangeable, you can use either in this dish.

1 tablespoon olive oil

3 cups fresh corn kernels (6 large ears) or 16- or 20-ounce package frozen whole-kernel corn, thawed

1 medium red bell pepper, finely diced

1/4 cup minced red onion

1/2 fresh jalapeño pepper, seeds and ribs discarded, minced

2 tablespoons dry white wine (regular or nonalcoholic) (optional)

2 teaspoons fresh lime juice

6 medium fresh basil leaves, finely chopped, or 1/2 teaspoon dried, crumbled

3 or 4 sprigs of cilantro, coarsely chopped, or 1/8 teaspoon dried coriander seeds, crushed

3 sprigs of fresh thyme, stems removed, or 1/2 to 1 teaspoon dried, crumbled

1 small garlic clove, crushed

1/4 teaspoon salt

1/4 teaspoon pepper, or to taste

Heat a large skillet over medium heat. Pour the oil into the skillet and swirl to coat the bottom. Cook the corn, bell pepper, onion, and jalapeño for 2 to 3 minutes, or until tender. Remove the skillet from the heat and let the mixture cool for about 10 minutes.

Stir in the remaining ingredients. Transfer to a glass dish. Cover and refrigerate for 30 minutes to 2 days.

calories 73
protein 2 g
carbohydrates 13 g
 fiber 2 g
 sugars 4 g
cholesterol 0 mg
total fat 2.5 g
 saturated 0.5 g
 polyunsaturated 0.5 g
 monounsaturated 1.5 g
sodium 82 mg

dietary exchange
1 starch

Tabbouleh

Serves 8

This very refreshing summer salad is good with lamb or grilled Turkey Fillets with Fresh Herbs (page 264).

Salad
- ½ cup fine bulgur
- 2 bunches of fresh parsley
- 1 medium red bell pepper, diced
- 1 medium cucumber, peeled, seeded, and cubed
- 4 medium green onions (green and white parts), finely chopped
- ⅓ cup chopped fresh mint

- ½ teaspoon pepper
- ¼ teaspoon salt
- ❖
- Juice of 2 medium lemons
- 2 tablespoons olive oil (extra-virgin preferred)
- 1 to 2 medium garlic cloves, crushed or minced
- 18 cherry tomatoes

Put the bulgur in a large bowl. Add hot water to cover. Let stand for about 30 minutes. Drain and squeeze dry. Return to the bowl and fluff with a fork.

Meanwhile, snip enough parsley leaves to measure 2 cups. Stir the parsley and remaining salad ingredients into the prepared bulgur.

In a small bowl, whisk together the lemon juice, olive oil, and garlic. Pour over the salad and toss. Cover and refrigerate for 3 to 4 hours.

To serve, quarter the tomatoes. Stir into the salad.

Cook's Tip on Bulgur

Bulgur, also known as bulgur wheat or wheat bulgur, consists of cooked wheat kernels that are dried and coarsely broken or ground into grain. It lends a delicious nutty flavor and texture to food.

calories 89
protein 3 g
carbohydrates 13 g
  fiber 4 g
  sugars 2 g
cholesterol 0 mg
total fat 4.0 g
  saturated 0.5 g
  polyunsaturated 0.5 g
  monounsaturated 2.5 g
sodium 90 mg

dietary exchange
½ starch
1 vegetable
½ fat

Wild Rice Salad with Cranberry Vinaigrette

Serves 4

Wild rice, actually a long-grain marsh grass, is the primary ingredient in this elegant salad.

1 cup cooked wild rice	1/4 cup thinly sliced celery
1/3 cup chopped dried mixed fruit	1/4 cup sweetened cranberry juice
2 tablespoons pecan chips, dry-roasted	2 teaspoons red wine vinegar
3 tablespoons finely chopped red onion	1/2 teaspoon grated peeled gingerroot
	1/2 teaspoon toasted sesame oil

In a medium bowl, gently toss the ingredients.

Time-Saver

If you don't want to cook the wild rice yourself, you can buy precooked wild rice at health food stores.

calories 117
protein 2 g
carbohydrates 21 g
  fiber 3 g
  sugars 8 g
cholesterol 0 mg
total fat 3.0 g
  saturated 0.5 g
  polyunsaturated 1.0 g
  monounsaturated 1.5 g
sodium 29 mg

dietary exchange
1 fruit
1/2 starch
1/2 fat

Italian Rice Salad with Artichokes

Serves 6

This salad reflects the red, white, and green of the Italian flag.

Salad

- 8 ounces uncooked arborio rice
- 9-ounce package frozen artichoke hearts, thawed
- 4 medium Italian plum tomatoes
- 1 cup frozen green peas, thawed (about 5 ounces)
- 1/4 cup diced red onion

Dressing

- 2 tablespoons shredded or grated Parmesan cheese
- 2 tablespoons fresh lemon juice
- 1 tablespoon chopped fresh basil or 1 teaspoon dried, crumbled
- 1 tablespoon olive oil (extra-virgin preferred)
- 1 medium garlic clove, minced
- 1/2 teaspoon sugar
- 1/4 teaspoon salt
- 1/8 teaspoon pepper

Prepare the rice using the package directions, omitting the salt and margarine. Let cool to room temperature.

Meanwhile, drain the artichoke hearts. Blot dry with paper towels. Cut each piece in half. Put in a large bowl.

Cut the tomatoes in half lengthwise, then into thin slices. Stir the tomatoes, cooled rice, peas, and onion into the artichokes.

In a food processor or blender, process the dressing ingredients for 20 seconds. Pour over the salad. Using a rubber scraper, stir gently. Cover and refrigerate for several hours before serving.

Cook's Tip on Arborio Rice

Arborio rice absorbs more flavor than other rice. It is also what gives this dish its creaminess. Look for it in supermarkets, Italian markets, and health food stores.

calories 220
protein 6 g
carbohydrates 41 g
  fiber 6 g
  sugars 4 g
cholesterol 1 mg
total fat 3.0 g
  saturated 0.5 g
  polyunsaturated 0.5 g
  monounsaturated 2.0 g
sodium 179 mg

dietary exchange
2 1/2 starch
1 vegetable

Sixteen-Bean Salad

Serves 4

Here's one way to eat your soup with a fork! Using soup mix provides real variety with a minimum of effort.

1 cup 16-bean soup mix, sorted for stones and shriveled beans and rinsed

1/2 cup peeled (if desired), seeded, and chopped tomato

1/3 medium red bell pepper, chopped

1/3 medium yellow bell pepper, chopped

3 medium green onions (green and white parts), thinly sliced

1/4 cup fat-free, low-sodium salsa, such as Salsa Cruda (page 502)

1 tablespoon snipped fresh cilantro

1/8 teaspoon pepper

4 cups torn mixed salad greens

Discard the seasoning packet from the soup mix. Cook the beans until just tender using the package directions, omitting the salt. Drain and let cool for about 30 minutes, or until room temperature.

In a large bowl, gently toss together the beans and the remaining ingredients except the salad greens. Cover and refrigerate for 4 hours, stirring occasionally.

To serve, place 1 cup salad greens on each plate. Spoon the bean mixture over the salad greens.

Cook's Tip

For a really quick lunch, wrap some of the leftovers in a fat-free flour tortilla (look for the lowest sodium available) and zap it in the microwave until it is warm.

calories 202
protein 14 g
carbohydrates 37 g
  fiber 12 g
  sugars 5 g
cholesterol 0 mg
total fat 1.0 g
  saturated 0.0 g
  polyunsaturated 0.5 g
  monounsaturated 0.5 g
sodium 96 mg

dietary exchange
2 starch
1 1/2 vegetable
1 1/2 very lean meat

Marinated Pasta Salad

Serves 8

This is a wonderful make-ahead dish to take to potluck gatherings.

8 ounces dried pasta, such as rotini, farfalle, or ziti

8 ounces fresh asparagus (6 to 10 spears) or 10-ounce package frozen asparagus, thawed

1/2 medium red bell pepper, very thinly sliced

1/2 cup very thinly sliced zucchini

1/2 cup finely chopped red onion

1 medium rib of celery, thinly sliced

1/4 cup fat-free or low-fat Italian salad dressing

3 tablespoons white wine vinegar

2 tablespoons finely snipped fresh parsley

1/4 teaspoon salt

1/4 teaspoon dried bouquet garni or dried thyme, crumbled

1/8 teaspoon coarsely ground pepper

Crushed red pepper flakes or red hot-pepper sauce, to taste

Prepare the pasta using the package directions, omitting the salt and oil. Drain, rinse, and let cool. Transfer to a large bowl.

Meanwhile, trim the asparagus and cut into 1-inch pieces. Steam for 5 minutes, then plunge into a bowl of ice water to stop the cooking. Drain.

Add the asparagus and remaining ingredients to the pasta. Toss well. Cover and refrigerate for 2 to 8 hours.

calories 127
protein 5 g
carbohydrates 26 g
  fiber 2 g
  sugars 3 g
cholesterol 0 mg
total fat 0.5 g
  saturated 0.0 g
  polyunsaturated 0.0 g
  monounsaturated 0.0 g
sodium 190 mg

dietary exchange
1 1/2 starch
1 vegetable

Greek Pasta Salad

Serves 8

Enhanced with feta cheese and fresh dillweed, this winning pasta-vegetable combination is sure to bring compliments.

Salad

- 12 ounces dried tricolor rotini
- 1¼ cups frozen baby green peas, thawed
- 1 medium red bell pepper, diced
- ⅔ cup unpeeled seeded and diced cucumber
- 4 medium green onions (green and white parts), thinly sliced
- 4 ounces fat-free feta cheese, crumbled

Dressing

- ½ cup fat-fat or low-fat cottage cheese
- ½ cup fat-free or light plain yogurt
- ¼ cup fat-free or light mayonnaise dressing
- ¼ cup thinly sliced green onions (green part only)
- 1 to 2 tablespoons finely snipped fresh dillweed
- ¼ teaspoon pepper

Prepare the pasta using the package directions, omitting the salt and oil. Drain. Transfer to a large bowl.

Stir in the remaining salad ingredients. Set aside.

In a food processor or blender, process the cottage cheese, yogurt, mayonnaise, and ¼ cup green onions until smooth.

Stir in the dillweed and pepper. Stir into the pasta mixture. Cover and refrigerate for about 30 minutes, or until chilled.

Cook's Tip on Dillweed

Formerly used in charms against witchcraft, dillweed now leads a less exotic existence. It's used primarily to flavor pickles, sauces, and soups. Because its leaves are feathery, fragrant dillweed also makes a pretty garnish.

calories 223
protein 13 g
carbohydrates 41 g
  fiber 3 g
  sugars 7 g
cholesterol 1 mg
total fat 1.0 g
  saturated 0.0 g
  polyunsaturated 0.5 g
  monounsaturated 0.0 g
sodium 373 mg

dietary exchange
2½ starch
1 vegetable
½ very lean meat

Salmon and Orzo Salad

Serves 4

Made with petite orzo pasta, crunchy cucumbers, healthful salmon, and a burst of lemon, this dish gives you an enjoyable variation of tuna-pasta salad. Serve it with sliced kiwifruit on the side.

1 cup dried orzo
7.1-ounce vacuum-sealed pouch pink salmon, flaked
¹/₄ medium English cucumber or ¹/₂ medium standard cucumber, diced
2 medium green onions (green and white parts), thinly sliced

¹/₂ cup fat-free or light mayonnaise dressing
1 teaspoon grated lemon zest
2 tablespoons fresh lemon juice
1 teaspoon dried dillweed, crumbled
¹/₂ teaspoon lemon pepper, or ¹/₄ teaspoon black pepper and ¹/₂ teaspoon grated lemon zest

Prepare the orzo using the package directions, omitting the salt and oil. Drain in a colander and rinse with cold water to cool. Transfer to a medium bowl. Let cool for 10 minutes.

Gently stir in the remaining ingredients. Serve immediately or cover and refrigerate for up to three days.

calories 254
protein 15 g
carbohydrates 39 g
  fiber 2 g
  sugars 7 g
cholesterol 18 mg
total fat 2.5 g
  saturated 1.0 g
  polyunsaturated 0.5 g
  monounsaturated 0.0 g
sodium 508 mg

dietary exchange
2¹/₂ starch
1¹/₂ very lean meat

Fresh Salmon Salad

Serves 6

When served on dark, crisp greens, this salad is especially attractive. You can grill the salmon instead of baking it if you prefer.

Vegetable oil spray (olive oil flavor preferred)

1½ pounds salmon steaks, ¾ to 1 inch thick

2 tablespoons fresh lemon juice

½ teaspoon dried thyme, crumbled

¼ teaspoon black pepper, or to taste

2 medium ribs of celery, diced

½ medium red bell pepper, diced

½ cup finely diced onion

½ cup fat-free or light mayonnaise dressing

10 small black olives, thinly sliced (optional)

Juice of 1 medium lemon

2 tablespoons finely snipped fresh parsley

¼ teaspoon red hot-pepper sauce, or to taste

Preheat the oven to 450°F. Lightly spray an ovenproof 13 × 9 × 2-inch glass baking dish with vegetable oil spray.

Rinse the salmon and pat dry with paper towels. Pour 2 tablespoons lemon juice over the salmon. Lightly spray one side of the salmon with vegetable oil spray. Sprinkle with the thyme and black pepper. Put the salmon in the baking dish.

Bake for 10 minutes, or until the salmon flakes easily when tested with a fork.

Carefully remove the skin and bones from the salmon. Put the salmon in a medium bowl and flake with a fork.

Stir in the remaining ingredients. Cover and refrigerate for several hours before serving.

calories 173
protein 23 g
carbohydrates 7 g
  fiber 1 g
  sugars 5 g
cholesterol 59 mg
total fat 4.5 g
  saturated 0.5 g
  polyunsaturated 1.5 g
  monounsaturated 1.5 g
sodium 304 mg

dietary exchange
1 vegetable
3 lean meat

Salade Niçoise

Serves 12

Toss this traditional French salad in our flavorful vinaigrette. With crusty French bread on the side and fresh fruit salad, you have a splendid meal.

Dressing

- ¼ cup white wine vinegar
- 2 tablespoons Dijon mustard
- 2 tablespoons fat-free, low-sodium chicken broth, such as on page 45
- 1 tablespoon olive oil
- 2 teaspoons chopped fresh thyme or 1 teaspoon dried, crumbled
- 3 medium garlic cloves, minced
- 1 teaspoon sugar
- ½ teaspoon pepper, or to taste

Salad

- 2 pounds fresh green beans, trimmed and cut into 1-inch pieces
- 3 6-ounce cans albacore tuna, packed in distilled or spring water, rinsed, drained, and flaked
- 5 medium red potatoes, cooked and sliced (about 5 cups)
- 4 medium ribs of celery, sliced
- 1 pint cherry tomatoes
- 1 large red onion, sliced and separated into rings
- 1 medium green bell pepper, cut into rings
- 1 medium red bell pepper, cut into rings
- 10 large black olives, sliced
- 10 large stuffed green olives, sliced
- ⅓ cup snipped fresh parsley
- 2 medium green onions (green and white parts), finely chopped
- 2 tablespoons chopped fresh basil or 2 teaspoons dried, crumbled

In a small bowl, whisk together the dressing ingredients. Cover and refrigerate.

Steam the green beans for 6 to 8 minutes, or until tender-crisp. Put in a large bowl.

Stir the remaining salad ingredients into the beans.

Pour the dressing on the salad and toss.

calories 192
protein 14 g
carbohydrates 26 g
  fiber 6 g
  sugars 6 g
cholesterol 18 mg
total fat 4.0 g
  saturated 0.5 g
  polyunsaturated 1.0 g
  monounsaturated 2.0 g
sodium 255 mg

dietary exchange
1 starch
2 vegetable
1½ lean meat

Curried Tuna Salad

Serves 4

A quick lunch for four, this salad features a mild tuna mixture seasoned with a sweet curry mayonnaise and crunchy celery, water chestnuts, and red bell peppers. Clusters of seedless red grapes make an attractive accompaniment.

Tuna Salad

- 1/2 cup plus 2 tablespoons fat-free or light mayonnaise dressing
- 1 tablespoon sugar (plus 1 teaspoon if using light mayonnaise)
- 2 teaspoons curry powder
- 1/8 teaspoon cayenne
- 2 6-ounce cans albacore tuna, packed in distilled or spring water, rinsed, drained, and flaked

- 8-ounce can sliced water chestnuts, rinsed and drained
- 1 medium red bell pepper, chopped
- 1 1/2 medium ribs of celery, chopped

  ❖

- 8 red leaf lettuce leaves
- 4 slices pineapple, fresh or canned in their own juice
- 2 tablespoons pecan pieces, dry-roasted

In a medium bowl, whisk together the mayonnaise, sugar, curry powder, and cayenne.

Stir in the remaining tuna salad ingredients.

To serve, line the plates with lettuce. Place the pineapple in the center of the plates. Top each pineapple slice with a scoop of tuna salad. Sprinkle with the pecans.

calories 253
protein 22 g
carbohydrates 26 g
  fiber 5 g
  sugars 17 g
cholesterol 36 mg
total fat 5.5 g
  saturated 1.0 g
  polyunsaturated 2.0 g
  monounsaturated 2.0 g
sodium 426 mg

dietary exchange
1/2 fruit
1/2 other carbohydrate
1 1/2 vegetable
3 lean meat

Picante Shrimp with Broccoli and Snow Peas

Serves 4

Sit back and enjoy the rave reviews when you serve this dish at your next luncheon.

2 cups broccoli florets

1 cup fresh snow peas, trimmed and cut crosswise in half

12 ounces frozen cooked peeled shrimp, thawed

1/2 cup red bell pepper strips

Dressing

1/4 cup picante sauce

1/4 cup fat-free or low-fat Italian salad dressing

3/4 teaspoon grated peeled gingerroot

3/4 teaspoon low-salt soy sauce

❖

4 romaine leaves

1/2 cup cucumber sticks

Steam the broccoli for 2 minutes. Add the snow peas and steam for 5 minutes, or until the vegetables are tender-crisp. Place in a colander and rinse with cold water to stop the cooking process. Transfer to a large bowl.

Stir the shrimp and bell pepper strips into the broccoli and snow peas.

In a small bowl, whisk together the dressing ingredients. Pour over the shrimp mixture. Cover and refrigerate for 2 hours, stirring occasionally.

To serve, line salad plates with the romaine. Stir the cucumber strips into the salad. Spoon onto the plates.

Cook's Tip on Steaming Vegetables

If you don't own a vegetable steamer, you can use a spaghetti cooker or set a metal colander or sieve in a saucepan. The boiling water shouldn't touch the vegetables.

calories 127
protein 20 g
carbohydrates 8 g
 fiber 2 g
 sugars 3 g
cholesterol 166 mg
total fat 1.5 g
 saturated 0.5 g
 polyunsaturated 0.5 g
 monounsaturated 0.0 g
sodium 572 mg

dietary exchange
1 1/2 vegetable
3 very lean meat

Mexican Shrimp Salad

Serves 6

Spicy shrimp and a bed of jícama and raw spinach are the stars of this salad. Try it with chilled Cucumber Watercress Soup (page 52).

2¹/₂ quarts water

1¹/₂ pounds raw medium shrimp in shells

2 teaspoons liquid crab-and-shrimp boil

4 medium green onions (green and white parts), sliced

¹/₂ cup fat-free or light mayonnaise dressing

¹/₃ cup fat-free or light plain yogurt

2 tablespoons chili sauce

1 tablespoon chopped fresh cilantro (optional)

2 teaspoons prepared white horseradish

1 teaspoon chili powder

¹/₂ teaspoon grated lime zest
Red hot-pepper sauce to taste

3 cups coarsely chopped fresh spinach leaves

¹/₂ medium jícama (about 12 ounces)

Pour the water into a large saucepan and bring to a boil over high heat. Add the shrimp and crab-and-shrimp boil. Return to a boil, remove from the heat, and set aside for 5 minutes, or until the shrimp turn pink. Drain in a colander and run under cool water. Peel, devein, and cut the shrimp in half lengthwise (to retain the C shape).

In a large bowl, stir together the green onions, mayonnaise, yogurt, chili sauce, cilantro, horseradish, chili powder, lime zest, and hot-pepper sauce.

Stir in the shrimp. Cover and refrigerate for at least 2 hours.

To serve, put the spinach and jícama in a large bowl. Toss. Arrange the mixture on plates. Top with the shrimp mixture.

calories 148
protein 20 g
carbohydrates 12 g
 fiber 4 g
 sugars 7 g
cholesterol 166 mg
total fat 1.0 g
 saturated 0.5 g
 polyunsaturated 0.5 g
 monounsaturated 0.0 g
sodium 553 mg

dietary exchange
1¹/₂ vegetable
¹/₂ other carbohydrate
3 very lean meat

Curried Chicken Salad

Serves 6

Chill this salad and serve it on a bed of lettuce, or heat it gently and serve it over cooked rice or noodles.

Dressing

- 1/2 cup fat-free or light mayonnaise dressing
- 1 tablespoon fresh lemon juice
- 2 teaspoons plain rice vinegar or white vinegar
- 1/2 teaspoon curry powder
- 1/4 teaspoon salt
- 1/8 teaspoon black pepper
- 1/8 teaspoon cayenne

Chicken Salad

- 4 cups cubed cooked skinless chicken breasts, cooked without salt, all visible fat discarded
- 4 medium ribs of celery, chopped
- 8 thin strips green bell pepper (optional)

In a large bowl, whisk together the dressing ingredients.

Stir in the chicken and celery. Cover and refrigerate for at least 30 minutes.

To serve, garnish with the bell pepper.

Cook's Tip on Rice Vinegar

Used in Chinese and Japanese cooking, rice vinegar is slightly milder than most North American vinegars. Unless a recipe specifies black rice vinegar, use white or red rice vinegar. The black has a distinctive, heavier flavor; the red and the white are interchangeable. We call for plain rice vinegar because the seasoned varieties are high in sodium.

calories 180
protein 29 g
carbohydrates 4 g
  fiber 1 g
  sugars 3 g
cholesterol 79 mg
total fat 3.5 g
  saturated 1.0 g
  polyunsaturated 0.5 g
  monounsaturated 1.0 g
sodium 356 mg

dietary exchange
4 very lean meat

Chicken Vegetable Salad

Serves 6

Serve this crunchy mixture over salad greens or in pita bread.

2 cups diced cooked skinless chicken or turkey breast, cooked without salt, all visible fat discarded

1/2 medium cucumber, peeled and diced

1 medium rib of celery, diced

1/2 cup sliced water chestnuts, rinsed and drained

1/4 medium green bell pepper, diced

1/4 cup chopped pimiento

2 medium green onions (green and white parts), sliced

1/4 cup fat-free or light mayonnaise dressing

2 tablespoons capers, rinsed and drained

1/4 teaspoon paprika

---

calories 104
protein 15 g
carbohydrates 5 g
  fiber 2 g
  sugars 2 g
cholesterol 40 mg
total fat 2.0 g
  saturated 0.5 g
  polyunsaturated 0.5 g
  monounsaturated 0.5 g
sodium 209 mg

dietary exchange
1 vegetable
2 very lean meat

---

tuna vegetable salad

calories 100
protein 14 g
carbohydrates 5 g
  fiber 2 g
  sugars 2 g
cholesterol 24 mg
total fat 2.0 g
  saturated 0.5 g
  polyunsaturated 0.5 g
  monounsaturated 0.5 g
sodium 228 mg

dietary exchange
1 vegetable
2 very lean meat

In a large bowl, stir together the chicken, cucumber, celery, water chestnuts, bell pepper, pimiento, green onions, and mayonnaise.

Sprinkle with the capers and paprika.

Tuna Vegetable Salad
Substitute two 6-ounce cans albacore tuna, packed in distilled or spring water, rinsed, drained, and flaked, for the chicken.

Cajun Chicken Salad

Serves 5

Need a little spice in your life? Try this bed of mixed greens piled high with roasted red bell peppers, mushrooms, and strips of Triple-Pepper Chicken.

Dressing
- 1/4 cup plus 2 tablespoons cider vinegar
- 1 tablespoon olive oil (extra-virgin preferred)
- 3 medium garlic cloves, minced
- 1/2 tablespoon sugar
- 1/2 teaspoon red hot-pepper sauce
  ❖
- 8 ounces button mushrooms, sliced

- 7.2-ounce jar roasted red bell peppers, rinsed, drained, and thinly sliced, or 1 large red bell pepper, roasted and thinly sliced
- 3 medium green onions (green and white parts), chopped
- 6 cups torn mixed greens
- 4 cooked Triple-Pepper Chicken breast halves (page 237)

In a small bowl, whisk together the dressing ingredients until well blended.

In a large, shallow glass baking dish, stir together the mushrooms, peppers, and green onions. Pour the dressing over all, stirring to coat. Let stand for 20 minutes.

To assemble, arrange 1 1/2 cups mixed greens on each plate. Cut the chicken into thin strips. Stir into the mushroom mixture. Spoon over the mixed greens.

Cook's Tip

You can make the mushroom mixture up to 8 hours in advance. Cover and refrigerate it until serving time.

calories 187
protein 24 g
carbohydrates 11 g
 fiber 3 g
 sugars 4 g
cholesterol 52 mg
total fat 6.0 g
 saturated 1.0 g
 polyunsaturated 1.0 g
 monounsaturated 3.0 g
sodium 258 mg

dietary exchange
3 vegetable
3 lean meat

Asian Chicken and Rice Salad

Serves 8

Made in a ring mold, this salad is a worthy centerpiece for a luncheon. Or serve it in edible bowls—hollowed-out tomatoes or bell pepper halves.

Salad

- 3 cups cooked long-grain rice (about 1 cup uncooked)
- 10-ounce package frozen green peas, thawed
- 1½ pounds diced cooked skinless chicken breasts (cooked without salt), all visible fat discarded
- 4 medium green onions (green and white parts), sliced
- 1 medium rib of celery, diced
- 2 tablespoons diced green bell pepper

Dressing

- ¼ cup plain rice vinegar
- 2 tablespoons acceptable vegetable oil
- 2 tablespoons dry sherry
- 1 tablespoon low-salt soy sauce
- 1 tablespoon Dijon mustard
- ¼ teaspoon hot-pepper oil (optional)
- ⅛ teaspoon ground ginger

❖

Vegetable oil spray (optional)
Sprigs of fresh cilantro (optional)

In a large bowl, toss together the salad ingredients.

In a small bowl, whisk together the dressing ingredients. Pour over the salad. Toss well.

If using a ring mold, lightly spray with vegetable oil spray. Spoon the salad into the mold, packing firmly. Cover with plastic wrap. Refrigerate for at least 30 minutes. Turn the salad out onto the serving platter. Place the cilantro in the center.

If using the bowl, cover it with plastic wrap. Refrigerate for at least 30 minutes. Mound the salad on plates. Garnish each serving with cilantro.

calories 288
protein 30 g
carbohydrates 23 g
  fiber 3 g
  sugars 3 g
cholesterol 72 mg
total fat 7.0 g
  saturated 1.0 g
  polyunsaturated 2.0 g
  monounsaturated 3.0 g
sodium 198 mg

dietary exchange
1½ starch
3½ lean meat

Island Chicken Salad
with Fresh Mint

Serves 4

Light and utterly refreshing, this salad begins with Sweet-Spice Glazed Chicken on a bed of mixed greens. Mango and kiwifruit with a bit of jalapeño heat surround it, and a cooling sweet citrus dressing and fresh mint top it.

½ cup fresh lime juice

3 tablespoons sugar

2 teaspoons acceptable vegetable oil

1 to 2 fresh jalapeño peppers (optional)

4 cups torn mixed greens

4 cooked Sweet-Spice Glazed Chicken breast halves (page 234), cut into thin strips

1½ to 2 cups diced mango (2 to 3 medium)

3 green kiwifruit, peeled and diced

¼ cup chopped fresh mint leaves

In a small bowl, whisk together the lime juice, sugar, and oil until the sugar is dissolved.

Wearing gloves, discard the seeds and ribs of the peppers. Finely chop the peppers.

To assemble, place 1 cup mixed greens on each plate. Top with the chicken. Arrange the mango and kiwifruit around the chicken. Sprinkle the jalapeño over the fruit. Drizzle the lime mixture over the salad. Sprinkle with the mint. Serve immediately.

Cook's Tip on Cutting Mangoes

To cut a mango, lay it on its flattest side. Cutting horizontally, slice off the top half of the mango. (The large pit won't "let go" of the flesh, so you can't cut the fruit exactly in half.) Turn the mango so the pit side is down. Slice off the top part of the second side, near the pit. Trim and discard all the peel from the three pieces. Cut off the flesh still on the pit. Slice, chop, or dice all the flesh.

calories 368
protein 29 g
carbohydrates 45 g
  fiber 5 g
  sugars 37 g
cholesterol 66 mg
total fat 7.0 g
  saturated 1.0 g
  polyunsaturated 2.0 g
  monounsaturated 3.0 g
sodium 110 mg

dietary exchange
1½ fruit
1½ other carbohydrate
3 lean meat

Turkey on a Bed
of Sliced Tomatoes

Serves 4

Serve leftover cooked turkey in a refreshingly simple salad of mixed greens and sweet red onions, tossed with a vinaigrette and prettily arranged on slices of vine-ripened tomatoes.

4 cups torn mixed greens or romaine	2 tablespoons cider vinegar
12 ounces boneless, skinless cooked turkey breast, cooked without salt, cut into 1-inch pieces	1½ tablespoons olive oil (extra-virgin preferred)
⅓ cup thinly sliced red onion	1 medium garlic clove, minced
2 teaspoons capers, rinsed and drained	¼ teaspoon pepper
	12 slices tomato
	Pepper to taste

In a large bowl, toss together the greens, turkey, onion, and capers.

In a small bowl, whisk together the vinegar, oil, garlic, and pepper. Stir into the turkey mixture.

To serve, arrange 3 tomato slices on each dinner plate, spoon the salad on top, and sprinkle with the pepper.

Cook's Tip on Capers

Capers are the flavorful flower buds of a prickly bush native to the Mediterranean and Asia. Found with the pickles and olives at the supermarket, capers most often are packed in brine. Always rinse them to remove excess salt before using. Cut large capers in half if you wish.

calories 192
protein 27 g
carbohydrates 6 g
  fiber 2 g
  sugars 3 g
cholesterol 73 mg
total fat 6.5 g
  saturated 1.0 g
  polyunsaturated 1.0 g
  monounsaturated 4.0 g
sodium 107 mg

dietary exchange
1 vegetable
3 lean meat

Grilled Flank Steak Salad with Sweet-and-Sour Sesame Dressing

Serves 4

Leftover steak is a rare occurrence. If you plan ahead, however, you'll have some Grilled Lemongrass Flank Steak (page 292) to use in this salad of colorful vegetables and earthy wild rice. A sweet-and-sour dressing melds the varied flavors and textures.

Sweet-and-Sour Sesame Dressing
- 1 tablespoon sesame seeds
- 1/2 teaspoon grated lemon zest
- 2 tablespoons fresh lemon juice
- 2 tablespoons plain rice vinegar
- 1 tablespoon Chinese plum sauce
- 1 tablespoon light brown sugar

❖

- 4 cups shredded napa cabbage (12 to 16 ounces)
- 2 cups cooked wild rice, chilled
- 4 medium spears fresh asparagus, trimmed and cooked
- 8 cherry tomatoes (gold preferred)
- 1/2 medium cucumber, thinly sliced
- 1/2 medium red bell pepper, thinly sliced
- 1/2 medium red onion, thinly sliced
- 6 to 8 ounces grilled flank steak, thinly sliced against the grain, warm or chilled

Heat a small skillet over medium heat. Dry-roast the sesame seeds for 1 to 3 minutes, or until golden, stirring occasionally. Transfer to a medium bowl and let cool for 5 minutes.

Add the remaining dressing ingredients. Whisk together.

To serve, arrange the cabbage on a large platter. Mound the rice in the center of the cabbage. Decoratively arrange the asparagus, tomatoes, cucumber, bell pepper, and red onion on the cabbage. Lay the beef slices on the rice. Drizzle the dressing over all.

calories 265
protein 20 g
carbohydrates 32 g
 fiber 4 g
 sugars 10 g
cholesterol 33 mg
total fat 7.0 g
 saturated 2.5 g
 polyunsaturated 1.0 g
 monounsaturated 2.5 g
sodium 84 mg

dietary exchange
1 1/2 starch
1 1/2 vegetable
2 lean meat

Warm Orzo Salad with
Black Beans and Ham

Serves 4

Bright yellow pasta, dark black beans, and colorful bell peppers make this currylike salad beautiful. It's a great one-dish meal to take on a picnic or pack for brown bag lunches.

Vegetable oil spray
1 medium onion, diced
1 medium garlic clove, minced
2 large red or yellow bell peppers or a combination, seeded and diced
1/2 cup dry white wine (regular or nonalcoholic) or fat-free, low-sodium chicken broth, such as on page 45
1/2 to 1 cup frozen whole-kernel corn
1 cup dried orzo or dried pastina

2 tablespoons red wine vinegar
2 teaspoons olive oil
1 teaspoon ground cumin
1/2 teaspoon ground turmeric
1/8 to 1/4 teaspoon crushed red pepper flakes
15-ounce can no-salt-added black beans, rinsed and drained
1 cup minced lower-sodium, low-fat ham or turkey ham (about 4 1/2 ounces)

Lightly spray a large nonstick skillet with vegetable oil spray. Cook the onion and garlic over medium-high heat for 3 minutes, stirring occasionally.

Reduce the heat to medium. Stir in the bell peppers. Cook for 2 to 3 minutes.

Pour in the wine. Cook for 5 minutes, or until the peppers are very soft and most of the wine has evaporated.

Stir in the corn. Cook for 1 to 2 minutes, or just until heated through.

Prepare the orzo using the package directions, omitting the salt and oil. Drain well.

In a large bowl, stir together the vinegar, oil, cumin, turmeric, and red pepper flakes. Stir in the beans, ham, bell pepper mixture, and orzo. Serve warm or at room temperature.

calories 388
protein 19 g
carbohydrates 65 g
fiber 8 g
sugars 10 g
cholesterol 14 mg
total fat 4.5 g
saturated 1.0 g
polyunsaturated 1.0 g
monounsaturated 2.5 g
sodium 274 mg

dietary exchange
3 1/2 starch
2 vegetable
2 very lean meat

Southwestern
Pork Salad

Serves 6

From the tangy vinaigrette to the hearty black beans, this is a delicious portable salad. Try it at your next picnic, or take it to a potluck dinner. The garnish of orange slices and grapes makes a nice contrast to the salad.

2 cups cubed cooked pork tenderloin, cooked without salt, all visible fat discarded

1 cup Cuban Black Beans (page 379) or canned no-salt-added black beans (about ¹/₂ 16- to 17-ounce can), rinsed and drained

4 medium green onions (green and white parts), finely chopped

¹/₂ medium green or red bell pepper, chopped

1 small garlic clove, minced

Dressing

¹/₄ cup snipped fresh parsley

¹/₄ cup cider vinegar

2 tablespoons fat-free, low-sodium chicken broth, such as on page 45

1¹/₂ tablespoons sugar

2 teaspoons olive oil (extra-virgin preferred)

¹/₂ teaspoon dried oregano, crumbled

¹/₂ teaspoon dry mustard

❖

1 cup cherry tomatoes, quartered

6 medium black olives, chopped

3 cups salad greens
Orange slices (optional)
Green grapes (optional)

In a large bowl, stir together the pork, beans, green onions, bell pepper, and garlic.

In a small bowl, whisk together the dressing ingredients. Pour over the pork mixture, tossing to coat. Cover and refrigerate for at least 30 minutes, stirring occasionally.

Immediately before serving, gently stir in the tomatoes and olives. Spoon over the salad greens. Garnish with the orange slices and grapes.

calories 240
protein 21 g
carbohydrates 28 g
fiber 4 g
sugars 9 g
cholesterol 42 mg
total fat 5.0 g
saturated 1.0 g
polyunsaturated 0.5 g
monounsaturated 2.5 g
sodium 86 mg

dietary exchange
1¹/₂ starch
1 vegetable
2¹/₂ lean meat

Double Spinach
Tortellini Salad

Serves 6

For double the flavor, combine spinach tortellini and frozen chopped spinach. Serve this hearty salad with colorful fresh fruit.

9-ounce package fresh spinach-and-cheese tortellini
10-ounce package frozen chopped spinach
1 medium zucchini, thinly sliced (about 1 cup)
1 medium yellow summer squash, thinly sliced (about 1 cup)
1 large carrot, thinly sliced
1 large yellow or red tomato, diced

Dressing
1/2 cup fat-free, low-sodium chicken broth, such as on page 45
1/3 cup white wine vinegar
1 tablespoon olive oil
2 teaspoons sugar
2 medium garlic cloves, minced
1 teaspoon dried oregano, crumbled
1 teaspoon dried basil, crumbled
1/4 teaspoon pepper

Prepare the tortellini using the package directions, omitting the salt and oil. Drain well. Transfer to a large bowl and let cool for 10 minutes.

Meanwhile, prepare the spinach using the package directions, omitting the salt and margarine. Squeeze out the excess water.

Add the zucchini, yellow squash, carrot, and tomato to the tortellini. Gently toss to partially combine.

In a small bowl, whisk together the dressing ingredients. Pour over the pasta mixture. Toss gently. Serve immediately or cover and refrigerate until needed, up to three days.

calories 191
protein 8 g
carbohydrates 29 g
 fiber 5 g
 sugars 5 g
cholesterol 16 mg
total fat 5.5 g
 saturated 2.5 g
 polyunsaturated 0.5 g
 monounsaturated 1.5 g
sodium 241 mg

dietary exchange
1 1/2 starch
1 1/2 vegetable
1 fat

Marinated White Beans and Cucumber with Basil

Serves 4

This filling salad will become a favorite entrée in the summertime, when tomatoes, cucumbers, and basil are plentiful and bursting with flavor.

19-ounce can no-salt-added cannellini beans, rinsed and drained
4 medium tomatoes, chopped
2 medium cucumbers, peeled and chopped
1/3 cup chopped red onion
2 1/2 to 3 tablespoons white wine vinegar

2 tablespoons finely chopped fresh basil or 1 1/2 to 2 teaspoons dried, crumbled
1 1/2 tablespoons olive oil (extra-virgin preferred)
1 medium garlic clove, crushed
1/4 teaspoon salt
Pepper to taste

In a large bowl, toss together the beans, tomatoes, cucumbers, and onion.

In a small bowl, whisk together the remaining ingredients. Pour over the salad. Cover and refrigerate for 1 to 2 hours, stirring occasionally.

Variation
Instead of chopping the tomatoes, make tomato cups to hold the salad. Slice the top off each tomato; discard the tops. Scoop out and discard the pulp. Spoon the bean mixture into each cup.

calories 192
protein 7 g
carbohydrates 28 g
  fiber 7 g
  sugars 4 g
cholesterol 0 mg
total fat 6.0 g
  saturated 1.0 g
  polyunsaturated 1.0 g
  monounsaturated 4.0 g
sodium 415 mg

dietary exchange
1 starch
2 vegetable
1/2 very lean meat
1 fat

Curried Rice
and Bean Salad

Serves 6

Make this your entrée, accompanied by Easy Refrigerator Rolls (page 532) and fresh tomato and cucumber slices.

Salad

- 3 cups cooked brown rice
- 1½ cups canned no-salt-added kidney beans, rinsed and drained
- 2 medium ribs of celery, diced
- 4 medium green onions (green and white parts), chopped
- ½ medium green bell pepper, diced
- ¼ cup snipped fresh parsley

Dressing

- ¼ cup fat-free or light mayonnaise dressing
- ¼ cup fat-free or light plain yogurt
- 2 teaspoons curry powder
- Dash of pepper

In a large bowl, stir together the salad ingredients.

In a small bowl, whisk together the dressing ingredients. Pour over the salad. Stir well.

Cook's Tip on Brown Rice

Brown rice is a whole-grain rice. Its bran covering provides color, fiber, and an extra helping of vitamins and minerals, compared with white rice. The bran also doubles the cooking time. White rice has had the bran removed.

calories 194
protein 7 g
carbohydrates 38 g
  fiber 6 g
  sugars 4 g
cholesterol 0 mg
total fat 1.0 g
  saturated 0.0 g
  polyunsaturated 0.5 g
  monounsaturated 0.5 g
sodium 116 mg

dietary exchange
2½ starch
½ very lean meat

Curried Quinoa Salad with Cranberries and Almonds

Serves 4

Toss quinoa (KEEN-wah) with a sweet soy and curry sauce, then top it with toasted almonds for this entrée salad.

2 cups water
1 cup uncooked quinoa
2 tablespoons low-salt soy sauce
1 tablespoon cider vinegar
1 tablespoon honey
1/2 teaspoon curry powder
1/4 teaspoon crushed red pepper flakes, or to taste
1/2 medium green bell pepper, chopped

1 medium rib of celery, finely chopped
8-ounce can sliced water chestnuts, rinsed and drained
1/2 cup dried cranberries or mixed dried fruit
1/2 teaspoon grated orange zest
1/4 cup sliced almonds, dry-roasted

In a medium saucepan, bring the water to a boil over high heat. Stir in the quinoa. Reduce the heat and simmer, uncovered, for 15 minutes, or until the water is absorbed. Remove from the heat and let cool.

Meanwhile, in a small bowl, stir together the soy sauce, vinegar, honey, curry powder, and red pepper flakes until completely blended.

In a large bowl, stir together the remaining ingredients except the almonds. Gently stir in the cooled quinoa, then the soy sauce mixture.

To serve, sprinkle with the almonds.

Cook's Tip on Quinoa

Serve quinoa hot or cold, press it into molds to serve as timbales, make it into a curry, or add vegetables and herbs to give it a Mediterranean or all-American flavor. Serve it for breakfast, lunch, or dinner.

Time-Saver

A quick way to cool cooked quinoa is to spread it in a thin layer on a baking sheet that's on a cooling rack.

calories 287
protein 8 g
carbohydrates 53 g
  fiber 7 g
  sugars 16 g
cholesterol 0 mg
total fat 5.5 g
  saturated 0.5 g
  polyunsaturated 2.0 g
  monounsaturated 2.5 g
sodium 226 mg

dietary exchange
2 starch
1 fruit
1 1/2 vegetable
1 fat

Couscous Salad

Serves 4

You can save time by using bagged spinach for this entrée salad. Simply chop what you need and save the rest for tomorrow night's salad.

1 cup water
3/4 cup uncooked couscous
1 cup shredded fat-free mozzarella
1 cup diced seeded tomatoes
1/2 cup finely snipped fresh parsley
12 kalamata olives, finely chopped
1 teaspoon grated lemon zest

2 tablespoons fresh lemon juice
1/2 medium garlic clove, minced
1/4 teaspoon salt
1/4 teaspoon crushed red pepper flakes
2 cups coarsely chopped fresh spinach leaves

In a small saucepan, bring the water to a boil over high heat. Remove from the heat. Stir in the couscous. Let stand, covered, for 5 minutes, or until the liquid is absorbed. Fluff the couscous with a fork. Spread the couscous in a thin layer on a baking sheet or sheet of aluminum foil. Let stand for 5 minutes, or until cooled.

Meanwhile, in a large bowl, stir together the remaining ingredients except the spinach. Add the couscous. Toss gently to blend.

Add the spinach and toss gently.

calories 217
protein 14 g
carbohydrates 32 g
    fiber 4 g
    sugars 2 g
cholesterol 5 mg
total fat 3.5 g
    saturated 0.5 g
    polyunsaturated 0.5 g
    monounsaturated 2.5 g
sodium 694 mg

dietary exchange

2 starch
1 vegetable
1 lean meat

Zesty Tomato Dressing

Serves 10; 2 tablespoons per serving

Fresh lemon juice and dry mustard make this dressing sparkle.

1 cup no-salt-added tomato juice
2 medium green onions (green and white parts), thinly sliced
2 tablespoons fresh lemon juice
2 tablespoons red wine vinegar
1 teaspoon dried parsley, crumbled

1 teaspoon sugar
1/2 teaspoon dried oregano, crumbled
1/2 teaspoon dry mustard
1/2 teaspoon low-salt soy sauce
1/4 teaspoon pepper

In a medium bowl, whisk together the ingredients. Cover and refrigerate for up to three days.

calories 10
protein 0 g
carbohydrates 2 g
  fiber 1 g
  sugars 2 g
cholesterol 0 mg
total fat 0.0 g
  saturated 0.0 g
  polyunsaturated 0.0 g
  monounsaturated 0.0 g
sodium 10 mg

dietary exchange
Free

Chunky Cucumber
and Garlic Dressing

Serves 6; 2 tablespoons per serving

Be as cool as a cucumber on a hot summer day and serve this dressing on your favorite salad or a grilled chicken, pork, or beef pita sandwich.

½ cup fat-free or light plain yogurt	½ teaspoon dehydrated onion flakes
½ medium cucumber, peeled and chopped	¼ teaspoon garlic powder
1 tablespoon sugar	¼ teaspoon pepper
1 tablespoon acceptable vegetable oil	1 tablespoon red wine vinegar

In a small bowl, whisk the yogurt until smooth.

Whisk in the remaining ingredients except the vinegar.

Gradually whisk in the vinegar until combined. Cover and refrigerate for at least 4 hours.

calories 43
protein 1 g
carbohydrates 4 g
  fiber 0 g
  sugars 4 g
cholesterol 0 mg
total fat 2.5 g
  saturated 0.0 g
  polyunsaturated 0.5 g
  monounsaturated 1.5 g
sodium 16 mg

dietary exchange
½ fat

Ranch-Style Herb Dressing

Serves 8; 2 tablespoons per serving

Freshly made ranch-style dressing is delightful on a salad or baked potato or as a dip for vegetables.

3/4 cup fat-free or low-fat cottage cheese

1/3 cup fat-free or low-fat buttermilk

1 1/2 tablespoons finely chopped onion

2 tablespoons fat-free or light mayonnaise dressing

2 tablespoons finely snipped fresh parsley

1 teaspoon dried dillweed, crumbled

1 teaspoon dried basil, crumbled

1/2 teaspoon dried oregano, crumbled

1/4 teaspoon garlic powder

1/8 teaspoon salt

Dash of red hot-pepper sauce

In a food processor or blender, process the cottage cheese, buttermilk, onion, and mayonnaise until smooth.

Add the remaining ingredients and process for 10 seconds. Cover and refrigerate for at least 1 hour.

Cook's Tip

For a richer flavor—but a dressing with a higher calorie count—increase the amount of mayonnaise and reduce the amount of cottage cheese.

calories 25
protein 3 g
carbohydrates 2 g
  fiber 0 g
  sugars 2 g
cholesterol 1 mg
total fat 0.0 g
  saturated 0.0 g
  polyunsaturated 0.0 g
  monounsaturated 0.0 g
sodium 151 mg

dietary exchange
1/2 very lean meat

Poppy Seed Dressing
with Kiwifruit

Serves 8; 2 tablespoons per serving

Serve this delicately sweet dressing over a crisp lettuce and jicama salad, seasonal fresh fruit, or fat-free or low-fat cottage cheese or frozen yogurt.

3/4 cup pineapple juice

1 tablespoon cornstarch

2 green kiwifruit

2 tablespoons honey

1 tablespoon fresh lime juice

1 teaspoon poppy seeds

In a small saucepan, whisk together the pineapple juice and cornstarch. Bring to a boil over medium-high heat, whisking occasionally for 3 to 4 minutes, or until the mixture thickens. Spoon into a small bowl and let cool at room temperature for 5 minutes. Cover and refrigerate until cold, at least 15 minutes.

Meanwhile, peel and coarsely dice the kiwifruit.

Spoon the cold pineapple mixture into a food processor or blender. Add the kiwifruit, honey, and lime juice. Process until smooth (except the seeds). Pour the dressing into a bowl.

Stir in the poppy seeds. Serve immediately or cover and refrigerate for up to five days.

Cook's Tip on Kiwifruit

Choose kiwifruit that yields to gentle pressure (it should not be soft or mushy). If the kiwifruit is extremely firm, let it sit on the counter for a few days to ripen. Although the fuzzy skin is almost always removed, it is edible, as are the tiny black seeds.

calories 46
protein 0 g
carbohydrates 11 g
  fiber 1 g
  sugars 9 g
cholesterol 0 mg
total fat 0.0 g
  saturated 0.0 g
  polyunsaturated 0.0 g
  monounsaturated 0.0 g
sodium 2 mg

dietary exchange
1 fruit

Lemon Dressing

Serves 8; 2 tablespoons per serving

Tangy and flavorful, this dressing is a rousing accompaniment for salads and other fresh vegetables.

1/2 cup fresh lemon juice
2 tablespoons water
1 tablespoon snipped fresh parsley
1 tablespoon snipped or chopped fresh oregano

1 tablespoon olive oil (extra-virgin preferred)
1 tablespoon honey
1 tablespoon Dijon mustard
2 medium garlic cloves, minced
1/2 teaspoon fennel seeds, crushed

In a small bowl, whisk together the ingredients.

Cook's Tip on Fennel

Known primarily as an Italian herb and spice, fennel has a delicate anise flavor. The two main kinds of fennel both have feathery leaves and celerylike stems. Garden, or common, fennel produces the fennel seed that is used as a spice. Fennel seeds resemble caraway seeds and are usually ground before using. Florence fennel, or finocchio, is prized for the thickened leaf stalks that form a bulb at the base. The bulb and stems of both kinds can be used like a vegetable, raw or cooked, much as celery is used. The leaves can be snipped and used for flavoring. Add to cooked dishes at the last minute so the flavor doesn't dissipate.

calories 32
protein 0 g
carbohydrates 4 g
  fiber 0 g
  sugars 3 g
cholesterol 0 mg
total fat 2.0 g g
  saturated 0.0 g
  polyunsaturated 0.0 g
  monounsaturated 1.5 g
sodium 39 mg
dietary exchange
1/2 fat

seafood

Ginger Broiled Fish

Bronzed Catfish with Remoulade Sauce

Baked Catfish

Catfish Po' Boy with Zesty Slaw Topping

Crispy Cajun Catfish Nibbles with Red Sauce

Cod and Vegetables in Lemony Cream Sauce

Poached Fish

Cod Baked with Vegetables

Fish Fillets in Foil

Seared Fish with Rosemary Aïoli

Fish Fillets with Zesty Rosemary Oil

So Simple, So Fast, So Good Fillets

Fish Fillets with Asparagus

Haddock with Tomatoes and Ginger

Mediterranean Fish

Coconut-Rum Baked Fish

Teriyaki Halibut

Fish Tacos with Pico de Gallo

Orange Roughy with Tomatoes and Spinach

Dilled Orange Roughy with Lemon-Caper Sauce

Salmon with Cucumber-Dill Sauce

Baked Salmon with Cucumber Relish

Broiled Salmon with Citrus Salsa

Grilled Salmon

Salmon Cakes

Salmon Alfredo

Snapper with Fresh Tomatoes and Capers

Mushroom-Stuffed Fish Rolls

French-Style Braised Fish Fillets

Crispy Baked Fillet of Sole

Sole Baked with Mushrooms

Bay-Style Fillets

Sole with Walnuts and White Wine

Sole with Parsley and Mint

Stovetop Fish with Vegetable Rice, Mexican Style

Tex-Mex Tilapia

Baked Tilapia with Sausage-Flecked Rice

Baked Tilapia with Tarragon Bread Crumbs

Tilapia Amandine

Greek Fish Fillets

Crisp Pan-Seared Trout with Green Onions

Braised Tuna Steaks with Orange-Cranberry Glaze

Sesame Tuna with Pineapple Sauce

Grilled Tuna with Pineapple-Nectarine Salsa

Tuna and Soba Noodles

Stuffed Shells with Albacore Tuna and Vegetables

Tuna Chili

Tuna Salad Pitas

Linguine with White Clam Sauce

Crabmeat Maryland

Crab Primavera Alfredo

Scallops and Asparagus in Wine Sauce

Oven-Fried Scallops with Cilantro and Lime

Shrimp and Okra Étouffée

Fiery Shrimp Dijon

Little Shrimp Cakes

Cioppino

Ginger Broiled Fish

Serves 8

Fresh ginger and wine are a winning combination in this simple fish dish.

Vegetable oil spray
2 pounds fish fillets or steaks, such as halibut, about ¾ inch thick
¾ cup dry white wine (regular or nonalcoholic)
2 medium green onions (green and white parts), chopped

1 tablespoon low-salt soy sauce
2 teaspoons grated peeled gingerroot
2 teaspoons prepared white horseradish, drained
1 teaspoon acceptable vegetable oil

Preheat the broiler. Lightly spray a broilerproof baking dish with vegetable oil spray.

Meanwhile, rinse the fish and pat dry with paper towels. Cut the fish into 8 equal portions.

In a small bowl, stir together the remaining ingredients.

Put the baking dish under the broiler for 1 to 2 minutes. Arrange the fish in a single layer in the preheated dish. Pour the green onion mixture over the fish.

Broil the fish about 2 inches from the heat for 5 minutes. Turn over carefully. Broil for 5 to 6 minutes, or until the fish flakes easily when tested with a fork.

with halibut

calories 150
protein 24 g
carbohydrates 1 g
  fiber 0 g
  sugars 0 g
cholesterol 36 mg
total fat 3.0 g
  saturated 0.5 g
  polyunsaturated 1.0 g
  monounsaturated 1.0 g
sodium 116 mg

dietary exchange
3 very lean meat

Cook's Tip on Gingerroot

You can find gingerroot in the produce section. Choose a root with smooth skin. To keep it from drying out, peel just as much as you need to grate, keeping a "handle" with the skin left on. Keep leftover unpeeled gingerroot wrapped in a paper towel and refrigerate it in a resealable plastic bag for up to three weeks. For longer storage, put peeled gingerroot in a small jar with a tight-fitting lid and cover the ginger with dry sherry. Refrigerate for up to three months. Both the ginger and the ginger-flavored sherry will be great for cooking.

Bronzed Catfish with Remoulade Sauce

Serves 4

The bronzing technique used in this recipe is similar to the blackening used for dishes such as blackened redfish. To get that bronzed look, however, the fish is cooked at a more moderate temperature, so the seasonings do not burn. Remoulade sauce lends its piquant flavor to this dish.

Remoulade Sauce

- 2 medium green onions (green and white parts), thinly sliced
- 1 small rib of celery, finely chopped
- 2 tablespoons snipped fresh parsley
- 2 tablespoons no-salt-added ketchup
- 1 tablespoon red wine vinegar
- 1 tablespoon Creole mustard
- 2 teaspoons low-sodium Worcestershire sauce

- 2 teaspoons olive oil
- 1 medium garlic clove, minced
- 1/2 teaspoon paprika
- 1/4 teaspoon salt
- ❖
- 4 catfish fillets (about 4 ounces each)
  Vegetable oil spray
- 4 teaspoons Creole or Cajun seasoning blend, divided use

In a medium bowl, stir together the remoulade sauce ingredients. Cover with plastic wrap and refrigerate for up to three days.

Rinse the fish and pat dry with paper towels. Lightly spray both sides with vegetable oil spray. Sprinkle 2 teaspoons seasoning evenly over one side of the fillets.

Heat a nonstick skillet over medium-high heat. Put the fish with the seasoned side down in the skillet. Cook for 5 minutes, or until golden brown on the seasoned side. Sprinkle the unseasoned side with the remaining 2 teaspoons seasoning. Turn the fillets over. Cook for 4 to 5 minutes, or until the bottom side is browned and the fish flakes easily when tested with a fork.

To serve, put the fish on a platter. Spoon the sauce over it.

calories 145
protein 19 g
carbohydrates 4 g
  fiber 1 g
  sugars 2 g
cholesterol 66 mg
total fat 5.5 g
  saturated 1.0 g
  polyunsaturated 1.0 g
  monounsaturated 2.5 g
sodium 590 mg

dietary exchange
1 vegetable
3 lean meat

Baked Catfish

Crisp on the outside and moist on the inside, these fish fillets go well with Baked Okra Bites (page 440).

Vegetable oil spray
3/4 cup fat-free or low-fat buttermilk
1/4 teaspoon salt
1/4 teaspoon red hot-pepper sauce
3 ounces fat-free, low-sodium whole-wheat crackers, crushed (about 30)

6 catfish fillets (about 4 ounces each)
1 tablespoon light tub margarine, melted
Vegetable oil spray
2 tablespoons snipped fresh parsley
6 lemon wedges (optional)

Preheat the oven to 400°F. Lightly spray a 13 × 9 × 2-inch baking dish with vegetable oil spray.

In a small, shallow dish, stir together the buttermilk, salt, and hot-pepper sauce. Put the cracker crumbs on a plate next to the dish.

Rinse the fish and pat dry with paper towels. Dip the fish in the buttermilk mixture, then in the crumbs to coat.

Put the fish in the baking dish. Drizzle with the margarine and lightly spray with vegetable oil spray.

Bake, uncovered, for 15 to 20 minutes, or until the fish flakes easily when tested with a fork.

To serve, sprinkle the fish with the parsley and garnish with the lemon wedges.

calories 190
protein 21 g
carbohydrates 11 g
  fiber 2 g
  sugars 2 g
cholesterol 67 mg
total fat 6.5 g
  saturated 1.5 g
  polyunsaturated 2.0 g
  monounsaturated 2.5 g
sodium 230 mg

dietary exchange
1 starch
3 lean meat

Catfish Po' Boy
with Zesty Slaw Topping

Serves 4

A New Orleans favorite gets a lean update with crispy baked catfish and a broccoli-slaw topping, kicked up with spicy seasonings.

¼ cup whole-wheat flour or all-purpose flour

1 teaspoon salt-free spicy all-purpose seasoning
Egg substitute equivalent to 1 egg, or 1 large egg, lightly beaten

¾ cup crushed cornflake cereal (about 2 cups flakes)

1 pound catfish fillets
Vegetable oil spray

Slaw Topping

4 cups broccoli slaw or shredded green cabbage

1 medium carrot, shredded

2 medium green onions (green and white parts), thinly sliced

2 tablespoons fat-free or light mayonnaise dressing

1 teaspoon white wine vinegar

1 teaspoon prepared white horseradish

½ teaspoon Creole or Cajun seasoning blend

❖

4 whole-wheat hoagie-style buns or whole-wheat hot dog buns

Preheat the oven to 400°F.

In a shallow bowl, stir together the flour and all-purpose seasoning. Put the egg substitute and cornflake crumbs in two separate shallow bowls. Set the three bowls with the flour mixture, egg substitute, and cornflake crumbs in a row, assembly-line fashion.

Rinse the fish and pat dry with paper towels. Cut the fish into 1-inch cubes. Coat in the flour mixture, then in the egg, then lightly in the cornflakes. Put the fish cubes on a baking sheet, spacing so they don't touch. Lightly spray with vegetable oil spray.

Bake for 10 to 12 minutes, or until the fish flakes easily when tested with a fork. Put the baking sheet on a cooling rack. Let cool for 5 minutes.

Meanwhile, in a medium bowl, stir together the slaw topping ingredients.

To assemble, place the fish on the bottom half of the buns. Top with the slaw and the tops of the buns.

calories 357
protein 28 g
carbohydrates 49 g
  fiber 8 g
  sugars 8 g
cholesterol 66 mg
total fat 5.5 g
  saturated 1.0 g
  polyunsaturated 2.0 g
  monounsaturated 1.5 g
sodium 542 mg

dietary exchange
3 starch
1 vegetable
3 very lean meat

Crispy Cajun Catfish Nibbles with Red Sauce

Serves 4

Do you like fried popcorn shrimp? Then you'll love these crisp bites of catfish. They're served with a zesty sauce similar to cocktail sauce.

Vegetable oil spray

Coating
3 tablespoons yellow cornmeal
1/2 teaspoon chili powder
1/2 teaspoon ground cumin
1/4 teaspoon salt
1/4 teaspoon garlic powder
1/8 teaspoon pepper

❖

1 pound catfish fillets

Egg substitute equivalent to 1 egg, or 1 large egg
1/2 cup cornflake crumbs

Red Sauce
1/4 cup no-salt-added ketchup
2 tablespoons white wine vinegar
2 tablespoons fresh lemon juice
1 tablespoon honey
1 tablespoon prepared white horseradish

Preheat the oven to 400°F. Lightly spray a baking sheet with vegetable oil spray. Set aside.

In a large resealable plastic bag, combine the coating ingredients.

Rinse the fish and pat dry with paper towels. Cut the fish into 1/2-inch pieces. Add the fish to the bag. Seal and turn to coat.

Pour the egg substitute into the bag. Seal and shake gently to coat.

Put the cornflake crumbs in a shallow bowl. Using a slotted spoon, add the fish to the cornflake crumbs, turning gently with the spoon to coat. Arrange the fish in a single layer on the baking sheet. Lightly spray the fish with vegetable oil spray.

Bake for 7 to 8 minutes, or until the fish flakes easily when tested with a fork.

Meanwhile, in a small bowl, whisk together the sauce ingredients. Serve with the fish.

calories 217
protein 22 g
carbohydrates 25 g
  fiber 1 g
  sugars 8 g
cholesterol 66 mg
total fat 3.5 g
  saturated 1.0 g
  polyunsaturated 1.0 g
  monounsaturated 1.0 g
sodium 404 mg

dietary exchange
1 1/2 starch
3 very lean meat

Cod and Vegetables in Lemony Cream Sauce

Serves 4

Baby carrots, pearl onions, red potatoes, and mild-flavored cod are enveloped in a velvety sauce. Serve this dish with a delicate salad, such as Wilted Baby Spinach with Pear and Goat Cheese (page 88).

1 1/2 cups fat-free, low-sodium chicken broth, such as on page 45

8 small red potatoes (about 8 ounces), halved

1 1/2 cups baby carrots

1 cup frozen pearl onions

1 teaspoon salt-free all-purpose seasoning

1/2 cup fat-free half-and-half

2 1/2 tablespoons all-purpose flour

2 tablespoons snipped fresh parsley

1 teaspoon grated lemon zest

1 medium garlic clove, minced

4 cod fillets (about 4 ounces each)

In a large skillet, stir together the broth, potatoes, carrots, onions, and all-purpose seasoning. Bring to a simmer over medium-high heat, stirring occasionally. Reduce the heat and simmer, covered, for 10 minutes, or until the vegetables are tender.

In a small bowl, whisk together the remaining ingredients except the fish (there may be a few lumps). Stir into the broth mixture. Simmer, covered, for 2 to 3 minutes, or until thickened, stirring occasionally.

Rinse the fish and pat dry with paper towels. Place the fish fillets in the skillet, spacing them evenly. Spoon the vegetable-sauce mixture on top. Simmer, covered, for 8 to 10 minutes, or until the fish flakes easily when tested with a fork.

calories 228
protein 26 g
carbohydrates 30 g
 fiber 3 g
 sugars 8 g
cholesterol 49 mg
total fat 1.0 g
 saturated 0.0 g
 polyunsaturated 0.5 g
 monounsaturated 0.0 g
sodium 126 mg

dietary exchange
1 starch
3 vegetable
3 very lean meat

Poached Fish

Serves 8

Poaching is an excellent way to cook lean fish because the procedure keeps the fish moist, and it works well with salmon and other fatty fish. Serve this simple dish with one of our sauces, such as Walnut Cream Sauce (page 491).

8 fish fillets, such as cod, sea bass, salmon, or tilapia (about 4 ounces each)
1 teaspoon acceptable vegetable oil
1 small onion, chopped
1 small rib of celery, chopped

1 cup dry white wine (regular or nonalcoholic) or hot water
2 tablespoons fresh lemon juice
1 bay leaf
   Pepper to taste
   Sprigs of fresh parsley (optional)

Rinse the fish and pat dry with paper towels.

Heat a large nonstick skillet over medium-high heat. Pour the oil into the skillet and swirl to coat the bottom. Cook the onion and celery for 2 to 3 minutes, or until soft.

Place the fish flat on top of the vegetables, or roll each fillet, securing it with a toothpick, and place the rolls on the vegetables. Add the remaining ingredients except the parsley. Bring to a simmer over medium-high heat. Reduce the heat and simmer, covered, for about 8 minutes, or until the fish flakes easily when tested with a fork.

To serve, carefully transfer the fish to a platter. Remove the toothpicks. Sprinkle the parsley over the fish.

calories 125
protein 21 g
carbohydrates 2 g
  fiber 0 g
  sugars 1 g
cholesterol 49 mg
total fat 1.5 g
  saturated 0.0 g
  polyunsaturated 0.5 g
  monounsaturated 0.5 g
sodium 67 mg

dietary exchange
3 very lean meat

Cook's Tip on Freezing Lemon Juice

Pour fresh lemon juice into the compartments of a plastic ice tray—each compartment holds about 1 tablespoon of juice—and freeze it. Remove the cubes and store them in a resealable plastic bag in the freezer. They'll be ready whenever you need them.

Cod Baked with Vegetables

Serves 6

This one-dish comfort meal preserves the mildness of cod yet is full of flavor.

Vegetable oil spray
2 cups cubed red potatoes (10 to 12 ounces), unpeeled
2 medium carrots, sliced
2 tablespoons light tub margarine, melted
2 tablespoons fresh lemon juice
¼ teaspoon salt
¼ teaspoon pepper
1½ pounds cod fillets

¼ teaspoon salt
¼ teaspoon pepper
4 medium green onions (green and white parts), sliced
2 tablespoons snipped fresh parsley or 2 teaspoons dried, crumbled
1 tablespoon finely snipped fresh dillweed or 1 teaspoon dried, crumbled

Preheat the oven to 400°F. Lightly spray a 13 × 9 × 2-inch baking dish with vegetable oil spray.

Put the potatoes and carrots in the baking dish.

In a small bowl, stir together the margarine, lemon juice, ¼ teaspoon salt, and ¼ teaspoon pepper. Pour over the vegetables.

Bake, covered, for 25 minutes.

Meanwhile, rinse the fish and pat dry with paper towels. Cut the fish into 2-inch pieces. Sprinkle with ¼ teaspoon salt, ¼ teaspoon pepper, and the green onions.

Stir the fish mixture into the cooked vegetables. Sprinkle with the parsley and dillweed.

Bake, covered, for 15 to 20 minutes, or until the fish flakes easily when tested with a fork.

Microwave Method
Prepare the vegetables and margarine mixture as directed. Cover the baking dish with vented plastic wrap and microwave at 100 percent power (high) for 8 to 10 minutes. Add the remaining ingredients and microwave, covered and vented, at 100 percent power (high) for 5 to 7 minutes.

calories 158
protein 22 g
carbohydrates 12 g
 fiber 2 g
 sugars 2 g
cholesterol 49 mg
total fat 2.5 g
 saturated 0.0 g
 polyunsaturated 0.5 g
 monounsaturated 1.0 g
sodium 297 mg

dietary exchange
½ starch
1 vegetable
3 very lean meat

Fish Fillets in Foil

Serves 4

Cooking fish in aluminum foil packets keeps the filling and the fillets moist. Custom-design your dinner by replacing the mushroom sauce with one of the variations below.

Vegetable oil spray

4 thin fish fillets, such as flounder
   (about 4 ounces each)

1/2 teaspoon pepper

Mushroom Sauce

1 teaspoon light tub margarine

1 tablespoon chopped shallots or
   green onions (green and white parts)

8 ounces button mushrooms, chopped

3 tablespoons dry white wine (regular
   or nonalcoholic)

1 tablespoon snipped fresh parsley

1 tablespoon fresh lemon juice

Preheat the oven to 400°F.

Lightly spray four 8-inch square pieces of heavy-duty aluminum foil with vegetable oil spray. Rinse the fish and pat dry with paper towels. Place a fillet on each piece of foil. Season with the pepper. Set aside.

For the mushroom sauce, heat a medium nonstick skillet over medium-high heat. In the skillet, melt the margarine and swirl to coat the bottom. Cook the shallots for 2 to 3 minutes, or until soft.

Add the mushrooms and cook for 5 minutes, stirring occasionally.

Stir in the remaining sauce ingredients. Cook for 2 to 3 minutes, or until most of the liquid has evaporated. Spoon the mushroom sauce over the fish. Seal the foil tightly.

Bake for 20 minutes. Being careful to avoid steam burns, open a foil packet and see if the fish flakes easily when tested with a fork. If it is not ready, reseal the packet and bake a little longer. Serve in the foil.

calories 131
protein 23 g
carbohydrates 3 g
 fiber 1 g
 sugars 1 g
cholesterol 54 mg
total fat 2.0 g
 saturated 0.5 g
 polyunsaturated 0.5 g
 monounsaturated 0.5 g
sodium 103 mg

dietary exchange
3 very lean meat

Variations

In place of the mushroom sauce, use any of the combinations listed below. Amounts of all the ingredients except margarine may be varied to suit individual taste. Use the margarine to dot each serving.

- Spinach, fresh or frozen, thawed and squeezed dry
  Fresh lemon juice
  Ground nutmeg
  1 teaspoon light tub margarine
- Tomato, thinly sliced or chopped
  Green onions, thinly sliced
  Basil, fresh and chopped or dried and crumbled
  Fresh lemon juice
  1 teaspoon light tub margarine
- Cucumber, thinly sliced
  Fresh lemon juice
  Fresh dillweed and/or parsley, snipped
  1 teaspoon light tub margarine
- Celery, thinly sliced
  Fresh lemon juice
  Thyme, fresh and chopped or dried and crumbled
  1 teaspoon light tub margarine
- Green onions, thinly sliced
  Carrots, very thinly sliced
  Curry powder
  Green bell pepper, thinly sliced
  1 teaspoon light tub margarine

Seared Fish
with Rosemary Aïoli

Serves 4

Aïoli (ay-OH-lee or I-OH-lee) is basically mayonnaise with herbs and fresh garlic. The use of a particular herb is generally what makes the big difference. Rosemary is the choice for this assertive entrée!

Rosemary Aïoli
- 1/4 cup fat-free or light sour cream
- 2 tablespoons fat-free milk
- 2 tablespoons fat-free or light mayonnaise dressing
- 1 medium garlic clove, minced
- 1/4 teaspoon dried rosemary, crushed
- 1/4 teaspoon salt

❖

- 4 grouper, tilapia, or other mild fish fillets (about 4 ounces each)
- 1/2 teaspoon paprika
- 1/4 teaspoon pepper
- 1/8 teaspoon salt

In a small bowl, stir together the aïoli ingredients. Set aside.

Rinse the fish and pat dry with paper towels. Sprinkle the paprika, pepper, and 1/8 teaspoon salt evenly over both sides of the fish. Rub lightly to coat.

Heat a 12-inch nonstick skillet over medium-high heat. Cook the fish for 3 minutes on each side, or until it flakes easily when tested with a fork.

To serve, place the fish on plates with the aïoli on the side.

calories 134
protein 23 g
carbohydrates 5 g
  fiber 0 g
  sugars 2 g
cholesterol 45 mg
total fat 1.0 g
  saturated 0.5 g
  polyunsaturated 0.5 g
  monounsaturated 0.0 g
sodium 357 mg

dietary exchange
1/2 other carbohydrate
3 very lean meat

Fish Fillets with Zesty Rosemary Oil

Serves 4

Just a tip of cider vinegar is added to heighten the flavor of this already-tasty fish dish. The sauce is very intense, so a little goes a very long way.

4   grouper, tilapia, or other mild fish
    fillets (about 4 ounces each)
1   tablespoon olive oil (extra-virgin
    preferred)
1   teaspoon grated lemon zest

1   tablespoon fresh lemon juice
1/2 teaspoon cider vinegar
1/2 medium garlic clove, minced
1/4 teaspoon salt
1/8 teaspoon dried rosemary, crushed

Rinse the fish and pat dry with paper towels.

Heat a 12-inch nonstick skillet over medium heat. Cook the fish for 3 minutes on each side, or until the fish flakes easily when tested with a fork. Transfer to a platter.

Meanwhile, in a small bowl, stir together the remaining ingredients.

To serve, drizzle the sauce over the fish.

calories 136
protein 22 g
carbohydrates 1 g
  fiber 0 g
  sugars 0 g
cholesterol 42 mg
total fat 4.5 g
  saturated 0.5 g
  polyunsaturated 0.5 g
  monounsaturated 2.5 g
sodium 206 mg

dietary exchange
3 lean meat

So Simple, So Fast, So Good Fillets

Serves 4

If you want something easy to prepare and easy to clean up, keep this recipe close at hand. You'll use it over and over and over again!

4 grouper, tilapia, or other mild fish fillets (about 4 ounces each)

$\frac{1}{2}$ teaspoon dried thyme, crumbled (optional)

$\frac{1}{4}$ teaspoon salt

$\frac{1}{4}$ teaspoon pepper

2 tablespoons light tub margarine

2 tablespoons snipped fresh parsley (optional)

1 medium lemon, quartered

Rinse the fish and pat dry with paper towels. Sprinkle both sides of the fish with the thyme, salt, and pepper.

Heat a 12-inch nonstick skillet over medium heat. Cook the fish for 3 minutes on each side, or until it flakes easily when tested with a fork.

Spread the margarine over the fish. Sprinkle with the parsley. Squeeze the lemon over all.

Cook's Tip

Using a larger skillet makes it easier to turn the delicate fillets.

calories 128
protein 22 g
carbohydrates 1 g
  fiber 0 g
  sugars 0 g
cholesterol 42 mg
total fat 3.5 g
  saturated 0.5 g
  polyunsaturated 1.0 g
  monounsaturated 1.5 g
sodium 251 mg

dietary exchange
3 very lean meat

Fish Fillets
with Asparagus

Serves 4

Fish and asparagus always pair well. Crown them with a rich-tasting topping, and you have a special treat.

Vegetable oil spray
4 mild fish fillets, such as haddock or cod (about 4 ounces each)
1 tablespoon fresh lemon juice
1/2 teaspoon pepper
Vegetable oil spray
12 medium spears cooked asparagus

Topping
1/3 cup fat-free or light sour cream
1/3 cup fat-free or light plain yogurt
2 teaspoons minced green onion (green part only)
2 teaspoons prepared white horseradish, drained
1/2 teaspoon dried dillweed, crumbled
White of 1 large egg

❖

2 tablespoons snipped fresh parsley

Preheat the broiler. Lightly spray a broiler pan and rack with vegetable oil spray.

Rinse the fish and pat dry with paper towels. Place the fish on the broiler rack. Pour the lemon juice over the fish, sprinkle with the pepper, and lightly spray with vegetable oil spray.

Broil about 6 inches from the heat for 4 minutes on each side, or until the fish almost flakes when tested with a fork. Remove from the broiler and top each fillet with 3 spears of asparagus.

Meanwhile, in a small bowl, whisk together all the topping ingredients except the egg white.

In another small bowl, beat the egg white until stiff peaks form. Fold into the sour cream mixture. Spread over each fillet to cover the fish and asparagus.

Broil about 6 inches from the heat for 1 to 2 minutes, or until golden brown.

Sprinkle with the parsley.

calories 153
protein 26 g
carbohydrates 9 g
 fiber 1 g
 sugars 4 g
cholesterol 68 mg
total fat 1.0 g
 saturated 0.0 g
 polyunsaturated 0.5 g
 monounsaturated 0.0 g
sodium 134 mg

dietary exchange
1/2 skim milk
3 very lean meat

Haddock with Tomatoes and Ginger

Serves 6

A citrusy tomato sauce with an Asian flair tops mild haddock fillets.

Vegetable oil spray
3 tablespoons all-purpose flour
Dash of pepper
6 haddock fillets (about 4 ounces each)
1 tablespoon acceptable vegetable oil
1 tablespoon grated peeled gingerroot
2 medium garlic cloves, minced

2 cups seeded, chopped tomatoes (about 4 medium)
2 or 3 medium green onions (green and white parts), sliced
1 cup fresh orange juice
1/2 cup dry white wine (regular or nonalcoholic)
1 1/2 tablespoons cornstarch
1 tablespoon low-salt soy sauce
1 tablespoon snipped fresh parsley

Preheat the oven to 350°F. Lightly spray a 13 × 9 × 2-inch baking dish with vegetable oil spray.

Combine the flour and pepper on a plate.

Rinse the fish and pat dry with paper towels. Coat the fillets in the flour mixture one at a time. Shake off any excess flour.

Heat a large nonstick skillet over medium-high heat. Pour the oil into the skillet and swirl to coat the bottom. Cook the fish for 1 minute on each side. Transfer the fish to the baking dish.

Bake for 10 to 15 minutes, or until the fish flakes easily when tested with a fork.

Meanwhile, add the gingerroot and garlic to the residual oil in the skillet. Cook over medium heat for 10 to 15 minutes. Stir in the tomatoes and green onions. Bring to a simmer. Simmer for 3 to 4 minutes.

In a small bowl, whisk together the remaining ingredients except the parsley. Add to the tomato mixture. Increase the heat to medium high and cook for 2 to 3 minutes, or until thickened, whisking constantly. Stir in the parsley. Spoon the sauce over the fish.

calories 192
protein 23 g
carbohydrates 13 g
  fiber 1 g
  sugars 6 g
cholesterol 65 mg
total fat 3.5 g
  saturated 0.5 g
  polyunsaturated 1.0 g
  monounsaturated 1.5 g
sodium 151 mg

dietary exchange
1/2 starch
1/2 fruit
3 very lean meat

Mediterranean Fish

Serves 6

You can use almost any fish fillets—thick or thin—in this dish.

Vegetable oil spray
1 medium onion, thinly sliced
1½ pounds fish fillets, such as halibut, sole, or orange roughy
2 large tomatoes, sliced, or 14.5-ounce can no-salt-added tomatoes, drained
6 ounces button mushrooms, sliced
½ medium green bell pepper, sliced
¼ cup snipped fresh parsley

½ cup dry white wine (regular or nonalcoholic) or fat-free, low-sodium chicken broth, such as on page 45
2 tablespoons fresh lemon juice
1 teaspoon fresh dillweed or ¼ teaspoon dried, crumbled
Black pepper to taste
½ cup plain dry bread crumbs
1 tablespoon olive oil
½ teaspoon dried basil, crumbled

Preheat the oven to 350°F. Lightly spray a 13 × 9 × 2-inch baking dish with vegetable oil spray.

Arrange the onion slices in the baking dish. Rinse the fish and pat dry with paper towels. Cut the fish into serving pieces if necessary. Place the fish on the onion slices.

In a medium bowl, stir together the tomatoes, mushrooms, bell pepper, and parsley. Spoon over the fish.

In a measuring cup, stir together the wine, lemon juice, dillweed, and black pepper. Pour over the fish. Cover the baking dish with aluminum foil.

Bake thicker fish, such as halibut, for 20 minutes. Bake thinner fish, such as sole or orange roughy, for 15 minutes.

Meanwhile, in a small bowl, stir together the remaining ingredients. Sprinkle over the fish and vegetables.

Bake, uncovered, for 5 to 10 minutes, or until the fish flakes easily when tested with a fork.

calories 229
protein 27 g
carbohydrates 14 g
 fiber 2 g
 sugars 4 g
cholesterol 36 mg
total fat 5.5 g
 saturated 1.0 g
 polyunsaturated 1.5 g
 monounsaturated 3.0 g
sodium 149 mg

dietary exchange
½ starch
1½ vegetable
3 lean meat

Coconut-Rum Baked Fish

Serves 4

One bite of this incredibly delicious fish will make you want to reserve passage on a Caribbean cruise. Stir-fried sugar snap peas and wedges of fresh pineapple make terrific accompaniments.

2 tablespoons rum or ¹/₂ teaspoon rum extract
1 teaspoon lime zest
1 tablespoon fresh lime juice
¹/₂ teaspoon coconut extract
1 pound halibut, orange roughy, or tilapia fillets
¹/₄ cup all-purpose flour
Egg substitute equivalent to 2 eggs, or 2 large eggs
¹/₃ cup dry plain bread crumbs
2 tablespoons shredded sweetened coconut
2 tablespoons chopped macadamia nuts
Vegetable oil spray

In a medium glass bowl, stir together the rum, lime zest, lime juice, and coconut extract.

Rinse the fish and pat dry with paper towels. Cut the fish into serving pieces if necessary. Add the fish to the rum mixture, turning to coat. Cover and refrigerate for 10 minutes to 1 hour.

Put the flour in one shallow bowl and the egg substitute in another. In a third shallow bowl, stir together the bread crumbs, coconut, and macadamia nuts. Set the bowls side by side, assembly-line fashion.

Preheat the oven to 400°F. Lightly spray a baking sheet with vegetable oil spray.

Remove a fillet from the marinade, shaking off any excess marinade. Lightly coat both sides of the fillet with flour, dip both sides in the egg substitute, and lightly coat both sides with the bread crumb mixture. Place the fillet on the baking sheet. Repeat with the remaining fillets. Discard any extra marinade. Lightly spray the fish with vegetable oil spray.

Bake for 10 to 12 minutes, or until the fish is light golden brown and flakes easily when tested with a fork.

calories 235
protein 29 g
carbohydrates 15 g
  fiber 1 g
  sugars 2 g
cholesterol 35 mg
total fat 7.0 g
  saturated 1.5 g
  polyunsaturated 0.0 g
  monounsaturated 2.5 g
sodium 209 mg

dietary exchange
1 starch
3 lean meat

Teriyaki Halibut

Serves 8

Steam some brown rice and bright-green snow peas to complement this dish.

Marinade
1/2 cup dry white wine (regular or
   nonalcoholic)
3 tablespoons low-salt soy sauce
1 tablespoon light brown sugar
1 teaspoon all-purpose flour
1 teaspoon acceptable vegetable oil

1/2 teaspoon dry mustard
❖
2 pounds halibut fillets
   Vegetable oil spray
6 slices pineapple, canned in their
   own juice

In a small saucepan, whisk together the marinade ingredients. Bring to a boil over medium-high heat. Reduce the heat and simmer for 3 minutes. Pour into a small bowl, cover, and refrigerate for 30 minutes to 1 hour.

Rinse the fish and pat dry with paper towels. Cut the fish into serving pieces if necessary. Put the fish in a large resealable plastic bag. Pour the marinade over the fish. Seal the bag. Turn several times to coat completely. Refrigerate for 15 minutes.

Preheat the broiler. Lightly spray a broiler pan and rack with vegetable oil spray.

Remove the fish from the marinade and put it on the rack. Pour the marinade into a small saucepan. Bring the marinade to a boil over medium-high heat. Boil for 5 minutes. Brush the fish with the hot marinade.

Broil the fish 5 to 6 inches from the heat for 5 minutes. Turn over and top with the pineapple. Broil for about 5 minutes, or until the fish flakes easily when tested with a fork.

Cook's Tip

Seafood doesn't need to marinate for long. Too much marinating time can cause it to become rubbery.

calories 173
protein 24 g
carbohydrates 8 g
   fiber 0 g
   sugars 6 g
cholesterol 36 mg
total fat 3.5 g
   saturated 0.5 g
   polyunsaturated 1.0 g
   monounsaturated 1.5 g
sodium 209 mg

dietary exchange
1/2 fruit
3 very lean meat

Fish Tacos
with Pico de Gallo

Serves 4

Fish tacos are all the rage at many restaurants. Our version includes a margarita-style marinade and fresh pico de gallo enhanced with the delicate crunch of jícama.

Pico de Gallo
1 fresh jalapeño
1 cup diced jícama
2 medium Italian plum tomatoes, diced
¼ small red onion, finely chopped
2 tablespoons coarsely chopped fresh cilantro
2 teaspoons fresh lime juice

❖

1 tablespoon tequila or dry white wine (regular or nonalcoholic) (optional)
1 tablespoon fresh lime juice
1 teaspoon grated orange zest
1 teaspoon acceptable vegetable oil
1 pound mahimahi, halibut, or tuna fillets
8 6-inch corn tortillas

Wearing gloves, discard the seeds and ribs of the jalapeño. Finely chop the jalapeño. Put in a medium glass bowl. Stir in the remaining pico de gallo ingredients. Cover and refrigerate until ready to assemble tacos, up to two days.

In a medium glass bowl, stir together the tequila, 1 tablespoon lime juice, orange zest, and oil.

Rinse the fish and pat dry with paper towels. Cut the fish into ¾-inch cubes. Add the fish to the marinade and stir to coat. Cover and refrigerate for 10 to 30 minutes.

Preheat the oven to 350°F.

Wrap the tortillas in aluminum foil. Bake for 5 minutes, or until warmed through. Remove the tortillas from the oven, leaving them in the foil.

calories 201
protein 23 g
carbohydrates 19 g
  fiber 4 g
  sugars 2 g
cholesterol 83 mg
total fat 3.0 g
  saturated 0.5 g
  polyunsaturated 1.0 g
  monounsaturated 1.0 g
sodium 150 mg

dietary exchange
1 starch
1 vegetable
3 very lean meat

Meanwhile, heat a large nonstick skillet over medium-high heat. Cook the fish with the marinade for 4 to 6 minutes, or until the fish flakes easily when tested with a fork and most of the liquid has evaporated. If there is excess liquid in the pan, increase the heat to high and cook for 1 to 2 minutes.

To assemble, spoon the fish down the center of each warm tortilla. Spoon the pico de gallo over the fish. Roll up the tortillas to enclose the filling. Place with the seam side down on a platter.

Orange Roughy with Tomatoes and Spinach

Serves 6

While this aromatic dish bakes, slice some crusty French bread and fresh strawberries to serve with it.

1 teaspoon olive oil	2 tablespoons finely snipped fresh dillweed
1 large onion, finely chopped	
3 medium garlic cloves, minced	2 tablespoons snipped fresh parsley
3 tablespoons water	2 tablespoons fresh lemon juice
28-ounce can no-salt-added Italian plum tomatoes, undrained	Vegetable oil spray
1/2 cup dry white wine (regular or nonalcoholic)	6 orange roughy fillets (about 4 ounces each)
10-ounce package fresh spinach, stems discarded, coarsely torn	1/2 teaspoon pepper
	2 tablespoons cornstarch (optional)
	2 tablespoons water (optional)

Preheat the oven to 400°F.

Heat a large nonstick skillet over medium-high heat. Pour the oil into the skillet and swirl to coat the bottom. Cook the onion and garlic for 2 minutes. Pour in 3 tablespoons water. Cook until the water evaporates, stirring constantly.

Stir in the undrained tomatoes and wine. Crush the tomatoes with a spoon. Cook, uncovered, over medium-high heat for 7 to 8 minutes, or until the liquid is reduced slightly.

Stir in the spinach. Cook, covered, for 3 to 5 minutes, or until the spinach is wilted. Remove from the heat.

Stir in the dillweed, parsley, and lemon juice.

Lightly spray an oblong, nonaluminum baking dish with vegetable oil spray. Pour half the sauce into the dish.

Rinse the fish and pat dry with paper towels. Place the fish on the sauce and sprinkle with the pepper. Fold each fillet in half and pour the remaining sauce over all. Cover the dish with aluminum foil.

calories 146
protein 21 g
carbohydrates 10 g
  fiber 3 g
  sugars 5 g
cholesterol 23 mg
total fat 2.0 g
  saturated 0.0 g
  polyunsaturated 0.0 g
  monounsaturated 1.0 g
sodium 212 mg

dietary exchange
2 vegetable
3 very lean meat

Bake for 15 to 18 minutes, or until the fish flakes easily when tested with a fork.

If a thicker sauce is desired, place the fish on a platter. Cover the platter with aluminum foil to keep warm. Pour the sauce into a nonstick skillet. Put the cornstarch in a cup or small bowl. Add the 2 tablespoons water, stirring to dissolve. Stir the cornstarch mixture into the sauce. Bring to a boil over medium-high heat. Cook until desired consistency, stirring constantly.

To serve, pour the sauce over the fish.

Cook's Tip on Cooking Wine

Avoid wine bottled and labeled as cooking wine. It's loaded with sodium. It won't do your dish—or your body—any good.

Time-Saver

Buy frozen chopped onions or freeze your own in a resealable plastic freezer bag. You don't even need to thaw them to use them. A bonus: Because of the extra moisture, you can reduce or eliminate the amount of oil or margarine needed for cooking the onions in most recipes. A second bonus is that the frozen onions actually take less time to cook than the fresh ones.

Dilled Orange Roughy with
Lemon-Caper Sauce

Serves 4

One skillet is all you need for cooking this fish, enveloped in a creamy lemon sauce. Serve with steamed asparagus.

¹/₄ cup all-purpose flour
1 tablespoon snipped fresh dillweed
   or 1 teaspoon dried, crumbled
¹/₄ teaspoon pepper
4 orange roughy fillets (about
   4 ounces each)
2 teaspoons olive oil

¹/₂ cup fat-free, low-sodium chicken
   broth, such as on page 45
1 teaspoon grated lemon zest
1 tablespoon fresh lemon juice
1 tablespoon capers, rinsed and
   drained

In a shallow dish, stir together the flour, dillweed, and pepper.

Rinse the fish and pat dry with paper towels. Coat both sides of the fish with the flour mixture. Shake off any excess.

Heat a large nonstick skillet over medium-high heat. Pour the oil into the skillet and swirl to coat the bottom. Cook the fish for 1 minute on each side, or until lightly browned.

Add the broth, lemon zest, lemon juice, and capers without stirring. Bring to a simmer. Reduce the heat and simmer, covered, for 7 to 8 minutes, or until the fish flakes easily when tested with a fork.

To serve, place the fish on a platter. Pour the sauce over all.

calories 130
protein 18 g
carbohydrates 7 g
  fiber 0 g
  sugars 0 g
cholesterol 23 mg
total fat 3.0 g
  saturated 0.5 g
  polyunsaturated 0.0 g
  monounsaturated 2.0 g
sodium 134 mg

dietary exchange
¹/₂ starch
3 very lean meat

Salmon with Cucumber-Dill Sauce

Serves 4

Serve this light entrée warm, at room temperature, or chilled.

4 salmon fillets (about 4 ounces each)
1 cup dry white wine (regular or nonalcoholic)
2 bay leaves
2 tablespoons finely snipped fresh dillweed or 2 teaspoons dried, crumbled
Pepper to taste

Cucumber-Dill Sauce

2 medium cucumbers, peeled, seeded, and cut into $^1/_2$-inch slices
1 medium rib of celery, including leaves, cut into $^1/_2$-inch slices
3 tablespoons snipped fresh dillweed or 1 tablespoon dried, crumbled
1 teaspoon olive oil (extra-virgin preferred)
$^1/_4$ teaspoon salt
Pepper to taste

Preheat the oven to 350°F.

Rinse the fish and pat dry with paper towels. Put the fish in a glass baking dish.

Pour the wine over the fish. Add the bay leaves. Sprinkle with the dillweed and pepper. Cover tightly with aluminum foil.

Bake the fish for 10 minutes per inch of thickness, or until it flakes easily when tested with a fork. Remove from the oven and keep covered.

Put the sauce ingredients in a large saucepan with enough water to barely cover the vegetables. Boil, covered, over high heat for about 30 minutes, or until the celery is soft, stirring occasionally.

Carefully ladle the sauce into a food processor or blender and process until smooth.

To serve, spoon half the sauce onto a platter. Place the fish on the sauce. Spoon the remaining sauce over the fish or serve on the side.

calories 163
protein 24 g
carbohydrates 5 g
fiber 1 g
sugars 3 g
cholesterol 59 mg
total fat 5.5 g
saturated 1.0 g
polyunsaturated 1.5 g
monounsaturated 2.0 g
sodium 236 mg
dietary exchange
1 vegetable
3 lean meat

Baked Salmon
with Cucumber Relish

Serves 4

The cool crispness of this dish is completely refreshing, even on the hottest days of summer.

Vegetable oil spray
4 salmon fillets (about 4 ounces each)
1/4 teaspoon pepper
1/4 teaspoon salt
1 fresh jalapeño
1/2 medium cucumber, peeled, seeded, and chopped

1/4 cup finely chopped red onion
1/2 cup fat-free or light plain yogurt
1 teaspoon grated lemon zest
1 tablespoon fresh lemon juice
1/4 teaspoon salt

Preheat the oven to 400°F. Line a baking sheet with aluminum foil. Lightly spray with vegetable oil spray.

Rinse the fish and pat dry with paper towels. Put the fish on the baking sheet. Sprinkle with the pepper and 1/4 teaspoon salt.

Bake for 20 minutes, or until the fish flakes easily when tested with a fork.

Meanwhile, wearing gloves, discard the seeds and ribs of the jalapeño. Finely chop the jalapeño. Put the jalapeño in a medium bowl. Stir the cucumber and red onion into the jalapeño.

In a small bowl, stir together the remaining ingredients.

To serve, place the fish on plates. Spoon 2 tablespoons yogurt mixture evenly over each fillet. Top each serving with 1/4 cup cucumber mixture, spooned crosswise over the fish for a pretty presentation.

calories 161
protein 25 g
carbohydrates 5 g
  fiber 1 g
  sugars 4 g
cholesterol 60 mg
total fat 4.0 g
  saturated 0.5 g
  polyunsaturated 1.5 g
  monounsaturated 1.0 g
sodium 391 mg

dietary exchange

1 vegetable
3 lean meat

Broiled Salmon
with Citrus Salsa

Serves 4

A delightfully minty fruit salsa dresses up just-about-foolproof broiled salmon. This so-easy entrée is ideal when you're entertaining.

Vegetable oil spray
4 salmon fillets (about 4 ounces each)
$1/4$ teaspoon salt
$1/4$ teaspoon pepper

Citrus Salsa

$1^1/2$ cups bottled mixed citrus, such as grapefruit and orange sections, in extra-light syrup, drained and finely chopped
$1/4$ cup finely chopped red onion
2 tablespoons chopped fresh mint
$1/4$ teaspoon crushed red pepper flakes

Preheat the broiler. Lightly spray a broiler pan and rack with vegetable oil spray.

Rinse the fish and pat dry with paper towels. Sprinkle the fish with the salt and pepper.

Broil for 5 minutes on each side, or until the fish flakes easily when tested with a fork.

Meanwhile, in a medium bowl, stir together the salsa ingredients.

To serve, place the fish on plates. Spoon the salsa over or beside the fish.

Cook's Tip on Bottled Citrus Sections

Check the supermarket's refrigerated produce section for this convenient product.

calories 177
protein 23 g
carbohydrates 11 g
 fiber 1 g
 sugars 8 g
cholesterol 59 mg
total fat 4.0 g
 saturated 0.5 g
 polyunsaturated 1.5 g
 monounsaturated 1.0 g
sodium 232 mg

dietary exchange
$1/2$ fruit
3 lean meat

Grilled Salmon

Summertime and the grilling is easy. Once the salmon soaks up the pineapple-lime marinade flavors, it's ready in almost no time.

Marinade
  6 ounces pineapple juice
  1/2 cup finely chopped onion
  1/2 teaspoon grated lime zest
  2 tablespoons fresh lime juice
  1 tablespoon grated peeled
     gingerroot
  1 tablespoon low-salt soy sauce

  2 medium garlic cloves, minced
  1 teaspoon hot-pepper oil (optional)
  1 teaspoon acceptable vegetable oil
  ❖
  6 salmon steaks or fillets (about
     4 ounces each)
     Vegetable oil spray

Put the marinade ingredients in a large resealable plastic bag.

Rinse the fish and pat dry with paper towels. Add to the marinade. Seal the bag. Turn several times to coat completely. Refrigerate for 15 minutes to 1 hour, turning occasionally.

Lightly spray the grill or a broiler pan and rack with vegetable oil spray. Preheat the grill on medium-high or preheat the broiler.

Remove the fish from the marinade; discard the marinade. Grill the fish or broil it 4 to 5 inches from the heat for 5 to 7 minutes on each side, or until the fish flakes easily when tested with a fork.

calories 133
protein 23 g
carbohydrates 0 g
  fiber 0 g
  sugars 0 g
cholesterol 59 mg
total fat 4.0 g
  saturated 0.5 g
  polyunsaturated 1.5 g
  monounsaturated 1.0 g
sodium 141 mg

dietary exchange
3 lean meat

Cook's Tip on Hot-Pepper Oil

Also called chili oil, this is vegetable oil flavored with hot red chile peppers. Commonly used in Chinese cuisine, it can be very hot. You can make your own by steeping crushed red pepper flakes in an acceptable vegetable oil.

Salmon Cakes

Serves 8

Remember salmon croquettes? Here's a distant cousin. Serve with a steamed green vegetable and corn on the cob.

1 pound salmon fillets with skin
Whites of 2 large eggs
1 teaspoon acceptable vegetable oil
1 small onion, finely chopped (white preferred)
1/2 teaspoon grated or minced peeled gingerroot
1 medium garlic clove, grated or minced
4 medium green onions (green and white parts), finely chopped
1 medium potato, cooked and mashed

Egg substitute equivalent to 1 egg, or 1 large egg, slightly beaten
2 to 3 tablespoons fresh lime juice
1 1/2 tablespoons capers, rinsed, drained, and chopped
1 tablespoon snipped fresh cilantro or 1 teaspoon dried, crumbled
1 tablespoon snipped fresh dillweed or 1 teaspoon dried, crumbled
1/2 teaspoon paprika
1/4 teaspoon pepper
1/4 teaspoon dry mustard
1/4 to 1/2 teaspoon cayenne

Rinse the fish and pat dry with paper towels. Steam the fish for 6 to 8 minutes, or until it flakes easily when tested with a fork. Transfer to a casserole dish or medium bowl. Cover and refrigerate until cool. Discard the skin. Flake the fish.

In a medium bowl, beat the egg whites until frothy.

Heat a small nonstick skillet over medium heat. Pour the oil into the skillet and swirl to coat the bottom. Cook the onion, gingerroot, and garlic for 2 to 3 minutes, or until the onion is soft. Stir into the egg whites.

Stir in the remaining ingredients and the salmon. Divide the mixture into 8 patties.

Heat a large nonstick skillet over medium-high heat. Cook the patties for 3 to 4 minutes on each side, or until heated through.

calories 111
protein 14 g
carbohydrates 8 g
  fiber 1 g
  sugars 2 g
cholesterol 30 mg
total fat 2.5 g
  saturated 0.5 g
  polyunsaturated 1.0 g
  monounsaturated 1.0 g
sodium 115 mg

dietary exchange
1/2 starch
2 very lean meat

Salmon Alfredo

Serves 4

The sauce in this high-protein dish is as rich-tasting as conventional Alfredo made with cream.

8 ounces salmon fillets with skin
8 ounces dried plain or spinach
    fettuccine or spaghetti
    Vegetable oil spray
3 medium garlic cloves, minced
    10.5-ounce package light firm tofu
$2/3$ cup fat-free milk

2 ounces low-fat cream cheese
$1/4$ to $1/2$ teaspoon white pepper
$1/8$ teaspoon ground nutmeg
$2/3$ cup frozen green peas, thawed
1 tablespoon shredded or grated
    Parmesan cheese
1 tablespoon fresh lemon juice

Rinse the fish and pat dry with paper towels. Steam or poach the fish for 6 to 8 minutes, or until it flakes easily when tested with a fork.

Meanwhile, prepare the pasta using the package directions, omitting the salt and oil. Drain. Cover and keep warm.

While the pasta cooks, spray a large saucepan with vegetable oil spray. Cook the garlic over medium-high heat for about 30 seconds. Remove from the heat.

In a food processor or blender, process the tofu and milk until smooth. Add the tofu mixture, cream cheese, pepper, and nutmeg to the garlic. Cook over medium-high heat for 2 to 3 minutes, or until the cream cheese is melted and the mixture is smooth, whisking constantly.

Stir in the peas, Parmesan, and lemon juice. Cook for 1 minute.

Remove the skin from the salmon. Flake the salmon into the tofu mixture. Stir. Heat through for about 1 minute.

To serve, spoon the pasta into a large bowl. Spoon the sauce over the pasta.

calories 385
protein 29 g
carbohydrates 50 g
  fiber 3 g
  sugars 6 g
cholesterol 42 mg
total fat 7.0 g
  saturated 3.0 g
  polyunsaturated 1.5 g
  monounsaturated 2.0 g
sodium 241 mg

dietary exchange
$3\frac{1}{2}$ starch
3 lean meat

Snapper with Fresh Tomatoes and Capers

Serves 4

You get maximum flavor for minimal effort when you prepare this attractive dish. The brief amount of cooking turns the fresh vegetables into an assertive sauce.

4 snapper fillets (about 4 ounces each)	1 teaspoon grated lemon zest
¹/₂ medium tomato, seeded, finely chopped	2 tablespoons fresh lemon juice
4 medium green onions (green and white parts), chopped	1 tablespoon olive oil (extra-virgin preferred)
2 tablespoons capers, rinsed and drained	1 medium garlic clove, minced
	³/₄ teaspoon dried oregano, crumbled
	¹/₄ teaspoon salt

Rinse the fish and pat dry with paper towels.

Heat a 12-inch nonstick skillet over medium-high heat. Cook the fish for 3 minutes.

Add the remaining ingredients. Cook for 3 minutes, or until the fish flakes easily when tested with a fork.

calories 157
protein 24 g
carbohydrates 3 g
  fiber 1 g
  sugars 1 g
cholesterol 42 mg
total fat 5.0 g
  saturated 1.0 g
  polyunsaturated 1.0 g
  monounsaturated 3.0 g
sodium 337 mg

dietary exchange
3 lean meat

Mushroom-Stuffed Fish Rolls

Serves 6

Bits of fresh vegetables fill these baked fish rolls.

Vegetable oil spray

6 thin mild fish fillets, such as sole or orange roughy (about 4 ounces each)

1 teaspoon light tub margarine

12 ounces button mushrooms, finely diced

8 medium green onions (green and white parts), thinly sliced

1/2 medium red bell pepper, diced

2 tablespoons minced fresh parsley

1/4 teaspoon salt

1/4 teaspoon pepper

2 to 3 tablespoons fresh lemon juice

1/2 cup dry white wine (regular or nonalcoholic)

2 tablespoons all-purpose flour

2 tablespoons cold water

3/4 teaspoon paprika

2 tablespoons minced fresh parsley

Preheat the oven to 350°F. Lightly spray a 9-inch round or square casserole dish with vegetable oil spray. Rinse the fish and pat dry with paper towels.

In a heavy nonstick skillet, melt the margarine over medium heat and swirl to coat the bottom. Cook the mushrooms, green onions, bell pepper, and 2 tablespoons parsley for 3 to 5 minutes, or until soft.

Sprinkle the salt and pepper on the fish. Spoon the mushroom mixture evenly down the center of each fillet. Starting at a short side, roll up jelly-roll style and secure with wooden toothpicks. Put the fish in the casserole dish. Sprinkle with the lemon juice. Pour the wine over all. Cover the dish with aluminum foil.

Bake for 25 to 35 minutes, or until the fish flakes easily when tested with a fork. Using a slotted spoon, transfer the fish to a platter. Remove the toothpicks. Cover the platter with aluminum foil to keep warm. Pour the cooking liquid into a small saucepan.

In a small bowl, whisk together the flour, water, and paprika. Add to the saucepan. Cook over medium heat for 2 minutes, or until thickened, stirring constantly.

To serve, top the fish with the sauce and parsley.

calories 163
protein 24 g
carbohydrates 9 g
 fiber 3 g
 sugars 3 g
cholesterol 54 mg
total fat 2.0 g
 saturated 0.5 g
 polyunsaturated 0.5 g
 monounsaturated 0.5 g
sodium 206 mg

dietary exchange
1½ vegetable
3 very lean meat

French-Style Braised Fish Fillets

Serves 4

This classic dish from France is simple to prepare in American kitchens.

1 pound sole, trout, or orange roughy
   fillets
6 sprigs of fresh thyme
4 sprigs of fresh parsley
1 bay leaf

Marinade

1 cup dry white wine (regular or
   nonalcoholic) or water
1 small onion, thinly sliced
1 medium carrot, thinly sliced

1 tablespoon fresh lemon juice
1 medium shallot, thinly sliced
1 teaspoon olive oil
1 medium garlic clove, minced
1/4 teaspoon salt
1/8 teaspoon pepper

❖

Lemon slices (optional)
Sprigs of fresh thyme (optional)

Rinse the fish and pat dry with paper towels. Put the fish in a large resealable plastic bag.

Using kitchen twine, tie 6 sprigs of thyme, 4 sprigs of parsley, and the bay leaf in a bunch. Add to the fish.

Pour the marinade ingredients into the bag. Seal it. Turn to coat the fish. Refrigerate for 30 minutes to 1 hour, turning occasionally.

Transfer the fish and the marinade to a shallow pan. Bring to a simmer over medium-high heat. Reduce the heat and simmer, covered, for 10 to 12 minutes, or until the fish flakes easily when tested with a fork. Using a slotted spoon, transfer the fish to plates. Discard the marinade.

To serve, garnish the fish with the lemon and thyme.

calories 103
protein 21 g
carbohydrates 0 g
  fiber 0 g
  sugars 0 g
cholesterol 54 mg
total fat 1.5 g
  saturated 0.5 g
  polyunsaturated 0.5 g
  monounsaturated 0.5 g
sodium 237 mg

dietary exchange
3 very lean meat

Crispy Baked Fillet of Sole

Serves 6

Fish fillets absorb Asian flavor from a soy sauce and gingerroot marinade then are coated with an aromatic crumb coating and baked for crispness. Steamed baby carrots and Fresh Green Beans with Water Chestnuts (page 411) complete the meal.

Marinade
- ³/₄ cup finely chopped onion
- 2 teaspoons grated lime zest
- ¹/₄ cup fresh lime juice
- 1 tablespoon grated peeled gingerroot
- 1 tablespoon acceptable vegetable oil
- 1 tablespoon low-salt soy sauce
- ¹/₄ teaspoon salt
- ¹/₄ teaspoon pepper
- ❖
- 1¹/₂ pounds sole or other thin fish fillets
- Vegetable oil spray
- 1¹/₄ cups plain dry bread crumbs
- 2 tablespoons snipped fresh parsley
- 2 tablespoons finely chopped green onion (green and white parts)

Combine the marinade ingredients in a large resealable plastic bag.

Rinse the fish and pat dry with paper towels. Add to the marinade. Seal the bag. Turn several times to coat the fish completely. Refrigerate for 15 minutes to 1 hour.

Preheat the oven to 450°F. Lightly spray a 13 × 9 × 2-inch baking dish with vegetable oil spray.

On a large plate, stir together the remaining ingredients. Remove the fish from the marinade. Discard the marinade. Coat the fish with the crumb mixture. Shake off any excess. Put the fish in the baking dish.

Bake, uncovered, for 15 to 18 minutes, or until the fish flakes easily when tested with a fork.

calories 195
protein 24 g
carbohydrates 17 g
  fiber 1 g
  sugars 1 g
cholesterol 54 mg
total fat 2.5 g
  saturated 0.5 g
  polyunsaturated 0.5 g
  monounsaturated 1.0 g
sodium 449 mg

dietary exchange
1 starch
3 very lean meat

Sole Baked with Mushrooms

Serves 6

Try this dish with a variety of exotic mushrooms—shiitake, oyster, porto-bello, golden Italian, or whatever looks fresh and appealing.

Vegetable oil spray
1½ pounds sole or other thin fish fillets
1 teaspoon light tub margarine
12 ounces button mushrooms, sliced
¼ cup snipped fresh parsley
1 tablespoon finely chopped onion
½ teaspoon pepper

¼ cup dry white wine (regular or nonalcoholic)
1 tablespoon light tub margarine
½ cup fat-free milk
1 tablespoon all-purpose flour
2 tablespoons snipped fresh parsley
¼ teaspoon paprika

Preheat the oven to 350°F. Lightly spray a 13 × 9 × 2-inch baking dish with vegetable oil spray. Rinse the fish and pat dry with paper towels.

In a medium nonstick skillet, melt 1 teaspoon margarine over medium-high heat and swirl to coat the bottom. Cook the mushrooms, ¼ cup parsley, and onion for 2 to 3 minutes, or until the onion is soft, stirring frequently.

Place half the fish in the baking dish and sprinkle with half the pepper. Spread the mushroom mixture over the fish. Top with the remaining fish and sprinkle with the remaining pepper. Pour the wine over all. Dot with 1 tablespoon margarine.

Bake, uncovered, for 15 minutes. Using a slotted spatula, transfer the fish and mushrooms to a platter. Reserve the liquid.

In a small saucepan, whisk together the milk and flour. Whisk in the reserved liquid. Cook over medium-high heat for 2 to 3 minutes, or until thickened, whisking constantly.

Place the fish back in the baking dish. Pour the sauce over the fish. Bake, uncovered, for 5 minutes.

To serve, sprinkle with 2 tablespoons parsley and the paprika.

calories 148
protein 24 g
carbohydrates 5 g
  fiber 1 g
  sugars 2 g
cholesterol 55 mg
total fat 2.5 g
  saturated 0.5 g
  polyunsaturated 0.5 g
  monounsaturated 1.0 g
sodium 128 mg

dietary exchange
1 vegetable
3 very lean meat

Bay-Style Fillets

Serves 4

Here is the recipe for people who think cooking fish is daunting. All you do is bake fish with one ingredient sprinkled on top, then melt margarine right on the fish for a sauce that practically makes itself.

Vegetable oil spray

4 thin fish fillets, such as sole or tilapia (about 4 ounces each)

1 teaspoon seafood seasoning

2 tablespoons light tub margarine

Preheat the oven to 350°F. Line a rimmed baking sheet with aluminum foil. Lightly spray with vegetable oil spray.

Rinse the fish and pat dry with paper towels. Arrange the fish on the baking sheet. Sprinkle with the seafood seasoning.

Bake for 10 minutes, or until the fish flakes easily when tested with a fork.

To serve, spread $1/2$ tablespoon margarine evenly over each serving.

calories 123
protein 21 g
carbohydrates 0 g
  fiber 0 g
  sugars 0 g
cholesterol 54 mg
total fat 3.5 g
  saturated 0.5 g
  polyunsaturated 1.0 g
  monounsaturated 1.5 g
sodium 252 mg

dietary exchange
3 lean meat

Sole with Walnuts and White Wine

Serves 4

White sauce with walnuts makes this dish something special. You can whip up the sauce as the fish bakes. Serve with sugar snap peas and fresh peach slices.

Vegetable oil spray
1 pound sole or other thin fish fillets
1/2 cup dry white wine (regular or nonalcoholic)
1/2 cup fat-free, low-sodium chicken broth, such as on page 45; fish stock; or clam juice
Dash of cayenne

Sauce

2 tablespoons light stick margarine
2 tablespoons all-purpose flour

1/2 cup fat-free, low-sodium chicken broth, such as on page 45; fish stock; or clam juice
1/2 cup dry white wine (regular or nonalcoholic)
1/4 cup fat-free milk
Dash of white pepper
1/4 cup chopped walnuts, dry-roasted

❖

Sprigs of fresh parsley (optional)

Preheat the oven to 325°F. Lightly spray a 9-inch round or square baking dish with vegetable oil spray.

Rinse the fish and pat dry with paper towels. Put the fish in the baking dish. Add the wine, broth, and cayenne. Cover the dish with aluminum foil.

Bake for 20 minutes, or until the fish flakes easily when tested with a fork.

Meanwhile, in a small saucepan, melt the margarine over low heat. Whisk in the flour. Cook for 1 minute, stirring occasionally. (Don't let the flour brown.)

Increase the heat to medium-high. Whisk in the broth, wine, milk, and white pepper. Cook for 3 to 4 minutes, or until the mixture thickens, stirring constantly. Add the walnuts. Reduce the heat and simmer for 1 minute.

To serve, arrange the fish on a platter. Pour the sauce over the fish. Garnish with the parsley.

calories 218
protein 24 g
carbohydrates 5 g
  fiber 1 g
  sugars 1 g
cholesterol 55 mg
total fat 9.0 g
  saturated 1.5 g
  polyunsaturated 5.0 g
  monounsaturated 1.5 g
sodium 145 mg

dietary exchange
1/2 starch
3 lean meat

Sole with Parsley and Mint

Serves 4

Serve this dish with or without the sauce—either way is easy and unusual.

1 pound sole or other thin fish fillets
Vegetable oil spray
2 tablespoons finely snipped fresh parsley
1 tablespoon chopped fresh mint
2 teaspoons acceptable vegetable oil
1 medium garlic clove, chopped

Sauce (optional)
1 teaspoon light tub margarine
1 medium green onion (green part only), chopped
1/2 cup dry white wine (regular or nonalcoholic)
1/4 cup water
1/4 teaspoon white pepper

calories 126
protein 22 g
carbohydrates 1 g
  fiber 0 g
  sugars 0 g
cholesterol 54 mg
total fat 3.5 g
  saturated 0.5 g
  polyunsaturated 1.0 g
  monounsaturated 1.5 g
sodium 94 mg

dietary exchange
3 lean meat

with sauce

calories 153
protein 22 g
carbohydrates 1 g
  fiber 0 g
  sugars 0 g
cholesterol 54 mg
total fat 4.0 g
  saturated 0.5 g
  polyunsaturated 1.0 g
  monounsaturated 2.0 g
sodium 104 mg

dietary exchange
3 lean meat

Preheat the broiler.

Rinse the fish and pat dry with paper towels. Lightly spray a broiler pan and rack with vegetable oil spray. Put the fish on the rack.

In a small bowl, stir together the parsley, mint, oil, and garlic (mixture will be pastelike). Rub the mixture on the fish.

Broil about 4 inches from the heat for 5 to 8 minutes, or until the fish flakes easily when tested with a fork.

In a medium nonstick skillet, melt the margarine over medium-high heat and swirl to coat the bottom. Cook the green onion for 1 to 2 minutes. Stir in the pan juices from the fish and the remaining sauce ingredients. Heat thoroughly. Pour over the fish.

Cook's Tip on White Pepper

Milder in flavor than black pepper, white pepper is often used because its color blends in with a white or light-colored sauce. You can buy whole white peppercorns or ground white pepper.

Stovetop Fish with Vegetable Rice, Mexican Style

Serves 4

Cumin-seasoned fillets and yellow rice tossed with fresh vegetables, cilantro, and lemon are a winning combination for those hot summer nights.

1/2 cup uncooked white rice
1/2 teaspoon ground turmeric (optional)
4 tilapia or other mild fish fillets (about 4 ounces each)
1/2 tablespoon ground cumin
1 teaspoon paprika
1/4 teaspoon salt
1/4 teaspoon cayenne

1 cup finely chopped green bell pepper or poblano pepper, seeds and ribs discarded
2 medium Italian plum tomatoes, seeded and chopped
1/3 cup snipped fresh cilantro
1 teaspoon grated lemon zest
3 tablespoons fresh lemon juice
1 tablespoon olive oil (extra-virgin preferred)
1/2 teaspoon salt

Prepare the rice using the package directions, adding the turmeric and omitting the salt and margarine.

Meanwhile, rinse the fish and pat dry with paper towels.

In a small bowl, stir together the cumin, paprika, 1/4 teaspoon salt, and cayenne. Sprinkle the mixture over one side of each fillet. Pat lightly with fingertips to help the mixture adhere.

Heat a 12-inch nonstick skillet over high heat. Cook the fish for 1 minute on each side. Reduce the heat to medium. Turn the fish. Cook for 2 minutes. Turn and cook for 1 minute, or until the fish flakes easily when tested with a fork.

Meanwhile, in a medium bowl, stir together the remaining ingredients.

To serve, place 1 fillet on each plate. Either spoon the rice beside the fish and top the rice with the vegetable mixture or combine the rice with the vegetable mixture and serve beside the fish.

calories 200
protein 19 g
carbohydrates 23 g
  fiber 1 g
  sugars 2 g
cholesterol 43 mg
total fat 4.5 g
  saturated 0.5 g
  polyunsaturated 0.5 g
  monounsaturated 3.0 g
sodium 471 mg

dietary exchange
1 starch
1 1/2 vegetable
3 lean meat

Tex-Mex Tilapia

Serves 4

Shredded zucchini, red onions, enchilada sauce, and green chiles perk up mild-flavored tilapia and keep it moist while it bakes. Serve with ice-cold wedges of juicy watermelon on the side.

4 tilapia fillets (about 4 ounces each)
1 teaspoon ground cumin
1 medium zucchini, shredded
1/2 medium red onion, thinly sliced
2 tablespoons canned chopped green chiles, rinsed and drained

2 tablespoons sliced black olives
10-ounce can enchilada sauce
1/2 cup fat-free or low-fat shredded Cheddar cheese

Preheat the oven to 400°F.

Rinse the fish and pat dry with paper towels.

Put the fish in a nonstick 8-inch square baking dish. Sprinkle with the cumin.

Arrange the zucchini, onion, green chiles, and olives on the fish. Pour the enchilada sauce over all. Cover with aluminum foil.

Bake for 35 to 40 minutes, or until the fish flakes easily when tested with a fork and the vegetables are tender. Remove from the oven and sprinkle with the cheese.

calories 147
protein 23 g
carbohydrates 9 g
  fiber 2 g
  sugars 4 g
cholesterol 45 mg
total fat 3.0 g
  saturated 0.0 g
  polyunsaturated 1.0 g
  monounsaturated 1.0 g
sodium 368 mg

dietary exchange
2 vegetable
3 very lean meat

Baked Tilapia with Sausage-Flecked Rice

Serves 4

It's amazing how such a small amount of low-fat sausage can have such a large impact on flavor. This dish is similar to what cooks in New Orleans fondly call "dirty rice."

¹/₃ cup uncooked rice
Vegetable oil spray
4 tilapia fillets (about 4 ounces each)
¹/₄ teaspoon dried thyme, crumbled
¹/₈ teaspoon salt
Paprika to taste
3 ounces low-fat bulk breakfast sausage

1 medium red bell pepper, finely chopped
¹/₂ cup finely chopped green onions (green and white parts)
¹/₄ cup finely snipped fresh parsley
¹/₈ teaspoon cayenne (optional)
¹/₄ teaspoon salt

Prepare the rice using the package directions, omitting the salt and margarine.

Meanwhile, preheat the oven to 400°F. Line a baking sheet with aluminum foil. Lightly spray with vegetable oil spray.

Rinse the fish and pat dry with paper towels. Put on the baking sheet. Sprinkle with the thyme, ¹/₈ teaspoon salt, and paprika.

Bake for 12 minutes, or until the fish flakes easily when tested with a fork.

Meanwhile, heat a 10-inch nonstick skillet over medium-high heat. Cook the sausage for 2 minutes, stirring to break up the larger pieces.

Stir in the bell pepper and green onions. Cook for 1 minute, or until the sausage begins to lightly brown, stirring constantly. Remove from the heat.

Stir the rice, parsley, cayenne, and ¹/₄ teaspoon salt into the sausage mixture.

To serve, place 1 fillet on each plate. Spoon ¹/₂ cup sausage-rice mixture beside or on top of the fish.

calories 161
protein 21 g
carbohydrates 15 g
  fiber 1 g
  sugars 1 g
cholesterol 53 mg
total fat 1.5 g
  saturated 0.5 g
  polyunsaturated 0.5 g
  monounsaturated 0.5 g
sodium 374 mg

dietary exchange
1 starch
3 very lean meat

Baked Tilapia with
Tarragon Bread Crumbs

Serves 4

This dish is a sophisticated way to get your cravings for fried fish under control.

Vegetable oil spray
4 tilapia fillets (about 4 ounces each)
2 tablespoons fat-free or light Italian salad dressing
1/2 cup grated plain soft bread crumbs
1/2 teaspoon dried tarragon, crumbled

Paprika to taste
1 tablespoon plus 1 teaspoon olive oil (extra-virgin preferred)
1/8 teaspoon salt
1/8 teaspoon pepper

Preheat the oven to 400°F. Line a baking sheet with aluminum foil. Lightly spray with vegetable oil spray.

Rinse the fish and pat dry with paper towels. Place the fish on the baking sheet. Spoon the dressing over the fish. Sprinkle with the bread crumbs and tarragon. Sprinkle with the paprika.

Bake for 12 minutes, or until the fish flakes easily when tested with a fork.

Drizzle the fish with the oil. Sprinkle with the salt and pepper.

Cook's Tip on Grated Bread Crumbs

Use a food processor or blender to quickly turn soft bread into grated bread crumbs.

calories 131
protein 17 g
carbohydrates 4 g
  fiber 0 g
  sugars 1 g
cholesterol 43 mg
total fat 5.5 g
  saturated 1.0 g
  polyunsaturated 0.5 g
  monounsaturated 3.5 g
sodium 239 mg

dietary exchange
3 lean meat

Tilapia Amandine

Serves 4

Worcestershire sauce and fresh lemon juice provide the flavor boosts for this delicate dish.

¼ cup all-purpose flour
½ teaspoon paprika
⅛ teaspoon pepper
4 tilapia fillets (about 4 ounces each)
¼ cup water
2 tablespoons fresh lemon juice

1 tablespoon light tub margarine
2 teaspoons low-sodium Worcestershire sauce
¼ teaspoon salt
¼ cup sliced almonds, dry-roasted

In a shallow pan or dish, stir together the flour, paprika, and pepper.

Rinse the fish and pat dry with paper towels. Dust both sides of the fish with the flour mixture.

Heat a 12-inch nonstick skillet over medium heat. Cook the fish for 5 minutes on each side, or until it flakes easily when tested with a fork. Using a metal spatula, transfer to a platter.

Meanwhile, in a small bowl, stir together the remaining ingredients. After the fish has been removed, pour the lemon juice mixture into the skillet, scraping the bottom and sides with a rubber scraper. Cook for 2 minutes, or until reduced to ¼ cup.

To serve, spoon the sauce over the fish. Sprinkle with the almonds.

calories 146
protein 18 g
carbohydrates 8 g
  fiber 1 g
  sugars 1 g
cholesterol 43 mg
total fat 5.0 g
  saturated 0.5 g
  polyunsaturated 1.5 g
  monounsaturated 3.0 g
sodium 201 mg

dietary exchange
½ starch
3 lean meat

Greek Fish Fillets

Serves 4

It can't get much easier than this, from the simple seasonings to the simple cleanup. All this and great flavor, too!

1 teaspoon dried oregano, crumbled
1 teaspoon salt-free lemon pepper
¼ teaspoon paprika
¼ teaspoon salt
4 fish fillets, such as tilapia, flounder, or red snapper (about 4 ounces each)

Vegetable oil spray
1 tablespoon plus 1 teaspoon olive oil (extra-virgin preferred)
1 medium lemon, quartered

Preheat the broiler.

In a small bowl, stir together the oregano, lemon-pepper, paprika, and salt.

Rinse the fish and pat dry with paper towels. Place the fish on a nonstick baking sheet. Lightly spray the fish with vegetable oil spray. Sprinkle the seasoning mixture over the fish.

Broil for 5 minutes, or until the fish flakes easily when tested with a fork. Transfer to a platter.

Drizzle the fish with the oil. Squeeze 1 lemon quarter over each piece.

calories 114
protein 16 g
carbohydrates 1 g
  fiber 0 g
  sugars 0 g
cholesterol 43 mg
total fat 5.5 g
  saturated 0.5 g
  polyunsaturated 0.5 g
  monounsaturated 3.5 g
sodium 175 mg

dietary exchange
3 lean meat

Crisp Pan-Seared Trout with Green Onions

Serves 4

Rich in omega-3 fatty acids, trout is dressed up for dinner with a crisp coat made of flour and Chinese five-spice seasoning. It's then topped with thinly sliced green onions and a drizzle of vinegar and soy sauce. Serve with soba noodles tossed with a small amount of toasted sesame oil.

3 tablespoons red wine vinegar
2 teaspoons low-salt soy sauce
1 teaspoon toasted sesame oil
1/4 cup all-purpose flour
1 teaspoon five-spice powder

4 rainbow, brook, or steelhead trout fillets with skin (about 4.5 ounces each)
2 teaspoons acceptable vegetable oil
Vegetable oil spray
8 medium green onions (green part only), thinly sliced

In a small bowl, stir together the vinegar, soy sauce, and sesame oil. Set aside.

In a shallow bowl, stir together the flour and five-spice powder.

Rinse the fish and pat dry with paper towels. Coat only the flesh side of the fish with the flour mixture.

Heat a large nonstick skillet over medium-high heat. Pour the oil into the skillet and swirl to coat the bottom. Cook the fish with the flesh side down for 3 to 4 minutes, or until browned. Remove the skillet from the heat.

Lightly spray the skin side of each fillet with vegetable oil spray. Cook with the skin side down for 3 to 4 minutes, or until the fish flakes easily when tested with a fork.

To serve, place the fish with the skin side up on a platter. Let cool for 1 minute. Using tongs, carefully peel off the skin. Turn the fish over so the seasoned side is up. Sprinkle with the green onions. Pour the vinegar mixture over all.

calories 235
protein 27 g
carbohydrates 11 g
  fiber 2 g
  sugars 2 g
cholesterol 75 mg
total fat 8.0 g
  saturated 1.5 g
  polyunsaturated 3.0 g
  monounsaturated 3.5 g
sodium 115 mg

dietary exchange
1/2 starch
1 vegetable
3 1/2 lean meat

Braised Tuna Steaks with
Orange-Cranberry Glaze

Serves 4

If you like just a blush of pink in the center of your tuna, this braising technique will help you still keep the fish moist.

$1/2$ teaspoon ground pink peppercorns
    or $1/4$ teaspoon black pepper
4 tuna steaks (about 4 ounces each)
1 teaspoon olive oil
1 teaspoon grated orange zest
$1/2$ cup fresh orange juice

$1/2$ cup unsweetened cranberry juice
2 tablespoons port (optional)
2 teaspoons light brown sugar
1 tablespoon coarsely chopped fresh rosemary or 1 teaspoon dried, crushed

Sprinkle the peppercorns over both sides of the tuna.

Heat a large nonstick skillet over medium-high heat. Pour the oil into the skillet and swirl to coat the bottom. Lightly brown the tuna steaks for 1 minute on each side.

Stir in the remaining ingredients. Bring to a simmer. Reduce the heat and simmer, covered, for 7 to 9 minutes, or until the steaks are cooked through (centers will be slightly pink). Transfer to a platter. Cover the platter with aluminum foil.

For the glaze, increase the heat to medium-high and cook the liquid until reduced by half (about $1/2$ cup).

To serve, pour the glaze over the tuna.

with port

calories 175
protein 27 g
carbohydrates 8 g
  fiber 0 g
  sugars 7 g
cholesterol 51 mg
total fat 2.5 g
  saturated 0.5 g
  polyunsaturated 0.5 g
  monounsaturated 1.0 g
sodium 47 mg

dietary exchange
$1/2$ fruit
3 very lean meat

Sesame Tuna
with Pineapple Sauce

Serves 4

Turmeric turns the rice a brilliant yellow, dressing up this dish so it's perfect for when you want to impress without a lot of effort.

1 cup uncooked instant brown rice
1/2 teaspoon ground turmeric (optional)
3 tablespoons sesame seeds
2 teaspoons all-purpose flour
1/4 teaspoon salt
1/4 teaspoon pepper
4 tuna steaks (about 4 ounces each)
1/2 cup pineapple juice

1 tablespoon sugar
1 tablespoon low-salt soy sauce
2 teaspoons cornstarch
1/2 teaspoon grated peeled gingerroot
1/4 teaspoon crushed red pepper flakes
Vegetable oil spray
1/4 cup finely chopped green onions (green and white parts) (optional)

In a small saucepan, prepare the rice using the package directions, but adding the turmeric and omitting the salt and margarine.

Meanwhile, in a shallow pan or dish, stir together the sesame seeds, flour, salt, and pepper.

Rinse the fish and pat dry with paper towels. Coat the fish with the mixture. Don't shake off any excess.

Heat a 12-inch skillet over medium-high heat. Remove from the heat and lightly spray with vegetable oil spray (being careful not to spray near a gas flame). Cook the tuna for 2 minutes on each side, or until very pink in the center. (Overcooking causes dryness and toughness.)

Meanwhile, in a small saucepan, stir together the pineapple juice, sugar, soy sauce, cornstarch, gingerroot, and red pepper flakes until the cornstarch is dissolved. Bring to a boil over medium-high heat. Cook for 1 minute, or until thickened, stirring frequently.

In a medium bowl, stir together the rice and green onions. Transfer to the center of a platter.

To serve, arrange the tuna around the rice. Spoon the sauce over the tuna.

calories 291
protein 31 g
carbohydrates 28 g
  fiber 1 g
  sugars 7 g
cholesterol 51 mg
total fat 5.5 g
  saturated 1.0 g
  polyunsaturated 2.5 g
  monounsaturated 2.0 g
sodium 293 mg

dietary exchange
1 1/2 starch
1/2 fruit
3 lean meat

Grilled Tuna with
Pineapple-Nectarine Salsa

Serves 4

Citrus-marinated tuna sizzles on the grill, then is topped with a cool, refreshing fruit salsa.

1 pound tuna or other firm-fleshed fish, such as halibut

Marinade
- 1 teaspoon grated lime zest
- 2 tablespoons fresh lime juice
- 2 tablespoons fresh orange juice
- 1 tablespoon snipped fresh cilantro
- 1 teaspoon acceptable vegetable oil
- 1/4 teaspoon salt
- 1/8 teaspoon pepper

Pineapple-Nectarine Salsa
- 1 medium nectarine, diced
- 8-ounce can pineapple tidbits in their own juice
- 1 medium kiwifruit, peeled and diced
- 2 tablespoons diced red onion
- 1 tablespoon snipped fresh cilantro
- 1 teaspoon fresh lemon juice

Rinse the fish and pat dry with paper towels. Cut into 4 pieces.

Combine the marinade ingredients in a large resealable plastic bag. Add the fish. Seal the bag and turn to coat the fish. Refrigerate for 15 minutes to 1 hour, turning occasionally.

Meanwhile, in a medium bowl, stir together the salsa ingredients. Cover and refrigerate.

Preheat the grill on medium-high.

Grill the fish for 5 to 7 minutes on each side, or until it is cooked through and flakes easily when tested with a fork.

To serve, place the fish on plates. Top with the salsa.

calories 187
protein 27 g
carbohydrates 16 g
  fiber 2 g
  sugars 13 g
cholesterol 51 mg
total fat 1.5 g
  saturated 0.5 g
  polyunsaturated 0.5 g
  monounsaturated 0.0 g
sodium 189 mg

dietary exchange
1 fruit
3 very lean meat

Tuna and Soba Noodles

Serves 4

Raise canned tuna to new culinary heights in this Asian-flavored dish. Made with Japanese buckwheat noodles (soba), it can be served warm or chilled. Serve mandarin oranges on the side.

8 ounces dried soba noodles or whole-wheat angel hair pasta

12 ounces canned albacore tuna in spring or distilled water, drained and flaked

4 medium green onions (green and white parts), thinly sliced

3 tablespoons plain rice vinegar

2 tablespoons low-salt soy sauce

1 tablespoon brown sugar

2 teaspoons toasted sesame oil

2 medium garlic cloves, minced

Prepare the noodles using the package directions, omitting the salt and oil. Drain in a colander. Transfer to a large bowl. (Let cool for 10 minutes if you will be serving the dish chilled.)

Add the remaining ingredients to the noodles, stirring gently to coat.

Serve warm or cover and refrigerate for at least 30 minutes.

calories 350
protein 29 g
carbohydrates 49 g
  fiber 3 g
  sugars 8 g
cholesterol 36 mg
total fat 5.0 g
  saturated 1.0 g
  polyunsaturated 2.0 g
  monounsaturated 1.5 g
sodium 595 mg

dietary exchange
3 starch
3 very lean meat

Stuffed Shells with Albacore Tuna and Vegetables

Serves 4

A tuna noodle casserole variation goes gourmet with an upscale, from-scratch white sauce enhanced with Dijon mustard.

12 large dried pasta shells (about 4 ounces)
1 cup fat-free, low-sodium chicken broth, such as on page 45
3 tablespoons all-purpose flour
1 cup fat-free half-and-half
2 teaspoons Dijon mustard
1 teaspoon salt-free all-purpose seasoning

$\frac{1}{8}$ teaspoon salt
1-pound package frozen mixed vegetables (any combination), thawed
2 6-ounce cans albacore tuna in distilled or spring water, drained and flaked
2 tablespoons shredded or grated Parmesan cheese

Prepare the pasta using the package directions, omitting the salt and oil. Drain in a colander. Set aside.

Preheat the oven to 350°F.

In a medium saucepan, whisk together the broth and flour. Bring to a simmer over medium-high heat, stirring occasionally. Reduce the heat and simmer for 1 to 2 minutes, or until thickened.

Stir in the half-and-half, mustard, all-purpose seasoning, and salt. Reduce the heat to medium-low. Cook for 1 minute, or until warmed through, stirring occasionally. Remove from the heat.

In a medium bowl, stir together $\frac{1}{4}$ cup sauce, the vegetables, and the tuna.

Spoon $\frac{1}{4}$ cup tuna mixture into each pasta shell. Place the shells with the open side up in a nonstick 13 × 9 × 2-inch baking pan.

Pour the remaining sauce over all. Sprinkle with the Parmesan. Cover the pan with aluminum foil.

Bake for 25 to 30 minutes, or until warmed through.

To serve, transfer 3 stuffed shells to each plate. Spoon the sauce over all.

calories 361
protein 33 g
carbohydrates 50 g
  fiber 5 g
  sugars 10 g
cholesterol 38 mg
total fat 4.5 g
  saturated 1.5 g
  polyunsaturated 1.5 g
  monounsaturated 1.0 g
sodium 580 mg

dietary exchange
2 starch
4 vegetable
3 very lean meat

Tuna Chili

Serves 4

Here's an easy way to work more seafood into your diet—a warming bowl of chili with tuna instead of beef.

2 teaspoons olive oil
1 medium onion, chopped
1 medium green bell pepper, chopped
2 medium garlic cloves, minced
4 medium tomatoes, chopped
1½ cups no-salt-added canned pinto beans, rinsed and drained
2 6-ounce cans albacore tuna in distilled or spring water, rinsed, drained, and flaked
⅔ cup Salsa Cruda (page 502) or picante sauce
½ tablespoon chili powder
1 teaspoon ground cumin
1 tablespoon plus 1 teaspoon shredded fat-free or low-fat Cheddar cheese
1 tablespoon plus 1 teaspoon sliced green onion (green and white parts)

In a large saucepan, stir together the olive oil, onion, bell pepper, and garlic. Cook over medium-high heat for 4 to 5 minutes, or until the onion begins to brown, stirring occasionally.

Stir in the tomatoes, beans, tuna, Salsa Cruda, chili powder, and cumin. Reduce the heat and simmer, covered, for 20 to 30 minutes, or until the vegetables are tender and the mixture is heated through.

To serve, ladle the chili into bowls. Top each serving with the cheese and green onion.

calories 283
protein 29 g
carbohydrates 30 g
  fiber 7 g
  sugars 11 g
cholesterol 36 mg
total fat 5.5 g
  saturated 1.0 g
  polyunsaturated 1.5 g
  monounsaturated 2.5 g
sodium 195 mg

dietary exchange
1 starch
3 vegetable
3 lean meat

Tuna Salad
Pitas

Serves 5

Cilantro and lemon zest liven up the tuna salad in this pita sandwich.

Tuna Salad

- 9 ounces canned albacore tuna in distilled or spring water
- 1/2 cup diced seeded tomato
- 1/4 cup diced seeded unpeeled cucumber
- 1/4 cup plus 2 tablespoons fat-free or light mayonnaise dressing
- 1/4 cup sliced green onions
- 1/4 cup fat-free or light plain yogurt
- 1 tablespoon finely snipped fresh cilantro
- 1/2 teaspoon grated lemon zest
- Dash of red hot-pepper sauce

❖

- 5 6-inch whole-wheat pita breads
- 5 small pieces of leaf lettuce

Rinse and drain the tuna. Put it in a medium bowl and flake it.

Stir in the remaining tuna salad ingredients. Cover and refrigerate until thoroughly chilled, at least 30 minutes.

Split each pita carefully around the top edge, about one third of the circumference of the bread. Put a lettuce leaf and about 1/2 cup tuna mixture in each pita.

calories 258
protein 19 g
carbohydrates 38 g
  fiber 5 g
  sugars 5 g
cholesterol 22 mg
total fat 3.0 g
  saturated 0.5 g
  polyunsaturated 1.0 g
  monounsaturated 0.5 g
sodium 531 mg

dietary exchange
2 1/2 starch
2 very lean meat

Linguine with White Clam Sauce

Serves 5

We suggest fresh green beans and Tomato-Basil Salad with Balsamic Dressing (page 95) to go with this longtime favorite.

4 ounces bottled clam juice
1/2 cup fat-free, low-sodium chicken broth, such as on page 45
1/2 cup dry white wine (regular or nonalcoholic)
8 ounces dried linguine
1 teaspoon olive oil
1/2 cup finely chopped onion

4 medium garlic cloves, minced
2 tablespoons all-purpose flour
2 6 1/2-ounce cans minced clams, rinsed and drained
2 tablespoons finely snipped fresh parsley
2 tablespoons shredded or grated Parmesan cheese

In a small saucepan, stir together the clam juice, broth, and wine. Bring to a boil over high heat. Boil for about 5 minutes, or until the mixture is reduced to 1 1/4 cups. Set aside.

Prepare the linguine using the package directions, omitting the salt and oil. Drain well.

Meanwhile, heat a small nonstick skillet over medium-high heat. Pour the oil into the skillet and swirl to coat the bottom. Cook the onion for 2 to 3 minutes, or until soft.

Stir in the garlic. Cook for 2 minutes.

Stir in the flour. Cook for 1 minute.

Pour in the hot clam juice mixture. Cook until thickened, 2 to 3 minutes, stirring constantly.

Stir in the clams and parsley. Cook for 2 minutes, or until the clams are heated through, stirring constantly.

To serve, spoon the pasta onto a platter. Spoon the sauce over the pasta. Sprinkle with the Parmesan.

calories 258
protein 12 g
carbohydrates 41 g
 fiber 2 g
 sugars 3 g
cholesterol 14 mg
total fat 2.5 g
 saturated 0.5 g
 polyunsaturated 0.5 g
 monounsaturated 1.0 g
sodium 501 mg

dietary exchange
3 1/2 starch
1 very lean meat

Crabmeat Maryland

Serves 8

Serving individual casseroles adds a special touch to any meal.

3 cups flaked crabmeat
Vegetable oil spray
2 tablespoons minced onion
2 cups fat-free milk
3 tablespoons all-purpose flour
1 medium rib of celery, finely chopped; 1 teaspoon celery flakes; or ¼ teaspoon celery seeds
2-ounce jar diced pimientos, drained (about ¼ cup)

2 tablespoons minced green bell pepper
1 tablespoon snipped fresh parsley
Dash of red hot-pepper sauce
2 tablespoons dry sherry
Egg substitute equivalent to 1 egg, or 1 large egg, beaten
¼ teaspoon pepper, or to taste
2 slices bread, lightly toasted and crumbled
Vegetable oil spray

Thaw the crabmeat if frozen or drain if canned. Remove any shells or cartilage from the fresh or frozen crabmeat. Set the crabmeat aside.

Preheat the oven to 350°F. Lightly spray eight individual casserole dishes with vegetable oil spray. Set aside.

Heat a large nonstick skillet over medium-high heat. Cook the onion for 2 to 3 minutes, or until soft, stirring occasionally.

In a medium bowl, whisk together the milk and flour. Stir into the onion. Cook for 3 to 5 minutes, or until thickened, stirring occasionally.

Stir in the celery, pimientos, bell pepper, parsley, and hot-pepper sauce. Remove the skillet from the heat.

Stir the sherry into the sauce.

Whisk a little sauce into the egg substitute. Slowly pour the egg mixture into the sauce, whisking constantly.

Stir in the pepper and crabmeat. Spoon into the casserole dishes. Sprinkle with the bread crumbs. Lightly spray the crumbs with vegetable oil spray.

Bake, uncovered, for 15 to 20 minutes, or until lightly browned.

calories 109
protein 14 g
carbohydrates 10 g
  fiber 1 g
  sugars 4 g
cholesterol 35 mg
total fat 1.0 g
  saturated 0.0 g
  polyunsaturated 0.5 g
  monounsaturated 0.0 g
sodium 258 mg

dietary exchange
½ starch
2 very lean meat

Crab Primavera Alfredo

Serves 4

Lump crabmeat is simply irresistible, especially when you serve it in a creamy sauce with tender vegetables over pasta.

4 ounces dried fettuccine
1 teaspoon olive oil
2 medium shallots, coarsely chopped
1/2 cup halved baby carrots (cut lengthwise)
8 ounces broccoli florets
1 medium yellow summer squash, thinly sliced

1/2 cup fat-free, low-sodium chicken broth, such as on page 45
1/2 cup fat-free half-and-half
1 1/2 tablespoons all-purpose flour
1/2 teaspoon dried dillweed, crumbled
2 tablespoons shredded or grated Parmesan cheese
6-ounce can lump crabmeat, gently rinsed and drained

Prepare the pasta using the package directions, omitting the salt and oil. Drain in a colander. Transfer to a medium bowl. Cover to keep warm.

Meanwhile, heat a large skillet over medium-high heat. Pour the oil into the skillet and swirl to coat the bottom. Cook the shallots for 1 to 2 minutes, or until soft.

Stir in the carrots and broccoli. Cook for 2 to 3 minutes, or until tender-crisp.

Stir in the squash. Cook for 2 to 3 minutes, or until the vegetables are tender.

In a small bowl, whisk together the broth, half-and-half, flour, and dillweed. Pour into the skillet. Bring to a simmer. Reduce the heat and simmer for 1 to 2 minutes, or until thickened, stirring occasionally.

Stir in the Parmesan. Carefully fold in the crabmeat so the lumps don't break up too much. Cook for 2 to 3 minutes, or until the mixture is warmed through, gently stirring occasionally.

To serve, spoon the pasta onto each plate. Top each serving with the crab mixture.

calories 232
protein 18 g
carbohydrates 34 g
 fiber 3 g
 sugars 6 g
cholesterol 40 mg
total fat 3.0 g
 saturated 1.0 g
 polyunsaturated 0.5 g
 monounsaturated 1.0 g
sodium 236 mg

dietary exchange
2 starch
1 vegetable
1 1/2 very lean meat

Scallops and Asparagus in Wine Sauce

Serves 4

A velvety sauce and tender asparagus complement the delicate flavor of scallops in this dish. Serve it with your favorite pasta.

1 pound sea or bay scallops
8-ounce bottle clam juice
1/2 cup dry white wine (regular or nonalcoholic)
3 tablespoons all-purpose flour
1/4 teaspoon pepper
6 ounces fresh asparagus, trimmed, or 4 ounces frozen asparagus, thawed

1 teaspoon light tub margarine
1/4 cup minced shallots (about 4 large)
3 tablespoons finely snipped fresh parsley
1 tablespoon fresh lemon juice

Rinse the scallops and pat dry with paper towels. Cut them in quarters if large. Set aside.

In a large saucepan, whisk together the clam juice, wine, flour, and pepper. Bring to a boil over medium-high heat. Boil for 4 to 5 minutes, or until the mixture is thickened, stirring occasionally. Set aside.

Cut the asparagus diagonally into 1-inch pieces. Steam the fresh asparagus until tender-crisp, about 2 minutes (don't cook frozen asparagus). Set aside.

In a small nonstick skillet, melt the margarine over medium-high heat, swirling to coat the bottom. Cook the shallots for 2 to 3 minutes, or until soft.

Stir the shallots and scallops into the clam sauce. Reduce the heat to medium and cook for 5 minutes, stirring frequently. Don't let the mixture come to a boil. Add the asparagus, parsley, and lemon juice. Cook for 2 to 3 minutes, or until the scallops are opaque and the mixture is heated. Be careful not to overcook.

calories 164
protein 21 g
carbohydrates 12 g
  fiber 1 g
  sugars 2 g
cholesterol 37 mg
total fat 1.5 g
  saturated 0.0 g
  polyunsaturated 0.5 g
  monounsaturated 0.5 g
sodium 573 mg

dietary exchange
1/2 starch
1 vegetable
3 very lean meat

Oven-Fried Scallops
with Cilantro and Lime

Serves 4

Tender, moist scallops soak in a fresh cilantro-buttermilk marinade with the bright taste of lime; then they're coated in crumbs and baked.

Vegetable oil spray
1/2 cup fat-free or low-fat buttermilk
2 tablespoons snipped fresh cilantro
2 tablespoons fresh lime juice
1/8 teaspoon salt
1/4 teaspoon pepper

1 pound sea scallops
1/2 cup plain dry bread crumbs
Dash of paprika
2 tablespoons fresh cilantro leaves (optional)
4 lime wedges (optional)

Preheat the oven to 400°F. Lightly spray a 9-inch round or square baking dish with vegetable oil spray.

In a small, shallow bowl, whisk together the buttermilk, cilantro, lime juice, salt, and pepper.

Rinse the scallops and pat dry with paper towels. Add the scallops to the buttermilk mixture and let soak for 10 minutes.

Put the bread crumbs on a plate. Roll the scallops in the crumbs. Shake off any excess.

Arrange the scallops in a single layer in the baking dish. Sprinkle with the paprika. Lightly spray the scallops with vegetable oil spray.

Bake for 10 to 13 minutes, or until opaque.

To serve, sprinkle the scallops with the cilantro leaves. Garnish with the lime wedges.

calories 153
protein 21 g
carbohydrates 13 g
  fiber 0 g
  sugars 0 g
cholesterol 37 mg
total fat 1.5 g
  saturated 0.5 g
  polyunsaturated 0.5 g
  monounsaturated 0.5 g
sodium 404 mg

dietary exchange
1 starch
3 very lean meat

Shrimp and Okra Étouffée

Serves 6

This heart-healthy version of étouffée (ay-too-FAY) is every bit as rich tasting as the classic dish. The secret is to make a roux with browned flour but no oil.

1½ cups uncooked instant brown rice
¼ cup all-purpose flour
1 teaspoon acceptable vegetable oil
1 medium green bell pepper, finely chopped
1 medium onion, finely chopped
1 medium rib of celery, finely chopped

2 cups fresh or frozen sliced okra
2 cups fat-free, low-sodium chicken broth, such as on page 45
2 teaspoons Creole or Cajun seasoning blend
1 pound peeled medium raw shrimp

Prepare the brown rice using the package directions, omitting the salt and margarine.

In a large nonstick skillet, cook the flour over medium heat for 8 to 10 minutes, or until browned, stirring occasionally. Transfer to a medium bowl. Let cool for 5 minutes.

Wipe the skillet clean with paper towels. Heat the skillet over medium heat. Pour the oil into the skillet and swirl to coat the bottom. Cook the bell pepper, onion, and celery for 2 to 3 minutes, or until tender-crisp.

Stir in the okra. Cook for 2 to 3 minutes (4 to 5 minutes if using frozen), or until the okra is tender-crisp.

Whisk the broth into the flour (there may be a few lumps). Stir the broth mixture and Creole seasoning into the vegetable mixture. Bring to a simmer over medium-high heat, stirring occasionally. Reduce the heat and simmer, covered, for 15 to 20 minutes, or until the flavors have blended.

Stir in the shrimp. Simmer, covered, for 2 to 3 minutes, or until the shrimp are pink on the outside and opaque in the center.

To serve, spoon the rice into each bowl. Ladle the shrimp mixture over each serving.

calories 198
protein 16 g
carbohydrates 28 g
 fiber 3 g
 sugars 3 g
cholesterol 111 mg
total fat 2.5 g
 saturated 0.0 g
 polyunsaturated 1.0 g
 monounsaturated 1.0 g
sodium 257 mg

dietary exchange
1½ starch
1 vegetable
2 very lean meat

Fiery Shrimp Dijon

Serves 4

The addition of fresh lime juice makes the other intense ingredients in this dish explode with flavor.

2	tablespoons light tub margarine	¼	teaspoon black pepper
2	tablespoons Dijon mustard	⅛	teaspoon salt
½	tablespoon dried tarragon, crumbled		Vegetable oil spray
¼	teaspoon cayenne	1	pound raw medium shrimp in shells
		2	medium limes, quartered

In a small bowl, stir together the margarine, mustard, tarragon, cayenne, black pepper, and salt.

Peel and rinse the shrimp. Pat dry with paper towels.

Heat a 12-inch skillet over medium heat. Remove from the heat and lightly spray with vegetable oil spray (being careful not to spray near a gas flame). Cook the shrimp for 3 minutes, or until opaque, stirring frequently.

Stir in the margarine mixture to coat the shrimp.

Serve with the lime wedges.

calories 118
protein 19 g
carbohydrates 2 g
  fiber 1 g
  sugars 1 g
cholesterol 166 mg
total fat 4.0 g
  saturated 0.5 g
  polyunsaturated 1.0 g
  monounsaturated 1.5 g
sodium 462 mg

dietary exchange
3 lean meat

Little Shrimp Cakes

Serves 4

Perfect for dinner, these shrimp cakes are also great for appetizers. Using lots of lemon really sets them apart.

1 pound raw medium shrimp in shells
1 cup grated plain soft bread crumbs
  Whites of 3 large eggs
1/2 medium red bell pepper, finely chopped
1 medium green onion, finely chopped (green and white parts)
2 tablespoons fat-free or light mayonnaise dressing

1/2 teaspoon low-sodium Worcestershire sauce
1/2 teaspoon seafood seasoning
1/8 to 1/4 teaspoon cayenne
4 teaspoons acceptable vegetable oil, divided use
2 medium lemons, quartered

Peel and rinse the shrimp. Pat dry with paper towels.

Heat a 12-inch nonstick skillet over medium heat. Cook the shrimp for 5 minutes, or until opaque, stirring frequently. Set aside in a single layer on a baking sheet or sheet of aluminum foil to cool quickly.

Meanwhile, in a medium bowl, stir together the bread crumbs, egg whites, bell pepper, green onion, mayonnaise dressing, Worcestershire sauce, seafood seasoning, and cayenne.

Finely chop the shrimp. Stir into the bread-crumb mixture. With your hands, shape into 16 small patties.

Heat the skillet over medium heat. Pour 2 teaspoons oil into the skillet and swirl to coat the bottom. Cook 8 patties for 3 minutes. Turn. Cook for 2 to 3 minutes, or until golden. Transfer to a plate. Cover with aluminum foil to keep warm. Repeat with the remaining oil and patties.

Serve with the lemon wedges.

calories 183
protein 22 g
carbohydrates 8 g
  fiber 1 g
  sugars 2 g
cholesterol 166 mg
total fat 6.0 g
  saturated 0.5 g
  polyunsaturated 2.0 g
  monounsaturated 3.0 g
sodium 415 mg

dietary exchange
1/2 starch
3 lean meat

Cioppino

Serves 10

Pronounced "chuh-PEE-noh," this Italian fish stew will be pronounced delicious by all who taste it.

1½ pounds red snapper or other firm white fish fillets, skin removed
½ tablespoon olive oil
1½ cups chopped onions
1 medium green bell pepper, coarsely chopped
3 medium garlic cloves, minced
4 cups chopped tomatoes
¼ cup dry red wine (regular or nonalcoholic)
¼ cup bottled clam juice

2 tablespoons snipped fresh parsley
2 bay leaves
¾ teaspoon dried basil, crumbled
¼ teaspoon pepper
3 or 4 dashes of red hot-pepper sauce
½ pound medium raw shrimp, peeled and deveined (13 to 15)
½ teaspoon salt
Juice of 1 medium lemon

Rinse the fish and pat dry with paper towels. Cut the fish into 2-inch cubes. Set aside.

Heat a heavy stockpot over medium heat. Pour the oil into the stockpot and swirl to coat the bottom. Cook the onions, bell pepper, and garlic for 5 minutes.

Add the tomatoes, wine, clam juice, parsley, bay leaves, basil, pepper, and hot-pepper sauce. Increase the heat to high and bring to a boil. Reduce the heat and simmer for 15 minutes.

Stir in the fish. Simmer for 25 minutes, stirring occasionally.

Stir in the shrimp. Simmer for 8 minutes, stirring occasionally.

Stir in the salt and lemon juice.

Time-Saver on Chopped Bell Peppers

Like chopped onions, chopped green bell peppers are available in the frozen food section of your supermarket. You can also seed and chop them yourself, then freeze them in a resealable plastic freezer bag.

calories 133
protein 20 g
carbohydrates 7 g
  fiber 2 g
  sugars 4 g
cholesterol 60 mg
total fat 2.5 g
  saturated 0.5 g
  polyunsaturated 0.5 g
  monounsaturated 1.0 g
sodium 242 mg

dietary exchange
1½ vegetable
2½ very lean meat

poultry

Chicken with Orange Sauce

Lemon-Herb Roast Chicken

Caribbean Grilled Chicken Breasts

Chicken with Apricot Glaze

Chicken Casserole
with Dilled Sherry Sauce

Rosemary Chicken

Mexican Chicken and Vegetables
with Chipotle Peppers

Chicken Stew
with Cornmeal Dumplings

Slow-Cooked Chicken Italian Style

Chicken Jambalaya

Crispy Baked Chicken

Sesame Chicken

Lemongrass-Lime Baked Chicken

Italian Chicken Roll-Ups

Chicken Scallops al Limone

Chicken Columbo

Sun-Dried Tomato and
Kalamata Olive Chicken

Chicken with One-Minute Tomato Sauce

Rosé Chicken with Artichoke Hearts
and Mushrooms

Burgundy Chicken with Mushrooms

Chicken with Bell Peppers
and Mushrooms

Chicken Southwestern

Chicken in White Wine and Tarragon

Stuffed Chicken with Blue Cheese

Sweet-Spice Glazed Chicken

Grilled Lemon-Sage Chicken

Spicy Grilled Chicken

Triple-Pepper Chicken

Lemon-Cayenne Chicken

Spicy Chicken and Grits

Sweet-and-Sour Baked Chicken

Chicken and Snow-Pea Stir-Fry

Chicken and Mushroom Stir-Fry

Broiled Chicken with
Hoisin-Barbecue Sauce

Italian Double Toss

Baked Chicken Parmesan

Chicken Stufino

Chicken Chili

Savory Microwave Chicken

Tandoori Ginger Chicken Strips

Boneless Buffalo Wings

Slow-Cooker White Chili

Chipotle Chicken Wraps

Chicken Fajitas

Chicken à la King

Chicken-Spinach Manicotti

Chicken and Broccoli in
Mushroom Sauce

Chicken Curry in a Hurry

Roasted Garlic-Lemon Turkey Breast

Turkey Fillets with Fresh Herbs

Turkey Rolls with Garden Pesto

Turkey Sausage Patties

Turkey Lasagna

Turkey Enchiladas

Turkey Loaf

Southwestern Turkey Wraps

Swiss Garden Wraps

Turkey with Vegetables and Brown Rice

Cornish Hens Provence Style

Stuffed Cornish Hens with
Orange-Brandy Sauce

Chicken with
Orange Sauce

Serves 4

Orange juice tenderizes and adds zip to this dish, which is browned, then finished on the stovetop or in the oven. Serve the chicken warm over yolk-free noodles or chill it to take on a picnic.

Vegetable oil spray
2¹/₂-pound chicken
¹/₂ teaspoon paprika
1 medium onion, sliced

Orange Sauce
¹/₂ cup frozen orange juice concentrate

¹/₃ cup water
2 tablespoons light brown sugar
2 tablespoons snipped fresh parsley
1 teaspoon low-salt soy sauce
1 teaspoon dry sherry
¹/₂ teaspoon ground ginger

Preheat the broiler. Preheat the oven to 350°F, if using. Lightly spray a baking sheet with vegetable oil spray.

Discard the skin and all the visible fat from the chicken. Cut the chicken into serving pieces. Sprinkle the chicken with paprika. Put the chicken on the baking sheet.

Broil the chicken about 6 inches from the heat for about 2 minutes on each side, or until lightly browned. For stovetop preparation, transfer the chicken to a Dutch oven or large, deep skillet. (For baking, transfer to a medium casserole dish.)

Top the chicken with the onion slices.

In a small bowl, whisk together the sauce ingredients. Pour over the chicken and onion.

Cook over medium-high heat until the sauce comes to a boil. Reduce the heat and simmer, covered, for 55 to 60 minutes, or until the chicken is tender and no longer pink in the center. Or bake, covered, for 55 to 60 minutes.

calories 263
protein 31
carbohydrates 24 g
  fiber 1 g
  sugars 22 g
cholesterol 95 mg
total fat 4.5 g
  saturated 1.0 g
  polyunsaturated 1.0 g
  monounsaturated 1.0 g
sodium 144 mg

dietary exchange

1 fruit
¹/₂ other carbohydrate
4 very lean meat

Lemon-Herb
Roast Chicken

Serves 6

Try this moist, delicately seasoned roast chicken for a Sunday dinner treat.

Vegetable oil spray
$\frac{1}{2}$ tablespoon dried thyme, crumbled
$\frac{1}{2}$ teaspoon dried basil, crumbled
$\frac{1}{2}$ teaspoon pepper
$\frac{1}{4}$ teaspoon salt
4-pound roasting chicken

2 medium garlic cloves, minced
1 lemon, cut into wedges
1 bay leaf
$\frac{1}{2}$ medium onion
$\frac{1}{2}$ cup dry white wine (regular or nonalcoholic)

Preheat the oven to 350°F. Lightly spray a roasting pan and rack with vegetable oil spray.

In a small bowl, stir together the thyme, basil, pepper, and salt.

Discard the giblets and all the visible fat from the chicken. Rub the outside with the herb mixture. Put the chicken with the breast side up on the rack in the roasting pan. Put the garlic, lemon, bay leaf, and onion in the chicken. Pour the wine into the pan. Lightly spray the outside of the chicken with vegetable oil spray.

Bake for 20 minutes per pound, or until the internal temperature reaches 180°F or the juices run clear when a thigh is pierced with a sharp knife.

Let rest for 15 minutes before carving. Discard the skin before serving the chicken.

Cook's Tip on Chicken Yields

A 4-pound chicken, cooked, yields about the following:

Breast meat:	*12 ounces*
Leg meat:	*4 ounces*
Thigh meat:	*6 ounces*
Wing meat:	*1$\frac{1}{2}$ ounces*
Back meat:	*2 ounces*
Total:	*25$\frac{1}{2}$ ounces*

calories 188
protein 31 g
carbohydrates 1 g
  fiber 0 g
  sugars 0 g
cholesterol 102 mg
total fat 4.5 g
  saturated 1.0 g
  polyunsaturated 1.0 g
  monounsaturated 1.5 g
sodium 210 mg

dietary exchange
4$\frac{1}{2}$ very lean meat

Caribbean Grilled Chicken Breasts

Serves 4

An important part of this delicious blend of flavors, bananas are easier to handle on the grill if they're slightly underripe.

Marinade
- 2/3 cup pineapple juice
- 2 tablespoons minced onion
- 2 tablespoons fresh lime juice
- 1 tablespoon curry powder
- 1 tablespoon honey
- 1/4 teaspoon salt
- 1/4 teaspoon pepper
- 1/4 teaspoon red hot-pepper sauce

❖

- 4 skinless chicken breast halves with bone (about 6 ounces each)
- 2 slightly underripe bananas, halved lengthwise and crosswise (8 pieces)

In a large resealable plastic bag, combine the marinade ingredients.

Discard all the visible fat from the chicken. Add the chicken to the marinade. Seal the bag and turn to coat. Refrigerate for 2 to 12 hours, turning occasionally.

Preheat the grill on medium.

Meanwhile, remove the chicken from the marinade. Pour the marinade into a small saucepan. Bring to a boil over high heat. Boil for 5 minutes. Set aside.

Grill the chicken on a covered grill for about 20 minutes, turning occasionally.

Brush the bananas generously with the marinade. Place on the grill. Grill the chicken and bananas for 10 to 15 minutes, or until the chicken is tender, turning the bananas once. Brush the chicken and bananas with the marinade before serving.

calories 253
protein 33 g
carbohydrates 26 g
  fiber 2 g
  sugars 21 g
cholesterol 79 mg
total fat 2.0 g
  saturated 0.5 g
  polyunsaturated 0.5 g
  monounsaturated 0.5 g
sodium 238 mg

dietary exchange
1½ fruit
3 very lean meat

Chicken with
Apricot Glaze

Serves 4

Steamed brown rice would complement this palate-pleaser nicely.

1/4 cup all-purpose flour
1/8 teaspoon white pepper
4 skinless chicken breast halves with bone (about 6 ounces each), all visible fat discarded
Vegetable oil spray
1 tablespoon acceptable vegetable oil
1/2 cup all-fruit apricot spread
16-ounce can apricot halves in extra-light syrup

2/3 cup pineapple juice
1 tablespoon dry sherry
2 teaspoons low-salt soy sauce
1 teaspoon dried marjoram, crumbled
1 teaspoon grated peeled gingerroot
1 teaspoon grated lemon zest
1/8 teaspoon red hot-pepper sauce
1 medium green bell pepper, diced

In a medium resealable plastic bag, combine the flour and white pepper. Add several pieces of chicken. Seal. Shake to coat. Shake off the excess flour. Put the chicken with the meatier side up on a plate. Repeat with the remaining chicken. Lightly spray the top with vegetable oil spray.

Heat a large nonstick skillet over medium-high heat. Pour the oil into the skillet and swirl to coat the bottom. Cook the chicken with the meatier side down for 5 to 6 minutes, or until browned. Remove from the heat. Lightly spray the top of the chicken with vegetable oil spray. Cover the chicken with the apricot spread.

Drain the apricots, reserving the liquid in a medium bowl. Quarter the apricots. Set the apricots aside.

Stir the pineapple juice, sherry, soy sauce, marjoram, gingerroot, lemon zest, and hot-pepper sauce into the apricot liquid. Stir into the chicken. Reduce the heat and simmer, covered, for 50 to 60 minutes, or until the chicken is tender and no longer pink in the center.

Stir in the bell pepper. Cook for 7 to 8 minutes.

Spoon the apricots and sauce over the chicken.

calories 381
protein 34 g
carbohydrates 48 g
  fiber 3 g
  sugars 35 g
cholesterol 79 mg
total fat 5.5 g
  saturated 0.5 g
  polyunsaturated 1.5 g
  monounsaturated 2.5 g
sodium 158 mg

dietary exchange
1/2 starch
2 1/2 fruit
4 lean meat

Chicken Casserole
with Dilled Sherry Sauce

Serves 4

With its creamy dill sauce, this quick casserole is a good dish for company.

Vegetable oil spray

2 medium potatoes, peeled and quartered

2 large carrots, cut into 2-inch pieces

2 medium onions, quartered

4 whole garlic cloves

4 skinless chicken breast halves with bone (about 6 ounces each)

^{1}/$_2$ cup dry sherry

^{1}/$_2$ teaspoon pepper

^{1}/$_2$ teaspoon dried dillweed, crumbled

1^1/$_3$ cups fat-free, low-sodium chicken broth, such as on page 45

^{1}/$_4$ cup all-purpose flour

^{1}/$_4$ cup water

2 tablespoons finely chopped green onions (green and white parts)

Preheat the oven to 350°F. Lightly spray a deep baking pan with vegetable oil spray.

Put the potatoes, carrots, onions, and garlic in the baking pan.

Discard all the visible fat from the chicken. Arrange the chicken over the vegetable mixture.

Pour the sherry over all, then sprinkle with the pepper and dillweed.

Bake, covered, for 50 to 55 minutes, or until the chicken is no longer pink in the center.

Transfer the chicken and vegetables to a platter, reserving ^{2}/$_3$ cup pan juices. Cover the platter with aluminum foil. Set aside.

In a small saucepan, whisk together the reserved pan juices and the broth.

In a small bowl, stir together the flour and water. Whisk into the pan juice mixture. Bring to a boil over medium-high heat, stirring constantly.

Stir in the green onions.

To serve, pour the sauce over the chicken and vegetables.

calories 304
protein 37 g
carbohydrates 32 g
  fiber 5 g
  sugars 9 g
cholesterol 79 mg
total fat 2.0 g
  saturated 0.5 g
  polyunsaturated 0.5 g
  monounsaturated 0.5 g
sodium 116 mg

dietary exchange
1^1/$_2$ starch
2 vegetable
4 very lean meat

Rosemary Chicken

Serves 8

While the chicken bakes, make the sauce, a salad, and a vegetable dish. Then sit down and enjoy a fine dinner.

Vegetable oil spray

8 skinless chicken breast halves with bone (about 6 ounces each)

2 tablespoons chopped fresh rosemary or 2 teaspoons dried, crushed

Vegetable oil spray

3 tablespoons all-purpose flour

1/2 cup fat-free, low-sodium chicken broth, such as on page 45

3/4 cup fat-free or light plain yogurt

1/4 cup dry white wine (regular or nonalcoholic)

1 tablespoon light tub margarine

1 teaspoon grated lemon zest

Pepper to taste

4 ounces sliced button mushrooms

Lemon twist (optional)

Sprig of parsley (optional)

Preheat the oven to 350°F. Lightly spray a 13 × 9 × 2-inch baking pan with vegetable oil spray.

Discard all the visible fat from the chicken. Rub the chicken with the rosemary. Lightly spray with vegetable oil spray. Place the chicken with the meaty side down in the pan.

Bake, covered, for 30 minutes.

Meanwhile, in a medium saucepan, whisk together the flour and broth. Cook over medium-high heat for 2 to 3 minutes, stirring occasionally. Reduce the heat to low.

Whisk in the yogurt, wine, margarine, lemon zest, and pepper. Remove from the heat.

Remove the pan from the oven. Drain. Turn over each breast. Cover with the mushrooms. Pour the sauce over all.

Bake, uncovered, for 30 to 45 minutes, or until the chicken is tender and no longer pink in the center.

Garnish with the lemon or parsley.

calories 188
protein 34 g
carbohydrates 5 g
  fiber 0 g
  sugars 2 g
cholesterol 79 mg
total fat 2.5 g
  saturated 0.5 g
  polyunsaturated 0.5 g
  monounsaturated 0.5 g
sodium 120 mg

dietary exchange
1/2 starch
4 very lean meat

Mexican Chicken and Vegetables with Chipotle Peppers

Serves 4 (plus 4 chicken breast halves and 1 cup tomato mixture reserved)

Chicken simmered with bell peppers and tomatoes, richly seasoned with chipotle peppers (smoked jalapeño peppers), and served over yellow rice will satisfy the most demanding Mexican-food enthusiast. The extra chicken and sauce are ready for use in Chipotle Chicken Wraps (page 255).

1½ cups water
4 dried chipotle peppers
8 skinless chicken breast halves with bone (about 6 ounces each), all visible fat discarded
 Vegetable oil spray (olive oil spray preferred)
2 large onions, chopped
4 medium garlic cloves, minced
 14.5-ounce can no-salt-added diced tomatoes, undrained

1 medium green bell pepper, chopped
½ tablespoon dried oregano, crumbled
1 cup uncooked rice
½ teaspoon ground turmeric
½ teaspoon salt
½ tablespoon olive oil (extra-virgin preferred)

Pour the water into a small saucepan and bring to a boil over high heat. Remove from the heat. Wearing gloves, add the chipotle peppers. Let stand for 30 minutes.

Meanwhile, lightly spray a Dutch oven with vegetable oil spray. Heat over medium-high heat for 1 minute. Add half the chicken with the meaty side down. Brown for 5 minutes. Turn the chicken. Cook for 3 minutes. Transfer to a plate. Set aside. Repeat with the remaining chicken.

Put the onions and garlic in the Dutch oven, scraping to dislodge any browned bits. Cook for 5 to 7 minutes, or until golden brown, stirring occasionally. Remove from the heat.

Drain the chipotle peppers, reserving the water. Wearing gloves, remove and discard the stems, seeds, and membranes from the peppers. Put the peppers and

calories 344
protein 27 g
carbohydrates 51 g
 fiber 4 g
 sugars 7 g
cholesterol 53 mg
total fat 3.5 g
 saturated 0.5 g
 polyunsaturated 0.5 g
 monounsaturated 1.5 g
sodium 365 mg

dietary exchange
2½ starch
3 vegetable
3 very lean meat

reserved water in a food processor or blender and process until smooth.

Add the pepper mixture, chicken and its juices, undrained tomatoes, bell pepper, and oregano to the onion mixture. Bring to a boil over medium heat. Reduce the heat and simmer, covered, for 20 minutes. Remove from the heat. Put the chicken on a plate. Let cool slightly.

Meanwhile, prepare the rice using the package directions, omitting the salt and margarine but adding turmeric.

When the chicken is cool enough to handle, debone it. Chop or shred the chicken.

Put 4 chicken breast halves and 1 cup tomato mixture in an airtight container. Refrigerate and reserve for Chipotle Chicken Wraps (page 255).

Return the remaining chicken to the Dutch oven. Stir in the salt. If necessary, reheat the chicken, covered, over medium heat until heated through, stirring frequently. Remove from the heat. Stir in the oil. Serve over rice.

Cook's Tip

This stew is even better if refrigerated overnight. It's a good dish to make on the weekend for a quick dinner (or two, if you also make the Chipotle Chicken Wraps) during the week. Just reheat the stew, add the oil, and serve over rice.

Cook's Tip on Handling Hot Chile Peppers

Hot chile peppers contain oils that can burn your skin, lips, and eyes. Wear rubber or plastic disposable gloves or wash your hands thoroughly with warm, soapy water immediately after handling peppers. Rinsing the peppers under water makes removing the seeds and ribs (the hottest part) easier. Examples of hot peppers are Anaheim, ancho, cascabel, cayenne, cherry, chipotle, habanero, Hungarian wax, jalapeño, poblano, Scotch bonnet, serrano, and Thai. A rule of thumb is that the smaller the pepper, the hotter it is.

Chicken Stew with
Cornmeal Dumplings

Serves 6

Chicken and dumplings is a family-style dish found on many southern dinner tables. This creamy version is full of lean chicken and vegetables, topped with fluffy cornmeal dumplings.

Stew
- 4 skinless chicken breast halves with bone (about 6 ounces each)
- 4¹/₂ cups water
- 1 bay leaf
- 1 teaspoon dried basil, crumbled
- 1 teaspoon dried oregano, crumbled
- ¹/₄ teaspoon salt
- ¹/₄ teaspoon ground sage
- ¹/₄ teaspoon pepper

Cornmeal Dumplings
- ¹/₂ cup all-purpose flour
- ¹/₃ cup cornmeal
- ¹/₄ cup snipped fresh parsley
- ¹/₂ tablespoon baking powder
- ¹/₄ teaspoon salt
- ¹/₈ teaspoon white pepper
- Egg substitute equivalent to 1 egg, or 1 large egg
- ¹/₄ cup fat-free milk
- 1 tablespoon acceptable vegetable oil

❖

- 1 medium zucchini, halved lengthwise and sliced
- 1 medium yellow summer squash, halved lengthwise and sliced
- 1 cup fat-free milk
- ¹/₂ cup all-purpose flour

Discard all the visible fat from the chicken. Put the chicken in a Dutch oven.

Stir together all the remaining stew ingredients. Bring to a boil over medium-high heat. Reduce the heat and simmer, covered, for 45 minutes, or until the chicken is tender and no longer pink in the center.

Meanwhile, for the dumplings, stir together the flour, cornmeal, parsley, baking powder, salt, and white pepper in a small bowl.

Whisk together the remaining dumpling ingredients. Add to the flour mixture, whisking just until moistened. Set aside.

Stir the zucchini and yellow squash into the stew mixture.

calories 261
protein 27 g
carbohydrates 28 g
  fiber 2 g
  sugars 4 g
cholesterol 54 mg
total fat 4.0 g
  saturated 0.5 g
  polyunsaturated 1.0 g
  monounsaturated 2.0 g
sodium 431 mg

dietary exchange
2 starch
3 very lean meat

Remove the bay leaf from the stew. Discard. Remove the cooked chicken from the stew. When the chicken is cool enough to handle, remove the meat from the bones. Cut the chicken into bite-size pieces (you should have 2$^1/_2$ to 3 cups). Set aside.

In a jar with a tight-fitting lid, combine the milk and flour. Cover and shake well. Add to the stew mixture. Cook over medium to medium-high heat for 5 minutes, or until thickened and bubbly, stirring constantly. Stir in the chicken.

Using a spoon, drop the dumpling batter in 6 mounds on the simmering stew. Reduce the heat and simmer, covered, for 10 to 12 minutes, or until a cake tester or toothpick inserted in one of the dumplings comes out clean. (Don't peek at the dumplings while they cook.) Ladle into bowls.

Slow-Cooked Chicken
Italian Style

Serves 4

Your home will be filled with the comforting aromas of an Italian kitchen when you prepare this tender chicken-and-vegetables combination. Fennel seed gives a hint of Italian sausage without the extra fat.

4 skinless chicken breast halves with bone (about 6 ounces each)
14.5-ounce can artichoke quarters, rinsed and drained
14.5-ounce can no-salt-added diced tomatoes, undrained
8-ounce can no-salt-added tomato sauce

2 tablespoons sliced green olives (not stuffed with pimientos), rinsed
1 teaspoon dried oregano, crumbled
1/2 teaspoon fennel seeds
1/4 teaspoon pepper
8 ounces sliced button mushrooms
2 cups frozen green beans

Discard all the visible fat from the chicken. Put the chicken in a slow cooker.

Add the artichokes, undrained tomatoes, tomato sauce, olives, oregano, fennel seeds, and pepper to the slow cooker. Cook, covered, on high for 3 hours or on low for 7 hours, or until the chicken is tender and the flavors have blended.

Stir in the mushrooms. Place the green beans on top; don't stir (this will help keep the acid in the tomatoes from changing the color of the beans). Cook on high for 1 hour or on low for 2 hours, or until the mushrooms are tender and the green beans are cooked through. Stir before serving.

calories 228
protein 31 g
carbohydrates 20 g
  fiber 5 g
  sugars 10 g
cholesterol 66 mg
total fat 2.5 g
  saturated 0.5 g
  polyunsaturated 0.5 g
  monounsaturated 1.0 g
sodium 489 mg

dietary exchange
4 vegetable
3 very lean meat

Chicken Jambalaya

Serves 4

Capture the flavors of Louisiana with this casserole. Your family will love the taste—and you'll love the simple preparation.

Vegetable oil spray

1 cup fat-free, low-sodium chicken broth, such as on page 45

1 cup dry white wine (regular or nonalcoholic)

1 large onion, chopped

1 medium green bell pepper, chopped

2 medium ribs of celery, chopped

1/4 cup snipped fresh parsley

1/2 teaspoon dried basil, crumbled

1/2 teaspoon dried thyme, crumbled

1 large bay leaf

1/4 teaspoon red hot-pepper sauce

15-ounce can no-salt-added diced tomatoes, undrained

1 cup uncooked rice

1/2 cup cubed low-sodium, low-fat ham

4 boneless, skinless chicken breast halves (about 4 ounces each)

Preheat the oven to 350°F. Lightly spray a 13 × 9 × 2-inch or 2-quart casserole dish with vegetable oil spray.

In a medium saucepan, stir together the broth, wine, onion, bell pepper, celery, parsley, basil, thyme, bay leaf, and hot-pepper sauce. Bring to a boil over medium-high heat, stirring occasionally. Remove from the heat.

Meanwhile, discard all the visible fat from the chicken.

Put the undrained tomatoes, rice, and ham in the casserole dish. Place the chicken on top. Pour the hot broth mixture over all.

Bake, covered, for 45 to 55 minutes, or until the chicken is no longer pink in the center and the rice is tender.

calories 319
protein 37 g
carbohydrates 29 g
fiber 2 g
sugars 3 g
cholesterol 84 mg
total fat 2.5 g
saturated 0.5 g
polyunsaturated 0.5 g
monounsaturated 0.5 g
sodium 208 mg

dietary exchange
1½ starch
1 vegetable
4 very lean meat

Crispy Baked Chicken

Serves 4

Remember when you didn't want to fry chicken because it was such a mess to clean up? Now you have two good reasons to cook this chicken— no pan to wash and a really moist low-fat "fried" chicken!

Vegetable oil spray
1 cup fat-free milk
1 cup cornflake crumbs (about 3 cups cornflakes)

1 teaspoon dried rosemary, crushed
1/2 teaspoon pepper
4 boneless, skinless chicken breast halves (about 4 ounces each)

Preheat the oven to 400°F. Line a 13 × 9 × 2-inch baking pan with aluminum foil. Lightly spray the foil with vegetable oil spray.

Pour the milk into a shallow bowl. In another shallow bowl, stir together the cornflake crumbs, rosemary, and pepper. Set the bowl with the milk, the bowl with the crumb mixture, and the baking pan in a row, assembly-line fashion.

Discard all the visible fat from the chicken. Dip the chicken into the milk, then into the crumb mixture. Let stand for 5 to 10 minutes so the coating will adhere. Arrange the chicken in the pan so the pieces don't touch.

Bake for 30 minutes, or until the chicken is no longer pink in the center and the crumbs form a crisp "skin."

calories 206
protein 28 g
carbohydrates 18 g
  fiber 0 g
  sugars 2 g
cholesterol 66 mg
total fat 1.5 g
  saturated 0.5 g
  polyunsaturated 0.5 g
  monounsaturated 0.5 g
sodium 234 mg

dietary exchange
1 starch
3 very lean meat

Sesame Chicken

Serves 4

Lemon juice and wine flavor meaty chicken pieces, and a light crust of sesame seeds keeps them moist. Serve with bok choy and have Claret-Spiced Oranges (page 620) for dessert.

Vegetable oil spray
1/3 cup all-purpose flour
1/4 teaspoon pepper
4 boneless, skinless chicken breast halves (about 4 ounces each)
Vegetable oil spray
1 tablespoon fresh lemon juice

1/4 cup sesame seeds, divided use
3 tablespoons minced green onions (green and white parts)
1/2 cup dry white wine (regular or nonalcoholic) (plus more as needed)

Preheat the oven to 375°F. Lightly spray a 13 × 9 × 2-inch baking pan with vegetable oil spray.

In a shallow bowl, stir together the flour and pepper. Discard all the visible fat from the chicken. Coat the chicken with the flour mixture, shaking off the excess. Lightly spray each piece with vegetable oil spray. Place with the sprayed side down in the baking pan so the pieces don't touch. Lightly spray the top of the breasts.

Sprinkle the lemon juice and half the sesame seeds over the chicken.

Bake for 30 minutes, or until lightly browned. Turn over the chicken. Sprinkle with the remaining sesame seeds and the green onions. Pour the wine around the chicken.

Bake for 30 to 45 minutes, or until the chicken is no longer pink in the center, basting occasionally.

calories 241
protein 30 g
carbohydrates 10 g
  fiber 1 g
  sugars 1 g
cholesterol 66 mg
total fat 6.5 g
  saturated 1.0 g
  polyunsaturated 2.5 g
  monounsaturated 2.5 g
sodium 80 mg

dietary exchange
1/2 starch
3 lean meat

Lemongrass-Lime
Baked Chicken

Serves 4

Are you ready for a flavor adventure? See the Cook's Tip on Lemongrass that accompanies this recipe to learn how to handle lemongrass, then prepare this delicious dish.

Vegetable oil spray
1 tablespoon fresh lemon juice
1 tablespoon fresh lime juice
1 teaspoon acceptable vegetable oil
1 medium garlic clove, minced

1/4 teaspoon pepper
2 stalks lemongrass or 1 tablespoon grated lemon zest
4 skinless, boneless chicken breast halves (about 4 ounces each)

Preheat the oven to 350°F. Lightly spray a 9-inch square baking pan or 1-quart casserole dish with vegetable oil spray.

In a small bowl, stir together the lemon juice, lime juice, oil, garlic, and pepper.

Remove the outer leaf of the lemongrass. Slice the bottom 6 to 8 inches of lemongrass crosswise into 1/2-inch pieces. Stir into the lemon juice mixture.

Discard all the visible fat from the chicken. Put the chicken in the baking pan. Pour the juice mixture over the chicken.

Bake, covered, for 30 minutes, or until tender and no longer pink in the center, basting occasionally. Bake, uncovered, for 10 minutes, or until brown.

Discard the lemongrass before serving the chicken.

calories 139
protein 26 g
carbohydrates 1 g
  fiber 0 g
  sugars 0 g
cholesterol 66 mg
total fat 2.5 g
  saturated 0.5 g
  polyunsaturated 0.5 g
  monounsaturated 1.0 g
sodium 74 mg

dietary exchange
3 very lean meat

Cook's Tip on Lemongrass

Look in the produce section of your grocery for lemongrass. Because it is tough and fibrous, lemongrass is not eaten; use the bottom 6 to 8 inches to impart the characteristic perfume and sour lemon flavor.

Italian Chicken Roll-Ups

Serves 4

Serve these attractive chicken rolls with a simple salad and fruit sorbet.

1 cup water
6-ounce can no-salt-added tomato paste
1 medium garlic clove, minced
3/4 teaspoon dried oregano, crumbled
3/4 teaspoon dried basil, crumbled
1/2 teaspoon dried marjoram, crumbled
1/4 teaspoon pepper, or to taste

1/4 teaspoon salt
4 boneless, skinless chicken breast halves (about 4 ounces each)
4 ounces fat-free or low-fat cottage cheese, drained (about 1/2 cup)
2 ounces shredded fat-free or part-skim mozzarella cheese

Preheat the oven to 350°F.

In a small saucepan, whisk together the water, tomato paste, and garlic.

In a small bowl, stir together the oregano, basil, marjoram, pepper, and salt. Add three fourths of the mixture to the saucepan. Bring to a boil over medium-high heat. Reduce the heat and simmer for 10 minutes, stirring occasionally.

Meanwhile, discard all the visible fat from the chicken. Put the chicken with the smooth side up between two pieces of plastic wrap. Using a tortilla press, the smooth side of a meat mallet, or a rolling pin, lightly flatten the breasts to a thickness of 1/4 inch, being careful not to tear the meat.

In a small bowl, stir together the remaining herb mixture and the cottage cheese. Leaving a 1/2-inch edge all around, spoon onto the chicken. From the narrow end, roll up each breast jelly-roll style.

Spoon half the tomato sauce into a 10 × 6-inch baking dish. Arrange the chicken rolls with the seam side down on the sauce. Spoon the remaining tomato sauce over the chicken rolls. Sprinkle with the mozzarella.

Bake for 45 minutes, or until the chicken is no longer pink in the center. If the chicken is getting too brown, cover for the last 10 minutes of baking.

calories 204
protein 36 g
carbohydrates 11 g
 fiber 3 g
 sugars 2 g
cholesterol 70 mg
total fat 1.5 g
 saturated 0.5 g
 polyunsaturated 0.5 g
 monounsaturated 0.5 g
sodium 519 mg

dietary exchange
2 vegetable
4 1/2 very lean meat

Chicken Scallops al Limone

Serves 6

This dish is very good over any kind of pasta. It also goes well with Asparagus par Excellence (page 408) or Tomato-Basil Salad with Balsamic Dressing (page 95).

1/4 cup plus 1 tablespoon all-purpose flour

1/2 teaspoon pepper

1/4 teaspoon salt

6 boneless, skinless chicken breast halves (about 4 ounces each), all visible fat discarded, flattened to 1/4-inch thickness

2 teaspoons olive oil

1 3/4 cups fat-free, low-sodium chicken broth, such as on page 45

1/4 cup fresh lemon juice

1/4 cup dry white wine (regular or nonalcoholic)

1 tablespoon finely snipped fresh parsley

6 thin lemon slices (optional)

In a large resealable plastic bag or paper bag, combine the flour, pepper, and salt. Add several pieces of the chicken. Seal the bag. Shake to coat the chicken. Shake off the excess flour. Set the chicken on a plate. Repeat with the remaining chicken.

Heat a large nonstick skillet over medium-high heat. Pour the oil into the skillet and swirl to coat the bottom. Cook half the chicken for 2 to 3 minutes, turning to brown on both sides. Transfer to a plate. Repeat with the remaining chicken.

Pour the broth, lemon juice, and wine into the skillet. Cook for 7 to 8 minutes, or until the sauce is reduced by about one third, scraping to dislodge any browned bits from the skillet.

Return the chicken to the skillet. Reduce the heat and simmer for 5 to 7 minutes, or until the sauce is slightly thickened, stirring occasionally. Using a slotted spoon or pancake turner, transfer the chicken to a platter.

Stir the parsley into the sauce. Pour over the chicken. Garnish with the lemon slices.

calories 175
protein 28 g
carbohydrates 6 g
  fiber 0 g
  sugars 1 g
cholesterol 66 mg
total fat 3.0 g
  saturated 0.5 g
  polyunsaturated 0.5 g
  monounsaturated 1.5 g
sodium 179 mg

dietary exchange
1/2 starch
3 very lean meat

Chicken Columbo

Serves 4

Seasoned wheat germ coats the chicken and gives it an interesting crunch and a lot of flavor. Shell pasta is a good accompaniment—it helps soak up the savory sauce.

1/2 cup fat-free milk
1/3 cup wheat germ or plain dry bread crumbs
1 teaspoon dried oregano, crumbled
1/2 teaspoon salt
1/4 teaspoon garlic powder
1/4 teaspoon onion powder
Pepper to taste
4 boneless, skinless chicken breast halves (about 4 ounces each)

1 tablespoon acceptable stick margarine
8 ounces button mushrooms, sliced
1/4 cup dry marsala or dry sherry
1/4 cup water
3 tablespoons no-salt-added tomato paste
2 tablespoons snipped fresh parsley

Pour the milk into a shallow bowl.

On a plate placed next to the milk, stir together the wheat germ, oregano, salt, garlic powder, onion powder, and pepper.

Discard all the visible fat from the chicken. Dip the chicken into the milk. Coat the chicken with the wheat-germ mixture, shaking off the excess.

In a large nonstick skillet, melt the margarine over medium-high heat and swirl to coat the bottom. Cook the chicken for 3 to 4 minutes on each side, or until golden.

In a medium bowl, stir together the remaining ingredients except the parsley. Pour over the chicken. Reduce the heat and simmer for 10 minutes, or until the chicken is no longer pink in the center.

To serve, sprinkle with the parsley.

calories 209
protein 30 g
carbohydrates 12 g
  fiber 2 g
  sugars 3 g
cholesterol 66 mg
total fat 3.5 g
  saturated 0.5 g
  polyunsaturated 1.0 g
  monounsaturated 0.5 g
sodium 399 mg

dietary exchange
1/2 starch
1 vegetable
3 very lean meat

Sun-Dried Tomato and
Kalamata Olive Chicken

Serves 4

Rich-tasting sun-dried tomatoes, Greek olives, and feta come together to make this simple, yet sensational, fare. (See photo on back cover.)

10 sun-dried tomato halves, chopped
1/4 cup boiling water
4 boneless, skinless chicken breast halves (about 4 ounces each)
1/2 teaspoon dried oregano, crumbled
12 kalamata olives, finely chopped
1/4 cup finely snipped fresh parsley

1/2 teaspoon dried oregano, crumbled
1/8 teaspoon crushed red pepper flakes
1 ounce fat-free or low-fat feta cheese, crumbled
1/8 teaspoon salt
2 teaspoons olive oil (extra-virgin preferred)

In a small bowl, stir together the sun-dried tomatoes and water. Let stand for 10 minutes. Drain. Return the tomatoes to the bowl.

Meanwhile, discard all the visible fat from the chicken. Put the chicken between two pieces of plastic wrap. Using a tortilla press, the smooth side of a meat mallet, or a rolling pin, flatten the chicken to a thickness of 1/4 inch, being careful not to tear the meat.

Sprinkle 1/2 teaspoon oregano over the chicken.

Stir the olives, parsley, 1/2 teaspoon oregano, and red pepper flakes into the tomatoes. Gently stir in the feta.

Heat a 10-inch nonstick skillet over medium-high heat. Cook the chicken for 3 minutes. Turn over and cook for 3 minutes, or until no longer pink in the center. Remove from the heat. Sprinkle the salt over the chicken.

To serve, put chicken on each plate. Top each serving with 1/4 cup tomato mixture. Drizzle each serving with 1/2 teaspoon oil.

calories 209
protein 29 g
carbohydrates 6 g
  fiber 1 g
  sugars 2 g
cholesterol 66 mg
total fat 7.0 g
  saturated 1.0 g
  polyunsaturated 1.0 g
  monounsaturated 4.5 g
sodium 444 mg

dietary exchange
1 vegetable
3 lean meat

Chicken with One-Minute
Tomato Sauce

Serves 4

Cooking the tomato sauce for only one minute lets the fresh taste prevail.

¹/₄ cup dry white wine (regular or nonalcoholic)
¹/₂ teaspoon grated lemon zest
2 tablespoons fresh lemon juice
2 teaspoons dried oregano, crumbled
4 boneless, skinless chicken breast halves (about 4 ounces each)

One-Minute Tomato Sauce
1 medium tomato, seeded, finely chopped
3 tablespoons capers, rinsed and drained
2 tablespoons finely chopped red onion
1 tablespoon olive oil (extra-virgin preferred)
2 medium garlic cloves, minced
¹/₄ teaspoon salt

In a large resealable plastic bag, combine the wine, lemon zest, lemon juice, and oregano.

Discard all the visible fat from the chicken. Add the chicken to the marinade. Seal the bag and turn to coat. Refrigerate for 8 hours, turning occasionally. Remove the chicken from the bag. Discard the marinade.

Heat a 10-inch nonstick skillet over medium-high heat. Cook the chicken for 3 minutes. Turn over and cook for 2 to 3 minutes, or until no longer pink in the center. Transfer to a platter.

Meanwhile, in a small bowl, stir together the tomato sauce ingredients.

Add the tomato mixture to the skillet, scraping to dislodge any browned bits. Cook over medium-high heat for 1 minute, or until the tomato is soft, stirring constantly.

To serve, spoon the sauce over the chicken.

calories 167
protein 27 g
carbohydrates 3 g
  fiber 1 g
  sugars 1 g
cholesterol 66 mg
total fat 5.0 g
  saturated 1.0 g
  polyunsaturated 0.5 g
  monounsaturated 3.0 g
sodium 398 mg

dietary exchange
3 lean meat

Rosé Chicken with Artichoke
Hearts and Mushrooms

Serves 4

Delicious as is, this one-skillet dish is also great over penne pasta.

1/4 cup all-purpose flour
4 boneless, skinless chicken breast
  halves (about 4 ounces each)
1/2 teaspoon olive oil
8 ounces button mushrooms,
  quartered (2 1/2 to 3 cups)
2 medium garlic cloves, minced
1/2 teaspoon olive oil
  9-ounce package frozen artichoke
  hearts, thawed and halved
  14.5-ounce can no-salt-added
  diced tomatoes, undrained

1/4 cup fat-free, low-sodium chicken
  broth, such as on page 45
1/4 cup rosé wine, dry white wine
  (regular or nonalcoholic), or dry
  vermouth
1 tablespoon fresh lemon juice
1 teaspoon dried oregano, crumbled
1/4 teaspoon salt
1/2 cup thinly sliced green onions
  (green part only)

Put the flour in a shallow bowl.

Discard all the visible fat from the chicken. Coat the chicken lightly with the flour, shaking off the excess.

Heat a large nonstick skillet over medium heat. Pour 1/2 teaspoon oil into the skillet and swirl to coat the bottom. Brown the chicken for 4 minutes on each side. Transfer to a plate.

Stir in the mushrooms, garlic, and 1/2 teaspoon oil. Cook, covered, for 7 minutes.

Stir in the artichoke hearts. Cook, uncovered, for 1 to 2 minutes, or until the juices have evaporated.

Stir in the chicken and the remaining ingredients except the green onions. Cook for 10 minutes, or until the chicken is no longer pink in the center.

Stir in the green onions. Cook for 1 minute.

calories 248
protein 32 g
carbohydrates 22 g
  fiber 8 g
  sugars 5 g
cholesterol 66 mg
total fat 3.0 g
  saturated 0.5 g
  polyunsaturated 0.5 g
  monounsaturated 1.0 g
sodium 301 mg

dietary exchange
1/2 starch
3 vegetable
3 very lean meat

Burgundy Chicken with Mushrooms

Serves 4

Company really goes for this—chicken smothered in mushrooms and a hint of burgundy, then sprinkled with fresh parsley and drizzled with olive oil. A bonus is that you can do most of the cooking before your guests arrive.

4 boneless, skinless chicken breast halves (about 4 ounces each)

8 ounces button mushrooms, sliced

1/4 cup finely chopped onion (yellow preferred)

2 medium garlic cloves, minced

2 tablespoons burgundy or other dry red wine (regular or nonalcoholic)

1/4 teaspoon salt

2 tablespoons finely chopped fresh parsley

2 teaspoons olive oil (extra-virgin preferred)

Discard all the visible fat from the chicken.

Heat a large nonstick skillet over medium-high heat. Cook the chicken for 5 minutes. Turn over and cook for 4 to 5 minutes, or until beginning to brown on the outside and no longer pink in the center. Transfer the chicken to a plate.

Scrape the skillet to dislodge any browned bits. Put the mushrooms, onion, garlic, and burgundy in the skillet. Stir together. Cook for 2 minutes.

Stir in the chicken and its juices. Cook for 5 minutes, or until the mushrooms just begin to brown slightly.

To serve, place the chicken on a platter. Spoon the mushroom mixture over the chicken. Sprinkle with the salt and parsley. Drizzle with the oil.

calories 171
protein 28 g
carbohydrates 4 g
  fiber 1 g
  sugars 2 g
cholesterol 66 mg
total fat 4.0 g
  saturated 0.5 g
  polyunsaturated 0.5 g
  monounsaturated 2.0 g
sodium 224 mg

dietary exchange
1 vegetable
3 very lean meat

Chicken with Bell Peppers and Mushrooms

Serves 6

Add a whole-grain roll and tossed salad with one of our dressings (pages 137-141) for a dinner to please the whole family.

1/3 cup all-purpose flour

1/4 teaspoon pepper

1/4 teaspoon salt

6 boneless, skinless chicken breast halves (about 4 ounces each)

2 teaspoons olive oil

8 ounces medium button mushrooms, quartered

1 1/2 medium red bell peppers, cut into strips

3 medium garlic cloves, minced

1 1/2 cups fat-free, low-sodium chicken broth, such as on page 45

1/3 cup white wine (regular or nonalcoholic)

2 tablespoons fresh lemon juice

1/2 cup sliced green onions (green and white parts)

Snipped fresh parsley

In a medium resealable plastic bag, combine the flour, pepper, and salt.

Discard all the visible fat from the chicken. Put the chicken with the smooth side up between two pieces of plastic wrap. Using a tortilla press, the smooth side of a meat mallet, or a rolling pin, lightly flatten the breasts to a thickness of 1/4 inch, being careful not to tear the meat.

Add several pieces of the chicken to the bag. Seal the bag and shake to coat the chicken. Shake off the excess flour. Set the chicken on a plate. Repeat with the remaining chicken.

Heat a large nonstick skillet over medium-high heat. Pour the oil into the skillet and swirl to coat the bottom. Cook half the chicken for 2 to 3 minutes, turning to brown lightly on both sides. Transfer to a plate. Repeat with the remaining chicken.

calories 197
protein 29 g
carbohydrates 10 g
  fiber 1 g
  sugars 2 g
cholesterol 66 mg
total fat 3.0 g
  saturated 0.5 g
  polyunsaturated 0.5 g
  monounsaturated 1.5 g
sodium 181 mg

dietary exchange
1/2 starch
3 very lean meat

Add the mushrooms, bell peppers, and garlic to the skillet. Reduce the heat to medium low. Cook, covered, for 7 to 9 minutes, stirring occasionally.

Pour in the broth, wine, and lemon juice. Add the chicken. Increase the heat to medium. Cook for 10 minutes, or until the sauce thickens slightly, stirring occasionally.

Stir in the green onions. Cook for 1 minute.

To serve, sprinkle with the parsley.

Veal with Bell Peppers and Mushrooms
Replace the chicken with 1¹/₂ pounds veal scallops.

with veal

calories 199
protein 26 g
carbohydrates 10 g
  fiber 1 g
  sugars 2 g
cholesterol 94 mg
total fat 5.0 g
  saturated 1.0 g
  polyunsaturated 0.5 g
  monounsaturated 2.0 g
sodium 205 mg

dietary exchange
¹/₂ starch
3 lean meat

Chicken Southwestern

Serves 6

Serve this spicy dish with warm corn tortillas and wedges of ice-cold watermelon. You can adjust the heat level by cutting back on the jalapeño (see Cook's Tip on Handling Hot Chile Peppers, page 213) and chili powder.

1¹/₂ cups orange, red, or yellow bell pepper strips or combination

2 teaspoons seeded and minced fresh jalapeño

¹/₂ cup diagonally sliced green onions (green and white parts)

6 boneless, skinless chicken breast halves (about 4 ounces each)

¹/₃ cup all-purpose flour

¹/₂ tablespoon chili powder

¹/₄ teaspoon pepper

¹/₄ teaspoon salt

2 teaspoons acceptable vegetable oil, divided use

28-ounce can no-salt-added whole tomatoes, undrained

1 teaspoon chili powder

¹/₄ teaspoon pepper

1 teaspoon grated lime zest

calories 203
protein 29 g
carbohydrates 14 g
  fiber 3 g
  sugars 4 g
cholesterol 66 mg
total fat 3.5 g
  saturated 0.5 g
  polyunsaturated 1.0 g
  monounsaturated 1.5 g
sodium 197 mg

dietary exchange
¹/₂ starch
1¹/₂ vegetable
3 very lean meat

Heat a large nonstick skillet over medium-high heat. Cook the bell pepper and jalapeño for 4 to 5 minutes, stirring occasionally.

Stir in the green onions. Cook for 1 minute. Transfer the mixture to a plate. Set aside.

Discard all the visible fat from the chicken. Put the chicken with the smooth side up between two pieces of plastic wrap. Using a tortilla press, the smooth side of a meat mallet, or a rolling pin, lightly flatten the breasts to a thickness of ¹/₂ inch, being careful not to tear the meat.

In a medium resealable plastic bag, combine the flour, ¹/₂ tablespoon chili powder, ¹/₄ teaspoon pepper, and salt.

Add several pieces of chicken. Seal the bag. Shake to coat the chicken. Shake off the excess flour mixture. Repeat with the remaining chicken.

Heat a large nonstick skillet over medium-high heat. Pour 1 teaspoon oil into the skillet and swirl to coat the bottom. Cook half the chicken pieces for 3 to 4 minutes on each side, or until lightly brown on both sides. Transfer to the plate with the bell pepper mixture. Repeat with the remaining oil and chicken.

Add the undrained tomatoes to the skillet, breaking up the whole tomatoes with a wooden spoon.

Stir in 1 teaspoon chili powder and $1/4$ teaspoon pepper. Reduce the heat and simmer for 3 to 4 minutes.

Stir in the lime zest. Stir in the bell pepper mixture and chicken. Increase the heat to medium and cook for 5 to 6 minutes, or until the chicken is no longer pink in the center and the mixture is heated through.

Chicken in White Wine
and Tarragon

Serves 4

Make a double batch of this fragrant chicken so you can pair it with angel hair pasta one night and still have enough for sandwiches later in the week.

4 boneless, skinless chicken breast halves (about 4 ounces each)
1 cup dry white wine (regular or nonalcoholic)

1 tablespoon dried tarragon, crumbled
4 medium garlic cloves, minced
1 teaspoon dry mustard
1/4 teaspoon pepper

Preheat the oven to 350°F.

Discard all the visible fat from the chicken. Place the chicken in a shallow broilerproof pan.

Pour the wine over the chicken.

In a small bowl, stir together the remaining ingredients. Rub on the chicken. Cover the pan with aluminum foil.

Bake for 35 minutes. Remove the foil. Turn the oven setting to broil. Broil the chicken about 5 inches from the heat for 2 to 3 minutes, or until lightly browned and no longer pink in the center.

calories 179
protein 27 g
carbohydrates 3 g
  fiber 1 g
  sugars 0 g
cholesterol 66 mg
total fat 2.0 g
  saturated 0.5 g
  polyunsaturated 0.5 g
  monounsaturated 0.5 g
sodium 78 mg

dietary exchange
3 very lean meat

Stuffed Chicken with Blue Cheese

Serves 4

Simply light the candles and impress your guests with this high-flavor, low-effort dish!

Vegetable oil spray
10-ounce package frozen chopped spinach, thawed and squeezed dry
1/2 cup finely chopped onion
2 teaspoons dried basil, crumbled
1/8 teaspoon crushed red pepper flakes
2 ounces blue cheese, crumbled (about 1/2 cup)
4 boneless, skinless chicken breast halves (about 4 ounces each)
1/8 teaspoon salt
Pepper to taste
Paprika to taste

Preheat the oven to 400°F. Line a baking sheet with aluminum foil. Lightly spray the sheet with vegetable oil spray.

In a small bowl, stir together the spinach, onion, basil, and red pepper flakes. Add the cheese. Toss gently to blend.

Discard all the visible fat from the chicken. Put the chicken between two pieces of plastic wrap. Using a tortilla press, the smooth side of a meat mallet, or a rolling pin, lightly flatten the breasts to a thickness of 1/4 inch, being careful not to tear the meat. Place the chicken with the smooth side down on the baking sheet.

Spoon the spinach mixture down the center of each breast. Press down on the mixture to pack. Roll the breasts jelly-roll style, placing them with the seam side down. Lightly spray the chicken rolls with vegetable oil spray. Sprinkle with the salt, pepper, and paprika.

Bake for 25 minutes, or until the chicken is no longer pink in the center.

Cook's Tip on Aluminum Foil

Using aluminum foil to protect baking sheets makes cleanup easy.

calories 201
protein 32 g
carbohydrates 5 g
  fiber 3 g
  sugars 2 g
cholesterol 76 mg
total fat 6.0 g
  saturated 3.0 g
  polyunsaturated 0.5 g
  monounsaturated 1.5 g
sodium 398 mg

dietary exchange
1 vegetable
3 1/2 lean meat

Sweet-Spice
Glazed Chicken

Serves 4 (plus 4 breast halves reserved)

Allspice, cloves, sweet-and-sour sauce, and a hint of bourbon sumptuously jazz up the glaze in this recipe. The extra chicken you cook is the main ingredient in Island Chicken Salad with Fresh Mint (page 127), an easy dinner for later in the week.

Vegetable oil spray

Glaze
1 cup sweet-and-sour sauce
1/4 cup bourbon
1 tablespoon plus 1 teaspoon low-sodium Worcestershire sauce
1 tablespoon plus 1 teaspoon acceptable vegetable oil

1 tablespoon cider vinegar
1/2 teaspoon crushed red pepper flakes
1/2 teaspoon ground allspice
1/2 teaspoon ground cloves
❖
8 boneless, skinless chicken breast halves (about 4 ounces each)

Preheat the broiler. Lightly spray the broiler pan and rack with vegetable oil spray.

In a small bowl, whisk together the glaze ingredients. Pour half the glaze into a cup.

Discard all the visible fat from the chicken. Put the chicken with the smooth side down on the broiler rack. Using a pastry brush, brush lightly with the glaze in the small bowl.

Broil 2 to 3 inches from the heat for 4 minutes.

Meanwhile, wash the pastry brush with hot, soapy water. Rinse and dry with paper towels.

Turn the chicken. Broil for 3 minutes. Brush the chicken with the remaining glaze in the small bowl. Broil for 2 to 3 minutes, or until the chicken is no longer pink in the center and begins to brown.

Wash and dry the pastry brush again.

Remove the chicken from the broiler. Brush with the glaze in the cup. Serve 4 breasts. Refrigerate the remaining breasts in an airtight container for up to three days for use in Island Chicken Salad with Fresh Mint.

calories 208
protein 26 g
carbohydrates 11 g
  fiber 0 g
  sugars 9 g
cholesterol 66 mg
total fat 4.0 g
  saturated 0.5 g
  polyunsaturated 1.0 g
  monounsaturated 1.5 g
sodium 88 mg

dietary exchange
1/2 other carbohydrate
3 very lean meat

Grilled Lemon-Sage Chicken

Serves 6

Fresh sage and rosemary impart a different flavor to grilled chicken. Tomato halves and corn on the cob can grill along with the chicken.

Marinade
- 1 teaspoon olive oil
- 1 teaspoon grated lemon zest
- 1/4 cup fresh lemon juice
- 1/4 cup chopped fresh sage leaves
- 1 tablespoon chopped fresh rosemary or 1 teaspoon dried, crushed
- 2 or 3 medium garlic cloves, minced

- 1 teaspoon black peppercorns, cracked
- 1/2 teaspoon salt

❖

- 6 boneless, skinless chicken breast halves (about 4 ounces each)
- 6 lemon slices, cut in half (optional) Fresh sage leaves (optional)

In a large resealable plastic bag, combine the marinade ingredients.

Discard all the visible fat from the chicken. Put the chicken with the smooth side up between two sheets of plastic wrap. Using a tortilla press, the smooth side of a meat mallet, or a rolling pin, lightly flatten the chicken to a thickness of 1/8 inch, being careful not to tear the meat. Add to the marinade. Seal the bag and turn to coat. Refrigerate for 30 minutes to 8 hours, turning occasionally. Discard the marinade.

Preheat the grill on medium-high.

Grill the chicken for 6 to 7 minutes on each side, or until no longer pink in the center.

To serve, garnish with the lemon slices and sage leaves.

calories 125
protein 26 g
carbohydrates 0 g
  fiber 0 g
  sugars 0 g
cholesterol 66 mg
total fat 1.5 g
  saturated 0.5 g
  polyunsaturated 0.5 g
  monounsaturated 0.5 g
sodium 268 mg

dietary exchange
3 very lean meat

Spicy Grilled Chicken

Serves 4 (plus 3 breast halves reserved)

This recipe will give you the basis for two easy dinners: grilled chicken for tonight and extra for whenever you want Chicken Fajitas (page 256) and a south-of-the-border fiesta.

Marinade
- 1 small onion, finely chopped
- 2 to 3 tablespoons fresh lime juice
- 2 tablespoons olive oil
- 1 to 2 tablespoons finely chopped fresh cilantro

- 1 small garlic clove, crushed
- 1/2 teaspoon chili powder
- Pepper to taste
- ❖
- 7 boneless, skinless chicken breast halves (about 4 ounces each)

In a large resealable plastic bag, combine the marinade ingredients.

Discard all the visible fat from the chicken. Add the chicken to the marinade. Seal the bag and turn to coat. Refrigerate for 2 to 3 hours, turning occasionally.

Preheat the grill on medium-high or preheat the broiler.

Grill the chicken or broil it about 6 inches from the heat for 6 to 7 minutes on each side, or until no longer pink in the center. Reserve 3 breast halves in an airtight container and refrigerate for up to three days for use in Chicken Fajitas.

calories 125
protein 26 g
carbohydrates 0 g
  fiber 0 g
  sugars 0 g
cholesterol 66 mg
total fat 1.5 g
  saturated 0.5 g
  polyunsaturated 0.5 g
  monounsaturated 0.5 g
sodium 74 mg

dietary exchange
3 very lean meat

Triple-Pepper Chicken

Serves 4 (plus 4 breast halves reserved)

Turn up the heat with a spicy paste of cayenne, lemon pepper, and black pepper! This recipe makes enough for two meals—use the extra chicken for Cajun Chicken Salad (page 125).

8 boneless, skinless chicken breast halves (about 4 ounces each)

Spice Rub

1 tablespoon chili powder
2 teaspoons fresh lime juice
1/2 tablespoon dried oregano, crumbled
2 medium garlic cloves, minced
1/2 teaspoon salt-free lemon pepper
1/2 teaspoon pepper

1/2 teaspoon onion powder
1/2 teaspoon ground cumin
1/2 teaspoon low-sodium Worcestershire sauce
1/2 teaspoon liquid smoke seasoning
1/4 teaspoon cayenne
❖
1 tablespoon plus 1 teaspoon acceptable stick margarine

Discard all the visible fat from the chicken. Put the chicken in a 12 × 8-inch glass baking dish.

In a small bowl, stir together the spice rub ingredients. Apply a thin paste to the chicken. Cover with plastic wrap and refrigerate for 4 hours.

Heat a large nonstick skillet over high heat. Heat half the margarine until medium brown. Add half the chicken. Immediately reduce the heat to medium. Cook for 4 minutes. Turn the chicken. Cook for 3 to 4 minutes, or until no longer pink in the center. Place on a plate. Cover with aluminum foil.

Increase the heat to high. Heat the remaining margarine until medium brown. Repeat the process.

Serve 4 breasts halves, refrigerating the remaining chicken in an airtight container for use in Cajun Chicken Salad.

Time-Saver

You can refrigerate the chicken with the rub for as little as 30 minutes. The flavor intensifies with the longer marinating, however.

calories 149
protein 27 g
carbohydrates 1 g
 fiber 1 g
 sugars 0 g
cholesterol 66 mg
total fat 3.5 g
 saturated 0.5 g
 polyunsaturated 1.0 g
 monounsaturated 1.5 g
sodium 107 mg

dietary exchange
3 very lean meat

Lemon-Cayenne Chicken

Serves 4

Cayenne and a tart lemon sauce provide the zip for these lightly breaded chicken breasts.

4 boneless, skinless chicken breast halves (about 4 ounces each)
1/2 cup all-purpose flour
3/4 teaspoon paprika
1/2 teaspoon salt
1/4 teaspoon cayenne
1/8 teaspoon black pepper

1 tablespoon olive oil
3 tablespoons water
1 tablespoon light tub margarine
1 teaspoon fresh lemon juice
2 tablespoons finely chopped fresh parsley

Discard all the visible fat from the chicken. Put the chicken with the smooth side up between two sheets of plastic wrap. Using a tortilla press, the smooth side of a meat mallet, or a rolling pin, lightly flatten the chicken to a thickness of 1/4 inch, being careful not to tear the meat.

In a shallow bowl, stir together the flour, paprika, salt, cayenne, and black pepper. Coat the chicken, shaking off any excess.

Heat a large nonstick skillet over medium-high heat. Pour the oil into the skillet and heat for 1 minute, or until hot. Cook the chicken for 8 minutes on each side, or until golden brown on the outside and no longer pink on the inside. Transfer the chicken to a platter.

calories 224
protein 28 g
carbohydrates 13 g
 fiber 1 g
 sugars 0 g
cholesterol 66 mg
total fat 6.0 g
 saturated 1.0 g
 polyunsaturated 1.0 g
 monounsaturated 3.5 g
sodium 389 mg

dietary exchange
1 starch
3 lean meat

Put the water, margarine, and lemon juice in the skillet, scraping to dislodge any browned bits. Bring the mixture to a boil. Boil for about 30 seconds, or until the sauce is slightly thickened.

To serve, drizzle the sauce over the chicken. Sprinkle with the parsley.

Spicy Chicken and Grits

Serves 4

Cooks who watch both their time and their saturated fat intake love boneless, skinless chicken breasts—they're fast and easy to prepare and are low in saturated fat. This recipe uses a spice rub for lots of flavor, adds soothing grits, and keeps everything savory and moist with a chicken broth sauce.

1 cup quick-cooking grits
4 cups fat-free, low-sodium chicken broth, such as on page 45
1 teaspoon paprika
1 teaspoon sugar
1/2 teaspoon black pepper
1/2 teaspoon cayenne

1 pound boneless, skinless chicken breasts
1 tablespoon olive oil
1 small onion, minced
1/2 medium green bell pepper, minced
1 medium garlic clove, minced
2 cups fat-free, low-sodium chicken broth, such as on page 45

Prepare the grits using the package directions, substituting 4 cups broth for water and omitting the salt and margarine. Cover. Set aside.

Meanwhile, in a small bowl, stir together the paprika, sugar, black pepper, and cayenne. Rub on the chicken to coat. Set aside.

Heat a large nonstick skillet over medium heat. Pour the oil into the skillet and swirl to coat the bottom. When the oil is hot, cook the onion, bell pepper, and garlic for 10 minutes, or until softened, stirring occasionally.

Meanwhile, discard all the visible fat from the chicken. Cut the chicken into thin slivers across the grain. Add to the vegetables. Cook over high heat for about 3 minutes, stirring often. Scrape the contents of the skillet onto a platter.

Pour 2 cups broth into the skillet. Boil rapidly for 5 minutes, or until the broth is reduced to 3/4 cup.

Return the chicken mixture to the skillet. Stir. Cook for 2 minutes, or until heated through.

To serve, spoon the grits onto plates. Spoon the chicken and broth over the grits.

calories 338
protein 33 g
carbohydrates 37 g
  fiber 2 g
  sugars 3 g
cholesterol 66 mg
total fat 5.5 g
  saturated 1.0 g
  polyunsaturated 1.0 g
  monounsaturated 3.0 g
sodium 113 mg

dietary exchange
2 starch
1 vegetable
3 very lean meat

Sweet-and-Sour
Baked Chicken

Serves 4

Serve this dish on a bed of fluffy rice so you don't miss a single drop of the fantastic sauce.

1 pound boneless, skinless chicken breasts	2 tablespoons frozen orange juice concentrate
8½-ounce can pineapple chunks in their own juice	1 tablespoon dry sherry
½ cup jellied cranberry sauce	1 teaspoon low-salt soy sauce
2 tablespoons light brown sugar	¼ teaspoon ground ginger
2 tablespoons plain rice vinegar or cider vinegar	2 tablespoons cornstarch
	2 tablespoons water
	1 medium green bell pepper, cut into thin strips

Preheat the oven to 350°F.

Discard all the visible fat from the chicken. Cut the chicken into ½-inch strips. Put the chicken in an 8-inch square nonstick baking pan. Set aside.

Drain the juice from the pineapple into a small saucepan. Set the pineapple chunks aside.

Put the saucepan over medium heat and whisk in the cranberry sauce, brown sugar, vinegar, orange juice concentrate, sherry, soy sauce, and ginger.

Put the cornstarch in a cup. Add the water, stirring to dissolve. Whisk into the juice mixture.

Increase the heat to medium-high. Cook for 3 to 4 minutes, or until thickened, stirring occasionally.

Stir in the pineapple chunks. Pour over the chicken.

Bake, covered, for 35 minutes, or until the chicken is no longer pink in the center. Add the bell pepper. Baste with the sauce.

Bake, uncovered, for 5 minutes.

calories 278
protein 27 g
carbohydrates 38 g
  fiber 2 g
  sugars 27 g
cholesterol 66 mg
total fat 1.5 g
  saturated 0.5 g
  polyunsaturated 0.5 g
  monounsaturated 0.5 g
sodium 119 mg

dietary exchange
½ starch
2 fruit
3 very lean meat

Chicken and
Snow-Pea Stir-Fry

Serves 6

This stir-fry highlights crunch from water chestnuts, celery, and snow peas.

1 cup uncooked rice
1 pound boneless, skinless chicken breasts
$\frac{1}{4}$ cup fat-free, low-sodium chicken broth, such as on page 45
1 tablespoon dry sherry
1 tablespoon low-salt soy sauce
1 teaspoon grated peeled gingerroot
1 medium garlic clove, minced
$\frac{1}{8}$ teaspoon hot-pepper oil (optional)
Vegetable oil spray
1 small onion, thinly sliced

1 medium rib of celery, thinly sliced
10-ounce package frozen snow peas
8-ounce can sliced water chestnuts, rinsed and drained
8-ounce can bamboo shoots, rinsed and drained
1 tablespoon cornstarch
1 teaspoon sugar
$\frac{1}{4}$ cup cold water
2 tablespoons slivered almonds, dry-roasted

Prepare the rice using the package directions, omitting the salt and margarine.

Meanwhile, discard all the visible fat from the chicken. Cut the chicken into thin slices.

In a small bowl, whisk together the broth, sherry, soy sauce, gingerroot, garlic, and hot-pepper oil. Set aside.

Heat a large, heavy skillet over high heat. Remove from the heat and lightly spray with vegetable oil spray. Cook the chicken for 4 minutes, stirring occasionally.

Stir in the onion and celery. Cook for 3 minutes, stirring occasionally.

Stir in the snow peas, water chestnuts, bamboo shoots, and broth mixture. Reduce the heat to medium and cook, covered, for 5 minutes.

Put the cornstarch and sugar in a cup. Add the water, stirring to dissolve. Pour over the chicken. Increase the heat to medium high and cook for 2 minutes, or until the sauce is thick, stirring occasionally. Spoon over the rice. Sprinkle with the almonds.

calories 266
protein 23 g
carbohydrates 37 g
  fiber 4 g
  sugars 4 g
cholesterol 44 mg
total fat 2.5 g
  saturated 0.5 g
  polyunsaturated 0.5 g
  monounsaturated 1.0 g
sodium 130 mg

dietary exchange
$1\frac{1}{2}$ starch
2 vegetable
2 very lean meat

Chicken and Mushroom Stir-Fry

Serves 6

This colorful blend of vegetables and chicken is delicious over brown rice or whole-wheat pasta.

1 pound boneless, skinless chicken breasts

1 tablespoon grated peeled gingerroot

1 tablespoon hot-pepper oil

3 medium garlic cloves, minced

1 teaspoon toasted sesame oil

2 tablespoons light brown sugar

2 tablespoons fat-free, low-sodium chicken broth, such as on page 45

2 tablespoons dry sherry

1 tablespoon low-salt soy sauce

1 tablespoon plain rice vinegar

1 teaspoon cornstarch

8 ounces button mushrooms, sliced

1 medium red bell pepper, diced

1 medium zucchini, diced

$^1/_2$ medium onion, sliced

8 cherry tomatoes, halved

Discard all the visible fat from the chicken. Cut the chicken into 1-inch cubes. Put in a large bowl.

Stir in the gingerroot, hot-pepper oil, garlic, and sesame oil. Cover and refrigerate for 15 minutes.

Meanwhile, in a small bowl, stir together the brown sugar, broth, sherry, soy sauce, vinegar, and cornstarch until the sugar and cornstarch dissolve. Set aside.

Heat a large nonstick skillet or wok over high heat. Cook the chicken with the marinade for 3 to 4 minutes, or until the chicken is lightly browned, stirring constantly.

Stir in the mushrooms, bell pepper, zucchini, and onion. Reduce the heat to medium-high and cook, covered, for 5 minutes, stirring occasionally.

Stir in the chicken broth mixture and cherry tomatoes. Cook for 3 to 4 minutes, or until the sauce is thick, stirring occasionally.

calories 166
protein 20 g
carbohydrates 12 g
  fiber 2 g
  sugars 8 g
cholesterol 44 mg
total fat 4.5 g
  saturated 0.5 g
  polyunsaturated 1.5 g
  monounsaturated 2.0 g
sodium 123 mg

dietary exchange
1 vegetable
$^1/_2$ other carbohydrate
2 lean meat

Beef-Vegetable Stir-Fry
Substitute 1 pound thinly sliced sirloin or eye-of-round steak, all visible fat discarded, for the chicken.

Cook's Tip on *Mise en Place*

The French phrase mise en place *(meez ahn plahs) means having all your ingredients ready (measured, sliced, melted, etc.) before you start cooking. This advance preparation probably is never more important than in stir-frying, in which the cooking steps must move very quickly.*

beef-vegetable stir-fry

calories 190
protein 19 g
carbohydrates 12 g
  fiber 2 g
  sugars 8 g
cholesterol 45 mg
total fat 7.5 g
  saturated 2.0 g
  polyunsaturated 1.5 g
  monounsaturated 3.5 g
sodium 118 mg

dietary exchange
1 vegetable
½ other carbohydrate
2 lean meat

Broiled Chicken with
Hoisin-Barbecue Sauce

Serves 4

Barbecue sauce acquires an Asian flair in this broiled chicken dish.

Vegetable oil spray (optional)
1 cup uncooked rice
1/2 teaspoon ground turmeric

Hoisin-Barbecue Sauce
1/4 cup hoisin sauce
2 tablespoons barbecue sauce
1 teaspoon sugar
1 teaspoon cider vinegar
3/4 teaspoon low-sodium
Worcestershire sauce

1/2 teaspoon grated peeled gingerroot
1/8 teaspoon cayenne
❖
1 pound boneless, skinless chicken breasts
1 cup frozen green peas, thawed and drained
1/4 cup finely snipped fresh cilantro or parsley

If using long metal skewers, lightly spray 8 skewers with vegetable oil spray. If using bamboo skewers, soak 8 skewers in cold water for at least 10 minutes.

Preheat the broiler. Line the broiler pan with aluminum foil. Lightly spray the broiler rack with vegetable oil spray and put in the pan.

Prepare the rice using the package directions, omitting the salt and margarine but adding the turmeric.

Meanwhile, in a small bowl, whisk together the sauce ingredients.

calories 353
protein 32 g
carbohydrates 49 g
 fiber 3 g
 sugars 8 g
cholesterol 66 mg
total fat 2.0 g
 saturated 0.5 g
 polyunsaturated 0.5 g
 monounsaturated 0.5 g
sodium 262 mg

dietary exchange
3½ starch
3 very lean meat

Discard all the visible fat from the chicken. Cut the chicken into 1-inch cubes. Thread onto the skewers. Put on the broiler rack.

Broil 2 to 3 inches from the heat for 3 minutes. Turn the skewers. Spoon the sauce over all. Broil for 3 minutes, or until the chicken is no longer pink in the center.

To serve, stir the peas into the rice. Spoon onto a platter. Arrange the skewers on the rice. Sprinkle the cilantro over all.

Curried Sweet-and-Sour Chicken

Substitute ³/₈ cup sweet-and-sour sauce for hoisin and barbecue sauces, and substitute 1 teaspoon curry powder for gingerroot.

Cook's Tip on Skewered Food

For a dramatic presentation, poke skewered items into a large, heavy vegetable. Try butternut squash, eggplant, or red cabbage. Slice a thin piece off the bottom so it will sit flat. Surround the vegetable with parsley sprigs or other fresh herbs. If you're serving fruit kebabs, stick them into a pineapple.

curried sweet-and-sour chicken
calories 363
protein 32 g
carbohydrates 51 g
fiber 3 g
sugars 10 g
cholesterol 66 mg
total fat 2.0 g
saturated 0.5 g
polyunsaturated 0.5 g
monounsaturated 0.5 g
sodium 126 mg
dietary exchange
3½ starch
3 very lean meat

Italian Double Toss

Serves 4; 1½ cups per serving

You'll want to dig down deep with every forkful so you don't miss out on any of the layers.

4 ounces dried penne pasta
¾ cup cherry tomatoes, quartered (about 3½ ounces)
6 kalamata olives, coarsely chopped
2 tablespoons chopped fresh basil leaves
1½ tablespoons capers, rinsed and drained
8 ounces boneless, skinless chicken breasts, all visible fat discarded, cut into thin strips
½ medium red bell pepper, cut into thin strips

1 small zucchini, cut lengthwise into eighths, then cut crosswise into 2-inch pieces
¼ medium onion, cut into ½-inch wedges (about 1 ounce)
1 medium garlic clove, minced
   Vegetable oil spray
¼ teaspoon salt
1 tablespoon olive oil (extra-virgin preferred)
2 ounces fat-free or low-fat feta, crumbled (about ½ cup)

Prepare the pasta using the package directions, omitting the salt and oil. Drain, reserving ¼ cup pasta water.

Meanwhile, in a small bowl, stir together the tomatoes, olives, basil, and capers. Set aside.

Heat a 12-inch nonstick skillet over medium-high heat. Cook the chicken for 3 to 4 minutes, or until no longer pink in the center, stirring frequently. Transfer the chicken to a plate.

Put the bell pepper, zucchini, onion, and garlic in the skillet. Lightly spray the vegetables with vegetable oil spray. Cook for 4 minutes, or until the pepper is just tender-crisp, stirring frequently.

Stir in the chicken, reserved pasta water, and salt.

To serve, spoon the pasta onto a platter. Top with the chicken mixture. Drizzle with the oil. Top with the tomato mixture. Sprinkle with the feta.

calories 251
protein 21 g
carbohydrates 28 g
  fiber 2 g
  sugars 4 g
cholesterol 33 mg
total fat 6.5 g
  saturated 1.0 g
  polyunsaturated 1.0 g
  monounsaturated 4.0 g
sodium 589 mg

dietary exchange
1½ starch
1 vegetable
2 lean meat

Baked Chicken Parmesan

Serves 6

Chicken pieces take a double dip (in buttermilk and in seasoned bread crumbs), then bake on a rack so they stay crisp all over.

Vegetable oil spray
4 slices whole-wheat bread
$1/4$ cup plus 2 tablespoons shredded or grated Parmesan cheese ($1^1/2$ ounces)
$1^1/2$ tablespoons finely snipped fresh parsley

$1/2$ tablespoon paprika
$3/4$ teaspoon garlic powder
$1/2$ teaspoon dried thyme, crumbled
$1/2$ cup fat-free or low-fat buttermilk
6 boneless, skinless chicken breast halves (about 4 ounces each)

Preheat the oven to 450°F. Lightly spray a rectangular baking sheet and slightly smaller cooling rack with vegetable oil spray. Put the rack on the baking sheet. Set aside.

In a food processor or blender, process the bread into fine crumbs. Pour into a shallow bowl. Stir the Parmesan, parsley, paprika, garlic powder, and thyme into the crumbs.

Pour the buttermilk into a shallow bowl.

Set the bowl with the buttermilk, the bowl with the crumbs, and the baking sheet and rack in a row, assembly-line fashion.

Discard all the visible fat from the chicken. Dip the chicken into the buttermilk, shaking off the excess liquid. Coat in the crumbs, shaking off excess crumbs. Put the chicken on the rack. Lightly spray each breast with vegetable oil spray.

Bake for 15 minutes. Turn over and bake for 10 minutes, or until no longer pink in the center.

calories 195
protein 30 g
carbohydrates 9 g
fiber 2 g
sugars 1 g
cholesterol 69 mg
total fat 3.5 g
saturated 1.5 g
polyunsaturated 0.5 g
monounsaturated 1.0 g
sodium 258 mg

dietary exchange
$1/2$ starch
3 very lean meat

Chicken Stufino

Serves 6

The taste of chicken slowly oven-braised in a tomato-rich sauce with vegetables is delicious enough. We go one more step and serve it all on a bed of tricolor pasta.

1 tablespoon all-purpose flour
1/2 teaspoon salt
1/4 teaspoon pepper, or to taste
1 1/2 pounds boneless, skinless chicken breasts
Olive oil spray
1 teaspoon olive oil
1 cup dry white wine (regular or nonalcoholic)
2 medium carrots, finely chopped
2 medium ribs of celery, finely chopped
1 medium onion, finely chopped
1 or 2 medium garlic cloves, minced
14.5-ounce can no-salt-added stewed tomatoes, crushed, undrained
12 ounces dried tricolor pasta shells
1 teaspoon salt-free Italian herb seasoning
1/4 cup snipped fresh parsley (optional)

In a small bowl, stir together the flour, salt, and pepper.

Discard all the visible fat from the chicken. Cut the chicken into large cubes. Put the chicken on a plate. Sprinkle with the flour mixture. Shake off the excess flour.

Heat a Dutch oven or heavy ovenproof skillet over medium-high heat. Remove from the heat and spray with olive oil spray (being careful not to spray near a gas flame). Pour the oil into the Dutch oven and swirl to coat the bottom. Brown the chicken quickly on all sides, 2 to 3 minutes.

Meanwhile, preheat the oven to 300°F.

Pour the wine into the Dutch oven, scraping to dislodge any browned bits.

Stir in the carrots, celery, onion, and garlic. Cook for 2 to 3 minutes, stirring occasionally.

Stir in the undrained tomatoes. Bring to a boil.

calories 452
protein 37 g
carbohydrates 63 g
fiber 4 g
sugars 8 g
cholesterol 66 mg
total fat 3.5 g
saturated 0.5 g
polyunsaturated 1.0 g
monounsaturated 1.0 g
sodium 303 mg

dietary exchange
3 1/2 starch
2 vegetable
3 very lean meat

Bake, covered, for 1 hour, or until the chicken is tender and no longer pink in the center.

Meanwhile, prepare the pasta using the package directions, adding the Italian herb seasoning and omitting the salt and oil. Drain in a colander.

To serve, put the pasta on plates. Top with the chicken mixture. Sprinkle with the parsley.

Veal Stufino

Replace the chicken with 1¹/₂ pounds boneless lean veal stew meat, all visible fat discarded, cut into bite-size pieces.

veal stufino

calories 454
protein 33 g
carbohydrates 63 g
  fiber 4 g
  sugars 8 g
cholesterol 94 mg
total fat 5.0 g
  saturated 1.0 g
  polyunsaturated 1.0 g
  monounsaturated 1.5 g
sodium 327 mg

dietary exchange
3½ starch
2 vegetable
3 lean meat

Chicken Chili

Serves 8

Corn and red bell pepper add a touch of color to this satisfying dish.

2 pounds boneless, skinless chicken breasts
1 teaspoon acceptable vegetable oil
1 large onion, finely chopped
4 medium garlic cloves, minced
1 cup dry white wine (regular or nonalcoholic)
8 ounces button mushrooms, thinly sliced (2½ to 3 cups)
2 15-ounce cans no-salt-added pinto beans, rinsed and drained
1½ cups frozen whole-kernel corn
1 medium red bell pepper, diced

4-ounce can diced green chiles, rinsed and drained
6 to 8 sprigs of fresh parsley
3 sprigs of fresh thyme
1 bay leaf
½ tablespoon ground cumin
½ tablespoon dried oregano, crumbled
½ teaspoon red hot-pepper sauce, or to taste
½ teaspoon salt
½ cup finely snipped fresh parsley

Discard all the visible fat from the chicken. Cut the chicken into 1½-inch cubes.

Heat a large stockpot over medium-high heat. Pour the oil into the pot and swirl to coat the bottom. Cook the onion for 2 to 3 minutes, or until soft.

Stir in the garlic. Cook for 1 minute.

Stir in the chicken, wine, and mushrooms. Reduce the heat to medium and cook, covered, for 5 minutes.

Stir half the beans into the chicken mixture. Mash the remaining beans and add to the pot.

Stir in the remaining ingredients except the snipped parsley. Reduce the heat and simmer for 20 minutes.

To serve, remove the sprigs of parsley and thyme and the bay leaf. Stir in the snipped parsley.

calories 297
protein 35 g
carbohydrates 29 g
  fiber 7 g
  sugars 6 g
cholesterol 66 mg
total fat 2.5 g
  saturated 0.5 g
  polyunsaturated 0.5 g
  monounsaturated 1.0 g
sodium 277 mg

dietary exchange
1½ starch
1 vegetable
4 very lean meat

Savory Microwave Chicken

Serves 6

Take advantage of the speedy microwave and prepare this chicken dish— complete with vegetables—in a snap.

1½ pounds boneless, skinless chicken breasts
2 cups fat-free, low-sodium chicken broth, such as on page 45
1 teaspoon light tub margarine
2 cups small broccoli florets
1 large onion, finely chopped
1 large carrot, sliced

1 teaspoon grated orange zest
1 cup fresh orange juice
2 tablespoons cornstarch
2 tablespoons dry sherry
1 tablespoon low-salt soy sauce
½ teaspoon garlic powder
¼ teaspoon salt
⅓ cup slivered almonds, dry-roasted

Discard all the visible fat from the chicken. Cut the chicken into 1-inch cubes.

Put 2 cups broth and the chicken in a microwave-safe casserole dish. Cook, covered, on 50 percent power (medium) for 5 minutes. Stir. Cook for 5 minutes. Drain the chicken, reserving 1 cup broth for the sauce. Transfer the chicken to a plate.

In the same casserole dish, melt the margarine on 100 percent power (high) for 20 seconds. Add the broccoli, onion, and carrot. Cook, covered, on 100 percent power (high) for 7 minutes. Remove from the microwave. Stir in the chicken.

In a microwave-safe bowl, stir together the reserved broth and the remaining ingredients except the almonds. Cook on 100 percent power (high) for 5 minutes. Stir into the chicken mixture.

Cook, covered, on 50 percent power (medium) for 3 minutes, or until heated through.

To serve, sprinkle with the almonds.

calories 231
protein 30 g
carbohydrates 15 g
  fiber 3 g
  sugars 8 g
cholesterol 66 mg
total fat 5.0 g
  saturated 0.5 g
  polyunsaturated 1.0 g
  monounsaturated 2.5 g
sodium 269 mg

dietary exchange
½ fruit
1½ vegetable
3 very lean meat
1 fat

Tandoori Ginger
Chicken Strips

Serves 4

A delicate, lemony marinade flavors tender strips of chicken.

3/4 cup coarsely chopped onion
1 tablespoon coarsely chopped
  peeled gingerroot
2 medium garlic cloves
1 cup fat-free or light plain yogurt
2 tablespoons fresh lemon juice
1 tablespoon paprika
1/2 tablespoon curry powder

1/2 teaspoon ground cumin
1/4 teaspoon salt
1/8 teaspoon cayenne
1 pound chicken tenders, all visible
  fat discarded
  Vegetable oil spray
1/8 teaspoon salt

In a food processor or blender, process the onion, gingerroot, and garlic until smooth. Add the yogurt, lemon juice, paprika, curry powder, cumin, 1/4 teaspoon salt, and cayenne. Process until well blended.

Put the chicken in a large resealable plastic bag. Pour the yogurt mixture over the chicken. Seal the bag. Turn several times to coat completely. Refrigerate for 4 to 8 hours, turning occasionally.

Preheat the broiler. Lightly spray the broiler rack and pan with vegetable oil spray.

Remove the chicken from the bag. Discard the marinade, leaving what clings to the chicken.

Broil the chicken about 4 inches from the heat for 6 minutes. Turn it over. Broil for 6 minutes, or until no longer pink in the center. Sprinkle with 1/8 teaspoon salt.

calories 125
protein 26 g
carbohydrates 0 g
  fiber 0 g
  sugars 0 g
cholesterol 66 mg
total fat 1.5 g
  saturated 0.5 g
  polyunsaturated 0.5 g
  monounsaturated 0.5 g
sodium 338 mg

dietary exchange
3 very lean meat

Cook's Tip

For peak flavor and texture, do not marinate longer than the suggested time.

Boneless Buffalo Wings

Serves 4

If it's a challenge to choose between the sauce coatings for these "wings," double the chicken and use both.

Vegetable oil spray (olive oil spray preferred)

8 chicken breast tenders (about 1 pound), all visible fat discarded

1/4 cup all-purpose flour

1 teaspoon salt-free all-purpose seasoning

Hot-Pepper Sauce Coating
1 tablespoon light tub margarine
1 teaspoon red hot-pepper sauce

or

Barbecue Sauce Coating
1/4 cup barbecue sauce
1 teaspoon low-salt soy sauce
1/2 teaspoon toasted sesame oil

Preheat the oven to 350°F. Lightly spray a baking sheet with vegetable oil spray.

Cut the chicken tenders in half crosswise.

In a large resealable plastic bag, combine the flour and all-purpose seasoning. Add several chicken tenders. Seal the bag. Shake to coat. Shake off any excess flour. Repeat with the remaining tenders. Arrange the chicken in a single layer on the baking sheet. Lightly spray the chicken with vegetable oil spray.

Bake for 20 to 25 minutes, or until no longer pink in the center and golden brown on the outside.

Meanwhile, for the coating of your choice, stir together the ingredients in a medium bowl. Add the warm chicken and toss to coat.

Cook's Tip

Keep in mind that bottled sauces such as hot-pepper sauce and barbecue sauce can be high in sodium, so check the labels and choose those with the lowest sodium available.

with hot-pepper sauce
calories 163
protein 27 g
carbohydrates 6 g
fiber 0 g
sugars 0 g
cholesterol 66 mg
total fat 2.5 g
saturated 0.5 g
polyunsaturated 0.5 g
monounsaturated 1 g
sodium 104 mg
dietary exchange
1/2 starch
3 very lean meat

with barbecue sauce
calories 171
protein 27 g
carbohydrates 8 g
fiber 0 g
sugars 2 g
cholesterol 66 mg
total fat 2.5 g
saturated 0.5 g
polyunsaturated 0.5 g
monounsaturated 0.5 g
sodium 234 mg
dietary exchange
1/2 starch
3 lean meat

Slow-Cooker
White Chili

Serves 6

Using bone-in chicken adds a savory quality to this cook-while-you-work dish. You can easily stretch the chili to serve more people by ladling it over rice.

Chili

1 pound dried navy or Great Northern beans, sorted for stones and shriveled beans and rinsed (about 2¼ cups)

1 pound skinless chicken thighs with bone, all visible fat discarded

6 cups fat-free, low-sodium chicken broth, such as on page 45

1 fresh jalapeño, seeds and ribs discarded, minced

2 4-ounce cans chopped green chiles, rinsed and drained

1 medium onion, chopped

4 medium garlic cloves, minced

2 teaspoons ground cumin

2 teaspoons dried oregano, crumbled

⅛ to ¼ teaspoon ground cloves

¼ teaspoon cayenne

❖

Fat-free, low-sodium salsa, such as Salsa Cruda (page 502) (optional)

Fat-free or light sour cream (optional)

Put the beans in a slow-cooker. Add the chicken and broth (don't stir).

Wearing gloves, discard the seeds and ribs of the jalapeño. Mince the jalapeño. Add with the remaining chili ingredients to the bean mixture. Cook on high for 10 hours, or until the beans and chicken are tender.

Remove and discard the bones from the chicken. Separate the chicken into bite-size pieces. Return the chicken to the chili.

To serve, ladle the chili into bowls. Top with the salsa and sour cream.

calories 372
protein 30 g
carbohydrates 51 g
 fiber 21 g
 sugars 5 g
cholesterol 38 mg
total fat 5.5 g
 saturated 1.5 g
 polyunsaturated 1.5 g
 monounsaturated 2.0 g
sodium 201 mg

dietary exchange
3 starch
1 vegetable
3 very lean meat

Chipotle Chicken Wraps

Serves 6

Smoky chicken saved from Mexican Chicken and Vegetables with Chipotle Peppers is rolled in flour tortillas with sour cream, cilantro, red onion, black olives, and freshly squeezed lime juice.

4 cooked chicken breast halves with bone and 1 cup tomato mixture reserved from Mexican Chicken and Vegetables with Chipotle Peppers (page 212)
6 8-inch fat-free or low-fat flour tortillas, warmed

1/2 cup fat-free or light sour cream
1/2 cup finely chopped red onion
1/4 cup chopped cilantro leaves (optional)
12 medium black olives, quartered
Pepper to taste
Fresh lime juice to taste

In a small saucepan, warm the reserved chicken and tomato mixture over medium heat for 10 minutes, or until heated through, stirring occasionally.

To assemble, layer as follows down the center of a tortilla: 1/4 cup chicken mixture (use a slotted spoon), 1 tablespoon sour cream, 1 tablespoon red onion, 1/2 tablespoon cilantro, 8 olive quarters, pepper, and lime juice. Fold the right third of the tortilla to the center. Fold the bottom half up to the top. Roll from the bottom edge up to the top. Repeat with the remaining ingredients.

calories 236
protein 20 g
carbohydrates 33 g
  fiber 3 g
  sugars 4 g
cholesterol 38 mg
total fat 2.0 g
  saturated 0.5 g
  polyunsaturated 0.5 g
  monounsaturated 0.5 g
sodium 457 mg

dietary exchange
2 starch
2 very lean meat

Chicken Fajitas

Serves 4

Spicy Grilled Chicken saved from another meal is the base for this super-speedy entrée.

1 teaspoon acceptable stick margarine
1 large onion, thinly sliced
1 large green bell pepper, thinly sliced
3 cooked chicken breast halves reserved from Spicy Grilled Chicken (page 236), thinly sliced

6 6-inch fat-free or low-fat flour tortillas or 3 pita breads, halved
1/3 cup fat-free, low-sodium salsa, such as Salsa Cruda (page 502)

Preheat the oven to 325°F.

In a large nonstick skillet, melt the margarine over medium-high heat and swirl to coat the bottom. Cook the onion and bell pepper for about 5 minutes, or until the onion is slightly brown, stirring constantly.

Stir in the chicken. Cook for 2 to 3 minutes, or until warmed through.

Meanwhile, wrap the tortillas or pita breads in aluminum foil. Warm in the oven for 6 to 8 minutes.

To serve, place the chicken strips down the center of the tortillas. Top with the onion, bell pepper, and salsa. Roll up jelly-roll style.

calories 266
protein 24 g
carbohydrates 36 g
 fiber 3 g
 sugars 5 g
cholesterol 49 mg
total fat 2.0 g
 saturated 0.5 g
 polyunsaturated 0.5 g
 monounsaturated 1.0 g
sodium 495 mg

dietary exchange
2 starch
1 vegetable
2½ very lean meat

Chicken à la King

Serves 6

An old standby gets a contemporary flavor with fragrant jasmine rice and oyster mushrooms. Feel free to substitute other mushrooms, such as shiitake or portobello.

1 cup uncooked jasmine or long-grain rice	1/4 teaspoon white pepper
1 teaspoon light tub margarine	1/3 cup all-purpose flour
8 ounces fresh oyster mushrooms or other exotic mushrooms, sliced	1/3 cup water
1/4 medium green bell pepper, diced	2 cups diced cooked skinless chicken breasts, cooked without salt
2 cups fat-free, low-sodium chicken broth, such as on page 45	7-ounce jar pimientos, drained and chopped
5-ounce can fat-free evaporated milk (2/3 cup)	2 tablespoons dry sherry (optional)
1/4 teaspoon salt	2 or 3 drops red hot-pepper sauce
	1 tablespoon snipped fresh parsley

Prepare the rice using the package directions, omitting the salt and margarine.

Meanwhile, in a large, heavy saucepan, melt the margarine over medium-high heat and swirl to coat the bottom. Reduce the heat to medium-low. Cook the mushrooms and bell pepper for 2 to 3 minutes, or until tender, stirring occasionally.

Whisk in the broth, milk, salt, and pepper.

In a small bowl, whisk together the flour and water. Whisk into the mushroom mixture. Bring to a boil over medium-high heat, stirring occasionally. Reduce the heat to medium-low. Cook for 2 to 3 minutes, or until thickened, stirring occasionally.

Stir in the chicken and pimientos. Heat through.

Stir in the sherry and hot-pepper sauce.

To serve, spoon the rice onto plates. Spoon the chicken mixture over the rice. Sprinkle with the parsley.

calories 264
protein 19 g
carbohydrates 38 g
fiber 3 g
sugars 3 g
cholesterol 35 mg
total fat 3.5 g
saturated 1.0 g
polyunsaturated 1.0 g
monounsaturated 1.5 g
sodium 193 mg

dietary exchange
2 starch
1 vegetable
2 very lean meat

Chicken-Spinach Manicotti

Serves 6

This recipe is a great way to use leftover cooked chicken.

Vegetable oil spray
12 dried manicotti shells

Filling

2 cups diced cooked skinless chicken breasts, cooked without salt
1½ cups fat-free or low-fat cottage cheese (about 12 ounces)
   10-ounce package frozen chopped spinach, thawed and squeezed dry
   Egg substitute equivalent to 3 eggs, or 3 large eggs
⅓ cup shredded or grated Parmesan cheese
2 teaspoons dried basil, crumbled
   Pepper to taste

Sauce

1 teaspoon olive oil
1 large onion, chopped
3 medium garlic cloves, minced
   14.5-ounce can no-salt-added diced tomatoes, undrained
1 cup water
   6-ounce can no-salt-added tomato paste
1 teaspoon salt-free Italian herb seasoning
1 teaspoon dried basil, crumbled
   ❖
3 tablespoons shredded or grated Parmesan cheese

Lightly spray a 13 × 9 × 2-inch pan with vegetable oil spray. Set aside.

Prepare the pasta using the package directions, omitting the salt and oil. Drain. Set aside.

Meanwhile, in a large bowl, stir together the filling ingredients. Set aside.

Heat the oil for the sauce in a medium saucepan over medium-high heat. Cook the onion for 2 to 3 minutes, or until soft.

Stir in the garlic. Cook for 1 minute.

Stir in the remaining sauce ingredients. Crush the tomatoes slightly with a wooden spoon. Reduce the heat and simmer for 8 to 10 minutes. Spread 1 cup sauce in the pan.

calories 363
protein 35 g
carbohydrates 43 g
  fiber 5 g
  sugars 8 g
cholesterol 47 mg
total fat 5.5 g
  saturated 2.0 g
  polyunsaturated 1.0 g
  monounsaturated 2.0 g
sodium 477 mg

dietary exchange
1 starch
3 vegetable
3½ lean meat

Preheat the oven to 375°F.

Stuff the shells with the filling. Place them on the sauce. Spoon the remaining sauce over the shells. Sprinkle with 3 tablespoons Parmesan.

Bake for 30 minutes, or until heated through.

Microwave Method

Prepare the shells as directed. Stir together the oil, onion, and garlic in a 1-quart microwave-safe bowl. Microwave on 100 percent power (high) for 3 minutes. Add the remaining sauce ingredients. Cook on 50 percent power (medium) for 10 minutes. Put half the sauce in a microwave-safe baking dish. Fill the shells as directed. Place them on the sauce. Cover with the remaining sauce. Top with 3 tablespoons Parmesan. Cover with vented plastic wrap and microwave on 50 percent power (medium) for 25 minutes. Let stand, covered, for 5 minutes.

Chicken and Broccoli
in Mushroom Sauce

Serves 6

Earthy mushrooms, bright-green broccoli, and creamy sauce form a succu-lent team in this casserole. If you're a cook on the run, see our Time-Saver below.

Vegetable oil spray
10 ounces fresh broccoli florets or 10-ounce package frozen broccoli florets
2 cups diced cooked skinless chicken breasts, cooked without salt

¹/₄ cup all-purpose flour
¹/₄ cup sliced green onions (green and white parts)
3 tablespoons shredded or grated Parmesan cheese
Dash of nutmeg

Sauce

1 teaspoon acceptable stick margarine
8 ounces button mushrooms, sliced
1¹/₃ cups fat-free, low-sodium chicken broth, such as on page 45
5-ounce can fat-free evaporated milk (²/₃ cup)

Topping

¹/₄ cup fresh bread crumbs (about ¹/₂ slice bread)
2 tablespoons finely snipped fresh parsley
1 teaspoon grated lemon zest

Lightly spray a 9-inch square baking pan with veg-etable oil spray.

Steam the broccoli until tender-crisp. Plunge into ice water to stop the cooking process. Drain. Pat dry with paper towels. Arrange in the baking pan.

Place the chicken over the broccoli. Set aside.

In a medium nonstick skillet, melt the margarine over medium heat and swirl to coat the bottom. Cook the mushrooms, covered, for 7 to 9 minutes, or until they have released their liquid. Increase the heat to high. Cook, uncovered, for 1 to 2 minutes to allow the liquid to evaporate.

calories 161
protein 18 g
carbohydrates 13 g
  fiber 2 g
  sugars 5 g
cholesterol 37 mg
total fat 4.5 g
  saturated 1.5 g
  polyunsaturated 1.0 g
  monounsaturated 1.5 g
sodium 143 mg

dietary exchange
¹/₂ starch
1 vegetable
2 lean meat

Preheat the oven to 375°F.

Pour the broth and milk into a medium saucepan. Whisk in the flour. Bring to a boil over medium-high heat. Cook for 3 to 4 minutes, or until thickened, stirring occasionally.

Stir in the green onions, Parmesan, nutmeg, and mushrooms. Pour over the chicken in the baking pan.

In a small bowl, stir together the topping ingredients. Sprinkle over the casserole.

Bake for 25 minutes.

Time-Saver

Substitute a 10.75-ounce can low-fat, low-sodium condensed cream of chicken soup mixed with 1/2 cup fat-free, low-sodium chicken broth for the broth-milk-flour sauce (no heating required). Add the cooked mushrooms, green onions, Parmesan, and nutmeg and proceed as directed.

Chicken Curry in a Hurry

Serves 4

Serve this quick and easy hit over steamed rice or rice pilaf. Offer small bowls of toppings such as sliced green onions or Cranberry Chutney (page 481).

Vegetable oil spray
1 teaspoon acceptable vegetable oil
2 cups diced cooked skinless chicken or turkey breast, cooked without salt
8 ounces button mushrooms, thinly sliced
1 small onion, chopped
3 tablespoons all-purpose flour

1 cup water
1 cup finely chopped apple (Granny Smith preferred) (about 1 medium)
1 cup fat-free, low-sodium chicken broth, such as on page 45
3/4 cup fat-free milk
1/4 cup snipped fresh parsley
1/2 tablespoon curry powder

Heat a large Dutch oven over medium-high heat. Remove from the heat and lightly spray with vegetable oil spray (being careful not to spray near a gas flame). Pour the oil into the pot and swirl to coat the bottom. Cook the chicken, mushrooms, and onion for 4 to 5 minutes, or until the chicken is warm and the vegetables are soft.

Put the flour in a small jar with a tight-fitting lid. Add the water. Shake well to combine. Pour the mixture into the pot.

Stir in the remaining ingredients. Bring to a boil over medium-high heat, stirring constantly. Reduce the heat and simmer for 3 minutes, or until the apple pieces are tender-crisp, stirring constantly.

Cook's Tip on Curry Powder

Make your own curry powder by mixing 1/2 teaspoon each of the ground forms of cardamom, cinnamon, cloves, and turmeric (the last gives curry powder its characteristic yellow color). Other spices commonly used are chiles, coriander, cumin, fennel seed, fenugreek, mace, nutmeg, red and black pepper, poppy and sesame seeds, saffron, and tamarind.

calories 209
protein 22 g
carbohydrates 16 g
  fiber 2 g
  sugars 8 g
cholesterol 53 mg
total fat 6.5 g
  saturated 1.5 g
  polyunsaturated 1.5 g
  monounsaturated 2.5 g
sodium 90 mg

dietary exchange
1/2 starch
1/2 fruit
3 lean meat

Roasted Garlic-Lemon Turkey Breast

Serves 8

A highly aromatic marinade of garlic, lemon, rosemary, thyme, and parsley flavors this roasted turkey breast. Save half the cooked turkey to use in Turkey on a Bed of Sliced Tomatoes (page 128).

Vegetable oil spray
3 1/2-pound frozen half turkey breast with skin, thawed (ask the butcher to cut)
2 tablespoons grated lemon zest
1/4 cup fresh lemon juice
3 tablespoons olive oil (extra-virgin preferred)

6 medium garlic cloves, minced
1/2 tablespoon Dijon mustard
3/4 teaspoon dried rosemary, crushed
1/2 teaspoon dried thyme, crumbled
1/2 teaspoon salt
1/2 cup snipped fresh parsley

Lightly spray a large glass baking dish with vegetable oil spray. Put the turkey in the baking dish.

In a small bowl, whisk together the remaining ingredients except the parsley. Stir in the parsley.

Gently loosen but don't remove the turkey skin, creating a pocket. Being careful to not break the skin, spoon the parsley mixture as evenly as possible under the skin. Gently pull the skin over any exposed meat. Cover tightly with plastic wrap and refrigerate for 8 to 12 hours.

Preheat the oven to 325°F.

Remove the plastic wrap. Bake the turkey for about 1 hour 45 minutes, or until it's cooked through and the juices run clear. Let stand on a cooling rack for 15 minutes for easy carving. Remove and discard the skin. Thinly slice the turkey.

calories 205
protein 33 g
carbohydrates 2 g
  fiber 1 g
  sugars 0 g
cholesterol 93 mg
total fat 6.5 g
  saturated 1.0 g
  polyunsaturated 1.0 g
  monounsaturated 4.0 g
sodium 228 mg

dietary exchange
4 lean meat

Turkey Fillets
with Fresh Herbs

Serves 6

No more dry turkey! The buttermilk tenderizes the fillets and keeps them moist as they cook. Refrigerate any leftovers and serve slices of chilled turkey over your favorite salad greens.

Marinade
- 2 cups fat-free or low-fat buttermilk
- 1 large onion, finely chopped
- 1 tablespoon finely chopped fresh dillweed
- 1 tablespoon finely chopped fresh tarragon
- 1 tablespoon finely chopped fresh cilantro
- 1 tablespoon finely chopped fresh rosemary
- 1 tablespoon acceptable vegetable oil
- 1 teaspoon pepper
- 1/4 teaspoon salt
- ❖
- 6 skinless turkey fillets (about 4 ounces each), about 3/4 inch thick, all visible fat discarded

In a large resealable plastic bag, combine the marinade ingredients.

Add the turkey to the marinade. Seal the bag and turn to coat. Refrigerate for 1 to 12 hours, turning the bag several times.

Preheat the grill on medium-high or preheat the broiler.

Remove the turkey from the marinade. Discard the marinade. Grill for 4 to 5 minutes on each side. Or broil about 6 inches from the heat for 5 to 7 minutes on each side. The turkey should be cooked through and no longer pink in the center.

Cook's Tip on Herbs

In most recipes, such as this one, you can substitute dried herbs for fresh, though the flavor won't be quite as good. The ratio is 1 teaspoon of dried herbs for 1 tablespoon of fresh herbs.

calories 125
protein 27 g
carbohydrates 0 g
  fiber 0 g
  sugars 0 g
cholesterol 77 mg
total fat 1.0 g
  saturated 0.5 g
  polyunsaturated 0.5 g
  monounsaturated 0.0 g
sodium 232 mg

dietary exchange
3 very lean meat

Turkey Rolls
with Garden Pesto

Serves 4

If you have any turkey rolls left over, slice them for great sandwiches.

Garden Pesto
- ½ cup packed fresh basil leaves
- 1 small tomato, peeled, seeded, and chopped
- 1 tablespoon pine nuts, dry-roasted
- 1 large garlic clove, minced
- 2 tablespoons shredded or grated Parmesan cheese
- ❖

- 2 8-ounce turkey tenderloins, halved lengthwise
- Vegetable oil spray
- 1 tablespoon honey
- 1 tablespoon low-salt soy sauce

Preheat the oven to 350°F.

In a food processor or blender, combine the pesto ingredients except the Parmesan and process until nearly smooth. Stir in the Parmesan.

Spread 1 rounded tablespoon pesto mixture on a piece of turkey. Roll up from one short end. Repeat with the remaining turkey. Set aside any remaining pesto.

Lightly spray an 8-inch square baking pan with vegetable oil spray. Place the turkey rolls with the seam side down in the pan.

In a cup or small bowl, stir together the honey and soy sauce. Brush on the turkey rolls.

Bake for 40 to 45 minutes, or until cooked through. Top the turkey rolls with the remaining pesto.

Cook's Tip on Peeling and Seeding Tomatoes

Plunge the tomatoes into boiling water for 10 to 15 seconds, then into ice water for about 1 minute. The skin will come off easily. Remove the cores and cut the tomatoes in half horizontally. With your fingers or a spoon, remove the seeds.

calories 171
protein 29 g
carbohydrates 7 g
  fiber 1 g
  sugars 5 g
cholesterol 79 mg
total fat 3.0 g
  saturated 1.0 g
  polyunsaturated 0.5 g
  monounsaturated 1.0 g
sodium 193 mg

dietary exchange
½ other carbohydrate
3 very lean meat

Turkey Sausage Patties

Serves 8

For brunch, serve this tasty, low-fat meat with Southern Raised Biscuits (see page 534) and Cranberry Chutney (see page 481). After you find out how good these patties are, you'll want to try them in sandwiches and even as a dinner entrée.

1 pound lean ground turkey breast, skin discarded before grinding
1/4 cup plain fine dry bread crumbs
1 tablespoon salt-free Italian herb seasoning
1 1/4 teaspoons ground coriander
1 teaspoon paprika

1/2 to 3/4 teaspoon cayenne
1/2 teaspoon ground cumin
1/2 teaspoon garlic powder
1/4 teaspoon pepper
1/4 teaspoon salt
1/2 cup fat-free, low-sodium chicken broth, such as on page 45

In a large bowl, stir together all the ingredients except the broth.

Add the chicken broth. Stir again. Let stand for 15 minutes.

Form into 8 patties, about 3/4 inch thick.

Heat a large nonstick skillet over medium heat. Cook the patties for 7 to 8 minutes on each side, or until done.

Cook's Tip on Ground Turkey Breast

Select a piece of skinless turkey breast and ask the butcher to grind it. The ground turkey already in the meat case often contains skin.

calories 80
protein 14 g
carbohydrates 3 g
  fiber 0 g
  sugars 0 g
cholesterol 39 mg
total fat 1.0 g
  saturated 0.0 g
  polyunsaturated 0.0 g
  monounsaturated 0.0 g
sodium 129 mg

dietary exchange
2 very lean meat

Turkey Lasagna

Serves 9

Here's the solution for what to take to potluck dinners.

Vegetable oil spray
8-ounce package dried lasagna noodles
1 pound lean ground turkey breast, skin discarded before grinding
8 ounces button mushrooms, sliced
$1/2$ cup chopped onion
3 medium garlic cloves, minced
3 cups no-salt-added tomato sauce
2 teaspoons dried basil, crumbled
$1/2$ teaspoon dried oregano, crumbled
Pepper to taste
10-ounce package frozen chopped spinach, thawed and squeezed dry
16 ounces fat-free or low-fat cottage cheese
Dash of nutmeg
8 ounces part-skim mozzarella cheese, shredded or grated

Preheat the oven to 375°F. Lightly spray a 13 × 9 × 2-inch baking dish with vegetable oil spray.

Prepare the noodles using the package directions, omitting the salt and oil.

Meanwhile, in a large nonstick skillet over medium-high heat, stir together the turkey, mushrooms, onion, and garlic. Cook the turkey for 8 to 10 minutes, or until no longer pink, stirring occasionally.

Reduce the heat to low and cook, covered, for 3 to 4 minutes, or until the mushrooms have released their liquid. Increase the heat to high and cook, uncovered, for 2 to 3 minutes, or until the liquid evaporates.

Stir in the tomato sauce, basil, oregano, and pepper. Reduce the heat to low. Cook for 5 to 6 minutes, or until heated through.

In a large bowl, stir together the spinach, cottage cheese, and nutmeg.

To assemble in the baking dish, layer, in order, one third cooked noodles, one half spinach mixture, one third turkey mixture, and one third mozzarella. Repeat. Finish with the remaining noodles, turkey, and mozzarella.

Bake, covered, for 35 to 40 minutes, or until the casserole is heated through and the mozzarella has melted.

calories 300
protein 29 g
carbohydrates 30 g
  fiber 3 g
  sugars 8 g
cholesterol 36 mg
total fat 5.5 g
  saturated 1.5 g
  polyunsaturated 1.5 g
  monounsaturated 2.0 g
sodium 339 mg

dietary exchange
$1/2$ starch
2 vegetable
3 lean meat

Turkey Enchiladas

Serves 4; 2 enchiladas per serving

Everything you'd expect from the whole enchilada—and more—is in these turkey enchiladas. Green chile enchilada sauce and sour cream are the toppers.

Vegetable oil spray

8 ounces lean ground turkey breast, skin removed before grinding

8 6-inch corn tortillas

1/2 15-ounce can no-salt-added black beans, rinsed and drained

1/2 cup frozen whole-kernel corn, thawed

1/2 cup shredded fat-free or low-fat Cheddar cheese

1/2 4-ounce can chopped green chiles, rinsed and drained (about 1/4 cup)

1 teaspoon chili powder

1/2 teaspoon ground cumin

1/4 teaspoon dried oregano, crumbled

1/4 teaspoon salt

4 ounces canned green chile enchilada sauce

1/2 cup fat-free or light sour cream

Preheat the oven to 350°F. Lightly spray an 8-inch square baking pan with vegetable oil spray.

In a large nonstick skillet, cook the turkey over medium-high heat for 7 to 8 minutes, or until browned on the outside and no longer pink in the center, stirring occasionally. Pour the turkey into a colander and rinse under hot water to remove excess fat. Drain well. Wipe the skillet with paper towels. Return the turkey to the skillet, but don't return to the heat.

Meanwhile, wrap the tortillas in aluminum foil. Bake for 5 minutes, or until warmed through. Remove the tortillas from the oven, leaving them in the foil.

Stir the beans, corn, cheese, chiles, chili powder, cumin, oregano, and salt into the turkey.

To assemble, spoon about 1/3 cup filling down the center of a tortilla. Roll up jelly-roll style and place with seam side down in the baking pan. Repeat with the remaining filling and tortillas. Pour the enchilada sauce over all. Cover with aluminum foil.

Bake for 25 minutes, or until the filling is warmed through. Spread the sour cream on top. Bake for 5 minutes, or until the sour cream is warmed through and flows over the enchiladas.

calories 265
protein 26 g
carbohydrates 35 g
  fiber 5 g
  sugars 5 g
cholesterol 46 mg
total fat 2.5 g
  saturated 0.5 g
  polyunsaturated 1.0 g
  monounsaturated 0.5 g
sodium 549 mg

dietary exchange
2 1/2 starch
3 very lean meat

Turkey Loaf

Serves 8

This meat loaf substitute is so moist that you'll gobble it up! Try it with Spinach-Chayote Salad with Orange Vinaigrette (see page 89).

Vegetable oil spray (optional)
4 slices whole-wheat bread
1/4 cup fat-free milk
2 pounds lean ground turkey breast, skin discarded before grinding
1 cup grated or finely chopped onion
1 cup canned no-salt-added stewed tomatoes, crushed, undrained
1 medium rib of celery, diced

1/2 medium red bell pepper, chopped
Egg substitute equivalent to 2 eggs, or 2 large eggs
1/4 cup minced fresh parsley
1 teaspoon seeded and finely minced fresh jalapeño, or to taste
1/4 teaspoon salt
1/4 teaspoon pepper
2 tablespoons no-salt-added ketchup

Preheat the oven to 350°F. Lightly spray a 10 1/2 × 5 1/2 × 2 1/2-inch loaf pan with vegetable oil spray, or use a nonstick loaf pan.

In a food processor or blender, process the bread into fine crumbs. Transfer to a shallow bowl. Stir in the milk. Let the crumbs soak for 5 minutes.

In a large bowl, gently but thoroughly stir together the remaining ingredients except the ketchup.

Drain the bread crumbs and squeeze out any excess milk to form a paste. Stir into the turkey mixture. Spoon into the loaf pan. Spread the ketchup over the loaf.

Bake, uncovered, for 1 hour 30 minutes, or until cooked through. Let stand for 5 to 10 minutes before serving.

calories 195
protein 31 g
carbohydrates 13 g
  fiber 2 g
  sugars 5 g
cholesterol 77 mg
total fat 1.5 g
  saturated 0.5 g
  polyunsaturated 0.5 g
  monounsaturated 0.5 g
sodium 251 mg

dietary exchange
1/2 starch
1 vegetable
3 1/2 very lean meat

Southwestern Turkey Wraps

Serves 4

These wraps get their kick from salsa and Dijon mustard and give you an easy way to use leftover turkey.

3 ounces fat-free or light cream cheese, softened

2 tablespoons fat-free, low-sodium salsa, such as Salsa Cruda (page 502)

2 tablespoons sliced green onion (green and white parts)

1 teaspoon Dijon mustard

4 8-inch fat-free or low-fat flour tortillas

1¹⁄₃ cups shredded lettuce

6 ounces very thinly sliced or finely chopped roasted turkey breast, skin and all visible fat discarded

¹⁄₄ cup shredded fat-free Cheddar cheese

4 strips red bell pepper, about ¹⁄₄ inch wide

In a small bowl, stir together the cream cheese, salsa, green onion, and mustard.

To assemble, spread 2 tablespoons of the cream cheese mixture over each tortilla. Layer ¹⁄₃ cup lettuce, one fourth of the turkey, 1 tablespoon Cheddar, and 1 red pepper strip over the cream cheese mixture. Roll to enclose the filling.

Wrap tightly in plastic wrap and refrigerate for several hours or until serving time.

calories 223
protein 23 g
carbohydrates 28 g
  fiber 3 g
  sugars 2 g
cholesterol 42 mg
total fat 1.0 g
  saturated 0.0 g
  polyunsaturated 0.0 g
  monounsaturated 0.0 g
sodium 560 mg

dietary exchange
2 starch
2¹⁄₂ very lean meat

Cook's Tip

Cut each tortilla roll into fourths to serve as appetizers.

Swiss Garden Wraps

Serves 4

Turkey and Swiss cheese team up with salad ingredients and tortillas for a yummy lunch treat.

2 tablespoons fat-free or light plain yogurt
2 1/2 teaspoons prepared mustard
1/4 teaspoon honey
1/4 teaspoon pepper
4 8-inch fat-free or low-fat flour tortillas, warmed
4 red leaf lettuce leaves
4 ounces thinly sliced cooked turkey breast, cooked without salt, skin and all visible fat discarded

4 3/4-ounce slices fat-free or low-fat Swiss cheese
1/2 cup finely chopped red onion
1/4 medium cucumber, peeled, cut horizontally into 8 slices, and halved
2 medium Italian plum tomatoes, each cut lengthwise into 8 slices
Pepper to taste (optional)

In a small bowl, whisk together the yogurt, mustard, honey, and 1/4 teaspoon pepper.

To assemble the wraps, spread one fourth of the mixture over each tortilla. Top each with 1 lettuce leaf, 1 ounce turkey, 1 slice cheese, 2 tablespoons red onion, 4 slices cucumber, and 4 slices tomato. Sprinkle with the pepper. Fold the sides of each tortilla toward the center, overlapping slightly. Place with the seam side down on a plate.

Cook's Tip on Tortillas

Warming tortillas makes them pliable and brings out the flavor. Wrap the tortillas in damp paper towels and microwave on 100 percent power (high) for 30 to 60 seconds. Or wrap them in aluminum foil and heat in a 325°F oven for 6 to 8 minutes.

calories 215
protein 20 g
carbohydrates 30 g
  fiber 3 g
  sugars 5 g
cholesterol 27 mg
total fat 1.0 g
  saturated 0.0 g
  polyunsaturated 0.0 g
  monounsaturated 0.0 g
sodium 566 mg

dietary exchange
1 1/2 starch
1 vegetable
2 very lean meat

Turkey with Vegetables and Brown Rice

Serves 4

Leftover turkey teams up with broccoli, carrots, brown rice, and a rich-tasting sauce in this stovetop meal in one.

1¼ cups fat-free, low-sodium chicken broth, such as on page 45
1 cup uncooked instant brown rice
1 cup broccoli florets
1 large carrot, thinly sliced
½ teaspoon dried basil, crumbled
10.75-ounce can low-fat, reduced-sodium condensed cream of chicken soup

1 cup diced cooked skinless turkey breast, cooked without salt (about 4 ounces)
½ cup fat-free half-and-half
2 tablespoons snipped fresh parsley or 2 teaspoons dried, crumbled
½ teaspoon dried oregano, crumbled

In a medium saucepan, bring the broth to a boil over high heat.

Stir in the brown rice, broccoli, carrot, and basil. Reduce the heat and simmer, covered, for 10 minutes, or until the vegetables and rice are tender.

In a separate medium saucepan, stir together the remaining ingredients. Heat the mixture over medium heat (so it warms gently and doesn't come to a simmer rapidly) for 8 to 10 minutes, or until warmed through, stirring occasionally and lowering the heat if necessary.

To serve, spoon 1 cup rice and vegetable mixture into each bowl. Ladle ½ cup turkey mixture over each serving.

calories 231
protein 17 g
carbohydrates 32 g
 fiber 2 g
 sugars 5 g
cholesterol 33 mg
total fat 4.0 g
 saturated 1.0 g
 polyunsaturated 1.0 g
 monounsaturated 0.5 g
sodium 375 mg

dietary exchange
2 starch
1½ very lean meat

Cornish Hens
Provence Style

Serves 4

You'll be amazed at how moist and tender a clay cooker keeps these hens.

2 Cornish game hens (about 14 ounces each), all visible fat, tails, and giblets discarded
1/2 teaspoon dried basil, crumbled
1/2 teaspoon dried thyme, crumbled
1/2 teaspoon salt
1/2 teaspoon pepper
1/2 pound boiling onions
8 medium garlic cloves, unpeeled
4 large sprigs of parsley

1/2 pound small red potatoes, halved
1 medium onion, sliced and separated into rings
1/4 teaspoon salt-free all-purpose seasoning
1/2 teaspoon pepper
1/4 teaspoon dried herbes de Provence or other dried herbs, crumbled
1 cup dry white wine (regular or nonalcoholic)

Soak a clay cooker in cold water for 15 minutes.

Meanwhile, season the hens inside and out with the basil, thyme, salt, and 1/2 teaspoon pepper.

Stuff the hens with boiling onions, garlic, and parsley. Put in the clay cooker. Put the potatoes and onion rings around the hens.

Sprinkle the all-purpose seasoning, 1/2 teaspoon pepper, and herbes de Provence over the hens and vegetables. Pour the wine into the clay cooker.

Put the clay cooker in a *cold* oven. If using an electric oven, set to 450°F. Bake for 1 hour 15 minutes, or until the juices from a pierced thigh run clear. If using a gas oven, set to 300°F. Increase the temperature 50 degrees every 10 minutes until it reaches 450°F. Cook for 1 hour 30 minutes, or until done.

Discard the stuffing. Cut the hens in half. Discard the skin. Serve the hens with the potatoes and onion rings.

Optional Cooking Method
Cook the hens, covered, at 350°F for 45 to 50 minutes. Uncover and cook for 5 to 10 minutes to brown.

calories 197
protein 19 g
carbohydrates 14 g
  fiber 2 g
  sugars 3 g
cholesterol 78 mg
total fat 3.0 g
  saturated 0.5 g
  polyunsaturated 0.5 g
  monounsaturated 1.0 g
sodium 357 mg

dietary exchange
1/2 starch
1 vegetable
2 1/2 very lean meat

Stuffed Cornish Hens with Orange-Brandy Sauce

Serves 12

Petite Cornish hens get four-star treatment with rice stuffing and brandied orange sections.

Vegetable oil spray
1⅓ cups uncooked long-grain and wild rice combination
1 teaspoon light tub margarine
1 medium onion, chopped
1 teaspoon dried sage, thyme, savory, or tarragon, crumbled
6 Cornish hens (about 14 ounces each), all visible fat, tails, and giblets discarded

Vegetable oil spray
½ cup fat-free, low-sodium chicken broth, such as on page 45
½ cup water
1 cup orange sections (1 to 2 medium)
¼ cup brandy

Preheat the oven to 350°F. Lightly spray a roasting pan and cooking rack(s) with vegetable oil spray.

Cook the rice until still slightly firm, using the package directions, omitting the salt and margarine and discarding the seasoning packet.

In a large skillet over medium-high heat, melt the margarine and swirl to coat the bottom. Cook the onion for 3 to 4 minutes, or until lightly browned.

Stir in the rice and sage. Remove from the heat.

Stuff the hens lightly with the rice mixture. Skewer or sew the cavities closed. Lightly spray the hens with vegetable oil spray. Put with the breast side up on the rack in the roasting pan.

Roast, uncovered, for 1 hour, or until the hens are done, basting occasionally with the broth.

Remove the hens from the pan. Cut in half along the backbone (kitchen scissors work well). Remove and discard the skin. Place the hens on a platter.

calories 159
protein 18 g
carbohydrates 11 g
 fiber 1 g
 sugars 3 g
cholesterol 78 mg
total fat 3.0 g
 saturated 0.5 g
 polyunsaturated 0.5 g
 monounsaturated 1.0 g
sodium 62 mg

dietary exchange
½ starch
2½ very lean meat

Heat the roasting pan, with juices, over medium-high heat. Add the water to the drippings, scraping to dislodge any browned bits from the pan.

Stir in the orange sections and brandy. Cook for 2 minutes, stirring constantly. Serve the sauce over the hens or on the side.

Cook's Tip on Savory

Native to the Mediterranean area, savory is an herb belonging to the mint family. Among the varieties are summer savory and winter savory, the latter of which is more pungent. Look for dried savory with the spices in the supermarket. To buy fresh savory, you may have to go to a specialty produce market. Use savory in poultry stuffings and dressings, in soups, and with ground beef and vegetables.

Cook's Tip on Sewing Poultry

Keep the stuffing moist in any kind of poultry by skewering or sewing the cavity. Pull it closed and weave a sharp, thin metal or wooden skewer into the skin at the sides of the cavity. (If using wooden skewers, be sure to soak them in cold water for at least 10 minutes first.) If you prefer, buy a large-eyed sewing needle at a craft or carpet store and thread it with thin kitchen twine. Sew the cavity closed.

meats

Fillet of Beef with Herbes de Provence

Beef Roast with Rosemary and Hoisin Sauce

Pot Roast Ratatouille and Pasta

Pepper-Coated Steak

Zesty Hot-Oven Sirloin

Brisket Stew, Slow and Easy

Rosemary-Sage Steak

Ginger-Lime Sirloin

Steak Marinated in Beer and Green Onions

Smothered Steak with Sangria Sauce

Shredded Beef Soft Tacos

Grilled Stuffed Flank Steak

Grilled Lemongrass Flank Steak

Greek-Style Eye-of-Round Steaks

Mediterranean Beef and Vegetable Stir-Fry

Beef Stroganoff

Beef Bourguignon

Portobello Mushrooms and Sirloin Strips over Spinach Pasta

Classic Chinese Beef Stir-Fry

Southwestern Beef Stir-Fry

Braised Sirloin Tips

Italian Beef Kebabs

Beef Skillet Oriental

Bowl of Red

Savory Beef Stew

Grilled Hamburgers with Vegetables and Feta

Mediterranean Meat Loaf

Philadelphia-Style Cheese Steak Wrap

Salisbury Steaks with Mushroom Sauce

Tex-Mex Lasagna

Beef and Pasta Skillet

Spaghetti with Meat Sauce

Beef and Noodle Casserole Dijon

Greek-Style Beef Skillet Supper

Glazed Meatballs on Water Chestnut and Bell Pepper Rice

Border Beef

Shepherd's Pie

Beef Tostadas

Meat with Bell Pepper and Tomato Sauce

Crustless Ham and Spinach Tart

New Orleans Muffaletta Wrap

Savory Black-Eyed Peas and Pasta

Bayou Red Beans and Rice

Marinated Pork Tenderloin

Orange Pork Medallions

Herb-Rubbed Pork Tenderloin with Dijon-Apricot Mop Sauce

Sweet-and-Sour Pork

Slow-Cooker Pork Roast with Orange Cranberry Sauce

Easy Barbecue-Sauced Pork Chops

Pork Chops Stuffed with Apricots and Walnuts

Jamaican Jerk Pork and Vegetables with Mango-Coconut Rice

Boneless Pork Ribs with Black Cherry Barbecue Sauce

Jollof Rice

Pork Stir-Fry with Crunchy Noodles

Louisiana Skillet Pork

Armenian Lamb Casserole

Moroccan-Style Lamb with Couscous

Venison Stew

Fillet of Beef with
Herbes de Provence

Serves 6

Black pepper, herbes de Provence, and a good measure of garlic flavor this tender cut of beef. Very easy and elegant—excellent for company.

1½-pound beef tenderloin, all visible fat and silver skin discarded
3 medium garlic cloves, minced
2 teaspoons dried herbes de Provence or mixed dried herbs, crumbled
1 teaspoon black pepper, or to taste

Vegetable oil spray (olive oil spray preferred)
2 medium carrots, finely diced
1 medium onion, sliced
¼ teaspoon salt
Sprigs of fresh parsley (optional)

Preheat the oven to 400°F.

Tie the meat in three or four places with kitchen twine. Rub the garlic all over the meat. Sprinkle with the herbes de Provence and pepper. Put in a heavy non-stick roasting pan. Lightly spray the roast with the olive oil spray.

Scatter the carrots and onion on and around the meat.

Cook, uncovered, for 25 to 30 minutes per pound for medium-rare, or to desired doneness. Remove from the oven and sprinkle with the salt.

Cover with aluminum foil and let stand for 10 to 15 minutes. Slice the roast. Garnish with the parsley.

calories 206
protein 24 g
carbohydrates 6 g
  fiber 2 g
  sugars 3 g
cholesterol 70 mg
total fat 9.0 g
  saturated 3.5 g
  polyunsaturated 0.5 g
  monounsaturated 3.5 g
sodium 168 mg

dietary exchange
1 vegetable
3 lean meat

Cook's Tip on Herbes de Provence

Herbes de Provence is a combination of herbs used quite frequently in southern France: basil, thyme, rosemary, marjoram, sage, and lavender. If you don't have herbes de Provence, use a combination of at least two of these, blended in equal amounts.

Beef Roast with Rosemary and Hoisin Sauce

Serves 8

Ingredients from several countries join forces to deliciously flavor a braised eye-of-round roast. For even more of a treat, prepare mashed potatoes spiked with wasabi or horseradish and top them with thin slices of beef and gravy.

Vegetable oil spray (olive oil spray preferred)
2-pound eye-of-round roast, all visible fat discarded
1 cup fat-free, no-salt-added beef broth, such as on page 44
2 tablespoons dry vermouth, dry white wine (regular or non-alcoholic), or fat-free, no-salt-added beef broth, such as on page 44

2 tablespoons hoisin sauce
1 tablespoon balsamic vinegar
2 teaspoons low-salt soy sauce
1 teaspoon dried rosemary, crushed
2 medium garlic cloves, minced
1 1/2 tablespoons cornstarch
1/4 cup water

Preheat the oven to 350°F.

Heat a Dutch oven over medium-high heat. Remove from the heat and lightly spray with vegetable oil spray (being careful not to spray near a gas flame). Brown the beef for 2 to 3 minutes on each side.

Stir in the broth, vermouth, hoisin sauce, vinegar, soy sauce, rosemary, and garlic. Bring to a simmer.

Bake, covered, for 1 hour 30 minutes to 2 hours, or until the beef is tender. Transfer the beef to a cutting board and cover with aluminum foil. Let stand for 15 minutes before cutting into thin slices. Cover and reserve the cooking liquid in the Dutch oven.

Put the cornstarch in a cup. Add the water, stirring to dissolve. Whisk into the cooking liquid. Bring to a simmer over medium-high heat. Reduce the heat and simmer for 1 to 2 minutes, or until the mixture has thickened, stirring occasionally.

To serve, ladle the gravy over the beef slices.

calories 162
protein 25 g
carbohydrates 4 g
  fiber 0 g
  sugars 2 g
cholesterol 58 mg
total fat 4.0 g
  saturated 1.5 g
  polyunsaturated 0.0 g
  monounsaturated 1.5 g
sodium 110 mg

dietary exchange
3 lean meat

Pot Roast Ratatouille and Pasta

Serves 8

Worthy of a special occasion, this dish can feature any pasta variety—from angel hair to shells to penne.

Vegetable oil spray (olive oil spray preferred)
1½-pound eye-of-round roast, all visible fat discarded
½ teaspoon salt-free all-purpose seasoning
¼ teaspoon pepper
2 cups chopped eggplant (about 10 ounces)
2 medium zucchini, sliced
5 medium Italian plum tomatoes, chopped

10.75-ounce can tomato puree
1 large onion, chopped (Spanish preferred)
2 medium ribs of celery, sliced
1 teaspoon dried oregano or salt-free Italian seasoning, crumbled
1 medium garlic clove, minced
1 bay leaf
¼ teaspoon dried basil, crumbled
8 ounces dried pasta

Preheat the oven to 350°F. Lightly spray a Dutch oven with olive oil spray.

Sprinkle the meat with the all-purpose seasoning and pepper. Put it in the Dutch oven and brown on all sides over medium-high heat, about 10 minutes.

Stir in the remaining ingredients except the pasta.

Bake, covered, for 2 hours 30 minutes, or until very tender.

Prepare the pasta using the package directions, omitting the salt and oil. Drain well.

Meanwhile, remove the roast from the sauce. Slice thinly across the grain, then slice into thin strips. Discard the bay leaf from the sauce.

To serve, spoon the pasta onto plates. Arrange the roast on the pasta. Top with the sauce.

calories 259
protein 24 g
carbohydrates 32 g
 fiber 4 g
 sugars 8 g
cholesterol 44 mg
total fat 4.0 g
 saturated 1.0 g
 polyunsaturated 0.5 g
 monounsaturated 1.5 g
sodium 70 mg

dietary exchange
1½ starch
2 vegetable
2½ very lean meat

Pepper-Coated Steak

Serves 4

In France, where it's called boeuf au poivre, *this steak is typically served with skillet-fried potatoes. For a more healthful option, choose one of the potato dishes you'll find in this cookbook (pages 451–456) and Hot and Spicy Watercress and Romaine Salad (page 86).*

4 beef tenderloin steaks (about 4 ounces each), all visible fat discarded

2 teaspoons coarsely ground black pepper

Vegetable oil spray

¼ cup brandy or unsweetened apple juice

5-ounce can fat-free evaporated milk

Sprinkle both sides of the meat with the pepper, pressing it into the surface.

Lightly spray a large skillet with vegetable oil spray. Heat over medium-high heat. Cook the meat for 5 minutes. Turn and cook for 3 to 5 minutes, or until the desired doneness. Transfer the meat to a plate. Cover with aluminum foil to keep warm. Remove the skillet from the heat; let cool for 1 minute.

Reduce the heat to low. Return the skillet to the heat. Gradually pour the brandy into the skillet. Cook for 1 minute, scraping to dislodge any browned bits.

Stir in the milk. Increase the heat to high and bring to a boil. Reduce the heat and simmer for 2 to 3 minutes, or until thickened, stirring frequently.

To serve, place the steaks on plates. Pour the sauce over the steaks.

Cook's Tip on Peppercorns

If you don't have a pepper mill, you can buy pepper already coarsely ground or use a mortar and pestle to crack whole peppercorns.

calories 244
protein 26 g
carbohydrates 5 g
  fiber 0 g
  sugars 4 g
cholesterol 72 mg
total fat 9.0 g
  saturated 3.5 g
  polyunsaturated 0.5 g
  monounsaturated 3.5 g
sodium 103 mg

dietary exchange
½ skim milk
3 lean meat

Zesty Hot-Oven Sirloin

Serves 4

This marinade is transformed into an intense and zesty sauce—a little goes a long way!

1-pound boneless sirloin steak, about 1 inch thick, all visible fat discarded

Marinade
2 tablespoons low-salt soy sauce
2 tablespoons balsamic vinegar
2 tablespoons fresh lemon juice
1 tablespoon low-sodium Worcestershire sauce

2 teaspoons dried oregano, crumbled
2 medium garlic cloves, minced
❖
Vegetable oil spray
1/4 cup water
1/2 tablespoon light tub margarine
1/4 teaspoon salt
1/4 teaspoon pepper
2 tablespoons finely snipped fresh parsley

In a large resealable plastic bag, combine the steak and marinade ingredients. Seal the bag and turn to coat. Refrigerate for 8 hours, turning occasionally.

Preheat the oven to 500°F.

Lightly spray a rimmed baking sheet with vegetable oil spray. Put the steak on the baking sheet, retaining the marinade.

Cook the steak on the top oven rack for 12 to 14 minutes, or until desired doneness.

Meanwhile, pour the marinade into a small saucepan. Add the water. Bring to a boil over high heat. Reduce the heat and simmer, uncovered, for 3 minutes, or until reduced to 1/4 cup. Remove from the heat. Add the margarine, salt, and pepper, stirring until the margarine has melted.

To serve, transfer the steak to a platter. Spoon the marinade over the steak. Sprinkle with the parsley.

calories 187
protein 25 g
carbohydrates 4 g
  fiber 0 g
  sugars 2 g
cholesterol 67 mg
total fat 7.0 g
  saturated 2.5 g
  polyunsaturated 0.5 g
  monounsaturated 3.0 g
sodium 427 mg

dietary exchange
3 lean meat

Brisket Stew, Slow and Easy

Serves 4

Slow cooking and a touch of sherry are the keys to the success of this comfort food. Serve as is or over no-yolk egg noodles.

2 medium carrots, cut into 1-inch pieces

1 medium onion, cut into 1/2-inch wedges

1 medium green bell pepper, cut into 1-inch pieces

1 medium rib of celery, cut into 1-inch pieces

1-pound flat cut beef brisket, all visible fat discarded

1/4 cup dry sherry or dry red wine (regular or nonalcoholic)

1 teaspoon very low sodium beef bouillon granules

1 teaspoon dried oregano, crumbled

2 tablespoons no-salt-added tomato paste

1 tablespoon sugar

1 tablespoon cider vinegar

2 teaspoons low-sodium Worcestershire sauce

3/4 teaspoon salt

1/4 teaspoon dried basil, crumbled

Put the carrots, onion, bell pepper, and celery in a slow cooker. Place the beef on the vegetables. Pour the sherry over all. Sprinkle with the bouillon granules and oregano.

Cook on high for 6 hours, or until the beef is tender. Transfer the beef to a cutting board. Let stand for 10 minutes before slicing.

In a small bowl, whisk together the remaining ingredients.

Stir the tomato-paste mixture into the vegetable mixture. Return the sliced beef to the slow cooker to heat for 5 minutes.

Cook's Tip

Purchase a 2 1/2-pound brisket. After you trim all the fat, the brisket should weigh about 2 pounds. Cut it in half and freeze one half to use later.

calories 208
protein 24 g
carbohydrates 16 g
 fiber 3 g
 sugars 10 g
cholesterol 67 mg
total fat 4.5 g
 saturated 1.5 g
 polyunsaturated 0.0 g
 monounsaturated 2.0 g
sodium 516 mg

dietary exchange
3 vegetable
3 lean meat

Rosemary-Sage Steak

Serves 4

Have a meat-and potatoes dinner with this herb-flavored steak, Rustic Potato Patties (page 454), and tossed salad.

1 pound boneless top sirloin steak, all visible fat discarded

Marinade

¼ cup chopped onion

2 tablespoons fresh lemon juice

1½ tablespoons dry white wine (regular or nonalcoholic)

1 tablespoon finely chopped fresh rosemary or 2 teaspoons dried, crushed

1 tablespoon finely chopped fresh sage or 2 teaspoons dried

½ tablespoon Dijon mustard

2 medium garlic cloves, minced

1 teaspoon olive oil

¼ teaspoon pepper

¼ teaspoon salt

Put the steak in a resealable plastic bag.

In a small bowl, stir together the marinade ingredients. Pour over the steak. Seal the bag and turn to coat. Refrigerate for 1 to 24 hours, turning occasionally.

Preheat the grill on medium-high.

Drain the steak, discarding the marinade.

Grill for 8 to 12 minutes on each side, or until desired doneness.

Cook's Tip on Fresh Rosemary

For a real taste treat, save woody, more mature rosemary stems to use as skewers. Strip the leaves to use in recipes such as this one. With a sharp object—a wooden or thin metal skewer works well—poke a hole through the foods you'll use for your kebabs. Thread the rosemary stem through the foods and grill or broil as usual.

calories 151
protein 24 g
carbohydrates 0 g
  fiber 0 g
  sugars 0 g
cholesterol 71 mg
total fat 5.5 g
  saturated 2.0 g
  polyunsaturated 0.0 g
  monounsaturated 2.5 g
sodium 234 mg

dietary exchange
3 lean meat

Ginger-Lime Sirloin

Serves 4

One great thing about this dish is that it can be prepared before you go to work or play.

Marinade
- 3 tablespoons sugar
- 3 tablespoons low-salt soy sauce
- 2 tablespoons cider vinegar
- 1 tablespoon fresh lime juice
- 1 teaspoon grated peeled gingerroot

- 1 medium garlic clove, minced
- 1/2 teaspoon crushed red pepper flakes
- ❖
- 1 pound boneless sirloin steak, about 1 inch thick, all visible fat discarded
- Vegetable oil spray

In a small nonmetallic bowl, stir together the marinade ingredients.

Put the steak in a large, resealable plastic bag.

Pour half the marinade into the bag. Seal the bag and turn to coat. Refrigerate for 8 hours, turning occasionally. Cover the remaining marinade with plastic wrap and refrigerate until needed.

Preheat the broiler. Lightly spray a broiler rack and pan with vegetable oil spray.

Put the steak on the broiler rack. Discard the marinade in the plastic bag.

Broil the steak 4 inches from the heat for 5 minutes. Turn. Broil for 8 minutes, or until desired doneness. Transfer the steak to a cutting board. Let stand for 5 minutes.

Meanwhile, in a small saucepan, bring the reserved marinade to a boil over high heat. Boil for 1 to 2 minutes, or until it measures about 2 tablespoons, stirring frequently. Remove from the heat.

Spoon the sauce over the steak. Cut into thin slices.

Cook's Tip

The steak is cooked longer on one side to allow it to blacken slightly.

calories 199
protein 25 g
carbohydrates 11 g
 fiber 0 g
 sugars 10 g
cholesterol 71 mg
total fat 5.5 g
 saturated 2.0 g
 polyunsaturated 0.0 g
 monounsaturated 2.5 g
sodium 346 mg

dietary exchange
1/2 other carbohydrate
3 lean meat

Steak Marinated in
Beer and Green Onions

Serves 8

Many Asian hosts serve beer rather than wine for special meals. It's no wonder that beer is often used in recipes, too. You'll savor each juicy bite of this Asian-flavored steak.

2 pounds boneless top sirloin steak, all visible fat discarded

Marinade
1½ cups light beer (regular or nonalcoholic)

4 medium green onions (green and white parts), minced

2 tablespoons light brown sugar

2 tablespoons dry sherry

1 tablespoon grated peeled gingerroot

1 tablespoon low-salt soy sauce

2 medium garlic cloves, minced

1 teaspoon crushed red pepper flakes

1 teaspoon acceptable vegetable oil

Dash of red hot-pepper sauce

Put the steak in a large resealable plastic bag.

In a medium bowl, stir together the marinade ingredients until the brown sugar is dissolved. Pour over the steak. Seal the bag and turn to coat. Refrigerate for 1 to 24 hours, turning occasionally.

Preheat the grill on medium high.

Drain the steak, discarding the marinade. Grill for 8 to 12 minutes on each side, or until desired doneness.

calories 153
protein 24 g
carbohydrates 0 g
  fiber 0 g
  sugars 0 g
cholesterol 71 mg
total fat 5.5 g
  saturated 2.0 g
  polyunsaturated 0.0 g
  monounsaturated 2.5 g
sodium 101 mg

dietary exchange
3 lean meat

Smothered Steak
with Sangria Sauce

Serves 4

Different and easy, this dish is great for company. Serve it over rice or pasta so you can enjoy all the sauce.

Sangria Sauce
- 1 cup sangría (white preferred)
- 1 medium tomato, chopped
- 1 small green bell pepper, chopped
- 1/4 cup golden raisins
- 1/4 cup dried apricots, coarsely chopped
- 1 large bay leaf

- 1 teaspoon dried basil, crumbled
- 1/2 teaspoon dried thyme, crumbled
- 1/4 teaspoon pepper, or to taste
- ❖
- Vegetable oil spray
- 4 thin slices sirloin steak (about 4 ounces each), all visible fat discarded

In a medium bowl, stir together the sauce ingredients.

Heat a large skillet over medium-high heat. Remove from the heat and lightly spray with vegetable oil spray (being careful not to spray near a gas flame). Brown the meat for 2 to 3 minutes on each side, or until desired doneness.

Pour the sauce into the skillet. Reduce the heat and simmer, covered, for 30 to 40 minutes, or until the meat is tender. Discard the bay leaf.

Time-Saver

Use cube steaks instead of sirloin steak and reduce the simmering time to 20 to 25 minutes.

calories 268
protein 26 g
carbohydrates 23 g
  fiber 2 g
  sugars 18 g
cholesterol 67 mg
total fat 6.5 g
  saturated 2.5 g
  polyunsaturated 0.5 g
  monounsaturated 2.5 g
sodium 76 mg

dietary exchange
1 1/2 fruit
3 lean meat

Shredded Beef
Soft Tacos

Serves 8

Let your slow cooker fix dinner while you're at work. Then give your family a Mexican feast of sirloin, onions, and bell peppers with cumin, all wrapped in warm tortillas. Serve with plenty of napkins!

1½ pounds boneless top sirloin steak or sirloin tip roast, all visible fat discarded

3 large onions, chopped

1 medium green bell pepper, chopped

¼ cup dry red wine (regular or nonalcoholic)

½ cup no-salt-added ketchup

2 tablespoons cider vinegar

6 medium garlic cloves, minced

2 teaspoons very low sodium beef bouillon granules

2 medium bay leaves

¾ teaspoon liquid smoke seasoning

½ teaspoon ground cumin

½ teaspoon red hot-pepper sauce

¼ teaspoon pepper

½ teaspoon ground cumin

1 teaspoon sugar (dark brown preferred)

8 8-inch fat-free or low-fat flour tortillas

Put the meat in a slow cooker. Add the onions and bell pepper.

In a medium bowl, whisk together the wine, ketchup, vinegar, garlic, bouillon granules, bay leaves, liquid smoke, ½ teaspoon cumin, hot-pepper sauce, and pepper. Pour the wine mixture into the slow cooker.

Cook on low for 9 hours, or until the meat is tender. Transfer the meat to a cutting board. Discard the bay leaves.

Using two forks, shred the meat. Return the meat to the slow cooker.

Add ½ teaspoon cumin and the sugar. Let stand for 1 hour so flavors will blend.

Preheat the oven to 325°F.

Wrap the tortillas in aluminum foil. Warm them in the oven for 6 to 8 minutes.

calories 296
protein 24 g
carbohydrates 39 g
  fiber 4 g
  sugars 8 g
cholesterol 52 mg
total fat 4.5 g
  saturated 1.5 g
  polyunsaturated 0.0 g
  monounsaturated 1.5 g
sodium 401 mg

dietary exchange
1½ starch
3 vegetable
2½ lean meat

To assemble, spoon the meat mixture down the center of each tortilla. Fold one end and each side of a tortilla toward the center. Repeat with the remaining tortillas.

Variation
Before folding the tortillas over the filling, add chopped tomatoes, shredded lettuce, and fat-free or low-fat Cheddar cheese. Or try salsa, fat-free or light sour cream, and fat-free or low-fat Cheddar.

Cook's Tip

If you can't find no-salt-added ketchup, use ¼ cup ketchup and 2 tablespoons water.

Grilled Stuffed Flank Steak

Serves 4

Grilling enthusiasts will enjoy adding this entrée to their repertoire. The moist stuffing is an unusual combination of vegetables, dried apricots, and chutney.

1 slice whole-wheat bread, torn into small pieces

1 large carrot, shredded

4 medium green onions (green and white parts), thinly sliced

1/2 cup coarsely chopped button mushrooms

1/4 cup coarsely chopped dried apricots

Egg substitute equivalent to 1 egg, or 1 large egg

2 tablespoons mango chutney

1 teaspoon salt-free all-purpose seasoning

Vegetable oil spray (olive oil spray preferred)

1-pound flank steak, all visible fat and silver skin discarded

In a small bowl, soak six 10-inch pieces of kitchen string in enough water to cover for 5 minutes (this will help keep the string from burning on the grill).

Meanwhile, in a medium bowl, stir together the bread pieces, carrot, green onions, mushrooms, apricots, egg substitute, chutney, and all-purpose seasoning until the ingredients are evenly distributed and the bread crumbs are moistened.

Lightly spray the grill rack with vegetable oil spray. Preheat the grill on medium high.

Using a long, sharp knife (a Chinese chef's knife works well), butterfly the steak. Starting at the widest edge, cut the steak almost in half parallel to your work surface (through the middle of the meat), stopping about 1/2 inch from the opposite edge so the two halves are still joined. Open the split steak (it will resemble a butterfly) and discard any visible fat or gristle. Place a piece of plastic wrap over the steak. With the flat side of a meat mallet, pound the steak to a thickness of 1/4 inch. Don't pound thinner than 1/4 inch.

calories 259
protein 25 g
carbohydrates 19 g
  fiber 3 g
  sugars 13 g
cholesterol 54 mg
total fat 8.5 g
  saturated 3.5 g
  polyunsaturated 0.5 g
  monounsaturated 3.5 g
sodium 149 mg

dietary exchange
1 fruit
1 vegetable
3 lean meat

Spoon the stuffing onto the center of the opened steak. Fold the long edges over the stuffing, enclosing it (the ends are not closed). Tie the steak at 2-inch intervals with the kitchen string. Lightly spray the outside of the steak with vegetable oil spray.

Grill the steak, turning every 10 minutes, for 40 to 45 minutes, or until the steak is browned on all sides and the stuffing reaches an internal temperature of 160°F. Transfer to a cutting board. Cover with aluminum foil. Let stand for 10 minutes before slicing crosswise into 8 pieces.

Time-Saver

Service attendants at the meat counter of your grocery can quickly butterfly a flank steak for you (usually at no extra charge), saving you time.

Grilled Lemongrass Flank Steak

Serves 4 (plus 6 to 8 ounces reserved)

Flank steak is marinated in a fragrant lemongrass mixture that also spot-lights delicate rice vinegar and zesty chili garlic sauce. Serve four people tonight and refrigerate the extra two servings to use in Grilled Flank Steak Salad with Sweet-and-Sour Sesame Dressing (page 129) later in the week.

Marinade
- 3 stalks of lemongrass
- 1/3 cup plain rice vinegar
- 3 medium garlic cloves, minced
- 1 teaspoon chili garlic sauce

- 1 teaspoon low-salt soy sauce
- 1 teaspoon acceptable vegetable oil
- ❖
- 1 1/2 pounds flank steak, all visible fat and silver skin discarded

Remove the outer leaf of the lemongrass. Slice the bottom 6 to 8 inches of lemongrass crosswise into 1/4-inch pieces. Put the sliced lemongrass and remaining marinade ingredients in a large resealable plastic bag.

Add the steak. Seal the bag and turn to coat. Refrigerate for 2 to 12 hours, turning occasionally.

Preheat the grill on medium-high.

Remove the steak from the marinade, discarding the marinade.

Grill for 8 to 9 minutes on each side, or until desired doneness. Let stand for 5 minutes.

Thinly slice the steak against the grain. Arrange 12 ounces cooked steak slices on a platter. Refrigerate the remaining steak, 6 to 8 ounces, in a resealable plastic bag for Grilled Flank Steak Salad.

calories 168
protein 22 g
carbohydrates 0 g
 fiber 0 g
 sugars 0 g
cholesterol 54 mg
total fat 8.0 g
 saturated 3.5 g
 polyunsaturated 0.5 g
 monounsaturated 3.5 g
sodium 115 mg

dietary exchange
3 lean meat

Cook's Tip on Chili Garlic Sauce

Not surprisingly, chili garlic sauce is made of pureed chiles and garlic. Look for it in the Asian section of the grocery store and in Asian markets. This sauce heightens the flavor of such dishes as soups, stir-fries, and dipping sauces.

Greek-Style
Eye-of-Round Steaks

Serves 4

When braised until fork-tender with ingredients popular in Greek cooking, lean eye-of-round steaks make an elegant entrée. This dish is even more delicious the next day, after the flavors have had a chance to marry.

Vegetable oil spray (olive oil spray preferred)

4 eye-of-round steaks (about 4 ounces each), all visible fat discarded

1 large green bell pepper, cut into 1-inch squares

1 cup frozen pearl onions, thawed

14.5-ounce can no-salt-added diced tomatoes, undrained

$1/2$ cup dry red wine (regular or non-alcoholic) or fat-free, no-salt-added beef broth, such as on page 44

2 tablespoons chopped kalamata olives

1 teaspoon grated lemon zest

1 tablespoon fresh lemon juice

1 teaspoon dried oregano, crumbled

$1/8$ teaspoon ground cinnamon

Heat a medium skillet over medium-high heat. Remove from the heat and lightly spray with vegetable oil spray (being careful not to spray near a gas flame). Cook the steaks for 2 to 3 minutes on each side, or until browned.

Stir in the bell pepper and onions. Cook for 1 to 2 minutes, or until the peppers are tender-crisp.

Stir in the remaining ingredients. Bring to a simmer over medium-high heat. Reduce the heat and simmer, covered, for 1 hour 30 minutes, or until the meat is tender, stirring occasionally.

calories 253
protein 27 g
carbohydrates 17 g
 fiber 3 g
 sugars 6 g
cholesterol 61 mg
total fat 6.5 g
 saturated 2.0 g
 polyunsaturated 0.5 g
 monounsaturated 3.0 g
sodium 194 mg

dietary exchange
3 vegetable
3 lean meat

Mediterranean Beef
and Vegetable Stir-Fry

Serves 4

When you spot a vibrant purple eggplant in the store, add it to your shopping cart. When you get home, turn to this recipe. A variety of vegetables and lean sirloin round out the dish.

1 pound boneless sirloin steak

2 medium shallots, coarsely chopped

1 small eggplant (about 1 pound), cut into $1/2$-inch cubes

2 tablespoons fat-free, low-sodium chicken broth, such as on page 45

14.5-ounce can artichoke hearts, rinsed, drained, and coarsely chopped

1 small yellow summer squash, cut into thin slices

14.5-ounce can no-salt-added diced tomatoes, undrained

$1/4$ cup coarsely chopped fresh basil leaves

2 tablespoons chopped kalamata olives

$1/4$ teaspoon salt

$1/4$ teaspoon pepper

If desired, put the steak in the freezer for 30 minutes for easier slicing. Discard all the visible fat. Cut the steak into thin strips.

Heat a nonstick wok or large nonstick skillet over medium-high heat. Cook the steak for 4 to 5 minutes, or until no longer pink in the center, stirring constantly. Transfer to a small bowl. Set aside.

In the same wok, cook the shallots for 1 minute, or until tender-crisp, stirring constantly.

Stir in the eggplant and broth. Cook for 4 to 5 minutes, or until the eggplant is tender, stirring constantly.

Stir in the artichoke hearts and squash. Cook for 2 to 3 minutes, or until the squash is tender-crisp, stirring constantly.

Stir in the remaining ingredients. Cook for 2 to 3 minutes, or until the mixture is almost warmed through, stirring constantly.

Stir in the reserved steak. Cook for 1 to 2 minutes, or until mixture is warmed through, stirring constantly.

calories 260
protein 29 g
carbohydrates 19 g
  fiber 6 g
  sugars 9 g
cholesterol 67 mg
total fat 8.0 g
  saturated 2.5 g
  polyunsaturated 0.5 g
  monounsaturated 4.0 g
sodium 507 mg

dietary exchange
4 vegetable
3 lean meat

Beef Stroganoff

Serves 6

Serve this perennial favorite over noodles or rice. Add Fresh Green Beans with Water Chestnuts (page 411) to complete the meal.

1 pound beef tenderloin, boneless round steak, or boneless sirloin
1/2 teaspoon pepper, or to taste
1 teaspoon acceptable vegetable oil
1/2 pound button mushrooms, sliced
1 medium onion, sliced
2 tablespoons all-purpose flour
2 cups fat-free, no-salt-added beef broth, such as on page 44

2 tablespoons no-salt-added tomato paste
2 tablespoons dry sherry
1 teaspoon dry mustard
1/4 teaspoon dried oregano, crumbled
1/4 teaspoon dried dillweed, crumbled
1/3 cup fat-free or light sour cream

If desired, put the meat in the freezer for 30 minutes for easier slicing. Discard all the visible fat and silver skin (if any). Slice the meat into thin strips about 2 inches long. Sprinkle with the pepper.

Heat a large, heavy skillet over medium-high heat. Pour the oil into the skillet and swirl to coat the bottom. Cook the mushrooms for 2 to 3 minutes, or until tender. Transfer to a plate.

Cook the onion in the same skillet for 3 to 4 minutes, or until brown. Add to the mushrooms.

Put the meat in the skillet and brown on all sides until rare, 2 to 3 minutes for tenderloin, 3 to 5 minutes for round steak or sirloin. Add to the mushrooms.

Put the flour in the skillet. Gradually pour in the broth, whisking constantly. Cook for 2 to 3 minutes, or until thickened, whisking constantly. Reduce the heat to low.

Whisk in the remaining ingredients except the sour cream. Stir in the mushroom mixture. Cook for 15 minutes.

Put the sour cream in a small bowl. Stir in a small amount of the meat mixture. Add to the skillet. Cook for 5 minutes, or until heated through, stirring occasionally.

calories 187
protein 19 g
carbohydrates 10 g
 fiber 1 g
 sugars 3 g
cholesterol 49 mg
total fat 7.0 g
 saturated 2.5 g
 polyunsaturated 0.5 g
 monounsaturated 3.0 g
sodium 70 mg

dietary exchange
1/2 starch
1 vegetable
2 1/2 lean meat

Beef Bourguignon

Serves 8

Like other stews, Beef Bourguignon tastes best when made ahead so the flavors have time to mingle. Serve it on brown rice or whole-wheat noodles.

Vegetable oil spray
1 teaspoon olive oil
5 medium onions, sliced
2 pounds boneless top sirloin roast (or other lean cut), all visible fat discarded, cut into 1-inch cubes
1 1/2 tablespoons all-purpose flour
1/4 teaspoon dried marjoram, crumbled
1/4 teaspoon dried thyme, crumbled

1/2 teaspoon pepper, or to taste
1 cup dry red wine (regular or nonalcoholic) (plus more as needed)
1/2 cup fat-free, no-salt-added beef broth, such as on page 44 (plus more as needed)
8 ounces button mushrooms
1/2 teaspoon salt

Heat a large, heavy skillet over medium-high heat. Remove from the heat and lightly spray with vegetable oil spray (being careful not to spray near a gas flame). Pour the oil into the skillet and swirl to coat the bottom. Cook the onions for 2 to 3 minutes, or until soft. Transfer the onions to a plate. Set aside.

Cook the beef cubes for 10 to 12 minutes, or until browned on all sides. Sprinkle with the flour, marjoram, thyme, and pepper. Stir well.

Stir in the wine and broth. Reduce the heat and simmer, covered, for 1 hour 30 minutes to 2 hours, or until almost tender. Add more wine and broth (2 parts wine to 1 part broth) as necessary to keep the beef barely covered.

Meanwhile, slice the mushrooms.

Return the onions to the skillet. Stir in the mushrooms and salt. Cook, covered, for 30 minutes, stirring occasionally. Add more wine and broth if necessary. The sauce should be thick and dark brown.

calories 225
protein 27 g
carbohydrates 12 g
  fiber 2 g
  sugars 6 g
cholesterol 69 mg
total fat 5.5 g
  saturated 2.0 g
  polyunsaturated 0.5 g
  monounsaturated 2.5 g
sodium 219 mg

dietary exchange
2 vegetable
3 lean meat

Portobello Mushrooms and Sirloin Strips over Spinach Pasta

Serves 4

Beef and robust, beefy-tasting portobello mushrooms, both marinated in red wine and seasonings, make a terrific combination.

12 ounces boneless top sirloin steak

Marinade
1/3 cup burgundy or other dry red wine (regular or nonalcoholic)
3 tablespoons low-salt soy sauce
3 tablespoons low-sodium Worcestershire sauce
6 medium garlic cloves, minced

2 teaspoons olive oil
1/2 tablespoon dried oregano, crumbled

❖

12 ounces portobello mushrooms, sliced
8 ounces dried spinach fettuccine

If desired, put the beef in the freezer for 30 minutes for easier slicing. Discard all the visible fat. Cut the beef into thin strips.

Combine the marinade ingredients in a large resealable plastic bag.

Add the mushrooms and beef to the marinade. Seal and turn to coat. Refrigerate for 30 minutes, turning the bag frequently.

Prepare the pasta using the package directions, omitting the salt and oil.

Meanwhile, heat a large nonstick skillet over medium-high heat for 1 minute. Using a slotted spoon, transfer half the beef mixture to the skillet. Cook for 4 minutes, or until the meat is no longer pink, stirring frequently. Transfer the meat to a plate and set aside. Cook the remaining beef mixture.

Return the reserved beef mixture with any juices to the skillet. Increase the heat to high. Boil for 5 minutes, stirring occasionally. Remove from the heat.

To serve, spoon the pasta onto plates. Spoon the beef mixture and sauce over the pasta.

calories 381
protein 29 g
carbohydrates 47 g
 fiber 4 g
 sugars 4 g
cholesterol 52 mg
total fat 7.5 g
 saturated 2.0 g
 polyunsaturated 1.5 g
 monounsaturated 3.5 g
sodium 381 mg

dietary exchange
3 starch
2½ lean meat

Classic Chinese Beef Stir-Fry

Serves 4

For Chinese comfort food at its best, serve lean beef and colorful vegetables in a soy-hoisin sauce over brown rice.

1 pound boneless sirloin steak

1 cup uncooked brown rice

1/2 cup fat-free, no-salt-added beef broth, such as on page 44

1 tablespoon low-salt soy sauce

2 teaspoons cornstarch

1 teaspoon toasted sesame oil

1/2 medium red bell pepper, thinly sliced

1 cup sugar snap peas, trimmed

4 ounces asparagus, trimmed, cut into 1-inch pieces

1/4 small jicama, peeled and diced, or 1/4 cup canned sliced water chestnuts, rinsed and drained

2 medium green onions (green and white parts), cut into 1-inch pieces

2 tablespoons chopped unsalted peanuts, dry-roasted

If desired, put the steak in the freezer for 30 minutes for easier slicing. Discard all the visible fat. Cut the steak into thin strips.

Meanwhile, prepare the brown rice using the package directions, omitting the salt and margarine.

In a small bowl, stir together the broth, soy sauce, cornstarch, and sesame oil until the cornstarch is dissolved. Set aside.

Heat a large nonstick skillet over medium-high heat. Cook the steak for 5 minutes, or until no longer pink in the center, stirring constantly. Transfer to a bowl.

Stir in the bell pepper. Cook for 1 to 2 minutes, or until tender-crisp, stirring constantly.

Stir in the peas, asparagus, jicama, and green onions. Cook for 1 to 2 minutes, or until tender-crisp, stirring constantly.

Stir in the broth mixture and steak. Cook for 2 to 3 minutes, or until the sauce is thickened and the mixture is warmed through, stirring constantly.

To serve, spoon the rice into bowls. Top each serving with the beef mixture. Garnish with the peanuts.

calories 326
protein 30 g
carbohydrates 27 g
  fiber 5 g
  sugars 3 g
cholesterol 67 mg
total fat 10.0 g
  saturated 3.0 g
  polyunsaturated 1.5 g
  monounsaturated 4.5 g
sodium 177 mg

dietary exchange
1 1/2 starch
1 vegetable
3 lean meat

Southwestern Beef Stir-Fry

Serves 4

Try this quick and easy dish if you already know how good chayote squash and tomatillos are—or if you want to learn.

1 cup uncooked instant brown rice
1 pound boneless sirloin steak
1 medium chayote, peeled, sliced, and seed discarded
1 medium zucchini, thinly sliced
5 medium tomatillos (about 4 ounces), paperlike skin discarded, rinsed, and quartered

14.5-ounce can no-salt-added diced tomatoes, undrained
2 tablespoons canned green chiles, rinsed and drained
1/2 teaspoon ground cumin
1/4 teaspoon salt

If desired, put the steak in the freezer for 30 minutes for easier slicing. Discard all the visible fat. Cut the steak into thin strips.

Prepare the rice using the package directions, omitting the salt and margarine.

Heat a nonstick wok or large nonstick skillet over medium-high heat. Cook the steak for 4 to 5 minutes, or until no longer pink in the center, stirring constantly. Transfer to a medium bowl.

Put the chayote, zucchini, and tomatillos in the wok. Cook for 3 to 4 minutes, or until the chayote and zucchini are tender-crisp, stirring constantly.

Stir in the undrained tomatoes, green chiles, cumin, and salt. Cook for 3 to 4 minutes, or until the chayote and zucchini are tender, stirring constantly.

Stir in the reserved steak. Cook for 2 minutes, or until the mixture is warmed through, stirring constantly.

To serve, spoon the rice onto plates. Top each serving with the steak mixture.

calories 299
protein 29 g
carbohydrates 28 g
 fiber 5 g
 sugars 4 g
cholesterol 67 mg
total fat 7.5 g
 saturated 2.5 g
 polyunsaturated 1.0 g
 monounsaturated 3.0 g
sodium 287 mg

dietary exchange
1 starch
3 vegetable
3 lean meat

Braised Sirloin Tips

Serves 8

For a real treat, try this dish with Wild Rice with Mushrooms (page 462).

2 pounds sirloin tip, all visible fat
   discarded, cubed
¹/₄ teaspoon pepper
1 small to medium onion, finely
   chopped
2 medium garlic cloves, minced
1¹/₄ cups fat-free, no-salt-added beef
   broth, such as on page 44

¹/₃ cup dry red wine (regular or
   nonalcoholic)
1 tablespoon low-salt soy sauce
2 tablespoons cornstarch
¹/₄ cup cold water
¹/₄ cup snipped fresh parsley

Heat a large nonstick skillet over medium-high heat.

Sprinkle the meat with the pepper. Cook the meat in the skillet for 8 to 10 minutes, or until well browned on all sides, stirring often.

Stir in the onion and garlic. Cook for 2 to 3 minutes, or until the onion is soft.

Pour in the broth, wine, and soy sauce. Bring to a boil. Reduce the heat and simmer, covered, for 1 hour 30 minutes, or until the meat is tender.

Put the cornstarch in a cup or small bowl. Add the water, stirring to dissolve. Slowly pour the mixture into the skillet, stirring constantly. Increase the heat to medium-high. Cook for 2 to 3 minutes, or until the gravy thickens, stirring constantly.

To serve, sprinkle with the parsley.

calories 188
protein 25 g
carbohydrates 4 g
  fiber 1 g
  sugars 1 g
cholesterol 67 mg
total fat 6.5 g
  saturated 2.5 g
  polyunsaturated 0.0 g
  monounsaturated 2.5 g
sodium 123 mg

dietary exchange
1 vegetable
3 lean meat

Italian Beef Kebabs

Serves 8

Get your guests in on the fun by letting them thread their own skewers.

Marinade
- 1 medium onion, finely chopped
- 3/4 cup dry red wine (regular or nonalcoholic)
- 2 tablespoons fat-free or light Italian salad dressing
- 1/4 cup low-sodium Worcestershire sauce
- 2 tablespoons low-salt soy sauce
- 1 teaspoon dried thyme, crumbled
- 1 teaspoon dried rosemary, crushed
- 1 teaspoon acceptable vegetable oil
- 1/2 teaspoon pepper

❖

- 1 1/2 pounds sirloin tip, all visible fat discarded, cut into 16 cubes
- 1 quart water
- 8 red potatoes (about 2-inch diameter), halved
- 8 boiling onions (about 1-inch diameter), peeled
- 16 medium button mushrooms
- 16 large cherry tomatoes
- 1 large green bell pepper, cut into 16 squares
- 2 tablespoons fat-free or light Italian salad dressing

Pour the marinade ingredients into a large resealable plastic bag. Add the beef to the bag. Seal and turn to coat. Refrigerate for about 8 hours. Drain, discarding the marinade.

Soak 8 wooden skewers in cold water for at least 10 minutes before using.

In a medium saucepan, bring the water to a boil over high heat. Parboil the potatoes for 3 minutes.

Add the onions. Boil for 1 1/2 minutes. Drain. Rinse the vegetables under cold water to stop the cooking. Cut the onions in half.

Preheat the grill on medium-high or preheat the broiler.

On each skewer, thread in order a meat cube, potato half, onion half, mushroom, cherry tomato, and bell pepper square. Repeat.

Grill the kebabs or broil 3 to 4 inches from the heat for 12 to 15 minutes, or until the desired doneness, turning often and basting with the dressing.

calories 202
protein 22 g
carbohydrates 17 g
  fiber 3 g
  sugars 5 g
cholesterol 50 mg
total fat 5.0 g
  saturated 2.0 g
  polyunsaturated 0.5 g
  monounsaturated 2.0 g
sodium 274 mg

dietary exchange
1/2 starch
2 vegetable
2 1/2 lean meat

Beef Skillet Oriental

Serves 4

The ingredients in this dish provide a pleasant color and flavor palette. Try this stir-fry over a bed of brown rice.

1/2 pound flank steak
2 teaspoons acceptable vegetable oil
1/4 cup chopped onion
1 or 2 medium garlic cloves, minced
2 cups small fresh cauliflower florets (about 1/2 medium head)
1 cup fat-free, no-salt-added beef broth, such as on page 44
1 small or medium red bell pepper, diced

3 ounces fresh snow peas, trimmed
2 tablespoons cold water
2 tablespoons dry sherry
1 tablespoon cornstarch
1 tablespoon low-salt soy sauce
1/2 tablespoon grated peeled gingerroot
1/8 teaspoon red hot-pepper sauce

Put the flank steak in the freezer for 30 minutes for easier slicing. Discard all the visible fat and silver skin. Slice the steak against the grain into strips 2 to 3 inches long and 1/2 to 1 inch wide.

Heat a nonstick electric skillet to 400°F or heat a large nonstick skillet over medium-high heat. Stir-fry half the beef for 3 to 4 minutes, or just until browned, stirring frequently. Remove and set aside. Repeat with the remaining beef.

Heat the oil in the skillet, swirling to coat the bottom. Cook the onion and garlic for 2 to 3 minutes, or until the onion is soft.

Stir in the cauliflower and broth. Cook for 2 minutes, stirring occasionally.

Stir in the bell pepper and snow peas. Cook for 1 minute.

In a small bowl, whisk together the remaining ingredients. Pour into the skillet.

Add the beef. Cook for 2 to 3 minutes, or until the sauce thickens.

calories 149
protein 14 g
carbohydrates 9 g
  fiber 3 g
  sugars 4 g
cholesterol 28 mg
total fat 5.5 g
  saturated 2.0 g
  polyunsaturated 0.5 g
  monounsaturated 2.5 g
sodium 165 mg

dietary exchange
2 vegetable
1 1/2 lean meat

Bowl of Red

Serves 6

Texans love to eat chili almost as much as they love to argue over which version is the best. This one has cubed beef and skips the beans.

Vegetable oil spray

Chili

 2 pounds boneless top round steak, all visible fat discarded, cut into ½-inch cubes
 6 ancho peppers
 2 fresh jalapeño or serrano peppers
 2 cups water
16 ounces dark or regular beer (regular or nonalcoholic)
    8-ounce can no-salt-added tomato sauce
 1 medium onion, chopped

 4 medium garlic cloves, minced
 2 tablespoons chili powder
 2 tablespoons ground cumin
 1 teaspoon ground coriander
 1 teaspoon dried oregano, crumbled
 ½ teaspoon salt
 ¼ teaspoon pepper
 ¼ teaspoon cayenne

❖

 ¼ cup plus 2 tablespoons fat-free or light sour cream (optional)
    Fresh cilantro, snipped (optional)

Heat a Dutch oven over medium-high heat. Remove from the heat and lightly spray with vegetable oil spray (being careful not to spray near a gas flame). Brown half the meat on all sides, stirring occasionally. Using a slotted spoon, transfer the meat to a plate. Brown the remaining meat. Return the first batch of meat to the Dutch oven.

Meanwhile, wearing gloves, discard the seeds and ribs of the peppers. Chop the peppers.

Stir the peppers and remaining chili ingredients into the browned meat. Bring to a boil over medium-high heat. Reduce the heat and simmer, covered, for 1 hour, stirring occasionally. Uncover and simmer for 15 to 30 minutes, or until the desired consistency, stirring occasionally.

To serve, ladle the chili into bowls. Top each serving with a dollop of sour cream. Sprinkle with cilantro.

calories 318
protein 38 g
carbohydrates 20 g
  fiber 6 g
  sugars 11 g
cholesterol 86 mg
total fat 7.5 g
  saturated 2.0 g
  polyunsaturated 1.0 g
  monounsaturated 2.0 g
sodium 327 mg

dietary exchange
4 vegetable
4½ lean meat

Savory Beef Stew

Serves 12

This exciting array of seasonings makes for an interesting stew. Try serving Whole-Wheat French Bread (page 512) with it.

Vegetable oil spray

2½ pounds eye-of-round roast, all visible fat discarded, cut into bite-size pieces

1 teaspoon olive oil

1 large onion, finely chopped

5½ cups fat-free, no-salt-added beef broth, such as on page 44

1 teaspoon dried thyme, crumbled

1 teaspoon dried marjoram, crumbled

1 medium bay leaf, broken in half

1 pound red potatoes

2 large carrots

8 ounces button mushrooms

1 medium red bell pepper, diced

4 medium green onions (green and white parts), thinly sliced

2 cups fat-free, no-salt-added beef broth, such as on page 44

¼ cup plus 2 tablespoons cornstarch

¼ cup no-salt-added tomato paste

1 teaspoon dried thyme, crumbled

1 teaspoon salt-free Italian seasoning, crumbled

¾ teaspoon pepper

½ teaspoon salt

Preheat the broiler.

Lightly spray a broiler pan and rack with vegetable oil spray. Broil the meat about 6 inches from the heat for 15 to 20 minutes, or until the meat is brown on all sides, turning occasionally.

Heat a stockpot over medium-high heat. Remove from the heat and lightly spray with vegetable oil spray (being careful not to spray near a gas flame). Pour the oil into the skillet and swirl to coat the bottom. Cook the onion for 2 to 3 minutes, or until soft.

Add the meat, any pan juices, 5½ cups broth, thyme, marjoram, and bay leaf. Increase the heat to high and bring to a boil. Reduce the heat and simmer, covered, for 1 hour 30 minutes, or until the meat is tender.

Meanwhile, cut the potatoes into chunks, slice the carrots, and quarter the mushrooms. Add to the pot. Simmer, covered, for 30 minutes.

Add the bell pepper and green onions.

calories 198
protein 24 g
carbohydrates 16 g
  fiber 3 g
  sugars 3 g
cholesterol 49 mg
total fat 4.0 g
  saturated 1.5 g
  polyunsaturated 0.0 g
  monounsaturated 1.5 g
sodium 175 mg

dietary exchange
½ starch
1 vegetable
3 lean meat

In a medium bowl, whisk together the remaining ingredients. Pour into the stew. Increase the heat to high and bring to a boil, stirring constantly. Reduce the heat to low. Cook for 5 minutes, or until thickened, stirring constantly. Remove the bay leaf before serving the stew.

Cook's Tip on No-Salt-Added Tomato Paste

Sometimes you can save money by reading nutrition labels. For instance, a can of tomato paste labeled "No salt added" may cost more than "regular" tomato paste with the same sodium content—about 20 milligrams per serving.

Cook's Tip on Red Bell Peppers

Buy red bell peppers when they're on sale and roast or broil them for later use. Freeze them in resealable freezer bags for up to four months.

Grilled Hamburgers
with Vegetables and Feta

Serves 6

The vegetables are built right into this hamburger, with a flavor boost from feta cheese.

Vegetable oil spray

Hamburgers

- 1 pound lean ground beef
- 2 cups shredded broccoli (broccoli slaw)
- 1 medium portobello mushroom, stem discarded, finely chopped

- ¼ cup fat-free or low-fat feta cheese, rinsed and drained
- ½ teaspoon lemon pepper

❖

- 6 whole-wheat hamburger buns

Lightly spray the grill rack with vegetable oil spray. Preheat the grill on medium-high.

In a medium bowl, combine the hamburger ingredients. Using your hands, shape into six patties.

Grill the hamburgers for 4 to 5 minutes on each side, or until no longer pink in the center (internal temperature should be 160°F).

To serve, place a patty on each bun.

Cook's Tip

Rather than the same old ketchup and mustard, try these topping ideas: Dijon mustard flavored with horseradish, fruit chutney, baby spinach, red onions, or sliced cooked beets (a popular topping in Australia—it's really good, mate!).

calories 263
protein 20 g
carbohydrates 24 g
  fiber 4 g
  sugars 3 g
cholesterol 43 mg
total fat 10.0 g
  saturated 3.0 g
  polyunsaturated 1.0 g
  monounsaturated 3.5 g
sodium 368 mg

dietary exchange
1½ starch
2½ medium-fat meat

Mediterranean
Meat Loaf

Serves 4

Here's how to get the taste of meatballs without the work.

8 ounces lean ground beef
4 ounces low-fat bulk breakfast sausage
1 medium green bell pepper, finely chopped
1/3 cup plain dry bread crumbs
1/3 cup fat-free, low-sodium spaghetti sauce

1/2 cup finely chopped onion
Whites of 2 large eggs
2 teaspoons dried basil, crumbled
1 teaspoon dried oregano, crumbled
1/3 cup fat-free, low-sodium spaghetti sauce

Preheat the oven to 350°F.

In a medium bowl, combine all the ingredients except 1/3 cup spaghetti sauce. (Your hands work well for this.)

On a nonstick baking sheet, shape the beef mixture into a 9 × 5-inch oval loaf. Top with the remaining 1/3 cup spaghetti sauce.

Bake for 50 minutes, or until the loaf reaches an internal temperature of 160°F and is no longer pink in the center. Let stand for 10 minutes before slicing.

Cook's Tip

Save time by doubling this recipe. Bake one loaf and freeze the other (uncooked) to use another day. When it's needed, simply thaw the loaf and bake.

calories 212
protein 19 g
carbohydrates 14 g
  fiber 2 g
  sugars 4 g
cholesterol 46 mg
total fat 7.5 g
  saturated 2.5 g
  polyunsaturated 0.5 g
  monounsaturated 2.5 g
sodium 345 mg

dietary exchange
1/2 starch
1 vegetable
2 1/2 lean meat

Philadelphia-Style Cheese Steak Wrap

Serves 6

When you wrap marinated beef, onions, and bell peppers in a tortilla with a bit of cheese, you have a modern twist on a classic.

12 ounces eye-of-round roast, all visible fat discarded

Marinade
1 tablespoon balsamic vinegar or red wine vinegar

2 teaspoons low-sodium Worcestershire sauce

1 teaspoon sugar

1 teaspoon dried oregano, crumbled

1 teaspoon olive oil

2 medium garlic cloves, minced

¼ teaspoon pepper

❖

1 small onion

1 medium green bell pepper

2 1-ounce slices fat-free sharp Cheddar cheese

6 6-inch fat-free or low-fat flour tortillas

If desired, put the roast in the freezer for 30 minutes for easier slicing. Discard all the visible fat from the roast. With a sharp knife, cut the meat against the grain into very thin slices, about ⅛ inch thick.

Meanwhile, combine the marinade ingredients in a large resealable plastic bag.

Add the meat to the marinade. Seal the bag and turn to coat. Marinate at room temperature for 10 minutes or refrigerate for up to 8 hours, turning occasionally.

Meanwhile, thinly slice the onion and bell pepper. Cut each piece of cheese into 3 slices. Set aside.

If using the oven method, preheat the oven to 350°F.

Preheat a nonstick griddle over medium-high heat. Brown the meat for 3 to 5 minutes, or until no longer pink, stirring occasionally. Put the meat in a bowl and cover with aluminum foil to keep warm.

Wipe the griddle with paper towels. Cook the onion and bell pepper for 5 to 6 minutes, or until soft, stirring occasionally.

calories 187
protein 18 g
carbohydrates 22 g
  fiber 2 g
  sugars 2 g
cholesterol 32 mg
total fat 2.5 g
  saturated 1.0 g
  polyunsaturated 0.0 g
  monounsaturated 1.0 g
sodium 358 mg

dietary exchange
1½ starch
2 lean meat

To assemble, place the tortillas in a large, shallow baking pan. Spoon the meat down the center of each tortilla. Top with the onion mixture and cheese. Cover with aluminum foil. Heat for 4 to 5 minutes. Roll up the tortillas jelly-roll style. Secure with toothpicks if desired.

To microwave, place 2 tortillas on a microwave-safe plate. Add the meat, onion mixture, and cheese as directed. Microwave (still flat) on 100 percent power (high) for 30 seconds. Roll the tortillas jelly-roll style over the filling. Secure with toothpicks if desired. Repeat with the remaining tortillas and filling.

Salisbury Steaks
with Mushroom Sauce

Serves 4

Use the soaking liquid from dried mushrooms in the sauce for this dressed-up hamburger patty. Complete the meal with Baked Fries with Creole Seasoning (page 453) and sliced tomatoes.

1/2 to 3/4 ounce dried mushrooms, any variety or combination
1 cup hot water

Meat Patties
12 ounces lean ground beef
1/2 medium onion, grated or minced
1 1/2 tablespoons all-purpose flour
1/2 tablespoon low-sodium Worcestershire sauce
1/2 teaspoon salt-free all-purpose seasoning
1/4 teaspoon dried thyme, crumbled

1/4 teaspoon salt
1/8 teaspoon pepper
2 tablespoons fat-free milk

❖

1/2 cup (about) fat-free, no-salt-added beef broth, such as on page 44
1/2 cup dry red wine (regular or nonalcoholic)
1/2 medium carrot, grated
2 to 3 tablespoons snipped fresh parsley

Put the mushrooms in a small bowl. Cover with hot water and let soak for 20 to 30 minutes.

Meanwhile, in a large bowl, stir together all the meat patty ingredients except the milk.

Add the milk and stir again. Shape into 4 patties. Set aside.

Drain the mushrooms, reserving the liquid. Chop the mushrooms and set aside. Strain the liquid through a coffee filter or paper towel into a liquid measuring cup. (This will remove any dirt.) Add enough broth to the strained liquid to make 1 cup.

Stir in the wine. Set aside.

Heat a heavy nonstick skillet over medium-high heat. Cook the beef patties for 5 to 6 minutes on each side, or until brown on both sides and no longer pink in the center. Reduce the heat to medium if the meat is

calories 215
protein 19 g
carbohydrates 8 g
fiber 2 g
sugars 2 g
cholesterol 49 mg
total fat 9.0 g
saturated 3.0 g
polyunsaturated 0.5 g
monounsaturated 3.5 g
sodium 227 mg

dietary exchange
1 1/2 vegetable
2 1/2 medium-fat meat

browning too quickly. Remove from the skillet and drain on paper towels. Discard any liquid left in the skillet.

Return the skillet to the heat. Put the mushrooms, wine mixture, and carrot in the skillet. Increase the heat to high and bring to a boil. Boil the liquid for 4 to 5 minutes, or until reduced by one third to one half.

Add the beef patties. Reduce the heat and simmer for 10 minutes. Sprinkle with the parsley.

Tex-Mex Lasagna

Serves 8; 1½ cups per serving

When planning a party for a hungry crowd or it's your turn to feed the soccer team, you will appreciate this easy-to-assemble and satisfying meal.

Vegetable oil spray
1 pound lean ground beef
14.5-ounce can no-salt-added tomatoes, undrained
½ cup salsa
¼ teaspoon salt
1 cup fat-free or low-fat ricotta cheese
1 teaspoon chili powder

1 teaspoon ground cumin
16 6-inch corn tortillas, halved
1 cup shredded low-fat Monterey Jack cheese
15-ounce can no-salt-added navy beans, rinsed and drained
1 cup frozen whole-kernel corn, thawed
¼ cup sliced black olives

Preheat the oven to 375°F. Lightly spray a 13 × 9 × 2-inch baking pan with vegetable oil spray.

In a large nonstick skillet, cook the beef over medium-high heat for 7 to 8 minutes, or until browned, stirring occasionally. Pour into a colander and rinse under hot water to remove excess fat. Drain well. Wipe the skillet with paper towels. Return the beef to the skillet.

Stir in the undrained tomatoes, salsa, and salt. Reduce the heat to medium-low and cook for 5 minutes or until warmed through, stirring occasionally. Turn off the heat, leaving the skillet on the stove.

In a small bowl, stir together the ricotta cheese, chili powder, and cumin.

To assemble, arrange 8 tortilla halves in the baking dish. (The tortillas may overlap slightly, and they will not completely cover the bottom.) Spread half the beef mixture over the tortillas. Sprinkle with half the Monterey Jack. Arrange 8 tortilla halves over the cheese. Spoon 1-tablespoon mounds of the ricotta mixture over the tortillas. Using a spatula, flatten each mound slightly. Top the ricotta mixture with the beans and corn.

calories 273
protein 24 g
carbohydrates 30 g
  fiber 5 g
  sugars 6 g
cholesterol 36 mg
total fat 6.0 g
  saturated 2.5 g
  polyunsaturated 1.0 g
  monounsaturated 2.0 g
sodium 423 mg

dietary exchange
2 starch
2½ lean meat

Make another layer of 8 tortilla halves. Spread the remaining meat mixture over the tortillas. Sprinkle with the remaining Monterey Jack. Top with a layer of the remaining 8 tortillas halves. Sprinkle with the olives. Cover with aluminum foil.

Bake for 30 minutes, or until warmed through. Let cool on a rack for 5 minutes before cutting.

Beef and Pasta Skillet

Serves 6

Serve this family-pleasing dish with steamed zucchini and a dessert of Fruit with Vanilla Cream (page 616).

8 ounces dried tricolor rotini (3 to 4 cups)
8 ounces button mushrooms, sliced
8 ounces lean ground beef
1 large onion, chopped
3 medium garlic cloves, minced
½ tablespoon salt-free Italian seasoning
½ tablespoon dried basil, crumbled
1 cup water

6-ounce can no-salt-added tomato paste
2 tablespoons shredded or grated Parmesan cheese
2 tablespoons finely snipped fresh parsley
1 teaspoon low-sodium Worcestershire sauce
¼ teaspoon salt

Prepare the pasta using the package directions, omitting the salt and oil. Drain well. Set aside.

In a 12-inch skillet, stir together the mushrooms, beef, onion, garlic, herb seasoning, and basil. Cook, covered, over medium-high heat for 8 to 10 minutes, or until the mushrooms have released their juices and are fully cooked, stirring occasionally.

In a small bowl, whisk together the remaining ingredients. Stir the mixture and the pasta into the skillet. Heat thoroughly.

calories 262
protein 16 g
carbohydrates 40 g
  fiber 4 g
  sugars 5 g
cholesterol 23 mg
total fat 5.5 g
  saturated 2.0 g
  polyunsaturated 0.5 g
  monounsaturated 2.0 g
sodium 187 mg

dietary exchange
2 starch
2 vegetable
1 lean meat

Spaghetti with Meat Sauce

Serves 8

Savory and traditional, this meat sauce is heavy on the vegetables. Team it with fruit for dessert and help the kids get their five-a-day servings.

Vegetable oil spray

Meat Sauce

1½ pounds lean ground beef
2 large onions, chopped
4 medium ribs of celery, chopped
1 medium green bell pepper, chopped
   28-ounce can no-salt-added Italian plum tomatoes, undrained
   6-ounce can no-salt-added tomato paste

1 tablespoon low-sodium Worcestershire sauce
1 teaspoon pepper
1 teaspoon dried oregano, crumbled
1 teaspoon dried basil, crumbled
1 teaspoon garlic powder
2 medium bay leaves
❖
16 ounces dried spaghetti
½ cup shredded or grated Parmesan cheese

Heat a stockpot over medium-high heat. Remove from the heat and lightly spray with vegetable oil spray (being careful not to spray near a gas flame). Cook the beef over medium-high heat until no longer pink, 10 to 12 minutes, stirring frequently. Put the beef in a colander and rinse under hot water to remove the excess fat. Wipe the pot with paper towels. Return the beef to the pot.

Stir in the onions. Cook over medium-high heat for 3 to 4 minutes, or until slightly brown.

Stir in the celery and bell pepper. Cook for 2 minutes.

Stir in the remaining sauce ingredients. Reduce the heat and simmer, covered, for 30 minutes to 2 hours (the longer the better), stirring occasionally.

Near serving time, prepare the spaghetti using the package directions, omitting the salt and oil. Drain well.

To serve, spoon the spaghetti onto plates. Ladle the sauce over the spaghetti. Sprinkle with the Parmesan.

calories 390
protein 28 g
carbohydrates 57 g
  fiber 5 g
  sugars 9 g
cholesterol 42 mg
total fat 5.5 g
  saturated 2.0 g
  polyunsaturated 0.5 g
  monounsaturated 2.0 g
sodium 239 mg

dietary exchange
3 starch
3 vegetable
2 very lean meat

Beef and Noodle Casserole Dijon

Serves 4

This satisfying casserole requires only one pan from start to finish. With fewer dishes to wash, you'll have the time to take a brisk walk around the block while the casserole bakes.

8 ounces lean ground beef
8 ounces frozen Italian-style mixed vegetables
1 cup water
1 cup fat-free, no-salt-added beef broth, such as on page 44
$1/2$ 10.75-ounce can low-fat, reduced-sodium condensed cream of mushroom soup
$1/2$ tablespoon Dijon mustard flavored with horseradish, or $1/2$ teaspoon Dijon mustard and $1/4$ teaspoon prepared white horseradish

$1/2$ teaspoon salt-free Italian seasoning
$1/2$ teaspoon onion powder
$1/4$ teaspoon garlic powder
$1/4$ teaspoon salt
$1/4$ teaspoon pepper
4 ounces dried no-yolk egg noodles
2 tablespoons plain dry bread crumbs
1 tablespoon shredded or grated Parmesan cheese

Preheat the oven to 350°F. Heat a nonstick Dutch oven over medium-high heat. Cook the beef for 8 to 10 minutes, or until no longer pink, stirring occasionally. Pour into a colander and rinse under hot water to remove excess fat. Drain well. Wipe the Dutch oven with paper towels. Return the beef to the Dutch oven.

Stir in the vegetables, water, broth, soup, mustard, Italian seasoning, onion powder, garlic powder, salt, and pepper. Bring to a simmer over medium-high heat.

Stir in the noodles.

Bake, covered, for 30 to 35 minutes, or until the noodles are tender.

Sprinkle with the bread crumbs and Parmesan.

calories 234
protein 16 g
carbohydrates 31 g
 fiber 3 g
 sugars 3 g
cholesterol 30 mg
total fat 3.5 g
 saturated 1.5 g
 polyunsaturated 0.0 g
 monounsaturated 1.0 g
sodium 448 mg

dietary exchange
2 starch
$1^{1}/2$ very lean meat

Greek-Style Beef
Skillet Supper

Serves 4

Classic Greek ingredients transform everyday ground beef into something spectacular!

1   pound lean ground beef
2   cups fat-free, no-salt-added beef broth, such as on page 44
    14.5-ounce can no-salt-added diced tomatoes, undrained
2   tablespoons chopped kalamata olives
1   teaspoon dried oregano, crumbled
1   teaspoon onion powder
1   teaspoon grated lemon zest

1   teaspoon fresh lemon juice
1/2 teaspoon garlic powder
1/4 teaspoon salt
1/4 teaspoon pepper
4   ounces dried whole-wheat pasta spirals (about 1 1/4 cups)
    10-ounce package frozen chopped spinach, thawed and squeezed dry
1/4 cup crumbled fat-free or low-fat feta cheese

In a large nonstick skillet, cook the beef over medium-high heat for 8 to 10 minutes, or until brown, stirring occasionally. Pour into a colander and rinse under hot water to remove excess fat. Drain well. Wipe the skillet with paper towels. Return the beef to the skillet.

Stir in the broth, undrained tomatoes, olives, oregano, onion powder, lemon zest, lemon juice, garlic powder, salt, and pepper. Bring to a simmer over medium-high heat.

Stir in the pasta. Reduce the heat and simmer, covered, for 10 minutes, or until the pasta is tender.

Stir in the spinach. Simmer, covered, for 1 to 2 minutes, or until warmed through.

To serve, ladle into bowls. Sprinkle each serving with the feta.

calories 296
protein 31 g
carbohydrates 32 g
  fiber 6 g
  sugars 5 g
cholesterol 51 mg
total fat 6.0 g
  saturated 2.0 g
  polyunsaturated 0.5 g
  monounsaturated 3.0 g
sodium 537 mg

dietary exchange
1 1/2 starch
1 1/2 vegetable
3 lean meat

Glazed Meatballs on Water Chestnut and Bell Pepper Rice

Serves 4 (plus 3 cups rice mixture reserved)

Yellow rice tossed with water chestnuts and bell peppers makes a bed for flavor-packed meatballs in this dish. The rice combination is equally good in Vegetarian Stir-Fry (page 362).

Meatballs
- 12 ounces lean ground beef
- 1 small red or green bell pepper or combination, finely chopped
- 1/3 cup uncooked quick-cooking oatmeal
- Whites of 2 large eggs
- 2 1/2 teaspoons low-salt soy sauce
- 2 teaspoons cornstarch
- 2 teaspoons grated orange zest
- 1/4 to 1/2 teaspoon crushed red pepper flakes

Water Chestnut and Bell Pepper Rice
- 3 cups water
- 1 1/2 cups uncooked rice
- 1/2 teaspoon ground turmeric
- 1 large red or green bell pepper or combination, finely chopped
- 8-ounce can sliced water chestnuts, rinsed and drained

Glaze
- 3 tablespoons grape jelly
- 2 tablespoons no-salt-added ketchup
- 1 tablespoon plus 2 1/2 teaspoons low-salt soy sauce
- 1 teaspoon sugar
- 1 teaspoon low-sodium Worcestershire sauce

calories 381
protein 23 g
carbohydrates 51 g
 fiber 3 g
 sugars 13 g
cholesterol 49 mg
total fat 9.5 g
 saturated 3.0 g
 polyunsaturated 0.5 g
 monounsaturated 3.5 g
sodium 359 mg

dietary exchange
3 starch
1 vegetable
2 1/2 lean meat

In a large bowl, combine the meatball ingredients. (Your hands work well for this.) Shape into 24 meatballs. Set aside.

For the rice, in a medium saucepan, bring the water to a boil over high heat. Stir in the rice and turmeric. Return to a boil. Reduce the heat and simmer, covered, for 20 minutes. Stir in the bell pepper and water chestnuts.

Meanwhile, heat a large nonstick skillet over medium-high heat for 1 minute. Cook the meatballs for 12 minutes, or until cooked through and browned (reduce the heat to medium if necessary). Turn the meatballs frequently (using two spoons works well). Drain on paper towels. Wipe the skillet with paper towels. Return the meatballs to the skillet.

In a small bowl, whisk together the glaze ingredients. Pour into the skillet. Using a rubber scraper, gently coat the meatballs. Cook over medium-high heat for about 2 minutes, stirring constantly until meatballs are well glazed. Remove from the heat.

Reserve 3 cups of rice mixture in an airtight container and refrigerate for up to three days for use in Vegetarian Stir-Fry (page 362). Place the remaining rice mixture on a serving platter and top with the meatballs.

Border Beef

Serves 4

Adding coffee granules to this satisfying dish gives it extra-rich color as well as deep flavor.

Vegetable oil spray
12 ounces lean ground beef
2 medium green bell peppers, chopped
1 large onion, chopped
10-ounce can diced tomatoes with lime juice and cilantro, undrained

1¹/₂ cups water
2 tablespoons chili powder
1 tablespoon instant coffee granules
1 tablespoon sugar
2¹/₂ teaspoons ground cumin, divided use
¹/₄ teaspoon salt

Heat a Dutch oven over medium-high heat. Remove from the heat and lightly spray with vegetable oil spray (being careful not to spray near a gas flame). Cook the beef for 2 to 3 minutes, or until no longer pink on the outside, stirring constantly. Pour into a colander and rinse under hot water to remove excess fat. Drain well. Wipe the Dutch oven with paper towels. Transfer the beef to a plate.

Lightly spray the Dutch oven with vegetable oil spray. Cook the peppers and onion over medium-high heat for 3 to 4 minutes, or until the onion is soft, stirring frequently.

Return the beef and any accumulated juices to the Dutch oven. Stir in the undrained tomatoes, water, chili powder, coffee granules, sugar, and 1¹/₂ teaspoons cumin.

Increase the heat to high and bring to a boil. Reduce the heat and simmer, covered, for 20 minutes. Remove from the heat.

Stir in the remaining 1 teaspoon cumin and the salt. Let stand, covered, for 10 minutes to absorb flavors.

calories 178
protein 18 g
carbohydrates 18 g
  fiber 4 g
  sugars 10 g
cholesterol 38 mg
total fat 4.0 g
  saturated 1.0 g
  polyunsaturated 0.5 g
  monounsaturated 1.5 g
sodium 533 mg

dietary exchange
3 vegetable
2 lean meat

Shepherd's Pie

Serves 6

This one-dish meal is for the meat and potato lovers in your family.

1 pound lean ground beef
1 cup fat-free, no-salt-added beef broth, such as on page 44
1 teaspoon pepper
2 medium bay leaves
2 whole cloves
Dash of dried thyme, crumbled
2 medium carrots, sliced
1 large onion, sliced
4 ounces button mushrooms, sliced
2 medium ribs of celery, diced
1 cup canned no-salt-added whole-kernel corn

Vegetable oil spray
1 tablespoon plus ³/₄ teaspoon all-purpose flour
¹/₂ cup fat-free, no-salt-added beef broth, such as on page 44
1 pound potatoes, peeled, cooked, and diced
¹/₂ cup fat-free milk
1 tablespoon light tub margarine
1 tablespoon snipped chives or green onions (green part only)
4 ounces fat-free or part-skim mozzarella cheese, shredded

In a large skillet, brown the beef over medium-high heat, stirring occasionally. Put the beef in a colander and rinse under hot water to remove excess fat. Wipe the skillet with paper towels. Return the beef to the skillet.

Stir in the 1 cup broth, pepper, bay leaves, cloves, and thyme. Reduce the heat and simmer, covered, for 30 minutes.

Stir in the carrots, onion, mushrooms, celery, and corn. Simmer, covered, for 4 to 5 minutes, or until the vegetables are tender. Remove the bay leaves and cloves.

Preheat the oven to 375°F. Lightly spray a medium casserole dish with vegetable oil spray.

Put the flour in a small bowl. Gradually add the ¹/₂ cup broth, whisking constantly to form a smooth paste. Stir into the beef mixture. Simmer for 5 minutes, or until slightly thickened. Pour into the casserole dish.

Mash the potatoes with the milk, margarine, and chives. Spread over the meat. Sprinkle with the cheese.

Bake for 10 minutes.

calories 246
protein 25 g
carbohydrates 31 g
  fiber 5 g
  sugars 8 g
cholesterol 38 mg
total fat 4.0 g
  saturated 1.0 g
  polyunsaturated 0.5 g
  monounsaturated 1.5 g
sodium 316 mg

dietary exchange
1¹/₂ starch
1¹/₄ vegetatble
3 very lean meat

Beef Tostadas

Serves 6

Almost as fast as fast food but much better for you.

6 6-inch corn tortillas
    Vegetable oil spray

Filling
1 pound lean ground beef
1 medium onion, finely chopped
1½ to 2 teaspoons chili powder
½ teaspoon ground cumin
½ teaspoon dried oregano, crumbled
½ teaspoon garlic powder
¼ teaspoon salt
    Dash of red hot-pepper sauce
    ❖

2 cups shredded lettuce
2 medium Italian plum tomatoes or
   1 large regular tomato, chopped
¾ cup fat-free, low-sodium salsa,
   such as Salsa Cruda (page 502)
¾ cup shredded fat-free or low-fat
   Cheddar cheese (about 3 ounces)

Preheat the oven to 450°F.

Put the tortillas on a heavy baking sheet. Lightly spray the tortillas with vegetable oil spray. Bake for 8 to 10 minutes, or until crisp.

Meanwhile, in a large nonstick skillet over medium-high heat, stir together the beef and onion. Cook until the meat is browned, 8 to 10 minutes, stirring occasionally. Pour the meat mixture into a colander and rinse under hot water to remove the excess fat. Wipe the skillet with paper towels. Return the meat to the skillet.

Stir the remaining filling ingredients into the meat mixture.

For each tostada, spread about ⅓ cup meat mixture over a crisped tortilla. Layer the remaining ingredients over the meat.

calories 167
protein 20 g
carbohydrates 14 g
  fiber 2 g
  sugars 4 g
cholesterol 37 mg
total fat 3.5 g
  saturated 1.0 g
  polyunsaturated 0.5 g
  monounsaturated 1.5 g
sodium 314 mg

dietary exchange
½ starch
1½ vegetable
2½ lean meat

Meat with Bell Pepper and Tomato Sauce

Serves 4

A simple bell pepper and tomato sauce works wonders with leftover beef, pork, or chicken and is also delicious over pasta.

12 ounces cooked lean beef, lean pork, or boneless, skinless chicken breasts, cooked without salt, all visible fat discarded

Bell Pepper and Tomato Sauce

1 medium green bell pepper, thinly sliced
1 medium onion, thinly sliced
1 teaspoon dried oregano, crumbled
1 medium garlic clove, minced
Vegetable oil spray
1/2 cup no-salt-added tomato sauce
1/2 cup water
1/2 teaspoon sugar
2 teaspoons olive oil (extra-virgin preferred)
1 teaspoon vinegar
1/2 teaspoon salt

Cut the meat diagonally into thin slices. Set aside.

Heat a 10-inch nonstick skillet over medium-high heat. Add the bell pepper, onion, oregano, and garlic. Lightly spray the vegetables with vegetable oil spray. Cook for 4 minutes, or until the onion is soft, stirring frequently.

Stir in the tomato sauce, water, and sugar. Reduce the heat and simmer, covered, for 10 minutes, or until reduced to 1 cup. Remove from the heat.

Stir in the oil, vinegar, and salt.

Add the meat to the skillet, spooning the sauce over the slices. Increase the heat to medium and cook, covered, for 5 minutes, or until warmed through.

Cook's Tip

Make the sauce ahead and store it in the freezer. It will be ready for a lightning-fast meal the next time you have extra cooked meat or poultry.

calories 216
protein 27 g
carbohydrates 8 g
  fiber 2 g
  sugars 5 g
cholesterol 76 mg
total fat 8.0 g
  saturated 2.5 g
  polyunsaturated 0.5 g
  monounsaturated 4.0 g
sodium 359 mg

dietary exchange
1 1/2 vegetable
3 lean meat

Crustless Ham
and Spinach Tart

Serves 6

This is a great brunch dish. Serve it with Southern Raised Biscuits (page 534) and Claret-Spiced Oranges (page 620).

Vegetable oil spray
1½ tablespoons shredded or grated Parmesan cheese
1 teaspoon olive oil
1 large onion, finely chopped
2 medium garlic cloves, minced
10-ounce package frozen chopped spinach, thawed and squeezed dry
3 slices (½ ounce each) lower-sodium, low-fat cracked-black-pepper ham, cut into strips

1¼ cups fat-free milk
Egg substitute equivalent to 3 eggs
¼ cup plus ½ tablespoon shredded or grated Parmesan cheese
1½ tablespoons all-purpose flour
1 tablespoon finely chopped fresh basil or 2 teaspoons dried, crumbled
½ teaspoon pepper
Dash of nutmeg

Preheat the oven to 350°F. Lightly spray a 9-inch glass pie pan with vegetable oil spray. Dust with 1½ tablespoons Parmesan.

Heat a medium nonstick skillet over medium-high heat. Pour the oil into the skillet and swirl to coat the bottom. Cook the onion for 2 to 3 minutes, or until soft, stirring occasionally.

Stir in the garlic. Cook for 1 minute.

Stir in the spinach and ham. Spread the mixture evenly in the pie pan.

In a medium bowl, whisk together the remaining ingredients. Pour over the spinach mixture.

Bake for 50 to 55 minutes, or until a knife inserted in the center comes out clean.

calories 102
protein 10 g
carbohydrates 10 g
  fiber 2 g
  sugars 5 g
cholesterol 8 mg
total fat 2.5 g
  saturated 1.0 g
  polyunsaturated 0.0 g
  monounsaturated 1.0 g
sodium 269 mg

dietary exchange
½ starch
1 vegetable
1 lean meat

New Orleans
Muffaletta Wrap

Serves 6

For a combination of Louisiana and Mexico, wrap the traditional stuffing ingredients of the popular New Orleans muffaletta—olive salad, meat, and cheese—in a flour tortilla.

1 medium carrot, diced

1 rib of celery, diced

1/2 medium red bell pepper, diced

2 ounces low-fat, lower-sodium ham, diced (1/2 cup)

1 medium green onion (green and white parts), thinly sliced

1/4 cup shredded fat-free or part-skim mozzarella cheese

4 medium pimiento-stuffed green olives, chopped

4 medium black olives, chopped

1 tablespoon olive oil

1 tablespoon red wine vinegar

1 medium garlic clove, minced

1/4 teaspoon dried oregano, crumbled

1/4 teaspoon pepper

1/4 teaspoon sugar

6 6-inch fat-free or low-fat flour tortillas

In a medium bowl, stir together all the ingredients except the tortillas.

To assemble, put a tortilla on a microwave-safe plate. Spoon 1/3 cup mixture down the middle of the tortilla. Microwave on 100 percent power (high) for 30 seconds. Roll the tortilla jelly-roll style over the filling, securing with a toothpick if desired. Repeat with the remaining ingredients.

calories 140
protein 6 g
carbohydrates 22 g
 fiber 2 g
 sugars 2 g
cholesterol 5 mg
total fat 3.0 g
 saturated 0.5 g
 polyunsaturated 0.5 g
 monounsaturated 2.0 g
sodium 482 mg

dietary exchange
1 1/2 starch
1/2 lean meat

Savory Black-Eyed Peas and Pasta

Serves 4

Here's what you can do with a little bit of the ham left over from your holiday dinner.

½ cup minced baked low-fat, lower-sodium ham

1 medium carrot, finely chopped

1 small onion, finely chopped

¼ cup minced fresh parsley

1 medium garlic clove, minced

15.5-ounce can no-salt-added black-eyed peas, rinsed and drained

2 cups fat-free, low-sodium chicken broth, such as on page 45

½ teaspoon dried thyme, crumbled

½ teaspoon dried basil, crumbled

½ teaspoon dried oregano, crumbled

½ teaspoon pepper

Dash of cayenne, or to taste

4 quarts water

8 ounces dried small shell pasta

Heat a large nonstick skillet over medium-high heat. Cook the ham, carrot, onion, parsley, and garlic over medium-high heat for 15 minutes, stirring occasionally.

Add the peas, broth, thyme, basil, oregano, pepper, and cayenne. Bring to a boil over medium-high heat. Reduce the heat and simmer, uncovered, for 15 minutes.

Meanwhile, in a stockpot, bring the water to a boil over high heat. Prepare the pasta using the package directions, omitting the salt and oil; cook until barely tender. Drain well. Return the pasta to the stockpot.

Stir the bean mixture into the pasta.

calories 351
protein 18 g
carbohydrates 66 g
 fiber 7 g
 sugars 9 g
cholesterol 8 mg
total fat 1.5 g
 saturated 0.5 g
 polyunsaturated 0.5 g
 monounsaturated 0.5 g
sodium 173 mg

dietary exchange

4 starch
1 vegetable
1 very lean meat

Bayou Red Beans
and Rice

Serves 8

This recipe will show you how easy it is to prepare Louisiana's most popular comfort food.

3   15.5-ounce cans no-salt-added red kidney beans, rinsed and drained
3   cups fat-free, low-sodium chicken broth, such as on page 45
    14.5-ounce can no-salt-added stewed tomatoes, undrained
1   cup chopped low-fat, lower-sodium ham

1   large onion, chopped
2   medium ribs of celery with leaves, chopped
2   teaspoons red hot-pepper sauce
1   medium garlic clove, minced
1/4 teaspoon black pepper
1   cup uncooked white rice

In a Dutch oven, stir together all the ingredients except the rice. Bring to a boil over high heat. Reduce the heat and simmer, covered, for 1 hour, or until the vegetables are tender, stirring occasionally.

Prepare the rice using the package directions, omitting the salt and margarine.

Using a potato masher, mash about one fourth of the bean mixture while it is in the pot. Stir the mixture. Cook over low heat for 10 minutes, stirring occasionally.

To serve, spoon the rice into bowls. Ladle the bean mixture over the rice.

calories 265
protein 16 g
carbohydrates 51 g
  fiber 8 g
  sugars 7 g
cholesterol 8 mg
total fat 0.5 g
  saturated 0.0 g
  polyunsaturated 0.0 g
  monounsaturated 0.5 g
sodium 201 mg

dietary exchange
3 starch
1 vegetable
1½ very lean meat

Marinated
Pork Tenderloin

Serves 4

Steamed brown rice and snow peas go well with this Asian-flavored pork.

Marinade
- 1 small onion, grated or minced
- ¼ cup low-salt soy sauce
- 1 tablespoon toasted sesame oil
- 2 teaspoons grated peeled gingerroot or ¾ teaspoon ground ginger
- 2 medium garlic cloves, crushed
- 1 teaspoon grated lemon zest

❖

- 1-pound pork tenderloin, all visible fat and silver skin discarded
- ¼ cup dry white wine (regular or nonalcoholic)
- ¼ cup honey
- 1 tablespoon dark brown sugar

In a large resealable plastic bag, combine the marinade ingredients.

Add the pork to the marinade. Seal the bag and turn to coat. Refrigerate for about 8 hours, turning occasionally.

Preheat the oven to 375°F.

Remove the pork from the marinade; drain well, discarding the marinade. Put the pork in a shallow nonstick baking pan.

In a small bowl, whisk together the remaining ingredients. Pour over the pork, turning to coat all sides.

Bake for 25 to 30 minutes, or until the internal temperature reaches 170°F. Remove from the oven and let rest for 5 minutes. Slice and serve.

calories 229
protein 24 g
carbohydrates 22 g
  fiber 0 g
  sugars 20 g
cholesterol 63 mg
total fat 4.0 g
  saturated 1.5 g
  polyunsaturated 0.5 g
  monounsaturated 1.5 g
sodium 438 mg

dietary exchange
1½ other carbohydrate
3 lean meat

Cook's Tip on Toasted Sesame Oil

Widely used in Asian and Indian cuisines, this polyunsaturated oil is also called Asian sesame oil and fragrant toasted sesame oil. Toasted sesame oil is darker and stronger in flavor than "plain" sesame oil.

Orange Pork Medallions

Serves 4

An unusual combination of flavors enhances this dish. It's very good served with Couscous with Vegetables (page 478).

Sauce
  Juice of 2 medium oranges
2½ tablespoons fresh lemon juice
 2 tablespoons all-fruit orange marmalade
 2 tablespoons minced fresh parsley
 1 tablespoon cornstarch
 2 teaspoons toasted sesame oil
¾ teaspoon prepared white horseradish

½ teaspoon ground cinnamon
½ teaspoon dried rosemary, crushed
¼ teaspoon pepper
❖
 1 pound pork tenderloin
 4 medium green onions (green and white parts), thinly sliced
 4 large sprigs of fresh parsley (optional)

In a small bowl, whisk together the sauce ingredients. Set aside.

Discard all the visible fat and the silver skin from the pork. Cut the pork into ½-inch-thick slices. Put the pork slices between sheets of plastic wrap. Flatten the pork lightly with the flat side of a meat mallet or with a rolling pin, hamburger press, or tortilla press.

Heat a large nonstick skillet over medium-high heat. Brown the pork quickly, about 2 minutes on each side.

Stir in the green onions. Cook for 1 minute, or until tender.

Stir in the sauce. Cook for 2 to 3 minutes, or until thickened, stirring constantly.

To serve, place the medallions and sauce on a serving platter. Garnish with the parsley.

calories 217
protein 24 g
carbohydrates 15 g
  fiber 2 g
  sugars 10 g
cholesterol 74 mg
total fat 6.5 g
  saturated 1.5 g
  polyunsaturated 1.5 g
  monounsaturated 2.5 g
sodium 67 mg

dietary exchange
1 fruit
3 lean meat

Herb-Rubbed
Pork Tenderloin with Dijon-Apricot Mop Sauce

Serves 8

A dry herb rub flavors the pork and makes a nice crust. You may want to stop right there, or you can go one step further and add the tangy mop sauce.

Herb Rub

- 1 tablespoon dried rosemary, crushed
- 1 tablespoon dried thyme, crumbled
- 1 tablespoon ground cumin
- 2 teaspoons coarsely ground pepper
- 2 teaspoons paprika
- 2 teaspoons celery seeds

❖

- 2 1-pound pork tenderloins, all visible fat and silver skin discarded
  Vegetable oil spray

Dijon-Apricot Mop Sauce

- 1 teaspoon acceptable vegetable oil
- 1 small onion, finely chopped
- 1/2 cup cider vinegar
- 1/4 cup honey
- 1/4 cup all-fruit apricot preserves
- 2 tablespoons Dijon mustard
- 1 teaspoon grated lemon zest
- 1 tablespoon fresh lemon juice

In a small bowl, stir together the rub ingredients. Using your hands or a spoon, rub the mixture evenly over the pork. Set aside.

Preheat the oven to 350°F or lightly spray the grill rack with vegetable oil spray and preheat the grill on medium-high.

For the mop sauce, heat a small saucepan over medium-high heat. Pour the oil into the pan and swirl to coat the bottom. Cook the onion for 2 to 3 minutes, or until soft, stirring occasionally.

Stir in the remaining sauce ingredients. Bring to a boil. Reduce the heat and simmer for 5 minutes, stirring occasionally. (You may wish to reserve 1/2 cup sauce to use as a dipping sauce for the cooked pork.)

If baking, lightly spray a broiling pan and rack with vegetable oil spray. Put the tenderloins on the rack in the pan. Bake for 30 minutes. Using a pastry brush or

---

calories 205
protein 23 g
carbohydrates 17 g
 fiber 2 g
 sugars 13 g
cholesterol 63 mg
total fat 5.0 g
 saturated 1.5 g
 polyunsaturated 0.5 g
 monounsaturated 2.0 g
sodium 127 mg

dietary exchange
1 other carbohydrate
3 lean meat

---

basting mop, baste on all sides. Bake for 10 minutes, then baste again. Bake for 10 to 15 minutes, or until the pork is no longer pink in the center or registers 165°F on a meat thermometer.

If grilling, grill the tenderloins for 10 minutes on each side (40 minutes total). Baste with the mop sauce. Grill for 2 to 3 minutes on each side, or until the pork is no longer pink in the center or registers 165°F on a meat thermometer.

Cook's Tip

Chicken, flank steak, and eye-of-round roast are delicious with both the rub and the mop sauce. Try the mop sauce on its own over vegetable kebabs, beef, poultry, firm fish fillets, or shrimp.

Cook's Tip on Leftover Meat

If you have any leftover meat, such as part of this pork tenderloin, or if you cook "planned-overs" to use in other meals, you can use them to make French bread sandwiches, top salads with them, toss them with cooked pasta, wrap them in tortillas with grilled vegetables, or add them to soup with yolk-free noodles.

Sweet-and-Sour Pork

Serves 4

You don't even need a wok to create this classic at home.

15-ounce can pineapple chunks in their own juice

Sauce

1 tablespoon plus 1 teaspoon plain rice vinegar or cider vinegar
2 teaspoons dry sherry
1 teaspoon low-salt soy sauce
1/8 teaspoon ground ginger
1/8 teaspoon ground allspice
1/8 teaspoon hot-pepper oil

2 teaspoons cornstarch
1/4 cup water

❖

12 ounces pork tenderloin
2 tablespoons minced leeks, green onions, or any combination
1/2 cup sliced green bell pepper
1 small onion, sliced
2 teaspoons snipped fresh parsley
1/8 teaspoon pepper

Drain the pineapple, reserving the juice. Add water to the reserved juice to make 1 cup.

In a small saucepan, stir together the pineapple juice, vinegar, sherry, soy sauce, ginger, allspice, and hot-pepper oil. Cook over medium-high heat for 3 to 4 minutes, or until the sauce comes just to a boil.

Meanwhile, put the cornstarch in a cup or small bowl. Add the water, whisking to dissolve.

When the pineapple juice mixture is hot, whisk in the dissolved cornstarch. Cook over medium heat for 1 to 2 minutes, or until the sauce begins to thicken, whisking constantly. Remove from the heat.

Discard all the visible fat and the silver skin from the pork. Cut the pork into 1/4-inch strips.

Heat a large nonstick skillet or wok over medium-high heat. Cook the pork for 3 to 4 minutes, or until no longer pink on the outside. Push to the side.

Reduce the heat to medium. Put the leeks, bell pepper, and onion in the skillet. Top with the pork. Sprinkle with the parsley and pepper. Cook for 4 to 5 minutes, or until the vegetables are tender-crisp and the pork is no longer pink in the center, stirring occasionally.

Stir in the sauce and pineapple. Heat through.

calories 192
protein 19 g
carbohydrates 22 g
 fiber 2 g
 sugars 15 g
cholesterol 55 mg
total fat 3.0 g
 saturated 1.0 g
 polyunsaturated 0.5 g
 monounsaturated 1.5 g
sodium 79 mg

dietary exchange
1 fruit
1 vegetable
2 1/2 lean meat

Slow-Cooker Pork Roast with
Orange Cranberry Sauce

Serves 8

This fork-tender pork roast features a built-in savory, slightly tart sauce. You will enjoy it any time of year, but especially during the summer because you won't need to heat up the kitchen.

1-pound boneless pork loin roast, all visible fat discarded

16-ounce can whole-berry cranberry sauce

2 teaspoons grated orange zest

1 cup fresh orange juice

1/2 cup water

2 tablespoons cider vinegar

2 medium shallots, coarsely chopped

1 tablespoon fresh rosemary, coarsely chopped, or 1 teaspoon dried, crushed

1/4 teaspoon pepper

Put all the ingredients in a slow cooker. Cook, covered, on high for 4 to 5 hours or on low for 8 to 10 hours, or until the pork is tender.

Transfer the pork to a cutting board, reserving the sauce. Cover the pork with aluminum foil and let stand for 10 to 15 minutes before slicing.

To serve, spoon the sauce over the pork slices or serve it on the side.

Cook's Tip

If you have leftover roast, try chopping some and combining it with whole-wheat pasta and broccoli with the sauce spooned on top. Or add a small amount of Dijon mustard to the sauce and use it as a dipping sauce for a sandwich of pork slices on whole-wheat bread or buns.

calories 179
protein 13 g
carbohydrates 25 g
 fiber 1 g
 sugars 17 g
cholesterol 36 mg
total fat 3.0 g
 saturated 1.0 g
 polyunsaturated 0.5 g
 monounsaturated 1.5 g
sodium 51 mg

dietary exchange
1/2 fruit
1 other carbohydrate
2 lean meat

Easy Barbecue-Sauced
Pork Chops

Serves 4

This a great recipe to keep on hand for those days when energy is low, but the need for comfort is high.

1/3 cup barbecue sauce

2 tablespoons all-fruit blackberry spread

2 teaspoons low-sodium Worcestershire sauce

1 teaspoon grated orange zest

1/2 teaspoon grated peeled gingerroot

4 boneless center-cut pork loin chops (about 4 ounces each), all visible fat discarded

In a small bowl, stir together all the ingredients except the pork.

Heat a 12-inch nonstick skillet over medium-high heat. Cook the pork for 4 minutes on each side, or until no longer pink in the center. Transfer the pork to a plate.

Add barbecue-sauce mixture to the skillet (no need to wipe clean first). Bring to a boil over medium-high heat, scraping the bottom of the pan. Reduce the heat to medium. Cook the sauce for 2 minutes, or until reduced to 1/4 cup.

To serve, spoon the sauce over the pork.

calories 207
protein 26 g
carbohydrates 8 g
  fiber 0 g
  sugars 6 g
cholesterol 62 mg
total fat 7.0 g
  saturated 2.5 g
  polyunsaturated 1.0 g
  monounsaturated 3.0 g
sodium 226 mg

dietary exchange
1/2 fruit
3 lean meat

Pork Chops Stuffed with Apricots and Walnuts

Serves 4

Slightly sweet, slightly tart filling permeates pork chops as they cook, and walnuts add a delicate crunch. Serve with whole-wheat bow-tie noodles and steamed green beans garnished with lemon zest.

4   boneless pork loin chops (about 4 ounces each), all visible fat discarded
1/2 cup chopped dried apricots
2   tablespoons chopped walnuts
1   tablespoon light brown sugar
1   tablespoon cider vinegar
1   teaspoon dried marjoram, crumbled
1/2 cup unsweetened apple juice
1/2 cup fat-free, low-sodium chicken broth, such as on page 45
1   tablespoon light maple syrup
1/4 teaspoon pepper

With a sharp knife, make a horizontal cut into the side of each pork chop to form a pocket for stuffing. Be careful not to cut through to the other side.

In a small bowl, stir together the apricots, walnuts, brown sugar, vinegar, and marjoram. Spoon about 2 tablespoons of this mixture into the pocket of each pork chop. Secure with wooden toothpicks.

Heat a large nonstick skillet over medium heat. Brown the pork chops for 1 minute on each side, or until golden brown. (Watch carefully. The brown sugar in the filling may seep out, which can make the pork burn more easily.)

Leaving the pork in the skillet, stir in the remaining ingredients. Increase the heat to medium-high and bring to a simmer. Reduce the heat and simmer, covered, for 30 minutes, or until the pork is no longer pink in the center and the stuffing is warmed through. Transfer to a platter. Discard the toothpicks. Cover the platter with aluminum foil.

Bring the cooking liquid to a simmer over medium-high heat. Reduce the heat and simmer for 5 minutes, or until the liquid is reduced to about 1/2 cup.

To serve, pour the sauce over the pork chops.

calories 277
protein 27 g
carbohydrates 22 g
  fiber 2 g
  sugars 19 g
cholesterol 62 mg
total fat 9.5 g
  saturated 2.5 g
  polyunsaturated 2.5 g
  monounsaturated 3.5 g
sodium 70 mg

dietary exchange
1 fruit
1/2 other carbohydrate
3 lean meat

Jamaican Jerk Pork and Vegetables with Mango-Coconut Rice

Serves 6

Jamaican jerk seasoning infuses this stewed pork dish with its rich flavor.

4 boneless pork loin chops (about 4 ounces each), all visible fat discarded, cut into ³/₄-inch cubes

2 teaspoons salt-free Jamaican jerk seasoning

¹/₂ medium onion, cut into 1-inch pieces

1 cup fat-free, low-sodium chicken broth, such as on page 45

2 teaspoons low-salt soy sauce

29-ounce can sweet potatoes in light syrup, rinsed and drained

3 cups frozen green beans

4 medium green onions (green and white parts), cut into 1-inch pieces

6-ounce can pineapple juice (about ³/₄ cup)

¹/₂ cup light coconut milk

1 cup uncooked instant brown rice

1 large mango, chopped

calories 407
protein 22 g
carbohydrates 65 g
  fiber 8 g
  sugars 38 g
cholesterol 42 mg
total fat 6.5 g
  saturated 2.5 g
  polyunsaturated 1.0 g
  monounsaturated 2.5 g
sodium 223 mg

dietary exchange
3 starch
1 fruit
1 vegetable
2 lean meat

Lightly rub the jerk seasoning into the pork.

Heat a large nonstick saucepan over medium-high heat. Brown the pork for 4 to 6 minutes, stirring occasionally.

Stir in the onion. Cook for 2 to 3 minutes, or until the onion is soft, stirring occasionally.

Stir in the broth and soy sauce. Bring to a simmer. Reduce the heat and simmer, covered, for 30 minutes, or until the pork is no longer pink in the center.

Stir in the sweet potatoes, beans, and green onions. Simmer, covered, for 8 to 10 minutes, or until the beans are tender. Set aside.

Meanwhile, in a medium saucepan, bring the pineapple juice and coconut milk to a simmer, covered, over medium-high heat.

Stir in the rice and mango. Reduce the heat and simmer, covered, for 10 minutes. Remove from the heat and let stand for 5 minutes. Fluff the mixture.

Serve the pork mixture over the rice.

Boneless Pork Ribs with Black Cherry Barbecue Sauce

Serves 4

If you crave tender pork ribs, you'll enjoy this boneless version. Lean pork loin with a zesty rub is braised to perfection and served with kicked-up barbecue sauce.

1/2 teaspoon ground cumin
1/2 teaspoon chili powder
1/2 teaspoon onion powder
1/2 teaspoon garlic powder
1/4 teaspoon pepper
 1 pound boneless pork loin chops, all visible fat discarded, cut into 16 1-inch-wide strips

Vegetable oil spray
1/4 cup barbecue sauce
1/4 cup all-fruit black cherry spread
 1 cup beer (light, regular, or nonalcoholic) or fat-free, low-sodium chicken broth, such as on page 45

In a medium bowl, stir together the cumin, chili powder, onion powder, garlic powder, and pepper. Add the pork. With a spoon or tongs, coat with the seasoning mix.

Heat a large skillet over medium-high heat. Remove from the heat and lightly spray with vegetable oil spray (being careful not to spray near a gas flame). Cook the pork for 2 to 3 minutes on each side, or until browned.

Pour the beer into the skillet. Bring to a simmer. Reduce the heat and simmer, covered, for 1 hour to 1 hour 30 minutes, or until desired tenderness (no stirring needed).

Using a slotted spoon, transfer the pork to a plate and cover with aluminum foil to keep warm.

Stir the barbecue sauce and jam into the beer. Cook over medium-low heat for 2 to 3 minutes, or until the mixture is warmed through, stirring occasionally.

To serve, spoon the sauce over the pork.

calories 241
protein 26 g
carbohydrates 13 g
 fiber 0 g
 sugars 10 g
cholesterol 62 mg
total fat 7.0 g
 saturated 2.5 g
 polyunsaturated 1.0 g
 monounsaturated 3.0 g
sodium 183 mg

dietary exchange
1 other carbohydrate
3 lean meat

Jollof Rice

Serves 6 (without optional ingredients)

Popular in western Africa, this dish will be a hit in your home as well.

1 fresh jalapeño

1 pound boneless center-cut pork loin chops (about 4 ounces each), all visible fat discarded, cut into ³/₄-inch cubes

1 medium bell pepper, diced (any color) (optional)

1 large carrot, thinly sliced (optional)

1 medium onion, chopped

2 medium garlic cloves, minced

2 cups fat-free, low-sodium chicken broth, such as on page 45

14.5-ounce can no-salt-added diced tomatoes, undrained

1 cup water

¹/₄ cup no-salt-added tomato paste

¹/₄ cup diced cooked low-sodium, low-fat ham (about 2 ounces)

1 teaspoon curry powder

¹/₂ teaspoon salt

¹/₄ teaspoon black pepper

1 bay leaf

2 cups uncooked quick-cooking brown rice

2 cups frozen green beans (optional)

1 cup frozen green peas (optional)

Garnishes (optional)

¹/₄ cup snipped parsley

1 cup chopped cooked cabbage

Whites of 4 large hard-cooked eggs

Wearing gloves, discard the seeds and ribs of the jalapeño. Dice the jalapeño. Set aside.

Heat a large nonstick saucepan or Dutch oven over medium-high heat. Cook the pork for 5 to 6 minutes, or until browned, stirring occasionally.

Stir in the bell pepper, carrot, onion, and garlic. Cook for 2 to 3 minutes, or until the onion is soft, stirring occasionally.

Stir in the broth, undrained tomatoes, water, tomato paste, ham, jalapeño, curry powder, salt, black pepper, and bay leaf. Simmer, covered, for 30 minutes to 1 hour, or until the pork is the desired tenderness.

Stir in the rice, beans, and peas. Simmer, covered, for 10 minutes, or until the rice is tender.

Put each garnish in a bowl. Serve with the pork.

calories 275
protein 23 g
carbohydrates 32 g
fiber 4 g
sugars 4 g
cholesterol 46 mg
total fat 6.0 g
saturated 1.5 g
polyunsaturated 1.0 g
monounsaturated 2.5 g
sodium 349 mg

dietary exchange
1¹/₂ starch
1¹/₂ vegetable
2¹/₂ lean meat

Pork Stir-Fry
with Crunchy Noodles

Serves 4

Lightly browned ramen noodles provide crunch for this colorful stir-fry.

12 ounces boneless pork sirloin cutlets
2 tablespoons sugar
2 tablespoons low-salt soy sauce
2 tablespoons dry sherry, or
   1 tablespoon fresh lemon juice
   and 1 tablespoon water
1 1/2 tablespoons cider vinegar
1 teaspoon grated peeled gingerroot
1 teaspoon toasted sesame oil
1/8 teaspoon crushed red pepper flakes

3 ounces ramen noodles, broken into small pieces, seasoning packet discarded
1 medium yellow or red bell pepper, cut into thin strips
1 medium onion, cut into 1/2-inch wedges
1 medium garlic clove, minced
   Vegetable oil spray
3 ounces fresh snow peas, trimmed

If desired, put the pork in the freezer for 30 minutes for easier slicing. Discard all the visible fat from the pork. Cut the pork into thin slices.

In a small bowl, stir together the sugar, soy sauce, sherry, vinegar, gingerroot, sesame oil, and red pepper flakes. Set aside.

Heat a 12-inch nonstick skillet over medium-high heat. Cook the noodles for 2 to 3 minutes, or until beginning to brown, stirring constantly. Transfer to a plate.

Put the pork in the skillet. Cook for 3 minutes, or until no longer pink in the center and beginning to brown, stirring frequently. Transfer the pork to a separate plate.

Put the bell pepper, onion, and garlic in the skillet. Lightly spray the vegetables with vegetable oil spray. Cook for 4 minutes, or until beginning to brown, stirring frequently.

Stir in the snow peas. Cook for 1 minute.

Stir in the pork and any accumulated juices. Cook for 1 minute, stirring frequently.

To serve, stir the soy sauce mixture and spoon over the pork mixture. Sprinkle with the noodles.

calories 295
protein 22 g
carbohydrates 28 g
  fiber 2 g
  sugars 11 g
cholesterol 54 mg
total fat 10.0 g
  saturated 4.0 g
  polyunsaturated 2.0 g
  monounsaturated 3.5 g
sodium 325 mg

dietary exchange
1 1/2 starch
1 vegetable
2 1/2 lean meat

Louisiana Skillet Pork

Serves 4

Deeply browned veggies with a hint of olive oil complement these Cajun-seasoned pork chops.

4 boneless center-cut pork chops (about 4 ounces each), all visible fat discarded
1 teaspoon Cajun seasoning
   Vegetable oil spray
1 cup frozen whole-kernel corn
1 medium red bell pepper, chopped
1 small zucchini, chopped

$^{1}/_{2}$ cup finely chopped onion
1 medium rib of celery, finely chopped
$^{1}/_{4}$ teaspoon black pepper
1 teaspoon olive oil (extra-virgin preferred)
$^{1}/_{2}$ teaspoon salt

Sprinkle the pork on both sides with the Cajun seasoning.

Heat a 12-inch nonstick skillet over medium-high heat. Cook the pork for 6 minutes on each side, or until no longer pink in the center. Remove from the heat. Transfer to a plate (don't scrape the skillet). Cover the plate with aluminum foil to keep warm.

Lightly spray any browned bits in the skillet with vegetable oil spray. Return to the heat. Cook the corn, bell pepper, zucchini, onion, celery, and black pepper for 4 minutes, or until the celery is tender-crisp and the vegetables begin to brown on the edges, stirring frequently. Remove from the heat.

Stir in the oil and salt.

To serve, place each pork chop on a plate. Spoon the vegetable mixture over the pork or to the side.

Cook's Tip

Be sure to remove the skillet from the heat before adding the olive oil so you get the maximum impact of the oil.

calories 229
protein 26 g
carbohydrates 14 g
  fiber 3 g
  sugars 3 g
cholesterol 65 mg
total fat 8.0 g
  saturated 2.5 g
  polyunsaturated 1.0 g
  monounsaturated 4.0 g
sodium 469 mg

dietary exchange
$^{1}/_{2}$ starch
1 vegetable
3 lean meat

Armenian Lamb Casserole

Serves 4

Tender chunks of lamb, cubes of vegetables, and lots of seasoning make this Middle Eastern dish a real winner.

1 pound lean lamb from loin or shoulder arm chop
Vegetable oil spray
1 teaspoon acceptable vegetable oil
1 medium onion, sliced
1 medium garlic clove, minced
1 cup canned no-salt-added tomatoes, undrained
1 medium eggplant, cut into cubes

1 medium green bell pepper, coarsely chopped
2 medium carrots, sliced
2 small zucchini, cut into cubes
$1/2$ cup sliced okra (6 to 7 small pods) (optional)
3 slices lemon
$1/2$ teaspoon paprika
$1/8$ teaspoon ground cumin
$1/8$ teaspoon pepper, or to taste

Remove and discard all the visible fat from the lamb. Cut the lamb into bite-size cubes.

Heat a stockpot, Dutch oven, or large, deep skillet over medium-high heat. Remove from the heat and lightly spray with vegetable oil spray (being careful not to spray near a gas flame). Pour the oil into the pot and swirl to coat the bottom. Thoroughly brown the lamb cubes on all sides, about 10 minutes, turning occasionally.

Stir in the onion and garlic. Cook for 3 to 4 minutes, or until slightly browned.

Stir in the undrained tomatoes. Reduce the heat to low. Cook, covered, for 1 hour, stirring occasionally and adding a small amount of water if necessary.

Preheat the oven to 350°F.

Stir the remaining ingredients into the pot. Bring to a boil. Transfer the mixture to a 3-quart ovenproof ceramic or glass casserole dish. (Don't use plain cast iron. It will discolor the vegetables.)

Bake, covered, for 1 hour, or until the vegetables are tender.

calories 271
protein 28 g
carbohydrates 22 g
  fiber 7 g
  sugars 13 g
cholesterol 73 mg
total fat 9.0 g
  saturated 3.0 g
  polyunsaturated 1.0 g
  monounsaturated 3.5 g
sodium 151 mg

dietary exchange
4$1/2$ vegetable
3 lean meat

Moroccan-Style Lamb with Couscous

Serves 4

Seasonings such as ginger, cumin, and garlic—along with tart lemon quarters and kalamata olives—make this lamb dish so tasty that you'll enjoy preparing it on a regular basis. The bonus juices capture all the flavors and soak into the fluffy couscous.

1 pound lean boneless lamb stew meat (from leg, loin, or shoulder arm chops), all visible fat discarded
1 cup baby carrots
1 medium onion, quartered
1 cup fat-free, low-sodium chicken broth, such as on page 45
1 medium lemon, quartered and seeded
1/4 cup chopped kalamata olives
2 medium garlic cloves, minced
1 teaspoon paprika
1 teaspoon ground cumin
1/2 teaspoon ground ginger
1/4 teaspoon ground turmeric (optional)
1/2 cup coarsely snipped fresh cilantro
1 cup uncooked couscous

Heat a large nonstick saucepan or Dutch oven over medium-high heat. Cook the lamb for 4 to 5 minutes, or until browned on the outside, stirring occasionally.

Stir in the carrots and onion. Cook for 2 to 3 minutes, or until the vegetables are tender-crisp.

Stir in the broth, lemon, olives, garlic, paprika, cumin, ginger, and turmeric. Bring to a simmer.

Reduce the heat and simmer, covered, for 1 hour. Stir in the cilantro. Simmer for 20 to 30 minutes, or until the lamb is tender.

Meanwhile, prepare the couscous using the package directions, omitting the salt and oil. Keep warm until ready to serve.

To serve, spoon the couscous onto each plate. Discard the lemon quarters from the lamb mixture. Ladle the lamb mixture over the couscous.

calories 382
protein 30 g
carbohydrates 42 g
 fiber 4 g
 sugars 5 g
cholesterol 74 mg
total fat 9.5 g
 saturated 2.5 g
 polyunsaturated 1.0 g
 monounsaturated 4.5 g
sodium 271 mg

dietary exchange
2½ starch
1 vegetable
3 lean meat

Venison Stew

Serves 8

If you have an excess of venison from a hunting trip, whether to the woods or a specialty grocery store, this simple recipe is a fine way to use it.

Vegetable oil spray
2 pounds breast or shoulder venison
2 tablespoons all-purpose flour
6 cups water or fat-free, no-salt-added beef broth, such as on page 44

$1/2$ teaspoon pepper
4 medium potatoes, peeled and diced
4 medium carrots, diced
4 medium onions, diced
2 medium turnips, diced

Preheat the broiler. Lightly spray a broiler pan and rack with vegetable oil spray.

Remove and discard all the visible fat from the venison. Cut the venison into 1-inch cubes.

Broil the venison about 6 inches from the heat for 15 to 20 minutes, or until brown on all sides, turning occasionally.

Put the meat in a large, heavy nonstick skillet. Sprinkle with the flour. Cook over medium-high heat for 2 minutes, stirring constantly.

Add the water and pepper. Bring to a boil, stirring constantly. Reduce the heat and simmer, covered, for 1 hour 30 minutes to 2 hours, or until the meat is just tender.

Stir in the remaining ingredients. Simmer, covered, for 30 minutes, or until the meat and vegetables are tender.

calories 247
protein 30 g
carbohydrates 27 g
  fiber 5 g
  sugars 10 g
cholesterol 96 mg
total fat 3.0 g
  saturated 1.0 g
  polyunsaturated 0.5 g
  monounsaturated 1.0 g
sodium 99 mg

dietary exchange
1 starch
$2^{1/2}$ vegetable
3 very lean meat

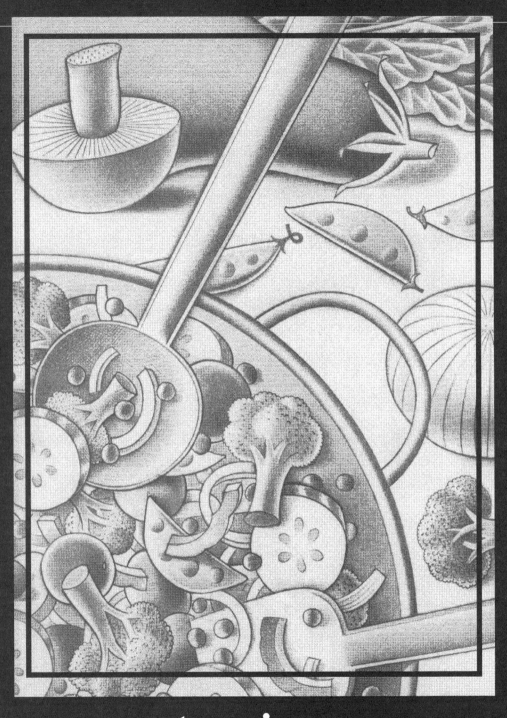

vegetarian entrées

Grilled Vegetable Pizza
with Herbs and Cheese

Serves 8

Fresh basil, goat cheese, and portobello mushrooms lend a gourmet touch to this grilled pizza.

2 cups all-purpose flour
1 cup whole-wheat flour
1 tablespoon olive oil
1 teaspoon salt-free Italian seasoning
 ¼-ounce package fast-rising yeast
1 cup warm water (120°F to 130°F)
 Vegetable oil spray
1 medium red onion, peeled, halved crosswise

2 medium portobello mushrooms, stems discarded
1 pound asparagus, trimmed (about 16 medium spears)
2 medium tomatoes (one red and one yellow preferred)
¼ cup coarsely chopped fresh basil leaves
4 ounces soft goat cheese

In a large bowl, stir together both flours. Remove 1 cup mixture.

Whisk the oil, Italian seasoning, and yeast into the remaining flour.

Pour in the warm water. Stir for 30 seconds. Gradually add some of the reserved flour mixture, beating with a spoon after each addition, until the dough starts to pull away from the side of the bowl. Add more flour as necessary to make the dough easy to handle (not sticky).

Lightly flour a flat surface. Turn out the dough. Gradually knead in enough of the remaining flour mixture until the dough is smooth and elastic, 6 to 8 minutes. Cover the dough with a dry dish towel. Let rest for 20 minutes. (You can cover the bowl with plastic wrap and refrigerate the dough for up to 24 hours. Remove the dough from the refrigerator 1 hour before shaping and grilling.)

While the dough is resting, lightly spray a large grill rack with vegetable oil spray. Preheat the grill on medium-high.

calories 242
protein 10 g
carbohydrates 41 g
 fiber 5 g
 sugars 4 g
cholesterol 5 mg
total fat 4.5 g
 saturated 2.0 g
 polyunsaturated 0.5 g
 monounsaturated 2.0 g
sodium 46 mg

dietary exchange
2½ starch
1 vegetable
½ lean meat
1 fat

Lightly spray all sides of the onion, mushrooms, and asparagus with vegetable oil spray.

Grill the onion for 10 minutes on one side. Turn the onion over.

Add the mushrooms with the cap side down. Grill for 5 minutes. Turn only the mushrooms.

Add the asparagus. Grill for 3 minutes. Turn only the asparagus. Grill for 2 to 3 minutes, or until all the vegetables are tender.

Transfer the vegetables to a cutting board. Let cool for 5 minutes. Coarsely chop the onion, dice the mushrooms, and cut the asparagus into 1-inch slices. Transfer to a large bowl.

Gently stir the tomatoes and basil into the vegetable mixture.

Meanwhile, lightly spray two medium baking sheets with vegetable oil spray. Divide the rested dough in half. Roll one half into a 9-inch round on a baking sheet. Repeat with the remaining dough on the second baking sheet. Lightly spray the top of the dough with vegetable oil spray. Put one of the dough rounds with the sprayed side down on the grill rack.

Grill, covered, for 3 to 4 minutes (watching carefully so it does not burn), or until golden brown. Using two large spatulas (or a spatula and tongs), turn the crust over. Spread half the vegetable mixture over the crust. Sprinkle with half the goat cheese.

Grill, covered, for 3 to 4 minutes, or until the crust is golden brown on the bottom, the vegetables are warmed through, and the cheese is slightly melted.

Using tongs, grasp the pizza and slide it onto a baking sheet. Transfer the pizza to a cooling rack. Let cool for 5 minutes before cutting into 4 slices.

Repeat with the remaining dough, vegetables, and cheese.

Artichoke-Tomato Pizza

Serves 6

By using refrigerated pizza dough, you can get dinner on the table in a flash.

Vegetable oil spray
1 refrigerated pizza crust in tube can
4 ounces part-skim mozzarella cheese or fat-free mozzarella-flavor soy cheese, shredded
2 tablespoons grated Parmesan or Romano cheese
3 medium Italian plum tomatoes, chopped

8-ounce package frozen artichoke hearts, thawed, drained, and chopped
1/2 cup thinly sliced red onion
1 teaspoon balsamic vinegar
1 medium garlic clove, minced
1/2 teaspoon salt-free Italian seasoning, crumbled

Preheat the oven using the pizza crust package directions. Line a baking sheet with aluminum foil. Lightly spray the foil with vegetable oil spray. Spread the pizza crust on the foil.

Bake for 7 minutes.

Sprinkle the mozzarella and Parmesan over the crust.

In a medium bowl, stir together the remaining ingredients except the Italian seasoning. Arrange the mixture on the cheese. Sprinkle with the herb seasoning.

Bake for 8 to 10 minutes, or until the cheese is bubbly.

Cook's Tip on Italian Plum Tomatoes

Also called Roma tomatoes, Italian plum tomatoes are shaped more like pears or eggs than plums. They are often tastier and less expensive than "regular" tomatoes.

calories 227
protein 12 g
carbohydrates 30 g
 fiber 4 g
 sugars 5 g
cholesterol 15 mg
total fat 7.0 g
 saturated 3.0 g
 polyunsaturated 0.0 g
 monounsaturated 0.5 g
sodium 527 mg

dietary exchange
1 1/2 starch
1 vegetable
1 1/2 medium-fat meat

Zucchini Linguini
with Walnuts

Serves 4

The generous amount of toasted walnuts gives this one-dish meal a warm and rustic character—just right for a cold or rainy night.

4 ounces dried linguini
2 medium zucchini, sliced
1 medium onion, thinly sliced
8 ounces sliced button mushrooms
1 tablespoon dried oregano, crumbled
4 medium garlic cloves, minced

1/4 teaspoon crushed red pepper flakes
Vegetable oil spray
1/2 cup chopped walnuts, dry-roasted
2 teaspoons olive oil (extra-virgin preferred)
1 teaspoon salt

Prepare the pasta using the package directions, omitting the salt and oil. Drain, reserving 1/2 cup pasta water.

Meanwhile, heat a 12-inch nonstick skillet over medium-high heat. Cook the zucchini and onion for 8 minutes, or until beginning to lightly brown on the edges, stirring frequently. Transfer to a plate.

Put the mushrooms, oregano, garlic, and red pepper flakes in the skillet. Lightly spray with vegetable oil spray. Cook for 4 minutes, or until beginning to lightly brown.

Stir the zucchini mixture into the mushroom mixture. Stir in the pasta and reserved pasta water. Cook for 30 seconds, or until most of the liquid has evaporated. Remove from the heat.

Stir in the walnuts, oil, and salt. Toss gently.

calories 275
protein 10 g
carbohydrates 34 g
  fiber 5 g
  sugars 6 g
cholesterol 0 mg
total fat 13.0 g
  saturated 1.5 g
  polyunsaturated 7.5 g
  monounsaturated 3.0 g
sodium 591 mg

dietary exchange
1 1/2 starch
2 vegetable
2 fat

Pecan-Topped Pasta with Vegetables

Serves 4

This pasta is piled high with colorful, sizzling veggies and a sprinkling of toasted pecans.

6 ounces dried rotini (whole-wheat preferred)
1½ cups finely chopped onion
1 medium red bell pepper, thinly sliced

1 cup matchstick-size carrot strips
Vegetable oil spray
½ teaspoon ground cumin
½ teaspoon salt
1½ ounces pecan pieces, dry-roasted

Prepare the pasta using the package directions, omitting the salt and oil. Drain in a colander.

Put the onion, bell pepper, and carrots in a 12-inch nonstick skillet. Lightly spray the vegetables with vegetable oil spray. Cook for 8 minutes, or until the onion is deeply browned, stirring frequently.

Stir in the cumin and salt. Cook for 30 seconds.

To serve, put the pasta on plates. Top with the vegetable mixture. Sprinkle the pecans over all.

calories 266
protein 9 g
carbohydrates 44 g
  fiber 8 g
  sugars 9 g
cholesterol 0 mg
total fat 8.5 g
  saturated 0.5 g
  polyunsaturated 2.5 g
  monounsaturated 4.0 g
sodium 309 mg

dietary exchange
2 starch
3 vegetable
3 fat

Spaghetti Cheese
Amandine

Serves 4

A textured sauce of cottage cheese, green peas, green onions, and Parmesan cheese tops bite-size pieces of spaghetti. Serve with sliced tomatoes, a tossed salad, or fresh fruit.

8 ounces dried spaghetti, broken into small pieces	2 tablespoons shredded or grated Parmesan cheese
1 cup frozen green peas, thawed	2 tablespoons fat-free milk
1 cup fat-free or low-fat cottage cheese	$1/2$ teaspoon salt-free Italian seasoning, crumbled
2 medium green onions (green part only), sliced	1 tablespoon light tub margarine Pepper to taste
	$1/4$ cup slivered almonds, dry-roasted

Prepare the spaghetti using the package directions, omitting the salt and oil. Drain well.

Meanwhile, in a medium bowl, stir together the peas, cottage cheese, green onions, Parmesan, milk, and herb seasoning.

In a large skillet, melt the margarine over medium-low heat. Stir in the spaghetti.

When the spaghetti is warm, stir in the cottage cheese mixture. Cook for 3 to 4 minutes, or until heated through, stirring occasionally.

To serve, stir in the pepper and sprinkle with the almonds.

calories 345
protein 19 g
carbohydrates 52 g
  fiber 4 g
  sugars 7 g
cholesterol 5 mg
total fat 6.5 g
  saturated 1.0 g
  polyunsaturated 1.5 g
  monounsaturated 3.0 g
sodium 306 mg

dietary exchange
$3^{1}/2$ starch
$1^{1}/2$ lean meat

Sesame-Peanut Pasta

Serves 4

This is so good—and quick, too! Serve it either hot or cold.

8 ounces dried spaghetti
2 medium green onions (green and white parts), thinly sliced
1/2 cup low-sodium vegetable broth, such as on page 46
3 tablespoons low-fat peanut butter

1 tablespoon plus 1 teaspoon cider vinegar or plain rice vinegar
1 teaspoon toasted sesame oil
1/8 to 1/4 teaspoon cayenne
1/8 teaspoon salt

Prepare the spaghetti using the package directions, omitting the salt and oil. Drain well.

Meanwhile, in a medium bowl, whisk together the remaining ingredients.

Transfer the spaghetti to a large platter. Stir the sauce into the spaghetti. Serve immediately for a hot entrée or cover and refrigerate for a cold entrée.

calories 275
protein 10 g
carbohydrates 45 g
  fiber 4 g
  sugars 4 g
cholesterol 0 mg
total fat 6.0 g
  saturated 1.0 g
  polyunsaturated 2.0 g
  monounsaturated 2.5 g
sodium 146 mg

dietary exchange
3 starch
1/2 very lean meat
1 fat

Spaghetti with
Zesty Marinara Sauce

Serves 8

This aromatic sauce turns any meal into an Italian feast. It freezes well for up to six months, so make extra for another time.

Zesty Marinara Sauce
- 1 teaspoon olive oil
- 1 large onion, finely chopped
- 2 large garlic cloves, crushed
  6-ounce can no-salt-added tomato paste
- 2 tablespoons minced fresh parsley
- 2 teaspoons sugar
- 1 1/4 teaspoons salt-free Italian seasoning, crumbled
- 1/2 teaspoon dried basil, crumbled
- 1/8 teaspoon salt
- 1/8 teaspoon crushed red pepper flakes, or to taste

- 1/4 teaspoon black pepper, or to taste
  14.5-ounce can no-salt-added tomatoes, crushed, undrained
- 1 cup water
  8-ounce can no-salt-added tomato sauce
- 1/4 cup dry red wine (regular or nonalcoholic)
- 1 medium bay leaf
  ❖
- 16 ounces dried spaghetti
- 1/2 cup shredded or grated Parmesan cheese

Heat a medium saucepan over medium-high heat. Pour the oil into the pan and swirl to coat the bottom. Cook the onion and garlic for 2 to 3 minutes, or until the onion is soft, stirring occasionally.

Whisk in the tomato paste, parsley, sugar, herb seasoning, basil, salt, red pepper flakes, and black pepper. Reduce the heat to medium-low and cook for 4 minutes, stirring often.

Stir in the remaining sauce ingredients. Increase the heat to high and bring to a boil. Reduce the heat and simmer, partially covered, for 1 to 1 hour 30 minutes. Remove the bay leaf.

Meanwhile, prepare the spaghetti using the package directions, omitting the salt and oil. Drain well. Stir in the Parmesan.

To serve, spoon the spaghetti onto plates. Ladle the sauce over the spaghetti.

calories 293
protein 11 g
carbohydrates 54 g
  fiber 4 g
  sugars 8 g
cholesterol 4 mg
total fat 3.0 g
  saturated 1.0 g
  polyunsaturated 0.5 g
  monounsaturated 1.0 g
sodium 195 mg

dietary exchange
3 starch
2 vegetable

Spaghetti with Perfect Pesto

Serves 6

This sauce is delicious—the mix of herbs is perfect!

12 ounces dried thin spaghetti

Pesto Sauce

2 cups firmly packed fresh spinach leaves (3 to 4 ounces)

1/2 cup firmly packed fresh basil leaves

1/2 cup firmly packed fresh parsley

1/4 cup low-sodium vegetable broth, such as on page 46

2 tablespoons pine nuts, dry-roasted

1/4 cup shredded or grated Parmesan cheese, or 2 tablespoons shredded or grated Parmesan cheese and 2 tablespoons shredded or grated Romano cheese

1 tablespoon olive oil

2 medium garlic cloves

Pepper to taste

1 to 2 tablespoons water (if needed)

Prepare the spaghetti using the package directions, omitting the salt and oil. Drain well.

Meanwhile, in a food processor or blender, process the sauce ingredients until almost smooth. If the mixture is too thick, add the water.

To serve, spoon the spaghetti onto plates. Ladle the sauce over the spaghetti.

Cook's Tip on Pine Nuts

Native to many parts of the world, pine nuts are the seeds found in the different varieties of pine tree. The difficulty in harvesting makes them rather expensive, but you use them in small quantities. Pine nuts—or pignoli—are traditionally used in pesto sauce. Also called piñons, they are very popular in southwestern cuisine. Store them in the refrigerator or freezer to keep them from turning rancid.

calories 265
protein 10 g
carbohydrates 44 g
 fiber 2 g
 sugars 2 g
cholesterol 2 mg
total fat 5.5 g
 saturated 1.0 g
 polyunsaturated 1.0 g
 monounsaturated 2.5 g
sodium 78 mg

dietary exchange
3 starch
1/2 fat

Thai-Style Vegetables with Pasta

Serves 4

Popular ingredients of Thai cuisine—such as fish sauce, with its salty-fermented flavor—blend well with whole-wheat pasta in this one-skillet dish. Serve it with juicy grapefruit slices on the side.

1 teaspoon acceptable vegetable oil
1/2 medium red bell pepper, cut into 1-inch squares
1 cup sliced shiitake mushrooms (3.2-ounce package)
2 medium shallots, coarsely chopped
1 1/2 cups low-sodium vegetable broth, such as on page 46
2 teaspoons fish sauce or low-salt soy sauce
2 teaspoons fresh lime juice
1 teaspoon light brown sugar

1 teaspoon ground dried lemongrass or 1 tablespoon finely chopped fresh lemongrass (cut from bottom end of stalk)
1/4 to 1/2 teaspoon dried crushed red pepper flakes
2 tablespoons chopped fresh basil leaves or 1/2 teaspoon dried, crumbled
3 ounces dried whole-wheat angel hair pasta
2 medium stalks of bok choy (green and white parts), coarsely chopped
1 cup fresh or frozen snow peas, trimmed if fresh

Heat a large skillet over medium-high heat. Pour the oil into the skillet and swirl to coat the bottom. Cook the bell pepper, mushrooms, and shallots for 2 to 3 minutes, or until tender-crisp, stirring occasionally.

Stir in the broth, fish sauce, lime juice, brown sugar, lemongrass, and red pepper flakes. If using dried basil, add here. Bring to a simmer. Reduce the heat and simmer, covered, for 3 minutes.

Stir in the pasta. Simmer, covered, for 4 to 5 minutes, or until the pasta is tender.

Stir in the bok choy, snow peas, and fresh basil. Simmer, covered, for 1 minute, or until the vegetables are tender-crisp.

calories 116
protein 5 g
carbohydrates 22 g
 fiber 4 g
 sugars 4 g
cholesterol 0 mg
total fat 1.5 g
 saturated 0.0 g
 polyunsaturated 0.5 g
 monounsaturated 0.5 g
sodium 249 mg

dietary exchange
1 starch
1 1/2 vegetable

Two-Cheese
Sour Cream Noodles

Serves 4

You'll need to save the empty containers to prove you didn't use high-fat ingredients to make this rich dish. For a nonvegetarian entrée, add cooked ground beef or steamed shrimp.

Vegetable oil spray
8 ounces dried yolk-free noodles
1½ cups fat-free or light sour cream
1 cup fat-free or low-fat cottage cheese, drained
¼ cup fat-free milk
2 medium garlic cloves, minced

1 teaspoon low-sodium Worcestershire sauce
⅛ teaspoon white pepper
¼ cup shredded or grated Parmesan cheese
1 tablespoon poppy seeds

Preheat the oven to 350°F. Lightly spray a 2-quart casserole dish with vegetable oil spray.

Prepare the noodles using the package directions, omitting the salt and oil. Drain well.

Meanwhile, in a large bowl, stir together the sour cream, cottage cheese, milk, garlic, Worcestershire, and pepper.

Stir in the noodles. Spoon into the casserole dish.

Bake, uncovered, for 15 minutes. Sprinkle with the Parmesan and poppy seeds. Bake for 5 minutes.

calories 396
protein 23 g
carbohydrates 64 g
  fiber 3 g
  sugars 10 g
cholesterol 21 mg
total fat 3.0 g
  saturated 1.0 g
  polyunsaturated 0.5 g
  monounsaturated 0.5 g
sodium 389 mg

dietary exchange
4 starch
2 very lean meat

Three-Cheese
Macaroni

Serves 6

This jazzed-up version of an old favorite is easy to put together. You don't even have to cook the macaroni before adding it to the casserole.

Vegetable oil spray
16-ounce can tomato puree
1 cup water
2 teaspoons salt-free Italian seasoning, crumbled
2 medium garlic cloves, minced
24 ounces fat-free or low-fat cottage cheese

1 large shallot, finely chopped
1 medium garlic clove, minced
8 ounces dried elbow macaroni (about 2 cups)
2 tablespoons shredded or grated Parmesan cheese
2 ounces fat-free or part-skim mozzarella cheese, sliced

Preheat the oven to 350°F. Lightly spray a 9-inch square casserole dish with vegetable oil spray.

In a medium bowl, stir together the tomato puree, water, herb seasoning, and 2 garlic cloves.

In another medium bowl, stir together the cottage cheese, shallot, and 1 garlic clove.

Spoon one third of the tomato mixture over the bottom of the casserole dish. In order, layer half the macaroni, all the cottage cheese mixture, one third of the tomato mixture, all the Parmesan, the remaining macaroni, and the remaining tomato mixture.

Bake, covered, for 1 hour. Uncover and top with the mozzarella. Bake, uncovered, for 5 minutes, or until the cheese is melted.

Let the casserole stand for 10 minutes before serving.

calories 271
protein 23 g
carbohydrates 41 g
  fiber 3 g
  sugars 9 g
cholesterol 8 mg
total fat 1.0 g
  saturated 0.5 g
  polyunsaturated 0.5 g
  monounsaturated 0.0 g
sodium 526 mg

dietary exchange
2 starch
2 vegetable
2 very lean meat

Mediterranean Linguini

Serves 4

If you're a fan of kalamata olives and capers, you'll rave about this easy, all-in-one dinner.

Vegetable oil spray
6 ounces dried linguini
1 medium green bell pepper, thinly sliced
1 medium red bell pepper, thinly sliced
1 medium onion, cut into 1/4-inch wedges
1 medium zucchini, cut lengthwise into eighths, then crosswise into 2-inch pieces

8 sun-dried tomato halves, chopped
1/4 cup finely snipped fresh parsley
3 tablespoons capers, rinsed and drained
12 kalamata olives, chopped
1 1/2 tablespoons dried basil, crumbled
1 medium garlic clove, minced
3/4 cup shredded fat-free or part-skim mozzarella cheese
2 tablespoons shredded or grated Parmesan cheese

Preheat the broiler. Lightly spray a broiler pan with vegetable oil spray.

Prepare the pasta using the package directions, omitting the salt and oil. Drain, reserving 1/2 cup pasta water.

Meanwhile, arrange the bell peppers, onion, and zucchini in a single layer in the broiler pan. Lightly spray the vegetables with vegetable oil spray.

Broil for 10 minutes. Stir. Broil for 4 minutes, or until the vegetables begin to deeply brown on the edges.

Meanwhile, in a small bowl, stir together the sun-dried tomatoes, parsley, capers, olives, basil, and garlic.

In a large, shallow bowl, gently stir together the pasta, reserved pasta water, broiled vegetables, and tomato mixture.

Add the mozzarella and Parmesan. Toss gently.

calories 298
protein 16 g
carbohydrates 48 g
  fiber 6 g
  sugars 8 g
cholesterol 6 mg
total fat 5.0 g
  saturated 1.0 g
  polyunsaturated 1.0 g
  monounsaturated 2.5 g
sodium 668 mg

dietary exchange
2 starch
3 vegetable
1 lean meat

Cook's Tip

Broiling the vegetables longer on one side allows them to brown to a deep rich color.

Tortellini and Vegetable Kebabs with Italian Pesto Salsa

Serves 6

These make-ahead kebabs of pasta and vegetables are perfect party food. Once assembled, they are ready to go without any last-minute cooking.

Kebabs
24 fresh cheese tortellini
   (about 1/2 9-ounce package)
24 small broccoli florets
24 cherry tomatoes

Pesto Salsa
   14.5-ounce can no-salt-added
   diced tomatoes, undrained

¹/₂ cup loosely packed fresh basil
   leaves
2 tablespoons shredded or grated
   Parmesan cheese
2 tablespoons pine nuts or walnuts,
   dry-roasted
1 tablespoon balsamic vinegar
1 medium garlic clove, minced

Prepare the tortellini using the package directions, omitting the salt and oil. One minute before the end of their cooking time, stir in the broccoli. Cook for 1 minute, or until the broccoli is tender-crisp. Drain in a colander.

Using twelve 8-inch wooden skewers, thread 2 tortellini, 2 broccoli florets, and 2 cherry tomatoes alternately on each skewer. (You may cover and refrigerate the kebabs for up to two days.)

For the pesto salsa, in a food processor or blender, process all salsa ingredients for 30 to 40 seconds, or until slightly chunky. Transfer to a serving bowl.

To serve, place the bowl of salsa in the middle of a platter and arrange the kebabs around it.

calories 130
protein 7 g
carbohydrates 20 g
  fiber 4 g
  sugars 6 g
cholesterol 10 mg
total fat 4.0 g
  saturated 1.5 g
  polyunsaturated 0.5 g
  monounsaturated 0.5 g
sodium 153 mg

dietary exchange
1 starch
1 vegetable
¹/₂ fat

Vegetable Biryani

Serves 6

Add a cucumber salad, such as a soothing raita, and you have a wonderful quick-and-easy meal.

2 cups uncooked long-grain rice (basmati preferred)

1/2 fresh jalapeño, finely chopped

2 tablespoons plus 1 teaspoon acceptable vegetable oil

1/2 tablespoon cumin seeds

1 large potato, peeled and cut into 1/2-inch pieces

2 medium carrots, cut into 1/2-inch pieces

12 to 14 cauliflower florets

3 tablespoons finely chopped fresh cilantro

1/2 tablespoon ground cumin

1 teaspoon salt

1 teaspoon finely grated peeled gingerroot

1 medium garlic clove, mashed

1/2 teaspoon ground turmeric

1/4 to 1/2 teaspoon cayenne

2³/4 cups water

Put the rice in a sieve and rinse under running water. Drain and put in a medium bowl. Add enough water to cover. Let soak for 20 minutes. Drain again in the sieve. Leave in the sieve for 20 minutes to soften.

Meanwhile, wearing gloves, discard the seeds and ribs of the jalapeño. Finely chop the jalapeño.

When the rice has softened, heat a Dutch oven or large, heavy saucepan over medium-high heat. Pour the oil into the pan and swirl to coat the bottom. Cook the cumin seeds for 5 to 6 seconds, or until they pop open.

Stir in the potato, carrots, and cauliflower. Cook for 1 minute. Reduce the heat to medium.

Stir in the rice and the remaining ingredients except the water. Cook for 2 minutes.

Stir in the water. Bring to a boil. Reduce the heat and simmer, covered, for 25 minutes. Turn off the heat and let stand, covered, for 5 minutes. Don't stir.

Fluff with a fork before serving.

calories 318
protein 6 g
carbohydrates 62 g
 fiber 3 g
 sugars 3 g
cholesterol 0 mg
total fat 6.0 g
 saturated 0.5 g
 polyunsaturated 1.5 g
 monounsaturated 3.5 g
sodium 412 mg

dietary exchange
4 starch
1/2 fat

Stuffed Peppers

Serves 8

Stuff bell pepper halves with a refreshing, crunchy combination of vegetables, rice, and water chestnuts. Experiment with different bell peppers—red, yellow, purple, orange, or white.

4 large bell peppers, any color or combination
1 teaspoon olive oil
2 medium tomatoes, chopped
1 medium yellow summer squash, diced
1 medium zucchini, diced
1 medium onion, diced

2 medium garlic cloves, minced
2 cups cooked brown rice
1/2 cup grated fat-free or low-fat Cheddar cheese
1/4 cup sliced water chestnuts, rinsed and drained (about 2 ounces)
1 cup no-salt-added tomato juice

Preheat the oven to 375°F.

Cut the peppers in half lengthwise, discarding the stems, ribs, and seeds.

Heat a large skillet over medium heat. Pour in the oil and swirl to coat the bottom. Cook the tomatoes, yellow squash, zucchini, onion, and garlic until the zucchini is tender-crisp, 3 to 4 minutes. Don't overcook.

In a medium bowl, stir together the rice, cheese, and water chestnuts. Gently stir into the skillet. Stuff the pepper halves with the vegetable mixture. Place in a 9-inch round or square casserole dish. Carefully pour tomato juice around the peppers.

Bake, uncovered, for 30 minutes.

calories 124
protein 6 g
carbohydrates 24 g
  fiber 4 g
  sugars 6 g
cholesterol 1 mg
total fat 1.5 g
  saturated 0.0 g
  polyunsaturated 0.5 g
  monounsaturated 0.5 g
sodium 63 mg

dietary exchange
1/2 starch
3 vegetable

Vegetarian Stir-Fry

Serves 4

Add some fresh vegetables, bamboo shoots, and seasonings to an already-prepared, already-tasty rice dish, and dinner is served.

3 tablespoons low-salt soy sauce
2½ teaspoons sugar
1 teaspoon low-sodium Worcestershire sauce
4 cups shredded cabbage (about 8 ounces)
1 large onion, chopped
1 medium carrot, shredded

8-ounce can bamboo shoots, rinsed and drained
2 medium garlic cloves, minced
1 teaspoon grated peeled gingerroot
1 tablespoon acceptable vegetable oil
3 cups reserved Water Chestnut and Bell Pepper Rice (page 318)

In a small bowl, stir together the soy sauce, sugar, and Worcestershire sauce. Set aside.

In a large bowl, stir together the cabbage, onion, carrot, bamboo shoots, garlic, and gingerroot.

Heat a nonstick wok or skillet over high heat. Pour the oil into the wok and swirl to coat the bottom. Heat the oil for 1 minute, or until it is very hot but not smoking. Cook the cabbage mixture for 2 minutes, stirring constantly.

Stir in the rice mixture. Cook for 2 minutes, stirring constantly. Remove from the heat.

Stir in the soy sauce mixture.

calories 233
protein 6 g
carbohydrates 45 g
 fiber 5 g
 sugars 10 g
cholesterol 0 mg
total fat 4.0 g
 saturated 0.5 g
 polyunsaturated 1.0 g
 monounsaturated 2.0 g
sodium 323 mg

dietary exchange
2 starch
3 vegetable
½ fat

Stuffed Zucchini

Serves 4

Brown rice flecked with color is used to stuff zucchini and transform it from its usual side-dish status to main-dish prominence. The chipotle pepper adds heat and a smoky quality.

4 small to medium zucchini

Stuffing
1 chipotle pepper canned in adobo sauce
2 teaspoons olive oil
1 medium red onion, finely chopped
1 large garlic clove, coarsely chopped
1 medium tomato, finely chopped
1/4 teaspoon salt
2 cups coarsely chopped fresh spinach leaves

4 large pimiento-stuffed green olives, coarsely chopped
2 tablespoons coarsely snipped cilantro
2 tablespoons white wine vinegar
3/4 teaspoon dried oregano, crumbled
1/4 teaspoon ground cumin
2 cups cooked brown rice
❖
1 cup water

Cut the zucchini in half lengthwise. Using a teaspoon, scrape out the seeds and just enough flesh to make a cavity for stuffing.

Wearing gloves, discard the stem of the chipotle pepper. Finely chop the pepper (no need to wipe off the sauce).

Heat a large, deep skillet over medium-low heat. Pour in the oil and swirl to coat the bottom. Cook the onion, garlic, chipotle, tomato, and salt for 5 to 7 minutes, or until the onion has softened, stirring occasionally.

Stir in the remaining stuffing ingredients. Cook for 3 to 4 minutes, or until the spinach is wilted, stirring frequently.

Preheat the oven to 400°F.

Stuff the zucchini with the spinach mixture. Place the zucchini in a single layer in a large baking pan. Carefully pour the water around—not on—the zucchini. Cover the pan tightly with aluminum foil.

Bake for 35 to 40 minutes, or until the zucchini is tender when tested with a fork inserted into the center.

calories 196
protein 6 g
carbohydrates 35 g
  fiber 6 g
  sugars 6 g
cholesterol 0 mg
total fat 4.5 g
  saturated 0.5 g
  polyunsaturated 1.0 g
  monounsaturated 2.5 g
sodium 393 mg

dietary exchange
1 1/2 starch
2 vegetable
1 fat

Spinach and Brown Rice Casserole

Serves 8

This casserole is a good way to use up leftover brown rice. Create a fruit parfait of bananas, mandarin oranges, and kiwifruit to serve with the casserole.

Vegetable oil spray
10 ounces fresh spinach or 10-ounce package frozen chopped spinach, thawed
3 cups cooked brown rice
2 cups fat-free or low-fat cottage cheese
Egg substitute equivalent to 1 egg, or 1 large egg
1 tablespoon all-purpose flour

1 tablespoon shredded or grated Parmesan cheese
1/2 teaspoon dried thyme, crumbled
Pepper to taste
1 teaspoon light tub margarine
2 medium onions, chopped
3 medium garlic cloves, minced
8 ounces button mushrooms, sliced
3 tablespoons shredded or grated Parmesan cheese
2 tablespoons sunflower seeds

Preheat the oven to 375°F. Lightly spray a 13 × 9 × 2-inch pan with vegetable oil spray.

If using fresh spinach, remove the large stems and tear the leaves into bite-size pieces. If using frozen spinach, squeeze out the moisture.

In a large bowl, stir together the rice, cottage cheese, egg substitute, flour, 1 tablespoon Parmesan, thyme, and pepper.

In a large saucepan, melt the margarine over medium-high heat. Cook the onions and garlic for 2 to 3 minutes, or until the onions are soft.

Reduce the heat to low. Stir in the spinach and mushrooms. Cook, covered, for 3 to 5 minutes.

Stir in the cottage cheese mixture. Spoon the mixture into the pan.

Sprinkle with the 3 tablespoons Parmesan and sunflower seeds.

Bake, uncovered, for 25 to 30 minutes.

calories 184
protein 14 g
carbohydrates 27 g
  fiber 4 g
  sugars 5 g
cholesterol 4 mg
total fat 3.0 g
  saturated 0.5 g
  polyunsaturated 1.0 g
  monounsaturated 1.0 g
sodium 286 mg

dietary exchange
1½ starch
1 vegetable
1½ very lean meat

Portobello Mushroom Wrap
with Yogurt Curry Sauce

Serves 8

A creamy curry sauce enhances this wrap featuring grilled portobellos.

Yogurt Curry Sauce
- 8 ounces fat-free or light plain yogurt
- 1 teaspoon curry powder
- 2 teaspoons fresh lemon juice
- 1 teaspoon sugar
- ❖
- 2 tablespoons balsamic vinegar
- 1 tablespoon olive oil
- 2 medium garlic cloves, minced
- 2 medium portobello mushrooms
- 2 cups cooked brown, wild, jasmine, or basmati rice

- 2 medium green onions (green and white parts), thinly sliced
- 1/4 cup shredded fat-free or part-skim mozzarella cheese or fat-free mozzarella-style soy cheese
- 1 medium Italian plum tomato, diced
- 1 teaspoon light brown sugar
- 1 teaspoon plain rice vinegar
- 8 6-inch fat-free or low-fat flour tortillas
- 16 medium asparagus spears, cooked until tender-crisp

In a small bowl, stir together the sauce ingredients. Cover and refrigerate for 30 minutes to two days.

In a resealable plastic bag, combine the vinegar, olive oil, and garlic. Cut each mushroom into 8 slices. Put into the bag. Seal. Turn to coat. Let marinate at room temperature for 10 to 15 minutes.

In a medium bowl, stir together the rice, green onions, mozzarella, tomato, brown sugar, and vinegar.

Preheat the grill on medium-high. Grill the undrained mushrooms for 1 to 2 minutes on each side, or until tender.

To assemble, put a tortilla on a microwave-safe plate. Put 2 mushroom slices in the center of the tortilla. Top with 2 asparagus spears and 1/4 cup rice mixture. Microwave on 100 percent power (high) for 30 seconds. Roll the tortilla jelly-roll style. Repeat with the remaining ingredients. Serve with the sauce.

calories 202
protein 8 g
carbohydrates 38 g
 fiber 3 g
 sugars 6 g
cholesterol 1 mg
total fat 2.5 g
 saturated 0.5 g
 polyunsaturated 0.5 g
 monounsaturated 1.5 g
sodium 333 mg

dietary exchange
2 starch
1 1/2 vegetable

Rice Sticks with Asian Vegetables (Pad Thai)

Serves 6

An exciting blend of taste, color, texture, and aroma comes together in pad thai, a popular dish from Thailand. This dish is fun to eat with chopsticks.

8 ounces dried flat rice sticks (rice-flour noodles)

2 tablespoons fresh lime juice

1 tablespoon sugar

2 teaspoons fish sauce or low-salt soy sauce

10.5-ounce package light firm tofu, diced

1 teaspoon acceptable vegetable oil

1/2 teaspoon crushed red pepper flakes

2 medium garlic cloves, minced

4 medium stalks of bok choy, stems and leaves thinly sliced

1 cup fresh sugar snap peas, trimmed

1/2 cup canned whole baby corn, drained

1 large carrot, cut into matchstick-size strips

1 tablespoon dry sherry (optional)

2 medium green onions (green and white parts), thinly sliced (optional)

2 tablespoons chopped peanuts (optional)

Lime wedges (optional)

Sprigs of fresh cilantro (optional)

Put the noodles in a large bowl with enough hot tap water to cover by 1 inch. Cover the bowl with plastic wrap and let the noodles soak for 15 to 20 minutes.

Meanwhile, stir together the lime juice, sugar, and fish sauce. Set aside.

Heat a large nonstick skillet on medium-high heat. Cook the tofu for 2 to 3 minutes, or until warmed through, stirring occasionally. Transfer to a bowl.

Pour the oil into the skillet and swirl to coat the bottom. Cook the red pepper flakes and garlic for 10 seconds.

Add the bok choy, peas, corn, and carrot. Cook for 1 to 2 minutes, or until tender-crisp, stirring occasionally.

calories 198
protein 7 g
carbohydrates 39 g
  fiber 3 g
  sugars 4 g
cholesterol 0 mg
total fat 1.0 g
  saturated 0.0 g
  polyunsaturated 0.5 g
  monounsaturated 0.5 g
sodium 245 mg

dietary exchange
2 1/2 starch
1/2 very lean meat

Drain the noodles. Stir the noodles, tofu, lime juice mixture, and sherry into the skillet. Cook for 2 to 3 minutes, or until the noodles are warmed through, stirring occasionally (noodles will get mushy if overcooked).

To serve, arrange the noodle mixture on a serving platter and garnish with the remaining ingredients.

Cook's Tip on Rice Sticks

Asian markets and some grocery and health food stores carry rice sticks, noodles made of rice flour and water. You can buy round or flat rice sticks in a variety of widths and even in some flavors. If you can't find the width you want, substitute a comparable pasta.

Cook's Tip on Fish Sauce

Look in the Asian section of the grocery for fish sauce. A very common ingredient in classic Thai and Vietnamese dishes, fish sauce has a very pungent aroma and adds a salty-fermented flavor. A little goes a long way to enhance and heighten the flavor of the dish.

with sherry and peanuts
calories 216
protein 8 g
carbohydrates 39 g
fiber 3 g
sugars 4 g
cholesterol 0 mg
total fat 2.5 g
saturated 0.5 g
polyunsaturated 1.0 g
monounsaturated 1.0 g
sodium 246 mg
dietary exchange
2½ starch
½ very lean meat

Vegetable and Kidney Bean Stew

Serves 6

Get to the root of good taste with this chunky stew, which features rutabagas, parsnips, and turnips. A hint of barley gives a nice texture. Serve with crusty whole-wheat bread.

4 cups low-sodium vegetable broth, such as on page 46
   15-ounce can no-salt-added kidney beans, rinsed and drained
   14.5-ounce can no-salt-added stewed tomatoes, undrained
1 large rutabaga (about 12 ounces), peeled and cut into 2-inch cubes
2 medium turnips (about 8 ounces), peeled and cut into 2-inch cubes

2 large parsnips (about 6 ounces), peeled and cut into 2-inch pieces
2 tablespoons uncooked pearl barley
1 teaspoon celery seeds
1 teaspoon dried thyme, crumbled
1 teaspoon prepared white horseradish (optional)
1/2 teaspoon dried sage
1/4 teaspoon pepper
1/4 teaspoon salt

Put the ingredients in a large stockpot or Dutch oven. Bring to a simmer over medium-high heat, stirring occasionally. Reduce the heat and simmer, covered, for 40 to 45 minutes, or until the vegetables and barley are tender.

calories 187
protein 9 g
carbohydrates 39 g
   fiber 11 g
   sugars 15 g
cholesterol 0 mg
total fat 0.5 g
   saturated 0.0 g
   polyunsaturated 0.0 g
   monounsaturated 0.0 g
sodium 179 mg

dietary exchange
2 starch
2 vegetable
1/2 very lean meat

Cheese-Topped Anaheims
with Pinto Rice

Serves 4

Instead of stuffing mild Anaheim peppers for this dish, you simplify and place the slit peppers on the filling. A splash of fresh lime juice adds just the right touch.

1 cup uncooked instant brown rice
4 medium Anaheim peppers
  Vegetable oil spray
  15-ounce can no-salt-added pinto beans, rinsed and drained
³/₄ cup finely chopped green onions (green and white parts)

1 tablespoon chili powder
2 teaspoons ground cumin
¹/₄ teaspoon salt
1 cup shredded fat-free or part-skim mozzarella cheese
¹/₈ teaspoon salt
1 medium lime, quartered

Prepare the rice using the package directions, omitting the salt and margarine.

Meanwhile, preheat the oven to 350°F. Lightly spray an 11 × 7 × 2-inch baking pan with vegetable oil spray.

Wearing gloves, discard the stems of the peppers. Halve the peppers lengthwise. Discard the seeds and ribs.

In the pan, stir together the rice, beans, green onions, chili powder, cumin, and ¹/₄ teaspoon salt. Arrange the peppers with the cut side down on top of the rice mixture, alternating the wide and narrow ends of the halves. Sprinkle the cheese evenly over all. Cover the pan with aluminum foil.

Bake for 45 minutes, or until the peppers are tender when pierced with a fork.

Sprinkle with ¹/₈ teaspoon salt. Squeeze the lime juice evenly over all.

Cook's Tip

If the peppers are too long for the pan, cut off any excess and use for another dish or freeze.

calories 261
protein 18 g
carbohydrates 45 g
  fiber 9 g
  sugars 7 g
cholesterol 5 mg
total fat 1.5 g
  saturated 0.0 g
  polyunsaturated 0.5 g
  monounsaturated 0.5 g
sodium 589 mg

dietary exchange
2¹/₂ starch
1¹/₂ vegetable
2 very lean meat

Hoppin' John

Serves 4

The certainty is that Hoppin' John always combines black-eyed peas with rice, onion, and herbs. The uncertainties are the history of the name and whether eating Hoppin' John on New Year's Day really brings good luck throughout the year. Regardless, your family will definitely feel lucky when you serve this southern dish.

1 cup uncooked rice
1 teaspoon acceptable vegetable oil
1 medium rib of celery, diced
1 small onion, sliced
2½ cups canned no-salt-added tomatoes, undrained

1 teaspoon chopped fresh basil leaves or ¼ teaspoon dried, crumbled
½ teaspoon dried rosemary, crushed
Pepper to taste
16-ounce can no-salt-added black-eyed peas, rinsed and drained

Prepare the rice using the package directions, omitting the salt and margarine.

Heat a large skillet over medium heat. Pour in the oil and swirl to coat the bottom. Cook the celery and onion for 2 to 3 minutes, or until the onion is soft, stirring frequently.

Stir in the remaining ingredients except the peas. Reduce the heat and simmer, uncovered, for 20 minutes, stirring occasionally.

Add the peas and cook, covered, over low heat for 5 minutes, or until heated through.

To serve, spoon the rice onto plates. Spoon the peas over the rice.

Cook's Tip on Mortar and Pestle

The mortar is a heavy bowl, and the pestle is the grinding tool—a handle with a large knob on the business end. They are wonderful for grinding spices. Put spices such as caraway seeds or herbs such as rosemary in the mortar and mash them against the bottom and side with the pestle until they are as fine as you want.

calories 289
protein 12 g
carbohydrates 59 g
 fiber 6 g
 sugars 8 g
cholesterol 0 mg
total fat 1.0 g
 saturated 0.0 g
 polyunsaturated 0.5 g
 monounsaturated 0.5 g
sodium 122 mg

dietary exchange
3½ starch
1 vegetable
½ very lean meat

Barbecued Lima Beans

Serves 6

Serve this sweet-and-sour bean dish, reminiscent of baked beans, at a cookout, on a vegetarian buffet, or as a main dish over rice.

1 pound dried baby lima beans, sorted for stones and shriveled beans and rinsed

4 cups fat-free, low-sodium chicken broth, such as on page 45

1 small onion
  Vegetable oil spray

3 tablespoons light brown sugar

2 tablespoons low-sodium Worcestershire sauce

1 teaspoon chili powder

1 teaspoon pepper

1 teaspoon dry mustard

8-ounce can no-salt-added tomato sauce

2 tablespoons vinegar

Put the beans in a stockpot or Dutch oven. Add water to cover by several inches. Bring to a boil over high heat. Remove from the heat, cover, and set aside for 1 hour. Drain the beans and return them to the stockpot.

Add the broth to just cover the beans (add water if needed). Bring to a boil over high heat. Reduce the heat and simmer, covered, for about 1 hour 15 minutes, or until tender, adding water if needed to keep the beans just covered. When the beans start to simmer, mince the onion.

Lightly spray a large skillet with vegetable oil spray. Cook the onion over medium-high heat for about 5 minutes, or until softened and browning. Stir the onion, brown sugar, Worcestershire sauce, chili powder, pepper, and mustard into the beans. Leave the beans uncovered for the remainder of their cooking time.

When the beans are tender, stir in the tomato sauce and vinegar.

calories 312
protein 17 g
carbohydrates 60 g
  fiber 17 g
  sugars 17 g
cholesterol 0 mg
total fat 1.0 g
  saturated 0.0 g
  polyunsaturated 0.5 g
  monounsaturated 0.0 g
sodium 53 mg

dietary exchange
4 starch
2 very lean meat

Mediterranean Lentils and Rice

Serves 4

Middle Eastern cuisine often combines sweet ingredients, such as cinnamon and currants, with more-savory ingredients, such as cumin and onion. That sweet and savory pairing "makes" this dish. Although the currants are so small that they aren't readily apparent, they add a depth and richness that's important.

1 medium onion, minced

2 teaspoons ground cumin

2 teaspoons ground cinnamon

1/2 teaspoon cayenne

3/4 cup dried lentils, sorted for stones and shriveled lentils and rinsed

2 cups low-sodium vegetable broth, such as on page 46, or water

14.5-ounce can no-salt-added crushed tomatoes, undrained

2 cups low-sodium vegetable broth, such as on page 46, or water

1 cup uncooked rice

1/2 cup water

1/3 cup dried currants

1/4 cup crumbled feta cheese

Heat a large nonstick skillet over medium heat. Add the onion, cumin, cinnamon, and cayenne. Cook for 10 minutes, or until the onion is soft.

Stir in the lentils and 2 cups broth. Increase the heat to medium-high and bring to a boil. Reduce the heat and simmer, covered, for 20 minutes.

Add the remaining ingredients except the feta. Increase the heat to medium-high and bring to a boil. Reduce the heat and simmer, covered, for 20 minutes, or until the rice and lentils are tender.

To serve, sprinkle with the feta.

calories 396
protein 18 g
carbohydrates 77 g
  fiber 15 g
  sugars 16 g
cholesterol 8 mg
total fat 2.5 g
  saturated 1.5 g
  polyunsaturated 0.5 g
  monounsaturated 0.5 g
sodium 150 mg

dietary exchange
4 starch
1/2 fruit
2 vegetable
1/2 very lean meat

Chick-Pea Pilaf

Serves 6

This pilaf is more chick-peas and green peas than quinoa. Feel free to double the amount of quinoa if you want to feed more people.

¹⁄₂ to ³⁄₄ cup dry-packed sun-dried tomatoes	1 large garlic clove, minced
1 cup boiling water	1 to 1¹⁄₂ teaspoons dried oregano, crumbled
1 cup uncooked quinoa	¹⁄₂ teaspoon crushed red pepper flakes
¹⁄₂ tablespoon olive oil	15.5-ounce can no-salt-added chick-peas, rinsed and drained
10-ounce package frozen green peas, thawed	3 ounces low-fat feta cheese

Put the tomatoes in a small bowl and add the boiling water. Set aside for about 10 minutes to soften.

Drain the tomatoes, saving the liquid in a 2-cup measuring cup. Chop the tomatoes and set aside.

Add enough water to the tomato liquid to equal 2 cups. Pour into a medium saucepan.

Rinse the quinoa under cold water; drain. Stir the quinoa into the saucepan. Bring to a boil over high heat. Reduce the heat and simmer, covered, for 15 minutes, or until all the liquid is absorbed.

Meanwhile, heat a large nonstick skillet over medium heat. Pour in the oil and swirl to coat the bottom. When the oil is hot, add the green peas, garlic, oregano, and red pepper flakes. Cook for 2 minutes, stirring occasionally. Stir in the chick-peas. Heat through, about 5 minutes.

To serve, stir together the tomatoes, quinoa, and chick-pea mixture. Spoon onto a large serving platter. Crumble the feta on top.

calories 338
protein 17 g
carbohydrates 53 g
  fiber 12 g
  sugars 7 g
cholesterol 5 mg
total fat 7.0 g
  saturated 1.5 g
  polyunsaturated 2.0 g
  monounsaturated 2.5 g
sodium 261 mg

dietary exchange
3¹⁄₂ starch
1 lean meat

Broccoli Rabe and Chick-Peas over Parmesan Toasts

Serves 6

You can serve this interesting one-dish meal of broccoli rabe and chick-peas (also called garbanzo beans) over penne pasta instead of toast for a nice change.

4 16-ounce cans no-salt-added chick-peas or 1 pound dried chick-peas, sorted for stones and shriveled beans

2 medium bunches broccoli rabe

1 tablespoon plus 2 teaspoons olive oil (extra-virgin preferred)

3 large garlic cloves, coarsely chopped

1 teaspoon fennel seeds

1/4 teaspoon crushed red pepper flakes

1/4 teaspoon salt

Pepper to taste

6 slices Italian or French bread, 1/2 inch thick (regular size, not baguette)

1 1/2 tablespoons shredded or grated Parmesan cheese

If using canned chick-peas, rinse, drain, and set aside. For dried chick-peas, prepare using the package directions, omitting the salt. Drain and set aside.

Meanwhile, remove and discard the bottom 4 inches of the broccoli rabe. Coarsely chop the remaining stems, leaves, and buds. Steam for 10 minutes. (If you don't have a two-tiered steamer, you'll need to do this in batches.)

Heat a stockpot over medium-low heat. Pour the oil into the pot and swirl to coat the bottom. When the oil is hot, stir in the broccoli rabe, garlic, fennel seeds, red pepper flakes, salt, and pepper. Cook, covered, for 15 minutes, stirring occasionally.

Preheat the broiler.

Stir the chick-peas into the broccoli rabe mixture. Cook, covered, for about 15 minutes, or until the broccoli rabe is the desired tenderness, stirring occasionally. Remove from the heat. Leave covered to keep warm.

calories 407
protein 20 g
carbohydrates 63 g
 fiber 14 g
 sugars 9 g
cholesterol 1 mg
total fat 9.5 g
 saturated 1.5 g
 polyunsaturated 3.0 g
 monounsaturated 4.0 g
sodium 316 mg

dietary exchange
4 starch
1 very lean meat
1 fat

Put the bread slices on a broilerproof baking sheet. Sprinkle the bread with the Parmesan. Broil about 4 inches from the heat for about 1 minute, or until the bread is golden brown and the cheese is melted.

To serve, arrange the toasts on a large, deep serving platter. Spoon the broccoli rabe mixture and liquid over the toasts.

Cook's Tip on Broccoli Rabe

Known by several other names—broccoli raab, broccoli rape, and rapini—broccoli rabe (rahb) is a bitter vegetable with a lemon-pepper taste. Look for deep, dark green leaves and buds (which look like tiny broccoli buds) with no trace of yellow (a sign of age). Broccoli rabe is rich in vitamin A.

Vegetable and Pinto Bean Enchiladas

Serves 8

These filling enchiladas offer not only vitamin-rich spinach and plump pinto beans but julienned vegetables as well. Chilled slices of fresh jícama with a squeeze of lime go well with these.

16 6-inch corn tortillas
1 teaspoon olive oil
1 medium carrot, cut into matchstick-size strips
2 medium leeks (white part only), thinly sliced, or 1/2 cup sliced onion
1 medium zucchini, cut into matchstick-size strips
15-ounce can no-salt-added pinto beans, rinsed and drained
10-ounce package frozen chopped spinach, cooked, drained, and squeezed dry
4 ounces fat-free or light cream cheese
1/2 cup salsa
1 teaspoon fresh lime juice
1/2 teaspoon salt
1/2 cup fat-free half-and-half
1 teaspoon ground cumin
1 cup shredded or grated low-fat Cheddar cheese

Preheat the oven to 350°F. Wrap the tortillas in aluminum foil.

Bake for 5 minutes, or until warmed through. Set aside, still in the foil, to keep warm.

Meanwhile, heat a medium nonstick skillet over medium-high heat. Pour the oil into the skillet and swirl to coat the bottom. Cook the carrot and leeks for 2 to 3 minutes, or until the carrot is tender-crisp, stirring occasionally.

Stir in the zucchini. Cook for 2 to 3 minutes, or until the zucchini is tender-crisp.

Stir in the beans, spinach, cream cheese, salsa, lime juice, and salt. Reduce the heat to medium-low and cook for 2 to 3 minutes, or until warmed through, stirring occasionally.

calories 213
protein 13 g
carbohydrates 31 g
fiber 6 g
sugars 6 g
cholesterol 10 mg
total fat 4.0 g
saturated 2.0 g
polyunsaturated 0.5 g
monounsaturated 1.0 g
sodium 470 mg

dietary exchange
1 1/2 starch
1 1/2 vegetable
1 lean meat

To assemble, spoon about $1/4$ cup filling down the center of a tortilla. Roll up jelly-roll style and place with seam side down in a nonstick $13 \times 9 \times 2$-inch baking pan. Repeat with the remaining filling and tortillas.

In a small bowl, stir together the half-and-half and cumin. Pour over the enchiladas. Sprinkle with the Cheddar cheese.

Bake for 15 to 20 minutes, or until the mixture is warmed through.

Enchilada Bake

Serves 6

Layers of vegetables, creamy sauce, beans, and tortillas make a tasty casserole that's even better the day after you prepare it.

Sauce

1 teaspoon light tub margarine
1 medium onion, chopped
½ medium green bell pepper, chopped
8 ounces button mushrooms, quartered
1 to 2 medium garlic cloves, minced
2 cups canned no-salt-added black or pinto beans, rinsed and drained
14.5-ounce can no-salt-added stewed tomatoes, undrained
½ cup dry red wine (regular or nonalcoholic)

2 to 3 teaspoons chili powder
1 to 2 teaspoons ground cumin
¼ teaspoon salt
❖
¾ cup fat-free or low-fat ricotta cheese
½ cup fat-free or light plain yogurt
Vegetable oil spray
6 6-inch corn tortillas, quartered
½ cup grated fat-free or part-skim mozzarella cheese
6 medium black olives, sliced

In a large saucepan, melt the margarine over medium-high heat. Swirl to coat the bottom. Cook the onion, bell pepper, mushrooms, and garlic for 2 to 3 minutes, or until the onion is soft.

Stir in the remaining sauce ingredients. Reduce the heat and simmer for 30 minutes.

Preheat the oven to 350°F.

In a small bowl, whisk together the ricotta and yogurt.

Lightly spray a 1½-quart casserole dish with vegetable oil spray. Place 3 tortillas in the dish. Top with half the sauce, half the mozzarella, and half the ricotta mixture. Repeat the layers. Top with the olives.

Bake, covered, for 15 to 20 minutes, or until heated through.

calories 224
protein 17 g
carbohydrates 33 g
  fiber 9 g
  sugars 9 g
cholesterol 5 mg
total fat 2.0 g
  saturated 0.5 g
  polyunsaturated 0.5 g
  monounsaturated 0.5 g
sodium 370 mg

dietary exchange
1½ starch
2 vegetable
1½ very lean meat

Cuban Black Beans

Serves 8

The green onions and vinegar give this dish its Cuban flavor. Serve with a crisp green salad and crunchy rolls for a colorful meatless meal.

2 cups dried black beans (about 1 pound), sorted for stones and shriveled beans and rinsed
Vegetable oil spray
1 teaspoon light tub margarine
2 medium onions, chopped
1/2 medium rib of celery, diced
1/2 medium lemon, quartered
1 tablespoon fresh savory or 1 teaspoon dried, crumbled

2 medium garlic cloves, minced
1 bay leaf
Pinch of ground ginger
1 1/2 cups uncooked rice
4 medium green onions (green and white parts), chopped (optional)
3 tablespoons red wine vinegar (optional)
2 medium oranges, sliced (optional)

Soak the beans using the package directions. Drain.

Heat a stockpot over medium-high heat. Remove from the heat and lightly spray with vegetable oil spray (being careful not to spray near a gas flame). Melt the margarine and swirl to coat the bottom. Cook the onions and celery for 2 to 3 minutes, or until the onions are soft.

Add the beans, lemon, savory, garlic, bay leaf, and ginger to the stockpot. Add water to cover by 2 inches. Stir well. Increase the heat to high and bring to a boil. Reduce the heat and simmer, covered, for 1 hour to 1 hour 30 minutes, or until the beans are tender. Discard the bay leaf and lemon.

Meanwhile, prepare the rice using the package directions, omitting the salt and margarine.

To serve, spoon the rice into bowls. Spoon the beans over the rice. Add green onions and vinegar to taste, or garnish with orange slices.

calories 298
protein 13 g
carbohydrates 60 g
  fiber 8 g
  sugars 9 g
cholesterol 0 mg
total fat 1.0 g
  saturated 0.0 g
  polyunsaturated 0.5 g
  monounsaturated 0.0 g
sodium 10 mg

dietary exchange
4 starch
1/2 very lean meat

Red Beans and Couscous

Serves 4

Go for a new spin on the classic red beans and rice with this quick and easy recipe. Serve the dish with slices of tomato and English cucumbers.

1 teaspoon olive oil
1/2 medium green bell pepper, chopped
1 medium rib of celery, chopped
1/2 medium onion, chopped
2 medium garlic cloves, chopped
2 cups low-sodium vegetable broth, such as on page 46

15-ounce can no-salt-added red beans, rinsed and drained
2 tablespoons imitation bacon bits
1 1/2 to 2 teaspoons Creole or Cajun seasoning blend
1 1/2 cups uncooked couscous (10-ounce box)

Heat a medium nonstick saucepan over medium-high heat. Pour the oil into the saucepan and swirl to coat the bottom. Cook the bell pepper, celery, onion, and garlic for 3 to 4 minutes, or until tender, stirring occasionally.

Stir in the broth, beans, bacon bits, and seasoning blend. Bring to a simmer. Reduce the heat and simmer, uncovered, for 1 to 2 minutes, or until the bacon bits are tender.

Stir in the couscous. Remove from the heat. Let stand, covered, for 5 minutes, or until the couscous has absorbed the liquid and is tender. Fluff with a fork and serve.

calories 373
protein 17 g
carbohydrates 72 g
 fiber 8 g
 sugars 5 g
cholesterol 0 mg
total fat 2.0 g
 saturated 0.0 g
 polyunsaturated 0.5 g
 monounsaturated 1.0 g
sodium 211 mg

dietary exchange
4 1/2 starch
1 vegetable
1/2 very lean meat

Quinoa with Black Beans and Seared Bell Pepper

Serves 4

Pine nuts add a bit of crunch and pizzazz to this filling dish.

²/₃ cup uncooked quinoa

1¹/₃ cups water

15-ounce can no-salt-added black beans, rinsed and drained

³/₄ cup frozen whole-kernel corn

Vegetable oil spray

1 large red bell pepper, cut into thin strips

2 medium onions, cut into thin strips

1 medium garlic clove, minced

2 tablespoons pine nuts, dry-roasted

1 tablespoon olive oil (extra-virgin preferred)

1 teaspoon ground cumin

³/₄ teaspoon salt

¹/₄ teaspoon crushed red pepper flakes

Rinse the quinoa in a colander to remove the bitter coating. Drain.

In a medium saucepan, bring the water to a boil over high heat. Stir in the quinoa. Return to a boil. Reduce the heat and simmer, uncovered, for 15 minutes, or until the water is absorbed.

Stir in the beans and corn. Remove from the heat. Cover to keep warm.

Meanwhile, heat a 12-inch skillet over medium-high heat. Remove from the heat and lightly spray with vegetable oil spray (being careful not to spray near a gas flame). Add the bell pepper, onions, and garlic. Lightly spray with vegetable oil spray. Cook for 8 minutes, or until deeply browned, stirring frequently.

Stir the pepper mixture and the remaining ingredients into the quinoa mixture.

Cook's Tip on Dry-Roasting Pine Nuts

To dry-roast pine nuts, heat a small ungreased skillet over medium-high heat. Dry-roast the pine nuts until they begin to lightly brown, 1 to 2 minutes, stirring constantly. Watch carefully so the nuts don't burn.

calories 316
protein 13 g
carbohydrates 53 g
  fiber 9 g
  sugars 10 g
cholesterol 0 mg
total fat 7.5 g
  saturated 1.0 g
  polyunsaturated 2.0 g
  monounsaturated 3.5 g
sodium 450 mg

dietary exchange
3 starch
2 vegetable
1 very lean meat
¹/₂ fat

Quinoa Pilaf with Tofu and Vegetables

Serves 4

The delicate flavor of quinoa is a nice change of pace in this Asian-inspired pilaf.

2 tablespoons slivered almonds
1/2 cup uncooked quinoa, rinsed and drained
1 cup low-sodium vegetable broth, such as on page 46
   12.3-ounce package light firm tofu, cubed

1-pound package frozen mixed stir-fry vegetables
2 teaspoons low-salt soy sauce
1 teaspoon toasted sesame oil
1 teaspoon chili paste

Heat a large nonstick skillet over medium heat. Dry-roast the almonds for 3 to 4 minutes, or until golden brown, stirring occasionally. Transfer to a small bowl.

Put the quinoa in the skillet. Increase the heat to medium-high. Dry-roast the quinoa for 3 to 4 minutes, or until it is lightly toasted and any excess water has evaporated (quinoa will not be golden brown), stirring occasionally.

Stir in the remaining ingredients. Bring to a simmer. Reduce the heat and simmer, covered, for 15 minutes, or until the quinoa is tender.

Stir in the almonds. Fluff the mixture with a fork.

Cook's Tip on Quinoa

Quinoa contains protein and all eight essential amino acids. Before cooking quinoa, rinse it to remove the protective coating, which imparts a bitter flavor.

calories 183
protein 12 g
carbohydrates 23 g
   fiber 4 g
   sugars 4 g
cholesterol 0 mg
total fat 5.5 g
   saturated 0.5 g
   polyunsaturated 2.0 g
   monounsaturated 2.0 g
sodium 209 mg

dietary exchange
1 starch
1 1/2 vegetable
1 very lean meat
1/2 fat

Curried Cauliflower and Tofu with Basmati Rice

Serves 6

The curry flavor here is so light and delicate that it makes this dish the introduction if your family hasn't tried curry.

1 tablespoon plus 2 teaspoons olive oil	1/8 teaspoon cayenne, or to taste
1 small head cauliflower, coarsely chopped	1 cup fat-free evaporated milk
12 spears asparagus, trimmed, cut into 1-inch pieces	1 medium apple (Fuji preferred), finely diced
12 fresh green beans, cut into 1-inch pieces	2 tablespoons mango chutney or honey
2 large tomatoes, cut into 1-inch wedges	1/4 teaspoon salt
1 large sweet onion, such as Texas Sweet, coarsely chopped	Pepper to taste
1/4 cup coarsely chopped fresh Italian, or flat-leaf, parsley	1 pound light firm tofu, cut into 1/2-inch cubes
1 tablespoon curry powder, or to taste	1 cup frozen green peas
	1/4 cup coarsely snipped cilantro
	3 cups cooked basmati rice
	2 tablespoons cashews, dry-roasted

Heat a stockpot over medium-low heat. Pour the oil into the pot and swirl to coat the bottom. When the oil is hot, stir in the cauliflower, asparagus, green beans, tomatoes, onion, parsley, curry, and cayenne. Cook, covered, for 15 minutes, or until the vegetables release their liquids, stirring occasionally.

Stir the evaporated milk, apple, chutney, salt, and pepper into the vegetable mixture. Cook, covered, for 10 to 12 minutes, or until the green beans are tender-crisp, stirring occasionally.

Gently stir in the tofu, peas, and cilantro. Cook, uncovered, for 5 minutes.

To serve, spoon the rice onto plates. Spoon the cauliflower mixture and liquids over the rice. Sprinkle with the nuts.

calories 330
protein 15 g
carbohydrates 54 g
  fiber 7 g
  sugars 18 g
cholesterol 2 mg
total fat 6.5 g
  saturated 1.0 g
  polyunsaturated 1.0 g
  monounsaturated 4.0 g
sodium 262 mg

dietary exchange
2 starch
1/2 skim milk
1/2 fruit
2 vegetable
1/2 very lean meat
1 fat

Meatless Moussaka

Serves 8

Traditional moussaka goes meatless in this tasty version.

Vegetable oil spray

2 pounds eggplant, peeled and thickly sliced

Sauce

1 teaspoon olive oil

1 large onion, finely chopped

3 medium garlic cloves, minced

14.5-ounce can diced no-salt-added tomatoes, undrained

1 cup water

6-ounce can no-salt-added tomato paste

2 teaspoons dried rosemary, crushed

2 tablespoons snipped fresh parsley

2 tablespoons snipped fresh mint

Filling

1 pound fat-free or low-fat cottage cheese

Egg substitute equivalent to 2 eggs, or 2 large eggs

2 tablespoons shredded or grated Parmesan cheese

1 teaspoon dried rosemary, crushed

½ teaspoon dried oregano, crumbled

½ teaspoon pepper, or to taste

❖

¼ cup shredded or grated Parmesan cheese

Preheat the broiler. Lightly spray a 13 × 9 × 2-inch glass baking dish with vegetable oil spray.

Put the eggplant slices on 2 large baking sheets. Lightly spray both sides of the slices with vegetable oil spray. Brown about 6 inches from the heat for 5 minutes on each side, or until the eggplant is tender.

Preheat the oven to 375°F.

In a large skillet, heat the oil over medium-high heat. Cook the onion and garlic for 3 minutes, or until soft.

Stir in the undrained tomatoes, water, tomato paste, and rosemary. Simmer for 10 minutes. Stir in the parsley and mint. Remove from the heat.

In a medium bowl, stir together the filling ingredients.

Spread half the sauce in the baking dish. Add half the eggplant. Spread the filling on top. Add the remaining eggplant, sauce, and Parmesan.

Bake, covered, for 45 minutes. Uncover and bake for 10 minutes, or until heated through.

calories 137
protein 12 g
carbohydrates 19 g
  fiber 5 g
  sugars 9 g
cholesterol 5 mg
total fat 2.0 g
  saturated 1.0 g
  polyunsaturated 0.0 g
  monounsaturated 1.0 g
sodium 317 mg

dietary exchange
4 vegetable
1 lean meat

Edamame and Vegetable Stir-Fry

Serves 6

The bright colors of jade-green edamame and vibrant cherry tomatoes really make this a show-stopper in a skillet, and a nutritious one to boot! Serve with Berry Explosion Salad (page 104).

1/2 cup low-sodium vegetable broth, such as on page 46
1 tablespoon hoisin sauce
2 teaspoons low-salt soy sauce
1 1/2 teaspoons cornstarch
1 teaspoon wasabi powder
1 teaspoon toasted sesame oil

16 ounces frozen shelled edamame (soybeans)
1 teaspoon acceptable vegetable oil
1/2 cup baby carrots, halved lengthwise
4 ounces baby pattypan squash
1 cup cherry tomatoes
2 medium green onions (green and white parts), thinly sliced

In a small bowl, whisk together the broth, hoisin sauce, soy sauce, cornstarch, wasabi powder, and sesame oil.

Prepare the edamame using the package directions, omitting the salt. Drain.

Meanwhile, heat a large nonstick skillet or wok over medium-high heat. Add the vegetable oil, swirling to coat the bottom. Cook the carrots for 3 to 4 minutes, or until tender-crisp, stirring constantly.

Stir in the squash. Cook for 2 to 3 minutes, or until tender-crisp, stirring constantly.

Stir in the sauce mixture and edamame. Cook until the mixture is thickened, 2 to 3 minutes, stirring occasionally.

To serve, stir in the cherry tomatoes and green onions.

calories 163
protein 11 g
carbohydrates 14 g
  fiber 7 g
  sugars 4 g
cholesterol 0 mg
total fat 7.0 g
  saturated 1.0 g
  polyunsaturated 3.0 g
  monounsaturated 2.0 g
sodium 79 mg

dietary exchange
1/2 starch
1 1/2 vegetable
1 very lean meat
1 fat

Eggplant Parmesan

Serves 6

Cooking the liquid out of the seasoned mushrooms raises their flavor level to new heights.

Vegetable oil spray (olive oil spray preferred)
1 medium eggplant (about 1¹/₂ pounds)
1 teaspoon olive oil
8 ounces button mushrooms, sliced
1 large onion, chopped
3 or 4 medium garlic cloves, minced
¹/₂ teaspoon salt-free Italian seasoning, crumbled

¹/₄ teaspoon salt
Pepper to taste
8-ounce can no-salt-added tomato sauce
4 ounces shredded fat-free or part-skim mozzarella cheese
¹/₄ cup shredded or grated Parmesan cheese

Preheat the broiler. Lightly spray a baking sheet, 13 × 9 × 2-inch baking pan, and 11 × 15-inch piece of aluminum foil with olive oil spray.

Peel the eggplant. Cut crosswise into ¹/₄-inch slices. Put the slices on the baking sheet.

Broil about 6 inches from the heat for 2 to 3 minutes on each side. Remove from the broiler and set the oven to 375°F.

In a large nonstick skillet, heat the oil over medium heat. Swirl to coat the bottom. Cook the mushrooms, onion, garlic, herb seasoning, and salt, covered, for 7 to 9 minutes, stirring occasionally. Increase the heat to high and cook, uncovered, for 2 to 3 minutes, or until the pan juices have evaporated, stirring frequently.

To assemble, spread 1 cup mushroom mixture in the baking pan. Cover with half the eggplant slices. Sprinkle with the pepper. Top with ¹/₂ cup tomato sauce and half the mozzarella. Repeat the layers except the cheese. Cover with the prepared foil.

Bake for 1 hour. Top with the remaining mozzarella and all the Parmesan. Bake, uncovered, for 5 to 8 minutes, or until the cheese is melted. Let cool for at least 10 minutes before cutting.

calories 109
protein 10 g
carbohydrates 14 g
  fiber 4 g
  sugars 8 g
cholesterol 6 mg
total fat 2.0 g
  saturated 0.5 g
  polyunsaturated 0.0 g
  monounsaturated 1.0 g
sodium 401 mg

dietary exchange
3 vegetable
1 very lean meat

Eggplant Zucchini Casserole

Serves 8

Put uncooked spaghetti right in the casserole. Everything bakes together—no spaghetti pot to wash!

Vegetable oil spray

Sauce
- 2 8-ounce cans no-salt-added tomato sauce
- 2 medium garlic cloves, crushed
- 2 teaspoons low-sodium Worcestershire sauce
- 1 teaspoon dried oregano, crumbled
- 1/2 teaspoon dried basil, crumbled
- 1/2 teaspoon dried marjoram, crumbled
- Pepper to taste

❖

- 1 medium eggplant, peeled and sliced
- 2 medium zucchini, sliced
- 4 ounces dried spaghetti, broken into thirds (about 1 cup)
- 3 medium ribs of celery, chopped
- 1 medium onion, chopped
- 1 medium green bell pepper, chopped
- 8 ounces fat-free or part-skim mozzarella cheese, cut into 18 small slices

Preheat the oven to 350°F. Lightly spray a 13 × 9 × 2-inch casserole dish with vegetable oil spray.

In a medium bowl, stir together the sauce ingredients.

In the casserole dish, arrange half the eggplant slices in a single layer. Top with half of each of the following, in order: zucchini, spaghetti, celery, onion, bell pepper, mozzarella, and tomato sauce mixture. Repeat the layers.

Bake, covered, for about 1 hour, or until the vegetables are tender.

calories 155
protein 13 g
carbohydrates 25 g
  fiber 5 g
  sugars 8 g
cholesterol 5 mg
total fat 0.5 g
  saturated 0.0 g
  polyunsaturated 0.0 g
  monounsaturated 0.0 g
sodium 383 mg

dietary exchange
1 starch
2 vegetable
1 very lean meat

Italian-Style Zucchini

Serves 6

When summer squash are at the peak of their season, try this layered casserole. Serve with juicy sliced nectarines and Marinated White Beans and Cucumber with Basil (page 133).

Vegetable oil spray

6 medium zucchini or yellow summer squash, thinly sliced

1 teaspoon olive oil

³/₄ cup sliced onion

2 large tomatoes or 4 Italian plum tomatoes, thinly sliced

1¹/₄ teaspoons dried basil, crumbled

1 teaspoon salt-free all-purpose seasoning

³/₄ teaspoon dried oregano, crumbled

4 ounces shredded fat-free or part-skim mozzarella

¹/₃ cup shredded or grated Parmesan cheese

2 tablespoons finely snipped fresh parsley

Preheat the oven to 375°F. Lightly spray a 2-quart casserole dish with vegetable oil spray.

Put the zucchini in a saucepan with water to cover by ¹/₂ inch. Bring to a boil over high heat. Reduce the heat and simmer for 4 to 5 minutes, or until tender. Drain well. Transfer to a large bowl.

Increase the heat to medium-high. Heat a small skillet. Pour the oil into the skillet and swirl to coat the bottom. Cook the onion for 2 to 3 minutes, or until soft. Add to the zucchini.

Stir in the tomatoes, basil, all-purpose seasoning, and oregano.

Spoon half the zucchini mixture into the casserole dish. Sprinkle with the mozzarella. Add the remaining zucchini mixture. Sprinkle with the Parmesan.

Bake, uncovered, for 25 to 30 minutes. Sprinkle with the parsley.

calories 103
protein 11 g
carbohydrates 12 g
  fiber 4 g
  sugars 6 g
cholesterol 7 mg
total fat 2.5 g
  saturated 1.0 g
  polyunsaturated 0.5 g
  monounsaturated 1.0 g
sodium 318 mg

dietary exchange
2 vegetable
1 lean meat

Spinach Ricotta Swirls

Serves 4

This dish will be a showstopper at your next dinner party.

8 dried lasagna noodles
   Vegetable oil spray (olive oil spray
   preferred)

Sauce
1 teaspoon olive oil
1 small or medium onion, finely
   chopped
2 large garlic cloves, minced
2 cups low-sodium vegetable broth,
   such as on page 46
   6-ounce can no-salt-added tomato
   paste

1 teaspoon salt-free Italian
   seasoning, crumbled
1/4 teaspoon salt

Filling
2 10-ounce packages frozen chopped
   spinach, thawed and squeezed dry
1 cup fat-free or low-fat ricotta
   cheese
2 tablespoons shredded or grated
   Parmesan cheese
1/4 teaspoon white pepper
1/8 teaspoon ground nutmeg

Prepare the noodles using the package directions, omitting the salt and oil. Drain. Place in a single layer on wax paper. Set aside.

Preheat the oven to 350°F. Lightly spray an 8-inch square baking dish with vegetable oil spray.

In a small nonstick saucepan, heat the oil over medium-high heat. Cook the onion and garlic for 2 to 3 minutes, or until the onion is soft, stirring occasionally.

Stir in the remaining sauce ingredients. Reduce the heat and simmer for 5 minutes, or until slightly thickened, stirring occasionally. Remove from the heat. Set aside.

Put the spinach in a large bowl. Stir in the remaining filling ingredients.

Spread a scant 1/3 cup filling lengthwise down each noodle, leaving a border on all sides. Roll up each noodle and place it on its side in the baking dish. (The rolled noodles shouldn't touch each other.)

Pour the sauce over the noodles.

Bake, covered, for 25 minutes, or until heated through.

calories 273
protein 20 g
carbohydrates 44 g
  fiber 8 g
  sugars 7 g
cholesterol 7 mg
total fat 3.5 g
  saturated 1.0 g
  polyunsaturated 1.0 g
  monounsaturated 1.0 g
sodium 463 mg

dietary exchange
1 1/2 starch
4 vegetable
1 1/2 very lean meat

Spinach Artichoke Gratin

Serves 6

Spinach, artichokes, and cheese—a perfect combination. As the mixture bakes to bubbly richness, prepare steamed carrots and tossed salad with one of our salad dressings (pages 137-141) to complete your meal.

Vegetable oil spray

16 ounces fat-free or low-fat cottage cheese

Egg substitute equivalent to 2 eggs, or 2 large eggs

3 tablespoons shredded or grated Parmesan cheese

1 tablespoon fresh lemon juice

$\frac{1}{8}$ teaspoon white pepper

$\frac{1}{8}$ teaspoon ground nutmeg

2 10-ounce packages frozen chopped spinach, thawed and drained

3 medium green onions, thinly sliced (green part only)

10-ounce package frozen artichoke hearts, thawed and drained

2 tablespoons shredded or grated Parmesan cheese

Preheat the oven to 375°F. Lightly spray a $1\frac{1}{2}$-quart baking dish with vegetable oil spray.

In a food processor or blender, process the cottage cheese, egg substitute, 3 tablespoons Parmesan, lemon juice, pepper, and nutmeg until smooth.

Squeeze the moisture from the spinach. Put the spinach in a large bowl.

Stir in the cottage cheese mixture and green onions. Spread half the mixture in the baking dish.

Cut the artichoke hearts in half. Pat dry with paper towels. Place in a single layer on the spinach mixture. Sprinkle with 2 tablespoons Parmesan. Cover with the remaining spinach mixture.

Bake, covered, for 25 minutes.

calories 128
protein 16 g
carbohydrates 13 g
 fiber 7 g
 sugars 3 g
cholesterol 6 mg
total fat 1.5 g
 saturated 1.0 g
 polyunsaturated 0.0 g
 monounsaturated 0.5 g
sodium 446 mg

dietary exchange
$2\frac{1}{2}$ vegetable
$1\frac{1}{2}$ very lean meat

Steamed Veggies with Herbed Cheese

Serves 4

You can serve these tender vegetables, topped with a rich-tasting, herbed cheese sauce, as a vegetarian entrée or as a side dish with almost anything—seafood, poultry, or meat.

1 large carrot, sliced into half-rounds
4 ounces broccoli florets (about 1 cup)
4 ounces cauliflower florets (about 1 cup)
1 medium zucchini, sliced into half-rounds
1 medium yellow summer squash, sliced into half-rounds

Sauce
2 tablespoons low-sodium vegetable broth, such as on page 46

2 medium shallots, finely chopped
1 cup fat-free milk
2 tablespoons all-purpose flour
1/8 teaspoon white pepper
2 ounces grated fat-free or low-fat sharp Cheddar cheese
2 tablespoons shredded or grated Parmesan cheese
1 tablespoon finely chopped fresh basil leaves
1/2 teaspoon finely chopped fresh rosemary

In a large pot, steam the carrot over medium-high heat for 5 minutes.

Add the broccoli, cauliflower, zucchini, and yellow squash. Steam for 10 minutes. Drain the vegetables and pat dry with paper towels. Place the vegetables on a serving plate. Cover the plate with aluminum foil to keep warm.

Meanwhile, heat the broth in a medium saucepan over medium heat. Cook the shallots for 2 to 3 minutes, stirring occasionally.

Whisk in the milk, flour, and pepper. Bring to a boil over medium-high heat and cook for 3 to 4 minutes, or until the mixture thickens, stirring occasionally.

Reduce the heat to low. Stir in the remaining ingredients. Cook for 1 to 2 minutes, stirring until the Cheddar melts. Pour over the vegetables.

calories 112
protein 11 g
carbohydrates 17 g
  fiber 4 g
  sugars 8 g
cholesterol 5 mg
total fat 1.0 g
  saturated 0.5 g
  polyunsaturated 0.0 g
  monounsaturated 0.5 g
sodium 195 mg

dietary exchange
1/2 starch
2 vegetable
1 very lean meat

Broiled Eggplant, Italian Style

Serves 4

Marinated eggplant, topped with tomato sauce and mozzarella and broiled, teams well with whole-wheat pita bread.

¹/₂ cup fat-free or light Italian salad dressing
1 teaspoon dried rosemary, crushed
¹/₄ teaspoon dried oregano, crumbled
1 large eggplant

8 ounces no-salt-added tomato sauce
¹/₂ teaspoon pepper, or to taste
¹/₂ cup grated fat-free or part-skim mozzarella cheese

Combine the salad dressing, rosemary, and oregano in a resealable plastic bag.

Peel the eggplant. Cut crosswise into ³/₄-inch slices. Add to the marinade. Seal the bag and turn to coat. Refrigerate for 1 hour. Drain, discarding the marinade.

Preheat the broiler.

Arrange the eggplant slices in one layer on a baking sheet. Broil about 6 inches from the heat for about 5 minutes on each side, or until tender and lightly browned.

Arrange alternate layers of the eggplant and tomato sauce in a broilerproof 8-inch square baking dish, lightly seasoning each layer with pepper. Top with the mozzarella.

Broil for about 2 minutes, or until the cheese is brown.

calories 108
protein 6 g
carbohydrates 20 g
 fiber 4 g
 sugars 11 g
cholesterol 3 mg
total fat 0.5 g
 saturated 0.0 g
 polyunsaturated 0.0 g
 monounsaturated 0.0 g
sodium 474 mg

dietary exchange
2 vegetable
¹/₂ other carbohydrate
¹/₂ very lean meat

Asparagus and Artichoke Quiche

Serves 6

This vegetable quiche sports a brown rice crust, which is very easy to assemble. Serve wedges of quiche with cool slices of honeydew melon.

1 1/4 cups low-sodium vegetable broth, such as on page 46
1 teaspoon salt-free all-purpose seasoning
1 cup uncooked instant brown rice
   Vegetable oil spray
   White of 1 large egg
8 medium asparagus spears, trimmed, cut into 1/4-inch slices

1 cup chopped canned artichoke hearts, rinsed and drained
2 medium Italian plum tomatoes, thinly sliced
1 cup fat-free half-and-half
   Egg substitute equivalent to 2 eggs, or 2 large eggs
1/4 cup shredded or grated Parmesan cheese
1/4 teaspoon pepper

In a medium saucepan, bring the vegetable broth and all-purpose seasoning to a simmer over medium-high heat. Stir in the rice. Reduce the heat and simmer, covered, for 10 minutes, or until the rice is tender. Transfer to a medium bowl. Refrigerate for 10 minutes to cool.

Preheat the oven to 400°F. Lightly spray a 9-inch pie plate with vegetable oil spray.

Stir the egg white into the cooled rice. Form a crust by pressing the rice mixture on the bottom and up the side of the pie pan.

Bake for 6 to 7 minutes, or until the rice is golden brown. Remove the crust from the oven. Reduce the oven temperature to 325°F.

In order, arrange the asparagus, artichokes, and tomatoes in even layers in the warm crust.

In a medium bowl, whisk together the remaining ingredients. Pour over the vegetables.

Bake for 40 to 45 minutes, or until the center is set (doesn't jiggle when gently shaken). Let cool for 10 minutes before cutting into wedges.

calories 135
protein 10 g
carbohydrates 22 g
 fiber 2 g
 sugars 5 g
cholesterol 2 mg
total fat 1.5 g
 saturated 0.5 g
 polyunsaturated 0.5 g
 monounsaturated 0.5 g
sodium 247 mg

dietary exchange
1 starch
1 vegetable
1/2 very lean meat

Tomato Quiche
in Couscous Crust

Serves 8

Serve a wedge of this dill-flavored quiche with fresh strawberries.

Crust
    Vegetable oil spray
1/2 cup low-sodium vegetable broth,
    such as on page 46
1/2 cup water
1/2 cup uncooked couscous
1/8 teaspoon ground turmeric
    White of 1 medium egg or
    2 tablespoons egg substitute

Filling
1 teaspoon olive oil
4 ounces button mushrooms, coarsely
    chopped

6 medium green onions (green and
    white parts), chopped
2 medium garlic cloves, minced
6 medium Italian plum tomatoes,
    thickly sliced
2 tablespoons shredded or grated
    Parmesan cheese
    Egg substitute equivalent to 3 eggs
    5-ounce can fat-free evaporated
    milk (2/3 cup)
1 tablespoon fresh dillweed or
    1 teaspoon dried, crumbled
1/4 teaspoon pepper

Preheat the oven to 400°F. Lightly spray a 9-inch pie pan with vegetable oil spray.

In a medium saucepan, bring the broth and water to a boil over medium-high heat. Stir in the couscous and turmeric. Remove from the heat and let stand, covered, for 5 minutes.

Stir the egg white into the couscous. Form a crust by pressing the mixture on the bottom and up the side of the pie pan.

Bake for 10 minutes. Remove the crust from the oven. Let cool completely, about 30 minutes.

Reduce the oven temperature to 350°F.

In a medium nonstick skillet, heat the oil over medium-high heat, swirling to coat the bottom. Cook the mushrooms, green onions, and garlic for 2 to 3 minutes, or until tender.

calories 101
protein 7 g
carbohydrates 15 g
  fiber 2 g
  sugars 5 g
cholesterol 2 mg
total fat 1.0 g
  saturated 0.5 g
  polyunsaturated 0.0 g
  monounsaturated 0.5 g
sodium 107 mg

dietary exchange
1/2 starch
1 vegetable
1/2 very lean meat

Arrange the tomato slices on the crust, cover with the mushroom mixture, and sprinkle with the Parmesan.

In a medium bowl, whisk together the remaining ingredients. Pour over the vegetables.

Bake for 40 to 45 minutes, or until a knife inserted in the center comes out clean.

Three-Cheese
Vegetable Strudel

Serves 4

Vegetables are cooked quickly in a skillet, seasoned and combined with beans, rolled with wafer-thin layers of phyllo dough, and baked. With dinner all wrapped up, the only challenge is picking out dessert.

1 teaspoon olive oil
1-pound bag frozen mixed vegetables (any combination)
1/4 cup coarsely chopped fresh basil leaves
2 tablespoons snipped fresh dillweed
1/4 teaspoon salt-free lemon pepper
15-ounce can no-salt-added navy beans, rinsed and drained

1 cup fat-free or low-fat ricotta cheese
1 cup shredded fat-free or part-skim mozzarella cheese
1/4 cup shredded or grated Romano cheese
6 sheets frozen phyllo dough, thawed
Vegetable oil spray

Heat a large nonstick skillet over medium-high heat. Pour the oil into the skillet and swirl to coat the bottom. Cook the vegetables for 8 to 10 minutes, or until tender and warmed through, stirring occasionally. (If there is excess liquid in the pan, increase the heat to high. Leaving the vegetables in the pan, cook for 2 to 3 minutes, or until the liquid has almost evaporated, stirring occasionally.) Remove from the heat.

Stir in the basil, dillweed, and lemon pepper. Let cool for 5 minutes.

In a medium bowl, stir together the beans, ricotta, mozzarella, and Romano cheese. Stir in the vegetables. Set aside.

Preheat the oven to 350°F.

Place one sheet of phyllo dough on a cutting board. Lightly spray the top with vegetable oil spray. Place another sheet of phyllo on top; lightly spray with vegetable oil spray. Repeat with a third sheet of phyllo. Leaving a 2-inch border along one wide end of the phyllo, spoon half the filling along that end. Fold the

calories 338
protein 29 g
carbohydrates 46 g
 fiber 9 g
 sugars 10 g
cholesterol 14 mg
total fat 4.0 g
 saturated 1.5 g
 polyunsaturated 0.5 g
 monounsaturated 2.0 g
sodium 666 mg

dietary exchange
2 starch
3 vegetable
2½ very lean meat

edge closest to the filling over the filling. Fold the short ends slightly toward the center and roll up from the wide end to enclose the filling. Place the strudel with the seam side down on a large nonstick baking sheet. Repeat with the remaining phyllo and filling, placing the second strudel about 2 inches from the first.

Lightly spray the tops and sides of the strudels with vegetable oil spray. Cut diagonal slits in the tops about 2 inches apart and about $1/2$ inch deep.

Bake for 30 to 35 minutes, or until the crust is golden brown and the filling is warmed through. Transfer the baking sheet to a cooling rack. Let cool for 10 minutes before cutting each strudel in half.

Carrot, Parsnip, and Potato Pancakes

Serves 6

Enjoy these wholesome, savory pancakes plain or with a dollop of fat-free sour cream or unsweetened applesauce.

2 medium carrots, peeled
1 medium parsnip, peeled
1 pound potatoes (about 3 medium), peeled
Egg substitute equivalent to 5 eggs
1 small onion, minced

3 tablespoons snipped fresh chives or green onions (green part only)
2 tablespoons all-purpose flour
2 tablespoons plain dry bread crumbs
1/4 teaspoon salt
Pepper to taste

Coarsely grate the carrots, parsnip, and potatoes using the large holes of a four-sided grater. Put the vegetables in a colander set in a large bowl.

Press down on the vegetables, squeezing out as much liquid as possible. Discard the liquid, and return the vegetables to the bowl.

Stir in the egg substitute, onion, chives, flour, bread crumbs, salt, and pepper.

Heat a large nonstick skillet over medium heat. Drop heaping tablespoons of batter onto the skillet, using the back of a spoon to flatten the pancakes slightly. Cook for 3 to 4 minutes, or until the bottoms are golden brown. Turn over each pancake and cook for about 3 minutes, or until golden brown. Transfer to a serving platter. Stirring to combine between batches as needed, cook the remaining batter. You should get about 24 pancakes.

Serve the pancakes hot or at room temperature by themselves or with the sour cream or applesauce.

calories 127
protein 8 g
carbohydrates 25 g
  fiber 4 g
  sugars 6 g
cholesterol 0 mg
total fat 0.5 g
  saturated 0.0 g
  polyunsaturated 0.0 g
  monounsaturated 0.0 g
sodium 232 mg

dietary exchange
1 1/2 starch
1 vegetable
1/2 very lean meat

Spinach Soufflé

Serves 4

Complement this airy soufflé with brilliantly colored Harvard Beets (page 418) and snow-white Parsnip Salad with Jícama and Apple (page 102).

Vegetable oil spray
2 tablespoons light stick margarine
2 tablespoons whole-wheat flour
1/2 cup fat-free milk
5 ounces frozen chopped spinach, cooked, drained, and squeezed dry

1 tablespoon finely chopped onion
1/4 teaspoon ground nutmeg
1/4 teaspoon pepper, or to taste
Whites of 6 medium eggs
3 tablespoons shredded or grated Parmesan cheese

Preheat the oven to 350°F. Lightly spray a 1³/₄-quart casserole dish with vegetable oil spray. Set aside.

In a small, heavy saucepan, melt the margarine over medium-high heat. Whisk in the flour. Cook for 1 minute, or until the mixture is smooth and bubbly, whisking constantly.

Remove from the heat and gradually whisk in the milk. Return to the heat and bring the mixture to a boil over medium-high heat, stirring constantly. Reduce the heat to low and cook for 1 minute, stirring occasionally. Remove from the heat.

In a large bowl, stir together the spinach, onion, nutmeg, and pepper. Stir in the milk mixture.

Beat the egg whites until stiff peaks form. Using a rubber scraper, fold gently into the spinach mixture. Pour the mixture into the casserole dish. Sprinkle with the Parmesan.

Bake for 35 minutes, or until the center is set (doesn't jiggle when the casserole is gently shaken). Serve immediately.

calories 95
protein 9 g
carbohydrates 7 g
 fiber 2 g
 sugars 2 g
cholesterol 3 mg
total fat 4.0 g
 saturated 1.5 g
 polyunsaturated 1.0 g
 monounsaturated 1.0 g
sodium 212 mg

dietary exchange
1/2 starch
1 lean meat

Spinach Roll
with Alfredo Sauce

Serves 3

This dish begins with a soufflé that's substantial enough to roll. Then it gets a rich and delicious Alfredo sauce. Even people who think they don't like spinach will love this dish.

Vegetable oil spray

Soufflé
Egg substitute equivalent to 2 eggs, or 2 large eggs
10-ounce package frozen chopped spinach, thawed and squeezed dry
2 tablespoons light stick margarine, melted
1 tablespoon fresh lemon juice
1/8 teaspoon pepper
1/8 teaspoon ground nutmeg, or to taste
Whites of 3 large eggs, stiffly beaten

Fat-Free Alfredo Sauce
5-ounce can fat-free evaporated milk
1/2 medium garlic clove, crushed
2 tablespoons shredded or grated Parmesan cheese
1/4 teaspoon salt-free Italian seasoning, crumbled
1/8 teaspoon pepper, or to taste
❖
1/2 teaspoon acceptable stick margarine
1/2 teaspoon fresh lemon juice
4 medium button mushrooms, sliced

Preheat the oven to 350°F.

Line an 8-inch square baking pan with cooking parchment or wax paper. Lightly spray with vegetable oil spray.

In a large mixing bowl, beat the egg substitute until foamy.

Stir in the spinach, 2 tablespoons margarine, 1 tablespoon lemon juice, pepper, and nutmeg.

Add one fourth of the egg whites, stirring well. Gently fold in the remaining egg whites, being careful not to deflate them. Spoon the mixture into the baking pan.

Bake for 10 to 12 minutes, or until the soufflé springs back when lightly touched in the center. Let cool for 10 minutes.

calories 155
protein 16 g
carbohydrates 12 g
  fiber 3 g
  sugars 7 g
cholesterol 4 mg
total fat 5.5 g
  saturated 1.5 g
  polyunsaturated 1.5 g
  monounsaturated 1.5 g
sodium 374 mg

dietary exchange
1/2 skim milk
1 vegetable
1 1/2 lean meat

Meanwhile, prepare the sauce. In a medium nonstick skillet, stir together the milk and garlic. Bring to a boil over medium-high heat, stirring frequently.

Stir in the remaining sauce ingredients. Reduce the heat to low and cook for 10 to 15 minutes, or until the cheese has melted, stirring frequently.

To remove the soufflé, invert the baking pan onto a flat surface. Roll up the soufflé, gently peeling the parchment while rolling. Place the soufflé with the seam side down on a serving platter.

In a small skillet over medium heat, melt $\frac{1}{2}$ teaspoon margarine. Stir in $\frac{1}{2}$ teaspoon lemon juice and the mushrooms. Cook for 3 minutes.

To serve, spoon the mushroom mixture over the spinach roll. Serve with the Alfredo sauce on the side.

Cook's Tip on Beating Egg Whites

Even a single drop of egg yolk will prevent egg whites from rising, so separate eggs very carefully. Crack the egg and drain the white into a small bowl. Pour the yolk into a separate bowl. Pour the white into the mixing bowl. That way you won't spoil the whole bowl of whites if a yolk breaks. If you do get a speck of yolk in the white, you can blot the yolk up with the corner of a paper towel.

Portobello Mushroom Ragout with Sun-Dried Tomato Polenta

Serves 4

Enjoy the rich, meaty flavor of giant portobello mushrooms over polenta, enhanced here with sun-dried tomatoes.

Ragout

- 1 tablespoon olive oil
- 3 medium portobello mushrooms, cut into ¹/₂-inch slices
- 1 medium sweet onion, such as Texas Sweet, cut into ¹/₄-inch rings
- 2 large garlic cloves, thickly sliced
- ¹/₄ cup coarsely chopped fresh Italian, or flat-leaf, parsley
- ¹/₄ cup firmly packed fresh basil leaves, coarsely chopped
- 2 teaspoons balsamic vinegar
- ¹/₄ teaspoon salt
  Pepper to taste

Polenta

- 2¹/₂ cups water
  12-ounce can fat-free evaporated milk
- 1 tablespoon no-salt-added tomato paste
- 5 dry-packed sun-dried tomato halves, thinly sliced
- 1 cup cornmeal (coarsely ground, finely ground, or combination)
- 2 tablespoons shredded or grated Parmesan cheese
  Pepper to taste

calories 276
protein 13 g
carbohydrates 48 g
  fiber 4 g
  sugars 14 g
cholesterol 5 mg
total fat 5.0 g
  saturated 1.0 g
  polyunsaturated 0.5 g
  monounsaturated 3.0 g
sodium 302 mg

dietary exchange
2 starch
¹/₂ skim milk
2 vegetable
¹/₂ fat

Heat a Dutch oven or large skillet over medium heat. Pour in the oil and swirl to coat the bottom. When the oil is hot, cook the mushrooms, onion, and garlic, covered, for 10 to 20 minutes, or until the mushrooms release their liquid, stirring occasionally.

Stir in the parsley, basil, vinegar, salt, and pepper. Cook, covered, for 5 minutes, or until the onion is soft, stirring occasionally. Set aside.

In a 4-quart pot or stockpot, stir together the water, milk, and tomato paste. Bring to a boil over high heat.

Stir in the tomatoes. Reduce the heat to medium.

Using a long-handled whisk, carefully stir the mixture to create a swirl. Slowly pour the cornmeal in a steady stream into the mixture, whisking constantly. After adding all the cornmeal, hold the pot steady and continue whisking for 1 to 2 minutes, or until the polenta is the desired consistency.

To serve, pour the polenta into a large, deep serving platter or bowl. Spoon the mushroom ragout and liquids over the polenta. Sprinkle with the Parmesan and pepper. Serve immediately.

Cook's Tip on Sweet Onions

Growing conditions make onions sweet, and the locale where they grow is usually reflected in the name. Some examples are Maui from Hawaii, Texas Sweets from Texas, Vidalia from Georgia, and Walla Walla from Washington. You might also want to try Oso Sweet from Chile and Rio Sweet from Mexico.

When the ones you like are in season, you may want to freeze a big batch to have on hand for cooking. Chop the onions, put them on a baking sheet, and freeze them. Seal the frozen onions in a resealable plastic freezer bag.

Time-Saver

Substitute 1 tube of prepared polenta with sun-dried tomatoes and garlic for the homemade polenta recipe above. Preheat the broiler. Line a baking sheet with aluminum foil. Lightly spray the foil with vegetable oil spray. Cut the polenta into 12 slices, and put them on the foil. Broil for 2 minutes on each side, or until heated through. Arrange 3 slices on each plate and top with ragout.

vegetables and side dishes

Artichoke Hearts Riviera

Asparagus par Excellence

Asparagus with Garlic and
Parmesan Bread Crumbs

Braised Barley and Corn with Tomatoes

Fresh Green Beans with Water Chestnuts

Dilled Green Beans

French-Style Green Beans
with Pimiento and Dill Seeds

Green Beans and Rice with Hazelnuts

Louisiana Beans Oregano

Mediterranean Lima Beans

Deviled Beets

Harvard Beets

Stir-Fried Bok Choy with
Green Onion Sauce

Broccoli with Plum Sauce

Crunchy Broccoli Casserole

Parmesan-Topped Broccoli and
Cauliflower

Brussels Sprouts and Pecans

Cabbage with Mustard-Caraway Sauce

Spiced Red Cabbage

Tangy Carrots

Honeyed Carrots

Baked Grated Carrots with Sherry

Cauliflower and Roasted Corn
with Chili Powder and Lime

Creole Celery and Peas

Swiss Chard, Southern Style

Braised Swiss Chard

Cajun Corn

Southwestern Creamy Corn

Grits Casserole with Cheese and Chiles

Creamy Kale with Red Bell Pepper

Kohlrabi Gratin

Mushrooms with Red Wine

Mushrooms with White Wine
and Shallots

Baked Okra Bites

Asian Linguini

Crispy Baked Onion Flower

Parmesan Parsnip Puree with
Leeks and Carrots

Black-Eyed Peas with Canadian Bacon

Savory Peas

French Peas

Sweet Lemon Snow Peas

Stir-Fried Sugar Snap Peas

Basil Roasted Peppers

Scalloped Potatoes

Potatoes with Leeks
and Fresh Herbs

Baked Fries with Creole Seasoning

Rustic Potato Patties

Baked Sweet Potato Chips

Orange Sweet Potatoes

Risotto with Broccoli and Leeks

Risotto Milanese

Middle Eastern Brown Rice

Mexican Fried Rice

Rice Italiano

Wild Rice with Mushrooms

Basil Spinach

Sophisticated Spinach

Gingered Acorn Squash

Acorn Squash Stuffed with
Cranberries and Walnuts

Butternut Mash

(continued on next page)

Artichoke Hearts
Riviera

Serves 6

Because you can prepare the sauce while the artichoke hearts cook, this elegant side dish is ready in minutes.

2 10-ounce packages frozen
    artichoke hearts

Sauce
1/2 cup dry vermouth or dry white
     wine (regular or nonalcoholic)
2 tablespoons light stick margarine
1 tablespoon snipped fresh parsley

1 tablespoon fresh lemon juice
1 medium garlic clove, crushed
1/2 teaspoon dry mustard
1/2 teaspoon dried tarragon, crumbled
     White pepper to taste
     ❖
     Snipped fresh parsley (optional)

Prepare the artichoke hearts using the package directions, omitting the salt and margarine. Drain.

Meanwhile, in a small saucepan, stir together the sauce ingredients. Bring to a boil over medium-high heat. Reduce the heat and simmer, covered, for 5 minutes.

To serve, pour the sauce over the cooked artichoke hearts. Sprinkle with the remaining parsley.

calories 96
protein 3 g
carbohydrates 12 g
  fiber 7 g
  sugars 3 g
cholesterol 0 mg
total fat 2.0 g
  saturated 0.5 g
  polyunsaturated 0.5 g
  monounsaturated 0.5 g
sodium 78 mg

dietary exchange
2 1/2 vegetable
1/2 fat

Asparagus par Excellence

Serves 6

Excellent indeed, this side dish not only tastes good but also looks festive, with its sprinkling of red pimiento and green parsley and tarragon. It's a wonderful accompaniment for turkey and dressing.

1/2 cup water
1 small onion, diced
1/2 medium green bell pepper, chopped
   Pepper to taste
2 10-ounce packages frozen
   asparagus spears

2 teaspoons finely snipped fresh
   parsley
2 teaspoons diced pimiento
1/2 teaspoon dried tarragon, crumbled

In a large skillet, bring the water, onion, bell pepper, and pepper to a boil over medium-high heat. Reduce the heat and simmer, covered, for 5 minutes.

Add the asparagus and cook, covered, for 5 minutes, or until tender-crisp.

To serve, drain and discard the liquid from the skillet. Place the asparagus mixture on a plate. Sprinkle with the pimiento and tarragon.

calories 34
protein 4 g
carbohydrates 7 g
  fiber 2 g
  sugars 3 g
cholesterol 0 mg
total fat 0.5 g
  saturated 0.0 g
  polyunsaturated 0.0 g
  monounsaturated 0.0 g
sodium 9 mg

dietary exchange
1 1/2 vegetable

Asparagus with Garlic and Parmesan Bread Crumbs

Serves 6

Seasoned bread crumbs blanket asparagus spears in this easy side dish.

Bread Crumbs
- 2 slices bread (whole-grain preferred), torn into 1-inch pieces
- 1 tablespoon light tub margarine
- 2 medium garlic cloves, minced
- 1/2 tablespoon dried oregano, crumbled
- 2 tablespoons shredded Parmesan cheese (don't use grated)

❖

- 1 1/4 pounds asparagus spears, trimmed
- 1/8 teaspoon salt

Put the bread in a food processor or blender and pulse until the texture of commercial bread crumbs.

In a large nonstick skillet, melt the margarine over medium-high heat. Swirl to coat the bottom. Cook the garlic for 10 seconds, stirring constantly.

Stir in the bread crumbs and oregano. Cook for 5 minutes, or until the crumbs are golden brown, stirring frequently. Remove from the heat.

Stir in the Parmesan.

Steam the asparagus for 3 minutes, or until just tender-crisp.

To serve, arrange the asparagus on a platter. Sprinkle with the salt. Top with the crumb mixture.

Mixed Squash with Garlic and Lemon Bread Crumbs

Substitute 2 medium yellow summer squash, thinly sliced, and 2 medium zucchini, thinly sliced, for the asparagus, and 1 tablespoon grated lemon zest for the Parmesan cheese.

calories 60
protein 4 g
carbohydrates 9 g
 fiber 3 g
 sugars 3 g
cholesterol 1 mg
total fat 1.5 g
 saturated 0.5 g
 polyunsaturated 0.5 g
 monounsaturated 0.5 g
sodium 136 mg

dietary exchange
2 vegetable
1/2 fat

with mixed squash

calories 47
protein 2 g
carbohydrates 8 g
 fiber 2 g
 sugars 2 g
cholesterol 0 mg
total fat 1.5 g
 saturated 0.0 g
 polyunsaturated 0.5 g
 monounsaturated 0.5 g
sodium 108 mg

dietary exchange
2 vegetable

Braised Barley and Corn with Tomatoes

Serves 4

Chase the winter blues away with this side dish of plump kernels of corn and barley stewed with tomatoes.

$1/2$ teaspoon olive oil

$1/4$ medium onion, chopped

1 cup fat-free, low-sodium chicken broth, such as on page 45

$1/2$ 14.5-ounce can no-salt-added diced tomatoes, undrained

$1/2$ teaspoon salt-free all-purpose seasoning

$1/8$ teaspoon pepper

$1/8$ teaspoon crushed red pepper flakes (optional)

$1/4$ cup uncooked pearl barley

1 cup frozen whole-kernel corn

Heat a large saucepan over medium heat. Pour the oil into the saucepan and swirl to coat the bottom. Cook the onion for 2 to 3 minutes, or until soft, stirring occasionally.

Stir in the broth, undrained tomatoes, all-purpose seasoning, pepper, and red pepper flakes. Increase the heat to medium high and bring to a simmer, stirring occasionally.

Stir in the barley. Reduce the heat and simmer, covered, for 30 minutes.

Stir in the corn. Simmer, covered, for 15 to 20 minutes, or until the barley is tender and the corn is warmed through.

calories 102
protein 4 g
carbohydrates 22 g
  fiber 4 g
  sugars 3 g
cholesterol 0 mg
total fat 1.0 g
  saturated 0.0 g
  polyunsaturated 0.5 g
  monounsaturated 0.5 g
sodium 29 mg

dietary exchange
1 starch
1$1/2$ vegetable

Fresh Green Beans
with Water Chestnuts

Serves 6

Wondering what to serve with an Asian entrée besides steamed rice? Here's your answer.

1¹/₂ pounds fresh green beans	1 tablespoon sesame seeds, dry-roasted
1¹/₂ teaspoons acceptable vegetable oil	¹/₂ teaspoon salt
1 teaspoon hot-pepper oil	
8-ounce can sliced water chestnuts, rinsed and drained	

In a large saucepan over high heat, bring to a boil enough water to cover the beans. Meanwhile, trim the beans and cut diagonally into 1¹/₂-inch pieces. Boil for 4 minutes. With a large slotted spoon, remove the beans from the pan. Plunge them into ice water to stop the cooking process. Drain.

Heat a large skillet over high heat. Pour both oils into the skillet and swirl to coat the bottom. Heat the water chestnuts for 1 minute, stirring constantly.

Stir in the sesame seeds, beans, and salt. Cook until heated through, stirring constantly.

Cook's Tip on Water Chestnuts

Grown in water and frequently used in Chinese cooking, water chestnuts are underground stems of a marsh plant. Fresh and unpeeled, they do resemble chestnuts. You can find the fresh ones in Chinese markets. Peel them and use either raw or cooked to add crunch to salads or stir-fry dishes. Water chestnuts are also available whole or sliced in cans.

calories 73
protein 3 g
carbohydrates 11 g
  fiber 5 g
  sugars 3 g
cholesterol 0 mg
total fat 3.0 g
  saturated 0.5 g
  polyunsaturated 1.0 g
  monounsaturated 1.5 g
sodium 204 mg

dietary exchange
2 vegetable
¹/₂ fat

Dilled Green Beans

Serves 6

The secret's in the broth. The green beans absorb the vegetable broth, infused with bell pepper, onion, and dill seeds, which have a more intense flavor than dillweed.

1 cup low-sodium vegetable broth, such as on page 46

$^{1}/_{4}$ medium green bell pepper, chopped

2 tablespoons chopped onion

$^{1}/_{2}$ teaspoon dill seeds

2 9-ounce packages frozen cut green beans

In a large saucepan over medium heat, cook all the ingredients except the green beans for 3 to 4 minutes, or until heated through.

Stir in the beans. Cook, covered, for 5 to 8 minutes, or until the beans are tender-crisp. Serve hot or refrigerate and serve chilled.

Variations

Experiment with different herbs and seeds to find out just how adaptable this recipe is. Substitute any of the following for the dill seeds: caraway, fennel, mustard, or coriander seeds; dried marjoram or oregano, crumbled; or dried rosemary, crushed.

calories 32
protein 1 g
carbohydrates 6 g
  fiber 2 g
  sugars 3 g
cholesterol 0 mg
total fat 0.0 g
  saturated 0.0 g
  polyunsaturated 0.0 g
  monounsaturated 0.0 g
sodium 4 mg

dietary exchange
1 vegetable

French-Style Green Beans
with Pimiento and
Dill Seeds

Serves 4

A touch of cider vinegar and dill seeds, plus a trio of chopped vegetables, adds sparkle to this side dish.

1 tablespoon light stick margarine	¹/₄ cup finely chopped onion
1 tablespoon water	2 tablespoons chopped pimiento
9-ounce package frozen French-style green beans	1 tablespoon cider vinegar
1 medium rib of celery, finely chopped	¹/₄ teaspoon dill seeds
	Pepper to taste

In a medium saucepan, heat the margarine and water over medium heat until the margarine melts. Swirl to coat the bottom.

Add the beans. Cook for 1 to 2 minutes, separating them with a fork. Reduce the heat to low and cook, covered, for 5 to 6 minutes, or until the beans are tender-crisp.

Stir in the remaining ingredients and heat thoroughly. (The celery and onion should remain crisp.)

calories 41
protein 1 g
carbohydrates 6 g
  fiber 2 g
  sugars 3 g
cholesterol 0 mg
total fat 1.5 g
  saturated 0.5 g
  polyunsaturated 0.5 g
  monounsaturated 0.5 g
sodium 29 mg

dietary exchange
1 vegetable

Green Beans and Rice
with Hazelnuts

Serves 8

Green onions and lemon enhance fluffy rice and green beans. Chopped hazelnuts and pimiento provide the crowning touch.

9-ounce package frozen French-style green beans or 16-ounce can no-salt-added French-style green beans

1½ tablespoons light tub margarine

2 cups cooked rice

3 tablespoons sliced green onions (green and white parts)

½ to 1 teaspoon fresh lemon juice
Pepper to taste

¼ cup chopped or sliced hazelnuts, dry-roasted

¼ cup chopped pimiento, drained

Prepare the frozen green beans using the package directions, omitting the salt and margarine, or heat the canned beans. Drain.

In a large saucepan, melt the margarine over medium heat. Swirl to coat the bottom. Stir in the beans, rice, green onions, lemon juice, and pepper. Cook until heated through, stirring occasionally.

To serve, sprinkle with the nuts and pimiento.

Cook's Tip on Hazelnuts, or Filberts

Traditionally used in many European dishes, hazelnuts, or filberts, are now produced in Washington and Oregon. They have a bitter brown skin that you'll want to remove. Put the nuts in a single layer on a baking pan and bake in a pre-heated 350°F oven for about 10 minutes. Let them cool for 1 to 2 minutes. While the hazelnuts are warm, put a handful in a dish towel and rub to remove the skin. Chop the nuts with a knife or in a food processor, if desired.

calories 94
protein 2 g
carbohydrates 14 g
  fiber 2 g
  sugars 1 g
cholesterol 0 mg
total fat 3.0 g
  saturated 0.0 g
  polyunsaturated 0.5 g
  monounsaturated 2.0 g
sodium 19 mg

dietary exchange
1 starch
½ fat

Louisiana Beans
Oregano

Serves 4

Try these green beans with blackened redfish or roast chicken.

1½ medium tomatoes, diced
1 medium rib of celery, diced
⅓ cup water
¼ medium green bell pepper, diced
2 tablespoons chopped onion
½ teaspoon garlic powder

½ teaspoon onion powder
½ teaspoon dried oregano, crumbled
⅛ teaspoon white pepper
⅛ teaspoon salt
    9-ounce package frozen Italian
    green beans

In a medium saucepan, stir together all the ingredients except the green beans. Bring to a boil over high heat. Reduce the heat and simmer, covered, for 10 minutes.

Increase the heat to medium. Add the beans, separating them with a fork. Cook, uncovered, for 5 to 8 minutes, or until the beans are tender-crisp, stirring occasionally.

calories 42
protein 2 g
carbohydrates 10 g
  fiber 3 g
  sugars 4 g
cholesterol 0 mg
total fat 0.5 g
  saturated 0.0 g
  polyunsaturated 0.0 g
  monounsaturated 0.0 g
sodium 89 mg

dietary exchange
2 vegetable

Mediterranean Lima Beans

Serves 4

Many typical ingredients of Mediterranean cooking—garlic, tomatoes, onion, and mint—flavor this dish.

10-ounce package frozen lima beans
1 teaspoon light tub margarine
¼ cup chopped onion
1 medium garlic clove, crushed
1 cup canned no-salt-added tomatoes, undrained
½ teaspoon dried mint, crumbled

Prepare the lima beans using the package directions, omitting the salt and margarine. Drain.

In a medium skillet, melt the margarine over medium-high heat. Swirl to coat the bottom. Cook the onion and garlic for 2 to 3 minutes, or until the onion is soft.

Stir in the lima beans, undrained tomatoes, and mint. Heat thoroughly.

calories 112
protein 7 g
carbohydrates 21 g
  fiber 5 g
  sugars 5 g
cholesterol 0 mg
total fat 0.5 g
  saturated 0.0 g
  polyunsaturated 0.0 g
  monounsaturated 0.0 g
sodium 90 mg

dietary exchange
1½ starch
½ very lean meat

Deviled Beets

Serves 6

Are you looking for safe, fun ways to get your children involved in cooking? Letting them skin the beets may be the answer. The kids might even decide to eat the fruits of their labor.

3 pounds fresh beets or 3 15-ounce cans no-salt-added beets, drained

2 tablespoons plain rice vinegar

1 tablespoon light brown sugar

1 tablespoon light stick margarine

1 teaspoon low-sodium Worcestershire sauce

$^1/_2$ teaspoon paprika

$^1/_4$ teaspoon dry mustard

$^1/_4$ teaspoon ground cloves

If using fresh beets, cut off all but 1 to 2 inches of the stems. Don't cut off the root end. Put the beets in a large saucepan. Cover with water and bring to a boil over medium-high heat. Reduce the heat and simmer, covered, for 30 to 40 minutes, or until a knife easily pierces the beets. Drain the beets. Let cool slightly. Slip the skins off.

For fresh or canned beets, dice the beets.

In a large saucepan over medium heat, stir together the remaining ingredients. After the margarine melts, gently stir in the beets. Cook until heated through.

Microwave Method
Cook and dice the beets as directed. In a 4-cup microwave-safe bowl, stir together the remaining ingredients. Heat on 100 percent power (high) for 2 minutes, stirring halfway through. Gently stir in the beets. Cook on 100 percent power (high) for 2 minutes.

Cook's Tip on Beets

Cooking time for whole beets depends on their size. If they are very large, they may have to cook for up to an hour.

calories 116
protein 4 g
carbohydrates 24 g
 fiber 6 g
 sugars 16 g
cholesterol 0 mg
total fat 1.5 g
 saturated 0.0 g
 polyunsaturated 0.5 g
 monounsaturated 0.5 g
sodium 192 mg

dietary exchange
5 vegetable

Harvard Beets

Serves 4

Vibrant purple beets in a sweet-and-sour sauce is a classic. Try this version with lean pork or chicken and add your favorite green vegetable.

2 pounds fresh beets or 2 15-ounce cans no-salt-added beets, drained

Sauce
1/3 cup fresh orange juice
2 tablespoons cider vinegar
1/2 teaspoon grated lemon zest
2 tablespoons fresh lemon juice
1 1/2 tablespoons sugar
1 teaspoon cornstarch
1/8 teaspoon garlic powder
1/8 teaspoon salt

If using fresh beets, cut off all but 1 to 2 inches of the stems. Don't cut off the root end. Put the beets in a large saucepan. Cover with water and bring to a boil over medium-high heat. Reduce the heat and simmer, covered, for 30 to 40 minutes, or until a knife easily pierces the beets. Drain the beets. Let cool slightly. Slip the skins off.

For fresh or canned beets, dice the beets.

In a large saucepan, whisk together the sauce ingredients. Bring to a boil over medium-high heat. Cook for 3 to 5 minutes, or until thickened, whisking occasionally.

Stir in the beets. Cook for 2 minutes, or until heated through.

Microwave Method
Cook and dice the beets as directed. Whisk together the sauce ingredients except the lemon zest in a microwave-safe bowl. Cook on 100 percent power (high) for 3 to 3 1/2 minutes, or until the sauce bubbles and is thick. Stir in the lemon zest and beets. Cook on 100 percent power (high) for 2 minutes.

calories 131
protein 4 g
carbohydrates 30 g
  fiber 7 g
  sugars 21 g
cholesterol 0 mg
total fat 0.5 g
  saturated 0.0 g
  polyunsaturated 0.0 g
  monounsaturated 0.0 g
sodium 250 mg

dietary exchange
5 vegetable
1/2 other carbohydrate

Stir-Fried Bok Choy with Green Onion Sauce

Serves 8

Vitamin-rich bok choy is cooked quickly, then combined with an Asian-influenced pestolike sauce. This side dish is great with grilled beef tenderloin or lean pork loin chops.

Green Onion Sauce
- ¼ cup fat-free, low-sodium chicken broth, such as on page 45
- 4 medium green onions (green and white parts), thinly sliced
- 2 tablespoons fresh snipped cilantro or parsley
- 1 tablespoon slivered almonds
- 1 teaspoon toasted sesame oil
- 1 teaspoon low-salt soy sauce
- ½ teaspoon cornstarch
- ½ teaspoon red chili paste (optional)

❖

- 1 teaspoon acceptable vegetable oil
- 8 medium stalks of bok choy (green and white parts), cut into 1-inch pieces

In a food processor or blender, process the sauce ingredients for 10 to 15 seconds, or until almost smooth.

Heat a wok or large nonstick skillet over medium-high heat. Pour the vegetable oil into the wok and swirl to coat the bottom. Cook the bok choy for 2 to 3 minutes, or until tender-crisp, stirring constantly.

Stir in the sauce. Cook for 1 to 2 minutes, or until the sauce is slightly thickened, stirring constantly.

calories 23
protein 1 g
carbohydrates 2 g
  fiber 1 g
  sugars 1 g
cholesterol 0 mg
total fat 1.5 g
  saturated 0.0 g
  polyunsaturated 0.5 g
  monounsaturated 1.0 g
sodium 29 mg

dietary exchange
½ fat

Broccoli with Plum Sauce

Serves 4

It's fun to experiment with seeds and spices to infuse flavor. In this dish, coriander seeds add a delightful lemonlike flavor.

1 medium lemon, thinly sliced
1-inch piece unpeeled gingerroot, thinly sliced
2 cups broccoli florets (about 8 ounces)

1/2 teaspoon coriander seeds, crushed using a mortar and pestle
2 tablespoons plum sauce
1 teaspoon low-salt soy sauce
1/2 teaspoon toasted sesame oil
2 teaspoons sesame seeds

In a medium saucepan, bring about 1/2 inch of water to a simmer over high heat. Add the lemon and gingerroot. Set a steamer basket in the water. (The water shouldn't touch the bottom of the basket.) Put the broccoli in the basket.

Sprinkle the coriander over the broccoli. Reduce the heat and simmer, covered, for 6 to 8 minutes, or until tender-crisp. Drain well, discarding the lemon and gingerroot.

Meanwhile, in a medium bowl, stir together the plum sauce, soy sauce, and sesame oil.

Stir the broccoli into the plum sauce mixture to coat.

Sprinkle with the sesame seeds.

calories 41
protein 2 g
carbohydrates 6 g
  fiber 1 g
  sugars 3 g
cholesterol 0 mg
total fat 1.5 g
  saturated 0.0 g
  polyunsaturated 0.5 g
  monounsaturated 0.5 g
sodium 90 mg

dietary exchange
1 vegetable
1/2 fat

Crunchy Broccoli Casserole

Serves 8

Put this attractive casserole together early in the day, refrigerate, then bake just in time for your dinner guests to enjoy.

Vegetable oil spray
1 bunch fresh broccoli (about 1³/₄ pounds)

Sauce

2 tablespoons fat-free, low-sodium chicken broth, such as on page 45
1 large onion, finely chopped
¹/₂ medium red bell pepper, diced
¹/₄ cup all-purpose flour
1 cup fat-free milk
2 cups fat-free, low-sodium chicken broth, such as on page 45

¹/₄ cup grated Romano or Parmesan cheese
1 tablespoon finely chopped fresh basil or 1 teaspoon dried, crumbled
¹/₄ teaspoon salt
¹/₈ teaspoon ground nutmeg
¹/₈ teaspoon white pepper

❖

1 cup unseasoned croutons, coarsely crushed
2 tablespoons finely chopped walnuts, dry-roasted

Preheat the oven to 400°F. Lightly spray a 13 × 9 × 2-inch baking dish with vegetable oil spray.

Peel any broccoli stems that seem tough. Cut the broccoli into 4-inch pieces. Steam for 4 minutes. Arrange in two lengthwise rows in the baking dish. Set aside.

In a medium saucepan, heat 2 tablespoons broth over medium-high heat. Add the onion and bell pepper and cook for 2 to 3 minutes, or until the onion is soft.

In a small bowl, whisk together the flour and milk. Whisk the milk mixture and 2 cups broth into the onion mixture. Reduce the heat to medium and cook, whisking constantly, until thickened.

Whisk in the remaining sauce ingredients. Pour over the broccoli.

In a small bowl, stir together the croutons and walnuts. Sprinkle over the broccoli and sauce.

Bake for 20 to 25 minutes, or until the sauce is bubbly.

calories 110
protein 7 g
carbohydrates 16 g
  fiber 4 g
  sugars 6 g
cholesterol 5 mg
total fat 3.0 g
  saturated 1.0 g
  polyunsaturated 1.0 g
  monounsaturated 0.5 g
sodium 194 mg

dietary exchange
¹/₂ starch
1¹/₂ vegetable
¹/₂ fat

Parmesan-Topped
Broccoli and Cauliflower

Serves 4

When you want a break from the typical steamed side dishes, turn to this nutmeg-tinged combination.

2 cups frozen chopped broccoli, thawed and drained

2 cups frozen chopped cauliflower, thawed and drained

1/2 10.75-ounce can low-fat, reduced-sodium condensed cream of mushroom soup

1/8 teaspoon ground nutmeg

2 tablespoons shredded or grated Parmesan cheese

1/8 teaspoon salt

Pepper to taste

In a 10-inch nonstick skillet, stir together the broccoli, cauliflower, mushroom soup, and nutmeg. Bring just to a boil over medium-high heat. Reduce the heat and simmer, covered, for 4 minutes, or until the broccoli is just tender-crisp. Remove from the heat.

Sprinkle with the Parmesan, salt, and pepper. Let stand, covered, for 2 minutes before serving.

calories 68
protein 5 g
carbohydrates 10 g
  fiber 4 g
  sugars 3 g
cholesterol 5 mg
total fat 2.0 g
  saturated 1.0 g
  polyunsaturated 0.5 g
  monounsaturated 0.5 g
sodium 297 mg

dietary exchange
2 vegetable
1/2 fat

Brussels Sprouts
and Pecans

Serves 8

Tender brussels sprouts swim in a creamy sauce in this change-of-pace dish.

Vegetable oil spray
2 10-ounce packages frozen brussels sprouts or 1½ pounds fresh brussels sprouts

Sauce

1 cup fat-free, low-sodium chicken broth, such as on page 45
⅔ cup fat-free evaporated milk
¼ cup all-purpose flour

¼ teaspoon salt
⅛ teaspoon pepper
2 tablespoons chopped pecans, dry-roasted

❖

2 teaspoons chopped fresh sage or ½ teaspoon dried
½ cup plain dry bread crumbs

Preheat the oven to 400°F. Lightly spray a 1½-quart casserole dish with vegetable oil spray.

Prepare the frozen brussels sprouts using the package directions, omitting the salt and margarine, or steam the fresh sprouts for 6 to 8 minutes, or until tender. Uncover the fresh sprouts briefly after 2 to 3 minutes to release the odor. Drain. Put in the casserole dish.

In a medium saucepan, whisk together the sauce ingredients except the pecans. Cook over medium-high heat for 3 to 4 minutes, or until the sauce comes to a boil and thickens, stirring occasionally. Remove from the heat.

Stir the pecans into the sauce. Pour over the brussels sprouts. Sprinkle with the sage and bread crumbs. Lightly spray with vegetable oil spray.

Bake for 10 minutes, or until the topping is lightly browned.

calories 101
protein 6 g
carbohydrates 16 g
  fiber 3 g
  sugars 4 g
cholesterol 1 mg
total fat 2.0 g
  saturated 0.5 g
  polyunsaturated 0.5 g
  monounsaturated 1.0 g
sodium 166 mg

dietary exchange
½ starch
1½ vegetable
½ fat

Cabbage with
Mustard-Caraway Sauce

Serves 8

The distinctive flavor of caraway combines with spicy mustard and tangy yogurt in a sauce that goes nicely with both cabbage and brussels sprouts. Poached fish or chicken is a nice contrast to this robust dish.

8 cups coarsely shredded cabbage (about 2-pound head or 1-pound bag shredded cabbage) or 1 1/2 pounds fresh brussels sprouts

Mustard-Caraway Sauce

2 cups fat-free, low-sodium chicken broth, such as on page 45

1 tablespoon plus 1 teaspoon spicy brown mustard

1 tablespoon cornstarch (2 tablespoons for brussels sprouts)

1/2 teaspoon caraway seeds, crushed

1/3 cup fat-free or light plain yogurt

1/2 teaspoon grated lemon zest

1/4 teaspoon salt

1/4 teaspoon pepper

Steam the cabbage for 5 minutes (6 to 8 minutes for brussels sprouts), or until tender-crisp. Drain. Set aside.

Meanwhile, in a large saucepan, whisk together the broth, mustard, cornstarch, and caraway seeds. Bring to a boil over medium-high heat, stirring occasionally. Cook for 1 to 2 minutes, or until thickened.

Stir in the remaining sauce ingredients. Reduce the heat to low and cook for 2 to 3 minutes.

Add the cabbage and stir until well coated. Cook for 2 to 3 minutes, or until heated through. Don't overcook.

calories 34
protein 2 g
carbohydrates 6 g
  fiber 2 g
  sugars 3 g
cholesterol 0 mg
total fat 0.5 g
  saturated 0.0 g
  polyunsaturated 0.0 g
  monounsaturated 0.0 g
sodium 151 mg

dietary exchange
1 vegetable

Cook's Tip on Caraway Seeds

The fruit of an herb in the carrot family, caraway seeds are very popular in German, Austrian, and Hungarian foods. To release their flavor, crush them in a mortar and pestle. In many recipes, you can substitute other seeds, such as fennel, cumin, or dill.

Spiced Red Cabbage

Serves 4

Celebrate Oktoberfest or any other winter occasion with this festive dish of red cabbage, apples, and spices. Try it with one of our pork recipes, beginning on page 328.

3 cups shredded red cabbage (about 12 ounces)
$1/2$ cup water (plus more as needed)
$1/4$ cup cider vinegar
$1/4$ teaspoon ground allspice

$1/4$ teaspoon ground cinnamon
$1/8$ teaspoon ground nutmeg
2 medium tart apples, peeled, cored, and diced
1 tablespoon sugar

In a large saucepan, stir together the cabbage, water, vinegar, allspice, cinnamon, and nutmeg. Cook, covered, over low heat for 15 minutes, stirring occasionally and adding 2 to 3 tablespoons water if needed during cooking.

Stir in the apples. Cook, covered, for 5 minutes. If necessary, uncover and cook until all the moisture has cooked away.

Stir in the sugar.

Cook's Tip on Apples

Tart apples include Granny Smith and Gravenstein. Among the varieties that are tart but have a hint of sweetness are Braeburn, Jonathan, McIntosh, pippin (or Newton pippin), and Winesap.

calories 70
protein 1 g
carbohydrates 18 g
  fiber 3 g
  sugars 14 g
cholesterol 0 mg
total fat 0.5 g
  saturated 0.0 g
  polyunsaturated 0.0 g
  monounsaturated 0.0 g
sodium 7 mg

dietary exchange
1 fruit
1 vegetable

Tangy Carrots

Serves 6

The sharp flavors of mustard and pepper meet the tang of lime juice in this unusual side dish. Serve it hot or cold.

1 pound baby carrots
1 large shallot, very thinly sliced

Sauce
1 tablespoon acceptable stick
   margarine

1 tablespoon coarsely ground
   mustard
2 teaspoons fresh lime juice
   Generous sprinkle of pepper
2 tablespoons minced fresh parsley

Steam the carrots and shallot for 8 to 10 minutes, or until tender. Set aside.

In a small skillet, melt the margarine over medium heat. Swirl to coat the bottom. Add the remaining sauce ingredients except the parsley. Cook until heated through, stirring constantly.

Transfer the sauce to a medium bowl. Stir in the parsley and carrot mixture. Serve hot or cover and refrigerate to serve chilled.

Microwave Method
Put the carrots and shallot in a microwave steamer with 2 tablespoons water. Cook on 100 percent power (high) for 6 to 7 minutes, or until tender. Remove from the microwave and set aside. Put the remaining ingredients except the parsley in a microwave-safe dish. Cook on 100 percent power (high) for 10 to 15 seconds, or just until hot. In a medium bowl, stir together the parsley, carrots, shallot, and sauce.

calories 43
protein 1 g
carbohydrates 7 g
   fiber 2 g
   sugars 4 g
cholesterol 0 mg
total fat 1.5 g
   saturated 0.0 g
   polyunsaturated 0.5 g
   monounsaturated 0.5 g
sodium 91 mg

dietary exchange
1½ vegetable
½ fat

Cook's Tip on Shallots

Shallots combine the flavor of onion and garlic but are milder than either. You can substitute 1 tablespoon minced onion for 1 large shallot.

Honeyed Carrots

Serves 4

A tantalizing glaze of honey and brown sugar coats tender carrots.

2 cups water
10 to 12 small carrots (about
    12 ounces)
2 tablespoons light stick margarine

1 tablespoon light brown sugar
1 tablespoon honey
2 tablespoons finely snipped fresh
    parsley or fresh mint

In a large saucepan, bring the water to a boil over medium-high heat. Cook the carrots for 15 minutes, or until tender. Drain.

Dry the pan. Melt the margarine over medium heat. Swirl to coat the bottom. Stir in the brown sugar, honey, and carrots. Reduce the heat to low and cook for 2 to 3 minutes, or until the carrots are well glazed, stirring frequently.

Sprinkle with the parsley.

calories 91
protein 1 g
carbohydrates 17 g
  fiber 3 g
  sugars 13 g
cholesterol 0 mg
total fat 3.0 g
  saturated 0.5 g
  polyunsaturated 1.0 g
  monounsaturated 1.0 g
sodium 70 mg

dietary exchange
1½ vegetable
½ other carbohydrate
½ fat

Baked Grated Carrots
with Sherry

Serves 6

Pop this casserole into the oven while you roast a chicken. Fix a salad while they cook, and an easy meal is ready.

3 cups grated carrots

2 tablespoons light stick margarine, melted

2 tablespoons dry sherry

1 tablespoon fresh lemon juice

1 tablespoon chopped chives or green onions (green part only)

Preheat the oven to 350°F.

In a 1-quart casserole dish, stir together all the ingredients except the chives. Sprinkle with the chives.

Bake, covered, for 30 minutes.

calories 45
protein 1 g
carbohydrates 6 g
  fiber 2 g
  sugars 4 g
cholesterol 0 mg
total fat 2.0 g
  saturated 0.5 g
  polyunsaturated 0.5 g
  monounsaturated 0.5 g
sodium 45 mg

dietary exchange

1 vegetable
½ fat

Cauliflower and Roasted Corn with Chili Powder and Lime

Serves 8

Roasting or grilling gives corn an intense flavor. Serve this unusual combination with Turkey Loaf (page 269).

2 medium ears of corn, husks and silks removed
4 cups cauliflower florets (about 1/2 medium head)
1/4 cup fat-free, low-sodium chicken broth, such as on page 45

2-ounce jar diced pimientos, drained
1 tablespoon fresh lime juice
1 tablespoon light tub margarine
1/4 teaspoon chili powder
1/4 teaspoon salt
1/8 teaspoon pepper

Preheat the oven to 400°F.

Put the corn on a baking sheet and roast, uncovered, for 15 minutes. Let cool on a cooling rack for 5 to 10 minutes. Slice the corn off the cob. Set aside.

In a large saucepan, bring the cauliflower and broth to a boil over medium-high heat. Reduce the heat to medium-low and cook, covered, for 10 to 15 minutes, or until the cauliflower is tender.

Meanwhile, in a small bowl, stir together the remaining ingredients.

Stir the pimiento mixture and roasted corn into the cauliflower. Cook, uncovered, over medium-low heat for 1 to 2 minutes, or until warmed through, stirring occasionally.

calories 40
protein 2 g
carbohydrates 8 g
 fiber 2 g
 sugars 3 g
cholesterol 0 mg
total fat 1.0 g
 saturated 0.0 g
 polyunsaturated 0.5 g
 monounsaturated 0.5 g
sodium 105 mg

dietary exchange
1/2 starch

Creole Celery and Peas

Serves 10

Different colors, shapes, and textures combine to add interest to this side dish.

1 teaspoon light tub margarine	¹/₄ teaspoon dried thyme, crumbled
1 medium onion, chopped	8 medium ribs of celery, cut on the diagonal
14.5-ounce can no-salt-added tomatoes, undrained	10-ounce package frozen green peas
¹/₂ teaspoon red hot-pepper sauce	

In a large skillet, melt the margarine over medium-high heat and swirl to coat the bottom. Cook the onion for 2 to 3 minutes, or until soft.

Meanwhile, drain the tomatoes, reserving the liquid. Stir the liquid from the tomatoes, hot-pepper sauce, and thyme into the onion. Bring to a boil.

Stir in the celery and peas. Reduce the heat and simmer, covered, for 10 minutes, or until the celery is barely tender.

Stir in the tomatoes and heat through.

calories 42
protein 3 g
carbohydrates 8 g
 fiber 3 g
 sugars 4 g
cholesterol 0 mg
total fat 0.5 g
 saturated 0.0 g
 polyunsaturated 0.0 g
 monounsaturated 0.0 g
sodium 99 mg

dietary exchange
¹/₂ starch

Swiss Chard, Southern Style

Serves 4

This peppery Swiss chard dish is rich in vitamins A and C, as well as iron. And it tastes good, too!

2 bunches Swiss chard (about 8 ounces each)
1 teaspoon acceptable vegetable oil
1 large onion, finely chopped
1/4 cup water

1 teaspoon liquid smoke seasoning
1/4 to 1/2 teaspoon crushed red pepper flakes
1 tablespoon imitation bacon bits

Remove the stems from the chard. Stack several leaves and cut crosswise into 1/2-inch slices. Repeat with the remaining leaves.

In a large saucepan, heat the oil over medium-high heat. Swirl to coat the bottom. Cook the onion for 2 to 3 minutes, or until soft.

Stir in the chard and remaining ingredients except the bacon bits. Cook, covered, for 5 to 7 minutes, or until the chard is wilted and tender.

Stir in the bacon bits.

Cook's Tip on Swiss Chard

When you want a serving of one of those famous vitamin-rich leafy green vegetables, Swiss chard fills the bill. It has dark green leaves with silvery or red stalks. Select fresh-looking, crisp greens and cook them within three days. Wash thoroughly to remove dirt and sand, and use as you would spinach.

calories 59
protein 3 g
carbohydrates 10 g
  fiber 3 g
  sugars 4 g
cholesterol 0 mg
total fat 2.0 g
  saturated 0.0 g
  polyunsaturated 0.5 g
  monounsaturated 1.0 g
sodium 273 mg

dietary exchange
2 vegetable
1/2 fat

Braised Swiss Chard

Serves 6

Summer is peak season for Swiss chard, so when you spot the large deep-green leaves with ruby red stems (or other varieties), pick up two bunches and get braising!

1 teaspoon olive oil
2 medium leeks (white part only), thinly sliced, or ½ cup sliced onion
2 medium garlic cloves, minced
½ cup fat-free, low-sodium chicken broth, such as on page 45
2 tablespoons chopped kalamata olives

1 teaspoon dried oregano, crumbled
¼ teaspoon pepper
2 bunches Swiss chard, stems discarded, coarsely chopped (about 1 pound)
3 tablespoons shredded or grated Parmesan cheese

Heat a large skillet over medium heat. Pour the oil into the skillet and swirl to coat the bottom. Cook the leeks and garlic for 2 to 3 minutes, or until the leeks are tender, stirring occasionally.

Stir in the broth, olives, oregano, and pepper.

Stir in half the Swiss chard. Reduce the heat and simmer, covered, for 1 minute, or until the Swiss chard is wilted. Add the remaining Swiss chard and simmer, covered, for 14 to 16 minutes, or until tender, stirring occasionally.

To serve, sprinkle with the Parmesan.

calories 63
protein 3 g
carbohydrates 8 g
  fiber 2 g
  sugars 2 g
cholesterol 2 mg
total fat 2.5 g
  saturated 0.5 g
  polyunsaturated 0.5 g
  monounsaturated 1.5 g
sodium 269 mg

dietary exchange
1½ vegetable
½ fat

Cajun Corn

Serves 4

Richly browned onions are simmered with sweet yellow corn and served with a colorful "butter" compound of Cajun seasonings.

1½ tablespoons light tub margarine
¼ teaspoon dried thyme, crumbled
½ teaspoon paprika
⅛ teaspoon black pepper
⅛ teaspoon cayenne
⅛ teaspoon salt

Vegetable oil spray
1½ large onions, chopped (yellow preferred)
¼ teaspoon sugar
3 cups frozen whole-kernel corn, thawed and drained

In a small bowl, stir together the margarine, thyme, paprika, pepper, cayenne, and salt. Set aside.

Lightly spray a large skillet, preferably cast iron, with vegetable oil spray. Heat over high heat for 1 minute. Cook the onions for 2 minutes, stirring constantly. Reduce the heat to medium.

Stir in the sugar. Cook for 3 minutes, or until the onions are golden brown, stirring frequently.

Stir in the corn. Cook for 3 minutes, stirring occasionally. Remove from the heat.

Stir in the margarine mixture.

calories 156
protein 5 g
carbohydrates 33 g
  fiber 5 g
  sugars 7 g
cholesterol 0 mg
total fat 2.5 g
  saturated 0.0 g
  polyunsaturated 1.0 g
  monounsaturated 1.0 g
sodium 113 mg

dietary exchange
2 starch
1 vegetable

Jalapeño Corn

Substitute crumbled dried oregano for thyme, and add ¼ teaspoon ground cumin to the margarine mixture. Add 2 seeded and finely chopped fresh jalapeño peppers (wear gloves when handling the peppers) when adding the corn to the skillet.

jalapeño corn

calories 159
protein 5 g
carbohydrates 34 g
  fiber 5 g
  sugars 7 g
cholesterol 0 mg
total fat 3.0 g
  saturated 0.0 g
  polyunsaturated 1.0 g
  monounsaturated 1.0 g
sodium 113 mg

dietary exchange
2 starch
1 vegetable

Southwestern
Creamy Corn

Serves 6

Try this creamy side dish, flecked with color, with Beef Tostadas (page 322).

1 teaspoon light tub margarine
$1/2$ large onion, finely chopped
$1/2$ medium red bell pepper, diced
4 ounces fat-free or light cream cheese
$1/4$ cup diced canned green chiles, rinsed and drained

$1/4$ cup fat-free milk
$1/2$ teaspoon pepper
$1/2$ teaspoon chili powder
2 cups frozen whole-kernel corn
2 teaspoons finely snipped fresh cilantro

In a large nonstick skillet, melt the margarine over medium-high heat. Swirl to coat the bottom. Cook the onion and bell pepper for 2 to 3 minutes, or until the onion is soft.

Reduce the heat to low. Stir in the cream cheese, chiles, milk, pepper, and chili powder. Cook for 2 to 3 minutes, or until the mixture is smooth, stirring constantly.

Stir in the corn. Cook for 2 to 3 minutes, or just until the corn is warmed through.

To serve, stir in the cilantro.

calories 86
protein 5 g
carbohydrates 16 g
 fiber 2 g
 sugars 3 g
cholesterol 4 mg
total fat 1.0 g
 saturated 0.0 g
 polyunsaturated 0.5 g
 monounsaturated 0.5 g
sodium 142 mg

dietary exchange
1 starch

Grits Casserole
with Cheese and Chiles

Serves 8

Grill pork tenderloins and a medley of fresh vegetables, add this filling side dish of dressed-up grits, and you'll have a fuss-free dinner for eight. The casserole is also excellent as a brunch dish.

Vegetable oil spray
2 cups fat-free, low-sodium chicken broth, such as on page 45
2 cups water
1 cup uncooked grits
1/2 cup fat-free milk
1/4 cup shredded or grated Parmesan cheese
2 3/4-ounce slices fat-free Swiss cheese, diced

2-ounce can chopped green chiles, rinsed and drained
1 tablespoon light tub margarine
2 medium garlic cloves, minced
1/4 teaspoon salt
1/8 teaspoon pepper
Egg substitute equivalent to 2 eggs, or 2 large eggs
1/2 teaspoon chili powder

Preheat the oven to 375°F. Lightly spray a 13 × 9 × 2-inch baking pan with vegetable oil spray. Set aside.

In a large saucepan, bring the broth and water to a boil over medium-high heat. Gradually whisk in the grits. Reduce the heat to low and cook, covered, for 5 minutes, whisking occasionally. Remove the saucepan from the heat.

Stir the milk, Parmesan and Swiss cheeses, chiles, margarine, garlic, salt, and pepper into the grits.

Stir in the egg substitute. Pour into the baking pan, smoothing the top with a spatula.

Sprinkle with the chili powder.

Bake, uncovered, for 45 minutes. Remove from the oven and let cool for 5 to 10 minutes before serving.

calories 114
protein 7 g
carbohydrates 18 g
  fiber 1 g
  sugars 1 g
cholesterol 3 mg
total fat 1.5 g
  saturated 0.5 g
  polyunsaturated 0.5 g
  monounsaturated 0.5 g
sodium 241 mg

dietary exchange
1 starch
1 very lean meat

Creamy Kale
with Red Bell Pepper

Serves 4

The creamy sauce in this dish complements the mild cabbage flavor of kale. Like other cabbage, kale goes well with pork, or try it with braised eye-of-round roast.

1 bunch kale (about 1¹/₂ pounds)
1 medium red bell pepper, diced
2 tablespoons water
1 tablespoon plus 1 teaspoon light stick margarine
1 tablespoon plus 1 teaspoon all-purpose flour

³/₄ cup fat-free milk
¹/₄ teaspoon salt
¹/₈ teaspoon black pepper
¹/₄ cup fat-free half-and-half
¹/₂ teaspoon sugar

Tear the kale leaves into small pieces. Discard the stalks. Put the kale and bell pepper in a large saucepan over medium-high heat. Add the water. Reduce the heat to low and cook, covered, for 5 to 6 minutes, or until the leaves are wilted.

In a large saucepan, melt the margarine over medium-high heat. Swirl to coat the bottom. Whisk in the flour. Cook for 1 minute, whisking constantly.

Whisk in the milk, salt, and black pepper. Cook until the mixture boils, whisking constantly. Remove from the heat.

Stir in the kale mixture, half-and-half, and sugar.

calories 148
protein 9 g
carbohydrates 26 g
  fiber 4 g
  sugars 8 g
cholesterol 1 mg
total fat 3.0 g
  saturated 0.5 g
  polyunsaturated 1.0 g
  monounsaturated 0.5 g
sodium 283 mg

dietary exchange
¹/₂ starch
4 vegetable
¹/₂ fat

Cook's Tip on Kale

Kale has deep green frilly leaves, usually tinged with blue or purple. In small amounts, this mild, cabbagy-tasting vegetable is good in tossed salad. Prepare it as you would spinach. The best kale is available in the winter. It's a good source of vitamins A and C, folic acid, calcium, and iron.

Kohlrabi Gratin

Serves 4

Although a member of the same family as turnips, kohlrabi is milder and sweeter. Here it is prepared like scalloped potatoes.

Vegetable oil spray
2 medium kohlrabi bulbs (about 1¼ pounds)
1 cup water

Sauce

1 teaspoon olive oil
2 large shallots, finely chopped
1 cup fat-free, low-sodium chicken broth, such as on page 45
½ cup fat-free evaporated milk

1½ tablespoons all-purpose flour
¼ teaspoon salt
¼ teaspoon pepper
1 tablespoon snipped fresh dillweed or 1 teaspoon dried, crumbled
2 tablespoons shredded or grated Parmesan cheese

❖

¼ cup plain dry bread crumbs

Preheat the oven to 350°F. Lightly spray a 1½-quart casserole dish with vegetable oil spray.

With a sharp knife, peel the kohlrabi and cut into ¼-inch slices. In a medium saucepan, bring the kohlrabi and water to a boil over high heat. Reduce the heat to medium-low and cook, covered, for 5 minutes, or until tender-crisp. Drain. Set aside.

For the sauce, pour the oil into the saucepan. Swirl to coat the bottom. Cook the shallots over medium-low heat for 1 to 2 minutes, stirring occasionally.

In a medium bowl, whisk together the broth, milk, flour, salt, and pepper. Add to the shallots and bring to a boil over medium-high heat, stirring occasionally. Reduce the heat to medium and cook for 1 to 2 minutes, or until the mixture thickens, stirring occasionally.

Stir in the dillweed and Parmesan. Remove from the heat.

Arrange half the kohlrabi in the casserole dish. Spoon on half the sauce. Repeat. Cover the dish with aluminum foil.

Bake for 20 to 25 minutes, or until the kohlrabi is tender. Sprinkle with the bread crumbs. Bake for 10 minutes.

calories 129
protein 8 g
carbohydrates 21 g
  fiber 5 g
  sugars 8 g
cholesterol 3 mg
total fat 2.5 g
  saturated 0.5 g
  polyunsaturated 0.5 g
  monounsaturated 1.0 g
sodium 318 mg

dietary exchange
½ starch
½ skim milk
1½ vegetable

Mushrooms
with Red Wine

Serves 4

Dress up mushrooms in a snap by cooking them quickly, then letting them absorb a delicate red wine sauce.

2 tablespoons dry red wine (regular or nonalcoholic)

2 teaspoons very low sodium beef bouillon granules

1 medium garlic clove, minced

1/2 teaspoon sugar

1/2 teaspoon dried thyme, crumbled

1 pound whole medium button mushrooms, quartered

1/4 cup snipped fresh parsley

2 teaspoons olive oil (extra-virgin preferred)

1/8 teaspoon salt

In a small bowl, stir together the wine, bouillon granules, garlic, sugar, and thyme.

Heat a 12-inch nonstick skillet over medium-high heat. Cook the mushrooms for 4 minutes, or until soft.

Stir in the wine mixture. Increase the heat to high and bring to a boil. Remove from the heat.

Stir in the parsley, oil, and salt. Let stand, covered, for 3 minutes.

calories 64
protein 4 g
carbohydrates 7 g
  fiber 2 g
  sugars 3 g
cholesterol 0 mg
total fat 2.5 g
  saturated 0.5 g
  polyunsaturated 0.5 g
  monounsaturated 1.5 g
sodium 82 mg

dietary exchange
1 vegetable
1/2 fat

Mushrooms with
White Wine and Shallots

Serves 4

Cook succulent mushrooms with shallots and wine, then reduce the juices to intensify the flavor. Serve as a side dish or spoon the mushrooms over lean broiled steak.

2 tablespoons light stick margarine
1/2 cup finely chopped shallots (about 8 large)
1 pound medium fresh button mushrooms, quartered

1/2 cup dry white wine (regular or nonalcoholic)
1 tablespoon finely snipped fresh parsley
Pepper to taste

In a large nonstick skillet, melt the margarine over medium-high heat. Swirl to coat the bottom. Cook the shallots for 2 to 3 minutes, stirring constantly.

Add the mushrooms and wine. Reduce the heat to medium and cook, covered, for 7 to 9 minutes. Increase the heat to high. Cook, uncovered, for 5 to 6 minutes, or until the juices have evaporated.

To serve, stir in the parsley and pepper.

calories 88
protein 4 g
carbohydrates 9 g
  fiber 2 g
  sugars 2 g
cholesterol 0 mg
total fat 3.0 g
  saturated 0.5 g
  polyunsaturated 1.0 g
  monounsaturated 1.0 g
sodium 46 mg

dietary exchange
2 vegetable
1/2 fat

Baked Okra Bites

Serves 4

These crisp okra bites are the perfect side dish with grilled fish, as part of a Southern-style summer menu, or instead of French fries with our lean hamburgers (page 306). Try them as a topping for a spinach and romaine salad, or sprinkle them on top of baked casseroles, too.

Vegetable oil spray
1/2 cup yellow cornmeal
1/4 cup all-purpose flour
1/2 teaspoon onion powder
1/2 teaspoon garlic powder
1/2 teaspoon Creole or Cajun seasoning
   or 1/2 teaspoon spicy salt-free
   all-purpose seasoning

8 ounces fresh okra, stems removed,
   cut into 1/2-inch slices, or 2 cups
   frozen sliced okra, thawed
Egg substitute equivalent to 1 egg,
   or 1 large egg, lightly beaten

Preheat the oven to 400°F. Lightly spray a large baking sheet with vegetable oil spray.

In a shallow bowl, stir together the cornmeal, flour, onion powder, garlic powder, and Creole seasoning.

Put the okra in a medium bowl. Pour in the egg substitute. Stir to coat.

Set the bowl with the okra, the bowl with the cornmeal mixture, and the baking sheet in a row, assembly-line fashion. Using a slotted spoon, transfer the okra in batches to the cornmeal mixture. Stir to coat all sides of the okra. After all the okra has been coated, discard any remaining egg substitute.

Arrange the okra in an even layer on the baking sheet (leave space between the pieces so they brown evenly). Lightly spray the tops of the okra with vegetable oil spray. Bake for 20 to 25 minutes, or until the okra is tender on the inside and crisp on the outside. Put the pan on a cooling rack. Let cool for 2 to 3 minutes before serving.

calories 120
protein 5 g
carbohydrates 24 g
   fiber 3 g
   sugars 2 g
cholesterol 0 mg
total fat 0.5 g
   saturated 0.0 g
   polyunsaturated 0.0 g
   monounsaturated 0.0 g
sodium 77 mg

dietary exchange
1 starch
1 1/2 vegetable

Asian Linguini

Serves 4

Serve this sassy side dish to dress up the simplest cuts of meats or poultry.

1³/₄ cups fat-free, low-sodium chicken broth, such as on page 45

2 ounces dried linguini, broken in half

1 large onion, thinly sliced

2 medium carrots, cut into matchstick-size strips

2 tablespoons low-salt soy sauce

2 tablespoons cider vinegar

1¹/₂ tablespoons sugar

¹/₈ teaspoon garlic powder

2 tablespoons peanuts or slivered almonds, dry-roasted

In a medium saucepan, bring the broth to a boil over high heat. Stir in the pasta. Return to a boil. Reduce the heat to medium and cook for 5 minutes, or until the pasta is tender. Don't drain.

Meanwhile, in a large nonstick skillet over medium-high heat, cook the onion and carrots for 6 minutes, or until tender-crisp, stirring frequently.

In a small bowl, stir together the soy sauce, vinegar, sugar, and garlic powder.

To serve, add the pasta and any remaining liquid to the onion mixture. Pour in the soy sauce mixture. Toss gently to blend. Transfer to a serving bowl. Sprinkle with the peanuts.

calories 144
protein 5 g
carbohydrates 26 g
  fiber 3 g
  sugars 11 g
cholesterol 0 mg
total fat 2.5 g
  saturated 0.5 g
  polyunsaturated 1.0 g
  monounsaturated 1.0 g
sodium 222 mg

dietary exchange
1 starch
2 vegetable
¹/₂ fat

Crispy Baked
Onion Flower

Serves 4

If you like onion rings, you will have fun making and eating this spectacular onion flower. Serve it with a lean grilled hamburger or chicken breast.

1 large yellow onion (about 1¼ pounds) or 2 medium yellow onions (about 10 ounces each)
4 cups water
Vegetable oil spray
¼ cup all-purpose flour

½ tablespoon salt-free all-purpose seasoning
3 tablespoons egg substitute
½ cup cornflake crumbs (1½ cups cornflakes)

Trim the root end of the onion. Peel the onion. Put it with the root end down on a cutting board. With a long, sharp knife, leaving the onion intact, cut it into quarters almost to the root stem end. Still leaving the onion intact, carefully cut it into eighths, then into sixteenths.

Pour the water into a medium saucepan and bring to a boil over high heat. Reduce the heat to medium-high. Add the onion and cook for 7 minutes (5 minutes for medium onions). Turn the onion over halfway through the cooking time. Remove the onion with a slotted spoon. Drain in a colander.

Put the onion in a bowl with enough ice-cold water to cover by 1 inch. Refrigerate for at least 2 hours.

Preheat the oven to 350°F. Lightly spray a baking sheet with vegetable oil spray.

Drain the onion with the cut side down in the colander. Pat dry with paper towels.

In a large resealable plastic bag, combine the flour and all-purpose seasoning.

Put the onion in the bag. Seal the bag. Carefully shake and move the bag around and upside down to coat the onion. You may have to slightly open the onion through the bag to coat the middle.

calories 94
protein 4 g
carbohydrates 20 g
  fiber 1 g
  sugars 4 g
cholesterol 0 mg
total fat 0.0 g
  saturated 0.0 g
  polyunsaturated 0.0 g
  monounsaturated 0.0 g
sodium 105 mg

dietary exchange
1 starch
1 vegetable

Pour the egg substitute into the bag. Repeat the process to coat the onion. Remove the onion from the bag. Place the onion on a cutting board or platter.

Sprinkle the cornflake crumbs evenly over the onion. Slightly open the onion to coat the middle. Place the onion on the baking sheet.

Bake the large onion for 1 hour 20 minutes, the medium onions for 1 hour. Place on a plate. Serve warm. If desired, have a pair of kitchen scissors handy so you can easily remove the crispy onion petals.

Cook's Tip

To keep from cutting all the way through the onion, insert a metal skewer horizontally through the onion, just below where you want to finish cutting. As you cut the onion, the skewer will stop your knife.

Parmesan Parsnip Puree
with Leeks and Carrots

Serves 6

Parsnips have a sweet, slightly peppery taste. Puree them with carrots, leeks, and Parmesan cheese for a pale gold side dish similar in texture to mashed potatoes.

1 pound parsnips, peeled and cut crosswise into 1/2-inch pieces

2 small carrots, peeled and cut crosswise into 1/2-inch pieces

2 large leeks (white part only), thinly sliced crosswise

1/2 cup fat-free, low-sodium chicken broth, such as on page 45

2 tablespoons shredded or grated Parmesan cheese

1 tablespoon light tub margarine

1/4 teaspoon salt

1/2 cup fat-free, low-sodium chicken broth, such as on page 45

2 tablespoons thinly sliced almonds, dry-roasted

In a large saucepan, bring the parsnips, carrots, leeks, and 1/2 cup broth to a boil over high heat. Reduce the heat to medium-low and cook, covered, for 10 minutes, or until tender. Remove from the heat. Let cool for 5 minutes.

In a food processor or blender, process the parsnip mixture and remaining ingredients except the almonds until smooth.

To serve, spoon into a serving bowl. Sprinkle with the almonds.

calories 109
protein 3 g
carbohydrates 20 g
 fiber 5 g
 sugars 6 g
cholesterol 1 mg
total fat 2.5 g
 saturated 0.5 g
 polyunsaturated 0.5 g
 monounsaturated 1.5 g
sodium 164 mg

dietary exchange
4 vegetable
1/2 fat

Cook's Tip on Parsnips

Parsnips look like pale carrots and are in the same family. Whether you bake, sauté, roast, steam, or boil them, parsnips are sweet and aromatic. They turn mushy quickly, though, so don't overcook them. Look for firm parsnips without pitting. Don't worry if they're large—bigger size doesn't mean parsnips won't be tender. Wrapped in plastic wrap and refrigerated, parsnips will keep for several weeks to several months.

Black-Eyed Peas
with Canadian Bacon

Serves 8

In the South, black-eyed peas are traditionally served on New Year's Day to bring good luck throughout the coming year. This tasty version will bring you compliments no matter when you serve it.

¹/₂ pound dried black-eyed peas, sorted for stones and shriveled peas and rinsed	3 ounces no-salt-added tomato paste
2 ounces Canadian bacon	1 small bay leaf
1 medium onion	1 small garlic clove, chopped
1 medium rib of celery	¹/₈ teaspoon cayenne
	Pepper to taste

Put the peas in a large saucepan and add water to cover. Let soak for 45 minutes.

Meanwhile, dice the Canadian bacon and chop the onion and celery.

Drain the peas. Return them to the saucepan. Add enough fresh water just to cover.

Stir in the other ingredients. Bring to a boil over medium-high heat. Reduce the heat and simmer, covered, for 3 hours, or until tender.

Cook's Tip on Canadian Bacon

Canadian bacon is really more like ham than like bacon. It has much less fat than bacon. Fully cooked when you buy it, Canadian bacon can be sliced and used as you would cooked ham.

calories 121
protein 9 g
carbohydrates 21 g
  fiber 4 g
  sugars 3 g
cholesterol 4 mg
total fat 0.5 g
  saturated 0.5 g
  polyunsaturated 0.0 g
  monounsaturated 0.0 g
sodium 115 mg

dietary exchange
1 starch
1¹/₂ vegetable
¹/₂ very lean meat

Savory Peas

Enliven the flavor of peas with bacon, Italian herbs, and nutmeg.
Serve with mashed potatoes and Smothered Steak with Sangria Sauce
(page 287).

3 pounds fresh green peas in shells or
  16-ounce package frozen green
  peas
2 strips lower-sodium bacon or
  3 tablespoons imitation bacon bits
1 teaspoon light tub margarine

6 medium green onions (green and
  white parts), finely chopped
1 teaspoon salt-free Italian
  seasoning, crumbled
1/4 teaspoon nutmeg, or to taste (fresh
  preferred)

Shell the peas if using fresh. Put the peas in a medium saucepan with enough water to cover by about 1/2 inch. Bring to a boil over high heat. Reduce the heat and simmer, covered, for 5 to 8 minutes, or until the peas are tender-crisp. If using frozen peas, prepare using the package directions, omitting the salt and margarine.

Meanwhile, cook the bacon until crisp. Drain well; pat dry with paper towels. Dice the bacon.

In a large skillet, melt the margarine over medium-high heat and swirl to coat the bottom. Cook the green onions for 1 to 2 minutes, or until soft.

Reduce the heat to low. Stir in all the other ingredients and heat through.

calories 92
protein 5 g
carbohydrates 15 g
  fiber 5 g
  sugars 6 g
cholesterol 2 mg
total fat 1.5 g
  saturated 0.5 g
  polyunsaturated 0.5 g
  monounsaturated 0.5 g
sodium 44 mg

dietary exchange
1 starch

Cook's Tip on Grinding or Grating Nutmeg

Freshly ground or grated nutmeg is stronger and spicier than bottled ground nutmeg and makes a great difference in a recipe. It's best to use a nutmeg grinder, similar to a pepper mill, or nutmeg grater, but you can use a knife. Frequently sprinkled on (low-fat) eggnog, nutmeg can also spice up tomato sauce or soup, mashed potatoes, cheese dishes, spinach dishes, and sweet breads and other baked goods.

French Peas

Serves 6

Tender peas, wilted lettuce, and crunchy water chestnuts provide a variety of textures in this side dish. For a quick trip to Paris, serve this with French-Style Braised Fish Fillets (page 175).

10-ounce package frozen green peas	3 tablespoons fat-free, low-sodium chicken broth, such as on page 45
1 tablespoon acceptable vegetable oil	1 teaspoon all-purpose flour
1 cup finely shredded lettuce	8-ounce can sliced water chestnuts, rinsed and drained
2 medium green onions (green and white parts), diced	Pepper to taste

Prepare the peas using the package directions, omitting the salt and margarine. Drain. Set aside.

Heat a large saucepan over low heat. Pour the oil into the pan and swirl to coat the bottom. Cook the lettuce and green onions for 1 to 2 minutes, stirring occasionally.

In a small bowl, whisk together the broth and flour. Add to the lettuce mixture. Increase the heat to medium and cook for 2 to 3 minutes, or until thickened, stirring occasionally.

Stir in the peas, water chestnuts, and pepper. Heat through.

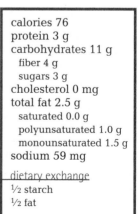

calories 76
protein 3 g
carbohydrates 11 g
  fiber 4 g
  sugars 3 g
cholesterol 0 mg
total fat 2.5 g
  saturated 0.0 g
  polyunsaturated 1.0 g
  monounsaturated 1.5 g
sodium 59 mg

dietary exchange
1/2 starch
1/2 fat

Sweet Lemon
Snow Peas

Serves 4

Chinese snow pea pods are quickly steamed (just 2 minutes), then splashed with spicy-sweet, lemony soy sauce mixture.

2   tablespoons sugar
2   tablespoons low-salt soy sauce
1   teaspoon grated lemon zest
2   tablespoons fresh lemon juice

$^1/_4$ teaspoon crushed red pepper flakes
9   ounces fresh or frozen snow peas, trimmed if fresh

In a small bowl, stir together all the ingredients except the snow peas.

In a medium saucepan, steam the snow peas for 2 minutes, or until just tender-crisp. Drain well. Transfer to a rimmed plate or shallow dish.

Pour the sauce evenly over the snow peas. Do not stir.

Cook's Tip on Lemon Zest

You can grate the zest of several lemons at one time and store what you don't need in the freezer. Having zest on hand whenever you need it will save you time and money.

calories 58
protein 2 g
carbohydrates 12 g
 fiber 2 g
 sugars 9 g
cholesterol 0 mg
total fat 0.0 g
 saturated 0.0 g
 polyunsaturated 0.0 g
 monounsaturated 0.0 g
sodium 198 mg

dietary exchange
1 starch

Stir-Fried
Sugar Snap Peas

Serves 4

Crispy-sweet sugar snap peas with an Asian-style sauce and toasted almonds are a snap to make and a real treat at any meal. Serve with grilled pork or poached fish, as well as with Asian entrées.

3 tablespoons fat-free, low-sodium chicken broth, such as on page 45
1 teaspoon low-salt soy sauce
$\frac{1}{2}$ teaspoon cornstarch
$\frac{1}{2}$ teaspoon light brown sugar
$\frac{1}{4}$ teaspoon toasted sesame oil

$\frac{1}{8}$ teaspoon crushed red pepper flakes (optional)
8 ounces sugar snap peas (about 1 cup)
1 medium garlic clove, minced
1 tablespoon sliced almonds, dry-roasted

In a small bowl, whisk together the broth, soy sauce, cornstarch, brown sugar, sesame oil, and red pepper flakes until the cornstarch is dissolved.

Heat a nonstick wok or medium nonstick skillet over medium heat. Cook the peas and garlic over medium-high heat for 1 to 2 minutes, or until tender-crisp, stirring constantly.

Pour the broth mixture into the wok. Reduce the heat and simmer until thickened.

To serve, sprinkle with the almonds.

calories 42
protein 2 g
carbohydrates 7 g
  fiber 2 g
  sugars 3 g
cholesterol 0 mg
total fat 1.0 g
  saturated 0.0 g
  polyunsaturated 0.5 g
  monounsaturated 0.5 g
sodium 34 mg

dietary exchange
$\frac{1}{2}$ starch

Basil Roasted Peppers

You'll find many uses for these roasted peppers in your cooking, or serve them cold as a garnish.

Vegetable oil spray
6 firm medium red bell peppers
1/4 cup plus 1 tablespoon olive oil
1/4 cup red wine vinegar
2 tablespoons finely chopped fresh basil leaves

3 or 4 medium garlic cloves, minced
1/2 teaspoon black pepper, or to taste
1/4 teaspoon salt

Preheat the broiler. Lightly spray a broiling pan and rack with vegetable oil spray.

Put the peppers on the rack in the pan. Broil the peppers about 2 inches from the heat for 1 to 2 minutes on each side, or until lightly charred. Seal in a large resealable plastic bag or put in a large bowl and cover with plastic wrap. Let cool for 5 to 10 minutes. Remove and discard the skin, core, ribs, and seeds. Rinse the peppers under cold water and pat dry with paper towels. Cut into strips 1/2 inch wide.

In a medium bowl, stir together the remaining ingredients. Stir in the peppers. Cover and refrigerate for 30 minutes to 8 hours. Drain, discarding the marinade. Refrigerate the drained peppers in an airtight container for up to five days or freeze for up to four months.

calories 24
protein 1 g
carbohydrates 6 g
 fiber 2 g
 sugars 2 g
cholesterol 0 mg
total fat 0.0 g
 saturated 0.0 g
 polyunsaturated 0.0 g
 monounsaturated 0.0 g
sodium 75 mg

dietary exchange
1 vegetable

Scalloped Potatoes

Serves 6

*Just out of the oven, these potatoes are a beautiful golden brown with a
slight crunch on top. Serve with lean grilled pork chops and Asparagus par
Excellence (page 408) or take to a potluck for plenty of compliments.*

Vegetable oil spray

Sauce
2 tablespoons light stick margarine
1 large onion, finely chopped
1/4 cup all-purpose flour
2 cups fat-free milk
1/4 cup fat-free half-and-half
3 tablespoons finely snipped fresh
parsley

1/8 teaspoon salt
1/8 to 1/4 teaspoon white pepper

❖

2 pounds baking potatoes, peeled
and thinly sliced
1/8 teaspoon salt
1/8 teaspoon white pepper
2 tablespoons grated Romano or
Parmesan cheese

Preheat the oven to 325°F. Lightly spray an 8-inch square
baking dish with vegetable oil spray. Set aside.

In a medium saucepan, melt the margarine over medium-
high heat. Swirl to coat the bottom. Cook the onion for
2 to 3 minutes, or until soft.

Whisk in the flour. Cook for 1 minute.

Whisk in the milk. Cook for 3 to 4 minutes, or until the
sauce is thickened, whisking constantly.

Whisk in the remaining sauce ingredients. Remove from
the heat.

Arrange the potatoes in the baking dish. Sprinkle with
1/8 teaspoon salt and 1/8 teaspoon pepper.

Pour the sauce over the potatoes. Sprinkle with the
Romano.

Bake, uncovered, for 1 hour 30 minutes.

calories 204
protein 10 g
carbohydrates 40 g
  fiber 4 g
  sugars 11 g
cholesterol 5 mg
total fat 2.5 g
  saturated 1.0 g
  polyunsaturated 0.5 g
  monounsaturated 0.5 g
sodium 215 mg

dietary exchange
2 starch
1/2 skim milk
1 vegetable

Potatoes with Leeks
and Fresh Herbs

Serves 8

While this one-skillet side dish simmers, it will fill your kitchen with a tantalizing aroma. And the dish tastes even better than it smells.

Vegetable oil spray (olive oil spray preferred)

2 medium leeks (white part only), sliced

2 medium garlic cloves, crushed

1 cup fat-free, low-sodium chicken broth, such as on page 45

1/2 cup snipped fresh parsley

1/4 cup dry white wine (regular or nonalcoholic) (optional)

2-ounce jar diced pimientos, rinsed and drained (about 1/4 cup)

2 tablespoons snipped fresh dillweed

1 tablespoon chopped fresh sage or thyme

2 teaspoons grated lemon zest

Pepper to taste

6 medium potatoes (about 2 pounds)

Heat a large skillet over medium heat. Remove from the heat and lightly spray with vegetable oil spray (being careful not to spray near a gas flame). Cook the leeks and garlic for 2 to 3 minutes, or until soft, stirring occasionally.

Stir in the remaining ingredients except the potatoes. Remove from the heat.

Peel and thinly slice the potatoes. Arrange on the leek mixture.

Bring the potato mixture to a boil over medium-high heat. Reduce the heat and simmer, covered, for 20 minutes, or until the potatoes are tender.

calories 95
protein 4 g
carbohydrates 24 g
  fiber 3 g
  sugars 3 g
cholesterol 0 mg
total fat 0.0 g
  saturated 0.0 g
  polyunsaturated 0.0 g
  monounsaturated 0.0 g
sodium 11 mg

dietary exchange
1 1/2 starch

Cook's Tip

If you have any potatoes left over, combine them with lightly cooked fresh button mushrooms and egg substitute or egg whites to make a wonderful frittata or omelet for breakfast, brunch, lunch, or dinner.

Baked Fries
with Creole Seasoning

Serves 4

These spice-flecked, crisp fries will perk up your taste buds. Serve them with a lean grilled hamburger and a thick slice of onion on a toasted whole-wheat bun.

4 medium unpeeled russet potatoes
($1^1/_4$ to $1^1/_2$ pounds)

Creole or Cajun Seasoning
$1/_2$ teaspoon chili powder
$1/_2$ teaspoon ground cumin
$1/_2$ teaspoon onion powder

$1/_2$ teaspoon garlic powder
$1/_2$ teaspoon paprika
$1/_2$ teaspoon black pepper
$1/_4$ teaspoon salt
$1/_8$ teaspoon cayenne (optional)
❖
Vegetable oil spray

Cut the potatoes into long strips about $1/_2$ inch wide. In a large bowl, let them soak for 15 minutes in enough cold water to cover by 1 inch.

Meanwhile, in a small bowl, stir together the seasoning ingredients. Set aside.

Preheat the oven to 450°F. Lightly spray a large baking sheet with vegetable oil spray.

Drain the potatoes and pat dry with paper towels. Spread the potatoes in a single layer on the baking sheet. Lightly spray the tops with vegetable oil spray. Sprinkle with the seasoning mixture.

Bake for 30 to 35 minutes, or until crisp.

Cook's Tip on Creole or Cajun Seasoning

To save time in the future, double or triple the seasoning mixture in this recipe and keep it in a container with a shaker top. This seasoning is excellent in Creole or Cajun dishes and on seafood, chicken, beef, vegetables, or garlic toast (made with light margarine, of course!).

calories 106
protein 4 g
carbohydrates 27 g
  fiber 3 g
  sugars 3 g
cholesterol 0 mg
total fat 0.0 g
  saturated 0.0 g
  polyunsaturated 0.0 g
  monounsaturated 0.0 g
sodium 150 mg

dietary exchange
2 starch

Rustic Potato Patties

Serves 5

Black pepper and cayenne heat up these potato patties, which get their texture from the skins.

4 cups water
1 pound red potatoes, unpeeled, diced
1/2 cup minced onion
1/4 cup plus 2 tablespoons fat-free evaporated milk
White of 1 large egg

1/2 teaspoon salt
1/8 teaspoon black pepper
1/8 teaspoon cayenne
1/4 cup all-purpose flour
1 tablespoon acceptable vegetable oil, divided use

Preheat the oven to warm or 140°F.

In a medium saucepan, bring the water to a boil over high heat. Add the potatoes and return to a boil. Reduce the heat and simmer, uncovered, for 7 to 8 minutes, or until tender but not mushy. Drain well. Return the potatoes to the pan or put in a large mixing bowl. Beat until no lumps remain.

Add the onion, milk, egg white, salt, black pepper, and cayenne. Beat until well blended.

Beat in the flour.

Pour 1/2 tablespoon oil into a large nonstick skillet. Swirl to coat the bottom. Heat over medium-high heat for about 2 minutes, or until hot. Spoon five 1/3-cup mounds of the potato mixture (about half) into the skillet. Using the back of a fork, flatten slightly until about 1/2 inch thick. Cook for about 9 minutes, turning once. Put the patties on an oven-safe platter. Set in the oven. Repeat the process (you should get 10 patties), heating the oil over medium-high heat for 30 seconds.

calories 134
protein 5 g
carbohydrates 24 g
  fiber 2 g
  sugars 5 g
cholesterol 1 mg
total fat 3.0 g
  saturated 0.0 g
  polyunsaturated 1.0 g
  monounsaturated 1.5 g
sodium 266 mg

dietary exchange
1 1/2 starch
1/2 fat

Time-Saver

Since you'll beat the cooked potatoes, you may wonder why you dice them first. It doesn't take long to dice them in the food processor, and using small pieces saves cooking time.

Baked Sweet Potato Chips

Serves 4

When you want to add a bit of flair to your meal, these sweet potato chips do it in a colorful, nutritious way. They're a great side dish for glazed ham with cranberries or roasted chicken with sugar snap peas.

Vegetable oil spray

Seasoning

1 teaspoon dried rosemary, crushed

1 teaspoon dried parsley, crumbled

1/2 teaspoon dry mustard

1/4 teaspoon paprika

1/4 teaspoon salt

1/4 teaspoon pepper

❖

2 medium sweet potatoes, unpeeled

Preheat the oven to 450°F. Lightly spray a baking sheet with vegetable oil spray.

In a small bowl, stir together the seasoning ingredients.

Cut the potatoes crosswise into 1/8-inch-thick slices. Put in a single layer on the baking sheet. Lightly spray the tops with vegetable oil spray. Sprinkle with the seasoning mixture.

Bake for 25 minutes, or until tender-crisp.

calories 69
protein 1 g
carbohydrates 17 g
  fiber 2 g
  sugars 4 g
cholesterol 0 mg
total fat 0.0 g
  saturated 0.0 g
  polyunsaturated 0.0 g
  monounsaturated 0.0 g
sodium 168 mg

dietary exchange
1 starch

Orange Sweet Potatoes

Serves 6

High in nutrition and smart for your heart, these sweet potatoes go well with lean pork or poultry. Add a dark green vegetable for color contrast and even more nutrients.

4 medium sweet potatoes, unpeeled, or 2 16-ounce cans
   Vegetable oil spray
1/2 cup fresh orange juice

2 tablespoons light brown sugar
1/4 to 1/2 teaspoon grated orange zest
1/4 teaspoon ground cinnamon
2 dashes of bitters (optional)

If using fresh sweet potatoes, fill a stockpot with enough water to just cover the sweet potatoes. Bring to a boil over high heat. Cook the potatoes for 30 minutes, or until tender. Discard the skins. If using canned potatoes, drain.

Preheat the oven to 350°F. Lightly spray a 1-quart casserole dish with vegetable oil spray.

In a large mixing bowl, mash the sweet potatoes.

Add the remaining ingredients and beat until fluffy. Spread the mixture in the casserole dish.

Bake, covered, for 25 minutes, or until heated through.

Cook's Tip on Bitters

Developed in South America as a tonic and digestive aid, bitters are an alcoholic mix of aromatic plant products. Although many recipes call for small amounts of bitters, most people think of using them in mixed drinks, such as Manhattans or old-fashioneds. The name only partially describes the flavor; bitters can provide a nicely intense pizazz to a number of dishes.

calories 114
protein 2 g
carbohydrates 29 g
  fiber 3 g
  sugars 11 g
cholesterol 0 mg
total fat 0.0 g
  saturated 0.0 g
  polyunsaturated 0.0 g
  monounsaturated 0.0 g
sodium 32 mg

dietary exchange
2 starch

Risotto with Broccoli and Leeks

Serves 8

Three basics for a creamy risotto are using arborio rice, gradually adding the liquid as you cook, and doing plenty of stirring. You can transform this side dish into a main dish by adding cubes of leftover skinless chicken or turkey breast.

2 medium leeks
3½ cups fat-free, low-sodium chicken broth, such as on page 45
½ cup white wine (regular or nonalcoholic) or fat-free, low-sodium chicken broth
2 teaspoons chopped fresh thyme or ½ teaspoon dried, crumbled
¼ teaspoon salt
⅛ teaspoon pepper
1 teaspoon olive oil
3 medium garlic cloves, minced
1 cup uncooked arborio rice
1 pound fresh or 13 to 14 ounces frozen broccoli florets, cooked and drained
¼ cup shredded or grated Parmesan or Romano cheese

Trim the root ends off the leeks. Cut a 2- to 3-inch section of the white part from each leek. Cut the sections in half lengthwise, then cut crosswise into thin slices. Put the leeks in a small colander. Rinse well under cold water. Drain.

In a large liquid measuring cup or other container with a handle and pouring spout, stir together the broth, wine, thyme, salt, and pepper. Set aside.

Heat a deep skillet over medium-high heat. Put the oil, leeks, and garlic in the skillet. Cook for 2 to 3 minutes, or until the leeks are tender, stirring occasionally.

Stir in the rice. Cook for 1 to 2 minutes, or until lightly toasted, stirring constantly.

Pour about ½ cup broth mixture into the skillet. Cook, uncovered, until the liquid is absorbed, stirring occasionally. Repeat the procedure until you've used all the liquid (the process takes 20 to 30 minutes). Reduce the heat to medium if the rice sticks excessively to the skillet.

Stir in the broccoli and Parmesan. Cook over medium heat for 1 to 2 minutes, or until the broccoli is warmed through, stirring occasionally.

calories 166
protein 6 g
carbohydrates 30 g
  fiber 3 g
  sugars 2 g
cholesterol 2 mg
total fat 1.5 g
  saturated 0.5 g
  polyunsaturated 0.0 g
  monounsaturated 0.5 g
sodium 147 mg

dietary exchange
1½ starch
1½ vegetable

Risotto Milanese

Serves 8

The key ingredient in any risotto is arborio rice. This delectable rice releases its starch, giving risotto and other dishes a creaminess that no other rice provides. Saffron traditionally flavors Risotto Milanese.

- 2 tablespoons acceptable stick margarine
- 1½ cups uncooked arborio rice
- 3 medium green onions (green and white parts), finely chopped
- ¼ cup dry white wine (regular or nonalcoholic)

- 4 cups fat-free, low-sodium chicken broth, such as on page 45
- 2 medium fresh button mushrooms, chopped
- ⅛ teaspoon saffron or ½ teaspoon ground turmeric
- 1 tablespoon shredded or grated Parmesan cheese

In a large, heavy saucepan, melt the margarine over medium heat and swirl to coat the bottom. Add the rice and green onions. Cook for 2 to 3 minutes, or until the rice is milky, stirring constantly with a wooden spoon.

Add the wine. Continue to cook for 2 to 3 minutes, or until the wine is absorbed, stirring constantly.

Stir in the remaining ingredients except the Parmesan. Bring to a boil over medium-high heat, stirring occasionally. Reduce the heat to low and cook, covered, for 20 minutes, or until the liquid is absorbed. Sprinkle with the Parmesan.

calories 188
protein 4 g
carbohydrates 35 g
fiber 1 g
sugars 1 g
cholesterol 0 mg
total fat 1.5 g
saturated 0.5 g
polyunsaturated 0.5 g
monounsaturated 0.5 g
sodium 44 mg

dietary exchange
2½ starch

Cook's Tip on Saffron

Saffron comes from the pistil of a particular crocus. Each flower has three threads called stigmas, and it takes more than 14,000 stigmas to make one ounce of saffron. That's why saffron is so expensive. You can buy saffron in powder form or in threads. The threads are fresher and more flavorful. Crush them just before you use them.

Middle Eastern
Brown Rice

Serves 8

Oranges and raisins add an interesting element to wholesome brown rice.

1 tablespoon light tub margarine	$^2/_3$ cup golden raisins
1 medium onion, minced	Zest of 1 medium orange, minced
2 medium ribs of celery, minced	(1 to 2 tablespoons)
2 cups uncooked brown rice	2 medium oranges, peeled and cut
3 cups water	into small pieces
2 cups fat-free, low-sodium chicken	$^1/_8$ teaspoon ground cloves
broth, such as on page 45	Sprigs of fresh mint (optional)

In a large saucepan, melt the margarine over medium-high heat. Swirl to coat the bottom. Cook the onion and celery for 3 minutes.

Stir in the rice. Cook for 2 minutes.

Stir in the water, broth, raisins, and orange zest. Bring to a boil. Reduce the heat and simmer, covered, for 40 to 45 minutes.

Stir in the oranges and cloves. Garnish with the mint.

Cook's Tip on Raisins

Seedless raisins are made from seedless grapes. Golden raisins and dark raisins are made from the same grape but dried differently. The golden ones are dried by artificial heat, and dark raisins are left in the sun for several weeks to achieve their deep color. This means that golden raisins are moister. If you need to chop raisins, freeze them first. They'll be easier to cut. If you're baking with raisins, coat them with some of the flour before adding to the batter. This will keep them from sinking to the bottom.

calories 248
protein 5 g
carbohydrates 54 g
  fiber 5 g
  sugars 14 g
cholesterol 0 mg
total fat 2.0 g
  saturated 0.5 g
  polyunsaturated 0.5 g
  monounsaturated 1.0 g
sodium 35 mg

dietary exchange
2$^1/_2$ starch
1 fruit

Mexican Fried Rice

Serves 6

Slightly brown the rice before cooking it to impart a mildly toasted flavor. Serve with fat-free refried beans and Chicken Fajitas (page 256) for a Tex-Mex feast.

1 teaspoon acceptable vegetable oil
1 cup uncooked long-grain rice
2 cups fat-free, low-sodium chicken broth, such as on page 45
⅔ cup canned chopped green chiles, rinsed and drained

4 to 5 medium green onions (green and white parts), thinly sliced
½ cup diced tomatoes
1 medium garlic clove, minced

Heat a large, heavy nonstick skillet over medium-high heat. Pour the oil into the skillet and swirl to coat the bottom. Cook the rice for 2 to 3 minutes, or until golden brown, stirring constantly.

Stir in the remaining ingredients. Reduce the heat and simmer, covered, for 30 minutes, or until the rice is tender and the liquid is absorbed. Fluff with a fork.

calories 127
protein 3 g
carbohydrates 27 g
  fiber 2 g
  sugars 1 g
cholesterol 0 mg
total fat 1.0 g
  saturated 0.0 g
  polyunsaturated 0.5 g
  monounsaturated 0.5 g
sodium 103 mg

dietary exchange
1½ starch
1 vegetable

Rice Italiano

Serves 6

Here's a twist on spaghetti with tomato sauce that's less messy. The rice absorbs the sauce, making it dripless but retaining all the flavor of Italy.

1 tablespoon light tub margarine
4 ounces fresh button mushrooms, sliced
1 small onion, chopped
1/4 medium green bell pepper, chopped
16-ounce can no-salt-added tomatoes, undrained

1/2 cup water
1 cup uncooked long-grain rice
2 tablespoons snipped fresh parsley
1/4 teaspoon dried basil, crumbled
1/4 teaspoon dried oregano, crumbled
Pepper to taste

In a large, deep skillet, melt the margarine over medium heat and swirl to coat the bottom. Cook the mushrooms, onion, and bell pepper for 3 to 4 minutes, or until the onion is tender and lightly browned.

Stir in the undrained tomatoes and water. Increase the heat to medium high and bring to a boil.

Stir in the remaining ingredients. Reduce the heat and simmer, covered, for 30 minutes, or until the rice is tender and the liquid is absorbed.

calories 135
protein 4 g
carbohydrates 29 g
  fiber 1 g
  sugars 4 g
cholesterol 0 mg
total fat 1.0 g
  saturated 0.0 g
  polyunsaturated 0.0 g
  monounsaturated 0.5 g
sodium 75 mg

dietary exchange
1 1/2 starch
1 1/2 vegetable

Wild Rice
with Mushrooms

Serves 6

The nutty flavor of wild rice pairs nicely with earthy mushrooms. Serve this dish with lean venison or Cornish game hens.

1¹/4 cups uncooked wild rice (4 ounces)
¹/4 teaspoon salt
2 tablespoons light tub margarine
8 ounces medium fresh button mushrooms, quartered
¹/4 cup dry white wine (regular or nonalcoholic)

¹/4 teaspoon salt
5 to 6 medium green onions (green and white parts), sliced
2 tablespoons white wine Worcestershire sauce
1 tablespoon finely chopped fresh sage

Prepare the rice using the package directions, decreasing the salt to ¹/4 teaspoon and omitting the margarine.

In a large nonstick skillet, melt the margarine over medium heat and swirl to coat the bottom. Cook the mushrooms, wine, and ¹/4 teaspoon salt, covered, for 5 minutes. Increase the temperature to high. Cook, uncovered, for 2 to 3 minutes, or until the juices evaporate.

Reduce the heat to medium. Stir in the green onions. Cook for 2 minutes, stirring occasionally.

Stir in the rice and remaining ingredients.

calories 158
protein 6 g
carbohydrates 30 g
  fiber 3 g
  sugars 3 g
cholesterol 0 mg
total fat 2.0 g
  saturated 0.0 g
  polyunsaturated 0.5 g
  monounsaturated 1.0 g
sodium 283 mg

dietary exchange
2 starch

Basil Spinach

Serves 4

The addition of basil and garlic gives this ultra-quick side dish the taste of Italy in a matter of seconds.

2 tablespoons light tub margarine
1 teaspoon dried basil, crumbled
1 medium garlic clove, minced

9 ounces fresh spinach
¼ teaspoon salt

Heat a 12-inch nonstick skillet over medium-high heat. Cook the margarine, basil, and garlic, stirring until the margarine is melted.

Stir in the spinach. Cook for 45 seconds, or until just wilted, stirring constantly. Don't overcook. Remove from the heat.

Gently stir in the salt.

calories 36
protein 2 g
carbohydrates 3 g
  fiber 2 g
  sugars 0 g
cholesterol 0 mg
total fat 2.5 g
  saturated 0.0 g
  polyunsaturated 0.5 g
  monounsaturated 1.5 g
sodium 241 mg

dietary exchange
½ fat

Sophisticated Spinach

Serves 4

This recipe is elegant enough to serve when entertaining but easy enough for a weeknight after a mad-dash day.

1 large onion, chopped
10-ounce package frozen chopped spinach, thawed and squeezed dry
3/4 cup fat-free half-and-half
1 1/2 ounces fat-free or light cream cheese, cut into small pieces

1 medium garlic clove, minced
1/4 teaspoon salt
1 tablespoon shredded or grated Parmesan cheese

In a 10-inch nonstick skillet over medium heat, cook the onion for 3 to 4 minutes, or until soft, stirring occasionally.

Stir in the spinach, half-and-half, cream cheese, and garlic to blend well. Reduce the heat and simmer, covered, for 5 minutes. Remove from the heat.

Stir in the salt. Sprinkle with the Parmesan.

Cook's Tip

Be sure to include the Parmesan. This tasty cheese acts as a sponge, absorbing some of the liquid.

calories 84
protein 8 g
carbohydrates 15 g
  fiber 3 g
  sugars 6 g
cholesterol 2 mg
total fat 0.5 g
  saturated 0.5 g
  polyunsaturated 0.0 g
  monounsaturated 0.0 g
sodium 324 mg

dietary exchange
1 1/2 vegetable
1/2 skim milk

Gingered Acorn Squash

Serves 4

You could almost serve this luscious vegetable dish for dessert!

Vegetable oil spray
2 acorn squash (about ¾ pound each)
8-ounce can pineapple tidbits in their own juice, drained

3 tablespoons raisins (optional)
2 tablespoons light brown sugar
1 tablespoon light tub margarine, melted
1 teaspoon grated peeled gingerroot

Preheat the oven to 400°F. Lightly spray a 13 × 9 × 2-inch baking dish with vegetable oil spray.

Cut each squash in half. Scoop out and discard the seeds and strings. Put the squash halves with the cut side up in the baking dish.

In a small bowl, stir together the remaining ingredients. Spoon the mixture into each squash cavity. Carefully pour a small amount of water around the squash.

Bake, covered, for 45 minutes.

calories 110
protein 1 g
carbohydrates 27 g
  fiber 2 g
  sugars 16 g
cholesterol 0 mg
total fat 1.5 g
  saturated 0.0 g
  polyunsaturated 0.5 g
  monounsaturated 0.5 g
sodium 34 mg

dietary exchange
1 starch
1 fruit

Time-Saver for Acorn Squash

To make acorn squash easier to cut, pierce it in several places with the tip of a knife. Put the squash on a paper towel in the microwave and cook on 100 percent power (high) for about 5 minutes. Handle carefully. Cut into halves and remove the seeds and strings with a spoon. Reduce the baking time to 50 to 60 minutes or the microwaving time to 8 to 10 minutes.

with raisins

calories 133
protein 1 g
carbohydrates 33 g
  fiber 3 g
  sugars 21 g
cholesterol 0 mg
total fat 1.5 g
  saturated 0.0 g
  polyunsaturated 0.5 g
  monounsaturated 0.5 g
sodium 34 mg

dietary exchange
1 starch
1 fruit

Acorn Squash Stuffed with Cranberries and Walnuts

Serves 6

A bounty of ingredients, including wine-red dried cranberries, fills mellow squash for a delectable dish.

3 small acorn squash (about 4 inches in diameter)

Stuffing

1 cup cooked brown rice

1 cup unseasoned croutons

1 medium onion, finely chopped

1/2 cup fat-free, low-sodium chicken broth, such as on page 45

1/4 cup dried cranberries

2 tablespoons chopped walnuts, dry-roasted

1 tablespoon light tub margarine

1 teaspoon dried sage

1/2 teaspoon dried thyme, crumbled

1/4 teaspoon dried oregano, crumbled

1/4 teaspoon salt

1/4 teaspoon pepper

❖

1/4 cup water

Preheat the oven to 400°F.

Cut each squash in half. Scoop out and discard the seeds and strings.

In a large bowl, stir together the stuffing ingredients. Fill the squash halves loosely with the stuffing mixture.

Pour the water into a 13 × 9 × 2-inch casserole dish. Place the squash halves with the filled side up in the dish.

Bake, covered, for 1 hour to 1 hour 15 minutes, or until the squash is tender when pierced with the tip of a knife.

Microwave Method

Put the acorn squash halves (unstuffed) with the cut side down in a microwave-safe dish. Add 1/4 cup water. Cover with plastic wrap and cook on 100 percent power (high) for 5 minutes. Carefully remove the plastic wrap (steam from the pan is hot). Remove the squash from the dish, leaving the water in the dish. Fill the squash halves loosely with the stuffing mixture. Return to the dish and cover with plastic wrap. Cook on 100 percent power (high) for 10 to 12 minutes, or until the squash is tender when pierced with the tip of a knife.

calories 193
protein 4 g
carbohydrates 40 g
fiber 5 g
sugars 10 g
cholesterol 0 mg
total fat 3.0 g
saturated 0.5 g
polyunsaturated 1.5 g
monounsaturated 1.0 g
sodium 158 mg
dietary exchange
2 1/2 starch
1/2 fruit

Butternut Mash

Serves 8

Savory spices and a spark of lime boost the flavor of yellow-orange butternut squash. Serve this side dish with pork roast or seared chicken breasts.

2¹/₂-pound butternut squash (1 medium)
1 cup water
¹/₄ cup fat-free half-and-half
2 medium garlic cloves, minced

2 teaspoons fresh lime juice
1 teaspoon ground cumin
1 teaspoon olive oil
¹/₄ teaspoon salt
¹/₄ teaspoon pepper

Cut the squash in half lengthwise (see Cook's Tip on Winter Squash, page 59) and remove the seeds. Place with the cut side up in a large microwave-safe container. Pour the water around the squash. Cover the container with plastic wrap. Microwave on 100 percent power (high) for 14 to 15 minutes, or until the squash is tender. Let cool for 3 to 4 minutes.

Meanwhile, in a small saucepan, cook the remaining ingredients over low heat for 2 to 3 minutes, stirring occasionally. Cover the pan.

Scoop the flesh from the squash into a medium bowl. Pour in the half-and-half mixture. Mash with a potato masher until smooth.

Cook's Tip

To roast the squash instead, cut it in half vertically (see Cook's Tip on Winter Squash, page 59) and scoop out the seeds. Place the squash with the cut side up on a nonstick baking sheet. Bake uncovered, for 1 hour, or until tender, in a preheated 350°F oven.

calories 66
protein 2 g
carbohydrates 15 g
  fiber 4 g
  sugars 4 g
cholesterol 0 mg
total fat 0.5 g
  saturated 0.0 g
  polyunsaturated 0.0 g
  monounsaturated 0.5 g
sodium 86 mg

dietary exchange
1 starch

Pattypan Squash
with Apple-Nut Stuffing

Serves 4

Here's a summertime version of stuffed squash. Like its wintertime counterpart, stuffed acorn squash, it goes well with poultry and pork.

4 medium pattypan squash, unpeeled

2 medium baking apples, such as Rome Beauty, chopped

2 tablespoons chopped walnuts or pecans

¹/₄ cup dried currants or dried cranberries

2¹/₂ tablespoons light brown sugar

Liquid margarine spray

Preheat the oven to 350°F.

Cut the squash horizontally into halves. Scoop out and discard the seeds. Put the squash with the cut side down in a 13 × 9 × 2-inch glass baking dish.

Bake for 30 minutes.

Meanwhile, in a small bowl, stir together the remaining ingredients except the margarine. Spoon into the squash halves. Spray with the margarine spray.

Bake with the stuffed side up for 30 minutes, or until tender.

calories 162
protein 3 g
carbohydrates 35 g
  fiber 7 g
  sugars 27 g
cholesterol 0 mg
total fat 3.0 g
  saturated 0.5 g
  polyunsaturated 2.0 g
  monounsaturated 0.5 g
sodium 8 mg

dietary exchange
1¹/₂ fruit
2 vegetable
1 fat

Cook's Tip on Pattypan Squash

A white summer squash, pattypan looks something like a scalloped flying saucer with a stem. Its unique shape makes it perfect for stuffing. Use as you would yellow summer squash or zucchini.

Yellow Summer Squash
Casserole with
Crunchy Crust

Serves 6

Tender cooked and mashed yellow summer squash is enhanced with fresh sage, then baked with a bagel topping that becomes crunchy. The flavors are similar to bread stuffing with all the goodness of vegetables.

1/2 teaspoon olive oil
1/2 large onion, thinly sliced
1 pound yellow summer squash, diced
2 tablespoons fat-free, low-sodium chicken broth, such as on page 45
3/4 teaspoon chopped fresh sage or 1/4 teaspoon dried
1 medium garlic clove, minced
1/8 teaspoon salt

1/8 teaspoon pepper
1/2 4-inch whole-wheat bagel, crumbled into small pieces, or 1 1/4 cups soft whole-wheat bread crumbs
1/8 cup shredded or grated Parmesan cheese
1 teaspoon olive oil
Vegetable oil spray (olive oil spray preferred)

Heat a medium saucepan over medium heat. Pour 1/2 teaspoon olive oil into the saucepan and swirl to coat the bottom. Cook the onion for 2 to 3 minutes, or until soft. Increase the heat to medium-high and cook for 7 to 10 minutes, or until the onion is a deep golden brown, stirring occasionally.

Stir in the squash, broth, sage, garlic, salt, and pepper and bring to a simmer. Reduce the heat and simmer, covered, for 10 to 12 minutes, or until the squash is tender.

Meanwhile, preheat the oven to 375°F.

In a medium bowl, stir together the bagel pieces, Parmesan, and 1 teaspoon olive oil.

Using a potato masher, mash together the squash and onion mixture until slightly chunky. Pour the mixture into an 8-inch square baking dish. Spread the bagel topping over the squash. Lightly spray with vegetable oil spray.

Bake for 25 to 30 minutes, or until the topping is golden brown and the squash mixture is warmed through.

calories 64
protein 3 g
carbohydrates 10 g
  fiber 3 g
  sugars 3 g
cholesterol 1 mg
total fat 2.0 g
  saturated 0.5 g
  polyunsaturated 0.0 g
  monounsaturated 1.0 g
sodium 129 mg

dietary exchange
1/2 starch
1 vegetable

Creole Squash

Serves 10

This layered vegetable casserole would be super with Baked Catfish (page 146).

Sauce
- 1 large fresh button mushroom, sliced
- 2 tablespoons chopped onion
- 2 tablespoons chopped green bell pepper
- 1 teaspoon light tub margarine
- 2 cups drained canned no-salt-added stewed tomatoes or 2 large fresh tomatoes, chopped

Pepper to taste

❖

- 6 medium yellow summer squash, cubed
- Vegetable oil spray
- 1/2 cup plain dry bread crumbs
- 1 tablespoon light tub margarine

calories 65
protein 2 g
carbohydrates 12 g
  fiber 3 g
  sugars 5 g
cholesterol 0 mg
total fat 1.0 g
  saturated 0.0 g
  polyunsaturated 0.5 g
  monounsaturated 0.5 g
sodium 67 mg

dietary exchange
2½ vegetable

creole eggplant

calories 60
protein 2 g
carbohydrates 11 g
  fiber 3 g
  sugars 5 g
cholesterol 0 mg
total fat 1.0 g
  saturated 0.0 g
  polyunsaturated 0.5 g
  monounsaturated 0.5 g
sodium 67 mg

dietary exchange
2 vegetable

In a medium saucepan, cook the mushroom, onion, bell pepper, and margarine over low heat for 5 minutes, stirring occasionally.

Stir in the tomatoes and pepper. Simmer, uncovered, for 30 minutes, or until the sauce is thickened, stirring occasionally.

Meanwhile, in a medium saucepan, boil the squash in a small amount of water over medium-high heat for 10 minutes, or just until tender. Drain.

Preheat the oven to 350°F. Lightly spray an 11 × 7 × 2-inch casserole dish with vegetable oil spray.

To assemble, alternate the layers of squash and sauce in the casserole dish, starting with the squash and ending with the sauce. Sprinkle with the bread crumbs. Dot with the margarine.

Bake for 30 minutes, or until bubbling.

Creole Eggplant
Substitute about 1½ pounds eggplant, sliced or cubed, for the squash and proceed as directed above.

Scalloped Squash

Serve this herb-flecked dish with Tilapia Amandine (page 185) and fresh green beans.

1 teaspoon light tub margarine	1 teaspoon dried basil, crumbled
1 large onion, finely chopped	1 teaspoon dried thyme, crumbled
1¹/₂ pounds yellow summer squash, sliced	1 teaspoon dried marjoram, crumbled
	¹/₄ teaspoon salt
²/₃ cup fat-free, low-sodium chicken broth, such as on page 45	1³/₄ cups seasoned croutons
	¹/₄ cup snipped fresh chives

In a large saucepan, melt the margarine over medium-high heat and swirl to coat the bottom. Cook the onion for 2 to 3 minutes, or until soft.

Add the squash, broth, basil, thyme, marjoram, and salt. Reduce the heat to medium. Cook, covered, for 10 minutes, or until the squash is tender.

Meanwhile, put the croutons in a plastic bag and crush with a mallet or rolling pin. Stir into the squash mixture. If the mixture is too dry, stir in a small amount of hot water.

Stir in the chives.

calories 95
protein 3 g
carbohydrates 16 g
  fiber 4 g
  sugars 5 g
cholesterol 1 mg
total fat 2.5 g
  saturated 0.5 g
  polyunsaturated 0.5 g
  monounsaturated 1.5 g
sodium 253 mg

dietary exchange
¹/₂ starch
2 vegetable
¹/₂ fat

Golden Lemon-Crumb Tomatoes

Serves 4

Don't leave out the grated lemon zest—it gives this dish its special flavor.

1/2 cup plain fresh soft bread crumbs

2 tablespoons finely snipped fresh parsley

1/2 teaspoon dried basil, crumbled

1/2 teaspoon grated lemon zest

2 ounces fat-free or low-fat feta cheese, crumbled

Vegetable oil spray

2 large tomatoes (about 8 ounces each), halved crosswise

1 1/2 tablespoons fresh lemon juice

1/8 teaspoon salt

Preheat the oven to 350°F.

In a small bowl, stir together the bread crumbs, parsley, basil, and lemon zest. Toss gently.

Add the feta. Toss gently.

To assemble, lightly spray a 9-inch pie pan with vegetable oil spray. Place the tomato halves in the pie pan. Spoon the lemon juice over the halves. Top the tomatoes with the bread-crumb mixture. Liberally spray with vegetable oil spray.

Bake for 30 minutes, or until the tomatoes are tender when pierced with a fork and beginning to lightly brown.

Sprinkle with the salt. Let stand for 10 minutes before serving.

calories 52
protein 4 g
carbohydrates 9 g
  fiber 1 g
  sugars 4 g
cholesterol 0 mg
total fat 0.5 g
  saturated 0.0 g
  polyunsaturated 0.0 g
  monounsaturated 0.0 g
sodium 332 mg

dietary exchange
1 1/2 vegetable
1/2 very lean meat

Italian
Vegetable Bake

Serves 4

Try different kinds of mushroom and vary the herbs and vegetables to "invent" different side dishes from this basic recipe.

Vegetable oil spray (olive oil spray preferred)

8 to 10 ounces fresh mushrooms, any variety or combination, sliced

1 small zucchini, thinly sliced

4 medium Italian plum tomatoes, sliced

2 small green onions (green and white parts), thinly sliced

3 tablespoons fat-free or light Italian salad dressing

2 teaspoons chopped fresh basil leaves or 1/2 teaspoon dried, crumbled

2 teaspoons chopped fresh oregano or 1/2 teaspoon dried, crumbled

1/2 medium garlic clove, minced

Preheat the oven to 350°F. Lightly spray an 8-inch square baking dish with vegetable oil spray.

Make one layer each of the mushrooms, zucchini, tomatoes, and green onions in the baking dish.

In a small bowl, stir together the remaining ingredients. Drizzle over the vegetables. Cover with aluminum foil. Bake for 25 minutes, or until the vegetables are tender.

To serve, use a slotted spoon to remove the vegetables from the liquid.

calories 47
protein 3 g
carbohydrates 9 g
  fiber 2 g
  sugars 4 g
cholesterol 0 mg
total fat 0.5 g
  saturated 0.0 g
  polyunsaturated 0.0 g
  monounsaturated 0.0 g
sodium 173 mg

dietary exchange
2 vegetable

Grilled Vegetable Medley
with Balsamic Dressing

Serves 16

You'll be glad this versatile recipe makes so much. Enjoy the veggies warm with whatever you grill for your entrée, then serve them chilled for another meal. See the Cook's Tip for ways to finish what's left.

Vegetable oil spray (olive oil spray preferred)

1 small unpeeled eggplant, cut crosswise into 1/2-inch slices

1 large red bell pepper, halved, seeds and ribs discarded

1 medium yellow summer squash (about 8 ounces), cut crosswise into 1/2-inch slices

1 medium zucchini (about 8 ounces), cut crosswise into 1/2-inch slices

1 medium onion, cut into 1-inch slices

1 large portobello mushroom, stem discarded, cut into 1-inch slices

Balsamic Dressing

2 tablespoons red currant jelly

2 tablespoons balsamic vinegar

1 tablespoon coarsely chopped fresh rosemary

2 medium garlic cloves, minced

1/4 teaspoon pepper

Lightly spray the grill rack with vegetable oil spray. Preheat the grill on medium-high.

Lightly spray both sides of the eggplant, bell pepper, yellow squash, zucchini, onion, and mushroom slices with vegetable oil spray.

Grill the vegetables for 3 to 4 minutes on each side, or until browned.

Meanwhile, in a large bowl, whisk together the dressing ingredients. Add the grilled vegetables and stir to coat. Serve warm or chilled.

Cook's Tip

If you have any leftovers, add 2 cups cooked chicken to 2 cups grilled vegetables (with dressing) and serve over brown rice or mixed greens. Another idea is to coarsely chop grilled vegetables (with dressing) and mix into your favorite meat loaf recipe.

calories 27
protein 1 g
carbohydrates 6 g
  fiber 2 g
  sugars 4 g
cholesterol 0 mg
total fat 0.0 g
  saturated 0.0 g
  polyunsaturated 0.0 g
  monounsaturated 0.0 g
sodium 2 mg

dietary exchange
1 vegetable

Roasted Veggies
with Sesame Seeds

Serves 4; ½ cup per serving

Roasting carrots, zucchini, and onion brings out their natural richness. A sprinkling of sesame seed adds a nice crunchiness.

2 medium carrots, quartered diagonally

1 medium zucchini, quartered and cut into 2-inch pieces, or 1 medium red bell pepper, cut into thin strips

1 medium onion, cut into ½-inch wedges

1 tablespoon sesame seeds
   Vegetable oil spray

1 tablespoon sugar

1½ tablespoons low-salt soy sauce

1 tablespoon cider vinegar

Preheat the oven to 425°F.

Arrange the carrots, zucchini, and onion on a nonstick baking sheet in a single layer. Sprinkle with the sesame seeds. Lightly spray the vegetables with vegetable oil spray.

Bake for 8 minutes. Stir. Bake for 8 more minutes, or until the vegetables begin to brown on the edges.

Meanwhile, in a small bowl, stir together the remaining ingredients.

To serve, transfer the vegetables to a rimmed platter or shallow bowl. Spoon the soy sauce mixture over all. Don't stir.

Cook's Tip on Roasting Vegetables

It's important to arrange vegetables in a single layer when roasting to allow them to brown properly.

calories 68
protein 2 g
carbohydrates 13 g
  fiber 2 g
  sugars 9 g
cholesterol 0 mg
total fat 1.5 g
  saturated 0.0 g
  polyunsaturated 0.5 g
  monounsaturated 0.5 g
sodium 163 mg

dietary exchange
3 vegetable

Vegetable Stir-Fry

Serves 8

It's easy to master the technique of stir-frying. Then you can prepare this dish and many others for quick meals.

1 pound fresh broccoli
1 teaspoon light stick margarine
1 teaspoon acceptable vegetable oil
1 pound carrots, thinly sliced
12 ounces fresh button mushrooms, thinly sliced

2 to 3 medium green onions (green and white parts), thinly sliced
2 tablespoons dry sherry
1 tablespoon fresh lemon juice
1 teaspoon ground nutmeg
1 teaspoon dried thyme, crumbled
Pepper to taste

Separate the broccoli florets so they are of small, uniform size. Peel the tough stems. Cut the stems into 2-inch pieces.

In a large skillet or wok, heat the margarine and oil over medium heat. Swirl to coat the bottom. Stir-fry the broccoli, carrots, mushrooms, and green onions for 5 minutes, or until the vegetables are tender-crisp, stirring constantly.

Stir in the remaining ingredients.

calories 66
protein 4 g
carbohydrates 12 g
  fiber 4 g
  sugars 6 g
cholesterol 0 mg
total fat 1.5 g
  saturated 0.0 g
  polyunsaturated 0.5 g
  monounsaturated 0.5 g
sodium 42 mg

dietary exchange
2½ vegetable

Southwestern Ratatouille

Serves 8

Southwestern spices combine with traditional Provençal vegetables in this version of ratatouille.

1 medium eggplant, peeled and diced	3 sprigs of fresh thyme, leaves removed and crushed, or
1/4 teaspoon salt	1/2 teaspoon dried, crumbled
1 teaspoon olive oil	1/4 teaspoon crushed red pepper flakes
1 medium onion, finely chopped	4 large tomatoes, seeded and chopped
1 medium red or green bell pepper, cut into thin strips	2 medium zucchini, sliced
2 tablespoons minced garlic	2 tablespoons minced fresh parsley
2 teaspoons dried oregano, crumbled	1 1/2 tablespoons shredded or grated Parmesan cheese
2 teaspoons chili powder	
2 teaspoons ground cumin	

Put the eggplant in a colander. Sprinkle with salt. Let stand for 30 minutes. Rinse well and pat dry with paper towels.

Heat a large skillet over medium-high heat. Pour the oil into the skillet and swirl to coat the bottom. Cook the onion, bell pepper, and garlic for 2 minutes, or until tender-crisp.

Stir in the oregano, chili powder, cumin, thyme, and red pepper flakes.

Stir in the tomatoes. Reduce the heat and simmer for 4 to 5 minutes.

Stir in the eggplant and zucchini. Simmer, covered, for 20 minutes.

To serve, stir in the parsley and Parmesan, or cover and refrigerate to serve chilled.

Cook's Tip on Eggplant

Salting eggplant and letting it stand awhile before rinsing helps draw out the bitterness and excess moisture.

calories 70
protein 3 g
carbohydrates 14 g
  fiber 4 g
  sugars 7 g
cholesterol 1 mg
total fat 1.5 g
  saturated 0.5 g
  polyunsaturated 0.5 g
  monounsaturated 0.5 g
sodium 109 mg

dietary exchange
3 vegetable

Couscous with Vegetables

Serves 4

Vivid green peas, velvety mushrooms, and fresh parsley are a terrific combination in this quick dish.

1/2 cup uncooked couscous

1 cup frozen green peas, thawed and drained, or any other quick-cooking vegetable

1/2 cup minced onion

2 medium fresh button mushrooms, thinly sliced

2 tablespoons dry white wine (regular or nonalcoholic)

1/2 teaspoon crushed garlic or 1/4 teaspoon garlic powder

2 tablespoons finely snipped fresh parsley

1/2 teaspoon dried basil, crumbled

1/8 teaspoon pepper

Prepare the couscous using the package directions, omitting the salt and oil.

Meanwhile, in a medium nonstick saucepan, cook the peas, onion, mushrooms, wine, and garlic over medium-high heat for 3 to 5 minutes, stirring often.

Stir the parsley, basil, and pepper into the pan.

To serve, stir together all the ingredients in a large bowl.

calories 124
protein 5 g
carbohydrates 24 g
 fiber 4 g
 sugars 4 g
cholesterol 0 mg
total fat 0.5 g
 saturated 0.0 g
 polyunsaturated 0.0 g
 monounsaturated 0.0 g
sodium 34 mg

dietary exchange
1 1/2 starch

Corn Bread Dressing

Serves 8

No one can resist this southern side dish. You'll get lots of flavor but very little fat in each golden spoonful.

Vegetable oil spray

3 cups crumbled Southern-Style Corn Bread (page 518)

2 cups fat-free, low-sodium chicken broth, such as on page 45

1 cup fat-free, no-salt-added cracker crumbs

3 medium ribs of celery, finely chopped

1 medium onion, finely chopped

Whites of 2 medium eggs or egg substitute equivalent to 1 egg

½ teaspoon pepper, or to taste

½ teaspoon dried sage or poultry seasoning

Preheat the oven to 350°F. Lightly spray a 9-inch round or square baking dish with vegetable oil spray.

In a large bowl, stir together the remaining ingredients. Pour into the baking dish.

Bake, covered, for 45 minutes.

Optional Cooking Method
Stuff the dressing loosely in the cavity of a 10- to 12-pound turkey just before roasting.

Cook's Tip on Poultry Seasoning

You can buy this salt-free herb mixture in the spice area of the supermarket or make your own. Experiment with proportions of dried sage, marjoram, thyme, and parsley, with perhaps some dried savory and pepper.

calories 167
protein 6 g
carbohydrates 31 g
  fiber 2 g
  sugars 3 g
cholesterol 1 mg
total fat 2.5 g
  saturated 0.5 g
  polyunsaturated 1.0 g
  monounsaturated 1.5 g
sodium 322 mg

dietary exchange
2 starch

Apple Dressing

Serves 12

For a warming fall or winter meal, serve this apple-sage dressing with Orange Sweet Potatoes (page 456) and a roast turkey breast or pork tenderloin.

Vegetable oil spray
1 teaspoon light tub margarine
1/4 cup chopped onion
1/2 medium rib of celery, chopped
4 cups toasted bread cubes or 6 cups fresh bread cubes

1 cup diced unpeeled apple
1/2 teaspoon poultry seasoning
1/2 teaspoon dried sage
Pepper to taste
1/2 cup fat-free, low-sodium chicken broth, such as on page 45

calories 63
protein 2 g
carbohydrates 12 g
 fiber 1 g
 sugars 2 g
cholesterol 0 mg
total fat 1.0 g
 saturated 0.0 g
 polyunsaturated 0.5 g
 monounsaturated 0.0 g
sodium 113 mg

dietary exchange
1 starch

Preheat the oven to 350°F. Lightly spray a 13 × 9 × 2-inch baking dish with vegetable oil spray.

In a small skillet, melt the margarine over medium-high heat. Swirl to coat the bottom. Cook the onion and celery for 5 minutes, or until soft. Transfer to a large bowl.

Stir the remaining ingredients except the broth into the bowl. Gently stir in the broth. Transfer to the baking dish.

Bake, covered, for 45 minutes.

dressing with mixed dried fruits

calories 106
protein 2 g
carbohydrates 23 g
 fiber 2 g
 sugars 11 g
cholesterol 0 mg
total fat 1.0 g
 saturated 0.0 g
 polyunsaturated 0.5 g
 monounsaturated 0.5 g
sodium 114 mg

dietary exchange
1 starch
1/2 fruit

Dressing with Mixed Dried Fruits

Omit the diced apple. In a small saucepan, stir together 1 cup chopped dried fruits, such as apricots, prunes, or peaches, or a combination, and 1/2 cup dried cranberries or raisins. Add water to cover. Simmer, covered, for 20 minutes. Drain. Let cool slightly. Proceed as directed.

Cranberry Chutney

Serves 16

Especially good with curried meat dishes, this chutney also pairs well with turkey and chicken. The serving size is more for a condiment than a true side dish.

16 ounces whole fresh cranberries (4 cups)
8 ounces dates, chopped
1¼ cups water
1 cup sugar
1 cup golden raisins
¾ cup cider vinegar
¼ cup fresh orange juice

1 tablespoon grated lemon zest
½ teaspoon salt
½ teaspoon ground cinnamon
½ teaspoon ground ginger
¼ teaspoon ground allspice
⅛ teaspoon ground cloves
¼ to 1 teaspoon crushed red pepper flakes

In a large saucepan, stir together the ingredients. Bring to a boil over medium-high heat. Reduce the heat and simmer, covered, for 15 minutes, stirring occasionally.

Transfer to a glass jar with a tight-fitting lid and refrigerate. Use within two weeks.

Cook's Tip

For a longer shelf life, spoon the mixture into hot sterilized jars. Follow the jar manufacturer's directions for sealing the jars. Process for 10 minutes in a boiling water bath (the water should cover the jars by 1 to 2 inches). Remove the jars from the water. Let cool for at least 12 hours at room temperature. Then check to be sure the seal is tight (there should be no air pocket when you press the center of the lid).

calories 140
protein 1 g
carbohydrates 37 g
  fiber 3 g
  sugars 32 g
cholesterol 0 mg
total fat 0.0 g
  saturated 0.0 g
  polyunsaturated 0.0 g
  monounsaturated 0.0 g
sodium 75 mg

dietary exchange
1½ fruit
1 other carbohydrate

Baked Curried Fruit

Serves 8

When the weather turns cold, serve this spicy fruit for brunch or instead of salad at dinner. It's excellent with baked ham or pork tenderloin.

15-ounce can peaches in fruit juice
14.5-ounce can Bing cherries in heavy syrup
15.25-ounce can pineapple chunks in their own juice
11-ounce can mandarin oranges in water or light syrup
Vegetable oil spray

$^1/_2$ cup firmly packed light brown sugar
$^1/_2$ tablespoon curry powder
Juice of 1 medium lemon (about 2 tablespoons)
1 tablespoon plus 1 teaspoon light tub margarine

Put a colander in a large bowl to collect the liquid that will drain out. (Make sure the colander will not sit in the drained juices.) Pour the peaches, cherries, pineapple, and mandarin oranges into the colander. Cover and refrigerate for 1 hour, or until all the juice has drained.

Preheat the oven to 300°F. Lightly spray a shallow 12 × 8 × 2-inch casserole dish with vegetable oil spray. Spoon the fruit into the dish.

In a small bowl, stir together the brown sugar and curry powder. Sprinkle over the fruit.

Sprinkle the fruit with the lemon juice. Dot with the margarine.

Bake, covered, for 45 minutes, or until heated through.

calories 150
protein 1 g
carbohydrates 36 g
  fiber 1 g
  sugars 32 g
cholesterol 0 mg
total fat 1.0 g
  saturated 0.0 g
  polyunsaturated 0.0 g
  monounsaturated 0.5 g
sodium 31 mg

dietary exchange
1$^1/_2$ fruit
1 other carbohydrate

Caramelized
Pineapple Spears

Serves 4

The natural sugars of fresh pineapple turn a rich golden brown, lightly caramelizing the outside of each spear.

16 whole cloves
1/3 whole ripe pineapple, peeled and cut into 4 spears
2 tablespoons light tub margarine

1 tablespoon firmly packed dark brown sugar
1/4 teaspoon ground allspice or cinnamon

Evenly space and insert 4 cloves on one side of each pineapple spear.

Heat a 10-inch nonstick skillet over medium-high heat. Cook the margarine, brown sugar, and allspice, stirring until the margarine is melted.

Add the pineapple spears with the clove side down. Cook for 2 minutes. Reduce the heat to medium. Turn the spears. Cook for 6 minutes, or until tender, turning twice.

To serve, transfer the spears to a serving dish. Remove the cloves. Using a rubber scraper, scrape any glaze remaining in the skillet and drizzle over the spears. Serve warm or at room temperature.

Cook's Tip on Pineapple

One way to choose a ripe pineapple is to use your sense of smell. A ripe pineapple has a distinct "pineapple" scent. If it's not ripe, place it on your kitchen counter for a few days, then check again.

calories 53
protein 0 g
carbohydrates 8 g
  fiber 1 g
  sugars 8 g
cholesterol 0 mg
total fat 2.5 g
  saturated 0.0 g
  polyunsaturated 0.5 g
  monounsaturated 1.5 g
sodium 47 mg

dietary exchange
1/2 fruit
1/2 fat

Baked Pears with Honey Almonds

Serves 4

Curry coupled with drizzles of honey makes these baked pears a great side dish with chicken or pork or the perfect ending for any meal.

2 large pears (about 1 pound total), halved and cored
¼ cup finely chopped dried apricots
1 teaspoon light tub margarine
¼ teaspoon curry powder

1 tablespoon fresh lemon juice
2 tablespoons slivered almonds, dry-roasted
1 tablespoon plus 1 teaspoon honey

Preheat the oven to 350°F.

In a pie pan or shallow pan, arrange the pears with the cut side up. Fill each pear half with 1 tablespoon apricots.

In a small bowl, stir together the margarine and curry powder. Spoon on each pear half.

Drizzle the lemon juice over the pears. Cover the pan with aluminum foil.

Bake for 40 minutes, or until the pears are tender when pierced with a fork.

Sprinkle with the almonds. Drizzle with the honey.

Cook's Tip

Using almond slivers rather than the thin slices gives a crunchier texture to this dish.

calories 131
protein 2 g
carbohydrates 29 g
 fiber 4 g
 sugars 22 g
cholesterol 0 mg
total fat 2.5 g
 saturated 0.0 g
 polyunsaturated 0.5 g
 monounsaturated 1.5 g
sodium 9 mg

dietary exchange
2 fruit
½ fat

Microwave
Baked Apple Slices

Serves 4

This dish is so easy, you'll want to make it every time you serve pork chops or ham or baked chicken or meat loaf—you get the idea! It's even great as a quick dessert.

Vegetable oil spray
1 pound unpeeled apples, cored and cut into ¹/₂-inch wedges
1¹/₂ tablespoons sugar

1 tablespoon light tub margarine
¹/₂ teaspoon ground cinnamon
¹/₄ teaspoon vanilla extract

Lightly spray a 9-inch glass baking dish with vegetable oil spray. Arrange the apples in the dish. Cover with plastic wrap.

Microwave at 100 percent power (high) for 2¹/₂ minutes, or until just tender. Remove from the microwave.

Add the remaining ingredients, stirring until the margarine is completely melted.

calories 91
protein 0 g
carbohydrates 21 g
  fiber 3 g
  sugars 17 g
cholesterol 0 mg
total fat 1.5 g
  saturated 0.0 g
  polyunsaturated 0.5 g
  monounsaturated 0.5 g
sodium 23 mg

dietary exchange
1 fruit
¹/₂ other carbohydrate

sauces and
gravies

Basic Gravy

Serves 8; 2 tablespoons per serving

Adjust the amount of flour according to whether you want thin, medium, or thick gravy. This recipe doubles or triples well.

2 to 4 tablespoons all-purpose flour

1 cup fat-free, low-sodium chicken broth or fat-free, no-salt-added beef broth, such as on pages 44 and 45; defatted meat drippings; or a combination, divided use

calories 12
protein 1 g
carbohydrates 2 g
fiber 0 g
sugars 0 g
cholesterol 0 mg
total fat 0.0 g
saturated 0.0 g
polyunsaturated 0.0 g
monounsaturated 0.0 g
sodium 3 mg
dietary exchange
Free

In a medium skillet over medium-high heat, cook the flour for 5 to 6 minutes, or until lightly colored, stirring occasionally.

Pour half the broth into a jar with a tight-fitting lid. Add the flour. Cover tightly. Shake until the mixture is smooth. Pour into the skillet.

Add the remaining broth. Bring to a simmer over medium heat. Cook until the desired consistency, whisking constantly.

mushroom gravy
calories 13
protein 1 g
carbohydrates 2 g
fiber 0 g
sugars 0 g
cholesterol 0 mg
total fat 0.0 g
saturated 0.0 g
polyunsaturated 0.0 g
monounsaturated 0.0 g
sodium 4 mg
dietary exchange
Free

Mushroom Gravy
In a small skillet over medium heat, cook ¹/₄ cup sliced fresh button mushrooms (about 1 ounce) in 2 tablespoons of the same liquid as used in the gravy. Stir into the cooked gravy.

Creamy Chicken Gravy

Serves 8; 2 tablespoons per serving

Everyone needs a recipe for basic chicken gravy. This one is about as simple as a recipe can be.

1 cup fat-free, low-sodium chicken broth, such as on page 45, or defatted chicken drippings

1/4 cup fat-free milk
2 tablespoons all-purpose flour
1/2 teaspoon pepper, or to taste

In a medium saucepan, warm the broth over medium heat.

Put the remaining ingredients in a small bowl and whisk until smooth, or put in a jar with a tight-fitting lid and shake until smooth. Gradually whisk into the chicken broth. Cook over medium heat for 3 to 5 minutes, or until thickened, whisking constantly.

calories 11
protein 1 g
carbohydrates 2 g
  fiber 0 g
  sugars 0 g
cholesterol 0 mg
total fat 0.0 g
  saturated 0.0 g
  polyunsaturated 0.0 g
  monounsaturated 0.0 g
sodium 7 mg

dietary exchange
Free

Basic White Sauce

Serves 8; 2 tablespoons per serving

Here's an easy, fat-free version of classic white sauce. For the basic sauce, use 2 tablespoons of flour; for a thick sauce, use 3 to 4 tablespoons.

1 cup fat-free milk
2 to 4 tablespoons all-purpose flour

$^1/_4$ teaspoon salt
Dash of white pepper, or to taste

In a small saucepan, whisk together the ingredients. Bring just to the boiling point over medium-high heat, stirring occasionally. Reduce the heat to medium and cook for 1 to 2 minutes, or until thickened, stirring occasionally.

Cook's Tip

For a different flavor, add a hint of curry, dillweed, or nutmeg.

calories 21
protein 1 g
carbohydrates 4 g
 fiber 0 g
 sugars 2 g
cholesterol 1 mg
total fat 0.0 g
 saturated 0.0 g
 polyunsaturated 0.0 g
 monounsaturated 0.0 g
sodium 89 mg

dietary exchange g
Free

Walnut Cream Sauce

Serves 8; 2 tablespoons per serving

A delicious toasted walnut flavor permeates this rich-tasting sauce. It's perfect with poached chicken or grilled fish.

2 tablespoons chopped walnuts
   Vegetable oil spray
1 medium shallot, finely chopped
1 cup fat-free milk
1½ tablespoons all-purpose flour

1 teaspoon Creole mustard or coarse-grained mustard
½ teaspoon dried marjoram, crumbled
¼ teaspoon salt
2 tablespoons shredded or grated Romano cheese

In a medium saucepan, dry-roast the walnuts over medium heat for 3 to 4 minutes, or until golden brown. (Watch carefully so they don't burn.) Remove the pan from the heat.

Lightly spray the tops of the walnuts with vegetable oil spray. Return the pan to the heat. Stir in the shallot. Cook for 2 minutes, or until the shallot is tender-crisp, stirring occasionally.

Add the remaining ingredients except the cheese, whisking until the flour is dissolved (there may be a few lumps). Increase the heat to medium-high and bring to a simmer, whisking occasionally. Reduce the heat and simmer for 2 to 3 minutes, or until thickened, whisking occasionally.

Remove from the heat.

Add the Romano cheese, whisking constantly until the cheese is melted.

calories 35
protein 2 g
carbohydrates 3 g
  fiber 0 g
  sugars 2 g
cholesterol 2 mg
total fat 1.5 g
  saturated 0.5 g
  polyunsaturated 1.0 g
  monounsaturated 0.5 g
sodium 115 mg

dietary exchange
½ fat

Sour Cream Sauce
with Dill

Serves 8; 2 tablespoons per serving

Enjoy this sauce three ways. Try the dill sauce over grilled or poached salmon, the garlic variation over boiled red potatoes, and the blue cheese version over steamed broccoli.

8 ounces fat-free or light sour cream
1 tablespoon snipped fresh dillweed
1 tablespoon minced green onions
   (green part only)

$^1/_2$ teaspoon pepper
2 to 3 tablespoons fat-free milk
   (optional)

---

with dill or garlic

calories 33
protein 2 g
carbohydrates 6 g
  fiber 0 g
  sugars 2 g
cholesterol 4 mg
total fat 0.0 g
  saturated 0.0 g
  polyunsaturated 0.0 g
  monounsaturated 0.0 g
sodium 23 mg

dietary exchange
$^1/_2$ starch

In a medium bowl, whisk together all the ingredients except the milk. Thin the mixture with the milk, if desired. Cover and refrigerate.

For each variation, stir the listed ingredients into the above before refrigerating.

Sour Cream Sauce with Garlic

Serves 8; 2 tablespoons per serving

1 tablespoon minced onion
1 tablespoon finely snipped fresh parsley
$^1/_4$ teaspoon garlic powder
   Dash of red hot-pepper sauce

---

with blue cheese

calories 35
protein 2 g
carbohydrates 5 g
  fiber 0 g
  sugars 2 g
cholesterol 5 mg
total fat 0.5 g
  saturated 0.5 g
  polyunsaturated 0.0 g
  monounsaturated 0.0 g
sodium 54 mg

dietary exchange
$^1/_2$ starch

Sour Cream Sauce with Blue Cheese

Serves 10; 2 tablespoons per serving

3 tablespoons crumbled blue cheese
1 tablespoon minced green onions (green part only)
$^1/_4$ teaspoon low-sodium Worcestershire sauce

Creamy Dijon-Lime Sauce

Serves 6, 2 tablespoons per serving

Serve this terrifically quick sauce at room temperature over chilled vegetables, such as fresh tomato slices or slightly steamed and chilled asparagus, or heat it to serve over steamed vegetables. Some possibilities are broccoli, cauliflower, lima beans, green beans, or carrots.

1/3 cup fat-free or light plain yogurt
1 tablespoon plus 1 teaspoon Dijon mustard
1 teaspoon fresh lime juice

1/8 teaspoon salt
1 tablespoon olive oil (extra-virgin preferred)

In a small bowl, whisk together all the ingredients except the oil until smooth.

If using over chilled vegetables, stir in the oil. If using over hot cooked vegetables, put the sauce in a small saucepan over medium-low heat and heat through. Don't allow to boil. Remove from the heat. Stir in the oil.

Cook's Tip

You'll get a more pronounced flavor from the olive oil by adding it after you take the sauce off the heat.

calories 32
protein 1 g
carbohydrates 2 g
  fiber 0 g
  sugars 1 g
cholesterol 0 mg
total fat 2.5 g
  saturated 0.5 g
  polyunsaturated 0.0 g
  monounsaturated 1.5 g
sodium 127 mg

dietary exchange
1/2 fat

Mild Mustard
Sauce

Serves 4; 2 tablespoons per serving

Buttermilk gives this sauce a gentle zing that complements just about any vegetable. Serve it chilled over cold or room temperature blanched vegetables or warm over hot cooked vegetables.

1/3 cup fat-free or low-fat buttermilk
2 tablespoons fat-free or light mayonnaise dressing

1 teaspoon prepared mustard

In a medium bowl, whisk together the ingredients until smooth.

Refrigerate the sauce in an airtight container until chilled if using over cold or room-temperature vegetables. Heat the sauce in a small saucepan over low heat for 2 to 3 minutes, or until warm, to spoon over hot vegetables.

calories 17
protein 1 g
carbohydrates 2 g
  fiber 0 g
  sugars 2 g
cholesterol 1 mg
total fat 0.0 g
  saturated 0.0 g
  polyunsaturated 0.0 g
  monounsaturated 0.0 g
sodium 98 mg

dietary exchange
Free

Red Bell Pepper Hollandaise

Serves 10; 2 tablespoons per serving

This sauce is excellent on cauliflower, asparagus, or broccoli. Add some chopped fresh herbs, such as parsley, basil, or lemon thyme, and serve it with seafood or chicken.

1 large red bell pepper
Egg substitute equivalent to 2 eggs, or 2 large eggs
¼ cup acceptable stick margarine, melted
3 tablespoons fresh lemon juice

¼ cup fat-free, low-sodium chicken broth, such as on page 45
1 tablespoon cornstarch
1 teaspoon chili powder
⅛ teaspoon cayenne

Preheat the broiler. Broil the bell pepper on the broiler pan about 4 inches from the heat, turning until the bell pepper is charred all over. Put the bell pepper in a plastic or paper bag. Close the bag. Set aside for 5 to 20 minutes. Rinse the bell pepper with cold water, discarding the skin, core, seeds, and stem. Pat dry with paper towels.

Warm the egg substitute in a microwave on 20 percent power (low) for 1 minute, or put the carton in 1 inch of warm water for 2 to 3 minutes. If using eggs, put in a bowl of warm tap water for 2 to 3 minutes. Discard the water.

Pour the warm egg substitute or eggs into a food processor or blender. With the motor running, add the margarine in a thin stream.

Add the bell pepper and lemon juice. Process on high for 1 minute, or until smooth.

In a small saucepan, whisk together the remaining ingredients.

Add the egg mixture and bring to a boil over medium-high heat, whisking occasionally. When the mixture starts to thicken, whisk constantly. Remove from the heat when thickened. Serve warm or cover and refrigerate to serve cold.

calories 36
protein 2 g
carbohydrates 3 g
 fiber 0 g
 sugars 1 g
cholesterol 0 mg
total fat 2.5 g
 saturated 0.5 g
 polyunsaturated 0.5 g
 monounsaturated 0.5 g
sodium 59 mg

dietary exchange
½ fat

Mock Hollandaise Sauce

Serves 8; 2 tablespoons per serving

By using chicken broth and a small amount of oil instead of lots of butter, you can prepare a low-fat hollandaise sauce that will dress up many dishes in your repertoire.

1 tablespoon cornstarch	2 tablespoons egg substitute or 1 egg yolk, lightly beaten
1 tablespoon acceptable vegetable oil	
3/4 cup fat-free, low-sodium chicken broth, such as on page 45	1 to 2 tablespoons fresh lemon juice

In a small saucepan, whisk together the cornstarch and oil. Cook over low heat for 1 minute, or until smooth, whisking constantly.

Whisk in the broth. Increase the heat to medium-high. Cook for 3 to 4 minutes, or until the mixture thickens, whisking constantly. Remove from the heat.

Stir a small amount of the sauce into the egg yolk. Slowly pour the egg mixture into the remaining sauce. Cook over low heat for 1 minute, whisking constantly. Remove from the heat.

Stir in the lemon juice.

Cook's Tip on Juicing Lemons

Before you cut a lemon, let it reach room temperature if it's been refrigerated. Then roll it on the counter while pressing down hard with your hand. This will cause the lemon to release more of its juice.

calories 23
protein 1 g
carbohydrates 1 g
  fiber 0 g
  sugars 0 g
cholesterol 0 mg
total fat 2.0 g
  saturated 0.0 g
  polyunsaturated 0.5 g
  monounsaturated 1.0 g
sodium 10 mg

dietary exchange
Free

Mock Béarnaise Sauce

Serves 8; 2 tablespoons per serving

Turn poached fish or steamed vegetables into something special with this elegant sauce.

1/4 cup white wine vinegar

1/4 cup dry white wine (regular or nonalcoholic) or dry vermouth

1 tablespoon minced shallot or green onion (green part only)

1 tablespoon minced fresh tarragon or 1 teaspoon dried, crumbled

1/8 teaspoon white pepper

1 tablespoon cornstarch

1 tablespoon acceptable vegetable oil

3/4 cup fat-free, low-sodium chicken broth, such as on page 45

2 tablespoons egg substitute or 1 egg yolk, lightly beaten

In a small saucepan, whisk together the vinegar, wine, shallot, tarragon, and pepper. Bring to a boil over medium-high heat, whisking constantly. Cook for 4 to 5 minutes, or until the liquid is reduced to about 2 table-spoons. Set aside.

In a small saucepan, whisk together the cornstarch and oil. Cook over low heat for 1 minute, or until the mixture is smooth, whisking constantly.

Whisk in the broth. Increase the heat to medium-high. Cook for 3 to 4 minutes, or until the mixture thickens, whisking constantly. Remove from the heat.

Whisk a small amount of the sauce into the egg substitute. Whisk the egg mixture slowly into the remaining sauce. Cook over low heat for 1 minute, whisking constantly. Remove from the heat.

Whisk the vinegar mixture into the sauce.

calories 31
protein 1 g
carbohydrates 2 g
  fiber 0 g
  sugars 0 g
cholesterol 0 mg
total fat 2.0 g
  saturated 0.0 g
  polyunsaturated 0.5 g
  monounsaturated 1.0 g
sodium 11 mg

dietary exchange
1/2 fat

Alfredo Sauce

Serves 4; ½ cup per serving

Versatile Alfredo sauce can go from topping pasta and layering lasagna to being ladled over savory crepes.

1 cup fat-free, low-sodium chicken
  broth, such as on page 45
1 cup fat-free half-and-half
2½ tablespoons all-purpose flour
1 medium garlic clove, minced

¼ teaspoon salt
⅛ teaspoon pepper
¼ cup shredded or grated Parmesan
  cheese

In a medium saucepan, whisk together all the ingredients except the Parmesan. Bring to a simmer over medium-high heat, stirring occasionally. Reduce the heat and simmer for 2 to 3 minutes, or until thickened. Remove from the heat.

Add the Parmesan, stirring constantly until the cheese is melted.

calories 82
protein 7 g
carbohydrates 12 g
  fiber 0 g
  sugars 4 g
cholesterol 4 mg
total fat 1.5 g
  saturated 1.0 g
  polyunsaturated 0.0 g
  monounsaturated 0.5 g
sodium 297 mg

dietary exchange
1 skim milk

Quick Madeira Sauce

Serves 8; 2 tablespoons per serving

Serve this flavorful sauce with pheasant or other game.

1¼ cups fat-free, low-sodium chicken
broth, such as on page 45
⅓ cup Madeira or port

2 teaspoons cornstarch
1 tablespoon Madeira or port

In a small saucepan, stir together the broth and ⅓ cup Madeira. Bring to a boil over high heat. Boil for 3 to 4 minutes to reduce rapidly to 1 cup (no stirring needed).

Put the cornstarch in a cup or small bowl. Add 1 table-spoon Madeira, whisking to dissolve. Whisk the mixture into the sauce. Cook over medium heat for 1 to 2 minutes, or until thickened, whisking constantly.

Cook's Tip on Madeira and Port

Either Madeira or port will make this a rich-tasting sauce. Madeira varies from very dry to very sweet. Port is sweet. You may want to experiment with different types to see which you like best.

calories 22
protein 0 g
carbohydrates 2 g
 fiber 0 g
 sugars 1 g
cholesterol 0 mg
total fat 0.0 g
 saturated 0.0 g
 polyunsaturated 0.0 g
 monounsaturated 0.0 g
sodium 5 mg

dietary exchange
Free

Speedy Marinara Sauce

Serves 4; ½ cup per serving

A combination of fresh and canned tomatoes gives this zesty marinara sauce a slow-cooked flavor.

2 medium tomatoes
1 teaspoon olive oil
2 medium shallots, finely chopped
2 medium garlic cloves, minced
   14.5-ounce can no-salt-added diced tomatoes, undrained
2 tablespoons no-salt-added tomato paste

1 tablespoon capers, rinsed and drained
1 teaspoon dried oregano, crumbled
½ teaspoon dried basil, crumbled
¼ to ½ teaspoon crushed red pepper flakes
¼ teaspoon salt

Fill a medium saucepan to three quarters full of water. Bring to a boil over high heat.

Cut a small *x* in the bottom of each fresh tomato. Carefully put the tomatoes into the water one at a time. Reduce the heat to medium-high. Cook for 1 minute, or until the tomato skins start to loosen. Using a slotted spoon, put the tomatoes on a cutting board. Let cool for 5 minutes.

Meanwhile, heat a medium saucepan over medium heat. Pour the oil into the pan and swirl to coat the bottom. Cook the shallots and garlic for 2 to 3 minutes, or until tender, stirring occasionally.

Stir in the remaining ingredients. Increase the heat to medium-high and bring to a simmer, stirring occasionally.

Meanwhile, peel and dice the fresh tomatoes. Stir into the sauce. Reduce the heat and simmer, uncovered, for 15 to 20 minutes, or until the flavors have blended, stirring occasionally.

calories 60
protein 2 g
carbohydrates 12 g
  fiber 3 g
  sugars 6 g
cholesterol 0 mg
total fat 1.5 g
  saturated 0.0 g
  polyunsaturated 0.0 g
  monounsaturated 1.0 g
sodium 259 mg

dietary exchange
2½ vegetable
½ fat

Tomato Sauce

Serves 16; ¼ cup per serving

Serve this easy sauce over stuffed bell peppers, meat loaf, or stuffed cabbage.

28-ounce can no-salt-added Italian
plum tomatoes, undrained
1 large onion, diced
3 tablespoons no-salt-added tomato
paste

2 medium garlic cloves, minced
½ teaspoon pepper, or to taste
½ teaspoon dried oregano, crumbled
½ teaspoon dried basil, crumbled

In a heavy saucepan, stir together the ingredients. Bring to a boil over medium-high heat. Reduce the heat and simmer, covered, for 20 minutes.

calories 17
protein 1 g
carbohydrates 4 g
 fiber 1 g
 sugars 2 g
cholesterol 0 mg
total fat 0.0 g
 saturated 0.0 g
 polyunsaturated 0.0 g
 monounsaturated 0.0 g
sodium 41 mg

dietary exchange
Free

Creole Sauce
Add 1 diced medium green bell pepper, 2 ounces sliced fresh button mushrooms, and 1 medium rib of celery, chopped. Cook as directed.

creole sauce

calories 20
protein 1 g
carbohydrates 4 g
 fiber 1 g
 sugars 2 g
cholesterol 0 mg
total fat 0.0 g
 saturated 0.0 g
 polyunsaturated 0.0 g
 monounsaturated 0.0 g
sodium 44 mg

dietary exchange
Free

Salsa Cruda

Serves 6; 2 tablespoons per serving

To serve this zippy salsa as a dip for your next party, simply double or triple the quantities listed. It also works as a terrific topping for many Mexican dishes, such as Beef Tostadas (page 322).

1 fresh jalapeño
1 large tomato, seeded and diced
2 tablespoons finely chopped onion

1 teaspoon finely snipped fresh cilantro, or to taste
1 to 2 teaspoons fresh lime juice
1/8 teaspoon salt

Wearing gloves, discard the seeds and ribs of the jalapeño. Chop the pepper and measure 1 teaspoon; put in a medium bowl. Save the remaining pepper for another use.

Stir in the remaining ingredients. Cover and refrigerate.

Cook's Tip

For a different texture, combine the ingredients in a food processor or blender and process until fairly smooth.

calories 9
protein 0 g
carbohydrates 2 g
  fiber 0 g
  sugars 1 g
cholesterol 0 mg
total fat 0.0 g
  saturated 0.0 g
  polyunsaturated 0.0 g
  monounsaturated 0.0 g
sodium 51 mg

dietary exchange
Free

Tomatillo-Cilantro Salsa
with Lime

Serves 8; 2 tablespoons per serving

Small green tomatoes known as tomatillos (tohm-ah-TEE-ohs) join fresh cilantro, lime juice, and a bit of jalapeño for this winning salsa. Serve it as a dip for baked tortillas or with main dishes from the grill.

1 fresh jalapeño
8 ounces tomatillos, papery skin discarded (5 to 6 medium)
1/2 cup snipped fresh cilantro
2 tablespoons chopped green onions (green and white parts)

1 tablespoon fresh lime juice
1/8 teaspoon salt
1 tablespoon olive oil (extra-virgin preferred)

Wearing gloves, discard the seeds and ribs of the jalapeño. Quarter the jalapeño.

In a food processor or blender, process the jalapeño and the remaining ingredients except the oil until smooth. Pour into a small bowl.

Stir in the oil. Serve or, for a stronger flavor, cover and refrigerate for up to two days.

Variation

Replace the tomatillos with 2 small to medium finely chopped tomatoes (about 8 ounces) and replace the lime juice with 2 tablespoons cider vinegar. Don't use a food processor or blender with this variation. The color will be less brilliant if you do. Just chop the jalapeño and stir all the ingredients together.

Cook's Tip on Tomatillos

Choose firm tomatillos with close-fitting papery skin. Remove the brown skins and thoroughly rinse the tomatillos before cooking.

calories 26
protein 0 g
carbohydrates 2 g
 fiber 1 g
 sugars 0 g
cholesterol 0 mg
total fat 2.0 g
 saturated 0.5 g
 polyunsaturated 0.5 g
 monounsaturated 1.5 g
sodium 37 mg

dietary exchange
1/2 fat

with tomatoes

calories 23
protein 0 g
carbohydrates 2 g
 fiber 0 g
 sugars 1 g
cholesterol 0 mg
total fat 2.0 g
 saturated 0.0 g
 polyunsaturated 0.0 g
 monounsaturated 1.5 g
sodium 40 mg

dietary exchange
1/2 fat

Chocolate Sauce

Serves 8; 2 tablespoons per serving

Need a chocolate fix? Serve this sauce warm or cold over almost any flavor of fat-free or low-fat frozen yogurt.

2 tablespoons acceptable stick margarine

2 tablespoons unsweetened cocoa powder

$\frac{1}{2}$ cup sugar

2 tablespoons white corn syrup

$\frac{1}{4}$ cup fat-free evaporated milk

1 teaspoon vanilla extract

In a small saucepan, melt the margarine over medium-high heat. Swirl to coat the bottom of the pan.

Whisk in the cocoa powder, sugar, and corn syrup.

Pour in the milk and bring to a boil, whisking constantly until smooth. Remove from the heat.

Whisk in the vanilla.

Cook's Tip on Cocoa Powder

Cocoa powder has much less fat than chocolate, which contains mostly saturated fat. To substitute cocoa for chocolate in baking, use 3 tablespoons of cocoa powder plus 1 tablespoon of acceptable vegetable oil for 1 ounce of unsweetened baking chocolate. You'll cut the total fat by about 50 percent.

calories 89
protein 1 g
carbohydrates 18 g
  fiber 0 g
  sugars 16 g
cholesterol 0 mg
total fat 1.5 g
  saturated 0.5 g
  polyunsaturated 0.5 g
  monounsaturated 0.5 g
sodium 34 mg

dietary exchange
1 other carbohydrate
$\frac{1}{2}$ fat

Raspberry Port Sauce

Serves 4; 2 tablespoons sauce per serving

For a simple yet sophisticated dessert, serve this sauce over poached fruit, angel food cake, fat-free pound cake, or fat-free or low-fat vanilla frozen yogurt or ice cream.

$3/4$ cup frozen unsweetened raspberries, blueberries, or combination

2 tablespoons port

$1^{1}/_{2}$ tablespoons sugar

$1/2$ tablespoon cornstarch

$1/4$ teaspoon vanilla extract

In a small saucepan, stir together all the ingredients except the vanilla until the cornstarch is dissolved completely. Bring to a boil over medium-high heat. Cook for 30 to 45 seconds, or until slightly thickened. Remove from the heat.

Stir in the vanilla. Let stand for 15 minutes to absorb flavors. Serve at room temperature or refrigerate in an airtight container and serve cold.

calories 49
protein 0 g
carbohydrates 10 g
  fiber 1 g
  sugars 7 g
cholesterol 0 mg
total fat 0.0 g
  saturated 0.0 g
  polyunsaturated 0.0 g
  monounsaturated 0.0 g
sodium 1 mg

dietary exchange
$1/2$ fruit

Easy Jubilee Sauce

Serves 13; 2 tablespoons per serving

This sauce is so easy to put together. Keep the ingredients and some fat-free or low-fat ice cream on hand for unexpected company.

16-ounce jar all-fruit black cherry spread

¹/₄ cup port
¹/₂ teaspoon almond extract

In a small bowl, stir together the ingredients. Serve immediately or cover and refrigerate to serve cold.

Cook's Tip

This sauce is named for the classic cherries jubilee, which is flambéed and served over ice cream. This one is quicker, and there's no fire to put out.

calories 81
protein 0 g
carbohydrates 19 g
  fiber 0 g
  sugars 17 g
cholesterol 0 mg
total fat 0.0 g
  saturated 0.0 g
  polyunsaturated 0.0 g
  monounsaturated 0.0 g
sodium 0 mg

dietary exchange
1¹/₂ fruit

Orange Sauce

Serves 8; 2 tablespoons per serving

This sauce is scrumptious over Easy Apple Cake (page 567), Delicious Rice Pudding (page 611), angel food cake, or gingerbread.

2 cups fresh orange juice
1 tablespoon cornstarch
1 tablespoon water
1 tablespoon sugar

1 tablespoon fresh lemon juice
2 teaspoons acceptable stick margarine
$\frac{1}{2}$ teaspoon grated orange zest

In a small saucepan, cook the orange juice over medium heat until reduced by half.

Put the cornstarch in a cup or small bowl. Add the water, whisking to dissolve.

Whisk in a little orange juice. Pour the cornstarch mixture into the remaining juice.

Whisk in the sugar. Cook for 1 to 2 minutes, or until thick. Remove from the heat.

Whisk in the remaining ingredients.

calories 43
protein 0 g
carbohydrates 9 g
  fiber 0 g
  sugars 8 g
cholesterol 0 mg
total fat 0.5 g
  saturated 0.0 g
  polyunsaturated 0.0 g
  monounsaturated 0.0 g
sodium 7 mg

dietary exchange
$\frac{1}{2}$ fruit

breads and
breakfast dishes

Basic Bread

Serves 32; 1 slice per serving

Sharpen your culinary skills with this step-by-step bread recipe. You'll even get a bit of exercise from lively kneading.

1/4 cup lukewarm water
   (105°F to 115°F)
2 1/4-ounce packages active dry yeast
1 3/4 cups fat-free milk
2 1/2 tablespoons sugar
2 tablespoons acceptable vegetable
   oil

4 cups all-purpose flour
1 teaspoon salt
2 cups all-purpose flour (plus more
   as needed)
Vegetable oil spray

Pour the water into a large mixing bowl. Add the yeast. Stir to dissolve. Let stand for 5 minutes.

Stir the milk, sugar, and oil into the yeast mixture.

Gradually stir 4 cups flour and salt into the yeast mixture. Beat with a mixer or sturdy spoon for about 30 seconds, or until smooth.

Gradually add some of the remaining flour, beating after each addition, until the dough starts to pull away from the side of the bowl. Add more flour if necessary to make the dough stiff enough to handle.

Lightly flour a flat surface. Turn out the dough. Knead for 6 to 8 minutes, gradually adding enough of the remaining flour to make the dough smooth and elastic. (The dough shouldn't be dry or stick to the surface. You may not need all the flour, or you may need up to 1/2 cup more if the dough is too sticky.)

Lightly spray a large bowl with vegetable oil spray. Turn the dough to coat all the sides. Cover the bowl with a damp dish towel. Let the dough rise in a warm, draft-free place (about 85°F) for about 1 hour, or until doubled in bulk.

Punch down the dough. Divide in half. Shape into loaves. Lightly spray two 9 × 5 × 3-inch loaf pans with vegetable oil spray. Put the dough into the loaf pans. Cover each with a damp dish towel. Let the dough rise in a warm,

calories 103
protein 3 g
carbohydrates 20 g
  fiber 1 g
  sugars 2 g
cholesterol 0 mg
total fat 1.0 g
  saturated 0.0 g
  polyunsaturated 0.5 g
  monounsaturated 0.5 g
sodium 80 mg

dietary exchange
1 1/2 starch

draft-free place (about 85°F) for about 30 minutes, or until doubled in bulk.

Preheat the oven to 425°F.

Bake the loaves for 15 minutes. Reduce the heat to 375°F. Bake for 30 minutes, or until the bread registers 190°F on an instant-read thermometer or sounds hollow when rapped with knuckles. Turn the bread onto cooling racks. Let cool for 15 to 20 minutes before cutting.

Herb Bread
Just before kneading, add to the dough 2 teaspoons caraway seeds; $1/2$ teaspoon ground nutmeg; $1/2$ teaspoon dried rosemary, crushed; and $1/4$ teaspoon dried thyme, crumbled. Proceed as directed.

Cook's Tip on Breadmaking

The more you practice, the easier it will be to develop a feel for when the dough has the proper consistency. If you knead in too much flour or overknead the dough, it will feel dry and stiff, and the resulting loaf can be heavy. If you use too little flour or don't knead the dough enough, your loaf won't retain its shape during baking.

Resist the urge to knead the dough completely flat against your counter or board. This can cause your dough to become sticky.

For basic kneading, fold the dough toward you. Using the heels of one or both hands, push the dough forward and slightly down in almost a rocking motion. Rotate the dough a quarter-turn and repeat. Follow this procedure until the dough is smooth and elastic. Add small amounts of flour when the dough starts to stick to the counter. Make note of the time you start, and knead for the amount of time called for in your recipe.

Whole-Wheat
French Bread

1 slice per serving

You'll love the versatility of this nutty flavored bread. Make a standard loaf in your bread machine, or use the dough cycle and shape the dough into baguettes to bake in your oven.

	1-POUND MACHINE (12 servings)	**1$^1/_2$-POUND MACHINE** (18 servings)	**2-POUND MACHINE** (24 servings)
Whole-wheat flour	1$^1/_4$ cups	2 cups	2$^1/_2$ cups
Bread flour	1 cup	1$^1/_2$ cups	2 cups
Fat-free dry milk	1 tablespoon	1$^1/_2$ tablespoons	2 tablespoons
Salt	$^1/_2$ teaspoon	$^3/_4$ teaspoon	1 teaspoon
Acceptable vegetable oil	1 tablespoon	1$^1/_2$ tablespoons	2 tablespoons
Honey	1 tablespoon	1$^1/_2$ tablespoons	2 tablespoons
Water	1 cup less 1 table- spoon	1$^1/_3$ cups	1$^7/_8$ cups
Active dry yeast	1 teaspoon	1$^1/_2$ teaspoons	2 teaspoons

Put the ingredients in the bread machine container in the order given or using the manufacturer's directions. When adding the yeast, use a small spoon to make a well in the dry ingredients. Put the yeast in the well.

Select the basic/white bread cycle. Proceed as directed. When the bread is done, let cool on a cooling rack.

1-pound loaf	1$^1/_2$-pound loaf	2-pound loaf
calories 102	calories 104	calories 102
protein 3 g	protein 4 g	protein 3 g
carbohydrates 19 g	carbohydrates 20 g	carbohydrates 19 g
fiber 2 g	fiber 2 g	fiber 2 g
sugars 2 g	sugars 2 g	sugars 2 g
cholesterol 0 mg	cholesterol 0 mg	cholesterol 0 mg
total fat 1.5 g	total fat 1.5 g	total fat 1.5 g
saturated 0.0 g	saturated 0.0 g	saturated 0.0 g
polyunsaturated 0.5 g	polyunsaturated 0.5 g	polyunsaturated 0.5 g
monounsaturated 0.5 g	monounsaturated 0.5 g	monounsaturated 0.5 g
sodium 101 mg	sodium 101 mg	sodium 101 mg
dietary exchange	dietary exchange	dietary exchange
1$^1/_2$ starch	1$^1/_2$ starch	1$^1/_2$ starch

Herb Cheese Bread

1 slice per serving

All the herb flavor bakes into this bread, making every morsel delectable.

	1-POUND MACHINE (12 servings)	1½-POUND MACHINE (18 servings)	2-POUND MACHINE (24 servings)
Water	½ cup	¾ cup	1 cup
Fat-free or light plain yogurt	½ cup	¾ cup	1 cup
Bread flour	2¼ cups	3¼ cups plus 2 tablespoons	4½ cups
Parmesan cheese	2 tablespoons	2½ tablespoons	3 tablespoons
Green onions	2 tablespoons	3 tablespoons	4 tablespoons
Olive oil	1 tablespoon	1½ tablespoons	2 tablespoons
Sugar	1 tablespoon	1½ tablespoons	2 tablespoons
Rosemary	1½ teaspoons fresh	2¼ teaspoons fresh	1 tablespoon fresh
Dillweed	1½ teaspoons fresh	2¼ teaspoons fresh	1 tablespoon fresh
Basil	1½ teaspoons fresh	2¼ teaspoons fresh	1 tablespoon fresh
Fat-free dry milk	1 tablespoon	1½ tablespoons	2 tablespoons
Salt	1 teaspoon	1½ teaspoons	2 teaspoons
Pepper	¼ teaspoon	½ teaspoon	¾ teaspoon
Active dry yeast	1½ teaspoons	2 teaspoons	1 tablespoon

Follow the manufacturer's instructions for the regular baking cycle.

1-pound loaf	1½-pound loaf	2-pound loaf
calories 119	calories 119	calories 118
protein 4 g	protein 4 g	protein 4 g
carbohydrates 21 g	carbohydrates 21 g	carbohydrates 21 g
fiber 1 g	fiber 1 g	fiber 1 g
sugars 3 g	sugars 3 g	sugars 2 g
cholesterol 1 mg	cholesterol 1 mg	cholesterol 1 mg
total fat 2.0 g	total fat 2.0 g	total fat 2.0 g
saturated 0.5 g	saturated 0.5 g	saturated 0.5 g
polyunsaturated 0.5 g	polyunsaturated 0.5 g	polyunsaturated 0.5 g
monounsaturated 1.0 g	monounsaturated 1.0 g	monounsaturated 1.0 g
sodium 219 mg	sodium 217 mg	sodium 216 mg
dietary exchange	dietary exchange	dietary exchange
1½ starch	1½ starch	1½ starch

Focaccia

Serves 16; 1 wedge per serving

Delicious on its own, useful for getting that last bite of spaghetti sauce, and even a double for pizza crust, this popular flatbread from Italy serves many purposes.

1½ cups bread flour or all-purpose flour

¼ cup semolina flour or all-purpose flour

¼ cup soy flour or all-purpose flour

1 package fast-rising yeast

1 tablespoon olive oil

2 teaspoons salt-free Italian seasoning, crumbled

1 teaspoon garlic powder

¼ teaspoon salt

1¼ cups warm water (120°F to 130°F)

1 cup bread flour or all-purpose flour

Flour for kneading and rolling dough

Vegetable oil spray (olive oil spray preferred)

1 tablespoon pine nuts (optional)

1 teaspoon dried rosemary, crushed

In a large bowl, stir together 1½ cups bread flour, semolina flour, soy flour, yeast, olive oil, Italian seasoning, garlic powder, and salt.

Pour the water into the flour mixture. Stir with a sturdy spoon for 30 seconds.

Gradually add some of the remaining 1 cup bread flour, beating after each addition, until the dough starts to pull away from the side of the bowl. Add more flour if necessary to make the dough stiff enough to handle.

Lightly flour a flat surface. Turn out the dough. Knead for 6 to 8 minutes, gradually adding enough of the remaining flour to make the dough smooth and elastic. (The dough shouldn't be dry or stick to the surface. You may not need all the flour, or you may need up to ½ cup more if the dough is too sticky. See Cook's Tip on Breadmaking, page 511.) Cover the dough with a dish towel. Let rest for 10 minutes.

Lightly spray a 14-inch pizza pan with vegetable oil spray. Press the dough to the edges with your fingers. Lightly spray with vegetable oil spray. Press in the pine nuts. Sprinkle with the rosemary. Cover with a dish towel. Let rise for 30 minutes.

calories 101
protein 4 g
carbohydrates 18 g
  fiber 1 g
  sugars 1 g
cholesterol 0 mg
total fat 1.5 g
  saturated 0.0 g
  polyunsaturated 0.0 g
  monounsaturated 0.5 g
sodium 38 mg

dietary exchange
1 starch

Preheat the oven to 375°F.

Bake for 20 to 25 minutes, or until golden brown. Let cool on a cooling rack for at least 10 minutes before cutting.

Bread Machine Instructions

Follow the manufacturer's instructions for the regular baking cycle. For a flat loaf, use the bread machine only to mix the dough, following the manufacturer's directions for the dough cycle. Remove the dough when it is ready. Shape it. Sprinkle with the pine nuts and rosemary. Bake as directed above. For a regular loaf, add the pine nuts and rosemary with the other ingredients.

	1-POUND MACHINE (12 servings)	1½-POUND MACHINE (18 servings)	2-POUND MACHINE (24 servings)
Water	³/₄ cup	1¹/₄ cups	1¹/₂ cups
Bread flour or all-purpose flour	1²/₃ cups	2¹/₂ cups	3¹/₃ cups
Semolina flour or all-purpose flour	3 tablespoons	¹/₄ cup	¹/₃ cup
Soy flour or all-purpose flour	3 tablespoons	¹/₄ cup	¹/₃ cup
Active dry yeast	2 teaspoons	2¹/₂ teaspoons	1 tablespoon
Olive oil	2¹/₄ teaspoons	1 tablespoon	1¹/₂ tablespoons
Salt-free Italian seasoning, crumbled	1¹/₂ teaspoons	2 teaspoons	1 tablespoon
Garlic powder	³/₄ teaspoon	1 teaspoon	1¹/₂ teaspoons
Salt	¹/₈ teaspoon	¹/₄ teaspoon	¹/₂ teaspoon

Focaccia Sandwich Loaves

Lightly spray two baking sheets with vegetable oil spray. Let the dough rest for 10 minutes. Divide into 8 pieces. Shape into disks. Put on the baking sheets. Cover each with a dish towel. Let rise for 30 minutes. Bake as directed for 15 to 20 minutes, or until golden brown. Let cool. Slice in half horizontally. Serves 16.

> **1-pound bread machine**
>
> calories 93
> protein 4 g
> carbohydrates 17 g
> fiber 1 g
> sugars 1 g
> cholesterol 0 mg
> total fat 1.0 g
> saturated 0.0 g
> polyunsaturated 0.0 g
> monounsaturated 0.5 g
> sodium 26 mg
>
> dietary exchange
> 1 starch

Jalapeño Cheese Bread

Serves 20; 1 slice per serving

Smoked paprika lends an interesting touch to this easy-to-prepare quick bread.

Vegetable oil spray
3 cups all-purpose flour (plus more as needed)
1 teaspoon baking soda
1/2 teaspoon baking powder
1 cup shredded fat-free or low-fat Cheddar cheese

2 tablespoons pickled jalapeños, rinsed, drained, and chopped
1 1/2 cups beer (light, regular, or nonalcoholic) or fat-free or low-fat buttermilk
1 tablespoon olive oil
1/2 teaspoon smoked or regular paprika (optional)

Preheat the oven to 350°F. Lightly spray a large baking sheet with vegetable oil spray.

In a large bowl, whisk together the flour, baking soda, and baking powder.

Stir in the Cheddar and jalapeños. Make a well in the center.

Pour the beer and oil into the well. Stir until the flour absorbs the liquids (the mixture will be slightly sticky). Spoon the dough onto the center of the baking sheet.

With lightly floured hands, shape the dough into a 9 × 6-inch oval loaf. Sprinkle with the paprika.

Bake for 40 to 45 minutes, or until the loaf is golden brown and sounds hollow when tapped with knuckles. Transfer to a cooling rack. Let cool for at least 15 minutes before cutting into 20 slices.

Cook's Tip on Smoked Paprika

Smoked paprika, which comes from Spain, is like chipotle peppers without the heat. You can find it in gourmet grocery stores or through online mail-order sources. Use it to enhance refried beans, dips, rice dishes, and marinades.

calories 89
protein 4 g
carbohydrates 15 g
  fiber 1 g
  sugars 0 g
cholesterol 1 mg
total fat 1.0 g
  saturated 0.0 g
  polyunsaturated 0.0 g
  monounsaturated 0.5 g
sodium 136 mg

dietary exchange
1 starch

Nutmeg Bread

Serves 16; 1 slice per serving

This bread freezes well and makes a great gift, whether to welcome a new neighbor, take to a holiday party, or just to brighten someone's day.

Vegetable oil spray
3/4 cup sugar
1/4 cup acceptable stick margarine
Egg substitute equivalent to 1 egg, or 1 large egg, well beaten
1/4 cup unsweetened applesauce

2 cups sifted all-purpose flour
1 teaspoon ground nutmeg
1/2 teaspoon baking powder
1/2 teaspoon baking soda
1 cup fat-free or low-fat buttermilk

Preheat the oven to 350°F. Lightly spray a 9 × 5 × 3-inch loaf pan with vegetable oil spray.

In a large mixing bowl, cream the sugar and margarine.

Add the egg substitute and applesauce. Beat well.

Put the remaining ingredients except the buttermilk in a medium bowl. Sift together twice.

Alternately add the flour mixture and buttermilk to the sugar mixture, beginning and ending with the flour and stirring after each addition. Pour the batter into the loaf pan.

Bake for 45 to 60 minutes, or until a cake tester or toothpick inserted in the center comes out clean. Let cool in the pan for 10 minutes, then turn the bread onto a cooling rack.

calories 129
protein 3 g
carbohydrates 23 g
  fiber 1 g
  sugars 11 g
cholesterol 1 mg
total fat 3.0 g
  saturated 0.5 g
  polyunsaturated 0.5 g
  monounsaturated 1.5 g
sodium 112 mg

dietary exchange
1 1/2 starch
1/2 fat

Southern-Style Corn Bread

Serves 8

Buttermilk and all-purpose seasoning make this corn bread recipe stand out.

1 tablespoon acceptable vegetable oil
1 cup fat-free or low-fat buttermilk
  Egg substitute equivalent to 1 egg,
  or 1 large egg
1¼ cups yellow or white cornmeal
1 cup frozen or canned no-salt-
  added whole-kernel corn, thawed if
  frozen, drained

1 teaspoon baking powder
1 teaspoon sugar (optional)
¼ teaspoon baking soda
¼ teaspoon salt
¼ teaspoon salt-free all-purpose
  seasoning

calories 126
protein 4 g
carbohydrates 24 g
  fiber 2 g
  sugars 2 g
cholesterol 1 mg
total fat 2.5 g
  saturated 0.5 g
  polyunsaturated 1.0 g
  monounsaturated 1.0 g
sodium 222 mg

dietary exchange
1½ starch

Mexican-Style

calories 124
protein 5 g
carbohydrates 22 g
  fiber 2 g
  sugars 3 g
cholesterol 2 mg
total fat 2.5 g
  saturated 0.5 g
  polyunsaturated 0.5 g
  monounsaturated 1.5 g
sodium 248 mg

dietary exchange
1½ starch

Set the oven at 400°F. Pour the oil into a 10-inch skillet with a heatproof handle. Heat in the preheating oven. Don't forget it! (When the oven temperature reaches 400°F, remove the skillet.)

Meanwhile, in a small bowl, whisk together the buttermilk and egg substitute.

In a large bowl, stir together the remaining ingredients. Make a well in the center.

Pour the buttermilk mixture into the well. Whisk gently.

Whisk in the hot oil from the skillet. Pour the mixture into the hot skillet. Spread to cover the bottom.

Bake for 20 minutes, or until the top is golden brown and the edges pull away from the pan.

Mexican-Style Corn Bread
Just before adding the hot oil, add ½ cup grated onion; ⅓ cup fresh or frozen whole-kernel corn, thawed; ¼ cup grated fat-free or low-fat sharp Cheddar cheese; and ½ to 1 finely chopped fresh jalapeño, seeds and ribs discarded (see Cook's Tip on Handling Hot Chile Peppers, page 213).

Peppercorn-Dill Flatbread

Serves 15; 4 pieces per serving

Enjoy flatbread as a snack by itself or with a heart-healthy dip or spread, such as Roasted-Pepper Hummus (page 14).

1½ cups all-purpose flour
1 cup whole-wheat flour
½ cup soy flour or all-purpose flour
1 tablespoon olive oil
2 teaspoons celery seeds
2 teaspoons dried dillweed, crumbled
2 teaspoons baking powder

1 teaspoon coarsely ground pepper
1 teaspoon sugar
½ teaspoon baking soda
¼ teaspoon salt
1¼ cups fat-free or low-fat buttermilk
Flour for rolling out dough
Vegetable oil spray

In a large mixing bowl, stir together the flours, oil, celery seeds, dillweed, baking powder, pepper, sugar, baking soda, and salt. Make a well in the center.

Pour the buttermilk into the well. Stir until the mixture forms a ball.

Lightly flour a flat surface. Turn the dough out. Knead for 2 minutes. Set the floured surface aside. Return the dough to the mixing bowl. Cover the dough with a dry dish towel. Let the dough rest for 10 to 15 minutes.

Preheat the oven to 400°F. Lightly spray two large baking sheets with vegetable oil spray.

Lightly flour the flat surface again if more flour is needed. Roll out the dough to ⅛-inch thickness. Using a pizza cutter or sharp knife, cut the dough into strips about 1½ inches wide by 4 inches long (you should get about 60). Place the strips on baking sheets. Prick each strip with a fork.

Bake for 15 minutes, or until crispy. Put the baking sheets on cooling racks. Let cool for 15 to 20 minutes. Store the flatbread in an airtight container for up to seven days.

calories 103
protein 5 g
carbohydrates 18 g
 fiber 2 g
 sugars 2 g
cholesterol 1 mg
total fat 1.5 g
 saturated 0.5 g
 polyunsaturated 0.0 g
 monounsaturated 1.0 g
sodium 169 mg

dietary exchange
1 starch

Zucchini Bread
with Pistachios

Serves 32; 1 slice per serving

Some surprise ingredients—shredded Fuji apple, extra-light olive oil, and pistachios—add a fruity nuance, color, and crunch to this zucchini bread.

Vegetable oil spray
2 cups all-purpose flour
1 cup whole-wheat flour
1 cup sugar
1/2 cup firmly packed light brown sugar
1/4 cup chopped unsalted pistachio nuts
1 teaspoon ground cinnamon
1 teaspoon baking powder
1 teaspoon baking soda

1/4 teaspoon salt
2 cups shredded zucchini (about 12 ounces)
1 medium Fuji or Granny Smith apple, peeled and shredded (about 1 cup)
Egg substitute equivalent to 3 eggs, or 3 large eggs
1/2 cup unsweetened apple juice
2 tablespoons extra-light olive oil or other acceptable vegetable oil

Preheat the oven to 375°F. Lightly spray two 8¹/₂ × 4¹/₂ × 2¹/₂-inch loaf pans with vegetable oil spray.

In a medium bowl, stir together both flours, both sugars, pistachios, cinnamon, baking powder, baking soda, and salt until evenly distributed.

Add the remaining ingredients. Stir until the mixture is just moistened and evenly distributed. Don't overmix. Pour the batter into the loaf pans.

Bake for 55 to 60 minutes, or until a cake tester or toothpick inserted in the center comes out clean. Remove the bread from the pans. Let cool on a cooling rack for 20 minutes before cutting into slices.

calories 100
protein 2 g
carbohydrates 20 g
 fiber 1 g
 sugars 11 g
cholesterol 0 mg
total fat 1.5 g
 saturated 0.0 g
 polyunsaturated 0.5 g
 monounsaturated 1.0 g
sodium 87 mg

dietary exchange
1¹/₂ starch

Cook's Tip

You can bake this bread in two 8-inch square baking pans (lightly sprayed with vegetable oil spray) for 35 to 40 minutes, or until a cake tester or toothpick inserted in the center comes out clean. Cool as directed in the recipe above.

Savory Walnut Bread

Serves 16; 1 slice per serving

Here's a simple way to celebrate the robust flavor of walnuts.

Vegetable oil spray
2 cups all-purpose flour
2 teaspoons baking powder
1/2 cup firmly packed light brown sugar
1/2 teaspoon salt
1/4 teaspoon baking soda

1 cup fat-free milk
Egg substitute equivalent to 1 egg, or 1 large egg, beaten until slightly thickened and light yellow
1/2 cup finely chopped walnuts, dry-roasted

Preheat the oven to 350°F. Lightly spray an 8 1/2 × 4 1/2 × 2 1/2-inch loaf pan with vegetable oil spray. Set aside.

In a large bowl, sift together the flour, baking powder, brown sugar, salt, and baking soda.

In another large bowl, whisk together the milk and egg substitute.

Add the flour mixture and walnuts to the milk mixture, stirring until just moistened. Pour into the loaf pan.

Bake for 40 minutes, or until a cake tester or toothpick inserted in the center comes out clean. Loosen the loaf from the sides of the pan with a metal spatula. Remove the bread from the pan. Let cool right side up on the cooling rack.

Cook's Tip on Baking Powder and Baking Soda

Baking powder usually is mixed in with other dry ingredients. It reacts and leavens when heated or when liquid is added. Baking soda is also a leavener. If the two are combined, the baking powder helps leaven in the mixing and baking stage, and the baking soda helps neutralize acidic ingredients, such as fruit juices, molasses, and cranberries, so they don't interfere with the baking powder.

calories 115
protein 3 g
carbohydrates 20 g
  fiber 1 g
  sugars 8 g
cholesterol 0 mg
total fat 2.5 g
  saturated 0.5 g
  polyunsaturated 2.0 g
  monounsaturated 0.5 g
sodium 172 mg

dietary exchange
1 1/2 starch
1/2 fat

Velvet Pumpkin Bread

Serves 16; 1 slice per serving

The name says it all—this bread has a wonderful texture. And just wait till you smell it baking!

Vegetable oil spray
1 cup canned pumpkin
1/3 cup fat-free milk
Egg substitute equivalent to 2 eggs, or 2 large eggs, slightly beaten
2 tablespoons acceptable stick margarine
1 tablespoon acceptable vegetable oil
2 cups all-purpose flour

2 teaspoons baking powder
1 teaspoon ground cinnamon
1/2 teaspoon ground ginger
1/4 teaspoon ground nutmeg
1/4 teaspoon salt
1/2 cup chopped pecans, dry-roasted
1/2 cup sugar
1/2 cup firmly packed light brown sugar

Preheat the oven to 350°F. Lightly spray a 9 × 5 × 3-inch loaf pan with vegetable oil spray. Set aside.

In a medium bowl, whisk together the pumpkin, milk, egg substitute, margarine, and oil.

In a large bowl, sift together the flour, baking powder, cinnamon, ginger, nutmeg, and salt.

Stir the remaining ingredients into the flour mixture. Make a well in the center of the flour mixture.

Pour the pumpkin mixture all at once into the well. Stir until just moistened. Don't overmix. Pour the batter into the loaf pan.

Bake for 1 hour, or until a cake tester or toothpick inserted in the center comes out clean. Turn out onto a cooling rack.

calories 158
protein 3 g
carbohydrates 27 g
  fiber 1 g
  sugars 14 g
cholesterol 0 mg
total fat 4.5 g
  saturated 0.5 g
  polyunsaturated 1.5 g
  monounsaturated 2.0 g
sodium 129 mg

dietary exchange
2 starch
1/2 fat

Bananas Foster Bread

Serves 16; 1 slice per serving

You'll love how this bread captures the flavor of a classic New Orleans dessert, bananas Foster.

Vegetable oil spray
1½ cups all-purpose flour
½ cup sugar
2 teaspoons baking powder
1 teaspoon baking soda
¼ teaspoon salt
3 medium very ripe bananas, mashed (about 1½ cups)
Whites of 4 large eggs
½ cup wheat germ
¼ cup fat-free or low-fat buttermilk
¼ cup unsweetened applesauce
1 tablespoon acceptable vegetable oil
1 teaspoon rum extract
½ teaspoon ground cinnamon
½ teaspoon imitation butter flavoring
¼ cup firmly packed light brown sugar

Preheat the oven to 350°F. Lightly spray an 8½ × 4½ × 2½-inch loaf pan with vegetable oil spray.

In a large bowl, sift together the flour, sugar, baking powder, baking soda, and salt.

Add the remaining ingredients except the brown sugar. Stir until just combined. Don't overmix. Pour into the loaf pan.

Sprinkle the brown sugar over the batter.

Bake for 1 hour, or until a cake tester or toothpick inserted in the center comes out clean. Let cool in the pan for at least 10 minutes. Turn out onto a cooling rack.

calories 130
protein 3 g
carbohydrates 27 g
  fiber 1 g
  sugars 15 g
cholesterol 0 mg
total fat 1.5 g
  saturated 0.0 g
  polyunsaturated 0.5 g
  monounsaturated 0.5 g
sodium 196 mg

dietary exchange
2 starch

Whole-Wheat
Apricot Bread

Serves 16; 1 slice per serving

Bits of dried apricot flavor each bite of this quick bread. You may be tempted to dunk your slice in hot tea or flavored coffee.

Vegetable oil spray
1 cup chopped dried apricots (see Cook's Tip on Cutting Sticky Foods, page 10)
1 cup whole-wheat flour
1 cup all-purpose flour
1/2 cup sugar
1/2 cup finely chopped walnuts, dry-roasted

2 teaspoons baking powder
1/4 teaspoon baking soda
1/2 cup fat-free evaporated milk
Egg substitute equivalent to 1 egg, or 1 large egg, slightly beaten
1/2 cup unsweetened applesauce
1 tablespoon acceptable vegetable oil

Preheat the oven to 350°F. Lightly spray a 9 × 5 × 3-inch loaf pan with vegetable oil spray.

In a large bowl, stir together the apricots, flours, sugar, nuts, baking powder, and baking soda.

In a small bowl, whisk together the remaining ingredients. Add to the apricot mixture. Stir just until well blended. Don't overmix. Pour into the loaf pan.

Bake for 40 to 50 minutes, or until a cake tester or toothpick inserted in the center comes out clean. Turn out onto a cooling rack. Let cool completely, about 1 hour, before slicing.

calories 146
protein 4 g
carbohydrates 26 g
 fiber 2 g
 sugars 13 g
cholesterol 0 mg
total fat 3.5 g
 saturated 0.5 g
 polyunsaturated 2.0 g
 monounsaturated 1.0 g
sodium 99 mg

dietary exchange
2 starch
1/2 fat

Orange Wheat Bread

Serves 16; 1 slice per serving

The orange zest makes this bread smell wonderful as it bakes.

Vegetable oil spray
2 cups all-purpose flour
$1/2$ cup whole-wheat flour
$1/2$ cup wheat germ
$1/2$ cup sugar
$1/4$ cup chopped walnuts, dry-roasted
1 tablespoon baking powder

$1/2$ teaspoon baking soda
2 tablespoons grated orange zest
1 cup fresh orange juice
$1/3$ cup unsweetened applesauce
Egg substitute equivalent to 1 egg, or 1 large egg, beaten
1 tablespoon acceptable vegetable oil

Preheat the oven to 350°F. Lightly spray a 9 × 5 × 3-inch loaf pan with vegetable oil spray.

In a large bowl, stir together the flours, wheat germ, sugar, walnuts, baking powder, and baking soda.

Add the remaining ingredients, stirring just until blended. Don't overmix. Pour into the loaf pan.

Bake for 55 minutes, or until a cake tester or toothpick inserted in the center comes out clean. Turn out onto a cooling rack or plate immediately. Serve warm, or let cool completely and wrap tightly in aluminum foil or plastic wrap. Refrigerate for up to four days.

calories 139
protein 4 g
carbohydrates 26 g
  fiber 2 g
  sugars 9 g
cholesterol 0 mg
total fat 2.5 g
  saturated 0.5 g
  polyunsaturated 1.5 g
  monounsaturated 1.0 g
sodium 140 mg

dietary exchange
$1^1/2$ starch

Cranberry Bread

Serves 16; 1 slice per serving

Slow down the kids with a slice of this bread and a glass of orange juice on their way to see what Santa brought.

Vegetable oil spray
2 cups all-purpose flour
2/3 cup firmly packed light brown sugar
2 teaspoons baking powder
1/2 teaspoon baking soda
1/4 teaspoon salt
1/4 teaspoon ground allspice

1 cup fresh cranberries, chopped
2 teaspoons grated orange zest
3/4 cup fresh orange juice
Egg substitute equivalent to 1 egg, or 1 large egg
1 tablespoon acceptable vegetable oil
2 teaspoons vanilla extract

Preheat the oven to 350°F. Lightly spray an 8½ × 4½ × 2½-inch loaf pan with vegetable oil spray.

In a large bowl, stir together the flour, brown sugar, baking powder, baking soda, salt, and allspice. Make a well in the center.

In a medium bowl, stir together the remaining ingredients. Pour the cranberry mixture into the well. Stir just until blended. Don't overmix. Pour into the loaf pan.

Bake for 50 to 60 minutes, or until a cake tester or toothpick inserted in the center comes out clean. Turn out onto a cooling rack.

Cook's Tip on Cranberries

Look for fresh cranberries from October through December. Buy a few extra bags (they'll freeze for up to 12 months) so you can enjoy the berries throughout the year.

calories 111
protein 2 g
carbohydrates 23 g
  fiber 1 g
  sugars 11 g
cholesterol 0 mg
total fat 1.0 g
  saturated 0.0 g
  polyunsaturated 0.5 g
  monounsaturated 0.5 g
sodium 149 mg

dietary exchange
1½ starch

Applesauce Raisin Bread with Streusel Topping

Serves 16; 1 slice per serving

Serve a warm slice of this bread with a steaming cup of orange tea and a cinnamon stick stirrer.

Vegetable oil spray

Bread
- 1 cup unsweetened applesauce
- 1/2 cup sugar
- 1/4 cup firmly packed light brown sugar
- Egg substitute equivalent to 1 egg, or 1 large egg
- 2 tablespoons fat-free milk
- 1 tablespoon acceptable vegetable oil
- 2 cups all-purpose flour
- 2 teaspoons baking powder
- 1 teaspoon ground cinnamon
- 1/4 teaspoon salt
- 1/4 teaspoon ground nutmeg
- 1/8 teaspoon ground cloves
- 1/2 cup raisins

Topping
- 2 tablespoons light brown sugar
- 2 tablespoons uncooked quick-cooking oatmeal
- 2 tablespoons chopped pecans, dry-roasted
- 1 tablespoon acceptable stick margarine
- 1/2 teaspoon ground cinnamon

Preheat the oven to 350°F. Lightly spray a 9 × 5 × 3-inch loaf pan with vegetable oil spray.

In a large mixing bowl, whisk together the applesauce, sugars, egg substitute, milk, and oil.

In a medium bowl, sift together the remaining bread ingredients except the raisins.

Stir in the raisins. Pour into the applesauce mixture. Beat until well blended. Pour into the loaf pan.

In a small bowl, stir together the topping ingredients. Sprinkle over the batter.

Bake for 50 to 60 minutes, or until a cake tester or toothpick inserted in the center comes out clean. Turn out onto a cooling rack.

calories 146
protein 2 g
carbohydrates 30 g
  fiber 1 g
  sugars 16 g
cholesterol 0 mg
total fat 2.0 g
  saturated 0.0 g
  polyunsaturated 0.5 g
  monounsaturated 1.0 g
sodium 114 mg

dietary exchange
2 starch

Apple Coffee Cake

Serves 9

You'll love the crisp crumb topping and moist center of this coffee cake.

Vegetable oil spray

Topping

1/3 cup firmly packed dark brown sugar

1/3 cup uncooked quick-cooking oatmeal

1 1/2 tablespoons all-purpose flour

1 teaspoon ground cinnamon

1 tablespoon acceptable stick margarine, melted

Coffee Cake

1 1/2 cups all-purpose flour

1/2 cup sugar

2 1/2 teaspoons baking powder

1/2 teaspoon ground cinnamon

3/4 cup fat-free milk

1 medium Granny Smith apple, grated

1/4 cup unsweetened applesauce

White of 1 large egg, beaten until frothy

1/4 teaspoon vanilla extract

Preheat the oven to 375°F. Lightly spray a 9-inch square baking pan with vegetable oil spray.

In a small bowl, stir together the topping ingredients except the margarine.

Stir in the margarine. Set aside.

In a large bowl, sift together the flour, sugar, baking powder, and cinnamon.

In a small bowl, stir together the remaining coffee cake ingredients. Add to the flour mixture. Stir just until the dry ingredients are moistened. Don't overmix. Pour into the baking pan. Sprinkle with the topping.

Bake for 30 to 35 minutes. Let cool on a cooling rack for about 30 minutes.

calories 194
protein 4 g
carbohydrates 43 g
  fiber 2 g
  sugars 23 g
cholesterol 0 mg
total fat 1.0 g
  saturated 0.0 g
  polyunsaturated 0.5 g
  monounsaturated 0.5 g
sodium 165 mg

dietary exchange
3 starch

Banana Raisin Coffee Cake
with Citrus Glaze

Serves 12

This delectable coffee cake tastes best when eaten within a few hours of baking.

1/2 cup golden raisins

1/4 cup unsweetened apple juice

1/2 cup fat-free or low-fat buttermilk

   Whites of 2 large eggs

3 tablespoons honey

1 tablespoon acceptable vegetable oil

2 cups all-purpose flour or bread flour

1/2 tablespoon baking powder

1 teaspoon baking soda

1/4 cup firmly packed light brown sugar

1/2 teaspoon ground ginger

1/2 teaspoon ground cinnamon

   Vegetable oil spray (optional)

2 medium bananas, mashed (about 1 cup)

1 1/4 cups confectioners' sugar, sifted

2 teaspoons fresh orange juice

2 teaspoons fresh lemon juice

Preheat the oven to 350°F.

In a small bowl, stir together the raisins and apple juice. Let stand for 5 minutes.

In a large bowl, whisk together the buttermilk, egg whites, honey, and oil. Stir the raisin mixture into the buttermilk mixture.

In a large bowl, sift together the flour, baking powder, and baking soda.

Stir in the brown sugar, ginger, and cinnamon. Add the brown sugar mixture and bananas to the raisin mixture. Stir just until moistened. Don't overmix. Spoon into a nonstick Bundt pan or a 9-inch tube pan lightly sprayed with vegetable oil spray.

Bake for 30 to 35 minutes, or until a cake tester or toothpick inserted in the center comes out clean.

In a small bowl, whisk together the confectioners' sugar, orange juice, and lemon juice until smooth. Drizzle over the warm coffee cake.

calories 209
protein 3 g
carbohydrates 47 g
  fiber 1 g
  sugars 30 g
cholesterol 0 mg
total fat 1.5 g
  saturated 0.0 g
  polyunsaturated 0.5 g
  monounsaturated 0.5 g
sodium 189 mg

dietary exchange
3 starch

Quick Orange Streusel Cake

Serves 9

This cake is scented with orange zest and juice—definitely worth waking up to!

Vegetable oil spray

Topping

- ¼ cup chopped dry-roasted pecans or walnuts
- ¼ cup firmly packed light brown sugar
- 2 tablespoons all-purpose flour
- 1 tablespoon acceptable stick margarine, melted

Cake

- 2 cups all-purpose flour
- ⅓ cup sugar
- 2 teaspoons baking powder
- ¼ teaspoon baking soda
- ¼ teaspoon salt
- ½ cup fat-free milk
- 2 teaspoons grated orange zest
- ½ cup fresh orange juice
- ⅓ cup unsweetened applesauce
  Egg substitute equivalent to 1 egg, or 1 large egg
- 1 tablespoon acceptable vegetable oil
- 1 teaspoon vanilla extract

Preheat the oven to 375°F. Lightly spray an 8-inch square baking pan with vegetable oil spray.

In a small bowl, stir together the topping ingredients. Set aside.

In a large bowl, sift together the 2 cups flour, sugar, baking powder, baking soda, and salt. Make a well in the center.

In a medium bowl, whisk together the remaining cake ingredients. Pour into the well. Stir just to blend well, until no flour is visible. Pour into the baking pan. Spread evenly.

Crumble the topping over the batter.

Bake for 28 to 33 minutes, or until a cake tester or toothpick inserted in the center comes out clean.

calories 222
protein 5 g
carbohydrates 40 g
  fiber 1 g
  sugars 17 g
cholesterol 0 mg
total fat 5.0 g
  saturated 0.5 g
  polyunsaturated 1.5 g
  monounsaturated 2.5 g
sodium 241 mg

dietary exchange
2½ starch
½ fat

Orange Pull-Apart
Breakfast Bread

Serves 16

A traditional favorite, this bread is made with small pieces of buttermilk biscuits dipped in cinnamon sugar, layered, and baked with an orange-flavored brown sugar sauce. Use a Bundt pan if you want to make a spectacular presentation at your next brunch.

Vegetable oil spray
3 10-count cans refrigerated buttermilk biscuits
1/3 cup sugar
1 teaspoon ground cinnamon
1/4 teaspoon ground nutmeg

1/4 cup firmly packed light brown sugar
3 tablespoons acceptable stick margarine
1/2 teaspoon ground cinnamon
2 teaspoons orange extract

Preheat the oven to 350°F. Lightly spray a 10-inch Bundt pan or 9-inch round cake pan with vegetable oil spray.

Cut each biscuit into quarters with a sharp knife or kitchen scissors.

In a small bowl, stir together the sugar, 1 teaspoon cinnamon, and nutmeg. Coat the biscuit pieces. Layer in the pan.

In a small saucepan, stir together the brown sugar, margarine, and 1/2 teaspoon cinnamon. Cook over low heat for 2 to 3 minutes, or until the margarine has melted and the sugar is dissolved, stirring occasionally.

Stir in the orange extract. Pour over the biscuits.

Bake for 30 to 35 minutes, or until the biscuits are cooked through. Let cool in the pan on a cooling rack for 2 to 3 minutes. Invert onto a large plate. Let cool for at least 10 minutes before slicing. Serve warm.

calories 152
protein 3 g
carbohydrates 28 g
  fiber 1 g
  sugars 9 g
cholesterol 0 mg
total fat 3.0 g
  saturated 0.5 g
  polyunsaturated 0.5 g
  monounsaturated 1.5 g
sodium 554 mg

dietary exchange
2 starch

Easy Refrigerator Rolls

Serves 36; 1 roll per serving

Enjoy these yeast rolls at your convenience. Mix and refrigerate the simple dough. When you want homemade rolls, shape them, let them rise, bake them, and enjoy!

¹/₄ cup lukewarm water (105°F to 115°F)
   ¹/₄-ounce package active dry yeast
   Whites of 2 large eggs
¹/₄ cup acceptable vegetable oil
¹/₂ cup sugar

1 teaspoon salt
1 cup lukewarm water (105°F to 115°F)
4 cups whole-wheat or all-purpose flour (plus more as needed)
   Vegetable oil spray

Pour ¹/₄ cup water into a small bowl. Add the yeast. Stir to dissolve. Let stand for 5 minutes, or until the mixture bubbles.

Pour the egg whites into a large bowl. Whisk lightly.

Add the following ingredients in order, stirring after each addition: oil, sugar, yeast mixture, salt, 1 cup water, and flour. Cover the dough and refrigerate for 12 hours to 4 days.

Lightly spray a baking sheet with vegetable oil spray. Make 36 rolls in your favorite shape. Put the rolls on the baking sheet. Cover with a dry dish towel. Let the rolls rise in a warm, draft-free place (about 85°F) for 2 hours.

Preheat the oven to 375°F.

Bake for 10 minutes.

calories 71
protein 2 g
carbohydrates 13 g
  fiber 2 g
  sugars 3 g
cholesterol 0 mg
total fat 2.0 g
  saturated 0.0 g
  polyunsaturated 0.5 g
  monounsaturated 1.0 g
sodium 69 mg

dietary exchange
1 starch

Yogurt
Dinner Rolls

Serves 18; 1 roll per serving

Tangy yogurt and fragrant herbs flavor these wheat-and-white rolls.

$^1/_4$ cup lukewarm water (105°F to 115°F)

2 tablespoons sugar

$^1/_4$-ounce package active dry yeast

1 cup fat-free or light plain yogurt

Egg substitute equivalent to 1 egg, or 1 large egg

2 tablespoons acceptable stick margarine, melted

2 tablespoons grated or minced onion

2 teaspoons dried basil, crumbled

1 teaspoon dried oregano, crumbled

$^3/_4$ cup whole-wheat flour

$^3/_4$ cup all-purpose flour

$^1/_2$ teaspoon salt

$^3/_4$ cup whole-wheat flour

$^1/_2$ cup all-purpose flour

Vegetable oil spray

Flour for hands

Pour the water, sugar, and yeast into a medium bowl. Stir to dissolve. Let stand for 5 minutes, or until the mixture bubbles. Stir in the yogurt, egg substitute, margarine, onion, basil, and oregano.

In a large mixing bowl, stir together $^3/_4$ cup whole-wheat flour, $^3/_4$ cup all-purpose flour, and salt.

Blend in the yogurt mixture. Using an electric mixer, beat on low speed for 30 seconds, then beat on high speed for 3 minutes. Stir in the remaining flours. (The dough will be moist and sticky.)

Lightly spray a large bowl with vegetable oil spray. Add the dough. Turn to coat. Cover with a damp dish towel. Let rise in a warm, draft-free place (about 85°F) for $1^1/_2$ hours. Punch down the dough. Lightly spray a 13 × 9 × 2-inch baking pan with vegetable oil spray. Lightly flour hands. Form the dough into 18 balls. Put on the pan. Cover with a dry dish towel. Let rise in a warm, draft-free place (about 85°F) for 40 minutes.

Preheat the oven to 400°F. Bake for 15 minutes.

calories 94
protein 4 g
carbohydrates 17 g
  fiber 2 g
  sugars 3 g
cholesterol 0 mg
total fat 1.5 g
  saturated 0.5 g
  polyunsaturated 0.5 g
  monounsaturated 1.0 g
sodium 98 mg

dietary exchange
1 starch

Southern
Raised Biscuits

Soak up some heart-healthy gravy with these full-flavored biscuits.

1 cup fat-free or low-fat buttermilk, slightly warmed
¼-ounce package active dry yeast
2½ cups all-purpose flour
¼ cup sugar

½ teaspoon baking soda
½ teaspoon salt
¼ cup acceptable vegetable oil
Flour for kneading
Vegetable oil spray

Pour the buttermilk into a small bowl. Add the yeast and stir to dissolve. Let stand for 5 minutes, or until the mixture bubbles.

In a large bowl, stir together 2½ cups flour, sugar, baking soda, and salt.

Add the buttermilk mixture and oil to the flour mixture. Stir gently and quickly until mixed.

Lightly flour a flat surface. Turn out the dough. Knead gently 20 to 30 times. Roll out or pat to ¼-inch thickness. With a floured 1-inch biscuit cutter, cut out 60 biscuits. Lightly spray each biscuit with vegetable oil spray.

Lightly spray a baking sheet. Put 30 biscuits on it. Put a second biscuit on top of each. Cover with a dry dish towel. Let the dough rise in a warm, draft-free place (about 85°F) for about 2 hours.

Preheat the oven to 375°F. Bake for 12 to 15 minutes.

calories 65
protein 1 g
carbohydrates 10 g
  fiber 0 g
  sugars 2 g
cholesterol 0 mg
total fat 2.0 g
  saturated 0.0 g
  polyunsaturated 0.5 g
  monounsaturated 1.0 g
sodium 69 mg

dietary exchange
½ starch
½ fat

Cold-Oven Popovers

Serves 12; 1 large popover per serving

This recipe is really cheap entertainment! If your oven has a window and a light, you and your children will want to watch as the batter bubbles up.

Vegetable oil spray
Whites of 6 large eggs
2 cups fat-free milk
2 tablespoons acceptable vegetable oil

1 tablespoon acceptable stick margarine, melted
2 cups sifted all-purpose flour
1/4 teaspoon salt

Lightly spray a 12-cup popover pan with vegetable oil spray.

In a medium bowl, beat the egg whites lightly with a fork.

Add the milk, oil, and margarine, stirring well.

In a large mixing bowl, stir together the flour and salt. Gradually add the milk mixture, beating with an electric mixer after each addition until well blended. Mix on high speed for 1 to 2 minutes.

Fill each popover cup half full of batter and put in a *cold* oven. Set the oven to 400°F. Bake the popovers for 45 to 60 minutes, or until a light golden color.

Cook's Tip

If you don't have a popover pan, substitute 12 large (about 9-ounce) or 18 medium (about 5-ounce) custard cups lightly sprayed with vegetable oil spray. Muffin tins won't give you consistent results.

calories 123
protein 5 g
carbohydrates 18 g
  fiber 1 g
  sugars 3 g
cholesterol 1 mg
total fat 3.0 g
  saturated 0.5 g
  polyunsaturated 1.0 g
  monounsaturated 1.5 g
sodium 104 mg

dietary exchange
1 starch
1/2 fat

Parmesan-Herb
Breadsticks

Serves 18; 1 breadstick per serving

Nothing soaks up the last spoonful of spaghetti sauce or gravy quite like these soft homemade breadsticks.

Vegetable oil spray
2 cups all-purpose flour
1 cup whole-wheat flour
2 tablespoons minced green onions (green part only) or snipped chives
1 tablespoon snipped fresh dillweed or 1 teaspoon dried, crumbled
1 teaspoon baking soda

1/2 teaspoon baking powder
1/4 teaspoon salt
1/4 teaspoon pepper
1 1/2 cups fat-free or low-fat buttermilk
2 tablespoons olive oil
2 tablespoons shredded or grated Parmesan cheese

Preheat the oven to 350°F. Lightly spray a large baking sheet with vegetable oil spray.

In a large bowl, whisk together both flours, green onions, dillweed, baking soda, baking powder, salt, and pepper. Make a well in the center.

Pour the buttermilk and oil into the well. Stir just until moistened (don't overmix).

With floured hands, divide the dough into 18 pieces. Shape each piece into a 4-inch-long cylinder (slightly wetting your hands with cold water will help keep the dough from sticking). Place the cylinders about 1 inch apart on the baking sheet. Sprinkle with the Parmesan.

Bake for 20 to 22 minutes, or until golden brown. For a slightly crispy outside, transfer the rolls onto a cooling rack. Let cool for 5 minutes before serving. For a slightly warmer and less crispy roll, put them in a bread basket lined with a dish towel, cover, and let rest for 5 minutes.

calories 97
protein 3 g
carbohydrates 17 g
  fiber 1 g
  sugars 1 g
cholesterol 1 mg
total fat 2.0 g
  saturated 0.5 g
  polyunsaturated 0.0 g
  monounsaturated 1.0 g
sodium 147 mg

dietary exchange
1 starch

Muffins

Serves 12

Muffins aren't just for breakfast and brunch. They are so easy to make that you can enjoy them anytime.

Vegetable oil spray
2 cups sifted all-purpose flour
2 tablespoons sugar
1 tablespoon baking powder
1/4 teaspoon salt

1 1/4 cups fat-free milk
1/4 cup unsweetened applesauce
Egg substitute equivalent to 1 egg, or 1 large egg
1 tablespoon acceptable vegetable oil

Preheat the oven to 425°F. Lightly spray a 12-cup muffin tin with vegetable oil spray.

In a large bowl, sift together the flour, sugar, baking powder, and salt. Make a well in the center.

In a medium bowl, whisk together the remaining ingredients. Pour into the well. Whisk just enough to moisten the flour. Don't overmix. The batter should be lumpy.

Fill the muffin cups two-thirds full.

Bake for 20 to 25 minutes, or until a cake tester or toothpick inserted in the center comes out clean.

calories 108
protein 4 g
carbohydrates 20 g
  fiber 1 g
  sugars 4 g
cholesterol 1 mg
total fat 1.5 g
  saturated 0.0 g
  polyunsaturated 0.5 g
  monounsaturated 0.5 g
sodium 195 mg

dietary exchange
1 1/2 starch

Fruit Muffins

Add 1/2 cup fruit, such as blueberries, to the batter. Or fill the muffin cups one-third full, put 1 teaspoon of all-fruit spread in the center of each, and cover with the remaining batter.

fruit muffins
with blueberries

calories 112
protein 4 g
carbohydrates 21 g
  fiber 1 g
  sugars 5 g
cholesterol 1 mg
total fat 1.5 g
  saturated 0.0 g
  polyunsaturated 0.5 g
  monounsaturated 0.5 g
sodium 195 mg

dietary exchange
1 1/2 starch

Whole-Wheat Muffins

Serves 12

Serve these fragrant muffins with Curried Chicken Salad (page 123).

Vegetable oil spray
1 cup whole-wheat flour
³/₄ cup all-purpose flour
¹/₄ cup wheat germ
¹/₄ cup sugar
2¹/₂ teaspoons baking powder
¹/₂ teaspoon ground cinnamon
¹/₄ teaspoon salt
¹/₈ teaspoon ground cloves

1 cup fat-free milk
¹/₃ cup unsweetened applesauce
¹/₂ cup grated zucchini
Egg substitute equivalent to 1 egg, or 1 large egg
1 tablespoon acceptable vegetable oil
1 teaspoon grated orange zest
3 tablespoons dry-roasted chopped walnuts (optional)

calories 112
protein 4 g
carbohydrates 21 g
 fiber 2 g
 sugars 7 g
cholesterol 0 mg
total fat 1.5 g
 saturated 0.0 g
 polyunsaturated 0.5 g
 monounsaturated 1.0 g
sodium 172 mg

dietary exchange
1¹/₂ starch

with nuts

calories 124
protein 4 g
carbohydrates 21 g
 fiber 2 g
 sugars 7 g
cholesterol 0 mg
total fat 3.0 g
 saturated 0.5 g
 polyunsaturated 1.5 g
 monounsaturated 1.0 g
sodium 173 mg

dietary exchange
1¹/₂ starch
¹/₂ fat

Preheat the oven to 375°F. Lightly spray a 12-cup muffin tin with vegetable oil spray.

In a large bowl, stir together the flours, wheat germ, sugar, baking powder, cinnamon, salt, and cloves. Make a well in the center.

In a medium bowl, whisk together the remaining ingredients except the walnuts. Pour into the well.

Add the walnuts. Stir just enough to moisten the flour. Don't overmix; the batter should be lumpy. Pour the batter into the muffin cups.

Bake for 20 to 25 minutes, or until the muffins are firm. Remove from the oven. Let the muffins stand for a few minutes in the pan before serving.

Time-Saver on Roasted Nuts

For dry-roasted nuts ready at a moment's notice, prepare extras for storing in an airtight container in the freezer. You don't even need to thaw them.

Buttermilk Bran Muffins

Serves 12

Pack a muffin and fruit juice or fat-free milk for a snack at work or school. Save a few muffins for a later date. They'll keep in the freezer for up to four months.

1 cup fat-free or low-fat buttermilk
3/4 cup bud-type bran cereal
1/3 cup sugar
1/2 cup raisins
1/2 cup shredded carrots
1/4 cup unsweetened applesauce
   Egg substitute equivalent to 1 egg, or 1 large egg

1 tablespoon acceptable vegetable oil
1/2 teaspoon vanilla extract
1 cup all-purpose flour
1/2 cup oat bran flour
2 teaspoons baking powder
1/2 teaspoon ground cinnamon
1/4 teaspoon ground nutmeg

Preheat the oven to 375°F. Line a 12-cup muffin tin with bake cups.

In a medium bowl, whisk together the buttermilk, cereal, sugar, raisins, carrots, applesauce, egg substitute, oil, and vanilla. Let stand for about 10 minutes.

In a large bowl, stir together the remaining ingredients. Make a well in the center.

Pour the buttermilk mixture into the well. Stir just enough to moisten the flour. Don't overmix; the batter should be lumpy. Fill the muffin cups two-thirds full of batter.

Bake for 20 to 25 minutes, or until a cake tester or tooth-pick inserted in the center comes out clean.

calories 137
protein 4 g
carbohydrates 27 g
   fiber 3 g
   sugars 13 g
cholesterol 1 mg
total fat 2.0 g
   saturated 0.5 g
   polyunsaturated 0.5 g
   monounsaturated 1.0 g
sodium 125 mg

dietary exchange
2 starch

Oat Bran Fruit Muffins

Serves 18

Do your heart a favor and start your day off right with a proper breakfast. One of these muffins, a cold glass of fat-free milk, and a bowl of sliced strawberries would fit the bill.

1 1/2 cups high-fiber oat-bran cereal
3/4 cup all-purpose flour
3/4 cup whole-wheat flour
1/2 cup raisins
1/2 cup chopped dates
1/2 cup chopped prunes
2 teaspoons baking powder
1 teaspoon baking soda
1 teaspoon ground cinnamon

1 cup fat-free or low-fat buttermilk
1/2 cup honey
Egg substitute equivalent to 2 eggs, or 2 large eggs, well beaten
1/4 cup firmly packed dark brown sugar
3 tablespoons acceptable vegetable oil

Preheat the oven to 400°F. Line a 12-cup and a 6-cup muffin tin with bake cups.

In a large bowl, stir together the cereal, flours, raisins, dates, prunes, baking powder, baking soda, and cinnamon. Make a well in the center.

In a medium bowl, whisk together the remaining ingredients. Pour into the well. Stir just enough to moisten the flour. Don't overmix; the batter should be lumpy. Spoon into the muffin cups.

Bake for 20 to 25 minutes, or until a cake tester or toothpick inserted in the center comes out clean.

calories 158
protein 3 g
carbohydrates 32 g
  fiber 2 g
  sugars 20 g
cholesterol 1 mg
total fat 3.0 g
  saturated 0.5 g
  polyunsaturated 1.0 g
  monounsaturated 1.5 g
sodium 169 mg

dietary exchange
2 starch

Mini Strawberry-Orange Muffins

Serves 12

Fresh strawberries add the perfect amount of moisture to these delicious muffins. The orange zest heightens the flavor to jumpstart those sleepy mornings.

Vegetable oil spray
7.4-ounce package bran muffin mix (honey-bran variety preferred)
$2/3$ cup fat-free milk
$1/2$ tablespoon grated orange zest

$1/2$ teaspoon ground cinnamon
$3/4$ cup whole fresh strawberries, diced
$1/2$ tablespoon sugar
$1/4$ teaspoon ground cinnamon

Preheat the oven to 425°F. Lightly spray a 12-cup non-stick mini muffin tin with vegetable oil spray.

In a medium bowl, stir together the muffin mix, milk, orange zest, and $1/2$ teaspoon cinnamon until just blended. Don't overmix.

Fold in the strawberries. Don't overmix. Spoon the batter into each muffin cup.

Bake for 15 to 18 minutes, or until a cake tester or toothpick inserted in the center of a muffin comes out clean.

Meanwhile, in a small bowl, stir together the sugar and $1/4$ teaspoon cinnamon.

Put the muffin tin on a cooling rack. Sprinkle the muffins with the sugar mixture. Let stand for 5 minutes. Using a spoon or knife, carefully remove the muffins from the tin (they will be very moist). Let cool completely.

Cook's Tip

Be sure to use fresh strawberries for this recipe. Frozen strawberries will make these muffins soggy.

calories 83
protein 2 g
carbohydrates 14 g
 fiber 2 g
 sugars 7 g
cholesterol 2 mg
total fat 2.0 g
 saturated 0.5 g
 polyunsaturated 0.5 g
 monounsaturated 1.0 g
sodium 184 mg

dietary exchange
2 starch
$1/2$ fat

Blueberry Banana Muffins

Serves 12

A fruit-lover's dream, these muffins combine blueberries, banana, orange juice, and applesauce.

Vegetable oil spray
1 cup all-purpose flour
1/2 cup whole-wheat flour
1/2 cup wheat germ
1/3 cup firmly packed light brown sugar
1 tablespoon baking powder
1/2 teaspoon salt
1/2 teaspoon ground cinnamon

1/8 teaspoon ground nutmeg
1 medium banana
1/2 cup fresh orange juice
1/4 cup unsweetened applesauce
Egg substitute equivalent to 1 egg, or 1 large egg
1 tablespoon acceptable vegetable oil
1 cup fresh blueberries

Preheat the oven to 400°F. Lightly spray a 12-cup muffin tin with vegetable oil spray.

In a large bowl, stir together the flours, wheat germ, brown sugar, baking powder, salt, cinnamon, and nutmeg. Make a well in the center.

In a small bowl, mash the banana. Add the remaining ingredients except the blueberries. Whisk until well blended. Pour into the well. Stir just enough to moisten the flour. Don't overmix; the batter should be lumpy.

With a rubber scraper, carefully fold the blueberries into the batter. Pour the batter into the muffin cups.

Bake for 15 minutes, or until a cake tester or toothpick inserted in the center comes out clean.

calories 132
protein 4 g
carbohydrates 26 g
  fiber 2 g
  sugars 12 g
cholesterol 0 mg
total fat 2.0 g
  saturated 0.0 g
  polyunsaturated 0.5 g
  monounsaturated 1.0 g
sodium 234 mg

dietary exchange
1 1/2 starch

Poppy Seed Scones with Dried Cranberries

Serves 16

A cross between a cookie and a biscuit, a scone is perfect for teatime or with a piece of fruit after dinner. This porous Scottish classic is great for dunking in tea, coffee, or fat-free milk with a shot or two of fat-free chocolate syrup.

Vegetable oil spray
2 cups all-purpose flour
1/2 cup uncooked quick-cooking oatmeal
1/2 cup sugar
1 tablespoon poppy seeds
1 teaspoon baking powder
1/2 teaspoon baking soda

1/4 teaspoon salt
2 tablespoons acceptable stick margarine
1/2 cup dried cranberries
1/2 cup pineapple juice
Egg substitute equivalent to 1 egg, or 1 large egg
Flour for hands

Preheat the oven to 375°F. Lightly spray a baking sheet with vegetable oil spray.

In a large bowl, stir together 2 cups flour, oatmeal, sugar, poppy seeds, baking powder, baking soda, and salt.

Using a fork or pastry blender, cut the margarine into the flour mixture until crumbly.

Stir in the cranberries. Make a well in the center.

Pour the pineapple juice and egg substitute into the well. Stir until just combined. Don't overmix.

With floured hands, divide the dough in half. Shape into 2 balls. Put 4 to 5 inches apart on the baking sheet. Flatten each into a 6-inch disk. Cut each into 8 wedges with a sharp knife or pizza cutter. Don't separate the wedges.

Bake for 15 to 20 minutes, or until the edges are golden brown. Let cool for at least 5 minutes on a cooling rack. Separate the wedges with a knife or pizza cutter.

calories 118
protein 3 g
carbohydrates 24 g
 fiber 1 g
 sugars 10 g
cholesterol 0 mg
total fat 1.0 g
 saturated 0.0 g
 polyunsaturated 0.5 g
 monounsaturated 0.5 g
sodium 124 mg

dietary exchange
1 1/2 starch

Petite Cinnamon Swirls

Serves 12

This is the easy way to make "homemade" cinnamon rolls.

8-ounce tube refrigerated low-fat
crescent dinner roll dough
1 teaspoon ground cinnamon
2 teaspoons grated orange zest

¹/₃ cup raisins
¹/₂ cup confectioners' sugar
1 tablespoon fat-free milk

Preheat the oven to 375°F.

Unwrap the dough but don't separate it. Place the dough in one piece on a flat surface. In order, sprinkle with the cinnamon, orange zest, and raisins. Press gently into the dough.

Starting with one long end, roll up the dough jelly-roll style, making a log about 12 inches long. Using a serrated knife, cut crosswise into 12 slices. Place the dough slices about 1 inch apart on a nonstick baking sheet. Using the palm of your hand, gently press down on each roll to slightly flatten.

Bake for 10 to 11 minutes, or until just beginning to turn golden.

Meanwhile, in a small bowl, stir together the confectioners' sugar and milk until well blended. Spoon over the rolls as soon as they are removed from the oven.

calories 102
protein 2 g
carbohydrates 17 g
  fiber 0 g
  sugars 10 g
cholesterol 0 mg
total fat 3.0 g
  saturated 0.5 g
  polyunsaturated 0.0 g
  monounsaturated 0.0 g
sodium 157 mg

dietary exchange
¹/₂ starch
¹/₂ fruit
¹/₂ fat

Muesli

Serves 6; 1 cup per serving

For a change of pace, this no-cook creamy-textured dish incorporates the goodness of oatmeal, wheat germ, yogurt, and dried fruits. Prepare it the night before to save time in the morning.

1 cup uncooked quick-cooking oats
1 cup fat-free or light vanilla yogurt
1/2 cup fat-free milk
1/4 cup dried currants or raisins
1/4 cup chopped dried apricots

2 tablespoons toasted wheat germ
1 tablespoon honey
2 cups sliced fresh strawberries
2 tablespoons sliced almonds, dry-roasted

In a medium bowl, stir together the oats, yogurt, milk, currants, apricots, wheat germ, and honey. Cover and refrigerate for 2 hours (the oats should be plump and tender) to two days.

To serve, stir in the strawberries. Ladle the cereal into bowls. Sprinkle with the almonds.

calories 177
protein 7 g
carbohydrates 34 g
  fiber 4 g
  sugars 22 g
cholesterol 1 mg
total fat 2.5 g
  saturated 0.5 g
  polyunsaturated 1.0 g
  monounsaturated 1.0 g
sodium 41 mg

dietary exchange
1 starch
1 fruit
1/2 skim milk

Apple-Berry Couscous

Serves 6; 1¼ cups per serving

Start your day healthfully with this unusual combination of fresh and dried fruits plus couscous, a quick-cooking grain.

1 teaspoon acceptable vegetable oil
2 medium apples, such as Fuji, McIntosh, or Rome Beauty, cut into ½-inch pieces (about 2 cups)
¼ cup dried cherries or dried cranberries
¼ cup golden raisins
3 tablespoons dried currants

3 tablespoons light brown sugar
1 teaspoon ground cinnamon
2 cups unsweetened apple juice
½ cup water
1 teaspoon coarsely grated lime zest
3 tablespoons fresh lime juice
1⅔ cups uncooked couscous

Heat a large saucepan over low heat. Pour the oil into the pan and swirl to coat the bottom. Stir in the apples, cherries, raisins, currants, brown sugar, and cinnamon. Cook, covered, for 10 minutes, or until the apples have released some of their juices, stirring occasionally.

Stir in the remaining ingredients except the couscous. Increase the heat to high. Cover and bring to a boil.

Stir in the couscous. Cover the pan. Remove from the heat. Let stand for 15 minutes. Fluff with a fork before serving.

calories 335
protein 7 g
carbohydrates 75 g
 fiber 5 g
 sugars 33 g
cholesterol 0 mg
total fat 1.5 g
 saturated 0.0 g
 polyunsaturated 0.5 g
 monounsaturated 0.5 g
sodium 12 mg

dietary exchange
3 starch
2 fruit

Cook's Tip on Couscous

Couscous (KOOS-koos), which looks like tiny bits of pasta, is made from a coarse wheat flour called semolina. Couscous cooks quickly, making it a boon when you're in a hurry. The name "couscous" also refers to a stew made of the grain, lamb or chicken, and vegetables.

Apple Oatmeal Pancake

Serves 8

Here's a tasty breakfast dish for a cold Sunday morning.

Vegetable oil spray
1 tablespoon acceptable stick margarine
2/3 cup all-purpose flour
1/3 cup uncooked quick-cooking oatmeal
1 tablespoon light brown sugar
Egg substitute equivalent to 6 eggs
1 cup fat-free milk
1 tablespoon vanilla extract

1 teaspoon ground cinnamon
1/4 teaspoon salt
2 tablespoons light brown sugar
1/2 teaspoon ground cinnamon
3 large Red Delicious apples (about 1 1/2 pounds)
1 tablespoon acceptable stick margarine
1 tablespoon fresh lemon juice

Preheat the oven to 425°F. Lightly spray a 13 × 9 × 2-inch pan with vegetable oil spray. Melt 1 tablespoon margarine in the pan. Swirl to coat the bottom.

Using a food processor or blender, process the flour, oatmeal, and 1 tablespoon brown sugar until smooth.

Add the egg substitute, milk, vanilla, 1 teaspoon cinnamon, and salt to the flour mixture. Process until smooth. Pour into the hot pan. Bake for 25 minutes.

Meanwhile, in a small bowl, stir together 2 tablespoons brown sugar and 1/2 teaspoon cinnamon.

Peel, core, and slice the apples.

Melt 1 tablespoon margarine in a large nonstick skillet over medium heat and swirl to coat the bottom. Add the apples, gently stirring with a rubber scraper to prevent breakage. Sprinkle with the brown sugar mixture. Cook, covered, over medium heat for 7 to 8 minutes.

To serve, cut the pancake into 8 pieces. Place on plates. Stir the lemon juice into the apple mixture. Spoon over each portion.

calories 170
protein 7 g
carbohydrates 29 g
  fiber 2 g
  sugars 17 g
cholesterol 1 mg
total fat 2.5 g
  saturated 0.5 g
  polyunsaturated 0.5 g
  monounsaturated 1.0 g
sodium 211 mg

dietary exchange
1 starch
1 fruit
1/2 lean meat

Cinnamon Orange Pancakes

Serves 6; 2 pancakes per serving

Start the day off right with these yummy pancakes, served with Orange Sauce (page 507), light syrup, or cottage cheese topped with sliced bananas or strawberries.

1 cup whole-wheat flour
3/4 cup all-purpose flour
2 tablespoons wheat germ
1 tablespoon sugar
2 teaspoons baking powder
1 teaspoon ground cinnamon

1 cup fat-free milk
1 teaspoon grated fresh orange zest
3/4 cup fresh orange juice
Egg substitute equivalent to 1 egg, or 1 large egg
Vegetable oil spray

In a large mixing bowl, stir together the flours, wheat germ, sugar, baking powder, and cinnamon.

In a small bowl, whisk together the remaining ingredients except the vegetable oil spray. Pour into the flour mixture. Stir just until moistened. Don't overmix.

Preheat a griddle or large skillet over medium heat. Remove from the heat and lightly spray with vegetable oil spray (being careful not to spray near a gas flame).

Using a 1/4-cup measure, pour the batter onto the griddle. (You should have 12 pancakes.) Cook for 2 to 3 minutes, or until the tops are bubbly and the edges are dry. Turn over and cook for 2 to 3 minutes.

calories 177
protein 8 g
carbohydrates 36 g
  fiber 4 g
  sugars 8 g
cholesterol 1 mg
total fat 1.0 g
  saturated 0.0 g
  polyunsaturated 0.5 g
  monounsaturated 0.0 g
sodium 207 mg

dietary exchange
2 1/2 starch

Stacked Sausage and Eggs

Serves 4

Try this for an easy but hearty breakfast when you have out-of-towners visiting or for a midnight breakfast when the conversation never stops! Serve with whole-wheat English muffins.

4 ounces low-fat bulk breakfast sausage
1 cup sliced button mushrooms (about 2¹/₂ ounces)
¹/₂ large onion, chopped
¹/₂ medium green bell pepper, chopped
Egg substitute equivalent to 4 eggs, or 4 large eggs

3 tablespoons fat-free milk
¹/₂ teaspoon low-sodium Worcestershire sauce
¹/₈ teaspoon cayenne
¹/₈ teaspoon salt
2 tablespoons snipped fresh parsley

Heat a 12-inch nonstick skillet over medium-high heat. Cook the sausage for 2 to 3 minutes, or until no longer pink, stirring constantly. Transfer to a plate.

Put the mushrooms, onion, and bell pepper in the skillet. Cook for 4 minutes, or until the onion is soft. Transfer to the plate with the sausage. Cover to keep warm.

Meanwhile, in a small bowl, whisk together the egg substitute, milk, Worcestershire sauce, and cayenne.

Wipe the skillet with damp paper towels. Heat the skillet over medium heat. Cook the egg mixture for 2 minutes, stirring frequently.

Spoon the egg mixture onto a platter. Top with the sausage mixture. Sprinkle with the salt and parsley.

calories 90
protein 12 g
carbohydrates 6 g
  fiber 1 g
  sugars 4 g
cholesterol 14 mg
total fat 1.0 g
  saturated 0.0 g
  polyunsaturated 0.0 g
  monounsaturated 0.0 g
sodium 371 mg

dietary exchange
1 vegetable
1¹/₂ very lean meat

Peachy Stuffed French Toast

Serves 4; 1 piece per serving

Sandwich a peach filling infused with nutmeg and lemon zest between slices of whole-wheat bread and drizzle honey on top for a brunch delight.

2 tablespoons pecan pieces
  Vegetable oil spray
1 teaspoon light brown sugar
1/4 teaspoon ground cinnamon
2 tablespoons fat-free or light cream cheese, softened
  15-ounce can sliced peaches in extra-light syrup, drained and diced

1 teaspoon grated lemon zest
1/8 teaspoon ground nutmeg
4 slices whole-wheat, multigrain, or Texas toast–style bread, cut in half vertically
  Egg substitute equivalent to 2 eggs, or 2 large eggs
2 tablespoons fat-free milk
4 tablespoons honey

In a medium nonstick skillet, dry-roast the pecans over medium heat for 3 to 4 minutes, or until golden brown, stirring occasionally. Remove from the heat. Lightly spray the pecans with vegetable oil spray. Return the pan to the heat.

Stir in the brown sugar and cinnamon. Cook for 1 minute, or until the brown sugar is slightly dissolved, stirring occasionally. (Watch carefully so the mixture does not burn.) Transfer to a small plate. Set aside.

In a medium bowl, stir the cream cheese until smooth. Stir in the peaches, lemon zest, and nutmeg.

Put four pieces of bread on a flat surface, such as a cutting board. Spoon the peach mixture onto each piece. Top with the remaining bread.

In a shallow bowl, whisk together the egg substitute and milk. Dip the stuffed bread into the egg mixture to coat both sides. Let the excess drip off.

calories 225
protein 7 g
carbohydrates 42 g
  fiber 3 g
  sugars 28 g
cholesterol 1 mg
total fat 4.0 g
  saturated 0.5 g
  polyunsaturated 1.0 g
  monounsaturated 2.0 g
sodium 262 mg

dietary exchange
1 starch
1 fruit
1 other carbohydrate
1/2 lean meat

Heat a large nonstick griddle or skillet over medium-high heat. Put the bread on the griddle. Cook for 2 to 3 minutes, or until golden brown. Turn the bread over. Cook for 2 to 3 minutes, or until the bread is golden brown and the filling is warmed through.

To serve, transfer to plates. Sprinkle the toast with the pecans and drizzle with the honey.

Country-Style
Breakfast Casserole

Serves 10

For a special, no-fuss breakfast, prepare this casserole the night before.

Vegetable oil spray
8 ounces low-fat smoked link sausage
2 tablespoons maple syrup
2 pounds frozen country-style hash browns (no oil added)
2 cups fat-free milk
Egg substitute equivalent to 6 eggs, or 6 large eggs

2 1-ounce slices fat-free or low-fat American cheese, diced
1/4 cup shredded or grated Parmesan cheese
1/2 teaspoon dry mustard
1/4 teaspoon pepper
2 tablespoons finely snipped green onions (green part only) (optional)

Preheat the oven to 350°F. Lightly spray a 13 × 9 × 2-inch baking pan with vegetable oil spray.

Heat a medium skillet over medium-high heat. Cook the sausage for 3 to 4 minutes, or until browned, turning occasionally. Remove from the skillet and cut into bite-size pieces. Wipe the skillet with a paper towel. Return the sausage to the skillet.

Add the maple syrup to the sausage. Cook for 1 minute, stirring to coat. Arrange in a single layer in the baking pan.

Top the sausage with the hash browns.

In a medium bowl, whisk together the remaining ingredients except the green onions. Pour over the hash browns.

Bake for 1 hour, or until the center is set (doesn't jiggle when gently shaken). Sprinkle the green onions over the casserole. Let cool for at least 10 minutes before cutting.

calories 162
protein 12 g
carbohydrates 25 g
  fiber 1 g
  sugars 8 g
cholesterol 12 mg
total fat 1.5 g
  saturated 0.5 g
  polyunsaturated 0.0 g
  monounsaturated 0.0 g
sodium 430 mg

dietary exchange
1½ starch
1 lean meat

Cook's Tip

If you prepare this casserole ahead of time, cover it with plastic wrap and refrigerate. Put the cold casserole in a cold oven. Set the oven to 350°F and bake for 1 hour 10 minutes to 1 hour 15 minutes. Proceed as directed above.

Strata with Canadian Bacon, Spinach, and Tomatoes

Serves 4

Is this for breakfast, lunch, or dinner? Whatever time of day, this savory casserole will leave no question of how good it tastes, with colorful spinach and tomatoes, smoky Canadian bacon, and the distinctive flavor of Swiss cheese.

Vegetable oil spray
3 slices whole-wheat bread, cubed
  10-ounce package frozen chopped spinach, thawed and squeezed dry
2 medium Italian plum tomatoes, diced
1/2 cup diced lean low-sodium ham (about 3 ounces)

4 medium green onions (green and white parts), thinly sliced
1/4 cup shredded low-fat Swiss cheese
1/4 cup coarsely chopped fresh basil leaves
1 1/2 cups fat-free milk
  Egg substitute equivalent to 4 eggs, or 4 large eggs
1/4 teaspoon pepper

Preheat the oven to 350°F (unless you are preparing the strata mixture in advance; see the Cook's Tip). Lightly spray an 8-inch square baking pan with vegetable oil spray.

Put the English muffin cubes, spinach, tomatoes, Canadian bacon, green onions, Swiss cheese, and basil in the baking pan. Stir four to five times to distribute the ingredients evenly.

In a medium bowl, whisk together the remaining ingredients. Pour over the English muffin mixture.

Bake for 55 to 60 minutes, or until the center is set (doesn't jiggle when gently shaken). Let cool for 10 minutes before cutting into four squares.

Cook's Tip

If you prepare this casserole ahead of time, cover it with plastic wrap and refrigerate for up to 10 hours. Put the cold casserole in a cold oven, set the oven temperature to 350°F, and bake for 1 hour 5 minutes to 1 hour 10 minutes.

calories 191
protein 20 g
carbohydrates 23 g
  fiber 5 g
  sugars 9 g
cholesterol 15 mg
total fat 3.0 g
  saturated 1.0 g
  polyunsaturated 0.5 g
  monounsaturated 0.5 g
sodium 504 mg

dietary exchange
1 starch
1/2 skim milk
1 1/2 vegetable
2 very lean meat

Breakfast Pizzas

Serves 4

You'll need a knife and fork for these sky-high pizzas.

8 ounces fresh button mushrooms, sliced
1 medium green bell pepper, chopped
1 large onion, chopped
Egg substitute equivalent to 3 eggs
1/4 cup fat-free milk
1/2 cup no-salt-added tomato sauce

1 teaspoon salt-free Italian seasoning, crumbled
1/4 teaspoon crushed red pepper flakes
2 whole-wheat English muffins, halved and toasted
2 tablespoons shredded or grated Parmesan cheese

Heat a large nonstick skillet over medium-high heat for 1 minute. Cook the mushrooms for 4 minutes, or until soft, stirring occasionally.

Stir in the bell pepper and onion. Cook for 4 to 5 minutes, or until the onion is soft, stirring occasionally.

Meanwhile, in a small bowl, whisk together the egg substitute and milk.

Reduce the heat to medium. Stir the egg mixture into the mushroom mixture. Cook until the eggs are set, stirring occasionally with a rubber scraper. Remove from the heat.

In a small bowl, stir together the tomato sauce, Italian seasoning, and red pepper flakes.

To assemble, place a muffin half on each plate. Spoon 2 tablespoons tomato mixture over each muffin half. Top with the egg mixture. Sprinkle with the Parmesan.

calories 157
protein 11 g
carbohydrates 26 g
  fiber 4 g
  sugars 9 g
cholesterol 2 mg
total fat 1.5 g
  saturated 0.5 g
  polyunsaturated 0.5 g
  monounsaturated 0.5 g
sodium 268 mg

dietary exchange
1 starch
2 vegetable
1 very lean meat

Mexican Breakfast Pizzas

8 ounces fresh button mushrooms, sliced

1 medium green bell pepper, chopped

1 medium onion, chopped

Egg substitute equivalent to 3 eggs

¼ cup fat-free milk

½ cup no-salt-added tomato sauce

½ teaspoon ground cumin

¼ teaspoon crushed red pepper flakes

4 6-inch corn tortillas

¼ cup fat-free or light sour cream

1 tablespoon chopped fresh cilantro

Prepare the egg and vegetable mixture as directed above. Spoon the mixture onto the tortillas. Stir together the tomato sauce, cumin, and red pepper flakes. Spoon over the tortillas. Top each with sour cream and cilantro.

Mexican pizza

calories 127
protein 9 g
carbohydrates 21 g
 fiber 3 g
 sugars 9 g
cholesterol 3 mg
total fat 1.0 g
 saturated 0.0 g
 polyunsaturated 0.5 g
 monounsaturated 0.0 g
sodium 152 mg

dietary exchange
½ starch
2 vegetable
1 very lean meat

desserts

Angel Food Truffle Torte with Fruit Sauce

Angel Food Layers with Chocolate Custard and Kiwifruit

Lemon Roll with Blueberries

Chocolate Cherry Bundt Cake

Black Devil's Food Cake

Wacky Cake

Pineapple Paradise Cake

Nutmeg Cake

Easy Apple Cake

Carrot Cake

Double-Berry Snack Cake

Rum-Lime Pudding Cake

Peach Clafouti

Pumpkin Spice Cupcakes with Nutmeg Cream Topping

Spice Cupcakes with Vanilla Topping and Pineapple

Confectioners' Glaze

Seven-Minute Frosting

Key Lime Cheesecake

Chocolate Swirl Cheesecake

Pumpkin Pie

Frozen Mocha Yogurt Pie

Chocolate-Berry Pie

Crustless Apple Pie

Apple Raisin Crunch

Cherry Crisp

Deep-Dish Fruit Crisp

Peach-Cranberry Cobbler

Cherry-Filled Phyllo Rollovers

Oat Crumb Piecrust

Gingersnap and Graham Cracker Crust

Chocolate Oatmeal Cookies

Chewy Chocolate Chip Cookies

Ginger Cookies

Peanut Butter Cookies

Bourbon Balls

Sugar Cookies

Fudgy Buttermilk Brownies

Butterscotch Brownies

Apricot Raisin Bars

Raspberry Crumbles

Oatmeal Carrot Bar Cookies

Wafer Wedges

Sherry Thins

Apricot-Almond Biscotti

Cannoli Cream with Strawberries and Chocolate

Chocolate Crème Brûlée

Honey Almond Custards

Delicious Rice Pudding

Guiltless Banana Pudding

Vanilla Bread Pudding with Peaches

Cinnamon-Apple Dessert Tamales with Kahlúa Custard Sauce

Fruit with Vanilla Cream

Berries in Vanilla Sauce

Sweet and Fruity Salsa Bowl

Grapefruit Orange Palette

Claret-Spiced Oranges

Baked Ginger Pears

Golden Poached Pears

Fall Fruit Medley

Frozen Raspberry Cream

Spiced Skillet Bananas with Frozen Yogurt

Frozen Mini Key Lime Soufflés

Strawberries with Champagne Ice

Strawberry-Raspberry Ice

Strawberry-Banana Sorbet with Star Fruit

Tropical Breeze

Sunny Mango Sorbet

Tequila Lime Sherbet

Cardinal Sundae

Kiwifruit Sundaes

Angel Food Truffle Torte
with Fruit Sauce

Serves 12

Chocolate truffles are traditionally made with melted chocolate and cream. Our heart-healthy dessert incorporates layers of low-fat chocolate truffle filling between light layers of angel food cake. The cake nestles on a pool of marshmallow creme, strawberries, and passion fruit. Feel free to experiment with seasonal fruit for the sauce.

9-inch angel food cake

Filling
- 1/2 cup chocolate chips
- 8 ounces fat-free or light cream cheese, softened
- 1/4 cup sifted confectioners' sugar
- 2 tablespoons unsweetened cocoa powder (Dutch process preferred)
- 1 teaspoon vanilla extract

Sauce
- 2 ripe passion fruit (about 1 1/2 ounces each), 1/4 cup passion fruit nectar, or 1/4 cup passion fruit juice blend
- 1 cup marshmallow creme (4 ounces)
- 1 cup fresh strawberries

With a long, serrated knife, cut the cake horizontally into 4 equal layers.

In a small, heavy saucepan, heat the chocolate chips over low heat for 1 to 2 minutes, or until melted, stirring constantly. Using a rubber scraper, scrape the chocolate into a medium mixing bowl.

Stir the remaining filling ingredients into the chocolate. Beat with an electric mixer on medium-high speed for 2 minutes, or until smooth.

Place a layer of cake on a plate. Spread one third of the chocolate mixture over the layer. Repeat with the remaining cake and filling. Cover with plastic wrap and refrigerate for 30 minutes to four days.

Halve the passion fruit and scoop out the pulp with a spoon. Press the pulp through a fine sieve to remove the seeds; discard the seeds.

calories 174
protein 5 g
carbohydrates 33 g
  fiber 2 g
  sugars 26 g
cholesterol 3 mg
total fat 2.5 g
  saturated 1.5 g
  polyunsaturated 0.0 g
  monounsaturated 1.0 g
sodium 314 mg

dietary exchange
2 other carbohydrate
1/2 fat

In a food processor or blender, process the pulp, nectar, or juice; marshmallow creme; and strawberries until smooth (except the seeds).

To serve, spoon 2 to 3 tablespoons sauce onto a dessert plate. Swirl to coat the plate. Cut the cake into 12 slices. Place one slice on the prepared plate. Repeat with the remaining sauce and cake.

Cook's Tip on Passion Fruit

Passion fruit is available from spring to the beginning of fall. Ripe passion fruit is soft, heavy, and wrinkled. Unripe passion fruit has a much smoother appearance. The fruit will ripen in three to five days on the counter or in a paper bag.

Angel Food Layers with Chocolate Custard and Kiwifruit

Serves 6

Dark chocolate custard and jade-green kiwifruit nestle between layers of angel food cake in this decadent dessert.

Chocolate Custard

1 cup fat-free milk

1/2 cup sugar

Egg substitute equivalent to 1 egg, or 1 large egg

2 tablespoons unsweetened cocoa powder (Dutch process preferred)

2 tablespoons cornstarch

1 tablespoon all-purpose flour

1/2 teaspoon vanilla extract

❖

1/2 9-inch angel food cake

6 green kiwifruit, peeled and thinly sliced

3/4 cup strawberry glaze

1/2 cup frozen fat-free or low-fat whipped topping, thawed

In the top of a double boiler, whisk together all the custard ingredients except the vanilla. Set over a small amount of simmering water. Cook for 3 to 4 minutes, whisking occasionally until the mixture starts to thicken. Whisk constantly for about 1 minute, or until the custard is thick and smooth.

Stir in the vanilla. Cook for 1 minute, whisking occasionally. Remove the top of the double boiler and let the custard cool for 10 to 15 minutes. Place plastic wrap directly on the custard and refrigerate for up to four days.

To assemble, cut the cake into 6 slices; cut each slice in half crosswise. Put 1 piece of cake on a dessert plate. Arrange 3 slices of kiwifruit on the cake. Spread about 1/4 cup custard over the kiwifruit. Cover with another piece of cake. Spread 1/4 cup custard over the cake. Top with 3 or 4 slices of kiwifruit. Drizzle with about 2 tablespoons strawberry glaze. Top with 1 tablespoon whipped topping. Repeat with the remaining ingredients.

calories 276
protein 5 g
carbohydrates 62 g
 fiber 3 g
 sugars 50 g
cholesterol 1 mg
total fat 1.0 g
 saturated 0.0 g
 polyunsaturated 0.5 g
 monounsaturated 0.0 g
sodium 292 mg

dietary exchange
4 other carbohydrate

Lemon Roll
with Blueberries

Serves 16

Use angel food cake mix to create a sinfully delicious dessert? You bet! You won't believe this dessert until you try it.

22-ounce can lemon pie filling	2 cups fat-free or low-fat frozen whipped topping, thawed
16-ounce package angel food cake mix	1/4 teaspoon grated lemon zest
1 tablespoon confectioners' sugar	12 ounces fresh blueberries (1 1/2 cups)

Preheat the oven to 350°F. Line a 10 × 15-inch jelly-roll pan with wax paper.

In a large mixing bowl, stir together the pie filling and cake mix. Beat on medium for 5 to 7 minutes. Spoon into the pan. Using a rubber scraper, smooth the mixture. Bake for 25 to 30 minutes, or until a cake tester or toothpick inserted in the center comes out clean.

Sprinkle a dish towel with confectioners' sugar. Invert the cake onto the towel. Peel away and discard the wax paper. Neatly trim the edges of the cake roll. Starting from a short end, roll up the cake in the dish towel. Let cool on a cooling rack for 2 hours.

In a small bowl, stir together the whipped topping and lemon zest.

Unroll the cake and remove the dish towel. Spread the whipped topping over the cake; reroll. Freeze for about 2 hours, or until the whipped topping is firm.

To serve, cut into 16 slices. Sprinkle with the blueberries.

calories 189
protein 2 g
carbohydrates 42 g
  fiber 1 g
  sugars 30 g
cholesterol 0 mg
total fat 0.5 g
  saturated 0.0 g
  polyunsaturated 0.0 g
  monounsaturated 0.0 g
sodium 304 mg

dietary exchange
3 other carbohydrate

Chocolate Cherry Bundt Cake

Serves 12

A double dose of cherry, orange, and almond enhances chocolate cake.

Cake

1/2 cup dried cherries

1 tablespoon orange liqueur or fresh orange juice

18.25-ounce box chocolate cake mix

Egg substitute equivalent to 3 eggs, or 3 large eggs

1/4 cup unsweetened applesauce

1/4 cup fat-free or light sour cream

1 teaspoon grated orange zest

1/2 teaspoon almond extract

❖

1 cup confectioners' sugar, sifted

2 tablespoons unsweetened cocoa powder, sifted

1/4 cup maraschino cherry juice

1/4 cup sliced almonds, dry-roasted

In a small bowl, stir together the cherries and orange liqueur. Let stand, covered, for 10 minutes, or until the cherries absorb some of the liquid and become plump.

Preheat the oven to 350°F.

Prepare the cake using the package directions for a 12-cup Bundt cake, substituting the egg substitute for the whole eggs and the applesauce and sour cream for the oil. (If your cake mix lists different amounts for oil, whole eggs, or water, use those amounts.) Stir in the orange zest, almond extract, and soaked cherries with liquid. Bake using the package directions. Invert the baked cake on a cooling rack. Let cool for at least 15 minutes.

Meanwhile, in a small bowl, whisk together the confectioners' sugar and cocoa powder. Whisk in the cherry juice until smooth.

To serve, cut the cake into 12 slices. Drizzle with the sauce and sprinkle with the almonds.

Cook's Tip on Maraschino Cherry Juice

You can sometimes find bottled maraschino cherry juice with the canned fruit in the grocery. As an alternative, use the liquid that is in jars of maraschino cherries.

calories 282
protein 5 g
carbohydrates 55 g
 fiber 2 g
 sugars 35 g
cholesterol 1 mg
total fat 5.0 g
 saturated 1.5 g
 polyunsaturated 0.5 g
 monounsaturated 0.5 g
sodium 310 mg

dietary exchange
3 1/2 other carbohydrate
1 fat

Black Devil's Food Cake

Serves 20

When the chocolate urge hits, try this rich, moist cake, which goes together as quickly as it disappears! Frost it with Seven-Minute Frosting (page 576), dress it up with a dusting of confectioners' sugar, or enjoy it without any topping at all.

Vegetable oil spray
Flour for dusting pan
2 cups all-purpose flour
1³/₄ cups sugar
¹/₂ cup unsweetened cocoa powder
1 tablespoon baking soda

²/₃ cup unsweetened applesauce
1 cup fat-free or low-fat buttermilk
2 tablespoons acceptable vegetable oil
1 cup strong coffee

Preheat the oven to 350°F. Lightly spray a 13 × 9 × 2-inch pan with vegetable oil spray. Dust with flour; shake off the excess.

In a large mixing bowl, sift together 2 cups flour, sugar, cocoa powder, and baking soda.

Whisk in the remaining ingredients except the coffee.

In a small saucepan, bring the coffee to a boil over medium-high heat. Stir gently into the batter; the mixture will be soupy. Pour into the pan.

Bake for 35 to 40 minutes, or until a cake tester or toothpick inserted in the center comes out clean. Serve warm or let cool completely.

calories 143
protein 2 g
carbohydrates 30 g
 fiber 1 g
 sugars 19 g
cholesterol 1 mg
total fat 2.0 g
 saturated 0.5 g
 polyunsaturated 0.5 g
 monounsaturated 1.0 g
sodium 203 mg

dietary exchange
2 other carbohydrate
¹/₂ fat

Wacky Cake

Serves 9

Children love to make this cake—and the cleanup is so easy.

Vegetable oil spray
1¹⁄₂ cups all-purpose flour
1 cup sugar
¹⁄₄ cup unsweetened cocoa powder
1 teaspoon baking soda
1 teaspoon vanilla extract

1 teaspoon cider vinegar
2 tablespoons light stick margarine, melted
¹⁄₄ cup unsweetened applesauce
1 cup water

Preheat the oven to 350°F. Lightly spray an 8-inch square cake pan with vegetable oil spray.

Put the flour, sugar, cocoa powder, and baking soda in a sifter. Sift into the cake pan.

Make three wells in the flour mixture. Pour the vanilla into the first well, the vinegar into the second, and the margarine into the third.

Put the applesauce in a small bowl. Gradually stir in the water. Pour over the batter. Using a fork, stir together until entirely moist.

Bake for 30 minutes, or until a cake tester or toothpick inserted in the center comes out clean.

calories 187
protein 3 g
carbohydrates 41 g
  fiber 1 g
  sugars 23 g
cholesterol 0 mg
total fat 1.5 g
  saturated 0.5 g
  polyunsaturated 0.5 g
  monounsaturated 0.5 g
sodium 158 mg

dietary exchange
2¹⁄₂ other carbohydrate
¹⁄₂ fat

Pineapple Paradise Cake

Serves 12

Be prepared for oohhs *and* aahhs *when you present this taste of paradise!*

18.25-ounce box yellow cake mix
2 tablespoons unsweetened
  applesauce
Egg substitute equivalent to 3 eggs
1 teaspoon coconut extract
1/4 teaspoon ground nutmeg
  20-ounce can crushed pineapple in
  its own juice, undrained

2 tablespoons light brown sugar
2 tablespoons shredded sweetened
  coconut
2 tablespoons sliced almonds
1/4 cup unsifted confectioners' sugar
2 tablespoons rum or 1/2 teaspoon
  rum extract
2 medium mangoes, thinly sliced

Prepare the cake using the package directions, substituting applesauce for the oil and egg substitute for the whole eggs. (If your package lists different amounts for oil or eggs, use those amounts.) Add the coconut extract and nutmeg before mixing the batter. Spread the batter in two 8-inch round cake pans.

Drain the pineapple, reserving 1/2 cup juice. Place the pineapple on the cake batter. Sprinkle with the brown sugar.

Bake the cakes using the package directions, or until a cake tester or toothpick inserted in the center comes out clean. Cool according to the package directions.

If necessary, adjust the oven temperature to 350°F. Place the coconut and almonds in separate, even layers on a nonstick baking sheet.

Bake for 5 to 6 minutes, or until light golden brown. Put the baking sheet on a cooling rack.

In a small bowl, whisk together the reserved 1/2 cup pineapple juice, confectioners' sugar, and rum (the sugar may be slightly lumpy). Using a wooden skewer, cake tester, or toothpick, make 8 to 10 holes in the cooled cakes. Pour half the pineapple juice mixture over each cake to soak.

To assemble, place one cake layer on a platter. Arrange half the mango slices on the cake. Top with the second cake layer. Arrange the remaining mango in a decorative pattern. Sprinkle with the coconut and almonds.

calories 274
protein 4 g
carbohydrates 53 g
  fiber 2 g
  sugars 35 g
cholesterol 0 mg
total fat 5.0 g
  saturated 2.0 g
  polyunsaturated 1.0 g
  monounsaturated 1.5 g
sodium 310 mg

dietary exchange
2 1/2 starch
1 fruit
1/2 fat

Nutmeg Cake

Serves 16

The tempting aroma of nutmeg will fill the air as this cake bakes. The topping provides a satisfying crunchiness.

Vegetable oil spray
Flour for dusting baking pan

Cake

2 cups all-purpose flour
1 teaspoon baking powder
1 teaspoon baking soda
1 teaspoon ground nutmeg
1 cup sugar
1/2 cup unsweetened applesauce
Egg substitute equivalent to 2 eggs, or 2 large eggs
1 tablespoon acceptable vegetable oil
1 teaspoon butter flavoring

1 cup fat-free or low-fat buttermilk, at room temperature
1/2 teaspoon vanilla extract

Topping

2/3 cup uncooked quick-cooking oatmeal
1/3 cup firmly packed dark brown sugar
2 tablespoons finely chopped pecans, dry-roasted
1/2 teaspoon ground nutmeg
2 tablespoons light stick margarine, melted
3 tablespoons (about) fat-free milk

Preheat the oven to 350°F. Lightly spray a 13 × 9 × 2-inch baking pan with vegetable oil spray. Dust the pan with flour; shake off the excess. Set aside.

In a medium bowl, sift together 2 cups flour, baking powder, baking soda, and 1 teaspoon nutmeg.

In a large mixing bowl, beat the sugar, applesauce, egg substitute, oil, and butter flavoring until smooth.

Gradually add the flour mixture and the buttermilk alternately, beginning and ending with the flour; beat after each addition. Stir in the vanilla. Pour into the pan.

Bake for 30 to 35 minutes, or until a cake tester or toothpick inserted in the center comes out clean.

Meanwhile, in a small bowl, stir together the oatmeal, brown sugar, pecans, and nutmeg. Add the margarine.

Slowly add the milk, stirring constantly, until the mixture is spreading consistency (some milk may remain). Spread on the hot cake. Serve warm.

calories 172
protein 4 g
carbohydrates 33 g
 fiber 1 g
 sugars 19 g
cholesterol 1 mg
total fat 3.0 g
 saturated 0.5 g
 polyunsaturated 1.0 g
 monounsaturated 1.0 g
sodium 154 mg

dietary exchange
2 other carbohydrate
1/2 fat

Easy Apple Cake

Serves 9

Double your pleasure with apples two ways in this moist cake. Serve it with Orange Sauce (page 507) if desired.

Vegetable oil spray
2 cups diced apples (peeled or unpeeled)
$^3/_4$ cup sugar
$1^1/_2$ cups unsifted all-purpose flour
$^1/_2$ cup raisins
$^1/_2$ tablespoon pumpkin pie spice or apple pie spice

1 teaspoon baking powder
1 teaspoon baking soda
$^1/_4$ teaspoon salt
$^1/_3$ cup unsweetened applesauce
Egg substitute equivalent to 1 egg, or 1 large egg
1 tablespoon acceptable vegetable oil
1 teaspoon vanilla extract

Preheat the oven to 350°F. Lightly spray an 8-inch square cake pan with vegetable oil spray.

In a large bowl, stir together the apples and sugar. Set aside for about 10 minutes.

Meanwhile, in a medium bowl, stir together the flour, raisins, pumpkin pie spice, baking powder, baking soda, and salt.

Stir the remaining ingredients into the apple mixture. Gradually stir the flour mixture into the apple mixture; stir again. Spread the batter in the cake pan.

Bake for 35 to 40 minutes, or until a cake tester or toothpick inserted in the center comes out clean.

Cook's Tip on Pumpkin or Apple Pie Spice

If you can't find this mixture in the spice section or just prefer to make your own, start with four parts ground cinnamon, two parts each ground nutmeg and ground cloves, and one part each ground allspice and ground cardamom. Adjust the amounts to suit your taste.

calories 208
protein 3 g
carbohydrates 46 g
 fiber 2 g
 sugars 27 g
cholesterol 0 mg
total fat 2.0 g
 saturated 0.0 g
 polyunsaturated 0.5 g
 monounsaturated 1.0 g
sodium 275 mg

dietary exchange
3 other carbohydrate
$^1/_2$ fat

Carrot Cake

Serves 12

Enjoy a piece of this cake with hot tea for a lunchtime treat.

Vegetable oil spray
Egg substitute equivalent to 2 eggs, or 2 large eggs, beaten
1/2 cup sugar
1/2 cup unsweetened applesauce
1/2 cup fat-free or light plain yogurt
1/4 cup firmly packed light brown sugar

1 tablespoon acceptable vegetable oil
2 cups all-purpose flour
1 1/2 cups grated carrots
1/2 cup raisins (optional)
1/4 cup chopped walnuts, dry-roasted
1/2 tablespoon ground cinnamon
1 teaspoon baking soda

calories 174
protein 4 g
carbohydrates 33 g
 fiber 1 g
 sugars 16 g
cholesterol 0 mg
total fat 3.0 g
 saturated 0.5 g
 polyunsaturated 1.5 g
 monounsaturated 1.0 g
sodium 141 mg

dietary exchange
2 other carbohydrate
1/2 fat

with raisins

calories 194
protein 5 g
carbohydrates 38 g
 fiber 2 g
 sugars 20 g
cholesterol 0 mg
total fat 3.0 g
 saturated 0.5 g
 polyunsaturated 1.5 g
 monounsaturated 1.0 g
sodium 142 mg

dietary exchange
1/2 fruit
2 other carbohydrate
1/2 fat

Preheat the oven to 350°F. Lightly spray an 8-inch square cake pan with vegetable oil spray.

In a large bowl, whisk together the egg substitute, sugar, applesauce, yogurt, brown sugar, and oil.

In another large bowl, whisk together the remaining ingredients. Add to the liquid mixture and whisk until just combined. Don't overmix. Pour the batter into the cake pan.

Bake for 30 to 35 minutes, or until a cake tester or tooth-pick inserted in the center comes out clean.

Double-Berry
Snack Cake

Serves 12

Combine the berries from packaged blueberry muffin mix with frozen raspberries for a great glaze.

17.5-ounce package fat-free
blueberry muffin mix
1 cup water
Whites of 2 large eggs

Berry Sauce
1¹/₂ cups frozen unsweetened
raspberries
3 tablespoons sugar
2 teaspoons cornstarch
¹/₄ teaspoon almond extract

Preheat the oven to 400°F.

In a medium bowl, stir together the muffin mix (without the berries), water, and egg whites until just blended. Pour the batter into a 9-inch square nonstick baking pan.

Bake for 16 minutes, or until a cake tester or toothpick inserted in the center comes out clean. Put the pan on a cooling rack to cool slightly.

Meanwhile, in a small saucepan, stir together the reserved blueberries and their liquid, raspberries, sugar, and cornstarch until the cornstarch is completely dissolved. Bring to a boil over medium-high heat, stirring frequently. Cook for 1 minute, or until thickened slightly, stirring frequently. Remove from the heat. Let cool for about 10 minutes. Stir in the almond extract.

To serve, spoon the sauce over the cake. Cut into 12 squares.

Cook's Tip

Wrap any leftovers individually and freeze. Then you can thaw as many as you need whenever you want.

calories 146
protein 3 g
carbohydrates 34 g
  fiber 3 g
  sugars 18 g
cholesterol 0 mg
total fat 0.0 g
  saturated 0.0 g
  polyunsaturated 0.0 g
  monounsaturated 0.0 g
sodium 295 mg

dietary exchange
2¹/₂ starch

Rum-Lime Pudding Cake

Serves 9

Serve this dessert with glasses of pineapple-orange juice, decorated with paper umbrellas and slices of lime, to play up the feeling of being in the Caribbean.

Vegetable oil spray

$1/4$ cup plus 2 tablespoons egg substitute (3 ounces total)

$1^1/2$ cups fat-free milk

$2/3$ cup sugar

$1/4$ cup all-purpose flour

1 tablespoon grated lime zest

$1/3$ cup fresh lime juice

2 tablespoons acceptable stick margarine, melted and cooled

1 teaspoon rum extract

$1/8$ teaspoon salt

3 large egg whites

1 tablespoon sugar

Preheat the oven to 350°F. Lightly spray an 8-inch square baking pan with vegetable oil spray.

In a food processor or blender, process the egg substitute, milk, sugar, flour, lime zest, lime juice, margarine, rum extract, and salt until smooth. Pour into a large bowl.

In a medium bowl, beat the egg whites until soft peaks form. Add the 1 tablespoon sugar and beat until the whites are stiff. Stir about one third of the whites into the batter. Fold in the remaining whites. Pour the batter into the baking pan. Set the baking pan in a larger pan. Pour hot water to a depth of 2 inches in the larger pan.

Bake for 35 to 40 minutes, or until the center is set (doesn't jiggle when the pan is gently shaken). Serve warm, or cover and refrigerate to serve chilled.

calories 127
protein 4 g
carbohydrates 22 g
  fiber 0 g
  sugars 18 g
cholesterol 1 mg
total fat 2.5 g
  saturated 0.5 g
  polyunsaturated 0.5 g
  monounsaturated 1.5 g
sodium 123 mg

dietary exchange
$1^1/2$ other carbohydrate
$1/2$ fat

Peach Clafouti

Serves 8

A clafouti usually consists of a layer of batter topped with fresh fruit. Here, we've sandwiched the fruit between two layers of batter instead—a double treat.

Vegetable oil spray
1¼ cups fat-free milk
1 cup all-purpose flour
Egg substitute equivalent to 3 eggs
¼ cup firmly packed light brown sugar
1 tablespoon vanilla extract
1 teaspoon almond extract
½ teaspoon ground cinnamon

¼ teaspoon ground nutmeg or mace
¼ teaspoon salt
1½ pounds fresh peaches, peeled and sliced (about 3½ cups)

Topping
½ tablespoon sugar
¼ teaspoon ground cinnamon
3 tablespoons almonds or pine nuts, dry-roasted

Preheat the oven to 350°F. Lightly spray a 9-inch square baking pan with vegetable oil spray.

In a food processor or blender, process the milk, flour, egg substitute, brown sugar, vanilla, almond extract, ½ teaspoon cinnamon, nutmeg, and salt until smooth. Pour about ¼ cup batter into the baking pan.

Bake for 5 to 10 minutes, or until set (doesn't jiggle when gently shaken).

Arrange the peaches on the cooked batter. Pour the remaining batter on top.

Bake for 20 minutes.

Meanwhile, in a small bowl, stir together the sugar and ¼ teaspoon cinnamon. Sprinkle the almonds over the clafouti. Sprinkle the sugar mixture on top.

Bake for 40 minutes, or until the center is set (doesn't jiggle when the pan is gently shaken). Serve warm.

calories 164
protein 6 g
carbohydrates 31 g
  fiber 2 g
  sugars 17 g
cholesterol 1 mg
total fat 1.5 g
  saturated 0.0 g
  polyunsaturated 0.5 g
  monounsaturated 1.0 g
sodium 143 mg

dietary exchange
1 starch
½ fruit
½ other carbohydrate

Pumpkin Spice Cupcakes with Nutmeg Cream Topping

Serves 24

Doubly moist, these tasty cupcakes abound with the flavors of autumn.

Cupcakes
18.25-ounce box spice cake mix
1 cup canned pumpkin (not pumpkin pie filling)
1 cup unsweetened apple juice
Egg substitute equivalent to 2 eggs, or 2 large eggs
Whites of 2 large eggs
1 teaspoon vanilla, butter, and nut flavoring or vanilla extract

Nutmeg Cream Topping
8 ounces frozen fat-free or low-fat whipped topping, thawed
2 teaspoons ground nutmeg

Preheat the oven to 350°F.

In a large mixing bowl, stir together the cupcake ingredients. Using an electric mixer, beat on low for 30 seconds, scraping the side with a rubber scraper. Increase the speed to medium and beat for 2 minutes, scraping the side. Spoon into two 12-cup nonstick muffin pans.

Bake for 20 minutes, or until a cake tester or toothpick inserted in the center of the muffins comes out clean. Let cool on cooling racks for 15 minutes. Remove the cupcakes from the muffin pans and let cool completely.

Meanwhile, put the whipped topping in a medium bowl. Using a rubber scraper, gently fold the nutmeg into the whipped topping. Cover and refrigerate until ready to use.

When the cupcakes are completely cool, frost with the chilled topping.

Variation
Substitute a mixture of 2 teaspoons sugar and ¹/₂ teaspoon ground cinnamon for the Nutmeg Cream Topping. Sprinkle on the cupcakes.

calories 121
protein 2 g
carbohydrates 21 g
 fiber 1 g
 sugars 12 g
cholesterol 6 mg
total fat 2.5 g
 saturated 1.0 g
 polyunsaturated 0.0 g
 monounsaturated 1.0 g
sodium 186 mg

dietary exchange
1¹/₂ other carbohydrate
¹/₂ fat

Banana Spice Cupcakes

Substitute 1 cup very ripe, well-mashed bananas for the pumpkin. Bake as directed above or make a sheet cake and bake at 325°F in a 13 × 9 × 2-inch nonstick baking pan for 45 minutes, or until a cake tester or toothpick inserted in the center comes out clean. Cool completely and top with Nutmeg Cream Topping or cinnamon sugar (see Variation). Cut into 24 squares.

Cook's Tip

You can make the cupcakes up to 24 hours in advance. Put them in an airtight container or cover with plastic wrap and refrigerate or keep at room temperature. You can also make the topping up to 24 hours in advance. Refrigerate it separately. Frost the cupcakes up to 8 hours in advance; cover and refrigerate.

pumpkin spice with cinnamon sugar	banana spice cupcakes	banana spice with cinnamon sugar
calories 106	calories 126	calories 111
protein 2 g	protein 2 g	protein 2 g
carbohydrates 19 g	carbohydrates 23 g	carbohydrates 20 g
fiber 1 g	fiber 0 g	fiber 0 g
sugars 11 g	sugars 14 g	sugars 13 g
cholesterol 6 mg	cholesterol 6 mg	cholesterol 6 mg
total fat 2.5 g	total fat 2.5 g	total fat 2.5 g
saturated 1.0 g	saturated 1.0 g	saturated 1.0 g
polyunsaturated 0.0 g	polyunsaturated 0.0 g	polyunsaturated 0.0 g
monounsaturated 1.0 g	monounsaturated 1.0 g	monounsaturated 1.0 g
sodium 180 mg	sodium 185 mg	sodium 180 mg
dietary exchange	dietary exchange	dietary exchange
1 other carbohydrate	1½ other carbohydrate	1½ other carbohydrate
½ fat	½ fat	½ fat

Spice Cupcakes with Vanilla Topping and Pineapple

Serves 24

These moist, piled-high treats will bring you all the compliments you'll ever want. You'll make them over and over again.

18.25-ounce box spice cake mix
1¹/₃ cups water
Whites of 6 large eggs
³/₄ cup mashed ripe banana

Topping
1 cup fat-free or light vanilla yogurt
2 tablespoons confectioners' sugar

¹/₂ teaspoon vanilla extract
2 cups frozen fat-free or light whipped topping, thawed
❖
8-ounce can crushed pineapple in its own juice, drained

Preheat the oven to 325°F.

In a medium mixing bowl, stir together the cake mix, water, egg whites, and banana. Using an electric mixer, beat on low for 1 minute, or until moistened. Increase the speed to medium. Beat for 2 minutes. Spoon into two 12-cup nonstick muffin pans.

Bake for 18 minutes, or until a cake tester or toothpick inserted in the center comes out clean. Let cool on cooling racks for 15 minutes. Remove the cupcakes from the pans and let cool completely.

Meanwhile, using a rubber scraper, fold together the yogurt, confectioners' sugar, and vanilla in a medium bowl. Fold in the whipped topping. Cover with plastic wrap and refrigerate until needed.

To assemble, spoon 2 tablespoons whipped topping mixture over each cupcake. Spoon the pineapple on top.

Cook's Tip

You can top the cupcakes with the whipped topping mixture and pineapple, cover with plastic wrap, and refrigerate for up to 48 hours. Or refrigerate the cupcakes, topping, and pineapple in separate containers for up to four days and assemble when needed.

calories 129
protein 3 g
carbohydrates 23 g
 fiber 0 g
 sugars 15 g
cholesterol 6 mg
total fat 2.5 g
 saturated 1.0 g
 polyunsaturated 0.0 g
 monounsaturated 1.0 g
sodium 190 mg

dietary exchange
1¹/₂ other carbohydrate
¹/₂ fat

Confectioners' Glaze

Serves 16; 1 tablespoon per serving

Use this versatile glaze to frost and decorate cupcakes, cakes, or cookies. You can even drizzle it on graham crackers or toast.

1 cup confectioners' sugar, sifted	$1/4$ cup fat-free milk
$1/2$ teaspoon vanilla or rum extract	

In a small bowl, whisk together the confectioners' sugar and vanilla.

Gradually pour in the milk, whisking after each addition, until the desired consistency.

Lemon or Orange Confectioners' Glaze
Replace the milk with fresh lemon or orange juice.

Chocolate Confectioners' Glaze
Add 2 tablespoons unsweetened cocoa powder to the confectioners' sugar and proceed as directed.

	lemon or orange confectioners' glaze	chocolate confectioners' glaze
calories 31	calories 31	calories 34
protein 0 g	protein 0 g	protein 0 g
carbohydrates 8 g	carbohydrates 8 g	carbohydrates 8 g
fiber 0 g	fiber 0 g	fiber 0 g
sugars 7 g	sugars 7 g	sugars 7 g
cholesterol 0 mg	cholesterol 0 mg	cholesterol 0 mg
total fat 0.0 g	total fat 0.0 g	total fat 0.0 g
saturated 0.0 g	saturated 0.0 g	saturated 0.0 g
polyunsaturated 0.0 g	polyunsaturated 0.0 g	polyunsaturated 0.0 g
monounsaturated 0.0 g	monounsaturated 0.0 g	monounsaturated 0.0 g
sodium 2 mg	sodium 0 mg	sodium 2 mg
dietary exchange	dietary exchange	dietary exchange
$1/2$ other carbohydrate	$1/2$ other carbohydrate	$1/2$ other carbohydrate

Seven-Minute Frosting

Makes enough to frost a two-layer cake (12 servings)

Fluffy and rich tasting, this long-time favorite is especially impressive on devil's food cake.

1 1/2 cups sugar
1/3 cup water
    Whites of 2 large eggs

1/4 teaspoon cream of tartar
    or 1 tablespoon light corn syrup
1 teaspoon vanilla, rum, or sherry extract

calories 101
protein 1 g
carbohydrates 25 g
  fiber 0 g
  sugars 24 g
cholesterol 0 mg
total fat 0.0 g
  saturated 0.0 g
  polyunsaturated 0.0 g
  monounsaturated 0.0 g
sodium 10 mg

dietary exchange
1 1/2 other carbohydrate

In the top of a double boiler, stir together all the ingredients except the vanilla. With an electric mixer, beat on high for 1 minute. Put the top of the double boiler over a small amount of simmering water (don't let the water touch the top of the double boiler) and beat on high for 7 minutes, or until stiff peaks form. Remove the top of the double boiler from the heat.

Add the vanilla. Beat on high for 2 minutes, or until spreading consistency. Spread on a completely cooled cake.

Lemon-Flavored Seven-Minute Frosting
Substitute 1 tablespoon fresh lemon juice for the vanilla extract. Add 1/4 teaspoon grated lemon zest during the last minute of beating.

Seven-Minute Frosting with Fruit
Add 1 cup drained canned fruit, such as crushed pineapple, fruit cocktail, or mandarin oranges, to the cooked frosting, or substitute fruit flavoring, such as orange extract, for the vanilla extract.

seven-minute frosting with fruit

calories 112
protein 1 g
carbohydrates 28 g
  fiber 0 g
  sugars 27 g
cholesterol 0 mg
total fat 0.0 g
  saturated 0.0 g
  polyunsaturated 0.0 g
  monounsaturated 0.0 g
sodium 11 mg

dietary exchange
2 other carbohydrate

Key Lime Cheesecake

Serves 10

Try this light, refreshing dessert the next time Key limes are available.

4 cups fat-free or light plain yogurt without gelatin
   Vegetable oil spray
1 tablespoon light stick margarine
12 low-fat gingersnaps, finely crushed
1½ tablespoons grated lime zest
¼ cup lime juice (Key limes preferred)

1 tablespoon plus 2 teaspoons cornstarch
1 teaspoon vanilla extract
   Whites of 3 large eggs
½ cup sugar
½ cup plus 2 tablespoons fat-free or low-fat frozen whipped topping, thawed

Put a double-thick layer of fine-mesh cheesecloth or paper coffee filters in a rustproof colander. Set the colander in a bowl, leaving enough space for about 2 cups of whey (watery liquid) to drain out and not touch the colander. Pour the yogurt into the colander, cover with plastic wrap, and refrigerate for 8 to 10 hours.

After the yogurt has drained completely, preheat the oven to 375°F. Lightly spray a 9-inch springform pan with vegetable oil spray.

Melt the margarine. Put the gingersnap crumbs in a small bowl. Stir in the margarine. Press the mixture over the bottom of the pan.

Bake for 5 minutes. Let cool on a cooling rack. Reduce the oven temperature to 325°F.

In a large bowl, whisk together the drained yogurt, lime zest, lime juice, cornstarch, and vanilla.

In a medium mixing bowl, beat the egg whites until foamy. Add the sugar gradually, beating constantly until soft peaks form. Fold into the yogurt mixture. Spoon into the cooled crust.

Bake for 50 to 55 minutes, or until the center springs back when lightly pressed. Let stand until cool, about 15 minutes. Refrigerate for at least 2 hours.

To serve, cut the cheesecake into 10 wedges. Spoon whipped topping over each.

calories 130
protein 5 g
carbohydrates 24 g
  fiber 0 g
  sugars 18 g
cholesterol 1 mg
total fat 1.5 g
  saturated 0.5 g
  polyunsaturated 0.0 g
  monounsaturated 0.5 g
sodium 93 mg

dietary exchange
½ skim milk
1 other carbohydrate

Chocolate Swirl
Cheesecake

Serves 12

Swirl classic cheesecake batter with chocolate cheesecake batter, then add luscious caramel topping for good measure.

Vegetable oil spray
1/3 cup crushed chocolate graham cracker crumbs (about 9 small rectangles)
12 ounces fat-free cream cheese, softened
4 ounces light cream cheese, softened

3/4 cup sugar
Egg substitute equivalent to 3 eggs
8 ounces fat-free or light sour cream
1 teaspoon vanilla extract
1/3 cup unsweetened cocoa powder
1/4 cup fat-free caramel apple dip

Preheat the oven to 325°F. Lightly spray a 9-inch spring-form or 9-inch round cake pan with vegetable oil spray. If using the cake pan, line the bottom with cooking parchment or wax paper and lightly spray again. Sprinkle the graham cracker crumbs on the bottom of the pan. Set aside.

In a large mixing bowl, beat the cream cheeses and sugar on medium-high for 3 minutes, or until light and fluffy.

Add the egg substitute and beat on medium until mixed in.

Add the sour cream and vanilla. Beat on medium for 30 seconds, or until smooth. Remove 1 cup batter and set aside.

Stir the cocoa powder into the remaining batter. Beat on medium for 30 seconds, or until mixed in.

Pour half the chocolate batter into the pan (no need to spread over the bottom). Pour half the reserved white batter on the chocolate batter. Spoon half the caramel apple dip onto the white batter. Pour the remaining chocolate batter into the pan. Drop spoonfuls of the remaining white batter onto the chocolate batter in a cir-cular pattern. Spoon the remaining caramel apple dip on top. Gently shake the pan back and forth to distribute the

calories 173
protein 8 g
carbohydrates 26 g
  fiber 1 g
  sugars 20 g
cholesterol 15 mg
total fat 3.0 g
  saturated 1.5 g
  polyunsaturated 0.0 g
  monounsaturated 1.0 g
sodium 252 mg

dietary exchange
1½ other carbohydrate
1 lean meat

batter evenly. With a sharp knife, lightly swirl the batter to create a marbled effect. (Don't overswirl or you'll have no pattern.)

Bake for 55 minutes, or until the center is just set (doesn't jiggle when the pan is gently shaken). Put the pan on a cooling rack and let cool for 1 hour. Refrigerate for at least 3 hours. To serve, run a knife along the inside of the pan. Release the side of the springform pan or invert the cake pan onto a plate.

Cook's Tip on Slicing Cheesecake

To slice your cheesecake with ease, use a sharp knife dipped into hot water. Wipe the knife with a dish towel or paper towel after each slice; reheat the knife in hot water as needed.

Pumpkin Pie

Serves 8

Enjoy this American tradition any time of the year.

Crust

- $2/3$ cup all-purpose flour
- 3 tablespoons sugar
- 2 tablespoons light stick margarine, diced
- $1^1/2$ tablespoons fat-free milk

❖

- Vegetable oil spray
- 1 teaspoon all-purpose flour

Filling

- $2/3$ cup sugar
- $1/2$ teaspoon ground cinnamon
- $1/2$ teaspoon ground ginger
- $1/2$ teaspoon ground nutmeg
- Pinch of ground cloves
- $1^1/2$ cups canned pumpkin
- $1^1/2$ cups fat-free evaporated milk
- $1/4$ cup brandy
- Whites of 3 large eggs, slightly beaten
- 1 teaspoon vanilla extract
- $1/2$ teaspoon grated orange zest

In a food processor, process the crust ingredients until the dough begins to stick together. Form into a 4-inch disk. Cover with plastic wrap and refrigerate for 15 minutes.

Meanwhile, preheat the oven to 450°F. Lightly spray a 9-inch pie pan with vegetable oil spray.

Place a sheet of plastic wrap on a flat surface. Sprinkle with 1 teaspoon flour. Put the dough on the floured sur-face, press lightly, and turn the dough over (this allows some flour to stick to both sides). Cover with another sheet of plastic wrap. Roll into an 11-inch circle. Remove the top sheet of plastic wrap. Invert the dough into the pie pan. Remove the remaining plastic wrap. (Be careful not to stretch the dough or it will shrink when it bakes.) Trim the edges and flute with a fork or your fingers.

In a large mixing bowl, stir together the sugar, cinnamon, ginger, nutmeg, and cloves.

Add the pumpkin, milk, brandy, egg whites, vanilla, and orange zest. Beat until smooth. Pour into the pie shell.

Bake for 10 minutes. Reduce the heat to 325°F and bake for 45 minutes, or until a knife inserted in the center comes out clean.

calories 214
protein 7 g
carbohydrates 40 g
  fiber 2 g
  sugars 28 g
cholesterol 2 mg
total fat 2.0 g
  saturated 0.5 g
  polyunsaturated 0.5 g
  monounsaturated 0.5 g
sodium 99 mg

dietary exchange
$2^1/2$ other carbohydrate

Frozen Mocha Yogurt Pie

Serves 8

Kids—of every age—will have fun using chocolate syrup to decorate the dessert plates for this rich-tasting pie.

Vegetable oil spray
3/4 cup crushed chocolate graham crackers (about 5 rectangles)

Filling
2 cups fat-free or low-fat vanilla frozen yogurt, slightly softened

2 cups fat-free or low-fat coffee frozen yogurt, slightly softened
2 cups fat-free or low-fat chocolate frozen yogurt, slightly softened
1 cup fat-free chocolate syrup

Lightly spray a 9-inch pie pan with vegetable oil spray. Sprinkle with the graham cracker crumbs.

Put the vanilla yogurt on an 8-inch plate (such as a small dinner plate). Using a spoon or sturdy spatula, press down on the yogurt to cover the plate. (This will help when you put the yogurt in the pie pan.) Slip the vanilla yogurt layer into the pie pan. Using a spatula, carefully spread the yogurt over the bottom.

Repeat with the coffee yogurt, then with the chocolate yogurt. Cover with a double layer of plastic wrap and freeze for at least 2 hours.

To serve, cut the pie into 8 wedges. Drizzle 2 tablespoons chocolate syrup in a decorative pattern on a dessert plate. Place a pie wedge on the syrup. Repeat with the remaining syrup and pie.

Cook's Tip on Cutting Frozen Desserts

Dipping a sharp knife into hot water makes cutting frozen desserts easier.

calories 267
protein 6 g
carbohydrates 59 g
  fiber 0 g
  sugars 45 g
cholesterol 1 mg
total fat 1.5 g
  saturated 0.0 g
  polyunsaturated 0.0 g
  monounsaturated 0.5 g
sodium 113 mg

dietary exchange
4 other carbohydrate

Chocolate-Berry Pie

Serves 8

A delicate, crunchy meringue crust balances beautifully with a smooth chocolate layer and a topping of fresh berries.

Vegetable oil spray

Meringue Shell
Whites of 3 large eggs
1/4 teaspoon cream of tartar
2/3 cup sugar
1/4 teaspoon vanilla extract

Filling
1/3 cup unsweetened cocoa powder
2 tablespoons cornstarch
14-ounce can fat-free sweetened condensed milk
1 cup water
Egg substitute equivalent to 1 egg, or 1 large egg
1/2 teaspoon vanilla extract

❖

3/4 cup fresh raspberries or sliced fresh strawberries

Preheat the oven to 275°F. Lightly spray a 9-inch pie pan with vegetable oil spray.

In a medium mixing bowl, using an electric mixer on medium, beat the egg whites and cream of tartar until foamy.

Gradually add the sugar, beating on medium-high until stiff, glossy peaks form.

Add the vanilla and beat for 1 minute.

Spread the egg white mixture in the pie pan, building it up so the side is thicker than the bottom.

Bake for 1 hour 15 minutes, or until dry and a light creamy color. Let the meringue shell cool in the pan.

In a heavy medium saucepan, stir together the cocoa powder and cornstarch.

Whisk in the milk and water. Cook over medium-high heat until the mixture comes to a boil, whisking con-

calories 244
protein 7 g
carbohydrates 53 g
  fiber 2 g
  sugars 48 g
cholesterol 3 mg
total fat 0.5 g
  saturated 0.0 g
  polyunsaturated 0.0 g
  monounsaturated 0.0 g
sodium 88 mg

dietary exchange
3 1/2 other carbohydrate

stantly (don't use an electric whisk). Reduce the heat and boil gently for about 1 minute, or until thickened, whisking constantly. Continue to cook for 2 minutes, whisking constantly.

Whisk in the egg substitute. Cook for 1 minute, whisking constantly.

Whisk in the vanilla extract.

Pour the filling into a medium bowl. Place plastic wrap directly on the surface of the filling and let cool at room temperature for 30 minutes. Pour into the cooled meringue shell.

To serve, top with the berries.

Cook's Tip on Freezing Raspberries

Rinse raspberries gently in a bowl of cold water. Drain the berries and put them on paper towels to absorb the excess water. Put the berries in a single layer on a baking sheet and freeze. Transfer the berries to an airtight container or resealable plastic freezer bag and freeze for up to one year.

Crustless Apple Pie

Serves 8

Moist and rich, this pie is also easy and tasty—it's a real winner! Serve it warm or chilled.

Vegetable oil spray
Whites of 2 large eggs, or egg
  substitute equivalent to 1 egg
3/4 cup sugar
2 tablespoons light brown sugar
1 teaspoon baking powder
1 teaspoon vanilla extract

1/2 teaspoon ground cinnamon
1/2 teaspoon grated lemon zest
1/8 teaspoon ground nutmeg
1/2 cup all-purpose flour
1 cup diced peeled apples
1/4 cup chopped walnuts, dry-roasted

Preheat the oven to 350°F. Lightly spray an 8-inch pie pan with vegetable oil spray.

In a large mixing bowl, beat the egg whites, sugars, baking powder, vanilla, cinnamon, lemon zest, and nutmeg with an electric mixer until smooth and fluffy.

Stir in the flour just to blend. Beat until smooth and well blended.

Stir in the apples. Spoon into the pie pan.

Sprinkle the nuts over the apple mixture.

Bake for 30 minutes, or until golden brown. The pie will puff up as it cooks, then collapse as it cools.

calories 153
protein 2 g
carbohydrates 31 g
  fiber 1 g
  sugars 24 g
cholesterol 0 mg
total fat 2.5 g
  saturated 0.5 g
  polyunsaturated 2.0 g
  monounsaturated 0.5 g
sodium 77 mg

dietary exchange
2 other carbohydrate
1/2 fat

Apple Raisin Crunch

Serves 6

This versatile dessert is delicious as is or with fat-free ice cream or frozen yogurt.

Vegetable oil spray

Filling
2 pounds Granny Smith apples, peeled, cored, and sliced (about 5¹/₂ cups), or 2 20-ounce cans unsweetened sliced apples
¹/₂ cup raisins
¹/₂ cup fresh orange juice
¹/₃ cup sugar

¹/₄ teaspoon ground nutmeg

Topping
¹/₄ cup firmly packed dark brown sugar
³/₄ cup uncooked quick-cooking oatmeal
¹/₂ teaspoon ground cinnamon
2 tablespoons light stick margarine, melted

Preheat the oven to 350°F.

Lightly spray an 8-inch square baking pan with vegetable oil spray. Put all the filling ingredients except the nutmeg in the baking pan. Stir together.

Sprinkle the nutmeg over the apple mixture.

In a small bowl, stir together the topping ingredients. Sprinkle over the apple mixture.

Bake for 40 minutes. Let cool slightly before serving.

calories 258
protein 2 g
carbohydrates 59 g
  fiber 4 g
  sugars 47 g
cholesterol 0 mg
total fat 3.0 g
  saturated 0.5 g
  polyunsaturated 1.0 g
  monounsaturated 0.5 g
sodium 31 mg

dietary exchange
2 fruit
2 other carbohydrate
¹/₂ fat

Cherry Crisp

Serves 9

Sprinkle a crunchy oatmeal topping over juicy red cherries for a luscious dessert.

Vegetable oil spray

Topping
- ³/₄ cup uncooked rolled oats
- ¹/₃ cup all-purpose flour
- 2 tablespoons light stick margarine
- ¹/₄ cup sugar
- ¹/₄ cup firmly packed light brown sugar

Filling
- 2 16-ounce cans pitted tart red cherries in water
- ¹/₂ cup sugar
- 3 tablespoons cornstarch
- 1 tablespoon fresh lemon juice
- ¹/₄ teaspoon ground cinnamon
- ¹/₄ teaspoon ground nutmeg

Preheat the oven to 350°F. Lightly spray an 8-inch square baking pan with vegetable oil spray.

In a medium bowl, stir together the oats and flour.

Using a fork or pastry blender, cut in the margarine until the mixture is crumbly.

Stir in the ¹/₄ cup sugar and the brown sugar.

Drain the cherries, reserving the juice. Pour the juice into a medium saucepan.

Stir the ¹/₂ cup sugar, cornstarch, lemon juice, cinnamon, and nutmeg into the cherry juice. Cook over medium-high heat for 3 to 4 minutes, or until the sauce is thick and clear, whisking occasionally.

Stir in the cherries. Pour into the baking pan.

Sprinkle the topping over the cherry mixture.

Bake for 30 minutes, or until golden brown.

calories 189
protein 2 g
carbohydrates 42 g
 fiber 2 g
 sugars 30 g
cholesterol 0 mg
total fat 2.0 g
 saturated 0.5 g
 polyunsaturated 0.5 g
 monounsaturated 0.5 g
sodium 27 mg

dietary exchange
¹/₂ starch
¹/₂ fruit
2 other carbohydrate

Cook's Tip on Canned Cherries

It's a good idea to check canned cherries carefully before using them. Occasionally a pit is accidentally left in the can.

Deep-Dish Fruit Crisp

Serves 8

Take advantage of fresh fruits in season, but remember this recipe in the winter, too. The aroma of fruit and spices can help chase away those winter blahs.

Filling

6 cups fresh or unsweetened frozen fruit (blueberries, blackberries, cherries, peaches, raspberries, apples, apricots, or any combination)

1/4 cup all-purpose flour

1/4 cup firmly packed light brown sugar

2 teaspoons grated lemon zest

Topping

1/2 cup uncooked quick-cooking oatmeal

1/4 cup all-purpose flour

1/2 cup firmly packed light brown sugar

2 tablespoons light stick margarine

1/2 teaspoon ground cinnamon

1/4 teaspoon ground nutmeg or mace

1/4 teaspoon ground allspice

Preheat the oven to 350°F.

In a 9-inch deep-dish pie pan, stir together the filling ingredients.

In a small bowl, combine the topping ingredients with a fork, cutting the margarine into the other ingredients until slightly crumbly. Sprinkle over the fruit.

Bake for 30 to 35 minutes, or until golden brown.

calories 193
protein 3 g
carbohydrates 43 g
    fiber 5 g
    sugars 30 g
cholesterol 0 mg
total fat 2.0 g
    saturated 0.5 g
    polyunsaturated 0.5 g
    monounsaturated 0.5 g
sodium 30 mg

dietary exchange
1 fruit
2 other carbohydrate
1/2 fat

Peach-Cranberry Cobbler

Serves 8

The perfect end to any meal, this cobbler is light on sugar and loaded with flavor. Use cookie cutters to cut out shapes to fit a seasonal theme or just to make the cobbler decorative.

Vegetable oil spray

Piecrust
²/₃ cup all-purpose flour
3 tablespoons sugar
2 tablespoons acceptable stick margarine, diced
1½ tablespoons fat-free milk

Filling
5 cups sliced fresh peaches (about 3 pounds) or 5 cups frozen unsweetened sliced peaches, thawed

1 cup cranberries or blueberries, thawed if frozen
³/₄ cup firmly packed light brown sugar
2½ tablespoons all-purpose flour
1 to 2 teaspoons butter-rum flavoring or rum extract

❖

1 teaspoon all-purpose flour

Lightly spray a 9-inch square baking dish with vegetable oil spray.

In a food processor, process all the piecrust ingredients until the dough begins to stick together. Form the dough into a disk about 4 inches in diameter. Cover with plastic wrap. Refrigerate for 30 minutes.

Meanwhile, in a large bowl, combine the filling ingredients, gently stirring with a rubber spatula. Pour into the baking dish.

Preheat the oven to 375°F.

Place a sheet of plastic wrap on a flat surface. Sprinkle with 1 teaspoon flour. Put the dough on the floured surface, press lightly, and turn the dough over. Cover the dough with another sheet of plastic wrap. Roll out the dough to a circle 10 inches in diameter. Remove the top sheet of plastic wrap.

calories 224
protein 2 g
carbohydrates 48 g
  fiber 3 g
  sugars 35 g
cholesterol 0 mg
total fat 3.0 g
  saturated 0.5 g
  polyunsaturated 0.5 g
  monounsaturated 1.5 g
sodium 43 mg

dietary exchange
1 starch
1 fruit
1 other carbohydrate
½ fat

Using a cookie cutter, cut out the desired shapes. Combine and reroll the remaining bits of dough until all is used, making as many cutouts as possible. Gently place the cutouts over the fruit filling. Lightly spray the cutouts with vegetable oil spray.

Bake for 40 to 50 minutes, or until the filling is bubbly and hot and the crust is lightly browned. Let cool before serving.

Cherry-Filled
Phyllo Rollovers

Serves 4

You don't need chopsticks to enjoy these flaky dessert "egg rolls."

16-ounce can pitted tart red cherries in water, drained
1/4 cup sugar
1 tablespoon cornstarch
1 teaspoon vanilla extract
1/2 teaspoon almond extract
4 sheets frozen phyllo dough, thawed

Butter-flavored vegetable oil spray
1 teaspoon acceptable stick margarine, melted
2 teaspoons sugar
1/8 teaspoon ground cinnamon
1 teaspoon acceptable stick margarine, melted

Preheat the oven to 400°F.

In a small saucepan, stir together the cherries, 1/4 cup sugar, and cornstarch until the cornstarch is dissolved. Bring to a boil over medium-high heat, then stir. Boil for 1 to 2 minutes, or until thickened, stirring occasionally.

Stir in the vanilla and almond extracts.

Keeping the unused phyllo covered with a damp dish towel, lightly spray 1 sheet of dough with the vegetable oil spray. Working quickly, fold the dough in half, bringing the short ends together. Spoon one fourth of the cherry mixture about 4 inches from one end; fold that end over the cherry mixture. Fold the sides over the cherry mixture and roll up (should resemble an egg roll). Place with the seam side down on a nonstick baking sheet. Repeat with the remaining phyllo and cherry mixture.

Brush the tops of the rollovers with 1 teaspoon melted margarine.

Bake for 15 minutes.

Meanwhile, in a small bowl or cup, stir together the 2 teaspoons sugar and the cinnamon.

Place the rollovers on a cooling rack. Brush with 1 teaspoon margarine. Sprinkle with the cinnamon sugar. Let cool for 15 minutes.

calories 184
protein 2 g
carbohydrates 37 g
  fiber 2 g
  sugars 23 g
cholesterol 0 mg
total fat 3.0 g
  saturated 0.5 g
  polyunsaturated 0.5 g
  monounsaturated 1.5 g
sodium 123 mg

dietary exchange
1/2 fruit
2 other carbohydrate
1/2 fat

Oat Crumb Piecrust

Serves 8

This crust smells so wonderful as it bakes that you'll want to eat it even before adding the filling!

Vegetable oil spray
1 cup low-fat graham cracker crumbs (about 12 squares)
1/3 cup uncooked quick-cooking oatmeal
2 tablespoons sugar

1 teaspoon grated orange zest
1/2 teaspoon ground cinnamon
1/4 to 1/2 teaspoon grated lemon zest
2 1/2 tablespoons light stick margarine, melted

Preheat the oven to 375°F. Lightly spray a 9-inch pie pan with vegetable oil spray.

In a medium bowl, stir together the remaining ingredients except the margarine.

Stir in the margarine. Put the mixture in the pie pan. Using the back of a fork, press the mixture on the bottom and up the side of the pan to form a shell.

Bake for 8 to 10 minutes, or until lightly toasted. Let cool before filling.

calories 82
protein 1 g
carbohydrates 14 g
  fiber 1 g
  sugars 6 g
cholesterol 0 mg
total fat 2.5 g
  saturated 0.5 g
  polyunsaturated 0.5 g
  monounsaturated 0.5 g
sodium 68 mg

dietary exchange
1 starch
1/2 fat

Gingersnap and
Graham Cracker Crust

Serves 8

The flavorful pairing of gingersnaps and graham crackers makes this crust almost a dessert in itself. The corn syrup and apple juice bind the dough and make it easy to shape the piecrust.

³/₄ cup crushed low-fat graham crackers (about 9 squares)

³/₄ cup crushed low-fat gingersnaps (about 18 cookies)

2 tablespoons corn syrup

2 tablespoons unsweetened apple juice

In a medium bowl, stir together all the ingredients. Using your fingers, press the mixture evenly in a 9-inch pie pan.

The crust is ready to fill and bake. If you need a prebaked crust, bake it at 350°F for 10 minutes, then cool and fill.

calories 105
protein 1 g
carbohydrates 21 g
  fiber 0 g
  sugars 10 g
cholesterol 0 mg
total fat 2.0 g
  saturated 0.5 g
  polyunsaturated 0.0 g
  monounsaturated 1.0 g
sodium 98 mg

dietary exchange
1½ starch

Chocolate Oatmeal Cookies

Serves 30; 2 cookies per serving

When your sweet tooth craves a nibble of chocolate, try these cookies.

1½ cups firmly packed light brown sugar

½ cup sifted unsweetened cocoa powder

½ cup fat-free milk

¼ cup acceptable stick margarine, softened

¼ cup pureed dried plums or unsweetened baby food dried plums

2 teaspoons vanilla extract

1¾ cups all-purpose flour

2½ teaspoons baking powder

¼ teaspoon salt

1½ cups uncooked quick-cooking oatmeal

Preheat the oven to 350°F.

In a large mixing bowl, cream the brown sugar, cocoa powder, milk, margarine, dried plums, and vanilla.

In a small bowl, sift together the flour, baking powder, and salt. Beat into the brown sugar mixture.

Stir in the oatmeal.

Drop by teaspoonfuls onto ungreased baking sheets. (You should have about 60 cookies.)

Bake for 7 to 9 minutes, or until set in the center (the cookies don't jiggle when gently shaken).

calories 100
protein 2 g
carbohydrates 21 g
fiber 1 g
sugars 11 g
cholesterol 0 mg
total fat 1.0 g
saturated 0.5 g
polyunsaturated 0.5 g
monounsaturated 0.5 g
sodium 77 mg

dietary exchange
1½ other carbohydrate

Chewy Chocolate Chip Cookies

Serves 24; 2 cookies per serving

Soft, chewy, packed with chocolate—these cookies are delightful.

½ cup firmly packed light brown
   sugar
¼ cup sugar
1 large egg
3 tablespoons acceptable stick
   margarine, softened

1 teaspoon vanilla, butter, and nut
   flavoring or vanilla extract
¾ cup self-rising flour
⅓ cup chocolate mini morsels
   Vegetable oil spray

Preheat the oven to 350°F.

In a medium mixing bowl, stir together the sugars, egg, margarine, and flavoring just to blend. Using an electric mixer, beat until well blended.

Gradually add the flour to the batter, beating on low speed.

Using a rubber scraper, stir in the chocolate morsels, scraping the side of the bowl.

Liberally spray two nonstick baking sheets with vegetable oil spray. Spoon 12 slightly rounded teaspoons of dough onto one baking sheet. Bake for 9 minutes.

Meanwhile, on a second baking sheet, spoon out enough dough for 12 cookies.

When the cookies have baked for 9 minutes (they may not appear done), put the baking sheet on a cooling rack for 1½ minutes. Don't leave the cookies on the baking sheet more than 2 minutes; they will harden and crumble. Put a large piece of wax paper on the counter. Using a flat, thin metal spatula (plastic is too thick), gently transfer the first batch of cookies to the wax paper. When the cookies have cooled, place them between layers of wax paper to keep them from sticking together.

Repeat baking until all the dough is used.

calories 67
protein 1 g
carbohydrates 11 g
   fiber 0 g
   sugars 8 g
cholesterol 9 mg
total fat 2.5 g
   saturated 0.5 g
   polyunsaturated 0.5 g
   monounsaturated 1.0 g
sodium 74 mg

dietary exchange
½ other carbohydrate
½ fat

Ginger Cookies

Serves 30; 2 cookies or 1 gingerbread man per serving

If you like a spicy, soft cookie, you'll love these.

1 cup sugar	3 cups all-purpose flour
1/2 cup unsweetened applesauce	1 teaspoon baking soda
1/4 cup acceptable stick margarine	1 teaspoon ground cinnamon
Egg substitute equivalent to 1 egg, or 1 large egg, lightly beaten	1 teaspoon ground ginger
	Vegetable oil spray
1/4 cup molasses	

In a large bowl, beat the sugar, applesauce, and margarine with a sturdy spoon.

Beat in the egg substitute and molasses.

In another large bowl, sift together the remaining ingredients except the vegetable oil spray. Stir into the margarine mixture. Cover and refrigerate the dough for 2 hours, or until thoroughly chilled.

Preheat the oven to 350°F. Lightly spray baking sheets with vegetable oil spray.

Using a teaspoon, drop about 60 mounds of dough about 1 inch apart on the baking sheets.

Bake for 10 to 12 minutes.

calories 95
protein 2 g
carbohydrates 19 g
  fiber 0 g
  sugars 9 g
cholesterol 0 mg
total fat 1.5 g
  saturated 0.5 g
  polyunsaturated 0.5 g
  monounsaturated 1.0 g
sodium 65 mg

dietary exchange
1 other carbohydrate
1/2 fat

Gingerbread Men

Makes about 30 gingerbread men; 1 per serving
Prepare the dough as directed, increasing the flour to 3 1/2 cups. Lightly flour a flat surface and roll the chilled dough to 1/4-inch thickness. Cut out gingerbread men shapes with a 5-inch cookie cutter. Bake for 10 to 12 minutes at 350°F. Decorate with 1/2 cup Confectioners' Glaze (page 575).

gingerbread men

calories 111
protein 2 g
carbohydrates 22 g
  fiber 1 g
  sugars 11 g
cholesterol 0 mg
total fat 1.5 g
  saturated 0.5 g
  polyunsaturated 0.5 g
  monounsaturated 1.0 g
sodium 66 mg

dietary exchange
1 1/2 other carbohydrate
1/2 fat

Peanut Butter Cookies

Serves 30; 2 cookies per serving

Enjoy these cookies fresh from the oven with a glass of ice-cold fat-free milk.

Vegetable oil spray
$1/4$ cup acceptable stick margarine, softened
$3/4$ cup firmly packed light brown sugar
$1/2$ cup sugar
$1/3$ cup peanut butter

Egg substitute equivalent to 1 egg, or 1 large egg
$1/4$ cup unsweetened applesauce
$1/2$ teaspoon baking soda
$2^1/2$ cups all-purpose flour
1 teaspoon vanilla extract

Preheat the oven to 350°F. Lightly spray baking sheets with vegetable oil spray.

In a large mixing bowl, cream the margarine. Gradually add the sugars, beating after each addition, until creamy.

Add the peanut butter, egg substitute, applesauce, and baking soda; beat well.

Gradually add the flour to the batter, beating after each addition.

Stir in the vanilla.

Roll the dough into 60 balls about the size of a pecan or the bowl of a measuring teaspoon. Put on the baking sheets. Flatten the balls slightly with the back of a wet fork.

Bake for 12 to 15 minutes, or until light brown.

Cook's Tip on Cookie Dough

Cookies are easier to roll if you moisten your hands first with cold water. Also, dip your fork in cold water before flattening the cookies.

calories 97
protein 2 g
carbohydrates 18 g
  fiber 1 g
  sugars 9 g
cholesterol 0 mg
total fat 2.5 g
  saturated 0.5 g
  polyunsaturated 0.5 g
  monounsaturated 1.0 g
sodium 51 mg

dietary exchange
1 other carbohydrate
$1/2$ fat

Bourbon Balls

Serves 24; 2 cookies per serving

These tasty morsels are great for holiday parties.

3 cups finely crushed low-fat vanilla wafers

1 cup confectioners' sugar, sifted

$^1/_2$ cup chopped pecans, dry-roasted

3 tablespoons light corn syrup

$1^1/_2$ tablespoons unsweetened cocoa powder

6 tablespoons bourbon (plus more as needed)

$^1/_4$ cup sifted confectioners' sugar

In a large bowl, stir together all the ingredients except $^1/_4$ cup confectioners' sugar. Form the dough into about 48 small balls. (If the balls tend to crumble, stir in a few extra drops of bourbon.)

Put the $^1/_4$ cup confectioners' sugar on a saucer. Roll each ball in the sugar. Put the cookies in an airtight container and refrigerate for about one week to mellow before serving.

calories 102
protein 1 g
carbohydrates 16 g
  fiber 1 g
  sugars 11 g
cholesterol 5 mg
total fat 3.5 g
  saturated 0.5 g
  polyunsaturated 1.0 g
  monounsaturated 1.5 g
sodium 34 mg

dietary exchange
1 other carbohydrate
$^1/_2$ fat

Sugar Cookies

Serves 24; 2 cookies per serving

Make these cookies the next time you're home on a snowy day. For holidays, decorate them with Confectioners' Glaze (page 575).

1 cup sugar	1 teaspoon vanilla extract
1/3 cup acceptable stick margarine, softened	2 cups all-purpose flour
	2 teaspoons baking powder
Egg substitute equivalent to 1 egg, or 1 large egg	1/2 teaspoon salt
	1/8 teaspoon ground nutmeg
2 tablespoons fat-free milk	Vegetable oil spray

In a large mixing bowl, using an electric mixer, cream the sugar and margarine.

Beat in the egg substitute, milk, and vanilla.

In a medium bowl, sift together the remaining ingredients except the vegetable oil spray. Gradually add the sugar mixture, beating after each addition.

Cover and refrigerate the dough for 2 hours, or until thoroughly chilled.

Preheat the oven to 375°F. Lightly spray baking sheets with vegetable oil spray.

Form the dough into about 48 balls 1 inch in diameter; put on the baking sheets. Gently press your thumb in the center of each cookie, making a slight indentation.

Bake for 8 minutes, or until light brown. Remove the cookies from the baking sheets and let cool on cooling racks.

calories 95
protein 1 g
carbohydrates 17 g
 fiber 0 g
 sugars 8 g
cholesterol 0 mg
total fat 2.5 g
 saturated 0.5 g
 polyunsaturated 0.5 g
 monounsaturated 1.5 g
sodium 125 mg

dietary exchange
1 other carbohydrate
1/2 fat

Lemon Sugar Cookies
Substitute 2 tablespoons fresh lemon juice and 1 teaspoon grated lemon zest for the milk and vanilla.

Fudgy Buttermilk Brownies

Serves 16; 1 brownie per serving

Here's a wonderfully moist brownie to serve alone or topped with fat-free frozen yogurt.

Vegetable oil spray

Brownies
1 cup all-purpose flour
1 cup firmly packed light brown sugar
1/3 cup unsweetened cocoa powder
1/2 teaspoon baking soda
1/4 teaspoon salt
Whites of 2 large eggs, egg substitute equivalent to 1 egg, or 1 large egg

1/2 cup unsweetened applesauce
1/2 cup fat-free or low-fat buttermilk
2 teaspoons vanilla extract

Frosting
1 1/2 cups sifted confectioners' sugar
1/4 cup unsweetened cocoa powder
1 teaspoon vanilla extract
2 to 3 tablespoons fat-free milk

Preheat the oven to 350°F. Lightly spray a 9-inch square baking pan with vegetable oil spray.

In a medium bowl, stir together the flour, brown sugar, cocoa powder, baking soda, and salt.

In a small bowl, lightly whisk the egg whites. Whisk in the remaining brownie ingredients. Whisk into the flour mixture until well blended. Pour the batter into the baking pan.

Bake for 30 minutes. Let cool in the pan on a cooling rack.

In a small bowl, stir together the confectioners' sugar and cocoa powder.

Stir in the vanilla extract, then gradually stir in the milk until the frosting is spreading consistency. Spread over the cooled brownies. Cut into 16 squares.

calories 148
protein 2 g
carbohydrates 34 g
  fiber 1 g
  sugars 25 g
cholesterol 0 mg
total fat 0.5 g
  saturated 0.0 g
  polyunsaturated 0.0 g
  monounsaturated 0.0 g
sodium 98 mg

dietary exchange
2 1/2 other carbohydrate

Butterscotch Brownies

Serves 16; 1 brownie per serving

Serve these brownies with a cup of hot cocoa made with fat-free milk (you can even add a marshmallow or two).

Vegetable oil spray
1 cup firmly packed dark brown sugar
2 tablespoons acceptable stick margarine
Egg substitute equivalent to 1 egg, or 1 large egg

2 tablespoons unsweetened applesauce
1/2 teaspoon butter flavoring
1/2 teaspoon vanilla extract
3/4 cup sifted all-purpose flour
1 teaspoon baking powder

Preheat the oven to 350°F. Lightly spray an 8-inch square baking pan with vegetable oil spray.

In a large mixing bowl, cream the brown sugar and margarine with an electric mixer on medium-high.

Add the egg substitute, applesauce, butter flavoring, and vanilla. Beat on medium until smooth.

In a small bowl, sift together the flour and baking powder. Stir into the brown sugar mixture. Spread in the baking pan.

Bake for 20 to 25 minutes. Let cool slightly and cut into 16 bars.

Cook's Tip on Brown Sugar

You can interchange equal amounts of light brown and dark brown sugar. If a recipe calls for dark brown sugar and you prefer a less butterscotchy flavor, use light brown sugar and vice versa. To "make" light brown sugar, use half dark brown sugar and half white sugar.

calories 89
protein 1 g
carbohydrates 18 g
  fiber 0 g
  sugars 14 g
cholesterol 0 mg
total fat 1.5 g
  saturated 0.0 g
  polyunsaturated 0.5 g
  monounsaturated 1.0 g
sodium 61 mg

dietary exchange
1 other carbohydrate
1/2 fat

Apricot Raisin Bars

Serves 48; 1 cookie per serving

These bars make a welcome treat in lunch boxes or as an after-school snack.

6 ounces dried apricots, chopped	1 teaspoon baking powder
1 cup golden or dark raisins	1 1/4 cups uncooked quick-cooking oatmeal
1 3/4 cups unsweetened apple juice, divided use	3/4 cup firmly packed light brown sugar
3 tablespoons cornstarch	1/4 cup sugar
1/2 tablespoon grated lemon zest	2/3 cup light stick margarine
Vegetable oil spray	
1 1/2 cups all-purpose flour	

In a medium saucepan, stir together the apricots, raisins, and 1 1/2 cups apple juice. Cook over medium-low heat for 20 minutes, or until the fruit is tender.

In a small bowl, whisk together 1/4 cup apple juice, cornstarch, and zest. Whisk into the apricot mixture. Cook over medium-high heat for 2 to 3 minutes, or until the mixture thickens, stirring constantly. Remove from the heat and let cool.

Preheat the oven to 375°F. Lightly spray a 13 × 9 × 2-inch pan with vegetable oil spray.

Sift the flour and baking powder together into a large bowl.

Stir in the oatmeal and sugars.

Using a pastry blender or fork, blend in the margarine until the mixture is crumbly. Press about two thirds of the mixture in the pan.

Spread the fruit mixture over the crust. Top with the remaining oatmeal mixture.

Bake for 30 minutes, or until the crust is light golden. Cut into 48 bars.

calories 78
protein 1 g
carbohydrates 16 g
  fiber 1 g
  sugars 10 g
cholesterol 0 mg
total fat 1.5 g
  saturated 0.5 g
  polyunsaturated 0.5 g
  monounsaturated 0.5 g
sodium 30 mg

dietary exchange
1 other carbohydrate

Raspberry Crumbles

Serves 12; 1 cookie per serving

Serve this with plenty of napkins to catch those scrumptious crumbs. You won't want to miss a morsel.

3/4 cup all-purpose flour
3 tablespoons sugar
2 teaspoons grated lemon zest
1 tablespoon walnut chips
1/8 teaspoon ground nutmeg
1/4 cup acceptable stick margarine
2 ounces fat-free or light cream cheese

2 tablespoons fat-free milk
2 tablespoons confectioners' sugar
1/4 teaspoon vanilla extract
3 tablespoons all-fruit seedless raspberry spread

Preheat the oven to 350°F.

Lightly spoon the flour into measuring cups. Level with a knife.

In a small bowl, stir together the flour, sugar, lemon zest, walnuts, and nutmeg. Using a knife or pastry blender, cut in the margarine until the mixture resembles coarse crumbs. Press the mixture firmly and evenly in the baking pan.

Bake for 15 minutes, or until golden. Let cool completely on a cooling rack.

Meanwhile, put the cream cheese in a small microwave-safe bowl. Cover with plastic wrap. Microwave at 50 percent power (medium) for 20 to 30 seconds, or until soft. Whisk in the milk, confectioners' sugar, and vanilla until smooth. Cover and refrigerate for 30 minutes, or until firm.

Spread the cream cheese mixture over the crust.

Put the fruit spread in a small microwave-safe bowl. Microwave at 100 percent (high) for 10 seconds, or until slightly melted. Stir to melt completely. Drizzle over the cream-cheese mixture.

To serve, cut into 12 pieces.

calories 100
protein 2 g
carbohydrates 14 g
  fiber 0 g
  sugars 7 g
cholesterol 1 mg
total fat 4.5 g
  saturated 0.5 g
  polyunsaturated 1.0 g
  monounsaturated 2.0 g
sodium 69 mg

dietary exchange
1 starch
1/2 fat

Oatmeal Carrot Bar Cookies

Serves 24; 1 cookie per serving

Bursting with flavor, these cookies also boast the health benefits of oatmeal. Don't be surprised when you open the cookie jar and find only crumbs!

Vegetable oil spray
$1/2$ cup raisins
2 tablespoons acceptable stick margarine, at room temperature
$1/2$ cup firmly packed light brown sugar
$1/4$ cup unsweetened applesauce
Egg substitute equivalent to 1 egg, or 1 large egg
$1 1/4$ cups grated carrots
$1/2$ teaspoon ground cinnamon

$1/2$ teaspoon grated lemon or orange zest
$1/2$ teaspoon vanilla extract
$1/4$ teaspoon ground nutmeg
1 cup all-purpose flour
$1/2$ cup uncooked quick-cooking oatmeal
1 teaspoon baking powder
1 tablespoon sifted confectioners' sugar

Preheat the oven to 350°F. Lightly spray an $11 1/2 \times 7 1/2 \times 2$-inch baking pan with vegetable oil spray.

Put the raisins in a small bowl and cover with boiling water. Let soak for 15 minutes. Drain and set aside.

Meanwhile, in a large mixing bowl, cream the margarine and brown sugar until fluffy.

Add the applesauce and egg substitute. Beat well.

Stir in the carrots, cinnamon, lemon zest, vanilla, nutmeg, and raisins.

In a medium bowl, stir together the flour, oatmeal, and baking powder. Stir into the margarine mixture. Pour into the baking pan.

Bake for 20 to 25 minutes, or until the cookies are lightly golden. Let cool on a cooling rack.

To serve, sprinkle lightly with the confectioners' sugar. Cut into 24 bars.

calories 64
protein 1 g
carbohydrates 14 g
 fiber 1 g
 sugars 8 g
cholesterol 0 mg
total fat 0.5 g
 saturated 0.0 g
 polyunsaturated 0.0 g
 monounsaturated 0.0 g
sodium 36 mg

dietary exchange
1 other carbohydrate

Wafer Wedges

Serves 4; 3 cookies per serving

Try this no-frills cookie the next time you want just a bite of something sweet to go with a cup of hot tea or hot cider.

Vegetable oil spray
3 tablespoons firmly packed dark brown sugar
White of 1 large egg
1 tablespoon acceptable stick margarine, melted and slightly cooled

$^1/_2$ teaspoon vanilla, butter, and nut flavoring or 1 teaspoon vanilla extract
$^1/_4$ cup all-purpose flour
$^1/_4$ teaspoon ground cinnamon
$^1/_4$ teaspoon ground nutmeg

Preheat the oven to 375°F. Lightly spray a 9-inch glass pie pan with vegetable oil spray.

In a small bowl, whisk together the brown sugar, egg white, margarine, and flavoring until smooth.

Whisk in the remaining ingredients until well blended. Pour into the pie pan and smooth to cover the bottom.

Bake for 18 minutes, or until the edges begin to brown slightly. Let cool on a cooling rack for 10 minutes. Gently remove from the pan (the cookie will still be warm and slightly flexible). Cut into 12 wedges and let cool completely.

calories 101
protein 2 g
carbohydrates 16 g
  fiber 0 g
  sugars 10 g
cholesterol 0 mg
total fat 3.0 g
  saturated 0.5 g
  polyunsaturated 0.5 g
  monounsaturated 1.5 g
sodium 51 mg

dietary exchange
1 other carbohydrate
$^1/_2$ fat

Sherry Thins

Flavored with the sweet richness of cream sherry, these cookies are great for the holidays.

1 cup sugar	2 teaspoons baking powder
¼ cup acceptable stick margarine	½ teaspoon salt
Egg substitute equivalent to 1 egg, or 1 large egg	⅓ cup cream sherry
	Vegetable oil spray
1 teaspoon vanilla extract	Flour for rolling dough
3 cups sifted all-purpose flour	

In a large mixing bowl, cream the sugar and margarine until fluffy.

Beat in the egg substitute and vanilla.

In a large bowl, sift together 3 cups flour, baking powder, and salt. Add to the margarine mixture alternately with the sherry, beating after each addition. Cover and refrigerate the dough for at least 2 hours.

Preheat the oven to 375°F. Lightly spray baking sheets with vegetable oil spray.

Lightly flour a flat surface. Roll out half the dough. Cut out shapes with small cookie cutters. Repeat with the remaining dough. (You'll have about 60 cookies if using a 2-inch round biscuit cutter.) Place on baking sheets.

Bake for 5 to 7 minutes, or until the edges are light golden brown.

calories 81
protein 2 g
carbohydrates 16 g
  fiber 0 g
  sugars 7 g
cholesterol 0 mg
total fat 1.0 g
  saturated 0.0 g
  polyunsaturated 0.5 g
  monounsaturated 0.0 g
sodium 86 mg

dietary exchange
1 other carbohydrate

Apricot-Almond Biscotti

Serves 28; 1 cookie per serving

Biscotti are typically baked, sliced, and baked again, making them quite hard to bite into. They're perfect for dunking in hot tea or coffee for a midmorning treat or as a light dessert.

Vegetable oil spray
2 cups all-purpose flour
$^2/_3$ cup sugar
2 teaspoons baking powder
$^1/_4$ teaspoon salt
Egg substitute equivalent to 2 eggs, or 2 large eggs
2 tablespoons acceptable vegetable oil

2 tablespoons unsweetened applesauce
1 teaspoon grated lemon zest
$^1/_4$ teaspoon almond extract
$^3/_4$ cup finely chopped dried apricots (about 4 ounces)
$^1/_4$ cup chopped almonds, dry-roasted
Flour for kneading
$^3/_4$ cup sifted confectioners' sugar
2 to 3 teaspoons water

Preheat the oven to 350°F. Lightly spray a baking sheet with vegetable oil spray. Set aside.

In a medium bowl, stir together the flour, sugar, baking powder, and salt.

In a small bowl, whisk together the egg substitute, oil, applesauce, lemon zest, and almond extract.

Whisk the apricots and almonds into the egg mixture. Whisk the egg mixture into the flour mixture.

Lightly flour a flat surface; turn out the dough. Knead just until blended, 10 to 12 strokes. With slightly moistened hands, form into two 8-inch logs. Set the logs on the baking sheet. Slightly flatten to 2$^1/_2$-inch width.

Bake for 25 minutes. Reduce the oven temperature to 300°F. Let the biscotti cool on a cooling rack for 10 minutes.

Meanwhile, put the confectioners' sugar in a small bowl. Gradually stir in the water until the desired consistency. Brush on the logs. Cut into $^1/_2$-inch slices. Place the biscotti with the cut side down on the baking sheet.

Bake for 10 minutes. Turn the slices over. Bake for 10 minutes. Let cool on a cooling rack.

calories 91
protein 2 g
carbohydrates 18 g
  fiber 1 g
  sugars 10 g
cholesterol 0 mg
total fat 1.5 g
  saturated 0.0 g
  polyunsaturated 0.5 g
  monounsaturated 1.0 g
sodium 65 mg

dietary exchange
1 other carbohydrate
$^1/_2$ fat

Chocolate-Pecan Biscotti

Vegetable oil spray
1 1/2 cups all-purpose flour
2/3 cup firmly packed light brown sugar
1/2 cup unsweetened cocoa powder
2 teaspoons baking powder
1/4 teaspoon salt
Egg substitute equivalent to 2 eggs, or 2 large eggs
2 tablespoons acceptable vegetable oil

2 tablespoons unsweetened applesauce
1 teaspoon vanilla extract
1/2 cup finely chopped pecans, dry-roasted
Flour for kneading
3/4 cup sifted confectioners' sugar
2 to 3 teaspoons water

Preheat the oven and prepare the baking sheet as directed.

In a medium bowl, stir together the flour, brown sugar, cocoa powder, baking powder, and salt.

In a small bowl, whisk together the egg substitute, oil, applesauce, and vanilla.

Whisk the pecans into the egg mixture. Whisk the egg mixture into the flour mixture.

Proceed as directed above.

---

chocolate-pecan
biscotti

calories 90
protein 2 g
carbohydrates 15 g
  fiber 1 g
  sugars 9 g
cholesterol 0 mg
total fat 3.0 g
  saturated 0.5 g
  polyunsaturated 1.0 g
  monounsaturated 1.5 g
sodium 67 mg

dietary exchange
1 other carbohydrate
1/2 fat

Cannoli Cream with
Strawberries and Chocolate

Serves 4; 1 cup per serving

Creamy and elegant, this make-ahead dessert is just the way to end a meal for company.

1/4 cup cold fat-free milk
1 envelope unflavored gelatin
1/2 cup fat-free milk, boiling
3/4 cup fat-free or low-fat ricotta cheese
3/4 cup fat-free or low-fat cottage cheese

1/2 cup sugar
1 teaspoon vanilla extract
8 to 10 fresh or unsweetened frozen strawberries, thawed if frozen
3 tablespoons shaved sweet chocolate

Pour the cold milk into a food processor or blender. Sprinkle the gelatin over the milk. Let stand for 2 minutes.

Pour the boiling milk into the food processor or blender. Process for 1 minute, or until the gelatin is completely dissolved.

Add the ricotta cheese, cottage cheese, sugar, and vanilla. Process for 2 minutes. Divide the mixture evenly between two medium bowls.

Put the strawberries in the food processor or blender. Process until smooth (except the seeds). Fold into one bowl of pudding.

Stir the chocolate into the remaining bowl.

Alternate layers of strawberry pudding and chocolate pudding in stemmed dessert dishes or wineglasses until all the ingredients are used. Refrigerate for 3 hours, or until set.

calories 226
protein 15 g
carbohydrates 36 g
 fiber 1 g
 sugars 34 g
cholesterol 8 mg
total fat 2.0 g
 saturated 1.0 g
 polyunsaturated 0.0 g
 monounsaturated 0.5 g
sodium 266 mg

dietary exchange
2 1/2 other carbohydrate
2 very lean meat

Chocolate Crème Brûlée

Serves 10; ½ cup per serving

If crème brûlée is your favorite restaurant dessert, you will be pleased to know how easy it is to make at home. (See photo on back cover.)

3 cups fat-free half-and-half
½ cup unsweetened cocoa powder, sifted
   Egg substitute equivalent to 6 eggs
⅔ cup sugar

3 tablespoons plus 1 teaspoon mini chocolate chips
   Scant ½ cup sugar
1 cup fresh raspberries

Preheat the oven to 325°F.

In a medium microwave-safe bowl, whisk together the half-and-half and cocoa (the mixture will be lumpy). Cover with plastic wrap. Microwave on 100 percent power (high) for 1 minute to 1 minute 30 seconds, or until slightly warm. Whisk again to help dissolve the lumps.

Whisk in the egg substitute and ⅔ cup sugar. Pour ½ cup mixture into each of ten 6-ounce broilerproof custard cups.

Spoon 1 teaspoon chocolate chips into the middle of each custard cup. Place the custard cups on a 17 × 12 × 1-inch rimmed baking sheet or large baking pan. Fill the baking sheet half full with warm water, or fill the baking pan to a depth of 1 inch.

Bake for 30 to 35 minutes, or until the center is set (doesn't jiggle when gently shaken). Transfer the baking sheet to a cooling rack. Carefully transfer the custard cups to another cooling rack. Let cool for 15 minutes. Cover and refrigerate for 2 hours to 2 days.

At serving time, preheat the broiler.

Uncover the custard cups. Sprinkle 2 teaspoons sugar over each serving. Put the cups on a broilerproof pan.

Broil with the tops of the cups about 2 inches from the heat for 2 to 4 minutes, or until the sugar is caramelized (watch carefully so it does not burn).

To serve, put each custard cup on a plate. Garnish the crème brûlée with the raspberries.

calories 197
protein 10 g
carbohydrates 40 g
  fiber 2 g
  sugars 31 g
cholesterol 0 mg
total fat 1.5 g
  saturated 1.0 g
  polyunsaturated 0.0 g
  monounsaturated 0.5 g
sodium 148 mg

dietary exchange
1 skim milk
1½ other carbohydrate

Honey Almond Custards

Serves 6; ½ cup per serving

After a highly seasoned entrée, serve these honey-sweetened custards to balance the meal.

Vegetable oil spray
2 cups fat-free milk
Egg substitute equivalent to 3 eggs
¼ cup honey

2 teaspoons vanilla extract
¼ teaspoon almond extract
⅛ teaspoon salt

Preheat the oven to 350°F. Lightly spray six 6-ounce ovenproof custard cups with vegetable oil spray.

In a small saucepan, heat the milk over medium-high heat until very hot but not boiling, stirring constantly. Remove from the heat.

In a medium bowl, gently whisk together the remaining ingredients.

Gently whisk in the milk (don't create foam). Pour the mixture into the custard cups.

Place the cups in a large baking pan. Pour hot tap water into the pan to a depth of 1 inch.

Bake, uncovered, for 30 to 40 minutes, or until a knife inserted halfway between the cup and the center of the custard comes out clean (the center won't quite be firm).

Microwave Method
Prepare the custard mixture as directed. Pour into microwave-safe custard cups lightly sprayed with vegetable oil spray. Put the cups in a microwave-safe baking dish. Add the water as directed. Microwave on 100 percent power (high) for 12 to 15 minutes, or until the centers are just set (doesn't jiggle when gently shaken).

calories 91
protein 6 g
carbohydrates 16 g
  fiber 0 g
  sugars 16 g
cholesterol 2 mg
total fat 0.0 g
  saturated 0.0 g
  polyunsaturated 0.0 g
  monounsaturated 0.0 g
sodium 154 mg

dietary exchange
1 other carbohydrate
1 very lean meat

Delicious
Rice Pudding

Serves 6; ½ cup per serving

Enjoy this traditional comfort food unadorned, or try it with Easy Jubilee Sauce (page 506) as an interesting addition.

Vegetable oil spray
2 cups fat-free milk, heated
2 cups cooked rice
⅓ cup sugar
½ tablespoon vanilla extract
½ tablespoon grated lemon zest (optional)

1 teaspoon lemon extract (optional)
¼ teaspoon ground nutmeg
½ teaspoon ground cinnamon
Egg substitute equivalent to 1 egg, or 1 large egg

Preheat the oven to 350°F.

Lightly spray a 1-quart casserole dish with vegetable oil spray. Put the ingredients in the dish in the order listed. Stir well and cover. Set the dish in a large baking pan and pour hot tap water into the pan to a depth of 1 inch.

Bake for 1 hour, or until the mixture is thick. Serve warm or cover and refrigerate to serve chilled.

Cook's Tip on Bain-Marie

A bain-marie (bahn mah-REE), or water bath, is a technique for cooking custards and some other fragile foods. The container holding the food is placed in a larger pan (also called a bain-marie) that holds a small amount of hot, not boiling, water. (If the water starts to boil, add a little cold water.) The technique keeps the food from separating or curdling.

calories 149
protein 5 g
carbohydrates 30 g
　fiber 0 g
　sugars 15 g
cholesterol 2 mg
total fat 0.5 g
　saturated 0.0 g
　polyunsaturated 0.0 g
　monounsaturated 0.0 g
sodium 64 mg

dietary exchange
1 starch
1 other carbohydrate

Guiltless Banana Pudding

Serves 8; 1 cup per serving

It's so rich tasting and creamy that you'll wonder how this revised favorite can be guiltless.

1 cup fat-free milk
Small package fat-free, sugar-free vanilla instant pudding mix (1.5 to 1.7 ounces)
8 ounces frozen fat-free or low-fat whipped topping, thawed

$2/3$ cup fat-free sweetened condensed milk
2 tablespoons plus 1 teaspoon fresh lemon juice, or to taste
20 low-fat vanilla wafers, whole or crushed
2 medium bananas, sliced

calories 208
protein 4 g
carbohydrates 44 g
  fiber 1 g
  sugars 30 g
cholesterol 2 mg
total fat 1.0 g
  saturated 0.0 g
  polyunsaturated 0.0 g
  monounsaturated 0.0 g
sodium 238 mg

dietary exchange
3 other carbohydrate

In a large mixing bowl, whisk or beat the fat-free milk and pudding mix until thickened.

Fold in the whipped topping, condensed milk, and lemon juice. Layer half the vanilla wafers, half the bananas, and half the pudding mixture in an 8-inch square glass dish, glass serving dish, or individual bowls; repeat. Put plastic wrap directly on the surface of the pudding and refrigerate.

guiltless strawberry pudding

calories 215
protein 4 g
carbohydrates 43 g
  fiber 1 g
  sugars 27 g
cholesterol 2 mg
total fat 2.0 g
  saturated 0.5 g
  polyunsaturated 0.0 g
  monounsaturated 1.0 g
sodium 270 mg

dietary exchange
3 other carbohydrate
$1/2$ fat

Guiltless Strawberry Pudding
Replace the vanilla wafers with low-fat gingersnaps, and replace the bananas with 1 cup sliced fresh strawberries.

Vanilla Bread Pudding
with Peaches

Serves 6; 2½ × 4-inch piece bread pudding and ⅓ cup cooked peaches per serving

Like a soufflé, this bread pudding is puffy for only a moment. It is best when served fresh from the oven.

Bread Pudding
- 1 cup fat-free milk
- Whites of 3 large eggs
- ⅓ cup sugar
- 1 teaspoon vanilla, butter, and nut flavoring or vanilla extract
- ¾ teaspoon baking powder
- ¼ teaspoon ground cinnamon
- ⅛ teaspoon ground nutmeg
- 4 slices stale white bread, cut into cubes

❖
- ½ cup water
- 2 large peaches, peeled or unpeeled, thinly sliced (about 12 ounces)
- 2 tablespoons sugar

Preheat the oven to 375°F.

In a small bowl, whisk together the bread pudding ingredients except the bread.

Fold in the bread cubes just until coated. Don't overmix. Spoon into the baking pan.

Bake for 25 minutes, or until a sharp knife inserted in the center comes out clean.

Meanwhile, in a medium saucepan, bring the water to a boil over high heat. Stir in the peaches and sugar. Return to a boil. Reduce the heat and simmer, uncovered, for 4 minutes, or until just tender.

To serve, cut the bread pudding into 6 pieces. Transfer to dessert plates. Spoon ⅓ cup peaches over each serving.

calories 152
protein 5 g
carbohydrates 32 g
  fiber 2 g
  sugars 22 g
cholesterol 1 mg
total fat 0.5 g
  saturated 0.0 g
  polyunsaturated 0.5 g
  monounsaturated 0.0 g
sodium 200 mg

dietary exchange
1½ starch
½ fruit

Cinnamon-Apple
Dessert Tamales with
Kahlúa Custard Sauce

Serves 12

Tamales for dessert? A savory favorite turns into a luscious dessert with apples and cinnamon. The tamales are easy to make with our step-by-step instructions, whether you use the authentic dried corn husks or aluminum foil.

Vegetable oil spray (if using aluminum foil)

Filling
2 cups cornmeal
2 medium Granny Smith apples, peeled and diced
3/4 cup firmly packed light brown sugar
1/4 cup golden raisins
1 teaspoon ground cinnamon

1 cup mashed bananas (about 2)
3/4 cup fat-free milk

Kahlúa Custard Sauce
1 envelope (about 1 ounce) custard pudding dessert mix
2 1/2 cups fat-free milk
3 tablespoons sugar
2 tablespoons Kahlúa or strong brewed coffee
Sprigs of fresh mint (optional)

calories 227
protein 5 g
carbohydrates 52 g
  fiber 2 g
  sugars 31 g
cholesterol 1 mg
total fat 0.5 g
  saturated 0.0 g
  polyunsaturated 0.0 g
  monounsaturated 0.0 g
sodium 56 mg

dietary exchange
1 starch
1 fruit
1 1/2 other carbohydrate

Place 24 dried corn husks in enough cold water to cover. Let soak for 15 minutes. With your fingers, tear another 4 husks into 6 strips each. (Strips are used to tie tamales to hold them together.) Or lay twenty-four 5-inch squares of aluminum foil on a flat surface. Lightly spray one side of each square with vegetable oil spray.

In a large bowl, stir together the cornmeal, apples, brown sugar, raisins, and cinnamon.

Make a well in the center of the cornmeal mixture. Put the bananas and milk in the well. Stir until just combined.

Shake the excess water from 1 corn husk. Place a wide end closest to you and a narrower, pointed end to your right. Spoon about 2 tablespoons filling onto the center of the corn husk and spread it toward a wide end. Fold the left side of the husk over the filling and roll to the right (toward the point) to enclose. Fold the pointed end toward the open end of the tamale. Tie a corn-husk strip around the tamale to secure; set aside. (Don't tie too tightly—leave room for the tamale to expand.) If using aluminum foil, spoon the filling onto the center and fold the foil in half, crimping the edges to seal. Repeat with the remaining filling.

Put a steamer basket in a large stockpot. Add water to just below the basket. Bring to a simmer over high heat. Place the tamales in the basket with the open end up if using husks. The water shouldn't touch the bottom of the basket. Place a dish towel over the tamales (this will keep water from dripping on them while cooking). Reduce the heat to low and cook, covered, for 45 minutes.

Meanwhile, prepare the custard sauce according to the package directions (using mix, milk, and sugar). When the sauce is cooked, stir in the Kahlúa. Set aside.

Cool the tamales for at least 5 minutes before serving. Unwrap 2 tamales and place on a dessert plate. Ladle 1/4 cup sauce over the tamales and garnish with mint. Repeat with the remaining tamales, sauce, and mint.

Cook's Tip

To reheat, place wrapped tamales in a steamer basket over simmering water for 5 minutes, or microwave six at a time on a microwave-safe plate covered with plastic wrap on 100 percent power (high) for 30 to 60 seconds (leave in the husks but remove the foil).

Fruit with Vanilla Cream

Serves 4

A thick, cheesecake-flavored topping covers fresh or frozen fruit. If you wish, at serving time, randomly spear easy-to-bake Wafer Wedges (page 604) around the edge of the serving bowl or stick one wafer in each ramekin.

1/2 cup fat-free or light sour cream
1/4 cup sifted confectioners' sugar
2 teaspoons vanilla extract
3/4 cup frozen fat-free or low-fat whipped topping, thawed

8 ounces frozen unsweetened sliced peaches, slightly thawed, or peeled fresh peaches, strawberries, blueberries, raspberries, or a combination, diced
8 slices frozen unsweetened peaches, slightly thawed, or peeled fresh peaches

In a small bowl, whisk together the sour cream, confectioners' sugar, and vanilla until smooth.

Gently fold in the whipped topping.

Put the diced peaches in a decorative bowl or individual ramekins. Spoon the sour cream mixture over the fruit. Arrange the peach slices on top.

Serve at room temperature or cover and refrigerate for up to 2 hours.

calories 128
protein 3 g
carbohydrates 26 g
  fiber 2 g
  sugars 15 g
cholesterol 5 mg
total fat 0.5 g
  saturated 0.0 g
  polyunsaturated 0.0 g
  monounsaturated 0.0 g
sodium 33 mg

dietary exchange
1/2 fruit
1 other carbohydrate

Berries
in Vanilla Sauce

Serves 4

Summer fruits decoratively arranged on a bed of thick, sweet vanilla cream sauce—what a beautiful way to end a meal.

1 cup fat-free milk
3 tablespoons sugar
1/4 cup fat-free milk
1 tablespoon plus 1 teaspoon
   cornstarch

1 tablespoon vanilla extract
6 ounces fresh blueberries
8 ounces fresh strawberries, halved
1 whole strawberry with stem
   (optional)

In a small saucepan, whisk together the 1 cup milk and the sugar. Bring to a boil over medium-high heat, whisking occasionally.

Meanwhile, in a small bowl, whisk together the 1/4 cup milk and the cornstarch until the cornstarch is dissolved. Whisk into the sugar mixture. Cook for 2 to 3 minutes, or until thickened, whisking constantly. Remove from the heat. Whisk in the vanilla. Pour into a 10-inch quiche pan or onto a serving platter. Let cool for 20 minutes to set slightly.

Arrange the blueberries in a mound in the center of the pan. Circle with the strawberries. Place a whole strawberry or strawberry fan (see Cook's Tip on Strawberry Fans, below) on the blueberries. Cover with plastic wrap and refrigerate for about 2 hours.

Cook's Tip on Strawberry Fans

To make a strawberry fan, thinly slice the strawberry up to the stem (4 to 6 slices), but don't detach the stem. Gently press down with your fingertips to allow the slices to separate slightly to form a fan.

calories 123
protein 3 g
carbohydrates 26 g
  fiber 3 g
  sugars 20 g
cholesterol 2 mg
total fat 0.5 g
  saturated 0.0 g
  polyunsaturated 0.0 g
  monounsaturated 0.0 g
sodium 44 mg

dietary exchange
1/2 fruit
1 other carbohydrate

Sweet and Fruity
Salsa Bowl

Serves 4

Colorful fruit tossed with fresh mint and ginger comes alive with a splash of lemon.

5 ounces strawberries, cut into ¼-inch cubes (about 1 cup)

5 ounces mango, cut into ¼-inch cubes (about 1 cup)

1 green kiwifruit, peeled and cut into ¼-inch cubes

2 tablespoons chopped fresh mint

1 tablespoon sugar

½ teaspoon grated gingerroot

½ teaspoon grated lemon zest

1 tablespoon fresh lemon juice

2 cups fat-free or light vanilla or fruit-flavored yogurt

In a medium bowl, gently toss all the ingredients except the yogurt. Serve immediately, or cover with plastic wrap and refrigerate for up to 8 hours.

To serve, spoon ½ cup yogurt into each bowl or wine goblet. Top each serving with ½ cup fruit salsa.

Cook's Tip

You can find bottled precut mango in the refrigerated section of your supermarket's produce area.

calories 171
protein 7 g
carbohydrates 37 g
 fiber 2 g
 sugars 34 g
cholesterol 2 mg
total fat 0.5 g
 saturated 0.0 g
 polyunsaturated 0.0 g
 monounsaturated 0.0 g
sodium 88 mg

dietary exchange
1½ fruit
1 skim milk

Grapefruit Orange Palette

Serves 6

This is an artistic delight. Serve it as a late-night dessert or for Sunday brunch.

3 medium seedless oranges, peeled and chilled	¼ cup sifted confectioners' sugar
12 ounces frozen sweetened raspberries, thawed	3 medium pink or ruby red grapefruit, peeled, sectioned, and chilled
2 tablespoons black currant jelly or crème de cassis (black currant liqueur)	6 sprigs of fresh mint

Slice each orange into 5 slices crosswise, then cut each slice in half. Set aside.

In a food processor or blender, process the raspberries until smooth (except the seeds). Using a fine-mesh strainer, remove the seeds. Reserve the pulp in a small bowl; discard the seeds.

In a small microwave-safe bowl, microwave the jelly on 100 percent power (high) for 30 seconds.

Stir the jelly and confectioners' sugar into the raspberries.

For each serving, arrange one sixth of the grapefruit sections and 5 orange pieces alternately in a circular pattern (like flower petals) on a dessert plate. Drizzle the raspberry sauce in a circle over the fruit. Place a sprig of mint in the center. Repeat for each plate.

Cook's Tip

You can prepare the fruit and the sauce ahead of time. Cover and refrigerate the grapefruit sections, orange pieces, and pureed raspberries separately. Assemble just before serving.

calories 190
protein 2 g
carbohydrates 51 g
  fiber 12 g
  sugars 38 g
cholesterol 0 mg
total fat 0.0 g
  saturated 0.0 g
  polyunsaturated 0.0 g
  monounsaturated 0.0 g
sodium 1 mg

dietary exchange
3½ fruit

Claret-Spiced Oranges

Serves 6

Here's a light, lovely way to end a holiday meal.

4 medium oranges, peeled and sectioned
3/4 cup claret or other dry red wine (regular or nonalcoholic)
1/2 cup water

5 tablespoons sugar
3-inch cinnamon stick
1 tablespoon fresh lemon juice
2 whole cloves

Put the orange sections in a medium bowl.

In a small saucepan, stir together the remaining ingredients. Bring to a boil over medium-high heat. Reduce the heat and simmer for 5 minutes. Pour over the orange sections. Let cool slightly, then cover and refrigerate for at least 4 hours.

To serve, remove the cinnamon stick and cloves.

calories 108
protein 1 g
carbohydrates 25 g
 fiber 5 g
 sugars 20 g
cholesterol 0 mg
total fat 0.0 g
 saturated 0.0 g
 polyunsaturated 0.0 g
 monounsaturated 0.0 g
sodium 3 mg

dietary exchange
1 fruit
1/2 other carbohydrate

Baked
Ginger Pears

Serves 8

These Asian-influenced pears go nicely with a chicken or vegetable stir-fry.

8 canned pear halves in fruit juice

1/3 cup firmly packed light brown sugar

2 tablespoons chopped pecans, dry-roasted

1 teaspoon fresh lemon juice

1/4 teaspoon ground ginger, or chopped crystallized ginger to taste

Crystallized ginger (optional)

8 maraschino cherries (optional)

Preheat the oven to 350°F.

Drain the pears, reserving the juice. Arrange the pears with the cut side up in a baking dish just large enough to hold them.

In a small bowl, stir together the brown sugar, pecans, lemon juice, and ground ginger. Spoon into the pear halves.

Pour the reserved juice around the pears.

Bake for 15 to 20 minutes.

Serve warm or cover and refrigerate to serve chilled. Garnish with bits of crystallized ginger and maraschino cherries.

Microwave Variation
Drain the juice from the pears, reserving 1 cup. Arrange the pear halves with the cut side up in a glass pie pan. Prepare as directed. Microwave, uncovered, on 100 per-cent power (high) for 5 minutes. Let cool for at least 10 minutes before serving. Garnish with ginger and cherries.

Cook's Tip on Crystallized Ginger

Crystallized ginger has been cooked in a sugar syrup and coated with sugar. Look for it in the spice section at your supermarket.

calories 86
protein 0 g
carbohydrates 19 g
  fiber 1 g
  sugars 16 g
cholesterol 0 mg
total fat 1.5 g
  saturated 0.0 g
  polyunsaturated 0.5 g
  monounsaturated 1.0 g
sodium 7 mg

dietary exchange
1 fruit
1/2 other carbohydrate

Golden Poached Pears

Serves 6

Serve these delicately poached pears with a flute of sparkling wine or white grape juice. A great fall dessert!

6 Bartlett pears
1 tablespoon fresh lemon juice
2 12-ounce cans apricot nectar
½ cup sugar

1 teaspoon grated lemon zest
¼ cup fresh lemon juice
½ cup sherry (cream sherry preferred)
6 sprigs of fresh mint (optional)

Peel the pears. (Leave the cores and stems.) Sprinkle the pears with 1 tablespoon lemon juice to prevent discoloration.

In a large, deep saucepan, stir together the apricot nectar, sugar, lemon zest, and ¼ cup lemon juice. Bring to a boil over medium-high heat. Reduce the heat and simmer for 5 minutes.

Stir in the sherry.

Add the pears. Simmer for 20 to 25 minutes, or until just tender, basting and turning occasionally to cook evenly. (Cooking time may vary depending on the size and firmness of the pears.) Transfer the pears to a storage container.

Continue simmering the sauce until reduced by half. Pour the sauce over the pears, cover, and refrigerate.

To serve, spoon the syrup over the pears. Garnish with fresh mint.

calories 243
protein 1 g
carbohydrates 60 g
  fiber 5 g
  sugars 50 g
cholesterol 0 mg
total fat 1.0 g
  saturated 0.0 g
  polyunsaturated 0.0 g
  monounsaturated 0.0 g
sodium 5 mg

dietary exchange
3 fruit
1 other carbohydrate

Cook's Tip on Pears

Pears are ripe when they yield to gentle pressure at the stem end. The body of the pear will still be firm. To ripen pears, put them in a paper bag and fold the top down. To speed up the process, put an apple in the bag with them. A pear's skin toughens as it cooks, so always peel before cooking.

Fall Fruit Medley

This is a wonderful combination of seasonal fruits. Use the fruits listed or substitute whatever fruits are available.

2 medium apples, sliced
2 medium pears, sliced
1 Fuyu persimmon, sliced

5 ounces frozen sweetened raspberries, thawed and drained
¼ cup fresh orange juice
¼ cup kirsch (optional)

In a medium bowl, stir together the apples, pears, and persimmon.

Gently stir in the raspberries.

Pour in the orange juice and kirsch, stirring gently. Cover and refrigerate until needed.

Cook's Tip on Persimmons

A Fuyu persimmon resembles a squatty, reddish orange tomato in shape. Firm when ripe, it can be eaten whole or sliced and will be crisp and not astringent. Hachiya persimmons, on the other hand, are very bitter until they are completely soft.

calories 108
protein 1 g
carbohydrates 28 g
 fiber 5 g
 sugars 22 g
cholesterol 0 mg
total fat 0.5 g
 saturated 0.0 g
 polyunsaturated 0.0 g
 monounsaturated 0.0 g
sodium 1 mg

dietary exchange
2 fruit

.with kirsch

calories 133
protein 1 g
carbohydrates 31 g
 fiber 5 g
 sugars 25 g
cholesterol 0 mg
total fat 0.5 g
 saturated 0.0 g
 polyunsaturated 0.0 g
 monounsaturated 0.0 g
sodium 1 mg

dietary exchange
2 fruit

Frozen
Raspberry Cream

Serves 8

Sweet, tart berries combine with whipped topping for a dream of a dessert.

Whites of 2 large eggs, at room temperature
2 teaspoons water
1/8 teaspoon cream of tartar
3/4 cup sugar
10-ounce package frozen unsweetened raspberries or strawberries, thawed

1 tablespoon fresh lemon juice
1 cup frozen fat-free or low-fat whipped topping, thawed
8 fresh raspberries or strawberries (optional)
8 fresh sprigs of mint (optional)

In the top of a double boiler, beat together the egg whites, water, and cream of tartar. Cook over simmering water for 7 to 10 minutes, or until the mixture registers 160°F on an instant-read or candy thermometer. Pour into a large bowl.

Add the sugar 1 tablespoon at a time, beating constantly until smooth.

Stir in the berries and lemon juice. Beat until soft peaks form.

Fold in the whipped topping. Spoon into 8 goblets. Freeze for at least 8 hours.

To serve, place a berry and a mint sprig on each serving.

calories 115
protein 1 g
carbohydrates 28 g
  fiber 1 g
  sugars 22 g
cholesterol 0 mg
total fat 0.0 g
  saturated 0.0 g
  polyunsaturated 0.0 g
  monounsaturated 0.0 g
sodium 19 mg

dietary exchange
2 other carbohydrate

Time-Saver

Skip the freezing and just refrigerate the raspberry cream for 2 hours if you're pressed for time.

Spiced Skillet Bananas
with Frozen Yogurt

Serves 4

Sample a taste of the Deep South with these bananas in a brown sugar glaze.

1 tablespoon acceptable stick
   margarine
2 tablespoons dark brown sugar
2 cups sliced bananas (3 to
   4 medium)

¹/₂ teaspoon vanilla, butter, and nut
   flavoring or vanilla extract
2 cups fat-free or low-fat vanilla
   frozen yogurt

In a large nonstick skillet, melt the margarine over medium-high heat. Add the brown sugar, stirring until the mixture is bubbly and the sugar is dissolved.

Add the bananas, gently stirring to coat. Cook for 3 minutes, or until just softened and beginning to glaze and turn golden. Don't overcook, or the bananas will break down. Remove the skillet from the heat.

Gently stir in the flavoring.

Spoon the banana mixture over the frozen yogurt. Serve immediately.

calories 189
protein 4 g
carbohydrates 43 g
  fiber 2 g
  sugars 39 g
cholesterol 0 mg
total fat 1.5 g
  saturated 0.5 g
  polyunsaturated 0.5 g
  monounsaturated 0.5 g
sodium 62 mg

dietary exchange
1 fruit
2 other carbohydrate
¹/₂ fat

Spiced Skillet Apples with Frozen Yogurt
Replace the bananas with thinly sliced peeled apples, such as Red Delicious, and replace the vanilla, butter, and nut flavoring with apple pie spice (see Cook's Tip on Pumpkin or Apple Pie Spice, page 567). Cook for 6 to 8 minutes, or until the apples are just tender.

spiced skillet apples
with frozen yogurt

calories 150
protein 3 g
carbohydrates 33 g
  fiber 1 g
  sugars 32 g
cholesterol 0 mg
total fat 1.5 g
  saturated 0.5 g
  polyunsaturated 0.5 g
  monounsaturated 0.5 g
sodium 62 mg

dietary exchange
¹/₂ fruit
2 other carbohydrate
¹/₂ fat

Frozen Mini Key Lime Soufflés

Serves 8

No worries about these soufflés falling—they freeze in place. For a more dramatic presentation, use 2-ounce soufflé cups with collars. If you want a casual look use 4-ounce custard cups without collars.

14-ounce can fat-free sweetened condensed milk

1 teaspoon grated Key lime zest or lime zest

1/2 cup fresh Key lime juice (about 12 Key limes) or bottled Key lime juice

2 tablespoons powdered egg whites (pasteurized dried egg whites)

1/4 cup plus 2 tablespoons cold water

1 cup fat-free or low-fat frozen whipped topping, thawed

3 Key limes or 1 lime, cut into thin slices (optional)

To make cups for eight 2-ounce soufflé cups, cut aluminum foil into eight 8 × 2-inch strips. Wrap a strip around the rim of each soufflé cup to form a collar. Secure the foil with a piece of tape. This will give the illusion of a risen soufflé when the collar is removed.

In a medium bowl, whisk together the condensed milk, lime zest, and lime juice until slightly thickened.

In a separate medium bowl, whisk together the powdered egg whites and water. Let stand for 2 minutes, whisking occasionally, until the egg whites are completely dissolved and the mixture is slightly frothy. Using an electric hand mixer, beat on medium high for 2 to 3 minutes, or until the mixture reaches stiff peaks.

Using a rubber scraper, fold the whipped topping into the condensed milk mixture. Fold in the egg whites until just combined (mixture will be light and fluffy).

Spoon 1/2 cup mixture into each custard cup. Cover individually with aluminum foil. Freeze for at least 3 hours, or until firm (will keep for up to one month, covered in aluminum foil, in the freezer).

To serve, remove the foil collar. Garnish with the lime slices.

calories 166
protein 5 g
carbohydrates 35 g
  fiber 0 g
  sugars 32 g
cholesterol 3 mg
total fat 0.0 g
  saturated 0.0 g
  polyunsaturated 0.0 g
  monounsaturated 0.0 g
sodium 77 mg

dietary exchange
2½ other carbohydrate

Strawberries with Champagne Ice

Serves 14

The flavors of strawberries and champagne marry well in this cool, refreshing dessert.

2	medium oranges	2	cups champagne or other sparkling white wine
1	medium lemon		
1½	cups water	2	cups fresh strawberries
¾	cup sugar	1	cup champagne or other sparkling white wine
3	tablespoons orange-flavored liqueur	1	tablespoon sugar

With a vegetable peeler, peel the zest in strips from the oranges and lemon. Squeeze the juice from the oranges and lemon.

In a large saucepan, stir together the water, ¾ cup sugar, and citrus zest. Bring to a boil over medium-high heat; boil for 5 minutes. Remove from the heat. Discard the zest. Pour the liquid into a large bowl.

Stir the orange and lemon juices and liqueur into the sugar mixture. Cover and refrigerate for 2 hours.

Stir the 2 cups champagne into the juice mixture. Pour into an 8-inch square pan. Freeze for 2 hours 30 minutes to 3 hours, or until slushy.

Beat the juice mixture in a mixing bowl or process in a food processor or blender until smooth. Pour the mixture back into the pan and refreeze for 2 to 3 hours, stirring occasionally.

Meanwhile, hull the strawberries and cut in half. Put in a medium bowl.

Stir the 1 cup champagne and 1 tablespoon sugar into the strawberries. Cover and refrigerate for at least 2 hours.

To serve, place the strawberries in goblets and fill with champagne ice.

calories 103
protein 0 g
carbohydrates 16 g
  fiber 1 g
  sugars 15 g
cholesterol 0 mg
total fat 0.0 g
  saturated 0.0 g
  polyunsaturated 0.0 g
  monounsaturated 0.0 g
sodium 4 mg

dietary exchange
1 other carbohydrate

Strawberry-Raspberry Ice

Serves 8

A refreshingly cool double dose of berries, this ice looks attractive in chilled wine or champagne glasses with sprigs of fresh mint.

6 ounces frozen white grape juice concentrate

1 cup water

1 tablespoon confectioners' sugar

8 ounces frozen unsweetened strawberries, slightly thawed

6 ounces frozen sweetened raspberries, slightly thawed

6 ice cubes (about 1 cup)

Sprigs of fresh mint (optional)

In a food processor or blender, combine all the ingredients except the mint in the order listed. Process until smooth (except the seeds), stirring occasionally. Pour into a large resealable plastic bag and seal. Put the bag on its side in the freezer until the mixture freezes solid, at least 2 hours.

About 15 minutes before serving, remove the bag from the freezer and allow the ice to thaw slightly, mashing with a fork if needed. Spoon into chilled glasses and garnish with mint. Serve immediately.

calories 102
protein 0 g
carbohydrates 26 g
  fiber 2 g
  sugars 23 g
cholesterol 0 mg
total fat 0.0 g
  saturated 0.0 g
  polyunsaturated 0.0 g
  monounsaturated 0.0 g
sodium 10 mg

dietary exchange
1½ fruit

Strawberry-Banana Sorbet
with Star Fruit

Serves 5

Give your guests the star treatment—garnish this dessert with star fruit.

1 cup peach, apricot, or strawberry
  nectar or fresh orange juice
¼ cup sugar
1 cup sliced fresh strawberries
1 cup sliced bananas (1½ to
  2 medium)

2 tablespoons dry white wine
  (regular or nonalcoholic) or fresh
  orange juice
1 tablespoon fresh lemon juice
1 star fruit, or carambola
  Sprigs of fresh mint (optional)

In a small saucepan, stir together the nectar and sugar until the sugar is dissolved. Bring to a boil over medium-high heat. Reduce the heat and simmer for 5 minutes, stirring occasionally. Pour into a medium bowl and refrigerate for 10 to 15 minutes.

Meanwhile, in a food processor or blender, process the strawberries, bananas, wine, and lemon juice until smooth (except the seeds). Pour into the nectar mixture, stirring well.

Pour the mixture into an 8-inch square pan. Cover and put in the freezer for 2 hours, stirring every 30 minutes. Freeze without stirring for 4 to 5 hours, or until completely frozen.

To serve, trim the ends off the star fruit. Cut crosswise into thin slices. Remove the seeds. Using an ice cream scoop, fill dessert dishes or wineglasses with the sorbet. Garnish with the star fruit and mint.

Mango-Peach Sorbet with Star Fruit
Replace strawberries and bananas with 2 cups diced fresh mangoes (about 2 large) or one 14-ounce can mangoes, drained and diced.

calories 114
protein 1 g
carbohydrates 28 g
  fiber 2 g
  sugars 25 g
cholesterol 0 mg
total fat 0.5 g
  saturated 0.0 g
  polyunsaturated 0.0 g
  monounsaturated 0.0 g
sodium 5 mg

dietary exchange
1 fruit
1 other carbohydrate

**mango-peach sorbet
with star fruit**

calories 119
protein 1 g
carbohydrates 30 g
  fiber 2 g
  sugars 27 g
cholesterol 0 mg
total fat 0.5 g
  saturated 0.0 g
  polyunsaturated 0.0 g
  monounsaturated 0.0 g
sodium 6 mg

dietary exchange
1 fruit
1 other carbohydrate

Tropical Breeze

You'll think you've had a quick trip to the islands when you drink this creamy blend of tropical flavors. It's best when served in glasses that have been chilled in the freezer.

½ cup pineapple juice

2 cups fat-free or light vanilla yogurt

¾ cup very ripe mashed banana (about 1½ medium)

¼ cup confectioners' sugar

2 teaspoons vanilla extract

½ teaspoon coconut extract

8 ice cubes (about 1⅓ cups)

4 fresh pineapple spears (optional)

In a food processor or blender, combine all the ingredients except the pineapple spears in the order listed. Process until smooth. Pour into a large resealable plastic bag and seal. Put the bag on its side in the freezer until the mixture is very thick, about 1 hour.

To serve, spoon the mixture into glasses and garnish with the pineapple spears. If the mixture is too frozen to pour or spoon into glasses, return it to the processor or blender and process until slushy. Serve immediately.

calories 205
protein 7 g
carbohydrates 43 g
  fiber 1 g
  sugars 40 g
cholesterol 2 mg
total fat 0.5 g
  saturated 0.0 g
  polyunsaturated 0.0 g
  monounsaturated 0.0 g
sodium 86 mg

dietary exchange
1 fruit
2 other carbohydrate

Sunny Mango Sorbet

Serves 4

Thick, creamy, rich, tart, and sweet—this super simple sorbet is all these and more. Serve it in wineglasses or decorative bowls.

4 cups coarsely chopped mangoes (about 5 medium)	$^1/_2$ cup fresh lime juice
	2 tablespoons sugar

In a food processor or blender, process the ingredients until smooth. Pour into a large resealable plastic bag and seal. Put the bag on its side in the freezer for about 2 hours, or until thick. If the mixture is frozen solid, put the bag on the counter for about 30 minutes, then stir before serving.

Cook's Tip

If you want a completely smooth sorbet, strain the processed mixture before freezing.

calories 140
protein 1 g
carbohydrates 37 g
  fiber 3 g
  sugars 32 g
cholesterol 0 mg
total fat 0.5 g
  saturated 0.0 g
  polyunsaturated 0.0 g
  monounsaturated 0.0 g
sodium 4 mg

dietary exchange
2$^1/_2$ fruit

Tequila Lime Sherbet

Serves 6

Tequila and lime make a refreshing combination. Serve this sherbet after a spicy Tex-Mex meal.

2 tablespoons cold water	1 cup fat-free or light plain yogurt
1 envelope unflavored gelatin	1 tablespoon grated lime zest
1 cup water	1/2 cup fresh lime juice
3/4 cup sugar	1/3 cup tequila

In a cup or small bowl, combine 2 tablespoons water and gelatin (a fork works well). Set aside to let the gelatin soften.

In a medium saucepan, stir together 1 cup water and the sugar. Bring to a boil over medium-high heat. Boil for 5 minutes, stirring occasionally. Remove from the heat.

Whisk in the gelatin mixture and the remaining ingredients until smooth. Pour into an 8-inch square pan. Freeze for 2 hours 30 minutes to 3 hours, or until slushy.

In a food processor or blender, process the mixture until smooth. Return to the pan and freeze, about 6 hours. Remove from the freezer about 15 minutes before serving.

calories 158
protein 3 g
carbohydrates 30 g
  fiber 0 g
  sugars 28 g
cholesterol 1 mg
total fat 0.0 g
  saturated 0.0 g
  polyunsaturated 0.0 g
  monounsaturated 0.0 g
sodium 36 mg

dietary exchange
2 other carbohydrate

Cardinal Sundae

Serves 16

Frosty lime sherbet topped with a vibrant berry mixture makes a delicious treat with a beautiful color contrast.

¹/₂ cup frozen unsweetened strawberries, thawed	1 teaspoon cornstarch
¹/₂ cup frozen sweetened raspberries, thawed	¹/₄ teaspoon fresh lemon juice
	1 tablespoon currant jelly
	8 cups lime sherbet

Drain the strawberries and raspberries, reserving the juices. Set the berries aside.

In a small saucepan, whisk together the berry juices, cornstarch, and lemon juice. Bring to a boil over medium-high heat. Cook for 1 minute, whisking constantly.

Add the jelly, whisking until it melts. Remove from the heat.

Stir the berries into the sauce. Pour into a small bowl, cover, and refrigerate.

To serve, put ¹/₂ cup sherbet in each bowl. Top each serving with 1 tablespoon sauce. Cover and refrigerate any remaining topping.

calories 134
protein 0 g
carbohydrates 31 g
 fiber 0 g
 sugars 24 g
cholesterol 0 mg
total fat 0.0 g
 saturated 0.0 g
 polyunsaturated 0.0 g
 monounsaturated 0.0 g
sodium 35 mg

dietary exchange
2 other carbohydrate

Kiwifruit Sundaes

Serves 4

For variety, spoon this pretty sauce over angel food cake or pudding instead of frozen yogurt.

4 green kiwifruit, peeled
1/3 cup fresh orange juice
1/4 cup honey
2 teaspoons cornstarch
1 teaspoon grated orange zest

2 tablespoons fresh orange juice or orange liqueur
1/8 teaspoon almond extract
2 cups fat-free or low-fat frozen yogurt or ice cream

In a food processor or blender, process 2 kiwifruit until smooth (except the seeds). Slice the remaining kiwifruit and set aside.

In a microwave-safe bowl, whisk together the processed kiwifruit, 1/3 cup orange juice, honey, and cornstarch. Microwave, covered, on 100 percent power (high) for 3 minutes, stirring once.

Stir the orange zest, 2 tablespoons orange juice, and almond extract into the kiwifruit mixture.

To serve, spoon the frozen yogurt into dessert bowls. Spoon the sauce over the yogurt. Top with the sliced kiwifruit.

calories 210
protein 4 g
carbohydrates 51 g
  fiber 3 g
  sugars 46 g
cholesterol 0 mg
total fat 0.5 g
  saturated 0.0 g
  polyunsaturated 0.0 g
  monounsaturated 0.0 g
sodium 45 mg

dietary exchange
1 fruit
2½ other carbohydrate

appendixes

Appendix a
shopping with your health in mind

The next time you're waiting in line at the supermarket, take a look at what's in your grocery cart. This is where healthful eating begins—or doesn't. If your cart brims with fresh fruits and vegetables, whole-grain breads, low-fat dairy products, whole-grain pasta, dried beans, skinless chicken, and seafood, you are taking advantage of nature's bounty to eat well and take care of your heart.

Planning: Start off on the Right Foot

To make shopping easier, it's a good idea to plan your meals—at least the entrées —for the whole week. Variety is one of the keys to a healthful eating plan. Eating the same things day after day deprives you of many essential nutrients, and it's boring. As you plan a menu, try to choose something from each of the major food groups (pages xi–xiii, 641–647). Then, for the next day, pick something a little different in each group.

Shopping Guidelines

- Look for whole grains, whole-grain pasta, and brown and wild rices.
- Limit the daily amount of meat, seafood, or poultry to 6 ounces (cooked) per person.
- Include whole-grain bread or cereal products for satisfying bulk.
- Plan on including a variety of vegetables and fruits, including one serving of citrus fruit or a vegetable high in vitamin C and one serving of dark green, leafy vegetables or deep yellow vegetables each day.
- Be sure to use fat-free milk or other fat-free or low-fat dairy products.
- Use sweets sparingly. Enjoy delicious fruits instead.

Using a detailed list of what you need will save you time and help you cut down on impulse buying. Plan to do most of your shopping only once a week. Make it a habit to jot down the items you need to replace. Also, try not to shop on an empty stomach. When you're hungry, you may be guided by your impulses instead of your planned menus. Looking over sales fliers when planning your menu can help trim costs, but be sure to select only those sale items that fit into your dietary plan. If a food adds unnecessary calories, saturated fat, trans fat, or sodium to your table, it's not a bargain.

Read the Labels

With fresh produce and other foods that reach the supermarket in their natural, unaltered state, you have total control over how much fat and salt and how many calories you add in preparation. With packaged or prepared foods, however, the only way to be sure of what you're getting is to check the federally required nutrition label on each one. It tells you instantly how much fat and saturated fat a serving of the product contains; the number of calories per serving; the amount of cholesterol, sodium, and sugars; and the amount of total carbohydrates, dietary fiber, and protein. The content of all these nutrients is expressed in both weight (in grams or milligrams) and percentages of recommended daily amounts, based on a 2,000-calorie-per-day diet. The label also shows the content of some vitamins and minerals.

Nutrition Facts

Serving Size 1 cup (240mL)
Servings Per Container 8

Amount Per Serving

Calories 90 — Calories from Fat 0

	% Daily Value*
Total Fat 0g	0%
Saturated Fat 0g	0%
Cholesterol 5mg	0%
Sodium 125mg	5%
Total Carbohydrate 13g	4%
Dietary Fiber 0g	0%
Sugars 12g	
Protein 8g	

Vitamin A	10%	•	Vitamin C	2%
Calcium 30%	•	Iron 0%	•	Vitamin D 25%

*Percent Daily Values are based on a 2,000 calorie diet. Your daily values may be higher or lower depending on your calorie needs:

		Calories 2,000	2,500
Total Fat	Less than	65g	80g
Sat. Fat	Less than	20g	25g
Cholesterol	Less than	300mg	300mg
Sodium	Less than	2,400mg	2,400mg
Total Carbohydrate		300g	375g
Dietary Fiber		25g	30g

Calories per gram:
Fat 9 • Carbohydrate 4 • Protein 4

Packaged foods must also carry a list of all ingredients they contain. This list usually appears directly below the nutrition label. It gives all the ingredients by weight, starting with the heaviest. Obviously, if beef fat, butter, or vegetable shortening is at the top of the list, you can assume that the product is extremely high in fat. This fact will be amply reflected in the "Calories from Fat" and "% (of) Daily Value" shown at the top of the nutrition label.

Which Type of Fat—and How Much?

It's important to note the amounts of the different fats and cholesterol in a product, as shown on the Nutrition Facts label. Many packaged foods contain saturated, trans, polyunsaturated, and monounsaturated fats, but in varying amounts. Only saturated fat, trans fat, and dietary cholesterol raise blood cholesterol. In the typical American diet, the main sources of saturated fat are foods from animals. The only dietary source of cholesterol is animal products.

Watch for the foods in the following lists as you shop. If you see any of them in the ingredients list, especially as the first item listed, that product is likely to raise your blood cholesterol level if you make it part of your regular diet.

FOODS HIGH IN SATURATED FAT AND CHOLESTEROL	FOODS HIGH IN SATURATED FAT	FOODS HIGH IN TRANS FAT
Animal fats (bacon, beef, chicken, lamb, pork, turkey)	Cocoa butter	Partially hydrogenated vegetable oil
Butter	Coconut	Vegetable shortening
Cheese	Coconut oil	
Cream	Palm kernel oil	
Eggs or egg yolk solids	Palm oil	
Lard	Vegetable oil (could be coconut, palm, or palm kernel oil)	
Whole-milk solids		

Tropical oils, such as coconut, palm, and palm kernel, were once used in dozens of processed food products. Coconut oil and palm kernel oil are even more heavily saturated than butter or lard. Therefore, they pose a much greater health hazard. Palm oil is similar to butter and lard in saturated fat content. We strongly advise avoiding foods that include these oils.

Oils that stay liquid at room temperature are low in saturated fat and high in unsaturated fats (polyunsaturated and monounsaturated). These oils include canola, corn, olive, safflower, sesame, soybean, and sunflower. Including these oils as part of a diet low in saturated fat can help lower your cholesterol.

Margarines vary greatly in their fat composition. Select the ones with the lowest amounts of saturated and trans fats. That means choosing margarines that list liquid oils as their first ingredient. They are the lowest in saturated fat among the spreads that are 100 percent fat. Margarines listing partially hydrogenated oil as the first ingredient have more saturated fat. They also have more trans fats, which can raise blood cholesterol.

Trans fats are by-products created when the unsaturated fats in margarine are hydrogenated. Hydrogenation—adding hydrogen—converts liquid oils into a more stable form. This gives the product greater shelf life. It also makes the margarine harder and less likely to melt at room temperature.

You can tell a lot from the texture about how much trans fat a margarine contains. The softer the spread, the lower it is in trans fats. The harder it is, the more of these fats it contains. We still recommend margarine over butter, and the rule when buying margarine is "the softer the better." This includes sprays and liquid spreads that are primarily water and/or fat-free milk. They contain so little liquid vegetable oil that they can be classified as fat free. Use the lowest-fat margarine you can for spreading on such foods as bread, toast, or baked potatoes. For pan cooking, use a spray or liquid margarine or a little broth, wine, or water. For baking, use an acceptable liquid vegetable oil or solid margarine.

Food Certification Program

The American Heart Association Food Certification Program is designed to be an easy, reliable tool for grocery shoppers. The heart-check mark on food packages indicates that the product meets the American Heart Association food criteria for saturated fat and cholesterol. These criteria apply to healthy people over age two.

Heart-check products also meet the Federal Drug Administration criteria that allow food manufacturers to say on the package that the food may help reduce one's risk for heart disease. Visit *www.americanheart.org* for a list of certified products.

American Heart Association

Meets American Heart Association food criteria for saturated fat and cholesterol for healthy people over age 2.

Small Changes, Big Results

For many food shoppers, it's hard to break lifelong buying habits and eating patterns all at once. Few people are likely to make the switch from high-risk foods to heart-healthy foods overnight. Luckily, that isn't necessary. Making just a few minor changes can pay big health dividends when you reduce the saturated fat, trans fat, cholesterol, and calories in key food items.

For example, let's say you decide to try fat-free milk instead of the whole milk you've always bought. The chart below illustrates the dramatic savings you will see in calories, fat, and cholesterol.

PER 1-CUP SERVING	WHOLE MILK	FAT-FREE MILK
Calories	149.0 cal	86.0 cal
Protein	8.0 g	8.0 g
Carbohydrates	11.0 g	12.0 g
Total Fat	8.0 g	0.5 g
Saturated	5.0 g	0.5 g
Polyunsaturated	0.5 g	0.0 g
Monounsaturated	2.5 g	0.0 g
Cholesterol	34.0 mg	5.0 mg

If fat-free milk doesn't appeal to you, try drinking 2 percent milk for a couple of weeks, and then switch to 1 percent, then ½ percent, and finally to fat free. After getting used to fat-free milk, many people find that whole milk tastes too rich, almost like whipping cream. The benefits in health are well worth making the adjustment. With each small change in your shopping habits, you and your family will move a step closer to a heart-healthy eating plan.

What's a Serving?

When you're shopping, keep estimated portion sizes in mind. Serving sizes can be difficult to visualize. Few of us weigh or measure the food we eat. Most of us, however, can tell the difference between 1 cup and ½ cup. When you divide foods into servings or are counting your day's intake of nutrients, be honest about the size of the portions you eat. When you consume twice as much of a certain food as the listed serving size, you need to recognize that you are eating double the amount of calories, fats, cholesterol, sodium, and other nutrients. Restaurant portions are particularly large these days, making it easier to get used to eating more than you need. For example, a reasonable portion of cooked meat is about the size of a deck of cards or a computer mouse. (See pages xii and xiii for serving size charts.)

Shopping by Food Group

The tips that follow will help you make wise choices as you plan your meals. Remember that variety and balance are the keys to good nutrition and a satisfied palate.

VEGETABLES AND FRUITS

Fresh vegetables and fruits are high in fiber and vitamins, have little or no fat, and tend to be low in sodium. You can eat most of them freely as part of a balanced diet. In canning, packaging, and processing, however, many things can happen to fruits and vegetables. When shopping for foods in this category, here are a few thoughts to keep in mind.

- Vegetables prepared with butter, cream, or whole-milk cheese are likely to be high in saturated fat.
- Fried vegetables have much more saturated fat and many more calories than vegetables prepared without fat.
- Fruits that are fresh or canned in water are lower in calories than fruits canned in juice or in syrup. Drain fruits canned in syrup.
- Vegetables packed in brine, such as pickles and sauerkraut, are loaded with sodium. It helps to rinse brine-packed foods. Look for reduced-sodium pickles in some diet-food sections, too.
- All olives are high in fat, but much of it is unsaturated. They also are high in calories. Green olives are high in sodium (580 milligrams in 10 small ones), and black olives are moderately high (200 milligrams in 10 small ones). When you buy olives, check the labels carefully. Some brands of stuffed green olives are lower in fat than the plain ones.
- Coconut meat is high in saturated fat, and avocados are high in unsaturated fat but also high in calories. It's best to eat these foods in moderation.

BREADS, CEREALS, AND PASTA

Experiment freely with the many different kinds of whole-grain bread available. Although breads contain some sodium and a small amount of fat, they are full of flavor and nutritive value.

- Many commercially baked products (croissants, muffins, biscuits, and butter rolls) contain large amounts of saturated fat. It's much better to make your own. Use the recipes in this book (pages 510–544) or make your favorites, omitting or reducing the salt and using the ingredient substitutions listed on page 663 if needed.

- Check the labels on baked goods. If the foods are made with whole milk and dehydrated egg yolks, select them only occasionally.
- Some crackers are heavy in fats and oils, but stores also stock an increasing number of fat-free or reduced-fat varieties. Scandinavian-style rye crackers and other whole-grain crackers are often made without added fat or salt.
- For a low-sodium diet, use crackers with unsalted tops when recipes call for crackers or cracker crumbs.
- Cook brown rice, bulgur wheat, millet, or other whole grains in seasoned fat-free, low-sodium broth for a side dish or as part of an entrée. They're high in fiber, relatively low in calories, and economical.
- Hot cereals, rice, and pastas contain almost no sodium—if you cook them without salt.
- Read the ingredients lists and nutrition labels on dry cereals. Although most are low in saturated fat, some contain salt and a large quantity of sugar. Be moderate in the amount of sugar you add to cereals. (Sugar intake has not been directly linked to heart disease. However, the American Heart Association recommends a diet moderate in sugar because the additional calories can lead to obesity, which is a risk factor.) Some so-called natural cereals and granolas contain added salt, sugar, and saturated fat in the form of coconut or coconut oil. Remember that "natural" means different things to different people. It may mean only that the cereal contains whole, unmilled grains.

DAIRY PRODUCTS

Milk and other dairy products are the best source of calcium, are a good source of protein, and provide vitamins and minerals. They can be high in saturated fat, however, so look for fat-free and low-fat varieties.

- Although 2 percent milk is labeled "reduced-fat," it still contains almost half the fat of whole milk. Fat-free or ½ percent milk is much more suitable for a low-fat diet. Despite its name and rich taste, most buttermilk is very low in fat (it's made from cultured fat-free milk).
- The most readily available types of fat-free cheese include shredded Cheddar and mozzarella, sliced American and Swiss, cottage cheese, ricotta, and grated Parmesan. A number of low-fat cheeses also are available.
- Sour cream is available in both fat-free and low-fat versions.
- Creamy cheeses, such as Brie and processed cheese spreads, are high in

saturated fat. Save them for rare occasions. A good rule of thumb is to select cheese with 3 grams of fat or less per ounce.

- Choose from the wide selection of fat-free or low-fat dairy desserts, such as frozen and nonfrozen yogurt, ices, ice milk products, sorbet, and sherbet, as well as fat-free ice cream.
- Fat-free or low-fat nondairy coffee creamers and whipped toppings are available, replacing the products packed with coconut, palm, or palm kernel oil and loaded with saturated fat.

MEAT, POULTRY, AND SEAFOOD

Animal foods are the richest sources of protein, but many are also heavy in saturated fat and cholesterol. Seafood, chicken, turkey, and lean meats provide just as much protein as, but much less saturated fat than, fatty cuts of beef, lamb, and pork.

Meats

- Look for USDA Select or Choice grades of lean beef cuts, such as round steak, sirloin tip, tenderloin, or flank steak. Avoid cuts such as T-bones and rib eyes. Avoid Prime grade. It's heavily marbled, so it's high in saturated fat.
- Choose lean or extra-lean ground beef. If none of the ground meats is low enough in fat, select some lean steak, roast, or stewing beef and ask the butcher to remove all the visible fat and grind the meat for you.
- Serve liver, brains, kidneys, and sweetbreads only occasionally. They are high in cholesterol.
- Pork tenderloin, loin chops, center-cut ham, and Canadian bacon are good lean choices. Prepackaged hams usually have a fraction of the fat of whole hams and are labeled for fat and sodium content to eliminate guesswork.
- All cuts of veal are lean except the cutlets (ground or cubed) and breast.
- The lean cuts of lamb are leg, arm, shank, and loin.
- Some wild game, such as venison and rabbit, is very lean. Among the exotic meats also low in fat are ostrich, emu, and buffalo.
- Choose fat-free and low-fat varieties of cold cuts. Check the nutrition labels, however; some cold cuts are quite high in sodium.
- Substitute dried beans, peas, and lentils for meats in casseroles, stews, and soups. They're excellent protein sources and very economical.

Poultry

- Removing the skin from whole birds and pieces before eating the poultry greatly reduces the fat content. This is true for ground poultry as well. Chicken and turkey should be ground without the skin.

- Skinless white chicken meat has only half the fat of skinless dark meat.
- Goose, duck, and some processed poultry products are high in saturated fat. Cornish game hens are fairly high in cholesterol. Pheasant is lean.
- Some—but not all—commercial basting solutions in prebasted turkeys contain highly saturated fats. Even those that don't are usually high in sodium. You can baste your turkey with an unsalted, fat-free broth.
- You can substitute chicken or turkey breasts in recipes that call for veal steaks or cutlets. The taste and texture will be different, but the flavors will be excellent.

Seafood

- Try to eat fish that contain omega-3 fatty acids at least two times per week. Some good choices are Atlantic and coho salmon, albacore tuna, mackerel, lake and brook trout, and halibut.
- Fresh and frozen fish are good protein sources. So are tuna and salmon in foil packets, canned salmon, and tuna canned in distilled or spring water.
- Shrimp, lobster, crab, crayfish, and most other shellfish are very low in saturated fat. Shrimp and crayfish are higher in cholesterol than most other seafood, but lower in fat and cholesterol than most meats and poultry.
- Be aware that some types of fish may contain high levels of mercury, PCBs (polychlorinated biphenyls), dioxins, and other environmental contaminants. Shark, swordfish, tilefish (golden bass or golden snapper), and king mackerel are examples. Young children and women who are pregnant, planning to become pregnant, or nursing should avoid eating potentially contaminated fish.

EGGS AND EGG SUBSTITUTES

One large egg yolk contains about 213 milligrams of cholesterol, just over two thirds of the 300-mg daily recommended maximum. It's a good idea to limit your egg yolk consumption, including the egg yolks used in cooking. On the other hand, egg whites contain no cholesterol and are an excellent, inexpensive source of protein. In many recipes, you can substitute egg whites for whole eggs, using two egg whites for each whole egg. You can also use a commercial egg substitute. It's never safe to eat raw eggs or egg whites.

FATS AND OILS

The amount and the kinds of fat you consume are the major keys to staying within American Heart Association dietary recommendations. Include polyunsaturated and monounsaturated oils in your daily diet to replace saturated fats. If you are trying to lose weight, a reasonable total to aim for is 5 to 8 teaspoons of fat daily, which should include the hidden fat in baked and snack foods, as well as the fats used in cooking and the spreads you use on bread products. If your caloric intake is not a concern, you can consume a little more unsaturated fat as you replace the saturated fat in your diet.

Use the list below to identify the recommended fats and oils.

RECOMMENDED	FOR OCCASIONAL USE ONLY
Canola oil	Vegetable shortening
Olive oil	Regular stick margarine
Safflower oil	Butter
Sunflower oil	Bacon, salt pork
Corn oil	Chicken or turkey fat, meat fat
Sesame oil	Chocolate
Soybean oil	
Polyunsaturated margarine	

- Buy margarine in place of butter. Look for margarine with the lowest amounts of saturated and trans fats.
- Because light and fat-free margarines contain water, they can be difficult to use for baking. However, they are very useful as spreads and in a number of cooking procedures.
- Buy nonstick vegetable oil sprays to use in place of butter, margarine, or oil in cookware.
- Many commercial salad dressings contain large amounts of fat and salt. Try making your own salad dressings (see recipes pages 137–141), or use commercial fat-free or low-fat salad dressings.
- Chocolate, coconut, and coconut, palm, and palm kernel oils contain more saturated than unsaturated fat. When selecting commercial food items containing these ingredients, look at the nutrition labels. Select the foods with the lowest amounts of saturated fats, and use them in small quantities.
- For a flavor change, you can occasionally switch to peanut oil, especially for certain ethnic dishes.

SNACKS

A crisp red apple or a small dish of raspberry sorbet is a refreshingly delicious snack. Sometimes, though, you just want a typical snack food. In that case, it's best to make something yourself, using acceptable oil or margarine. If you do buy prepared snacks, read the labels and select from the many good products in the supermarket.

- Many nuts and seeds are available in their natural state: unsalted. These foods contain fat, but it's mostly the helpful unsaturated fat. If you're watching your weight, however, be aware that nuts are high in calories.
- You can make terrific cakes, pies, cookies, and puddings at home. (See the recipes in the "Desserts" chapter, pages 556–634, for some great suggestions.) Just use acceptable margarine or oil, fat-free milk, and egg substitute or egg whites. If you choose desserts that are high in calories, make them for special occasions.
- Chips fried in oil and high-fat snack crackers still outnumber the low-fat baked kinds, so check labels carefully. Some brands of baked tortilla chips have as little as 1 gram of fat per ounce (about 9 chips), and many pretzels are fat free. Among fried chips, look for those with small amounts of saturated and trans fats. It also helps to check the ingredients for a product with an acceptable vegetable oil listed first.

MISCELLANEOUS FOODS, FLAVORINGS, AND BEVERAGES

Lots of foods have more fat, calories, or sodium than you might expect. Always read the labels and choose your foods carefully.

- When your recipe calls for baking chocolate, substitute unsweetened cocoa powder and acceptable vegetable oil or margarine (see page 645). Chocolate and cocoa butter contain saturated fat, but most of the fat has been removed from cocoa powder.
- When you're thirsty, choose beverages that are low in calories, sodium, fat, and cholesterol. Examples include fat-free milk and water. (Watch for the high sodium levels in some drinks and mineral waters.)
- If you're trying to lose weight, avoid sugared carbonated sodas, syrupy fruit drinks, and beer, wine, and other alcoholic beverages. If you do drink alcohol, limit yourself to one drink a day if you're a woman and two drinks a day if you're a man. Alcoholic drinks contain empty calories that can sabotage your healthy eating plan. Heavy alcohol consumption is associated with high blood pressure and other severe health problems.
- If you're trying to cut down on salt, check the labels on commercial seasonings, condiments, and sauces that may contain a lot of sodium. These include soy sauce, steak sauce, ketchup, chili sauce, monosodium glutamate, meat tenderizer, pickles, relishes, flavored seasoning salts, bouillon

cubes, and salad dressings. Many of these items are available in low-sodium versions.

- Look for no-salt-added or reduced-salt versions of canned soups and canned vegetables.

Appendix b
cooking for a healthy heart

Some cooking methods, such as deep-fat frying, are guaranteed to add fat to any food. Fortunately, many more methods help retain vitamins and minerals and keep fat and calories to a minimum. Roasting, baking, broiling, braising, poaching, stir-frying, and microwaving are all good choices for heart-healthy cooking.

Techniques

Avoid any cooking method that adds fat or allows food to cook in its own fat. Instead, try these excellent techniques that enhance flavor and preserve nutrients. You'll soon find ways to cook your favorite dishes so they'll give you the flavor without the fat.

ROASTING

This slow, dry-heat method of cooking creates a delicious product—and keeps fat to a minimum.

If you're preparing a roast, trim as much fat as you can, but leave a very thin covering of fat across the top. Season the meat and place it with the fat side up on a rack in an uncovered roasting pan. The rack keeps the meat from sitting in its own fat drippings. Roast to the desired doneness in a preheated oven. If basting is needed, use a fat-free liquid, such as wine, tomato juice, or lemon juice. Be sure to remove the visible fat before eating the meat. (When roasting poultry, leave the skin on during cooking. Remove the skin before eating the poultry.)

Use a meat thermometer to test for doneness. Insert it in the center of the raw roast so the probe reaches the thickest part of the meat and does not rest in fat or on bone. When the thermometer shows the desired internal temperature, push it a little deeper into the meat. If the temperature drops, continue cooking until the thermometer reaches the correct temperature. If it stays the same, the meat is done.

Time the cooking to remove the roast from the oven 10 to 15 minutes before serving so the juices can redistribute throughout the meat. Then you'll be able to carve the meat easily.

Don't forget that roasting works very well with vegetables, too.

BAKING

Baking is another form of cooking that's excellent for poultry, seafood, and meat. It differs from roasting in that you don't use a rack to allow juices to drain, and you sometimes use a covered container and add liquid before cooking. The liquid adds flavor and helps keep the meat moist.

BRAISING OR STEWING

Braising is a great slow-cooking method to tenderize tougher cuts of meat. To braise, brown the meat on all sides, using vegetable oil spray or a minimum of vegetable oil. You can dredge the meat in seasoned flour instead of browning it if you prefer. Add a small amount of liquid (¼ to ½ cup) and whatever seasonings you wish, cover tightly, and simmer. For stewing, follow the same directions, but add water to cover.

The fat cooks out of the meat and into the liquid. It's a good idea to cook the meat a day ahead, then refrigerate it. After the chilled fat hardens, you can remove it easily before reheating the food. Also, the flavors of many braised and stewed dishes are improved after refrigerating.

Braising is also an excellent way to cook vegetables.

POACHING

Poaching is cooking by immersing in simmering liquid. It works particularly well with chicken and seafood. Place a single layer of food in a wide, shallow pan. Barely cover with liquid. Some good choices are water, fat-free milk, low-sodium broth, and wine. After cooking, you can reduce the liquid—that is, decrease the volume by boiling the liquid rapidly. This intensifies the flavor. You can thicken the reduced liquid to make a delicious sauce.

STEAMING

Food cooked in a basket over simmering liquid keeps its natural flavor, color, and vitamins and minerals.

A steam cooker is ideal, but you can also use a steamer basket that fits into a pot with a tight-fitting lid. If you don't have either of these, use a metal colander or anything else that will let steam cook the food. Just be sure the liquid doesn't touch the food.

Steaming is great for vegetables and fish. Bring a small amount of liquid, usually water or broth (about an inch), to a boil, then reduce the heat so the liquid simmers. You can add herbs or spices to the liquid for extra flavor. Put the food in the basket and cover the pot. In just a few minutes, vegetables will be tender-crisp and ready to eat. Fish takes a little longer, from 5 to 10 minutes, or until it flakes easily when tested with a fork. You can even use the liquid left in the pot for soup stock.

STIR-FRYING

This method cooks food quickly in a minimum of oil or broth. The high temperature and the constant stirring keep the food from sticking and burning. The sloping sides of a wok are designed especially for stir-frying, but you can also use a large frying pan.

The key to successful stir-frying is to dice or slice each food into small pieces before you heat the liquid in the wok.

Because the hottest area is at the base of the wok, cook each food quickly there. Push that food up on the side of the wok while you cook the next one.

Use an oil that won't smoke at high temperatures. (Fat that smokes releases undesirable chemicals and won't cook correctly.) Peanut oil, which smokes at 446°F, works best. Use only a small amount.

Stir-frying results in delicious dishes because the small pieces cook quickly, which preserves the color, flavor, and crispness of vegetables. It also seals in the natural juices of meats and seafood.

When your recipe calls for soy sauce, use the low-salt variety. This helps control the amount of sodium in your diet.

GRILLING OR BROILING

Placing food on a rack and cooking it over or under direct heat is an excellent way to help control the amount of fat in your diet. The fat drips away, either into the coals or into a broiling pan. Either way, much of the fat cooks out.

Skewered vegetables and chunks of meat taste great when browned over a flame or under the broiler. Steaks, seafood, and poultry are ideal, too. For extra flavor, marinate these foods and then baste with the marinade during cooking. This keeps the food moist. But be careful: Always boil the marinade for at least 5 minutes before using it for basting. Bacteria tend to grow in marinating meat mixtures, and boiling will kill the bacteria.

MICROWAVE COOKING

Microwaving is fast, easy, and so moisture-producing that it requires no added fats or oils. In fact, you can put some food between layers of paper towels so the fat drains as the food cooks. Cook foods in glass, paper, dishwasher-safe plastic, china, or earthenware containers. Using any type of metal—including aluminum foil—can be dangerous. Also, some types of plasticware will melt or warp in a microwave.

You can adapt conventional recipes for the microwave. Try to find a microwave recipe similar to the one you want to adapt and use it as a guide. If you don't find a similar recipe, cut the microwave cooking time to one fourth to one third of the conventional amount. If the food isn't ready, continue cooking it for short periods. Refer to your manufacturer's instructions for guidance.

Cooking Tips

Now that you know the basics of low-fat cooking, you're ready to specialize. We've compiled some specific fat-cutting techniques and some flavor-enhancing ideas you may want to try.

MEAT DRIPPINGS

While meat is cooking, a rich essence drips into the roasting or broiler pan along with the fat. To keep the essence without the fat, pour the contents of the pan—fat and all—into a cup or dish, cover it, and put it in the refrigerator. The next day you can easily remove the hardened fat, leaving only the flavorful juice. This juice adds zest to meat pies, soups, sauces, hash, or meat loaf.

GRAVY

You don't have to add meat fat to have a wonderfully thick gravy. Try this one and see what we mean. You'll need about 1 cup of clear, defatted broth, homemade, canned, or made from bouillon cubes. Pour ½ cup of the broth into a jar with a tight-fitting lid. Add 1 tablespoon of cornstarch, 1 tablespoon of flour, or 1 to 2 tablespoons of browned flour. (Browned flour gives the sauce a rich mahogany color.) Cover and shake until smooth. Heat the remaining broth in a saucepan. Shake and pour the cornstarch or flour mixture into the broth and simmer, adding seasonings as desired. Cook until the gravy is the consistency you want, whisking constantly.

BROTH

Once you taste homemade broth, the canned or bouillon-cube varieties will seem flavorless by comparison. Just remember to make the broth a day ahead so you can remove the fat after it cools and hardens in the refrigerator. Use broth to make soups or stews. If necessary, defat the finished dish. If you do use canned broth, choose a fat-free, low-sodium variety. Refrigerate the can before opening, then remove the fat that rises to the top before using the broth.

WINE AND OTHER ALCOHOLIC BEVERAGES

During cooking, most alcohol evaporates, leaving the flavor and tenderizing qualities. The wines and spirits you use for cooking don't have to be expensive, but they should be good enough to drink. Avoid using cooking wines, which are heavily laced with salt to keep people from drinking them.

VINEGAR

Good wine vinegars and herb vinegars are delicious substitutes for high-fat dressings on salads. Vinegar also is flavorful in other recipes, even some desserts.

WHOLE-GRAIN FLOUR

Keep whole-grain flour in the refrigerator for freshness. You can substitute 1 cup of whole-wheat pastry flour for 1 cup of all-purpose flour, or 1 cup of whole-wheat flour for ⅞ cup of all-purpose flour.

LOW-FAT COOKING TIPS

Whether you want to lower your blood cholesterol level or lose weight, these tips will make it easier.
- Trim all visible fat from meat before cooking except when roasting.
- Buy very lean ground beef, pork, chicken, and turkey. Ground meat is generally higher in fat than unground meat, except for very lean ground beef. For ground chicken or turkey, have the breast ground without any skin.
- When figuring serving sizes, remember that meat loses about 25 percent of its weight during cooking. (For example, 4 ounces of raw meat becomes about 3 ounces cooked.)
- Either buy skinless chicken parts or skin the chicken before cooking and remove all visible fat below the skin. Use paper towels or a clean cloth to take better hold of the skin. Be sure to scrub the cutting surface and utensils well with hot, sudsy water after preparing poultry for cooking. Leave the skin on for roasting, then remove it before serving the poultry.
- Fresh fish should be cooked for about 10 minutes per inch of thickness. Add 5 minutes to the total figure if the fish is wrapped in foil. Frozen fish requires about 20 minutes per inch of thickness, plus 10 minutes if it's wrapped in foil. Cooking time may vary, depending on the method used. Fish is done when the flesh is opaque and flakes easily when tested with a fork.
- Prepare scrambled eggs or omelets with no more than 1 egg yolk per portion. Add extra egg whites to make more generous servings, or use egg substitute.
- Before eating canned salmon, drain the liquid and remove the skin.

- Cut down on cholesterol by using more vegetables and less poultry or meat in soups, stews, and casseroles. Finely chopped vegetables are great for stretching ground poultry or ground meat, too.

Savor the Flavor: Easy Flavor Enhancers

Use your imagination to find easy ways to enhance the flavor of foods. Here are some ideas to get you started.

- Seal natural juices into foods by wrapping the foods in aluminum foil or cooking parchment before cooking. Or try wrapping foods in edible pouches made of steamed lettuce or cabbage leaves.
- Cook vegetables just until tender-crisp. Overcooked vegetables lose flavor, texture, and important nutrients.
- Sweeten plain fat-free yogurt with pureed fruit, unsweetened applesauce, or undiluted frozen orange juice. This will save you the extra sugar calories in some prepared fruit yogurts.

Ways to Spice Things Up

A creative cook can make cooking exciting, imaginative, and crowd-pleasing—without added salt or fat—by experimenting with seasonings. You'll find many combinations you'll want to experiment with.

Try these ideas to spice up your dishes for everyday as well as special occasions.

- Use fresh herbs whenever possible.
- Use fresh gingerroot and fresh horseradish for extra flavor. Grate fresh gingerroot with a ginger grater or a flat, sheet-type grater. Use a food processor to grate fresh horseradish.
- Use citrus zest, the colored part of the peel without the pith. It holds the true flavor of the fruit. Grate it with a zester, vegetable peeler, or grater.
- Dry-roast seeds, nuts, and whole or ground spices to bring out their full flavor. Cook them in a dry skillet or bake them on a baking sheet.
- Roast vegetables in a hot oven to caramelize their natural sugars and bring out their full flavor.
- Use vinegar or citrus juice as a wonderful flavor enhancer. Try vinegar on vegetables such as greens. Citrus juice works well on fruits such as melons and in place of dressing on salads. Either is great with fish.

- Use dry mustard for a zesty flavor in cooking, or mix it with water to make a very sharp condiment.
- Add fresh hot peppers for a little more "bite" in your dishes. To reduce the heat somewhat, don't use the membrane or the seeds. Remember: A small amount goes a long way. Wear rubber gloves or wash your hands thoroughly after handling the peppers. Skin, especially around the eyes, is very sensitive to the oil from hot peppers.
- Some vegetables and fruits, such as mushrooms, tomatoes, chile peppers, cherries, cranberries, and currants, have a more intense flavor when dried than when fresh. Use them when you want a burst of flavor. As a bonus, keep the flavored water they soaked in and use it for cooking.

Quick and Easy Foods

Sometimes the last thing you want to do on a busy day is cook. Here are some ideas for dealing with this dilemma without resorting to fast foods loaded with saturated fat and calories.

- Try cooking in quantity. Instead of one casserole, make two. Enjoy one right away and freeze one to use later. Let the second one thaw overnight in the refrigerator, then reheat it for your own nutritious version of fast food during the week. Soups, spaghetti sauce, meat and poultry dishes, and breads also freeze well. Preparing a roast, chicken, or turkey is another way to provide several family meals, including some delicious lunchbox sandwiches.
- A little advance preparation can cut cooking time way down. For example, make rice in large quantities and serve it with stir-fried vegetables and meats several times during the week. Clean and store salad greens in a plastic container with a tight-fitting lid—they'll stay fresh and crisp for about a week.
- Organize your kitchen. Arrange foods, utensils, and equipment so you can cook quickly and efficiently.
- Make sure your pantry, refrigerator, and freezer are stocked with easy-to-fix foods, such as canned and frozen vegetables, lean ground beef, fish fillets, and chicken.
- Keep a running shopping list so you can jot down needed items as you think of them.
- Before cooking, think through the recipe ingredients and preparation steps.
- Assemble equipment and ingredients before you begin cooking.

- If you're making a complex dish, prepare simple foods to go with it. For example, if your entrée needs a lot of attention, fix a simple salad or vegetable side dish. If your entrée is simple, create an interesting side dish.
- Cook vegetables in the microwave. It usually saves time, retains nutrients, and maximizes flavor. Microwaving is also great for heating leftover vegetables.
- Try microwave or quick stovetop versions of dishes you usually cook in the oven.
- Use other laborsaving devices, such as a food processor, convection oven, pressure cooker, or slow cooker.
- Cut down on food-transfer and cleanup time by using cookware in which food can be cooked, served, and stored.

Planned-Overs

When you prepare a dinner entrée, it's often just as easy to make extra. The suggestions that follow take that idea one more step. They use the "leftovers" in specific recipes designed around them, thus the name "planned-overs." When the week gets hectic, you'll really be glad you planned ahead.

- Roasted Garlic–Lemon Turkey Breast (page 263)
- Turkey on a Bed of Sliced Tomatoes (page 128)

Marinate turkey breast in a very aromatic combination of garlic, lemon, Dijon mustard, rosemary, and thyme. Serve warm sliced turkey for one meal. Add what's left to a salad of mixed greens, red onion, and capers to serve on tomato slices for a different meal.

- Triple-Pepper Chicken (page 237)
- Cajun Chicken Salad (page 125)

A spice rub of black pepper, lemon pepper, and cayenne, plus chili powder, lime, and other flavorful ingredients, heats up chicken breasts for one dinner. Save half the recipe for a speedy salad of mixed greens, roasted red bell peppers, mushrooms, and feta cheese to enjoy a few days later.

- Sweet-Spice Glazed Chicken (page 234)
- Island Chicken Salad with Fresh Mint (page 127)

First, have a meal of broiled chicken breasts with an incredible glaze of sweet-and-sour sauce and bourbon. Then, in a flash, create a beautiful salad with mango and kiwifruit for a change of pace.

- Glazed Meatballs on Water Chestnut and Bell Pepper Rice (page 318)
- Vegetarian Stir-Fry (page 362)

Prepare glazed meatballs with orange zest and crushed red pepper flakes and serve them over rice flavored with bell peppers and water chestnuts for one meal. Transform the extra rice from this meat-based meal into a totally different entrée by adding fresh gingerroot and stir-fried cabbage, carrots, and bamboo shoots.

- Mexican Chicken and Vegetables with Chipotle Peppers (page 212)
- Chipotle Chicken Wraps (page 255)

Start with a stew of chicken, bell peppers, tomatoes, and chipotle peppers. The planned-overs entrée is the chicken mixture rolled in corn tortillas along with sour cream, cilantro, olives, and lime juice.

- Grilled Lemongrass Flank Steak (page 292)
- Grilled Flank Steak Salad with Sweet-and-Sour Sesame Dressing (page 129)

Marinate flank steak in lemongrass, rice vinegar, and chili garlic sauce, and serve it hot off the grill. Plan to use part of the steak later in a salad of colorful vegetables, wild rice, and napa cabbage, topped with an Asian-inspired dressing.

Appendix c
menu planning

Dishes served at holidays and celebrations are traditionally high in fat and calories. More people are tempted to overeat at these special occasions than at any other time. The good news is that special-occasion food doesn't have to jeopardize your health to be special. You can take control of your holiday fare. Set a table of beautiful, taste-tempting foods that are low in fat and calories. Mix colors, blend flavors, and choose textures that create an appealing contrast. Since more people are eating light, your guests will appreciate your efforts.

We've developed the following menus to help you plan holiday and special-occasion meals, as well as "regular" meals, using recipes found in this cookbook. Feel free to mix and match these menus to suit your own taste. With a little creativity and skill, you can make each occasion an affair to remember.

New Year's Day Brunch
Country-Style Breakfast Casserole
Sliced Tomatoes*
Southern Raised Biscuits
Claret-Spiced Oranges

Chinese New Year
Lemongrass-Lime Baked Chicken
Asian Coleslaw
Fresh Green Beans with Water Chestnuts
Steamed Rice*
Baked Ginger Pears

Valentine's Dinner for Two
Linguine with White Clam Sauce
Tomato-Basil Salad with Balsamic
  Dressing
Dilled Green Beans
Cold-Oven Popovers
Chocolate Swirl Cheesecake

Snowy-Night Dinner
Lentil Chili Soup
Apple and Orange Slices*
Whole-Wheat French Bread
Pumpkin Spice Cupcakes with Nutmeg
  Cream Topping

Low-Fat Tuesday
Crispy Cajun Catfish Nibbles with Red
  Sauce
Steamed Grean Beans*
Baked Fries with Creole Seasoning
Apple Raisin Crunch

Easter Dinner
Slow-Cooker Pork Roast with Orange
  Cranberry Sauce
Hot and Spicy Watercress and Romaine
  Salad
Steamed Carrots*
Savory Peas
Yogurt Dinner Rolls
Angel Food Layers with Chocolate
  Custard and Kiwifruit

Cinco de Mayo Fiesta
Beef Tostadas
Salsa Cruda with Raw Vegetables
Zesty Corn Relish
Tequila Lime Sherbet

*Recipes not included.

Mother's Day Breakfast
Apple Oatmeal Pancake
Turkey Sausage Patties
Sparkling Cranberry Cooler

Kentucky Derby Dinner
Boneless Pork Ribs with Black Cherry
    Barbecue Sauce
Parsley Potato Salad
Baked Okra Bites
Nutmeg Cake

Memorial Day Picnic
Southwestern Turkey Wraps
Marinated Green Beans
Assorted Chilled Melon Slices*
Fudgy Buttermilk Brownies

Post-Tennis Lunch
Cucumber Watercress Soup
Asian Chicken and Rice Salad
Fat-Free Whole-Wheat Crackers*
Strawberry-Banana Sorbet with Star
    Fruit

Father's Day Dinner
Tilapia Amandine
Marinated Fresh Asparagus, Tomato, and
    Hearts of Palm Salad
Steamed Brown Rice*
Spiced Skillet Bananas with Frozen
    Yogurt

Labor Day Picnic
Southwestern Pork Salad
Multigrain Crackers*
Oatmeal Carrot Bar Cookies

Back-to-School Breakfast
Breakfast Pizzas
Assorted Fresh Fruit*

After the Football Game
Slow-Cooker White Chili
Confetti Coleslaw
Herb Cheese Bread
Fall Fruit Medley

Après Ski Dinner
Savory Beef Stew
Winter Fruit Salad with Spinach and
    Gorgonzola
Whole-Wheat Pasta*
Easy Apple Cake

Fourth of July Barbecue
Spicy Grilled Chicken
Italian Rice Salad with Artichokes
Grilled Zucchini*
Sunny Mango Sorbet

Dinner for a Busy Day
Grilled Flank Steak Salad with Sweet-
    and-Sour Sesame Dressing
Multigrain Rolls*
Fat-free Vanilla Frozen Yogurt* with
    Raspberry Port Sauce

Child's Birthday Party
Animal Crackers in My Fruit
Crispy Baked Chicken
Honeyed Carrots
Berry Good Smoothie
Black Devil's Food Cake

Summer Celebration
Grilled Salmon
Grilled Asparagus*
Couscous with Vegetables
Strawberries with Champagne Ice

*Recipes not included.

Thanksgiving Dinner
Flavorful Tomato Bouillon
Roast Turkey*
Basic Gravy
Apple Dressing
Steamed Broccoli*
Cranberry Orange Salad
Easy Refrigerator Rolls
Pumpkin Pie

Hanukkah Dinner
Herbed Mushroom Soup with Red Wine
Lemon-Herb Roast Chicken
Carrot, Parsnip, and Potato Pancakes
Asparagus with Garlic and Parmesan
    Bread Crumbs
Deep-Dish Fruit Crisp

Christmas Buffet Dinner Party
Fillet of Beef with Herbes de Provence
Scalloped Potatoes
Crunchy Broccoli Casserole
Baked Curried Fruit
Chocolate Crème Brûlée

Kwanzaa Super
Savory Black-Eyed Peas and Pasta
Tangy Cucumbers
Swiss Chard, Southern Style
Guiltless Banana Pudding

Vegetarian Feast
Minted Cantaloupe Soup with Fresh
    Lime
Spinach Roll with Alfredo Sauce
Sliced Tomatoes, Carrots, and
    Cucumbers*
Muffins
Frozen Raspberry Cream

Baby Shower
Smoked Salmon Party Dip
Plum Tomatoes with Blue Cheese
Skewered Chicken Strips with Soy-
    Peanut Marinade
Coconut Halibut Bites
Caramelized Pineapple Spears
Angel Food Truffle Torte with Fruit Sauce
Cherry Limeade Punch

*Recipes not included.

Appendix d
diet and health:
an ongoing relationship

Over the years, the connection between the foods we eat and our overall health has become clearer. Ongoing research will continue to bring us greater insight into the way our bodies work and how we can eat well to stay well. Thanks to recent advances in our understanding of heart disease, we know more than ever before about the risk factors that lead to disease and the ways we can change those risks.

Risk Factors for Heart Disease

The following are all major risk factors for heart disease:

- A diet rich in saturated and trans fats, cholesterol, and sodium
- Tobacco use
- High blood pressure
- Physical inactivity
- Obesity

Fortunately, these are also all things you can do something about. Following a healthy eating plan (see the American Heart Association recommendations on page x), quitting smoking, controlling your blood pressure, and getting enough exercise are the best ways you can avoid or lessen your risk for heart disease.

There are other risk factors we cannot change. Heredity and race can predispose certain people to heart problems. Men are more prone to heart attack earlier in life, although the death rate in women increases after menopause. Also, people who have diabetes are more likely to develop heart disease and stroke. If you fit into any of these categories, you need to be even more careful to eat well and stay fit.

Cholesterol, Heart Attack, and Diet

The cholesterol in your blood is carried in particles called lipoproteins. The measurement of total cholesterol includes both the low-density lipoproteins (LDLs, or "bad" cholesterol) and the high-density lipoproteins (HDLs, or "good" cholesterol).

A high level of LDL cholesterol in the blood is a major risk factor for coronary heart disease. When too much LDL cholesterol circulates in the blood, it can slowly build up in the walls of the arteries that feed the heart and brain. Together with other substances, it can form plaque, a thick, hard deposit that can clog those arteries. This condition is known as atherosclerosis. If a clot breaks off from the plaque and blocks a narrowed artery, it can cause a heart attack or stroke.

Many heart attacks in middle age and later in life are linked to long-term high blood levels of LDL cholesterol. How do our blood cholesterol levels get too high? Genetic factors can certainly play a part. Most high LDL levels, however, result from dietary habits.

The harmful LDL cholesterol that circulates in our blood comes from two primary sources. One is the cholesterol in the foods we eat. The other is the body, which manufactures cholesterol. When we eat a diet rich in saturated and trans fats, the body increases its production of LDL cholesterol. Reducing the amount of these fats in your diet will reduce the level of harmful LDL cholesterol. Current evidence indicates that more of the harm within the arteries is done by LDL cholesterol manufactured from saturated fat than by additional dietary cholesterol.

HDL cholesterol actually may help protect against heart attack by clearing fat from the bloodstream and removing excess cholesterol. Studies show that replacing saturated and trans fats with poly- and monounsaturated fats can reduce LDL without lowering levels of the helpful HDL cholesterol.

Be sure to talk with your doctor about your individual health needs. For more comprehensive information on diet and heart disease, as well as the latest news on ongoing research and new programs, visit the American Heart Association's Web site at *americanheart.org.*

Appendix e
equivalents and substitutions
Equivalents

ingredient	measurement
ALMONDS	1 OUNCE = ¼ CUP SLIVERS
APPLE	1 MEDIUM = ¾ CUP CHOPPED; 1 CUP SLICED
BASIL LEAVES, FRESH	⅔ OUNCE = ½ CUP, CHOPPED, STEMS REMOVED
BELL PEPPER, ANY COLOR	1 MEDIUM = 1 CUP CHOPPED OR SLICED
CARROT	1 MEDIUM = ⅓ TO ½ CUP CHOPPED OR SLICED; ½ CUP SHREDDED
CELERY	1 MEDIUM RIB = ½ CUP CHOPPED OR SLICED
CHEESE, HARD, such as PARMESAN	3½ OUNCES = 1 CUP SHREDDED; 4 OUNCES = 1 CUP GRATED
CHEESE, SEMIHARD, such as CHEDDAR, MOZZARELLA, OR SWISS	4 OUNCES = 1 CUP GRATED
CHEESE, SOFT, such as BLUE, FETA, OR GOAT	1 OUNCE CRUMBLED = ¼ CUP
CUCUMBER	1 MEDIUM = 1 CUP SLICED
LEMON JUICE	1 MEDIUM = 3 TABLESPOONS
LEMON ZEST	1 MEDIUM = 2 TO 3 TEASPOONS
LIME JUICE	1 MEDIUM = 1½ TO 2 TABLESPOONS
LIME ZEST	1 MEDIUM = 1 TEASPOON
MUSHROOMS (BUTTON)	1 POUND = 5 CUPS SLICED; 6 CUPS CHOPPED
ONIONS, GREEN	8 TO 9 MEDIUM = 1 CUP SLICED (GREEN AND WHITE PARTS)
ONIONS, WHITE or YELLOW	1 LARGE = 1 CUP CHOPPED 1 MEDIUM = ⅔ CUP CHOPPED 1 SMALL = ⅓ CUP CHOPPED
ORANGE JUICE	1 MEDIUM = ⅓ TO ½ CUP
ORANGE ZEST	1 MEDIUM = 1½ TO 2 TABLESPOONS
STRAWBERRIES	1 PINT = 2 CUPS SLICED OR CHOPPED
TOMATOES	2 LARGE, 3 MEDIUM, OR 4 SMALL = 1½ TO 2 CUPS CHOPPED
WALNUTS	1 OUNCE = ½ CUP CHOPPED

Ingredient Substitutions

You don't need to throw away old family recipes just because you want to eat healthfully. By making a few simple ingredient substitutions, you can fit almost any recipe into your eating plan.

recipe calls for	use
BROTH OR BOUILLON	Low-sodium bouillon granules or cubes, reconstituted according to package directions; homemade or commercially prepared fat-free, low-sodium broth.
BUTTER, MELTED BUTTER, or SHORTENING	Acceptable margarine or acceptable oil. When possible, use fat-free or light tub, light stick, or fat-free spray margarine. However, if the type of fat is critical to the recipe, especially in baked goods, you may need to use an acceptable stick margarine (see page xviii).
BUTTER OR OIL FOR SAUTÉING	Fat-free, low-sodium broth; vegetable oil spray; wine; fruit or vegetable juice.
CREAM	Fat-free half-and-half; polyunsaturated nondairy coffee cream; undiluted fat-free evaporated milk.
EGGS	Cholesterol-free egg substitutes; 2 egg whites for 1 whole egg.
EVAPORATED MILK	Fat-free evaporated milk.
FLAVORED SALTS, such as ONION SALT, GARLIC SALT, and CELERY SALT	Onion powder, garlic powder, celery seeds or flakes. Use about one fourth the amount of flavored salt indicated in the recipe.
ICE CREAM	Fat-free, low-fat, or light ice cream; fat-free or low-fat frozen yogurt; sorbet; sherbet.
OIL IN BAKING	Unsweetened applesauce.
SALT	No-salt-added seasoning blends.
TOMATO JUICE	No-salt-added tomato juice; 6-ounce can of no-salt-added tomato paste diluted with 3 cans of water.
TOMATO SAUCE	No-salt-added tomato sauce; 6-ounce can of no-salt-added tomato paste diluted with 1 can of water.
UNSWEETENED BAKING CHOCOLATE	3 tablespoons cocoa powder plus 1 tablespoon polyunsaturated oil or unsaturated, unsalted margarine for every 1-ounce square of chocolate.
VEGETABLE OIL FOR SAUTÉING or TO PREPARE PAN	Vegetable oil spray; fat-free or light tub, light stick, or fat-free spray margarine; acceptable margarine.
WHIPPING CREAM	Fat-free evaporated milk (thoroughly chilled before whipping).
WHOLE MILK	Fat-free milk.

Appendix f
american heart association national center and affiliates

For more information about our programs and services, call 1-800-AHA-USA1 (1-800-242-8721) or contact us online at *www.americanheart.org*. For information about the American Stroke Association, a division of the American Heart Association, call 1-888-4STROKE (1-888-478-7653).

National Center

American Heart Association
7272 Greenville Avenue
Dallas, TX 75231-4596
214-373-6300

Affiliates

GREATER MIDWEST AFFILIATE
Illinois, Indiana, Michigan, Minnesota, North Dakota, South Dakota, Wisconsin
Chicago, IL

GREATER RIVERS AFFILIATE
Delaware, Kentucky, Ohio, Pennsylvania, West Virginia
Columbus, OH

GREATER SOUTHEAST AFFILIATE
Alabama, Florida, Georgia, Louisiana, Mississippi, Puerto Rico, Tennessee
Marietta, GA

HEARTLAND AFFILIATE
Arkansas, Iowa, Kansas, Missouri, Nebraska, Oklahoma
Topeka, KS

HERITAGE AFFILIATE
Connecticut, Long Island, New Jersey, New York, Bronx, Queens, Richmond/ Staten Island
New York City, NY

MID-ATLANTIC AFFILIATE
Washington, D.C.; Maryland; North Carolina; South Carolina; Virginia
Glen Allen, VA

NORTHEAST AFFILIATE
Maine, Massachusetts, New Hampshire, New York State (excluding Heritage's designated areas), Rhode Island, Vermont
Framingham, MA

PACIFIC/MOUNTAIN AFFILIATE
Alaska, Arizona, Colorado, Hawaii, Idaho, Montana, New Mexico, Oregon, Washington, Wyoming
Seattle, WA

TEXAS AFFILIATE
Austin, TX

WESTERN STATES AFFILIATE
California, Nevada, Utah
Los Angeles, CA

Index

e

S

saffron, cook's tip on, 458

sage
  Grilled Lemon-Sage Chicken, 235
  Rosemary-Sage Steak, 284

salad dressing(s), 137–141
  buying, 645
  Chunky Cucumber and Garlic Dressing, 138
  Lemon Dressing, 141
  Poppy Seed Dressing with Kiwifruit, 140
  Ranch-Style Herb Dressing, 139
  Sweet-and-Sour Sesame Dressing, 129
  Zesty Tomato Dressing, 137
  see also specific salad recipes

salad(s), 86–136
  Artichoke and Hearts of Palm Salad, 90
  Asian Chicken and Rice Salad, 126
  Asian Coleslaw, 100
  Berry Explosion Salad, 104
  Brussels Sprouts Caesar-Style, 92–93
  Cajun Chicken Salad, 125
  Carrot Salad with Jícama and Pineapple, 103
  Chicken Vegetable Salad, 124
  Confetti Coleslaw, 101
  Couscous Salad, 136
  Cranberry Orange Salad, 107
  Curried Chicken Salad, 123
  Curried Quinoa Salad with Cranberries and Almonds, 135
  Curried Rice and Bean Salad, 134
  Curried Tuna Salad, 120
  Dijon-Marinated Vegetable Medley, 97
  Double Spinach Tortellini Salad, 132
  Fresh Fruit Salad Romanoff, 105
  Fresh Salmon Salad, 118
  Greek Pasta Salad, 116
  Grilled Flank Steak Salad with Sweet-and-Sour Sesame Dressing, 129
  Herbed Tomato Orzo Salad, 108
  Hot and Spicy Watercress and Romaine Salad, 86
  Island Chicken Salad with Fresh Mint, 127
  Italian Rice Salad with Artichokes, 113
  Marinated Fresh Asparagus, Tomato, and Hearts of Palm Salad, 91
  Marinated Green Beans, 94

Marinated Pasta Salad, 115
Marinated White Beans and Cucumber with Basil, 133
Mexican Shrimp Salad, 122
Mustard Potato Salad, 109
Parsley Potato Salad, 109
Parsnip Salad with Jícama and Apple, 102
Picante Shrimp with Broccoli and Snow Peas, 121
Roasted Beet and Orange Salad, 96
Salade Niçoise, 119
Salad Greens with Oranges and Strawberries, 87
Salmon and Orzo Salad, 117
Sixteen-Bean Salad, 114
Southwestern Pork Salad, 131
Spinach-Chayote Salad with Orange Vinaigrette, 89
Tabbouleh, 111
Tangy Cucumbers, 99
Tomato-Basil Salad with Balsamic Dressing, 95
Tossed Vegetables in Creamy Vinaigrette, 98
Tuna Vegetable Salad, 124
Turkey on a Bed of Sliced Tomatoes, 128
Warm Orzo Salad with Black Beans and Ham, 130
Wild Rice Salad with Cranberry Vinaigrette, 112
Wilted Baby Spinach with Pear and Goat Cheese, 88
Winter Fruit Salad with Spinach and Gorgonzola, 106
Zesty Corn Relish, 110

Salisbury Steaks with Mushroom Sauce, 310–311

salmon
  Baked Salmon with Cucumber Relish, 168
  Broiled Salmon with Citrus Salsa, 169
  Fresh Salmon Salad, 118
  Grilled Salmon, 170
  omega-3 fatty acids in, xiii
  Salmon Alfredo, 172
  Salmon and Orzo Salad, 117
  Salmon Cakes, 171
  Salmon with Cucumber-Dill Sauce, 167
  Smoked Salmon Party Dip, 6